The Ambivalent Character of Participation

Labour, Education & Society

Edited by György Széll,
Heinz Sünker, Anne Inga Hilsen
and Francesco Garibaldo

Volume 20

PETER LANG
Frankfurt am Main · Berlin · Bern · Bruxelles · New York · Oxford · Wien

Francesco Garibaldo
Volker Telljohann
(eds.)

The Ambivalent Character of Participation

New Tendencies
in Worker Participation in Europe

PETER LANG
Internationaler Verlag der Wissenschaften

Bibliographic Information published by the Deutsche Nationalbibliothek
The Deutsche Nationalbibliothek lists this publication in the Deutsche Nationalbibliografie; detailed bibliographic data is available in the internet at http://dnb.d-nb.de.

This book has been produced with financial support of the European Commission, Directorate General Employment, Social Affairs, and Equal Opportunities.

ISSN 1861-647X
ISBN 978-3-631-58943-4

www.peterlang.de

Contents

Wolfgang Potratz – An obituary

Our friend and colleague Wolfgang Potratz passed away on 13 February 2009 at the age of only 60. We have known Wolfgang Potratz as a farsighted and outstanding researcher.

Since 2000 Wolfgang Potratz was an active member of the international network *Regional and Local Development of Work and Labour (RLDWL)*. The conferences of the network benefited from the results of his multifaceted and extensive research activities. His most important work in recent years included research on health economics in the context of regional policies, information and communication technologies for active ageing, health care work in Europe and economic opportunities of an ageing society. In the past he also did extensive research on structures and processes of European regional policy as well as on enlargement and globalisation issues of the European Union.

Wolfgang Potratz' commitment was particularly directed towards the activities of the European section of RLDWL. When at the end of the Conference on "Globalisation, Company Strategies and Quality of Working Life in Europe" which took place in June 2003 in Bologna the European section of the Work and Labour network was set up Wolfgang was immediately elected a member of the steering committee. Also in 2004 he was actively involved in the international conference on "New Forms of Work Organisation and Industrial Relations. Where does Italy stand?". When it came to the preparation of the third European Conference in 2008 Wolfgang was again committed to contributing to the preparation of the event. The struggle against the disease, however, prevented him from participating in the "European Workplace Participation Forum".

Wolfgang's death represents a great loss for RLDWL. His cooperation in the network's activities was invaluable. RLDWL loses in Wolfgang Potratz not only a committed colleague on whose support we could always rely but also a wise and warm-hearted friend.

On behalf of the RLDWL Europe Steering Committee *Volker Telljohann*

Foreword

The *European Workplace Participation Forum – New Ways to Effective Forms of Worker Participation* was the fourth Conference since 1999 dealing with themes in the field of working conditions, employee participation and social cohesion organised by the international network Regional and Local Development of Work and Labour (RLDWL).

The aim of the Conference that took place from 24 to 26 September 2008 in Rome was to grasp the changes taking place in labour relations and, in particular, to collect and debate innovative participation experiences at the workplace as well as the relationship between different forms of participation. These developments were analysed in countries all over Europe in order to be able to examine the different framework conditions and in particular the role of the respective institutional context for the success of new participation experiences.

This volume assembles the contributions presented in the framework of the *European Workplace Participation Forum* which was organised along a number of critical thematic areas regarding worker participation. The contributions gave an overview on the new tendencies with regard to both the new contents and the evolving forms of participation processes. Concerning the content of participation, experiences regarding company performance, work organisation, health and safety as well as vocational training showed to be of growing importance. As to the forms of participation it was analysed which kind of institutional setting is needed to effectively promote cooperation between company-level actors. In particular, the development of new forms of participation, the relationship between different forms and levels of participation as well as the preconditions and procedures of participation at the workplace were aspects that were analysed in depth.

The Conference also contributed to the cooperation with the project WORK-IN-NET (Labour and innovation: Work-oriented innovations – a key to better employment, cohesion and competitiveness in a knowledge-intensive society). A special session was dedicated to the research on employee participation and the role of workplace research and development programmes. Opportunities provided by national and European-level research and development programmes for future research in the field of workplace participation were presented and discussed.

The final part of the Conference was dedicated to the identification of future research needs and the discussion about the possible contribution of innovative experiences of worker participation to the achievement of the goals set by the Lisbon Strategy and to the further development of the European Social Model.

The Conference as well as this volume were made possible by the financial support of the European Commission, DG Employment, Social Affairs and Equal Opportunities. Furthermore, we wish to thank the Hans-Böckler-Foundation, the Friedrich-Ebert-Foundation and the European Trade Union Institute for their practical and financial support.

Francesco Garibaldo *Volker Telljohann*

Introduction

Francesco Garibaldo

This book is based on a selection of the papers presented at the *European Workplace Participation Forum: new ways to effective forms of worker participation,* a conference held in Rome, in September 2008, sponsored and financed by the European Commission. The Conference was organized around three streams (articulated in twelve workshops); the first one concerned the institutional context at large, the second one focused on participation practices in the workplace and the third one on the new societal practices, such as the inter-company level and transnational experiments of participation and the corporate social responsibility experiences. The book is organized in a similar way and it collects some contributions from each stream; each stream is introduced by a short explanation of its rationale and a reporter comments the workshop outcomes. Furthermore, it includes a general conclusion.

The Forum was organized in an optimistic view. The main idea was that on the one hand, a highly skilled labour force as well as the quality of work have a decisive role in regard to improvements in productivity and innovation, on the other, that the effective utilisation of the staff concerning its competences, skills, creativity, flexibility, etc. to a large extent depends on the adequacy of the system of social regulation of work. There is growing evidence that worker participation can play an important role in the modernisation and performance of the workplace. In this context the role of participation appears to be of particular relevance as employees' motivation and commitment depend very much on their effective involvement and thereby on the adequacy of information and consultation processes.

Therefore a new mix of labour relations practices has now emerged where, in addition to forms of representative participation, workers' direct participation is supposed to be of increasing importance. The relationship between these two forms was posited to be not necessarily a conflictual one. In general, it was assumed that, in practice, industrial relations expertise has been progressing from the pure negotiation skills traditionally acquired by shop stewards and trade union officials and based on reactive strategies towards a new mix of consultation, cooperation and negotiation that combines reactive and proactive attitudes on the part of workers' representatives. In conclusion, the main idea underlying the streams dealt with by the conference was to show how forms of active partnership could lead to an improvement in company performance and then to contribute to mainstreaming this practises in Europe.

These optimistic assumptions have been damped down in the preparatory phase of the Forum, due to the possibility to start to collect new anecdotal evidence and facts in the framework of the project, by framing a rather different picture. This new awareness contributed to shape the opening speech on *Trends and challenges in the field of worker participation.* This speech, now a paper published in this book, took a critical approach on the very possibility to avoid a conflict between representative and direct participation.

The three streams, the eleven workshops and the more than sixty presented papers, provided delegates with the opportunity to acquire a European wide and in-depth understanding of the actual trends in this field. The resulting framework is ambivalent if not disappointing.

When the strategies of improving organizational performance through workplace participation – that is the outcome of stream two – are taken into consideration there is a clear lack of significant cases in the Eastern European States in and a North-South and West-East divide. As Paul Oehlke states:

"*It is no accident that this selection demonstrates that participative approaches, their contents, objectives and effects also depend on the respective systems of industrial relations, regional and national activities which are interrelated with the economic and political development on macro-level.*"

The new neo-liberal trends originated in the eighties all over Europe aimed at getting rid of the participative issues that after the Second World War were attempting at transferring objectives and procedures of political democracy into the economy. That cultural and political orientation have been aimed at

"*breaking and later on to balancing the dominance of big capital by introducing three elements of structural more or less interconnected change: democratic regulation of the economy on the basis of a broad public sector and an institutionalised participation of workers at company level reaching from involvement in social aspects of work until co-determination in economic decisions.*" (Paul Oehlke)

The rolling back strategies of the new "Supercapitalism", as Robert Reich nicknamed it, set in motion a down- and backward spirals of working and living standards, as many contributions documented in the Forum. The final social outcomes are, however, very different along the North-South and the West-East divide. As a matter of fact the neoliberal standards have been strongly supported in many European countries, through the launch of specific deregulation policies, justified by the necessity to cope with global competition. The case, at least up till now, of the Nordic countries looks more moderate, more aware of negative social consequences.

The management approaches in Europe in the last decades have been different along the North – South and the West – East divide but also within each macro areas and each country. Therefore it seems that the institutional context has been loosening relevance and the reason why this happened is the deregulation of the Industrial Relation systems, namely at the firm level, pursued from the majority of the European firms. In some countries this was easier because of policies supported by the public institutions but the trend is widespread all over Europe. So the main trend is that of purely cost-reducing strategies accompanied by restructuring the industrial relations systems in a very definitely non-participative way. At the same time many different examples of good participative practices in European firms were analysed in the Forum. In these cases what seems more relevant are the different policies implemented by firms, which are closely related to their specific market position. The restructuring of the Industrial Relations System is at the same time the consequence and the driver of the weakening of Trade Unions all over Europe. It is not only a matter of union density – very different in the different European macro areas and countries – but of effectiveness of Unions' actions. There are significant differences along the North-South and the West-East divide, also because of the differences in the governance system of the welfare provisions. However, the main trend is toward less relevance of Trade Unions as partners of the system, in favour of a kind of direct participation, which is unilaterally controlled by the management. Also in this case there are good participative practices based on a proactive role of Trade Unions, but this is not the mainstream.

Therefore national programmes supporting workplace research and development in Europe, as well as a European wide programme, are very instrumental to contribute to shift from scattered and fragmented best practices to a mainstream experience. Unfortunately these programmes are fragmented and unevenly developed across EU member states. Most of these activities, except those in Northern countries, have been rather modest in terms of their financial budgets, particularly compared to technology R&D programmes.

As far as the inter-company level and transnational experiments of participation and the corporate social responsibility experiences are concerned (stream III) the situation is still of an ambivalent nature. Following Pulignano comment we can take into consideration Ramsey ideas of cycles of control and the consequence that a win–win solution is not the natural outcome of an evolutionary process of participation, but, on the contrary there are initiators of a quest for participation with different, if not opposite interests, in each historical phase. As Pulignano states:

"Cycles must be understood as an attempt to correct the naïve position and optimism of those who cast their a-historical gaze upon developments in the 1970s and saw them as part of a theological process in which industry was becoming progressively more democratic. Patterns of participation have to be understood in their historical and sociological context."

Following the contributions to this stream this correction is indeed necessary. In this historical phase the initiator is the management and its interest is to mobilize the human potential of the work force – creativity, ingenuity, flexibility, etc. – and, with the same token, to reduce the role of Unions at the plant level. The forms of this cycle are therefore: capital-sharing through employee share schemes used to enhance labour performance and employer-initiated schemes based on task-centred employee involvement in areas narrowly identified as being of direct interests to employees of which empowerment and team-working are well-known examples. There are still different situations based on the possibility for employees, normally through collective action and means, of regulation over employment rights that may otherwise be restricted or denied to them in a free market system. These situations do not represent the mainstream in Europe today.

This is true for EWCs (European Work Councils) as well as of other instruments for workers' participation at the international level such as the International Framework Agreements (IFAs). It can be said that the case of EWCs and IFAs are still not so relevant for the vast majority of the work force in Europe but this is not the case when the value chain will be taken into consideration. The European industrial landscape is more and more characterised by a process of segmentation and polarisation of the labour market according to the new productive structure based on networks of firms, organised in layers hierarchically arranged. The position of each firm in these networks is very different depending on which of the different layers the firm belongs to. This process has produced a strong concentration starting from the industrial sector and spreading to the others economic sectors. Few economic players, competing each other in the different sectors, control mostly of the economic activities through complex and multilayered networks – value chains – of firms with an increasing level of operational integration. These complex European and transnational networks are very effective in taking critical decision on issues affecting the social life: employment levels, work life quality, a balance between private and work life, the quality of the natural environment, etc. This situation leads to increasing inequality of working conditions among firms, because of their relative positioning in the network, and consequently among employees, both in the industrial and non industrial sectors and in private and public firms. This new social and economic situation produces effects not only on income and wealth but also on employees' health and on their possibility of enjoying a fair balance between their working, social and private spheres of life. The possibility of a vertical form of representation of the work force through the value chain is a critical issue for the possibility of Trade Unions to have a say on the restructuring processes in the private but also in the public sectors. As a matter of fact Trade Unions need to overcome the fragmentation of the value chain in order to avoid new forms of social inequalities. It can be added that this difficulty to attain a vertical form of representation discloses strong contradictions with regards to the expectations generated in the public opinion concerning the application of European discourses and concepts, such as Corporate Social Responsibility (CSR) in the value supply chain. There is also a clear evidence hat the restructuring processes occurring today all over Europe in the private and in the public sectors can adversely affect the role of previous virtuous experiences. Another aspect that can be adversely affected is the problem of health and safety at work. Contrariwise the supposed process of ongoing improvement, for technological reasons of the work places, the deregulation of the labour contracts and of the Industrial Relation systems leads to old and new health and safety hazards.

In conclusion, the three streams have put into perspective the positive expectations that had been expressed during the design phase of the initiative, to a different extent and to different degrees of scepticism as to the quality of work life declared by enterprises and by trade unions involved in participative practices. Such evidence stems from multiple researches in the field and is unlikely to be put into question. Therefore, the point is to understand the reasons underlying this outcome; what are the forces involved in this domain? How are they connected to each other? Are there any positive countertrends? Etc. Many of these questions are raised by research. This research is less intended to provide a description and documentation of what exists – although necessary – and more oriented to provide a causal analysis. It should of course not be forgotten that the crisis, which was then seen as an incumbent threat rather than a true reality, has now burst out, putting en end to a long phase that has lasted almost a quarter of a century in Europe, with long-term structural effects.

A few facts can be regarded as acquired on the analytical and interpretation level.

First of all, it is clear that the idea of mainstreaming, namely the dissemination of positive practices is an abstract idea. It does not take into account the fact that there is a close relationship of a twofold correlation between each practice and set of circumstances that are independent from it. A few specific circumstances emerge, sometimes in competition between themselves, whose outcomes are sometimes difficult to foresee. The first group of circumstances in competition is represented by the matching between the institutional system and public policies vis-à-vis the corporate *governance*. The institutional system – i.e. the labour law and the competition criteria, the Industrial Relations system, etc. – and the industrial, tax and labour policies all push towards the identification of different areas on participation experiences in Europe. The forecast is now partially confirmed, with factual evidence being there, following the North-South and East-West divide; there are more positive and less isolated experiences in the North and in the West. At the same time, though, there are industrial approaches and organization models, which are led by the single market and global competition principles and overcome these historical differences. During the Nineties, the *Lean Production* and the *New Public Management* models have become a reference standard across Europe; they then joined forces with the de-regulation thrust of the labour market, according to the generalized flexibility theories, as the main way to increase employment. This corporate policy mix accompanied by a set of legislations aimed at supporting a more aggressive capitalism have called into question the historical differences between these political and geographical areas – Rhine Capitalism vs. Anglo-Saxon Capitalism, etc. – with a trend towards standardization. The same contradiction can be found in the European policies, which on the one hand have led to the creation of the juridical-regulatory infrastructure of the Europe style "supercapitalism" and on the other hand have launched policies promoting the "social dialogue", the European Works Councils, Corporate Social Responsibility, participation, etc. It should not be difficult to understand that the *business-oriented* thrust has prevailed over the other one.

The second group of circumstances is the national and the European level. Subsidiarity should be the guiding principle, as laid down by article 5 of the founding Treaty of the European Community, now known as the European Union, which stated:

"*The Community shall act within the limits of the powers conferred upon it by this Treaty and of the objectives assigned to it therein.*

In areas which do not fall within its exclusive competence, the Community shall take action, in accordance with the principle of subsidiarity, only if and in so far as the objectives of the proposed action cannot be sufficiently achieved by the Member States and can therefore, by reason of the scale or effects of the proposed action, be better achieved by the Community.

Any action by the Community shall not go beyond what is necessary to achieve the objectives of this Treaty"

This formal legal framework is then surmounted by a structure – in the economic activities – based on an extreme concentration of capitals, with the setting up of true European champions – in turn integrated on a global scale – organized according to oligopolistic formats. This concentration is not accompanied by a verticalization of the activities performed by each "champion" who, on the other hand, has organized its activity according to business networks, formally independent from one another, but closely integrated from the point of view of their activities. Hence, new labour regulation forms, which are not set by either the national or EU institutional levels, but by private actors. This regulation is indeed subjected to the global competition standards and gives rise to the relocation of labour to low-labour income countries, even within the European Union and uses the lack of any legally binding and strict European regulations, which would be against the deregulation that has been promoted over the past decades and the inability by trade unions to develop an initiative at the same geographical scale as the restructuring processes.

There is a problem of scale of action. In other words, if the phenomena that are described here have exceeded the previous regulation spheres to the point that they have led to the creation of brand new regulatory spaces that are more in compliance with real processes, should this *tuning in process* limit itself to the *business* or also to the more general institutional and social processes?

The consideration made by geographers about the use of transcalarity in the 19th century might be useful here, namely concerning a practice that was by the way widely spread in many international voluntary as well as social and political activist movements. Transcalarity is the shift from a scalar system made up of different layers, nested together into one another, like in a matrioska, (*nested scales*), to a transcalar system, i.e. a system connecting different independent or partially overlapping scalar systems, by connecting different layers of different scalar systems, regardless of their internal hierarchy. This is precisely the case of the European Union, with its hierarchically organized systems but with competing and overlapping spheres of influence – the *de facto* jurisdiction.

The question that arises here is: is it possible for the local level stakeholders to benefit from transcalarity to promote their strategies in a multiscalar way, namely at the different global levels, by skipping the typical intermediate levels of their own scalar structure? It is a possibility that has already been tried out by international activist and voluntary groups; does it only refer to them or does it point out new ways to implement political and social action beyond governance and administrative action?

Furthermore, an important characteristic of this type of multiscalar policies, at a local level, is that they are not obliged to move through a set of scalar levels, one within the other, from the local to the international one, but they can directly access to other local stakeholders similar in the same country or across borders. This possibility does not prevent powerful stakeholders to benefit from the presence of different jurisdiction scales to their advantage (Morrill, 1999) and the fact that the local resistance depends on how the State positions itself, by scaling the jurisdiction, administrative and regulatory tiers (Judd, 1998). On the contrary, it might also be the case that the conditions that have been analysed by Morrill and Judd, among others, force the problem. Why working through power relations structured within the State centred on a scale hierarchy? Why not jumping from the boat, if this is a possibility?[1]

1 Sassen S.(2003), Globalization or denationalization?, "Review of International Political Economy" Vol. 10, N. 1, p. 11.

This is exactly the scenario of a few social stakeholders, first of all trade unions, as well illustrated by the British case and by the insistence of the British government on the opting out clause, just to prevent such a "jump".

Hence, trade unions should build their own scope of action at a European scale but not as an additional space, but as the suitable scale to measure up with the real scale at which are determined working conditions.

Trade Unions have not managed so far to build this scale of action: on the other hand, if we look at the political and institutional level, we realize that the European democratic deficit turns into a power relations imbalance between Capital and Labour, at the European scale, due to the EU policies, when it comes to labour regulation.

If we then look at living and working conditions within enterprises it becomes ever more evident that the instrumental use by management of direct participation policies, to scale down or replace representative participation, we realize that it is also fuelled by the ineffectiveness of traditional trade union representation forms within enterprises. It is true that the plant-level representation forms are more oriented towards the collective regulation of questions that can be precisely defined upfront; different classes of phenomena exist in enterprises, which require a specific regulation especially when, as is now often the case, operational situations change very rapidly. The risk therefore is that company-level representation, when it exists and is able to do it, takes action to address the daily problems of workers but instead be absent or totally powerless on other aspects. They range from problems related to the regulation of work paces and the verification of ergonomic and safety conditions to the problems concerning the new work forms and/or the introduction of new equipment. For instance, the verification to assess whether a specific work position corresponds to the criteria defined by the OCRA methodology, to be regarded as ergonomically correct, might take many hours to a duly trained expert. A new debate is now opened on the new methods to be introduced for the computerisation of a work task, for it to be regarded not as a mere communication or training action, but rather as a participative design process, which might not be summarized by a delegate, but which would require the direct participation of the people who are actually going to be involved in this change. Hence, if trade unions wish to be able to address this whole set of issues, they have to rethink a mixed form of – either direct or representative – participation at the company level, by defining new spheres of action and the relationship between the two forms of participation. For this whole process to be realistic, the issue should be addressed within the Industrial Relations framework, which does not nevertheless seem to be the case at present.

I. Direct and indirect participation: reconcilable voices?

Direct and indirect participation: reconcilable voices? Report from Stream I

Erik Poutsma, Ulke Veersma

This chapter aims to give an overview of the experiences and arguments as presented at the Third_European Congress of the *Work and Labour Network European Workplace Participation Forum Congress*. Our main conclusion is that the debate evolved towards a broad view in which direct and indirect participation are seen as less conflicting than before. These forms of participation seem to be reconciled in a more balanced direction – both at a theoretical and a practical level a signs of convergence are observed. In practice, a main trend can be witnessed, where both forms of participation – at least potentially – support each other rather than substituting each other. It can thus be stated that the diverse channels of participation are more compatible than concluded in earlier debates. In this vein action research is proposed along three lines, which will be presented at the end of this chapter.

Since the nineties a debate has unfolded across the members states of the European Union focusing on the question until what extent and in what way direct participation would replace indirect forms of participation (EPOC Research Group, 1997; Wood and Fenton-O'Creevy, 2005). Both from the perspective of the 'high-performance workplace' literature in the US (Huselid 1995; Applebaum *et al.*, 2000; Osterman, 1994; Poutsma, Ligthart and Veersma, 2006) and the literature in the UK on the 'new employment relationships' and the flexible firm (Coller, 1996; Delbridge and Whitfield, 2001) there is more emphasis on direct participation as a means to create commitment of individual employees, to increase their motivation and thereby to enhance performance of individuals and organisations. Generally, this type of literature addresses the relevance of establishing long-term trust relationships with the new highly skilled workforce in many workplaces, specifically in the service sectors. Especially in countries with a lower level of institutionalization of employment relations, like Italy, direct participation is considered to be a potential threat. Established actors in the systems of employment relations fear their role to be substituted by the role of direct participation as management would pose a threat leading participation schemes and replacing the power of trade unions (see Telljohann). In the UK, with a highly scattered pattern of employment relations – fragmented at the company level and dependent on the local presence of trade unions –, trade unions fear the loss of 'voice' as the outcome of such a process. In this unitarist perspective trade unions would be endangered to lose their independent influence on employment conditions.

It is not only the fear of the role of institutional actors being taken over by manipulation of management as the main actor behind schemes of direct participation, but also the interests of specific groups of employees who are more vulnerable and whose interests are endangered when there is a high dependency on management (see Pollert). The study referred to makes also clear that, although the employment relationship seems to have been de-collectivised, there are still more informal grassroots responses to workplace grievances which means that the shift of power away from trade unions does not have to imply a withering away of collective voice and power. Also in the case of professionals and knowledge workers, who generally experience a high degree of direct participation, the possibility of generating and emerging collective voice is still very likely as is shown by Marsden (2007). A more balanced approach to the relationship between collective voice arrangements and direct participation may be persuasive, although this may be instigated on the basis of the existence of already a certain level of collective voice. Research in the UK revealed a new mood towards both state regulation and trade unions among managers, with several adopting the language of 'partnership' (Guest and Peccei, 1998; Gollan, 2001). Employee voice taking place through trade unions or direct participation is taken for granted and both are considered valuable in so far as it 'added value' to the business organization (Marchington, 2001; Ackers *et al.*, 2006).

The main debate in the workshop addressed the relations between trade unions and channels of direct participation. Specific attention was given to the possible strategies of trade unions to be deployed. Telljohann stresses in his paper the need for participation, triggered by the increasing demand for innovation and organisational change. The case of Italy shows evidence of direct participation following the rationale of intensified use and development of human capital. In this case direct participation seems to fulfill the need for skilled and specialized work rather than following the logic of integration of executive with decision making responsibilities at lower levels. It is also shown that direct participation may be doomed to fail when unilateral decisions for the introduction of direct participation undermines the relations of trust between the actors. Direct participation usually enhances productivity and adaptation to change and innovation, but, as concluded by Telljohann, it may also hamper existing – often low developed – institutional actors and employment relations to emphasise the need for a more sustainable approach.

Direct participation reflects not only the demands of new forms of work organisation but also the need for control, which may specifically affect the position of white-collar workers and their demands for interest representation. According to

Kratzer one may observe an ambivalent development: on the one hand white-collar-workers face an increasing responsibility and, due to that development, an increasing demand for self-rationalization and self-control – which is compensated by the opportunity to self organise working time and the course of daily work. On the other hand, however, these employees are confronted with an increasing workload and a much higher pressure on performance and simultaneously a loss of job security. A new pattern of performance management policy emerges at the company level which combines new forms of flexibility with insecurity and new strategies of management and control. The latter are often described as "participative management" or "indirect control". A tendency is observed towards an increase of such forms of direct participation and work councils and trade unions indeed have to cope with, or at least have to adjust to this trend. Recent developments undermine not only the assumption that more direct participation would directly lead to less representative participation, but also, certainly as convincingly, the assumption of better working conditions being a straightforward result of direct participation. Indeed, direct participation itself is obviously no protection against the risks of modern working life.

Even more, Gonzalez Menendez points to the reverse effect after researching direct participation and implementation strategies in Spain. Employers in Spain seem to be less inclined to support direct participation with the reason behind these discussions could open new issues and agendas (Blyton and Martinez Lucio, 1995). Gonzalez Menendez blames the culture of Spanish management, being reluctant to change and having a strong authoritarian attitude, as the main cause of inertia with regard to both direct and, possibly related to that, formal representative participation. As the Spanish case shows, trade unions would have little need to fear for substitution by direct participation, which means that *both* employers and trade unions have strategic choice to implement direct participation.

The debate then revolved around the question how direct and indirect participation could be combined successfully or how the conflict between direct and representative participation could be reconciled. As is argued by Hagen and Trygstad, such a combination could only be the outcome of a *localised* form of participation with a strongly multi-levelled model of employment relations in which various interests are mediated at various levels. Centrally bargained collective agreements and participation at the workplace should not be viewed as independent modes of participation with separate principles of participation, but they should be looked at as supporting each other and connecting between individual and representative participation. In the debate several participants gave evidence supporting such a thesis.

Hagen and Trygstad state that the development of direct participation, with its emphasis on individual responsible autonomy, may have positive performance outcomes due to increased flexibility within the work organisation. At the same time, however, this may lead to negative outcomes for individual employees due to the possible exploiting effects on individual employees and their health. After all, it is commonly known that stress is currently one of the main determinants of sickness leave. This may eventually lead to overall negative effects outweighing some of the advantages. Furthermore, direct participation and, as a consequence, individual flexibility in working conditions and labour terms appear rather costly to organise and employers may be aware of the benefits of higher levels of standardisation. As a consequence, both employers and employees may seek collective regulation safeguarding flexibility and security: hence the strategy of, what is labelled by Hagen and Trygstad 'local flexicurity'. Such a form of 'flexicurity' would enable increased flexibility at the company level, while arrangements are simultaneously linked to the institutional framework which could provide more security for individuals with reorganisations and various changes taking place.

The contrasting impact of the two discussed channels on performance, with low levels of representative participation and high levels of direct participation (or the other way around, high levels of representative participation with low levels of direct participation), points to the highly ambiguous outcomes from the two means of participation. The concept of flexicurity seems to offer a way out from the deadlock posed by the symmetric – opposing – direction of the impact of two channels of participation on performance, where representative participation provides more certainty and equality, whereas direct participation would enable flexibility and – freedom of – change. Flexicurity, as a concept applied to participation, suggests a balanced approach to, on the one hand, autonomy and freedom, i.e. flexibility, and, on the other hand, equality and consensus, i.e. security. It should however be noted that a coherent, transparent concept of flexicurity, which could be adapted in various settings of national models of employment relations, remains absent and still needs to be developed.

From the various papers a range of problems arose as impeding upon the introduction of direct participation when aiming at a successful outcome for both companies and employees. Trade unions may seek to preserve their position while occupying a monopoly as participation channel (cpr. Matey-Tyrowicz). At the company level, middle management may aim to preserve its interests and function within the company mediating between various layers of the organisation. This could, as Totterdill shows, impede upon the use and transfer of participation practices and its effectiveness. High-level management may therefore be willing to support direct participation, as it recognises the need for support with organisational change and strategy development, while middle management experiences its own role as becoming less indispensable and undermined by direct participation.

Direct participation may also be hampered by the control/regulation gap, which means that more control and autonomy is realized in the production process, whereas the regulation of behaviour of employees may increase and therefore also the work may be more intensified with different means of control on individual employees. This could also lead to more coercive forms of power being exercised on employees by integrating workers into fairly standardized (neo-Tayloristic) work systems (Dörhöfer; Gonzalez Menendez).

The debate then revolved around the question of the role of the institutional structures, regulation and possible changes due to EU directives. Clearly, the institutional context in EU member states is rather diverse, varying from voluntaristic to strongly institutionalised industrial relations and there are clearly strong path dependencies in this field. The question remains whether EU directives would make a difference. Although *European Works Councils (EWCs)*, *Information and Consultation bodies (ICE)* and representative bodies of *Health and Safety (H & S)* offer opportunities and challenges, especially – as shown by Kratzer – for white collar employees, the take up by unions is limited due to competition with non-union solutions leading to withdrawal behaviour and unions monopolising their role as the main institutional actor representing employees. This often leads to conflicts between unions on the one hand and non-union representation and works councils on the other hand, which creates chances for management to divide and rule. Another limitation to these strategies may be the lack of potential for transfer of these practices within multinational companies (Tholen; Meardi).

Despite the limitations and constraints there is empirical evidence that direct participation and representative participation may evolve in alternate patterns of participation forms. For Bulgaria Ribarova showed the possible emergence of hybrid forms of participation where union, non-union and works council structures are combined. In addition, a Hungarian survey showed that the combined structures of trade union representation and works councils are more effective in influencing decision making structures (Borbely). However, in other corners of the world of labour alternating channels of representation typically face managerial prerogatives and those forms have to cope with limited autonomy for employees and a lack of legitimacy and efficacy (Whittal / Tuckman).

The next issue to debate concerns the emphasis put on traditional structures and the attention for traditional categories of personnel, like the male dominated segments, and the focusing of direct participation on mainly professionals and knowledge workers. It was felt that more attention would be needed for the large groups of marginalised workers who possess a less powerful position with regard to participation. Baglioni and Leonardi called for more attention to diverse identities, a-typical workers, marginalised workers in peripherical segments of the labour market and the unorganised, non-dominant groups. De-collectivisation and individualisation and the increase of the unorganized do however not prevent the use of collective grassroots responses to problems – although until now generally with poor results (Pollert).

What could be learned from these debates and what should our future research entail? It becomes clear from the debate that participation is a social process, which is basically part of an exchange relationship. Therefore, it is principally pluralist and ambiguous in its meaning. Therefore, the development of a reconciliation of voices needs an action research approach to support a more balanced approach. The hybridisation of patterns of voice, with the diversity of approaches related to diverse identities of workers, requires an agenda that takes a bottom-up approach of organising and mobilising. In addition, the focus should be on the connection between union and non-union participation at various layers – the macro-level where institutional actors dominate and company-level individual and representative participation. We suggest research around the possible reconciliation between different channels of voice within three international focus groups.

The first group should focus on the process of developing 'effective' participation practices, where effectiveness is measured in terms of creating optimal benefits based on mutual interests, which means *local flexicurity* balancing democratic values and efficiency. The second group would focus on the alignment of alternating and complementary participation structures in terms of further institutionalisation of employment relations. The third group should focus on the non-dominant, largely unorganised groups with regard to interest representation in terms of organising and mobilising social movements.

All groups start from an international comparative perspective in order to identify national peculiarities and preconditions for effective employee participation. Such an approach would contribute to action research which is badly needed to fill the gap between the lack of experiences with other forms of participation and the past experiences through collective, institutionalised industrial relations. As promoted by the declaration of the *British Universities Industrial Relations (BUIRA)* this could enable the counterbalancing of the decline in democratic cultures and social participation (BUIRA 2008: 8-9). The transformation of the labour market, through fragmentation and individualisation of employment relations, urges such a research agenda. Recently, the financial crisis has clearly shown the deficit of the free market ideology, thereby underlining even more the need to question managerial prerogatives. The moment is obviously there to develop and implement this action research.

References

Ackers, P. / Marchington, M. / Wilkinson, A. / Dundon, T. (2006): 'Employee Participation in Britain: From Collective Bargaining & Industrial Democracy to Employee Involvement & Social Partnership: Two Decades of Manchester / Loughborough Research'. *Decision,* 33 (1): 75-88.

Appelbaum, E. / Bailey, T. / Berg, P. / Kalleberg, A.L. (2000), Manufacturing advantage: why high-performance and work systems pay off. ILR/Cornell University Press, Ithaca.

BUIRA (2008), What's the Point of Industrial Relations? A statement by the British Universities Industrial Relations Association.

Blyton, P. / Martinez Lucio, M. (1995): 'Industrial relations and the management of flexibility: factors shaping developments in Spain and the United Kingdom'. International Journal of Human Resource Management, 6 (2): 271-291.

Coller, X. (1996): 'Managing flexibility in the food-industry: a cross-national comparative case study in European multinational companies'. European Journal of Industrial Relations, 2 (2): 153-172.

Delbridge, R. / Whitfield, K. (2001): 'Employee perceptions of job influence and organizational participation'. Industrial Relations, 40 (3): 472-489.

EPOC Research Group (1997): New Forms of Work Organisation. Can Europe Realize its Potential? European Foundation for the Improvement of Living and Working Conditions, Dublin.

Gollan, P.J. (2001): Employee information and consultation: New directions in the UK and Europe, Research Report. Chartered Institute of Personnel and Development, London.

Guest, D. / Peccei, R. (1998): The Partnership Company: Benchmarks for the Future. Involvement and Participation Association, London.

Huselid, M.A. (1995): The impact of human resource management practices on turnover, productivity, and corporate financial performance. Academy of Management Journal, 38: 635–672.

Marchington, M. (2001): Management Choice and Employee Voice. CIPD, London.

Marsden, D. (2007): 'Individual employee voice: renegotiation and performance management in public services'. International Journal of Human Resource Management, 18(7): 1263-1278.

Osterman, P. (1994): 'How common is workplace transformation and who adopts it?'. Industrial and Labor Relations Review, 47 (2): 173-188.

Poutsma, E. / Ligthart, Paul / Veersma, Ulke (2006): The Diffusion of Calculative and Participative HRM Practices in European Firms. Industrial Relations. Vol. 45(2) 513-546.

Wood, S. / Fenton-O'Creevy, M. (2005): 'Direct involvement, representation and employee voice in UK multinationals in Europe'. European Journal of Industrial Relations, 10 (11): 27-50.

The role of the institutional context for participation and interest representation in Hungary and beyond

Szilvia Borbély

I. Descriptive part of presentation

1. Short history and main determinants

Hungary has a pluralistic employees' and employers' interest representation system. There are "greenfield" trade unions and employers' organisations, which have emerged after the change of regime. One of the most important events in dissolving the monolithic power structure took place on 18th May, 1988: it is the date of the foundation of the first trade union being organised outside the National Council of Trade Unions (the former monolithical trade union confederation, the SZOT). It was the Democratic Trade Union of Scientific Workers. Later, a liberal national trade union appeared outside the former structure, which was the Liga. In August 1989 the Workers Councils (MOSZ) (formerly operated during 1956) was reorganised. In October 1989 a new autonomous confederation of professional trade unions of public service employees (SZEF) was created in the place of Trade Unions of Public Employees. By the end of 1989 there were more than 50 professional unions and autonomous trade unions. It became also clear that life passed by the organisational form of the previous monolithical confederation, the National Council of Trade Unions (SZOT), the only national level trade union organisation before 1989. The need to create a new form with new working style led to the transformation of National Council of Trade Unions into the National Confederation of Hungarian Trade Unions (MSZOSZ) on 5th March, 1990. A former SZOT-member, the Chemical Workers Confederation, did not enter the new confederation, the MSZOSZ but laid down another new national confederation, the Autonomous Trade Unions.

Not only trade unions have emerged but also several organisations of employers' interest representation have appeared. The need for national level cross-sectoral tripartite interest reconciliation has raised and it has been established with the participation of six national Hungarian trade union confederations and nine employers' organisations (see later) and the representatives of the government. This first, national level Council of Interest Reconciliation operated from 1989 until 1999.

In spring 1999 – as a consequence of the new (right-wing) coalition Government – the almost 10 year's old interest reconciliation system was abolished and in April a totally new system of social dialogue started to exist in Hungary. *When the social partners took note of the Government's intention to dissolve the Interest Reconciliation Council, the negotiating partners signed the temporary Statues of National Labour Council thereby establishing the new tripartite forum. The MSZOSZ representatives asked for two weeks to consider the step to be taken, and then they also signed the document.* The National Labour Council was considered to be the legal successor of the Interest Reconciliation Council. In the same month, April, 1999 a totally new forum, the Economic Council was emerged, a forum on consultation on economic policy not only for employees and employers but also for other institutions like the trade chambers, representatives of multinational companies, bank sector, etc. The trade unions expressed their fear of consultation becoming too fragmented and also their discontent of the decision of the Government on setting up the Economic Council without *any consultation with the Interest Reconciliation Council.*

In 2002 the newly elected left-wing government (socialists in alliance with the free liberals) re-established the system of the original tripartite Interest Reconciliation Council, not at least to the request of trade unions in exchange of their political support. In July 2002 the new socialist coalition government and the social partners concluded on the agreement on the "renewal of the interest reconciliation process", including the renewal of the tripartite consultation and negotiation and – as a new phenomenon – the promotion of bipartite, autonomous social dialogue.

In sum, the present interest reconciliation system is based on the agreement concluded by the social partners in 2002 on the renewal of the cross-sectoral national tripartite consultation and negotiation and the promotion of bipartite, autonomous sectoral social dialogue. The programme of the Government for 2002-2006 explicitly stated: "the Government claims for consultation and negotiation with social partners, the continuous reconciliation of interests with trade unions, employer organisations as well as with civil (non-governmental) organisations." Since then the national level interest reconciliation has regained its role in the yearly wage proposal bargaining and proposal on the increase of minimum wage, and its role in consulting on macroeconomic and legislative questions having influence on employees and labour market.

2. *Elements of interest representation and the participation system in Hungary Institutional context for participation in Hungary – state and play*

In Hungary the different elements of industrial relations – including the participation system – do exist, like trade unions as bodies of interest-representation; workers' councils like main bodies of workers' participation; employees' participation in supervisory boards. As it was mentioned at macro-level there are six trade union confederations taking part in the macro-level cross-sectoral negotiation and social dialogue (public sector (SZEF, ÉSZT); competitive sector MSZOSZ (industry and services), Autonomous (public services), Liga (liberal) and Workers' Councils (Christian-democratic).

At mezzo-level there are the industrial federations, mostly members of one of the confederation. At micro-level there are the company level trade unions, as we could see the Labour code allows setting them up if the employees ask to do it.

In Hungary in the competitive sector the Labour Code (Act XXII of 1992) – amended several times – has served as legal framework to protect the employees' social and economic interests. Information and consultation rights of workers are regulated by the Labour Code. The EC Directive 2002/14/EC on information and consultation has been implemented by the Labour Code as well. According to the Labour Code trade unions may request information from employers on all issues related to the economic interests and social welfare of employees in connection with their employment and employers shall not refuse such information. Additionally, trade unions shall be entitled to express their position and opinion to the employer concerning any employer actions (decisions) and to initiate talks in connection with such actions. Labour Code also concerns the system of national level – cross-sectoral – interest reconciliation (that is the tripartite social dialogue), trade unions as interest representation organisation, and workers' councils as participation bodies of employees.

The Public Servants' Act (1992) covers public services in education, health, etc. and the Civil Servants' Act (1992) covers state administration, gives detailed description of job classification, salary scales, promotion (based on qualification and seniority).

2.1. *Tripartite cross-sectoral social dialogue*

Presently in the framework of the National Council for the Reconciliation of Interests social partners are granted the right to be informed, the right of opinion, and the right of consent.

Within the framework of the National Council for the Reconciliation of Interests the workers' negotiating group is composed of one representative from each of the six national trade union organisations as

- Autonomous Trade Unions Confederation
- Confederation of Unions of Professionals
- Democratic Confederations of Free Trade Unions
- National Confederation of Hungarian Trade Unions
- National Federation of Workers' Councils
- Forum for the Co-operation of Trade Unions

The employers' negotiating group is composed of one-one representatives of nine national employer organisations as

- Union of Agrarian Employers
- National Federation of Consumer Co-operative Societies and Trade Associations
- Hungarian Association of Craftsmen's Corporations
- National Federation of Traders and Caterers
- Hungarian Industrial Association
- National Federation of Agricultural Cooperators and Producers
- Confederation of Hungarian Employers and Industrialists
- National Association of Strategic and Public Utility Companies
- National Association of Entrepreneurs and Employers

The National Council for the Reconciliation of Interests is entitled to gather information on all economic, social and labour related issues that significantly affect the interests of employers or workers, directly or indirectly.

In the framework of the National Council for the Reconciliation of Interests social partners' right of opinion especially relates to "drafting laws", regulations and administrative actions regarding the world of work such as the Labour Code (XXII of 1992), the Act on Labour Inspection (LXXV of 1996), the Act on Labour Protection (XCIII of 1993), the Act on Promoting Employment (IV of 1991), the Act on Vocational Training (LXXVI of 1993), the Adult Training Act (CI of 2001), the Act on Strikes (VII of 1989), the Act on Wage Guarantee Fund (LXVI of 1994) and the Act on European Works Councils (XXI of 2003).

The Labour Code precisely lists the areas where governmental and ministerial decrees can only be issued with the consent of the social partners. This list includes:

- the national, statutory minimum wage, the maximum daily working hours and the number of public days off,

- the specific rules and measures on collective redundancies due to economic reasons, with a view to maintain or even increase employment also in these situations,
- the job classification system,
- the detailed rules of the compulsory reporting on collective agreements, and their registration,
- the justified derogations from the statutory minimum wage,
- the specific provisions on employment of people with disabilities,
- the register of occupations entitling to pre-retirement,
- any other specific derogation from the general statutory rules on employment.

Additionally, the Statute of the National Council for the Reconciliation of Interests provides right to consent for social partners in some other areas, such as:

- recommendations on principles and rules to be followed by the government and social partners
- alike; such as the recommendation on the annual average wage increase in the competitive sector;
- the rules of procedure and operation of the Labour Mediation and Arbitration Service, established by the OÉT, the Service's register of mediators and arbitrators, and the proposed appointment of the full time employees of the Service;
- the rules of procedure and operation of an institution to promote sectoral level social dialogue and consultation, and the proposed appointment of the head of the institution."[1]

Presently, at national level according to the Labour Code "The Government shall discuss issues of national significance pertaining to labour relations and employment relationships with the interest representation organizations of employees and employers through the National Council for the Reconciliation of Interests." (Section 16) The Government, with the agreement of the National Council for the Reconciliation of Interests, among other duties decrees the provisions for the mandatory minimum wage and the guaranteed wage minimum which is by now established in accordance with the level of education and/or vocational training of the employee required for a particular job or position, and the supervision of labour relations; further more it shall also submit recommendations to define the maximum duration of daily work time and to determine official holidays. The Government shall initiate wage negotiations on national level in the National Council for the Reconciliation of Interests.

---

1 http://www.szmum.gov.hu/main.php?folderID=16238&articleID=30381&ctag=articlelist&iid=1.

2.2. *Emerging sectoral level bipartite social dialogue*

One of the greatest shortcomings of the period following the change of regime is that no comprehensive system of sectoral collective agreements has evolved as a key regulative instrument of market economy.

"In Hungary the Phare twinning project number HU 0104-01 on 'The strengthening of the autonomous social dialogue' promoted the emergence of Sectoral Dialogue Committees since 2003. The Government has committed itself to the development and maintenance of the social dialogue, and in this framework the creation of system of Sectoral Dialogue is considered as a priority task.[2] According to the agreement between the social partners and government signed in March 2003 the Government takes responsibility to operate the Sectoral dialogue also after the end of Phare project (March 31, 2004). The Phare project firstly made an attempt to establish 18 Sectoral Dialogue Committees during the project period. Instead of 18 committees 20 Sectoral Dialogue Committees were set up until November 2003 and in another 9 sectors the partners have already signed an agreement to develop a committee. The need for such institution is indicated by the fact that by 2008 there are already 35 sectoral or subsectoral social dialogue committees in operation. The Sectoral Dialogue Committees has been set up in sectors or subsectores like agriculture, food, beverage, tobacco, mining, bakery, light industries (textile, cloths and leather), pharmaceuticals, metallurgy, electrical energy, construction, trade (possible subsectoral dialogue committee in the retail trade), tourism and catering, public catering (subsectorial committee), travel agencies (subsectoral committee), hotel (subsectoral committee), catering (subsectoral committee), air transportation (subsectoral committee), telecommunication, informatics (subsectoral committee), water supplying, settlement running, other communal services, rehabilitation employment, chemicals, mail services, Gas industry (subsectoral),

---

2 Ministry of Employment Policy and Labour
We should not forget that the European Commission and the European social partners (especially ETUC) have set serious requirements to the Hungarian social dialogue system. In the past period, they criticised the Hungarian practice of social dialogue on numerous occasions. The government jointly with the social partners enhanced to improve social dialogue. In this spirit a Phare project was proposed in order to strengthen the underdeveloped area of sectoral collective bargaining.
Accordingly, the specific tasks for the entire preparation period are as follows:
2/1: to strengthen the sectoral level of the Hungarian system of social dialogue through the establishment of so-called Sectoral Dialogue Committees
2/2: to extend the knowledge of the social partners concerning the European social dialogue and support their preparation for tasks awaiting them once Hungary becomes a member of the European Union.

railway transportation, mechanical industry, public road transportation (subsector),health sector, culture and arts, education.

On 2nd July, 2003 the Sectoral Council signed a framework agreement on the principles of operation of the Sectoral Dialogue Committees.[3] On its meeting in 27th October 2003 the National Interest Reconciliation Council agreed that the Sectoral Dialogue Committees (SDC) should emphasize on bargaining of the sectoral wage tariffs and concluding agreements on wage tariffs.

There are already some Hungarian Sectoral Dialogue Committees which take part in the European Sectoral Dialogue Committees (Joint Committee), like the Sectoral Dialogue committee in agriculture and catering since 1998, the electrical energy sector since 2000.

2.3. Social dialogue and workers' participation at company level

At company level the bodies of the workers' interest representation are the trade unions and shop stewards, meanwhile the workers' participation is realised first of all by the workers' councils.

2.3.1. Trade unions

Trade union rights

According to the Section (19) of Labour Code employees are entitled to organize trade unions within the labour organization and trade unions have the right to inform their members of their rights and obligations concerning their financial, social, cultural, as well as living and working conditions, furthermore to represent their members vis-a-vis the employers and before government agencies in matters concerning labour relations and employment.

The Labour Code – implementing the EU Directive on information and consultation – concerns the "*a)* 'employer's obligation to provide information to the trade union or workers' council (shop steward)'. This shall mean transmission of

---

3 According to it the partners on the two sides or recognise mutually each another as partners or if not, then on a base of a rather complicated calculation the partners should fulfil the representativity criteria. They are like:
- the participants must have legal personality and must have right to represent the employees' or employers' interests
- must operate legally at least already two years
- and other specific criteria like the result on the workers' councils election, number of trade unionists, active participation in the social dialogue, membership in organisation which takes part in the national level interest reconciliation council, membership in international trade union organisation for the employees' side.

information by the employer to the employees' representatives (as defined in the Act) relating to employment and labour relationships in order to enable them to acquaint themselves with the subject matter and to examine it so as to formulate an opinion; *b)* 'consultation' which shall mean the exchange of views and establishment of dialogue between the trade union or workers' council (shop steward) and the employer." (Section 15/B, Labour Code) Employers shall consult the local trade union branch prior to passing a decision in respect of any plans for actions affecting a large group of employees, in particular those related to proposals for the employer's reorganization, transformation, the conversion, privatization and modernization of a strategic business unit into an independent organization. (Section 21) Trade unions may request information from employers on all issues related to the economic interests and social welfare of employees in connection with their employment. If there is no workers' council at an employer, the employer shall inform the trade union: a) at least every sixth month regarding the fundamental issues affecting the employer's economic situation; and b) regarding the plans for major decisions pertaining to a significant modification of the employer's sphere of activities and investment projects; c) at least every sixth month regarding the trends in wages and salaries, liquidity related to the payment of wages, the characteristic features of employment, utilization of work time, and the characteristics of working conditions (section 22).

Trade union coverage and structure

The trade union coverage in Hungary is estimated to be around 13% in service sector, 15% in industry, near to 30% in the public sector.[4]

Characteristics of collective negotiation – as the main task of the trade unions

In Hungary there are no macro-level – cross-sectoral – collective agreements. As we could see, at macro-level the tripartite National Interest Reconciliation Council decides on minimum wages and gives yearly orientation figures for the next year wage increase.

Despite the effort to promote the bipartite sectoral level social dialogue and the possibility to extend the scope of the collective agreements sectoral collective agreements has been signed until now only in some sectors like in the bakery, electricity, construction and hotel and catering sector. (The minister in charge of employment and labour may extend the scope of the collective agreement to the

4 ",Industrial relations in Europe 2006", European Commission, 1.chapter, 1.2, "The social partners as membership organisations: an overview or forms and trends in the member states".

entire sector (or subsector), if so requested by the parties.) Supporting the collective and wage bargaining as the main tasks of trade unions is at company level. At the present time in Hungarian practice, negotiation is most common at enterprise level. According to the Labour Code trade unions shall be entitled to conclude collective bargaining agreements, which have to contain better conditions for the employers than what the Labour Code contains. In the competitive sector the agreements on wages are important part of the collective agreements. A collective agreement may be concluded, on the one hand, by an employer, an employer interest representation organization, or several employers, and on the other hand by a trade union or several trade unions. The collective agreements may be concluded at workplace (company) level or at branch (sectoral) level. A collective agreement shall also apply to the employees of the affected employer who are not members of the trade union concluding the collective agreement. (Section 36) Collective agreements may govern: a) rights and obligations originating from employment relationships, the method of exercising and fulfilling and the procedural order of such relationships; b) the relations between the parties to the collective agreement. (Section 30, Labour Code). The main topics included in the collective agreements are the wages and earnings, working conditions, working time and work organisation, health and safety issues. The wage agreements could refer to the average wage, the basic salary growth, a specific minimum wage. In case of collective agreements bound in public sphere the collective agreements covering more than one employer are bound always by employers as in this sphere we may not found employers' organisations. The wages in public administration and civil sector are regulated by strict wage tariffs.

Despite the existence of obligatory registering the figures in concern of coverage by collective agreement are uncertain. In the public information website of the Hungarian Information System of Industrial Relations in August 2008 the latest obtainable data are from 2004. According to the Register of Collective Agreements (operated in the Ministry of Labour) at company level 3293 agreements have been concluded, covering 886762 employees (around 30% of employees) (situation on 30th June 2004).[5] We have different figures if looking at the Labour Force Survey (KSH (2005), p. 51), from 3 246 662 employees 25.2% answered positively to the question of the survey whether there is a valid collective agreement at the workplace. 48.2% of the respondents answered that there isn't a valid agreement, and 26.6% don't know it. Near 50% of the employees are covered by collective agreement in sectors like energy, transport and telecommunications; around 40% of employees are covered in sectors of education, health and social services and mining. The less covered sectors are the building

5 http://www.szmm.gov.hu/mkir/doksik/ksz/2004/hatalyos_04.pdf.

industry (5.6%), the hotel and catering (7.9%) and trade and repair (8.8%). 34% of white collar and only 18.5% of blue collar workers are covered by valid collective agreement. 60% of the employees covered by collective agreement answered positively to the question whether working schedule and payment are influenced by the collective agreement or not.

2.3.2. Workers' councils

The main bodies of workers' participation are the workers' councils. The Labour Code of 1992 institutionalised workers' councils at workplace level and separated the authority of local union sections from that of workers' councils. The Labour Code originally gave the right of collective bargaining to trade unions, while workers' councils were designed to be information and consultation (participation) bodies. Separation was achieved originally by transferring information and consultation rights from unions to workers' councils.

In 2001, the right-wing government introduced a major amendment of the Hungarian Labour Code (as originally adopted by Act XXII 1992) introducing more flexibility in working time, and other areas and gave the right to workers' councils to conclude workplace agreement with the legal effect of a collective agreement if there was no union section at a given workplace. This decision shocked all trade unions as it meant to take the bargaining monopoly of the trade unions away.

In 2002 the newly elected left-wing government soon amended the Labour Code. Amending Act XIX of 2002 – supported by the trade unions – entered into effect on 1st September 2002. It repealed the amendment made by the previous right-wing government authorising workers' councils to conclude workplace agreement. So the trade union bargaining monopoly has been re-established. The amendment increased also the rights of trade unions at company level. The new amendment including employers' duty of consultation towards unions and maintaining the same towards workers' councils created a kind of double consultation duty, imposing the employer to consult with both trade union and workers' council. As all representative unions at a company have been entitled to consultation rights, the amendment could resulted several parallel channels of consultation.

At the present time (1) A workers' council shall be elected at all employers or at all of the employers' independent operational facilities (divisions) with more than fifty employees.

(2) A shop steward shall be elected at an employer or at an independent operational facility (division) of an employer with at least fifteen but no more than fifty-one employees. (Labour Code, Section 43). Workers' council members are elected by all employees.

Workers' council rights

The employer has to inform the workers' council at least in every 6 month on the business performance, liquidity of the company, wages and staff, use of working time, working conditions, persons working in tele-work and plans on serious change in the sphere of activity or investments (in accordance of the European Directive on Information and Consultation. Workers' councils shall be entitled to request information from the employers concerning all issues related to the employees economic and social interests in connection with employment, and with the observance of discrimination regulations. Employers may not refuse to disclose such information. The employer has to begin consultation with Workers' councils or in absence with committee set up by the local trade union in case of planning collective redundancies fifteen days prior to the decision and measures affecting major groups of employees (restructuring, reorganisation, privatisation)

In order to reach an agreement, the consultations shall cover

a) the possible ways of avoiding collective redundancies,
b) the principles of redundancies,
c) the means of mitigating the consequences, and
d) reducing the number of employees affected.

The employer must have the prior opinion of workers' council on

- *Holiday plans*
- *New methods of work organisation*
- *Internal regulations affecting the interests of employees*

A) Right of codetermination

According to the section 65 of Labour Code workers' councils shall have the right of codetermination with regard to a) the appropriation of welfare funds, and b) the utilization of welfare institutions and real property of such nature, as specified in the collective agreement.

B) Right of consultation

Employers shall consult the workers' council prior to adopting a decision in connection with a) plans for actions affecting a large group of employees, in particular those related to proposals for the employer's reorganization, transformation, the conversion, privatization and modernization of a strategic business unit into an independent organization; b) proposals for setting up a personnel records system; c) plans connected with employee training, proposals for the appropriation of job assistance subsidies for the betterment of employment conditions, and drafts of plans for early retirement; d) plans for actions pertaining to the occupational rehabilitation of persons who suffered some degree of health impairment or whose capacity to work has diminished; e) the plan for the annual vacation schedule; f) the introduction of new work organization methods and performance requirements; g) plans for internal regulations affecting the employees' substantive interests; h) tenders announced by the employer offering financial reward or recognition of exemplary performance.

C) Right of information

Employers shall notify the workers' council a) at least every sixth month regarding the fundamental issues affecting the employer's economic situation, and b) regarding the plans for major decisions pertaining to a significant modification of the employer's sphere of activities and investment projects; c) at least every sixth month regarding the trends in wages and salaries, liquidity related to the payment of wages, the characteristic features of employment, utilization of work time, and the characteristics of working conditions, d) at least every sixth month regarding the number of tele-workers and the description of the jobs they perform.

2.3.3. Supervisory boards

The other form of workers' participation is the presence in the Supervisory Boards. According to the Company Law (36 §. 1 point) the representative of employees has the right to take part in the Supervisory board in case c), that it concerns any company with staff over 200 persons. The employees' representative has no right to take part in the Board of directors. In case of right to participate in supervisory board, one third of the members of the Supervisory board are the representatives of employees. The number of members of the supervisory board is min 3- max 15 persons. As they are in minority and if their opinion differs from the opinion of the majority in the supervisory board, there is an obligation to make the minority's opinion known to the highest body (like board of directors) of the company. The employees' representative in the Supervisory board is nominated by the workers' council, following a consultation with the trade union/s at the workplace.

II. Analytical part of presentation

1. Practical effectiveness and promotion of workers participation rights and institutions

Are the highly developed and complex institutional and legal settings sufficient to perform efficient workers participation? How efficient is the Hungarian participation system? Is the trade union has effects on the management? *There was an attempt to obtain empirical evidences when a database (named* Berbarometer database) *was developed in Hungary in 2006/2007 within the framework of a European (EQUAL) project containing a sample of 10000 respondents.*[6]

1.1. About the database

The target population for the Hungarian survey was basically the

- Active-age population
- Population of the whole country
- All industries (based on NACE classification)
- All professions (professions based on ISCO classification) and
- Some pensioners of active-age were included

The first part of the survey (2500 questionnaires) was carried out by a professional team using their own sample. The second part of the survey was done by trade union activists. They covered the whole country guaranteeing territorial representativeness. While the first survey was realised mainly in bigger settlements (cities, towns, big villages), trade union activists reached small villages as well, covering all types of settlements. As a consequence of the fact that the second and bigger part of the survey was performed – under professional guidance – by trade union activist, the companies with trade union organisation are overrepresented within the sample. From our point of view it means that the present sample reflects the conditions well where trade union operates and – among others – we can look for the rate of trade unionisation and the rate of coverage by collective agreement in a company related to the workers' influence on management.

The sample reflects the fact well that despite the efforts to promote the sectoral level collective bargaining in Hungary the vast majority of collective agreements are signed at company (micro) level, yet. In our database the overwhelming majority of those who are covered by collective agreement are covered by company level agreement (91%).

6 See the project at www.berbarometer.com.

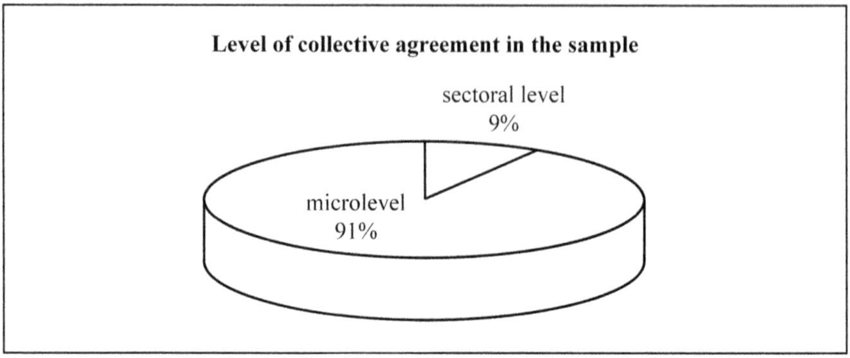

Source: Berbarometer database

1.2. Trade union effectiveness

Influence of trade union on the management

As we told previously the persons covered by trade unions and collective bargaining are overrepresented in the sample: 68% of them (6400 persons) work at a company where trade union organisation operates, 54% of them (around 500 persons) where workers' council organisation is present, 62% of them (around 6200 persons) are covered by collective agreement.

Distribution of persons answering "yes" or "no" to the related question

Answer	Trade union at the company	Collective agreement at the company	Influence of TU on the management	% of respondents influenced by collective agreement
No	28%	28%	41%	16%
Yes	68%	62%	45%	73%
doesn't concern or don't know	5%	10%	14%	12%

Source: Berbarometer database

Despite the high incidence of coverage by collective agreement and the high presence of both trade union and workers' council, only 45% of the respondents (a little more than 4000 persons) think that the trade union has influence on the management. Taking the high incidence of trade union presence into consideration we could not suppose that according to 41% of the respondents (around 3800 persons) the trade union has no influence on the management. We have to conclude that the influence of trade unions on the management is lower as it would follow from their presence at company level. On the other hand the percentage of coverage by collective agreement corresponds to the percentage of trade union coverage. To be fair we have to underline that in Hungary the main task of trade unions is to bargain the collective agreement; the employees' participation – which means directly influence the management – is carried out by such bodies like the workers' councils, or employees' delegates in supervisory boards.

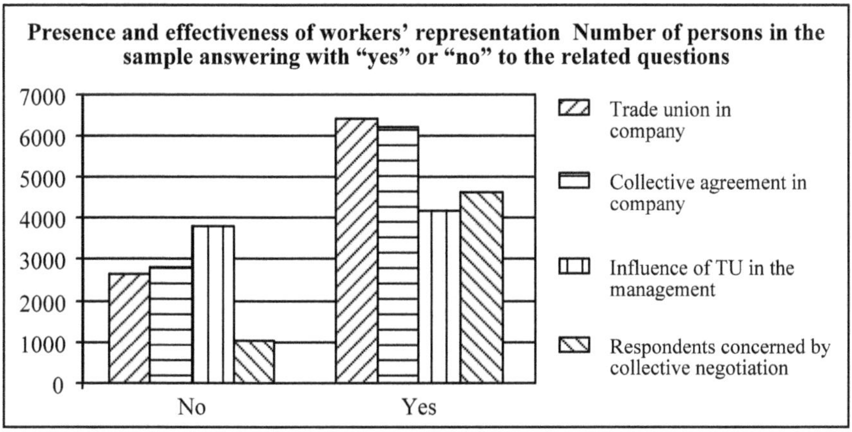

Source: Berbarometer database

Scope and content of collective agreement

In Hungary at a company the collective agreement is valid also in concern of employees who are not trade union members. According to the database a big amount of respondents (10%) do not have any idea whether they are covered or not by any collective agreements. 25% of the respondents do not know whether the valid collective agreement in his or her workplace regulates only wages or also the working conditions, and 12% do not know whether the collective negotiation concern them or not.

The trade unions have to draw the consequences: it is not enough to be present in the undertaking and to carry our collective bargaining or conclude collective agreement, it is also necessary to make their activity and results known, inform the trade union members and also the non-members. At the present time when trade union membership is constantly decreasing (because of different reasons) the PR and the dissemination of outcomes can be for example important tools to recruit new members.

Knowledge on the content of collective agreement

Sectors	**Number of respondents who does not know whether the collective agreement contains regulation on working conditions or not?**	**Total number of respondents to the question**	**% of those who are not informed in the total number of respondents**
competitive sphere	1321	5640	23%
public sector	601	2136	28%
non-profit sector	81	264	30%

Source: Berbarometer database

Employees in the competitive sector are the best informed on the content of collective agreement and so on the activity of trade unions and the less informed are those working in the non-profit sector: in the competitive sector 23% of all respondents are not informed about the content of the collective agreement, and in the non-profit sector 30% of the respondents.

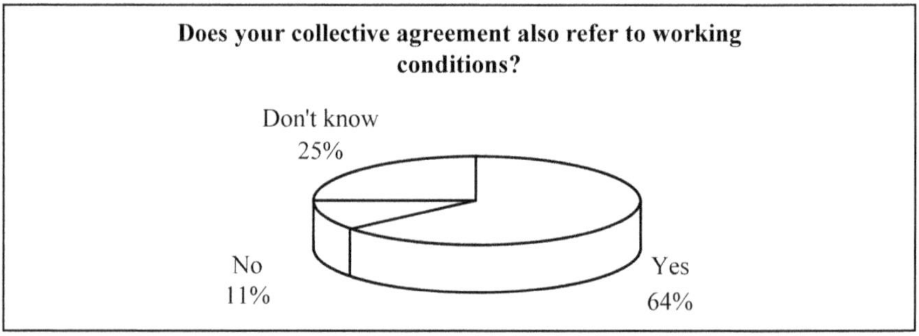

Source: Berbarometer database

In general the collective agreement contains a yearly renewed wage agreement and another agreement for more than one year including the regulation of other working conditions, the rights and duties of employees and trade unionists. 5265 persons responded positively and only 876 respondents answered negatively to the question whether or not the collective agreement regulated also the working conditions?

2. *Workers' councils: up and down.*

What are the Hungarian experiences of co-existence of trade unions (interest representation bodies) and workers' councils at workplace level? Are they competitive or cooperative?

The Labour Code approved in 1992 took the German model as a sample. The concept of workers' councils was not popular for the trade unions. Further, in 2001, the then right-wing government introduced a major amendment of the Labour Code which meant to increase the potential of workers' councils and decrease the potential of trade unions.

Since than the workers councils have been established. According to the before mentioned Berbarometer database more than half of the respondents answered positively to the question in concern of existence of workers' council at his or her company near to the rate of persons responding positively to the trade union presence in their workplace.

Does workers' council operate in your company?
Distribution of persons answering "yes" and "no" to the question

Answer	Number of respondents	%
No	3677	39%
Yes	5033	54%
doesn't concern	628	7%
Total	9338	100%

Source: Berbarometer database

The almost similar volume of presence of trade unions and workers' councils in workplaces is not incidental; it is favoured not only by the regulation (the obligation to establish workers' council over staff of 50 persons) and the practice (presence of trade unions in middle and big companies). There is also the fact that despite the original concept of the competitiveness of the two bodies, in practice in a big number of cases workers' councils have been established in companies where trade unions are active and in the majority of the cases the personnel of workers' councils and trade union organisations in the company overlaps one another.

Presence and effectiveness of workers' representation Number of persons in the sample answering with "yes" or "no" to the related questions

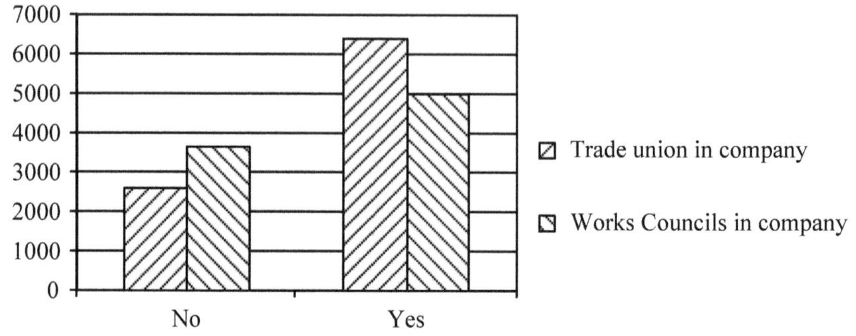

Source: Berbarometer database

The regulation of Labour Code in concern of election of members of workers' council also facilitates this kind of overlapping. According to it if there is no workers' council at an employer, the election committee shall be formed from the representatives of local trade union branches and/or the non-union employees. A local trade union branch may independently nominate a candidate among its members. (section 49).

Looking at the issue of competitiveness or cooperativeness of the two bodies we may put the question whether trade union influence on the management is higher in those companies where workers' council operates or not?

According to the BérBarometer database in 86% of the cases trade union has an influence on the management in those workplaces where both workers' council and trade union are present and in workplaces where only trade union was present it was only 14%! It clearly shows the synergy of the presence of the two bodies.

Influence of trade union on the management, number of respondents

Presence of employees' bodies	Trade union has influence on the management
Both workers' council and trade union are present	3468
Only trade union is present	573

Source: Berbarometer database

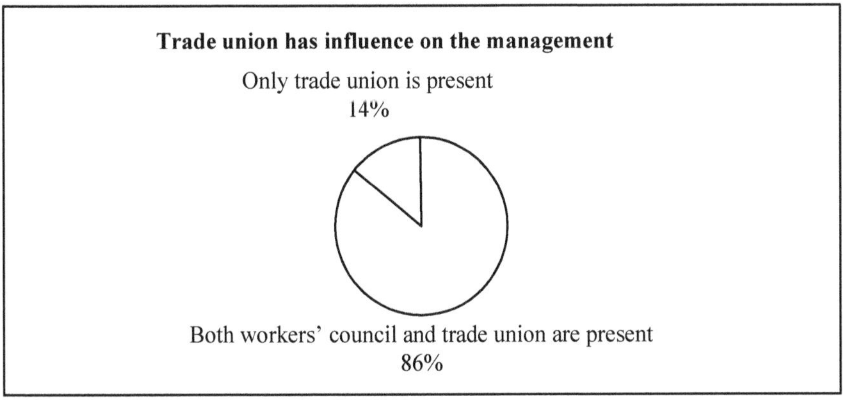

Source: Berbarometer database

The database contains answers to the question about the respondents worrying on their respective workplace. Does the joint presence of workers' body give a higher grade of security feeling?

Do you worry about your workplace?

	Number of persons responding that they absolutely worry	**all concerned respondents in the % of the total number of respective respondents**
Both workers' council and trade union are present	1478	32%
Only trade union is present	465	34%

Source: Berbarometer database

4664 persons responded to the question "Do you worry about your workplace?" who work at a company where both trade union and workers' council operates. 32% of them (1478 persons) answered that they were absolutely worrying about their workplace. 1353 persons responded to the question who worked in workplaces where only trade union operates. 34% of them (465 persons) responded that they are absolutely worrying about their workplace that is slightly more than in the previous case.

In Hungary in practice the coexistence of workers' council and trade union body at a workplace contributes to a better performance of interest representation and because of the frequent "personal union" they are cooperative and not competitive as it was supposed at the launching of the system.

The Berbarometer database also reveals that – despite the regulation – several times workers' councils are not established at companies with more than 50 employees. 1524 respondents, 41% of those who responded "no" to the question whether workers' council operates or not at his or her company – are employed at companies with more than 50 employees. The incidence is very high in the case of respondents working at companies of 50-250 employees (middle-size companies). Only 8% of the respondents work at big companies (with more than 500 employees) where workers' council does not operate.

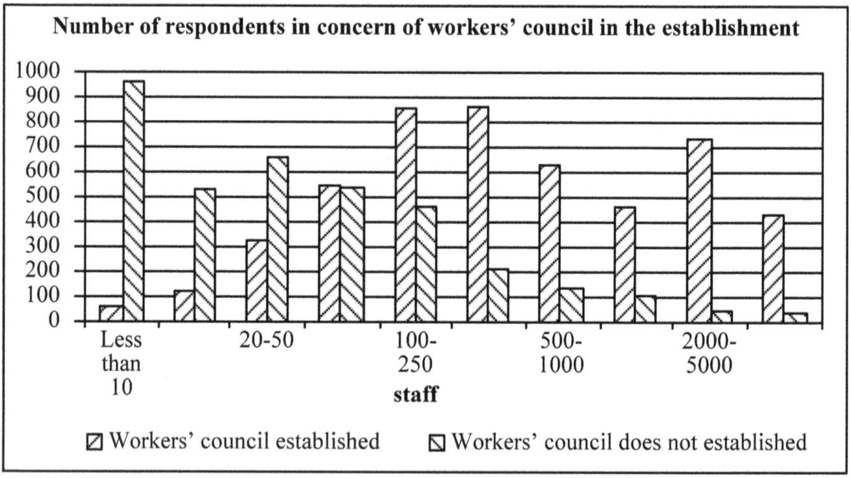

Source: Berbarometer database

How has the essence of European directive on information and consultation (IC) been implemented in the practice, or how does the concretisation of Labour Code perform? According to a survey on the content of collective agreements[7] we could differentiate 3 types of the implementation of IC directive by workers' councils and trade unions. According to the 1. type (well) operating workers' council and trade union operates; the information is predominantly given in written form and the president of the workers' councils may take part in the managerial meetings. According to the 2. type there is not any workers' council and the information flow is ad hoc and predominantly oral. In case of 3. type the workers' councils and trade

7 Analysis of Collective agreements, http://www.szmm.gov.hu/mkir/kszelemzesek.php.

unions are "overlapping"; information is given them at the same time, mainly orally.

In Hungary the other way of workers' participation is the presence in the Supervisory board. Taking part in the Supervisory board is a good source of information for the employees, but only if the information is disseminated after the meetings. The usefulness of taking part in the supervisory board for the employees depends not at least also on the personality of the nominated person, on which extent he or she makes use of the position, disseminates the information to the other employees.

4. *Solutions and lessons*

What is going wrong and how to solve it?

How the workers participation could be more effective? What are the main problems and obstacles? What measures would be beneficial? In what direction would it be useful to develop the institutional context and what else would be needed?

The growing flexibility of labour market and new types of work organisation (tele-work) and new types of works (IT sector) go on not only with decreasing membership but also with decreasing solidarity. The trade union membership is aging; there are difficulties to reach young generation. There is no strategy for example in concern of reaching and unionisation of growing strata of self-employed and/or employed in micro-and small enterprises. The training – which would prepare and coach the workers to take part in the institutions of participation and interest representation – is insufficient and fragmented.

We may lay down that in Hungary the regulations and the institutional context for the workers' participation and interest representation have been developed and are at disposal. The regulations need to be implemented in practice as much as possible. It is also sure that we need a complex workers' participation and interest representation strategy (based on well expressed values) instead of sporadic measures, we need a system with cooperative elements, we need solid research and training background, promoting communication among the bodies/institutions at the different levels, we need to find new ways to attract members, and new ways to disseminate real results of workers' participation. The institutional context for participation and interest representation is the primordial and basic condition to realise genuine interest protection of employees in every aspect at a company. As a conclusion, in Hungary it's time to look not only after hardware but also software in the workers' participation and interest representation process.

Sources

Berbarometer database, Budapest, EQUAL/H005 project, 2007, www.berbaro meter.com
EC Directive 2002/14/EC on information and consultation
Hungary: EU enlargement and the trade unions, South East Europe Review, SEER, Baden – Baden, 2000, number 1, ISSN 1435-2869, pp. 97-109
Industrial relations in Europe (2006), European Commission
Labour Force Survey (2005), Budapest KSH
Labour Code (Act XXII of 1992), Budapest

Informing and consulting employees in Poland – Problems of implementation of Directive 2002/14/EC

Maria Matey-Tyrowicz

1. Background

Poland has a well-known tradition of employee participation idea, which emerged as soon as in 1956, during the first great crisis of communism in Poland in the "Polish October 1956". It is famous for the establishment in the then socialist enterprises of spontaneous, authentic workers' councils, which unfortunately were eradicated soon after by the powerful communist authorities. The next attempt to advocate this democratic idea in the then failing communist system in Poland was the adoption, under pressure from the newly created "Solidarity" movement, in 1981, during the so-called "Solidarity carnival", of the Law on Workers' Self-Management in State-owned Enterprises), whose fruits were soon wiped away by the martial law. Parenthetically, the law is still in force in Poland today, but is applies only to state-owned enterprises, whose number has been seriously reduced as a result of privatization process and expansion of the newly-emerged market economy in Poland, so it lost any practical importance in contemporary economic reality of Poland.

The historical course of events in Poland – "Solidarity", its fight and systemic victory – resulted in the emergence in Polish political life of a sense of great social and economic importance of trade unions, of which sense "Solidarity" trade union has remained a guardian until now, although the apogee of this movement's force has passed. The historical importance of trade unions – from which both "Solidarity" and other most representative trade unions, including those of post-communist origin, derive their strength – affects the formation of the industrial relations model in Poland, as well as the substance of labour law and its particular institutions. This very phenomenon became apparent in the Polish approach to implementing the EU principle of informing and consulting employees, which – in the first legislative measure – was subordinated to "trade union monopoly", which was recently stigmatized by the Constitutional Tribunal, as we shall see further on.

What is characteristic is that such "uplift" or, as it is often called colloquially, "dictatorship" of trade unions in Poland concerns their political position and legal status in the country as such and does not translate directly into the actual importance of trade unions in enterprises, particularly in private ones, which are now the dominant sector of market economy in contemporary Poland (trade union membership in private enterprises is very low, ranging from 0% to 10%, with a very high number of enterprises where union do not exist at all). In addition, in contrast to the high formal position of the most representative nationwide trade unions, connected also with their participation in the main body for social dialogue in Poland – the Tripartite Commission for Social and Economic Matters – trade union's powers in enterprises, established for several decades in the Labour Code to protect employee rights, e.g. in the field of protection against unfair dismissal, are being gradually reduced or completely eliminated in subsequent labour law amendments undertaken under the pressure of free-market mechanisms.

2. The course of implementation of Directive 2002/14/EC in Poland

The adoption in the European Union of Directive 2002/14/EC on informing and consulting employees occurred at the time when in Poland employee participation was disappearing in the more and more numerous private enterprises. The state of law in this regard was as follows: 1/ the Polish Constitution of 1997 makes, in Art. 20, a general reference to solidarity, dialogue and cooperation between social partners as an element of social market economy, which is the grounds for the economic system of the Republic of Poland, however, the Constitution does not mention any other social partner on employee side apart from trade unions, 2/ although the Labour Code (adopted in 1974, amended many times, including a number of fundamental amendments after 1989) has included for several decades Art. $18^{(2)}$, according to which "employees shall participate in the management of an employing establishment within the scope of and according to the rules specified in separate provisions", however, these separate provisions comprised, until recently, only the Law of 1981 on Workers' Self-management in State-owned Enterprises, which applies only to state-owned enterprises. This means that until 2006 when the law of 7 April 2006 on informing and consulting employees (Polish Journal of Laws Nr 79/2006, item 550), implementing the Directive 2002/14/EC, has been adopted, there were no separate provisions, as mentioned in Art. $18^{(2)}$ of the Labour Code, which would concern employee participation in private enterprises.

Thus, until 2006, Poland lacked any legal regulations concerning employee participation in the majority private sector of the national economy or even an outline, enjoying broader public support, of a conception of their model, which would be desirable and feasible in the market economy. What is more, both social partners showed no interest in it: employers' circles, busy achieving their successes in gradual elimination of trade unions from workplaces, felt no need to replace them with any other representation on the employee side, while trade unions did not want any other employee representation to emerge and potentially threaten their tough-to-maintain existence in private enterprises.

The need to implement Directive 2002/14/EC in the Polish law appeared in the context of complete lack of conceptual preparedness and any agreements in the Polish social dialogue (the situation was in no way improved by the fact that earlier, as part of implementation of Directive 94/45/EEC on European Works Councils, the Polish Law of 5 April 2002 on European Works Councils (Polish Journal of Laws No. 62/2002, item 556) was adopted). Unsurprisingly, implementation in the Polish law of Directive 2002/14/EC was fraught with huge difficulties, resulting in over one year's delay in adoption of the relevant bill and the threat of the EU applying coercive measures. As the first stage, some nationwide social partners suggested that they saw a chance to negotiate, among themselves, the principles of future legal regulation implementing the Directive, which was readily supported by the state authorities, yet any attempts at negotiations proved a complete failure. In this situation, under the pressure of time and intervention of the European Commission, the matter was referred to the ordinary parliamentary path, in which at the turn of 2004 and 2005 work focused on four mutually competitive drafts of laws, submitted by the government, employers' organizations, most representative trade unions and a group of Deputies of the parliamentary Left. The key controversy among these drafts was who should represent employees in enterprises in which trade unions operate – the unions or representations especially elected for this purpose by the workers[1]. Trade unions fought to assure themselves the exclusive power ("monopoly") to exercise rights concerning employee information and consultation and finally reached the goal. The employers' attitude was characterized by reluctance to broadening trade union powers to include matters of information and consultation but, on the other hand, by the fear that establishing new employee representations will increase the costs of running enterprises and increase the risk of disclosing enterprise secrets. Adopted in such circumstances, facing EU sanctions for delay, the Law of 7 April 2006 on Informing and Consulting Employees is, as we shall see further on, a success of trade unions' pursuit to maintain exclusive powers of employee representation (at least in these enterprises where trade unions survived), which the employers accepted, eager to minimize the costs. The haste with which the law was

1 Cf. similarly J. Wratny: Zasada informacji i konsultacji pracowniczej w prawie europejskim. Uwagi dotyczące implementacji prawa europejskiego do prawa polskiego, [in:] "Informowanie i konsultacja pracowników w polskim prawie pracy", A. Sobczyk (ed.), Kraków 2008. Cf. also by the same author: Prawo pracowników do informacji i konsultacji w sprawach gospodarczych przedsiębiorstwa, "Praca i Zabezpieczenie Społeczne", June 2006, as well as L. Florek: Prawo pracowników do informacji konsultacji, "Monitor Prawa Pracy", 2006, No. 5.

worked on resulted, moreover, in various kinds of inconsistencies and legislative weaknesses that gradually came to light in the course of its application.

Upheld this way, trade unions' monopoly in the field of workers' representation was questioned in July 2008 by the Constitutional Tribunal as a result of complaint, filed by the Confederation of Polish Employers, about unconstitutionality of legal solutions of the 2006 law. Some legislative flaws in the law were removed after one year, by means of the law of 11 April 2008 on amendments to the 2006 law on Informing and Consulting Employees (Polish Journal of Laws No. 93/2008, item 584). This first amendment will be followed by ones needed as a result of the aforementioned judgment of the Constitutional Tribunal[2] and other apparent weaknesses of the Law.

The model of informing and consulting employees, outlined in the 2006 law, which consists in the formation of employees' councils under the auspices of representative trade unions (in enterprises where they exist) is nowadays, although with difficulties[3], implemented in Poland. What is interesting, out of some 2,500 councils registered by the Ministry of Labour as at the beginning of 2008, the majority were formed before the law's entry into force pursuant to the authorization to apply "pre-agreements", contained in Art. 5 of the Directive, probably with the aim to provide for independence from the statutory solutions.

3. Employees' Councils pursuant to the law of 7 April 2006 on informing and consulting employees

a) Scope of application of the law

From March 2008, the law has applied to enterprises which have more than 50 employees (between May 2006 and March 2008 it covered only enterprises with more than 100 employees). The law does not apply to state-owned enterprises;

2 Judgment of the Constitutional Tribunal of 1 July, 2008, Nr K 23/07 (Polish Journal of Laws Nr 120/2008, item 778). Text of Judgment without Grounds.

3 These difficulties are signalled by the Polish National Labour Inspectorate (see report prepared by the National Labour Inspectorate for the conference "Informowanie i konsultacja pracowników w prawie polskim – w drugą rocznicę uchwalenia ustawy" *[Informing and consulting employees in the Polish law – the second anniversary of adoption of the Law]*, Uniwersytet Jagielloński, Kraków, 9-10 May 2008), they were identified by participants of the aforementioned conference, many articles in periodicals, as well as preliminary research results of S.Partner, member of Syndex Group, *Monitoring ustawy z dn. 7 kwietnia 2006r. o informowaniu pracowników i przeprowadzaniu z nimi konsultacji* (unpublished).

they are still covered by the legal regulation contained in the law of 1981 on Workers' Self-management in State-owned Enterprises.

b) Scope of the duty of informing and consulting employees

According to the law, "informing" means transmission by the employer to the employees' council of data in order to enable them to acquaint themselves with the subject matter, while "consultation" means exchange of views and establishment of dialogue between the employer and the employees' council.

Information

The employer is under a duty to provide the employees' council with information[4] about: 1/ their employer's activities and economic situation, as well as probable developments in this field, 2/ situation, structure and probable development of employment and any measures aimed to maintain the level of employment, 3/ measures likely to lead to substantial changes in work organisation or in grounds for employment.

The employer should provide such information in case of anticipated changes or measures, as well as upon written request of the employees' council; the information must be provided at a time, in a form and scope to enable the employees' council to familiarize themselves with the subject matter, analyze the information and, in matters which require consultation, prepare for consultation.

In matters covered by the duty of information, the employees' council may submit an opinion; adoption of an opinion requires the consent of the majority of employees' council members, while each member may submit a dissenting opinion, with which the employer should be provided.

Consultation

The employer is under a duty to consult[5] the employees' council in matters of: 1/ situation, structure and probable development of employment and any measures aimed to maintain the level of employment, 2/ measures likely to lead to substantial changes in work organisation or in grounds for employment.

---

4 P. A. Sobczyk: *Przedmiot i procedura informowania rady pracowników* [in:] "Informowanie i konsultacja pracowników w polskim prawie pracy", op. cit., Kraków, 2008.

5 Cf. J. Stelina: *Pojęcie i procedura konsultacji z radą pracowników* [in:] "Informowanie i konsultacja....." op. cit.

Consultations should be held: 1/ at such time, in such fashion and to such extent as to enable the employer to take steps in matters covered by the consultation, 2/ at the relevant level of management, depending on the subject under discussion, 3/ on the basis of information supplied by the employer and of the opinion presented by the employees' council, as well as the dissenting opinion of a employees' council member, 4/ in such a way as to enable employees' council to meet with the employer to obtain a standpoint, with reasons, about their opinion, 5/ in such a way as to enable reaching an agreement between the employees' council and the employer.

The employees' council and the employer hold consultations in good faith and with respect for the parties' interests. This formula is, in the Polish labour law, a general clause describing how social partners should act in collective labour relationships.

When discharging its tasks, the employees' council may avail itself of assistance of persons having specialist knowledge.

c) *Protection of confidential information*

Members of employees' councils are obliged not to disclose information being an enterprise secret, obtained in connection with their function, if the employer stipulates the duty to keep such information confidential. The prohibition of disclosure of information applies also after one ceases to perform the function, but no longer than for 3 years.

In particularly justified cases, the employer may choose not to provide the employees' council with information whose disclosure might, according to objective criteria, seriously disturb the enterprise's operation or pose a threat of considerable loss. However, if the employees' council considers keeping by the employer the information confidential or not disclosing it to be contrary to the law, the council may file with the court a motion for release from the obligation of confidentiality or for an order to the employer to make information available or to hold consultation.

d) *Number of members in an employees' council*

Employees' councils should have, according to the law, between 3 and 7 members; the latter number applies to enterprises with more than 500 employees. However, pursuant to the statutory rule that each representative trade union operating in an enterprise has the right to appoint at least one council member and bearing in mind that it is permissible for enterprise trade unions' to determine jointly different rules of representation in the employees' council, the numbers of members in the councils may be different.

e) Monopoly of representative trade unions

We already mentioned that the law provides for exclusivity of **representative**[6] trade unions in the procedure of informing and consulting employees in enterprises where such unions exist. The law completely ignores trade unions which do not fit in the definition of "representativity" (see footnote 6), deriving them of any importance whatsoever in the procedure of informing and consulting employees. Also the rights of employees who do not belong to trade unions in such procedures in the enterprises where representative trade unions operate were seriously limited (see below, subsection f/ "Rules of appointing employees' councils"). These solutions of the law were questioned by the Constitutional Tribunal in the Judgment of 1 July 2008 and will have to change within 12 months, as otherwise they will lose binding force with expiration of this period[7]. Until this amendment, new councils may be formed pursuant to the provisions which were held unconstitutional and their fate should be determined by the legislative way when amending the law.

---

6 In the Polish labour law there are two definitions of trade union representativity: 1/ the first one resulting from the law of 2001 concerning the Tripartite Commission for Social and Economic Matters, which refers to the large nationwide unions, determining the criteria which entitle them to participate in the Tripartite Commission, 2/ the second one resulting from Art. $241^{(17)}$ and $241^{(25a)}$ of the Labour Code, the said articles determining the trade unions' capacity to enter into collective labour agreements. The representativity "for collective agreements" defined in these two articles involves, generally speaking, either being part of a structure or membership in a representative trade union for the purposes of the Tripartite Commission for Social and Economic Matters, or grouping at least 10% of all employees to be covered by the collective labour agreement, or, finally, grouping the highest number of such employees. In various contexts, labour law provisions refer to the notion of representativity "for collective agreements"; this is also the case of the law of 2006 on Informing and Consulting Employees. Cf. more on this issue A. Sobczyk: *Reprezentatywność organizacji związkowej a wybory rady pracowników*, "Praca i Zabezpieczenie Społeczne", March 2008.

7 However, since at the time of drafting this text no written reasons for this judgment of the Constitutional Tribunal have been published, the suggested directions of such changes are still unknown.

f) Rules of forming employees' councils

The law in its current version establishes three procedures for forming employees' councils, depending on whether in the enterprise a representative trade union exist. If there is a trade union meeting the criterion of representativity identified in Art. $241^{(17)}$ or $241^{(25a)}$ of the Labour Code (see note 6), members of the council are appointed by the board of this organization (trade union procedure), which as a rule means choosing them from among members of this trade union. If there are two or more representative trade unions, they should appoint the council jointly and if they fail to reach an agreement on this issue by the statutory deadline of 30 days, the council is elected by all employees, but only from among candidates put forward by the representative trade unions (mixed procedure). Only if there is no representative trade union in the enterprise, is the council elected by all workers from among candidates put forward by groups of 10 or 20 persons, depending on whether the enterprise has below or over 100 employees (staff's procedure). The last procedure is applied as well in cases when there are no trade unions at all, as in the event when existing trade unions do not meet the criterion of representativity.

According to the more and more widespread opinion among the public, confirmed by the judgment of the Constitutional Tribunal of 1 July 2008, it is only the last procedure ("staff's procedure") that does not discriminate employees who do not belong to trade unions (or belong to non-representative ones) when appointing and recalling the employees' council and assessing the results of its work. However, even in this case the trade unions' monopoly wins in the law, which stipulates that a council elected according to this procedure must be dissolved within 6 months if a representative trade union appears in an enterprise where no such union operated before. The Constitutional Tribunal's judgment of July 2008 questions in full the constitutionality of the "trade union procedure", questions in part the constitutionality of the "mixed procedure" (to the extent to which it limits candidates for members of the employees' council only to those put forward by representative trade unions) and questions in full the constitutionality of the order to dissolve a council elected in the mixed procedure if a representative trade union appears in an enterprise where no such union operated before.

Elections of members of the employees' council appointed in the "staff's' procedure" (when no representative trade union operates in the enterprise), or in the "mixed" procedure (when there are multiple representative trade unions in the enterprise, but they fail to agree on joint appointment of the employees' council) must be organized by the employer upon written request of at least 10% employees, giving notice about the election date and the deadline for putting forward candidates for council members in the way accepted in the given enterprise. The notice must be given at least 30 days before election day and the deadline for putting forward candidates is 21 days.

All employees, save for minor persons, have electoral franchise. The right to stand for election is enjoyed by employees who have worked with the given employer for at least one year, without interruptions, unless the employer has operated for less than one year. The right to stand for election is not enjoyed by the employee who manages the enterprise, his/her deputy, an employee being a members of a collective body managing the enterprise, the chief accountant, legal counsel or a minor employee.

The election of employees' council members is a direct one, held by secret ballot. The election is valid if at least 50% of the workers employed by the enterprise have cast votes. If less than 50% took part in the election, 30 days after the election day, another election is held, which is considered valid regardless of the number of employees casting votes. Those candidates who received the highest numbers of votes become members of the employees' council.

Membership of the council elected in the "staff's" procedure (see above) ceases in case of termination or expiration of employment, giving up the function or application for cessation of membership, signed by at least 50% of workers employed at the enterprise for at least 6 months. Membership of the council appointed according to the "trade union" or "mixed" procedures ceases upon termination or expiration of employment, giving up the function or the person being recalled by a representative trade union.

The employer cannot, without consent of the employees' council, to give notice or terminate the employment of the worker who is its member during his/her membership in the council. The employer cannot, without the council's consent, unilaterally change the terms of work or pay to the detriment of an employee who is a members of the employees' council during such membership.

g) *Rules of operation of the employees' councils*

Within 30 days after election of the employees' council, the employer convenes the first council meeting. From among its members, the employees' council elects the chairperson (whose powers are not set forth in the law) and adopts its by-laws.

The general guiding principle in this respect is the statutory formula (applicable in the whole field of collective labour law) that the employees' council and the employer – as social partners – act in good faith and with respect for the other party's interests.

The employees' council determines with the employer, by agreement[8]: 1/ the rules and procedure for transmitting information and holding consultations, 2/ the procedure of resolving disputes, 3/ the rules of incurring costs connected with election and activities of the council, in particular one elected in the "staff's" procedure, as well as other issues; the provisions of such agreements should ensure the conditions for informing and consulting at least equal to those set forth in the law and should take into account interests of the employer and the employees. If such decisions are not taken by agreement, the provisions of the law apply.

h) Penal sanctions

The law provides for penal sanctions for persons who render the establishment of an employees' council impossible, fail to organize the election of the council or render it difficult, fail to transmit information to the employees' council or to hold consultations with it in matters provided for by laws, as well as those who discriminate a member of the employees' council due to his/her performance of acts connected with informing and consulting.

4. Necessary rectifications in the hitherto implementation of Directive 2002/14/EC in Poland

According to the widespread opinion in Poland, the purpose of Directive 2002/14/EC concerning informing and consulting employees was not achieved in full through implementation of the Directive by the Polish law of 7 April 2006 due to lack of conceptual preparedness of the model of informing and consulting employees (or rather due to immature socioeconomic relations for the model). Many experts claim that the law is not sufficiently harmonized with the Polish legal system and gives the impression of it has been clumsily and hastily "super-imposed" on it. In fact, first of all, the solutions adopted in the law focus – because of trade unions' pressure – on putting the EU principle of informing and consulting employees to work for the interests of representative trade unions, neglecting the principle's purpose, that is, assuring **employees** access to vital information in an enterprise and the right to consultation on employer's measures which concern them. According to the wording of the law in the years 2006-2008,

---

8 P. B. Wagner: Porozumienia zawierane na gruncie ustawy o informowaniu pracowników i przeprowadzaniu z nimi konsultacji [in:] "Informowanie i konsultacja….", op.cit.

employees who do not belong to trade unions for whatever reasons, which make up a vast majority of all employed persons, have no influence on the composition of employees' councils, especially those appointed in the "trade union" procedure (over 80% of the existing councils were appointed, according to research[9], by representative trade unions), or on assessment of functioning of these councils and their individual members. Moreover, the law does not oblige the councils – regardless of the procedure of their appointment – to share with the workers, both those who belong to trade unions and those who do not, the information obtained from the employer, which excludes them completely from the sharing the benefits of the principle of informing and consulting employees. The last shortcoming was also stigmatized by the Constitutional Tribunal.

Currently it is not yet known whether the reasons for judgment of the Constitutional Tribunal will provide any recommendations for the Polish legislator as to how – when the law is amended – to correctly draw the demarcation line between rights of the trade unions and the bodies implementing the principle of informing and consulting employees, that is, how far the legislative operation to eliminate excesses of trade union "monopoly" should go, whether the problem will burden state authorities and parliamentary bodies, and whether and to what extent it will be possible to use the mechanisms of tripartite social dialogue (which proved powerless at the stage of preparing the law of 2006 when no constructive and generally acceptable solutions were found).

The theses, sometimes formulated in Poland, about the need to completely eliminate the influence of trade unions on the functioning of the procedure of informing and consulting employees seem too radical (if at all feasible). Research conducted under the auspices of trade unions has shown that councils appointed in the trade union procedure, using the direct expert assistance and financial support of trade unions, operate more actively and efficiently than those elected by workers, which justifies fears that their existence may be threatened in the long run if they are deprived of such support. In addition, according to trade union assessment, in the current socioeconomic reality and in the current state of law it is only trade unions that assure that employees' councils as a body are independent of the employer[10].

The complexity of this situation foretells that the Polish legislator has to solve serious dilemmas, of extreme importance for the future of Poland's social market economy by the deadline fixed by the Constitutional Tribunal, not longer than 12 months after the day of publication of the judgment with reasons (which has not taken place yet).

---

9 See "Związkowe przywileje zostaną ograniczone", *Rzeczpospolita* daily of 7 July 2008.
10 Ibid.

Institutional context of workers participation in Bulgaria – which way after joining the EU

Ekaterina Ribarova

Workers representation rights, including information, consultations and other forms of participation are the main challenge for modernization of Bulgarian industrial relations and implementation of the European acquits communitarian. The beginning of the story of Bulgarian experience in workers 'participation might be indicated even in the period before 1989. The discussion about the workers' participation, which has began in early 1990-s hasn't been finished yet now, even after transposition of all of the EU-directives into the Bulgaria law. There are too many different points of view, too many supports, hesitations and resistance, concerning mainly to the alternate workers representation (outside the trade union structures) and even more to the prospects for participation in decision-making at the company level.

Development of the debate of the workers' participation in Bulgaria – main trends, challenges and apprehensions

Pre-history in 1986-1989

In Bulgaria there have been some experiences of implementation of forms of workers' participation even in the period from 1986-1988. Under conditions of the centralized economy and lack of political democracy such forms look like strange phenomenon, but the fact is, that some of the governments of the former communists states from East Europe decided to start implementation of some forms of workers participation in 1980-s.

The reason for that was, firstly, the economical decline and the lack of motivation for work. Some leaders expected (currently looking naive) that such forms could help for the economical improvement and could promote enthusiasm for work. Secondly, the political system, ruled by only one party in all of this countries was fully discredited. The government leaders needed desperately some legitimacy, especially among the workers, because the main official philosophy of the communist regime was that this a "power of workers". However, in 1980-s already nobody believed in that and the communist leaders probably thought, that workers' participation forms could revive such believes. The third reason was the place and role of the trade unions. At this time they were also discredited, although they did have some social functions and lots of people still expected from them not only to implement such functions (often given to them by the government), but also to protect the workers and employees by the general employer- the communists state. There were also some trade union leaders in the beginning of the 80's, just after the "Solidarnost" appearance in Poland, who made some efforts to create some illusions that trade unions could be revived under the regime and that they could obtain more important role. There were also some early trade union reformists, who really believed that trade unions could be changed, but all of them knew this could be happened only under democracy and market economy, although no one could said this honestly to the public. The workers' participation forms implementation was also pushed by the coming on power of new leadership with in the former Sovjet union in 1985 and by the beginning of some reformist's steps.

Some efforts of implementation of various forms of workers' participation, together with forms for improvement motivation to work and initiatives, even for creating entrepreneurship were made in several East European countries, like Poland (just after abolishment of the military regime), Hungary, Rumania, Bulgaria, former Sovjet union after 1987 and former Tchehoslovakia . The former Yugoslavia had implemented such forms earlier, in 60-s, but it's development was different from the other East European countries. The countries, were such forms were not implement were the former DDR (East Germany) and Albania, but the last one was also different from the most of others.. In most of the countries there amendments of the labour law had been mad and also in some cases amendments of the commercial low.

In Bulgaria the problems of workers' motivation, workers' initiative and also of workers' participation had been discussed since the beginning of 1980-s on the level of communists' party leadership and government, but only in general, without any particular ideas. In 1986 finally an amendment of the Labour Code had been made and even in autumn 1986 a national campaign for meetings and elections of "self-managing" bodies was organised. According to the law, such structures should be established in all enterprises, with exception of traditional budget organisations like this in administration, education, health care, sport, culture and some other. The structures should be established at all levels – from the working teams, on the middle management levels, including also the level of enterprises. In fact this should be parallel to the trade union structures, because everywhere there should be held general assemblies (or assemblies of delegates) and team council or economic council meetings. On the level of working team there had been also direct participation foresight, because some rights for direct decision making, related to the production issues, labour and social issues had been given to the team assembly. The most radical decision was the requirement of election of managers at all levels, including supervisors, middle managers and directors of the enterprises. The organisation of campaign and election was assigned to the trade unions.

The first results, which appeared in 1986 campaign were more then expected and even dangerous for the communist leaders. Although all the meetings and elections were lead by the local party leaders, lot's of non-expected things were said by the workers and lot's of candidates for managers, in advance checked, discussed and nominated by the party leadership were not elected. There were even company directors, not elected, although at such level only one candidate could be nominated. As a consequence, two years later the campaign was organised again, but the election of the directors of the enterprises was not allowed. Since the beginning of 1989, the Bulgarian government implemented some new laws, related mostly to the companies and showing some elements of the early market behaviour. However, with some judicial tricks, like new Government Act, which neglected some of the new rights of participation, the government tried to avoid the process of "self-management", which was implemented by their own initiative. At the same time some attacks, pointed on the trade unions began at this time. Trade unions fall into new gap after "self-management" implementation. On the one hand they should organise the process and officially they seemed to obtain new functions. On the other hand, there were some trade union representatives, who already had understood, that trade unions need to have a new role – of protectors of working people. The implementation of the legal framework for workers' participation was for such leaders and experts a chance to express their opinions for a new trade unionism. There was a discussion in the former Trade Union Research Institute in autumn 1987, where new views have been expressed (mainly by the report of the director). However, as a result trade unions in a whole and trade union institutes in particular were attacked by the communists party leadership, including the replacement of director and nationalization of the building of the institute in 1988. The discussion on the workers' participation and the new role of trade unions had been stopped in 1988-1989.

Development of workers' representation and participation in 1989-2006

After the beginning of changes in the politics and economics in November 1989, the problems of workers' participation have been neglected for long time – in fact for most then 15 year. Even the legislative norms in the Labour Code have been abolished. There were several reasons for that, but the main one was related to the trade union revival. The trade union pluralism already had appeared and trade unions, both old and new had to work already under competition and voluntary choice of membership and they should fight both to protect their members and to keep them and to attract new members and their voice. To have another structure in the companies in 1990's was not comfortable for trade unions. However, even in 1992 there were some ideas, expressed by the first non-communists government (right-centered) to implement works' councils. Trade unions resisted very strongly to that, because they suspected the government tried to abolish trade union structure at the company level. In fact the project was withdrawed.

Probably the trade union leaders made a mistake, not asking this from the next government, ruling the country in 1993-1994. At this time the employers were not well organised, the government was established by a compromise between several political parties and needed support by social partners. Both government and employers could agree with suggestions for new forms of workers' representation and participation with giving more possibilities to the trade unions to influence this process. The reasons for resistance again were low workers' attitudes for participation and trade unions' needs to point more attention to other issues. According to the data from surveys, made in 1992-1995, in most cases workers preferred that the decision should be taken by the managers, because "this is their job and their obligation", they are likely to discuss some issues with their line managers, but mainly related to the wages and salaries[1]

At the same time, the issues of workers' representation structures and process, outside of the trade union representation could not be neglected. The process of transition to the market economy, privatisation and restructuring, appearance of many new enterprises, also implementation of new technologies and work organisation methods have challenged the industrial relations and the trade union activity. On the one hand, trade unions should extend their activity to solving the social consequences of privatisation and restructuring, but they practically could not oppose too much on the process in a whole. On the other hand, the legal framework, concerning privatisation process foresight some possibilities for workers

1 More particular comments on these issues could be find in "Стратегии на трудово и икономическо поведение в условията на приватизация и преструктуриране на икономиката" (Personal strategies of workers, employees and self-employed under privatisation and economical restructuring). E. Ribarova, N. Daskalova, T. Michailova (1994).ISTUR. S .(working paper in Bulgarian); see also "Алтернативни личностни и групови стратегии на оцеляване в условията на преструктуриране на икономиката" (Alternate personal and group strategies of survival under economical restructuring.) Y. Aroyo. E. Ribarova, N. Daskalova. T. Michailova (1995). ISTUR. National Research Foundation. S. (working paper in Bulgarian).

and employees to buy on less expensive prices not more then 20% of stocks or shares in cases of market or cash privatisation of the companies, where they have worked at least two years. Also all the workers and employees could attend the process of voucher privatisation, buying not only shares or stocks from their own companies. In cases of voucher privatisation of the companies where they have worked, they could also buy shares or stocks on lower level prices, but not more then 10% from all. However, in all cases they didn't have the right to vote in the general assembly of the shareholders or stockholders for the first 3 year. Another mechanism was so-called workers-management buy-out, which was used in 1993-2000, but the results were not acceptable.

On the third, in the privatised and new established private companies trade unions have been often clashed with radically new strategies and approaches in human recourses management and management of industrial relations. They should both study the new strategies and approaches (which are sometimes too sophisticated and pointed to the individual employees) and protect the collective interests of their members under the new conditions. They also should pay more attention on the collective bargaining process on the company level, because of employers' aspirations for deregulation of industrial relations.

The result of such aspiration were the new amendments of the Labour Code made in 2001. These amendments provided for the temporary character (for the period of 1-2 years)of collective agreements at all levels and possibilities of workers and employees, not covered by agreements, to join them consequently. Comparing to the time before 2001, trade unions should work more active and they needed better capacity. They used to suggest to the employers only annexes to the collective agreements, without organising whole new bargaining campaign. This was, of course a "lazy" approach, which could not continue more. At the same time trade union structures began to challenge by difficulties of organisational character, related to the decline of membership, lack of attitudes of existing members for struggle and support and lack of financial resources. Trade union structures at the company /organsation level in Bulgaria do have many rights (including mentioned above), for example to participate in the preparation of the company legal documents, like rules for company order, rules for wage and salary system, rules for health and safety at work, consultations for all the labour and social issues, representation of individual members, group of members at the court in cases of labour disputes.[2] Although that, it has been already clear even in the middle of 1990-s that not all the workers' problems could be solved only with the efforts of trade unions, even in the companies where they were strong.

---

2 See "Кодекс на труда" (Labour Code)(2006). S. (in Bulgarian).

The process of alternate representation has became already it's legal framework before the end of the century. An amendment on the Labour Code envisaged some functions of the general assembly of all the workers and employees in the company (or assembly of the delegates, when there are too many employed, shift work, several subsidiaries, situated at different places, even in different towns and some others.). The general assembly could take some decisions, like selection of the draft project for collective bargaining in cases, where more then one union in the company is and if there is no preliminary agreement between the unions. Also the assembly could decide how the money for social benefits should be used and to give opinion in relation to the changes of work organisation, work standards, working time. Some new representatives could be also elected and this right has been given to the general assembly also:

Firstly, it is possible to elect representatives of all the employed persons and they have the right to express the interests of personnel to the employer in relation to labour and social issues.[3] Secondly, according to the Commercial Law, in Limited Liability companies, having more then 50 employees its possible that one representative of the personnel participates in the meetings of shareholders and represents the interests of the employees, but having only a consultative vote. Also the managing bodies in every company should invite representative(s) of workers and employees at the meetings, when issues of labour or/and social affaires are discussing and they should consult the representative(s).[4] All this representatives are elected by the general assembly of personnel.[5]

However, these steps were only "cosmetic", in fact in most of the time the only real workers' representatives at the workplaces have been trade union structures and leaders. The representatives of the personnel in a whole have been elected in some companies, both in the companies with organised workers and in the companies free of unions. This representatives usually play the role of unions, if workers haven't been organised . In some cases they have had a role in the companies with union structures, for purposes of more detailed consultations, concerning questions, not put, or not agreed during the collective bargaining process. In the enterprises, where unions are strong, usually the representatives, participating in the shareholders' meetings or at the meetings of managing bodies with consultative vote are either trade union leaders, or trade union members. However they practically couldn't make any important influence on the decision, taken by the company bodies.

The discussion about workers' participation was raised again in 1997, together with coming on power of the new government, and when the preparation for joining

---

3 See "Кодекс на труда" (Labour Code)(2006). Sofia (in Bulgarian).

4 See the same.

5 See "Търговски закон" (Commercial Law).(1997). Sofia (in Bulgarian).

the EU has been started. Although it was right-centered, this government proclaimed that the partnership should be it's main mechanism and although it made some mistakes, it tried to keep the partnership until the end of it's mandate, having also former trade union leader as minister of labour and social affaires. The reason was that after national crises, caused by the former, socialists' government, the new government needed support both by the trade unions and employers to start finally the market reforms.

The preparation and implementation of the legal framework for workers participation had been put as a common purpose of the state and social partners in the Memorandum for priority common activities, signed by the government, employers' association and trade unions in autumn 1997. However, most of the purposes haven't been reached, mainly because of resistance, expressed by both sides-trade unions and employers. In 1997 the only step, which had been made, was the Law for Health and Safety at Work, where the election of Health and Safety committees by the workers was foresight and it was implemented in the companies with 50 and more employed persons. According to the law, one half of the members of such committees should be elected directly by the workers and employees, another could be nominate by the employer. In most of the companies with 50 and more employees such committees have been elected and in most of the cases they are dominated by the trade union members and leaders. However such committees not always have been worked effectively. Also in small and micro enterprises the groups for health and safety at work, foresight by the law, only rarely have been elected.

In 2000, Bulgaria ratified the Revised European Social Charter of the Council of Europe, including all the texts related to the information and consultation rights and this was also a new prerequisite for preparation for information and consultation systems at workplace. The resistance by both sides continued and didn't give any chance for starting the process. The main reasons for resistance, expressed by the trade union representatives were as follows:

- Firstly, the absence of readiness by the majority of workers and employees for participation, registered in the process of surveys (some mentioned above);
- Secondly, there were not enough qualified people for all the structures of representation;
- Thirdly, trade union representatives were afraid of possible collaboration of the new structures and representatives with the employers;
- Fourthly, the most strong expressed – the new representative bodies or structures might be used by the employers for neglecting and promotion of erosion of trade union structures in the companies;

- Fifthly, trade unionists in the companies as well as most of their leaders on the sector level were really afraid from competition between the main structures of representation. This was not said honestly, but it was the real reason;
- Sixthly, trade unionists had studied too much about the German model of workers' participation. In fact this model is good working in Germany, Austria and some other EU-member-states and it had been also implemented (not in a whole) in Hungary, Slovenia and Chroatia. This didn't mean that it should be directly implemented in Bulgaria and other East European states.

By the employers' side there were some various views. On the one hand, most of the employers opposed on the forthcoming implementation of the information and consultation systems, because they didn't believe that there were enough qualified workers and employees for such purposes. They also didn't won't to have too many structures of workers representation at the company level. Some of them were afraid from interference in their management issues in particular. Most of such employers, however, understood that the information and consultation will be implemented and at the beginning of the new millennium they usually said they would rather prefer to have trade unions as a main players in the information and consultation process. For a pity, this hadn't been used by trade unions because they rather preferred either not to have new representatives at the workplace, or at any case to prolong such decisions for "better" times.

Between the main reasons for that was also the position and behaviour of another group of employers, mainly representing big companies- privatised and new private. They tried to present the systems of information, consultation and participation, used in EU-member states as well as in some candidate countries at this time, as a main mechanism for neglecting trade unions. Such views, of course provoke reaction of more strong resistance by the side of trade unions.

At the same time in the second half of 1990-s some large multinational companies bought existing enterprises or established new subsidiaries in Bulgaria. Even in 1994-1995, there were some data about the process of information and consultation in such companies .According to the survey, made in Central and East European countries by the ILO and ETUI teams, the workers and employees in the MNC-s subsidiaries in most of the countries surveyed have been informed and consulted on issues of production increase, finance and investment, dismissals, short-time work, retirement issues and others.[6] Since 1996-1997 the foreign investments in Bulgaria had been extended and there were many subsidiaries of MNC-s, especially of some large and famous companies like Umicore (then Kumerio), InBef, Solvey, Karlsberg, Danone, Metro, Heidelberger Cement, Mirolio, Italcementi, Roka,

6 See P. Repo. Collective Bargaining in the Central Europe Subsidiaries of Multinationals. (1996). ETUI. Brussels.

Actavis, Coca-Cola, Haineken, ABB, Nestle, Kraft Foods International, Holderbank, Rover, American Standard, Kodak, Hyundai, Dewoo and others. In some of such companies practices of modern HRM, of industrial relations and also of informal information and consultation systems have been implemented.

The Institute for Social and Trade Union research (ISTUR) has made in 1998 and again in 2003 two surveys in more then 20 subsidiaries of MNCs in Bulgaria, with the supports of ILO and Fridrich Ebert Foundation. The data form the survey showed the process of development of views about information, consultation and workers' participation for more then 5 year. In 1998 the issue of information has been mostly related to the trade union representatives and they usually complained from "selected " by the employers' information, which was not always enough for their work. For example, the information about the content of privatisation contracts, even related to the employment issues hadn't been given to the trade unions. Most of information was expressed like "secret" and related to the company security.[7]

In 2003 the information and consultation already were treated in a context of all the workers and employees rights, not only of trade union representatives' rights. However, the information and consultation process still was mainly under trade union control and was implemented via meetings, committees for social partnership, health and safety committees. In some companies the general assembly also were used and forms of direct giving the information and consultations via meetings, collecting of employees' suggestions and others. The process in a whole included both issues, related to the labour, like health and safety at work, payment, social benefits, redundancies and some issues, more important for management like rules for company order and discipline at workplace, working time and organisation of work. The economical and financial issues were subject of exchange of information between the management and trade unions rarely and the consultations were excluded.[8]

In some subsidiaries the representatives of personnel (usually trade union leaders) had been elected as observers in the EWC (Umicore, Solvey, Danone, Mirolio, Nestle) in 1997-1998. Such practices provoked attitudes for implementing information and consultation systems in a whole. The data from ISTUR survey in

7 Мултинационалните компании в България- промени в индустриалните отношения и синдикатите (Multinational companies in Bulgaria-changes in the industrial relations and trade unions.) Gr. Gradev and others (1998). ISTUR. Fridrich Ebert Stiftung. pp 43-46 (in Bulgarian).

8 Мултинационалните компании –промени в индустриалните отношения и синдикатите-5 години по-късно(Multinational companies in Bulgaria-changes in the industrial relations and trade unions.-5 years later). L.Tomev and others.(2003) ISTUR. Fridrich Ebert Stiftung. pp 88-94 (in Bulgarian).

2003 expressed also some other trends. Although there were chances for representatives from some other companies (with exception of mentioned above) to participate in the EWC meetings with observers' status, they couldn't do this because of the local employers' resistance (this was mentioned for Kraft Foods International, Metro and some other companies) of even because of lack of support (or probably secret resistance) by the side of trade unions from the EU-member-states (this was mentioned as a reason for ImBev and other companies).[9]

The ISTUR survey in 2003 was added by the results form another parallel survey, collected by the CITUB experts from the MNC-s subsidiaries, including most of the companies, where the data of the first survey had been collected, as well as some other MNC-s subsidiaries, also not only owned by the EU-member-states investors and even several Bulgarian companies. The second survey (made in 2003) was a part of project of Extol-network, which is a partner of Irish trade union SIPTU. Project involved trade unions from most of the candidate countries at this time (excepting Hungary, Cyprus and Malta), together with Spain and Ireland. The data from the survey gave some details about the preparation and readiness of workers and employees, trade unions and managers for implementing information and consultation systems. In a whole most of the workers and employees didn't have any information about this possibilities. Managers were much better informed, but their views were various. Trade union representatives were also better informed, but some of them supported this process, some hesitated and some strongly resisted. It was interesting that even in companies like Solvey and Mirolio, where conditions for information and participation and for social dialogue were very good, the trade union leaders were not the main supporters of information and consultation process outside unions. The other trend was that both sides – workers and managers – didn't support workers participation in decision making at all.[10]

At the same time this trends were different and even opposed to another trends, which might be seen from another data. The survey of comparative human resources management, which had been made also in Bulgaria under the framework of Cranet in 1996, 1999, 2003-2006, expressed advantage in managers' attitudes for implementing financial participation schemes. In 2003-2006 in 29,1% from production companies (including manufacturing together with mines) profit sharing for workers and employees has been used, in 22,1% -stock options and in 19,8%-employee share schemes. The variable pay systems are

9 The same, pp 88-94.

10 Мултинационалните компании –промени в индустриалните отношения и синдикатите-5 години по-късно (Multinational companies in Bulgaria – changes in the industrial relations and trade unions. – 5 years later). L.Tomev and others. (2003) ISTUR. Fridrich Ebert Stiftung. pp 88-94 (in Bulgarian).

based on individual performance in 47, 7% from the companies, on company-wide performance in 40,7% and on team performance – in 22,1%. The main trends in 1996-2006 are decentralization of decision-making process, concerning to the pay-systems, growing correlation between pay and performance, extending scope of rewarding trough ownership and profit sharing schemes.[11] It seems, that some of managers were ready to implement financial participation, but still resisted to the information and consultation rights and participation in decision-making.

Implementation of European directives for information and consultation in Bulgaria

Final debate in 2005-2006

In 2005, just after signature of the accession treaty with the EU, preparation of the new legal framework has been started in Bulgaria. The government expressed the will to prepare the legislation, but only to make transposition of the texts of directives, not having in mind the particular situation of Bulgarian industrial relations system. They were in a hurry. Employers, comparing to the situation in 2001-2002 were ready to implement the new systems. They already didn't won't to have only a unions as a main partner, although they were ready for negotiation of mechanisms, involving trade unions in such process. Trade unions in a whole expressed their old apprehensions, sometimes even stronger, because during the last several years they have been challenged by more aggressive behaviour by the employers' side. There were several versions, suggested by the trade unions, preliminary created by their experts' teams and based on the results of common project with TUC-UK in 2006-2007. The main point of all of the trade union versions was the view, that trade unions should have the main role in the new systems of information and consultation. The strategy of trade unions was that the law should give the rights of information and consultations directly to their structures in the companies. However, this was not accepted neither by the employers, nor by the government. One of the reasons, which was expressed, was that there are a lot of companies, free of trade unions and their employees should have another rules for information and consultation. Another reason was, that even where there are unions, not all the people, working there are their members

11 Vatchkova E. Survey on Comparative Human Resource Management-National Report for Bulgaria CRANET 2006: Vatchkova E. Human Resource Management, Sofia 2007. Pp.189-196.

and trade unions don't have the full right to represent all people, working in the companies.

After many strong discussions the working group succeeded to bring to an end a draft amendment of the Labour Code, related to the all information and consultation rights at the national level. The law was a compromise between different points of view and in general was a direct transposition of the texts of Directive 14/2002 of the EU. The other directives, concerned to the information and consultation rights in the MNC-s, European Companies and European Co-operative Societies have been implemented through a separate Law for information and consultation of workers and employees in the multinational enterprises, groups of enterprises and European Societies (including European Companies and European Co-operative Societies).

The current legal framework of information and consultation rights in Bulgaria

The amendment of the Labour Code, made in 2006 foresight the creation of new structures-representatives of personnel for information and consultation, in relation to the Directive 14/2002 of the European Council. Such representatives (from 3 to 9 for every organisation) could be elected in all the companies, employed 50 and more persons and in all sectors, including public services and organisations, financed by the state and local budgets. Also in the companies' subsidiaries, having economical and financial independence workers and employees could elect their representatives(from 1 to 3). The period of time, when they could be representatives varies from 1 to 3 years, but there are no restrictions for re-election.

The functions, the rights and obligations of the representatives are the same like in the directive, including also the confidentiality of information. Representatives could obtain information on several main topics, like economical and financial issues, changes and development of employment and work organisation. They could also be consulted by the employer on employment issues and work organisation. They also could addressed another questions, related to the labour issues to the employer, when there are such problems. Employer should give the information, which is necessary in the shortest time. Information should be given and the consultation should be made before the decisions of managing bodies, related to the same issues. The representatives for information and consultation do have special protection against dismissals (like trade union representatives at the workplace), but they don't have legal rights for additional leave, reduced working time for implementing their functions and special education. This rights they could obtain either via collective bargaining, or via special agreements. The law foresight also possibility for trade unions or employer to suggest all the details of issues of organisation, conditions of work and activity of information and consultation in collective bargaining process or to negotiate for special agreement.

Representatives for information and consultations have to be elected by the general assembly of personnel (in some cases assembly of delegates) and by the general assembly of the personnel in the subsidiary. The nominations could be made by the individual employees or workers, by group of workers and employees or by the trade unions in the company. The mechanism of election should be decided by the assembly itself. When there is a suggestion and if the assembly decided, the rights both for nomination and for election of the representatives could be given to the trade unions in the company (nevertheless how many separate trade union structures there are). In such cases the assembly should only determine the time of mandate and the number of representatives.

In the law has been foresight also mechanisms for resign of representatives before finishing of their mandate, like legal prosecution, non implementation of their function, by their own will and others.[12]

Besides that, there are some other areas of information and consultations and some other rights, which have been kept for trade unions and for other representatives at the workplace. Trade unions should be always informed and consulted in cases of the change of employer, in cases of mass redundancies, when employer decide to implement prolongation of working time, or temporary part-time work for all employed or for some groups and any other questions, related to the working time. There are some other employees' and workers' representatives, which rights have been kept in the law and who could be elected even before the last amendments of the Labour Code in 2006. They are representatives for common labour and social issues, already mentioned above. They usually have been used as an alternate of trade unions (when in the company there are neither trade union structures, nor individual trade union members). Sometimes they exist together with trade union structures, especially when trade unions are week. Such representatives should be also informed and consulted in all the cases when trade unions should be informed and consulted, mentioned above. There could be an advantage in using such representatives in some cases, because there are no restrictions for their elections-they could be also elected in small and micro enterprises and also there are no restrictions in relation to their number.

At the same time the general assembly of personnel (or assembly of delegates) still does have some rights of information and consultations, like related to the changes in working standards, distribution of money for social benefits . It has also right to take decisions about social benefits.[13]

---

12 See "Кодекс на труда" (Labour Code) (2006). Sofia (in Bulgarian).

13 See "Кодекс на труда" (Labour Code) (2006). Sofia (in Bulgarian).

The framework of information and consultations at the workplace is a compromise between the government attitudes not to go very far away from the directive requirements, employers' strengths for more independence in decision-making and trade unions' wishes to be integrated in the process of information and consultations. Trade unions succeeded to obtain the rights for nomination of candidates and suggesting them to the general assembly and also to nominate and elect directly the representatives, when the general assembly decide to give this rights to them. However, they had tried to became exclusive rights for information and consultation process until the last moment and most of trade union representatives and leaders from all levels still think they had lost to much with such amendments in the Labour Code.

The first seminars and discussions, organised just after implementing the new law in 2006 and even some of practical results showed some gaps of the legal framework for information and consultations:

- There could be some problems in implementing the information and consultation systems in big national companies, both private and public owned, like Nation Company for Electricity, Bulgarian Telecom, state administration structures like National Tax Agency, National Agency for Social Assistance and others. The restriction of number of representatives to 9 gives no chance for all subsidiaries to have their representative at the company/organisation level, although they could have representatives in the subsidiaries also;
- There could be problems in election of representatives in some mobile structures like transport companies, especially in the see transport, because of difficulties to organise general assembly of personnel and even assembly of delegates and lack of alternate ways for election in the law;
- There could be some difficulties in relation to the confidentiality of information, which probably are not typical for Bulgaria. On the one hand, representatives have to inform workers and employees about the results of information and consultation meetings. On the other hand, they could be obliged by the employers not to disseminate part of information, when it has been expressed as confidential. On the third, employer could restrict any information he had decided, because of confidentiality, or also could refuse to give such information;
- There could be also some problems with organisation and self-organisation of representatives. They shouldn't be elected as a body, only as individual representatives. For such decision mainly trade unions have insisted, because of possibility of competition. However the representatives should work together and they should organise themselves.

Which concerns the implementation of other directives, related to the information and consultation process in the MNC-s and European Societies, the law in common was directly copied out from the texts of directives, with exception of some procedures for election and organsation. The law foresight all the cases of election of Special Negotiation Bodies, European Works Councils, Representative Bodies and participants in Supervisory /Managing bodies in the European companies and European co-operative societies. The representatives in the international companies should be elected on the same way like the representatives for national information and consultation systems. The general assemblies (or assemblies of the delegates) have to elected such representatives- members of the special negotiation bodies, of European works councils and of representative bodies in the European companies and European co-operative societies, but not the members of supervisory/ managing bodies, who should be elected by the representative bodies. The same like for the national representatives are the procedures for nominations and for election. Trade unions also could be given by the assemblies the rights to nominate and to elect directly such representatives. International representatives also obtained legal protection against dismissals, rights for paid free time during the working days for implementing their functions, paid leave for education and participation in the meetings. The issues of financing of their activity, especially of covering the costs for travel and accommodation and interpretation by the employers should be put on either in collective agreements, either in special agreements. However, for members of supervisory/managing bodies haven't been foresight special rights.[14]

One of the biggest gaps in the law is that it has been prepared, mainly having in mind the companies, whose headquarters are in Bulgaria. This does not correspond with the practice, because in Bulgaria there are still mainly subsidiaries of MNC-s. All the cases, when Bulgarian workers and employees should nominate their representatives for Special negotiation bodies, EWC or Representative bodies and representatives for Supervisory/Managing Bodies haven't been foresight. Of course, the laws of the countries, where the headquarters of the companies have been situated, standard rules and agreements, signed by the central managing bodies and special negotiation bodies could be used for such purposes. In Bulgarian law there are not even some orientation mechanisms. In such cases

14 See "Закон за информиране и консултиране на работниците и служителите от многонационалните предприятия, групи от предприятия и европейски дружества" (Law for information and consultations of the workers and employees from multinational enterprise, groups of enterprises and European societies). (2006). Sofia (in Bulgarian).

trade unions / or sometimes employers should make their own rules and give instructions to their members and representatives [15]

Information, consultation and participation at the workplace in Bulgaria – first results and problems

An overview of the structure of workers representation since 2007

The structure of workers' representation on the company/organisation level became too complicated. There are several types of companies/organisations regarding the various rights and bodies for representation, information and consultation and participation.

First, this are the small and micro companies, mostly private owned and acting in business sectors, employed less then 50 persons. In most of them, especially in micro-companies, employed less then 10 persons the representation and participation has been neglected. According to the law the workers and employees do have the right to call a general assembly and also to elect groups for health and safety at work. They could create trade unions or join other unions, or at least could elect representatives for common labour and social issues, which rights have been kept by Bulgarian law. In fact in most cases in such companies there are no structures of representation of any type. Sometimes there are trade unions, joining bigger trade union structures, but they usually have been inherited the old trade union structures in privatised companies. In the new established companies usually is too difficult for workers to create trade unions-either because of employers' resistance, or because of lack of will by most of employed. In some small companies sometimes there are trade union members, organised in regional or sector structures, or in both of them. Many small and micro companies are still in the "shadow economy" and their employers often violate the fundamental rights, like rights, related to the labour contracts, health and safety at work, working time, regularity of wages' payment. They usually resist both to the strengths for organising and to the will for establishment of non-union channels of information and consultations.

---

15 See "Закон за изменение и допълнение на Кодекса на труда. Закон за информиране и консултиране на работниците и служителите от многонационалните предприятия, групи от предприятия и европейски дружества. Сборник коментари" (Commentaries on the Labour Code Amendments and on the Law for Information and Cconsultation of the Workers and Employees from Multinational Enterprises, Groups of Enterprises and European Societies). Ch. Hristov, E. Ribarova and others. (2006). CITUB. Fridrich Ebert Stiftung. Sofia (in Bulgarian).

Second, these are most of organisations, financed by the state and local budgets or with mixed financing and also state and local administration. In most of them the main channels for representation and information and consultations are trade unions (with exception of the administration at highest level, where trade unions are very week). Employees in such organsations usually have all the rights for establishment of new channels for information and consultations, but not all of them have used these rights or if they had elected representatives, they often work only formally. They usually have elected health and safety committees (in organisations employed 50 or more persons). In some sectors like high education, research, culture, because of creative character of the activity, some of the employees or all of them often do have their particular rights for information, consultation and participation, including even election of managers. That's the reason that they don't pay too much attention to the other information and consultation rights.

Third, these are most of the private and public owned companies in business, employed 50 and more persons. The structures of representation there is the most complicated, because their employee do have more legal rights, then the others. In large part of such companies there are trade unions, but there are not everywhere strong. Trade unions are the most strong in so-called heavy industries like mines, metallurgy, building materials' manufacturing, weapon manufacturing and shipbuilding, but also in forestry, transport, road maintenance, water supply, electricity and heating production and supply and others. There are also trade unions in lot's of companies of machine-building, chemistry and pharmacy manufacturing, textile, clothing and shoes manufacturing, food industry, furniture and paper industries, telecommunications, construction and some others, but they are weaker. Also in some companies from distribution, tourism, banking, information technologies there are trade unions, but usually they are too week. In some of such companies there have been also representatives for common labour and social issues elected, nevertheless whether there are or not trade unions. There are also health and safety committees in most of companies of such group and also general assemblies have been called sometimes. In some companies also representatives with consultative vote sometimes attend the general assemblies of shareholders or meeting of managing bodies and they often are trade union leaders. Some of the companies of this group also use financial participation and in some cases direct information and consultation with workers and employees.

Workers and employees from such group do have the rights for new information and consultation representatives(according to the Directive 14/2002) and in some cases they have been elected, but not always working really.

In these companies there are problems, because of existing of too many structures (sometimes 4 or more different channels). Representatives from various structures often are one and the same and they often mix their work. Where trade unions are strong and the trade union density is high, usually trade unions have been well integrated in these structures and they practically control them and turn the activity on common purposes. In such cases the interaction of various structures is under co-ordination and doesn't mention to the workers' representation in a whole. However, where the trade unions are weaker, sometimes competition between the various structures and problems in interaction and information exchange appeared. By the side of employers the positions vary. Some employers try to use all structures for their purposes, not excluding also allowing the competition between them. Some other have been shocked be the needs to communicate with too much structures and to solve different problems and they even try to neglect all of them or at least trade unions. Another group tries to abolish sophistically trade unions, using the other structures.

Fourth, particular cases of the third group are MNC-s subsidiaries, where besides all the representatives, mentioned in the third group, there are also already members of EWC or of Special negotiation bodies in some of them. Particular for MNK also are the schemes of financial bonuses, like profit-sharing or stock options, as well as so-called direct participation, but only as information and consultations Means like information via inside computer network, collecting suggestions by workers and employees, meetings with workers, survey of the opinion of personnel have been used.

Usually problems in such group of companies should be the same, like for the third, but in some cases the organisation of representation and interaction has been made more effective. In most of subsidiaries of MNC-s in manufacturing there are strong or semi-strong trade unions, general assemblies and health and safety committees, in some of them there are already working representatives for information and consultations. The organisation and co-ordination has been made either by the strong and well organised trade union leaderships, or by HRM –department, or by both of them together, although they often do have contradictions and even conflicts in the collective bargaining process and in consultations for everyday labour and social issues. In some MNK subsidiaries, where there are no unions also formal channels for representation exists, but their work is not as much active.

Results from implementation of the EU-directives in Bulgaria – data from 2006-2008

For a pity, according to the data about the representative's election after 2006 the process has gone too slow. Trade unions (mainly Confederation of the Independent Trade Unions in Bulgaria – CITUB) collected some data from the companies, where there are their structures. For most of the companies, employed 50 or more persons, mainly where there are no trade unions, it's too difficult to collect data for information and consultation representatives. There isn't still national system of collecting such information.

The data, collected from the CITUB-structures in January 2008 expressed not very optimistic trends. Only in 137 companies, where CITUB does have sections there have been elected representatives for information and consultations. There are mainly in metallurgy, road transport, chemistry, food industry (including breweries), agriculture, banks and distribution. More then half of the representatives, which have been elected are trade union members or also trade union representatives from the CITUB- sections. Other representatives are members of other unions, there are also non-union members. There are also some non-official data for already elected representatives, collected from another branches like road maintenance, but they are not exact. In the companies of machine-building, electricity, telecommunications and posts, construction, forestry, where CITUB has sections, no election of representatives have been made at the time of the information collection. There are no data from companies of see transport, electronics, tourism, weapon manufacturing, education, co-operative societies.

As already mentioned, the most advanced in this process are the subsidiaries of MNC-s in metallurgy, chemistry, food industry, banks and some others. In March 2008 ISTUR made again small survey, based only on questionnaire for new forms of workers representation with the trade union leaders of CITUB-section in 15 MNC-s subsidiaries In 8 subsidiaries the representatives for information and consultation at national level were already elected. Some of them already had obtained some experience in EWC participation, like Solvey, Kumerio, Nestle. In most cases either the general assemblies gave the right for nomination and election directly to the trade union sections in the enterprises, or the representatives were nominated mainly by trade unions, but elected by the general assemblies (or assemblies of delegates). In most of the subsidiaries from such group-6, there were already procedures of information and consultations, mainly related to the employment issues and work organisation, but also in some cases related to the economical and financial issues. In two of subsidiaries special agreements, concerned to the organisation issues of the workers' representatives had been concluded. In most of the others this issues had been put into collective agreements with annexes. Most of trade union representatives declared that employers usually were ready to communicate with them and that they didn't refuse to give information, neither disturb their rights for information and consultations. In two of companies the representatives had been elected, but they hadn't began their real work at the moment of the survey.

In the other 7 subsidiaries the representatives were not elected yet at the time of the survey. The main reasons for that, mentioned by trade union leaders was as follows: trade unions didn't take any initiatives – in 6 from 7 cases; employers refused to call the general assemblies – in 5 cases; the workers didn't take initiative – in 1 case. "Employers didn't called the general assembly" could not be an excuse, because according to the law there are another ways for calling the assembly – either by the trade unions or by 1/10 from all the workers and employees in the company. Only in one case was mentioned that the employer disturb the rights for information and consultations (in Sheraton-Hotel, owned by the Grek Otel-Greece). It seems that in some cases trade unions are either not ready, or don't won't at all to have any "competition", represent by new system of information and consultations.

Which concerns the EWC members and members of Special negotiation bodies, the team of College for workers education, partner of the CITUB, surveyed all companies where they have been elected in February-March 2008. The survey was a part of project, worked together with CC.OO-Spain and other trade unions from EU-member states, which main purpose was to review the EWC in several member-states-old and new. The team surveyed practically all the subsidiaries in Bulgaria, where there had been members for EWC elected.

The undertakings that have elected representatives for the European Work Councils are a total number of 15 from several economic sectors and branches: light industry (textile and clothes); financial services; metallurgy, metal-work and machine-building including building of machines, electric appliances and electronics; food industry; chemical industry; production of building materials; trade; power engineering (electricity production and supply); information technologies and services. Besides the above mentioned sectors and branches there are another 15 subsidiaries of MNC in Bulgaria with functioning European Work Councils but with not elected Bulgarian representatives till now. Those subsidiaries are mainly from the above mentioned branches and sectors (financial services and banking, metal-work and machine-building, electricity production, distribution and supply, food industry, trade, tourism) and some more branches and sectors: construction and wood-processing. There are also four MNC-s with subsidiaries in Bulgaria in which the procedure for the establishment of European Work Councils has started – one in the pharmacy manufacturing and three more in the electricity production and supply and gas supply. In one of them – ENEL the representative for the Special negotiation body has been already elected.

The sectors and branches with subsidiaries from MNC-s have a considerable contribution to the economy. The average salaries in most of the subsidiaries are higher then the average salaries in the same sectors. The biggest group of enterprises that has elected Bulgarian representatives in the European Work Councils is from the sector food industry – 5. The sectors of machine-building and metal-work and chemical industry have 2 enterprises each with elected representatives in the European Work Councils. In the rest of the sectors and branches there is one enterprise in each with elected Bulgarian representatives.

In most of the enterprises that have elected representatives for the European Work Councils trade union organisations have existed. In one half of the enterprises that have established European Work Councils but have not elected Bulgarian representatives trade union organisations also have existed. In three of the enterprises that have started the election procedure for the European Works Councils there are structures of trade unions. As an average in the subsidiaries of the MNC in Bulgaria there is a higher percentage of the trade union density (average 46%) compared to the overall percentage of trade union density for the country which is about 18-19%.

In conclusion, most of trade union leaders at workplace still are afraid from the new forms of workers representation. This concerns both those, who already had organised election of new representatives and even already have taken control on this process and the others, who still try to postpone such election. Although there are some problems even in the MNC-s subsidiaries, the process of implementation of new information and consultation forms has been much more advanced then in most of the other companies. In the companies, where there is some experience in relation to the EWC, as well as in the companies, where this process has started in 2007-2008, there are also better results in relation to the national system of information and consultations. But in most of such companies trade unions also are either strong and with high density, or at least the employers do have respect on them.

Where are we going now ?

It seems that trade unions will be the main workers' and employees' representatives at the workplace in Bulgaria in the near future. Probably in some more companies from the business sectors the new forms will be implemented, but mainly where the trade unions are strong and not too much afraid from competition, or in some companies, free of unions in cases of employers' initiative. In some other MNC-s subsidiaries Bulgarian members of EWC will be elected. Probably the experience in some companies could give more new ideas for improvement of co-ordination and interaction between different structures.

One of the main reasons is also the lack of interest by the side of workers and employees themselves. They still haven't understood, that the process of information and consultations as well as the process of industrial relations in a whole are a part of the democracy. They usually prefer to have anybody to represent them, but representative(s) should take all the responsibility. Additional obstacles are again the legal framework restrictions. The law gives (in both cases-for national representatives and for EWC and other representative bodies' members) the rights, but it depends on the workers and employees how will they use their rights. Employers could no refuse to implement such structures according to the law, but they usually could not take initiative and they don't want very much to do that.

It seems that workers and employees, as well as trade union leaders and employers need more education and experience in relation to the information and consultation process. Some trade union representatives still don't understand they could use the process of information and consultation for their main purposes in collective bargaining process. Most of employers also could not seen the use of more channels for communication with personnel.

Which concerns the legal framework in general, it seems that some amendments are necessary. First, some new rights for workers and employees in the small and micro companies are necessary. They could elect representatives of common labour and social interests, but it would be better if this representatives will be particular foreseen for them. The personnel in medium and big companies doesn't need one more structure, because it has the rights to elect another structures.

Second, some more rights of the general assembly, especially for small and micro companies also could be foreseen . For example the rights for information and consultations, which have been foresight for the representatives in the companies, employed 50 or more persons, could be given to the general assemblies in small and micro companies.

Third, also some more details, related to the international channels for information and consultations are necessary, especially some mechanisms for employees in the subsidiaries of MNC-s and European Societies.

Finally, in commercial law some more rights for participation at the board level could be given. For example, all the companies could integrate personnel/ or trade union representatives in the process of decision –taking, in the first time only with consultative vote. But even this could be chance for obtaining more information by the side of workers and employees and for monitoring the process of company management.

Bibliography

Алтернативни личностни и групови стратегии на оцеляване в условията на преструктуриране на икономиката (Alternate personal strategies of survival under economical restructuring). *Aroyo, Y. / Ribarova, E. / Daskalova, N. / Michailova, T.* (1995): ISTUR. National Research Foundation. Sofia (working paper in Bulgarian)

Закон за информиране и консултиране на работниците и служителите от многонационалните предприятия, групи от предприятия и европейски дружества.Република България (Law for information and consultations of the workers and employees from multinational enterprise, groups of enterprises and European societies. Republic of Bulgaria) (2006): Sofia (in Bulgarian)

Закон за изменение и допълнение на Кодекса на труда. Закон за информиране и консултиране на работниците и служителите от многонационалните предприятия, групи от предприятия и европейски дружества. Сборник коментари (Commentaries on the Labour Code Amendments and on the Law for information and consultations of the workers and employees from multinational enterprise, groups of enterprises and European societies). *Hristov, Ch. / Ribarova, E.* and others (2006): CITUB. Fridrich Ebert Stiftung. Sofia (in Bulgarian).

Кодекс на труда. Република България. (Labour Code. Republic of Bulgaria) (2006): Sofi (in Bulgarian)

Мултинационалните компании в България- промени в индустриалните отношения и синдикатите (Multinational companies in Bulgaria-changes in the industrial relations and trade unions). *Gradev, Gr.* and others (1998): ISTUR. Fridrich Ebert Stiftung. Sofia (in Bulgarian)

Мултинационалните компании в България- промени в индустриалните отношения и синдикатите-5 години по-късно. (Multinational companies in Bulgaria – changes in the industrial relations and trade unions. – 5 years later). *Tomev, L.* and others (2003): ISTUR. Fridrich Ebert Stiftung. Sofia (in Bulgarian)

Repo P. Collective Bargaining in the Central Europe Subsidiaries of Multinationals (1996): ETUI. Brussels

Стратегии на трудово и икономическо поведение в условията на приватизация и преструктуриране на икономиката (Personal strategies of workers, employees and self-employed under privatisation and economical restructuring). *Ribarova, E. / Daskalova, N. / Michailova, T.* (1994): ISTUR. Sofia (working paper in Bulgarian).

Търговски закон. Република България (Commercial Law. Republic of Bulgaria) (1997): Sofia (in Bulgarian)

Vatchkova, E. Survey on Comparative Human Resource Management-National Report for Bulgaria CRANET 2006: *Vatchkova, E.*, Human Resource Management (2007): Sofia

Employee participation in new forms of organization and control opportunity for company health policies or potential for new burdens?

Nick Kratzer, Wolfgang Dunkel, Wolfgang Menz

1. Introduction

In the 1970s, participation still had the status of an alternative to Taylorist forms of organization and rationalization strategies. With the emergence of lean production and the approaches to organization that followed, it seemed to have established itself as a central component of "modern" management concepts. From the 1990s onwards, participation was considered to be not only an important way of improving employees' capacity to innovate and perform to the best of their abilities, but also a guarantor of their motivation, wellbeing, and health.

More recently, though, we have seen evidence of disillusionment. It is hardly possible to speak of an extensive and comprehensive dissemination of ambitious participatory structures of work and approaches to management, and there is even renewed talk of "intelligent Taylorism". In addition, in the framework of new forms of organization and control no reduction of physical workloads has occurred and there has even been a clear increase in psychological burdens. Classical ideas about the humane organization of work (more autonomy, more cooperation, more flexibility) seem to have had the opposite of the desired effect in the framework of new forms of organization and control: employees who enjoy their work, and are proud of the fact that they can work autonomously, nevertheless experience their scope of action as an excessive demand on their energies, cooperation as a burden, and flexibility as something that makes it impossible to reconcile the demands of work with their lives outside work. It now seems that "more freedom" has led to "more pressure", and employees seem to be "voluntarily risking their health" (Glißmann and Peters 2001).

This development seems contradictory when we consider it in the light of what we had previously learnt from scholarship in the fields of the sociology and psychology of work and ergonomic studies. These fields have up until now argued that participation, flexibility, and self-organization are the most important elements of a modern organization of work and of organization oriented towards the criteria of employees' capacity to perform and innovate and the promotion of their health. Does this mean that the concepts designed to foster a participatory organizational culture that allows the subjective potential of employees to blossom have failed? Or is the success of the concept of participation only possible if a high price is paid for it in practice – new and more extensive socio-psychological burdens and dangers to health?

This article takes this question as its starting point, and addresses the issue from a conceptual perspective informed by the sociology of work and industrial sociology. We begin with the discussion of the developments of the 1990s (first section). In the wake of the lean production debate, it seemed that approaches to organization such as "innovative organization of work" and "participatory management" had been successful across the board, and with them the direct participation of employees in the development of work, processes of change, and companies' decisions seemed to be on the way to establishing itself as the one-best-way of the organization and control of work. At the beginning of the new millennium, however, the win-win euphoria increasingly gave way to disillusionment. It is now taken for granted that employees participate to a greater extent than in the past, but in view of the renewed popularity of "intelligent" Taylorist solutions and the increase in workloads, especially in the psychological sense, one can only speak to a limited degree of a simultaneous advance of humanization across a broad front. Our second section therefore has the subtitle "From win-win euphoria to disillusionment", and here we examine the expectations and developments associated with, and the current state of, "innovative organization of work" and "participatory management". In the third section of the article, we suggest that a "semi-innovation" has taken place. The development of work and concepts of participatory management has come to a halt half way to its destination, and is currently even in danger of undermining its own basic principles – the capacity and preparedness of employees to perform to the best of their abilities. This can be seen most clearly in the rising level of burdens placed on, and dangers to, their health. In the fourth and final section, we argue that despite these problems the concept of participation should not be condemned prematurely as a failure; rather, it needs to be implemented more consistently and extended. We discuss this in conclusion by looking at the idea of setting up a system of "participatory health management".[1]

---

1 This article summarizes theoretical and empirical preparatory work and the preliminary findings of different ongoing research projects. It is principally based on the project "PARGEMA – Partizipatives Gesundheitsmanagement" (funded by the Federal Ministry of Education and Research under its funding programme "Prevention", and on the project C1, "Ökonomie und Arbeit im nachfordistischen Übergangsregime", which is part of the "Reflexive Modernization" Research Center in Munich.

2. Development of Work and Participatory Management in the 1990s: From Win-Win Euphoria to Disillusionment

2.1. From euphoria...

Since the mid-1980s, and since the 1990s at the latest, participation has been considered a central element in the "modern" organization of work (Dörre 2002). Since then, participation by employees, whether described as "participatory management" (Pekruhl 2001), "innovative organization of work" (Wengel et al. 2002), or "innovative industrial relations" (Schumann 2003; Kuhlmann 2004) has played a key role in the "modernization" of the organisation of work and of the structures of enterprises. But participation was certainly not discovered or invented when these concepts emerged in the 1990s – one of the traditional demands of the workers' movement and the trade unions is that employees should be involved in running their workplaces. In earlier decades, though, the "struggle to be involved" (Dörre 2002) was fought *against* resistance put up by the enterprises; in the 1990s, the enterprises went onto the offensive. Now management is demanding that employees should take more responsibility, show more initiative of their own, organize themselves to a greater extent, and think more about the future of the enterprise. And it is management, which, made more confident by current theories of management (and fashions), is setting about implementing and pushing through different forms of enhanced participation by employees. In this way, participation is becoming an important element in new management strategies designed to overcome problems and obstacles holding up Taylorist or Fordist conceptions of rationalization.

It is argued that these strategies are superior to Fordist-Taylorist approaches to rationalization because they are more flexible (and cheaper!) as ways of responding to the growing dynamism of markets and enterprises.[2] The second argument put forward in support of these strategies is that new arrangements for the organization of work are more efficient. Such arrangements are constituted by more extensive (direct) participation and a more comprehensive reliance on the (more or less) "whole person". This person is expected to participate actively, using his/her creative potential, in organizing his/her own work and reshaping the organization: "The key resource of the concept [innovative industrial relations] is the creative ability of every individual, the blossoming subjectivity

2 The significance of the need for greater flexibility, and the consequences of this for the development of organizations, are expressed in contemporary descriptions such as "the flexible, market-centred model of production" (Dörre and Röttger 2003) and "flexible capitalism" (Sennett 1998).

whose capacities are only used to an unsatisfactory extent or completely suppressed in the traditional organization of companies and work." (Schumann 2003, p. 51) "Participatory management uses and promotes, in a systematic way, the capacities and motivation of the employees in such a way as to continually optimise production and the development of goods and services." (Pekruhl 2001, p.10) "The involvement of those affected is the alpha and omega of the innovative organization of work ... Nearly all leading companies involve the people affected in the search for solutions." (Kiel and Kirner 2002)

The spread of management strategies and forms of organization oriented towards participation is not really the consequence of a change of values or culture, "rethinking" in the true sense of the word. It has more to do with a complex situation of upheaval in which the economy is at a transitional stage (Sauer 2005). With the emergence of "new conceptions of production" and the spread of "lean" conceptions of organization, the involvement of employees fits very well (or at least better than in earlier decades) into an overall conception of modernization which includes the restructuring of relations between enterprises (Altmann et al. 1986; Sydow and Windeler 1994; Sauer and Döhl 1997), the comprehensive reorganization of enterprise structures (Sauer and Döhl 1997), and the organization of work (Kern and Schumann 1984; Schumann et al. 1994; Nordhause-Janz and Pekruhl 2000; see also Kratzer 2003). Different approaches to rationalization and restructuring have now begun to interlock in a new way, and this is likely to have given the decisive impulse to an organization of work oriented towards the involvement of employees and "participatory management".

Accordingly, "innovative organization of work" and participatory management are not closed concepts. Each of them is an overarching concept covering conceptions, forms of organization, and management strategies which have a common feature: they are all attempts to use (more) "participation, cooperation and autonomy" (Nordhause-Janz and Pekruhl 2000) in order to give more scope to, and to harness within a company, the potential and resources of the employees. Individual elements of this overall strategy include (see, among others, Nordhause-Janz and Pekruhl 2000; Wengel et al. 2002; Sauer et al. 2005):

- *Teamwork*: This, at least in the most advanced forms of "structurally innovative teamwork" (Schumann and Gerst 1997), is based on the idea of greater direct participation in the carrying out of work (see also Pekruhl 2001; Nordhause-Janz and Pekruhl 2000, and others);
- *Project work and quality circles*: These are considered to be forms of systematic (individual) involvement of employees in institutions within companies (e.g. quality management, health and safety standards) or in reorganiza-

tion processes (on this point see Greifenstein et al. 1993; Wengel et al. 2002, p. 54 ff.);

- *Discussions with employees and surveys of their views* can be used as instruments providing for the direct individual involvement of employees in development processes within companies (Greifenstein et al. 1993; Wengel et al. 2002);
- Forms of *organization of working hours*, in which the concrete organization of working hours is left more or less in the hands of employees (this can range from working time accounts to trust based working time) (on this point see, for example, Lehndorff 2003; Kratzer and Sauer 2005);
- Finally, *changes of overall organization*: in addition to the setting up of profit centres, the dismantling of levels of hierarchy is considered to be particularly significant, because in both cases (and they are often combined) responsibility is delegated "downwards", to the parts of a company actually carrying out tasks (see also Wengel et al., 2002).

What was special about "participatory management" and "innovative organization of work" was that a new synthesis of rationalization and humanization was promised, and that the justification offered for this was not only normative but also, to the same and even a greater degree, functional. Publications in this field argue that what distinguishes participatory conceptions of work is that they lead to such impressive economic results precisely because they promote and make use of human resources, not in spite of this.[3] It is this synthesis of rationalization and humanization, which is held to be possible, that provides the idea of employees' participation with its discreet charm and was seen to justify a veritable "win-win" euphoria.

The idea of participation is associated with expectations about certain improvements – specific, reciprocal, positive correlations; in principle, there is also solid scientific evidence to support these expectations:

Participation and the success of enterprises: It is true that there is debate, or rather there is as yet no conclusive evidence, about whether there are direct connections between employees' involvement (i.e. collective, indirect, and formalized participation) and the economic development of an enterprise (capacity to innovate, capacity to formulate long-term strategies, sustainability, productivity), and if so what these connections are. Some scholars have, however, argued that complex chains of cause and effect make it reasonable to suppose that there are

3 This is probably what distinguishes the *social scientific* conceptions we are mainly dealing with here. Conceptions from the field of business management sound very similar, but they sometimes rest on slightly different foundations.

such effects, and that these are largely indirect (Kamp and Simon 2005; Blume and Gerstlberger 2007). There is, on the other hand, widespread agreement that direct, individual participation has "productive" effects – whether this is a matter of carrying out work (teamwork, job rotation) or of institutional involvement in processes of change (quality circles, the mechanism for making suggestions, etc.) (on this point, see Blume and Gerstlberger 2007).

Participation and motivation: On the assumption that everyone has a need to participate, one of the main arguments put forward in support of forms of organization of work and enterprises oriented towards the involvement of employees is that participation promotes motivation. One recent survey found that when a business is run on "colleague-oriented" lines, the employees complain less about obstacles making their jobs difficult, and are much more likely to feel that they are occupying themselves usefully and are able to influence their working situation (Barmer 2007). It is not easy to demonstrate empirically that this is actually the case, since the connections between needs, interests, motivating factors, and so on are complex. Nevertheless, there is a consensus that participation has a motivating effect and that it contributes both to the satisfaction of employees and to productivity (see, for example, Pekruhl 2001, p. 32 ff.). It is therefore also unsurprising that participation, for example in the form of "influence on the way of working", is seen – from the point of view of employees – as an important dimension of "good work" (Fuchs 2006).

Participation and health: The connection between participation and health is considered to be a central element of "human-oriented" organization of work. According to this school of thought, employees who enjoy a certain measure of autonomy in their work, or participation, are not only more productive, creative, and contented, but also healthier. Salutogenic potential is seen to exist if employees can be given opportunities to influence their working conditions and routines themselves in a positive way (Ulich 2005; Richter 2004; Lüders and Pleiss 1999). This is thus a matter of direct, individual involvement in the ways in which work is carried out and organized. In addition, scholars point to positive correlations between individual or collective involvement of employees in a company's health service and their health situation (Lenhardt 2006). Working conditions which correspond to this participatory model both make demands on and foster the competences and initiative of the employees. Restrictions ("obstacles") which contradict this model, on the other hand, lead to inefficient ways of working and increase the risk of psychosomatic illnesses and complaints (Oesterreich and Volpert 1999; Lenhardt 2006).

2.2 ... *to disillusionment*

The 1990s began with the lean production debate and ended with the shattering of the brief dream that virtual prosperity could be a permanent condition. In this period, much of what had been demanded for a long time but could not be implemented or pushed through seemed to become reality almost by itself. The costs of this were high (massive restructuring, staff cuts, widespread insecurity), but at least in the organization of work, progress in the sense of reconciliation between the economy and humanity and the opening up of quite new potential sources of productivity *and* individual development seemed to have arrived. The nature of "real" modernization, of "genuinely" innovative organization of work was clear, and the only remaining question seemed to be whether and to what extent enterprises and policy were already going about things the right way. So there was a great deal of measuring and drawing up of balances[4] in attempts to assess how widespread participation, cooperation, and autonomy already were and to what extent the hoped-for consequences and effects could be observed.

On the whole, the forms of work and organization which are said to involve at least some element of "innovative" organization of work are widespread, and in part they are already taken for granted. In production, hardly any work is performed that is *not* done "in teams" (whatever teamwork may consist of in particular cases), many employees take part at least occasionally in quality or health circles or projects, surveys of employees or discussions with them have become normality, working time accounts are widely used, hierarchies are flat, and so on (on these issues, see for example Sauer et al. 2005; Kratzer and Sauer 2005; Groß and Schwarz 2006). Wengel and his colleagues come to the following conclusion: "These figures show that, at the very least, things are on the move in a qualified minority of German enterprises, and we can conclude that the capacities and motivation of employees are being used to a greater extent" (Wengel et al. 2002, p. 61).

Nevertheless, the overall balance is negative. The state and dynamics of the spread of the innovative organization of work leaves something to be desired when one measures what has been achieved against the standard set by more ambitious conceptions. For one thing, this balance can be summed up by saying that in particular cases it is often unclear what is meant by "teamwork", "discussion among colleagues", etc. Secondly, the forms mentioned often meet no more

4 As for example in the projects that were part of the programme "Lessons Learned", funded by the Federal Ministry of Education and Research (see, for example, Wengel et al. 2002).

than the minimum criteria for innovative organization of work (see Wengel 2002; Schumann 2003).

In addition, not only is it the case that progress towards more participation and autonomy seems to have been slowed or even halted, it has frequently gone into reverse. Taylorist forms of work and principles of organization proved to be persistent (see Kurz 1998), or have even become stronger again in the shape of a new "industrialization" of work in service industries (see, for example, the discussions in Pohlmann et al. 2005) or as a "return to Taylorism" (Springer 1998). Klaus Dörre sums up the situation: "Two basic models in the development of participatory forms of work can be distinguished from one another. Various forms of involvement have been extended in a minority of companies, but stagnation and retrograde developments in industrial relations are dominant" (Dörre 2002, p.345). However, even if demanding forms of participation have not established themselves as *the* new mode of organization and rationalization, the active involvement of employees in rationalization is an essential structural feature of the "flexible, market-centred model of production" and so cannot easily be reversed. But there is a high price to be paid for this. Direct participation is often combined with a simultaneous erosion of individual participation and rights to participation, that is to say with a crisis in the functioning and legitimacy of the institutionalized representation of interests. And what is more, improved performance becomes the "absolutely dominant goal of participation. Other goals, such as the improvement of working conditions by means of intelligent forms of organization, are receiving less and less attention" (Dörre 2002, p. 386 ff.).

In practice, therefore, the innovative organization of work and participatory management are not living up to expectations when one measures them against the ambitious criterion that they should lead to an at least partial reconciliation between rationalization and humanization (which is constitutive of the idea of "innovative industrial relations", on this point see Schumann et al. 1994; Kuhlmann 2004). This can perhaps be seen most clearly in the development of workloads and the consequences of this for health, wellbeing, and the compatibility of work and life.

Some observers had hoped that physical burdens would cease to be an issue, but this has not happened. At the same time, we can observe massive increases in psychological and social burdens in the very places where the organization of work contains at least some participatory elements. The proportion of demanding activities, and the number of jobs where employees have the possibility of influencing working methods and the order in which they carry out tasks, are increasing to the same degree as pressure of work, time pressure, excessive burdens, and excessive demands, at the same time as working hours are getting longer and the proportion of working hours experienced as problematic is increasing (Lenhardt and

Priester 2005; Ahlers and Brussig 2004; Latniak and Gerlmaier 2006; Graß and Schwarz 2006; Fuchs 2006). Another way in which this development becomes visible is in the level of illness caused by work; this, at least, is how the steep increase in the proportion of psychological or psychiatric illnesses, which rose between 2001 and 2005 from 5.3% to 10.5% of working days lost because of illness (BauA 2007), has been interpreted.

This development must appear paradoxical when seen through the lenses of classical ideas about the humanization of work (Moldaschl 2001). A number of different attempts have been made to explain it.

The first explanation offered argues that the most important factor are the broader basic conditions in which participatory organization of work has been implemented, which mean that effects of participation that should reduce burdens or even act in a salutogenic way do not make themselves felt. The argument here is that participation is the right course to follow, but changed contextual factors endanger the success of participatory approaches. The factors identified include short-term utility calculations as a consequence of an enterprise policy that gives more weight to shareholders' interests, a phenomenon known as "shareholder value economy" (for example Schumann 1998), the obstructive activities of executives who are worried that their influence will decline, and the inertia of structures and cultures shaped by Fordism and Taylorism (for example Minssen 1999; Pekruhl 2002). In addition, it is suggested that employees are now more afraid of losing their jobs and that this factor is a burden which is increasingly outweighing the other influencing conditions (on this point, see also Dörre 2002; Fuchs 2006).

The second explanation starts from the forms of work themselves, and tries to identify specific burdens and new kinds of burden which result from the participatory organization of work itself. The most significant elements identified here are the growing demands being made on people's capacity to organize (themselves), increased pressure to obtain technical and social qualifications, the greater variety of sometimes contradictory demands being made in the workplace, burdens resulting from more personalized forms of cooperation and communication, and the absence of clearly defined boundaries between one's own responsibilities and those of others or between one's roles as an employee and as a person (for example Dörre 2002; Pröll and Gude 2003; Kratzer 2003; Peters and Sauer 2005; Krömmelbein 2005).

If one sums up the development of the participatory organization of work in the 1990s, two main results can be identified. Since the end of the new economy hype at the latest, the discussion has been dominated by increasing disillusionment about the extent, degree of diffusion, and repercussions of ambitious conceptions of participation. At the same time, however, the greater involvement of employees in the organization of work and in processes of rationalization and reorganization now seems to have become the normal state of affairs and must be seen as a trend that cannot easily be reversed. However, this trend has a number of consequences and side effects. Among these is the fact that the forms of participation that have been most successful in establishing themselves have been direct, weakly formalized and relatively unregulated, and these (together with the simultaneous weakening of institutional forms of participation and bodies as a result of the changed basic conditions) are tending to increase the pressure on employees to perform and to leave them largely at the mercy of the demands of a market-centred model of production – demands to which there may be no limit (Peters and Sauer 2005).

This has particular consequences for the development of working conditions and, above all, for workloads. It had been hoped that a salutogenic or at least a less burdensome organization of work would develop, and that this would also make it possible for the subjective potential and resources of employees to blossom and develop. But this has for the most part not happened, and the growth of psychological burdens is one of the most visible effects. The idea of greater involvement of employees is unlikely to have been the case of this in itself, since this would contradict everything we know about the ways in which participation improves motivation and has salutogenic effects. The question is not whether the participatory organization of work has failed, but rather to what extent, given the changes in basic conditions and the specific burdens that participatory forms of work may place on employees, there is still any prospect of working life being humanized. The basic conditions are no longer what they were in the postwar decades or the 1990s. It is no longer (just) a matter of debates about Taylorist forms of organization and principles of rationalization, as in the 1970s and 80s, nor is it (just) a matter of making more or less participatory arrangements while modernization processes take place almost by themselves, as in the 1990s. Today, what must be done is to implement and push through participation as a principle and conception, under the conditions of new forms of organization and control and against new market-centred, result-oriented rationalization strategies. In view of the findings on new risks to health and socio-psychological burdens, it is vital for performance policy and the organization of work to take forms that are good for employees' health and for health and safety standards to be adapted to the new conditions.

One possible answer to the problems encountered in implementing the conceptions of participation put forward so far *and* the changed conditions of today's world of work could be the idea of "participatory health management".[5]

5 When we speak of "participatory health management", we refer to conceptions, empirical findings, and approaches to organization that are currently being worked out

"Participatory health management" refers back to the conceptions already discussed here, "innovative organization of work" and "participatory management", in two ways. Initially, the idea is to broaden the conceptions of participation (and the goals they set themselves) that refer to the work process so that they apply to health and safety standards in companies. In a second step, it is necessary to go beyond these conceptions. Certain questions about direct participation, to which no satisfactory answers have yet been found, also arise in relation to the participation of employees in health and safety measures within companies – for example, questions about the conditions and possibilities of collective support for direct participation by individuals. If one looks more closely at these and other questions, something else becomes apparent: a conception such as participatory management contains specific inherent simplifications and contradictions, which are probably also ideological in nature and are currently becoming more obvious. One place where they become visible is at the boundaries of the implementation of "advanced" forms of new conceptions of management and control. At the same time, it becomes clear that these are no more than "semi-innovations" in the very places where they have been at least partially implemented, and as soon as one begins to ask questions about wellbeing and health. The goal of greater efficiency has been achieved, but at the cost of increased pressure to perform and new dangers to health. And finally, it becomes clear (not just in relation to the health question, but there too) that these conceptions cannot "resolve" the more fundamental conflicts and contradictions of work, and that they can even intensify such conflicts and set them in motion at a new level. The "weakness" of these conceptions lies in the fact that they provide "old" answers to new forms of control. This does not mean that these answers, as fundamental scientific findings (especially in the fields of "humanization research" and ergonomic studies) are obsolete, and it certainly does not mean that the intentions and demands associated with them are obsolete. What is needed, though, is a debate about the changed conditions and the possible change in the meaning of the demand for "participation" that would follow. As we have already said: the "right thing", the demand for more autonomy, participation, and opportunities to develop one's own capacities in work, does not therefore become false, but the conceptions designed to bring this about may under some circumstances not have the desired effects.

---

and tested in the framework of the project "PARGEMA – Partizipatives Gesundheitsmanagement". This project is being coordinated at the ISF Munich, and six institutes from the academic sphere and the world of practice as well as companies are involved. The project is funded by funded by the Federal Ministry of Education and Research under its funding programme "Prevention" and runs from June 2006 to November 2009.

For these reasons, we will start by discussing the "well-known" answers, after which we go on to present our own suggestions. These, though, should be understood as provisional hypotheses.

3. Participation in new forms of organization and control

New conceptions of control and management in which self-organization and taking responsibility for one's own work on the part of employees are constitutive components have to a considerable extent become established. A central element of these new conceptions of control and management is the "indirect control" of work and performance. Indirect control means that work continues to be coordinated, managed, and also controlled by the company and its management, but this is no longer done directly by means of detailed instructions and personal control by superiors. Instead, it is done "indirectly" by means of control of the basic conditions (e.g. budgets or the allocation of personnel) or by setting targets (e.g. turnover targets, delivery dates, customer satisfaction, etc.). The theoretical conception of "indirect control" confronts the old "command system" with a new principle of authority and control: instead of orders and obedience, a principle of control is introduced in which the management no longer exerts direct control but makes itself into a basic condition within which more or less autonomous employees act. This does not necessarily mean that employees enjoy more freedom of action at the level of work, since "liberation" from the hierarchy leads to the "bondage" of factors that cannot be influenced – set targets, personnel capacities, process standards, etc. (see Peters and Sauer 2005).

The new forms of control and organization are the changed organizational framework within which the subjective and health-promoting potential of "participatory" or "innovative" forms of organization of work can unfold further – or should be unfolded further. But indirect control, self-organization, and new autonomy are not miracle cures that will bring about innovative and flexible organization by themselves. If and how forms of indirect control or participatory organization of work are felt by employees to be burdens, and are associated with dangers to health, depends very much on the contextual conditions within the company and outside it (see for example Richter 2004; Pröll and Gude 2003). These conceptions therefore need to be developed further: findings from ergonomics, industrial medicine, and industrial psychology show that there is no doubt that these forms of control and organization have the capacity to allow the subjective and health-promoting potential of the new autonomy to unfold, but they can also endanger this potential. The relevant studies show that there is no doubt that new forms of control in organizations can lead both to an improvement in the positive criteria used to evaluate work (such as tasks which make it possible to develop capacities further) and to a strengthening of negative criteria such as time pressure and pressure to perform (e.g. Beiroth 2005), the endangering of social resources in the private family sphere, chronic disturbances of the rhythm of effort and relaxation, damage to social resources in the sphere of work, and the loss of (familiar) performance standards (Pröll and Gude 2003, p.165). New forms of control and organization lead to contradictory working conditions for employees. On the one hand, employees have more opportunities to act in ways they can organize themselves, with more scope to take their own decisions. The performance of tasks is experienced as meaningful, stimulating, and integral. On the other hand, we can observe serious psychological strains, especially as the result of time and performance pressure (Böllinger 2001; Bröder 2002; Gerlmaier 2003).

The result of the ambivalences of new forms of organization and control is that the original approaches to the participatory or innovative organization of work are no longer relevant, and we are now confronted with a *different organizational task*. It is no longer a question of ensuring that individual scope for action and organization is established as a productive and salotugenic potential. The question now is *how the productive and salutogenic potential of the new autonomy can be developed and encouraged against the background of a situation in which indirect forms of control are increasingly establishing themselves.*

4. From semi-innovation to "participatory health management"

It is clear that what we are dealing with is "semi-innovation". Enterprises are succeeding in their efforts to harness the performance-enhancing potential of "innovative organization of work", "participatory management", and so on, but the potential that might lead to improved health for employees is for the most part not being used. In most companies today, fewer employees are carrying out the same amount of work or even more. But the "other" side of innovation, the humanization of work, the promotion of wellbeing and health and the blossoming of the creative potential of workers seems to have fallen by the wayside. If one seeks explanations for this, one answer offered is that the innovative organization of work with its post-Taylorist features and new burdens is encountering a largely traditional conception of health and safety standards. Without accompanying innovations in this sphere, not only will "innovative organization of work" get stuck half way, it will even risk endangering its own foundations – the capacity and preparedness of employees to work efficiently and productively.

This means that "participatory management" must also provide for participation on questions to do with burdens and risks, wellbeing and health, and that "innovative organization of work" must be accompanied by innovative health and safety measures in which employees are involved to a greater degree. But what could this mean? What would a participatory health management look like, institutionally and in terms of content, that *also* gave a central role to the involvement of employees in questions to do with reducing burdens and improving health?

The first answer is as follows. Participatory health management means creating a new relationship between the organization of work and health and safety measures, and between direct and indirect participation. Seen from one perspective, this involves a broadening of the idea and aspirations of participation so that it is incorporated into health and safety standards. In "participatory management", employees are co-experts on matters relating to their own work, and now they must also have the possibility of being experts on their own health. And this entails the organization of or support for instruments, procedures, and institutions providing for greater direct and indirect involvement of employees in health and safety measures. Seen from the management perspective, it means that health, protection against risks, etc. themselves become dimensions of control for participatory management. The questions with which health and safety measures are concerned (protection against risks, the promotion of wellbeing and health, the sustainability of work, and so on) become questions of the control and organization of work. The interface between these two concerns is the subject of participation, i.e. in the final analysis the individual. Ideally, in participatory health management individuals become institutional actors of health and safety measures, and their individual interests become institutional dimensions of the control and organization of work. Participatory health management then means not just a new relationship between the organization of work and safety in the workplace, but also a new relationship between direct and indirect participation. Opportunities to participate should be created which go beyond the indirect involvement of workers councils, and which are safeguarded by collective agreements and supported by collective bodies whose central actors are now primarily the employees themselves (see also Dörre 2001).

The second answer starts from the conception itself, rather than from the institutional arrangements which accompany or integrate the "participatory management" of work processes or the extension of innovative work policy to include health and safety measures. We would like to put forward two hypotheses on this point.

Firstly, the conception of "participatory management" is not a model designed to challenge the Fordist-Taylorist principle of control, because its understanding of participation ("being involved in decisions") is an essentially Fordist one. Whereas "participatory management" provides for employees to be "involved" in decisionmaking (Pekruhl 2001, p. 10), in the new forms of control (let us call these "post-Fordist") it is the employees themselves who decide. However, they decide under conditions they cannot themselves influence, and which have been established by a combination of the market and the management. New forms of control change fundamentally the meaning of concepts like "participation" and "hierarchy". The question we need to look at is whether, under these conditions, "participation" is still the right concept; should we, perhaps, redefine it or replace it with a different concept?

Secondly, new and "innovative" conceptions of management or of the organization of work are not solutions to conflicts between different interests or to the problems of power and authority in companies. The idea that they might be is probably the greatest misunderstanding in relation to these concepts, and it is a "misunderstanding" that is sometimes deliberately propagated. However, they are the basis on which it is possible to reformulate the problems and for new conflict constellations, and they provide a new framework in which conflicts can take place, movement can occur, and difficulties can be dealt with. One example of this is the way new forms of control treat the individual as an object (the idea being to activate new working potential and new resources in the individual's lifeworld), but also as a subject of control (self-control, etc.). In this way, "classical" problems such as the control of performance or health and safety issues are individualized: pressure of work is interpreted as a matter of excessive demands made on the individual, and if an individual cannot do what is demanded of them this is interpreted as personal failure (someone is "badly organized"). Health risks seem to be mainly the responsibility of those affected. In this way health issues are no longer seen simply as collective problems (if this was ever simple), which are taken up by collective representative bodies on behalf of the employees in a procedure for resolving disputes; instead, they are dealt with, if at all, as individual issues. There is a danger that under the conditions of new forms of control, health questions will become taboo. Open criticism of working conditions within a company that present a danger to health risks being interpreted as an admission that the individual is not up to performing at the level required. This problem gets even worse if "company health cultures" are such that there is no space in which questions related to health and new kinds of burdens can be raised, and there is no way of addressing these issues. As a result, the possibility of illness is denied in organizational terms (Kocyba and Voswinkel 2007). This leads us to the question of collective support, and above all of new forms of movement that could represent interests and needs in companies.

This question is especially relevant to companies' performance policies and the two aspects of this that have been brought together here – demands made *on* workers and the demands of workers *themselves*. Under the conditions of new forms of control (including elements of "participatory management" or "innovative organization of work"), it is not just the demands made on workers that change (the debordering, flexibilization, or subjectivization of work – on this point see Kratzer 2003); the procedures and principles of the transformation of abstract performance expectations also become individual demands (the control of work). The conflict about the scale and sustainability of work is more sharply individualized through the increased demands made on workers and, at the same time, by the broader conception of the subject of control. What is missing here are individual and collective forms of the processing of the conflicts that arise.

Approaches to organization that (wish to) rise to these new challenges cannot concentrate on organization alone. They must also address the changed *conditions of organization* of new forms of organization and control, and there are at least four different ways in which they must do this.

- *Firstly*, in the case of indirect control organization and the individual stand in a direct relation to one another. Just as employees "internalize" the organization, so the organization becomes more "subjective", directly dependent on individual flexibility, creativity, and motivation. Because organization and individual behaviour are now so closely intertwined, it hardly makes sense any more to distinguish between conceptions of preventive health and safety standards oriented to relationships, i.e. those primarily referring to the organization, and conceptions oriented to behaviour, i.e. those primarily referring to individual actions. At the same time, however, it becomes clear when one looks at the findings of research on new forms of the organization and control of work that even though the individual person may now be more central, there is a need to go further and pay more attention to the organization of contextual conditions inside and outside companies (see also Ulich 2005).
- *Secondly*, as subjective potential and the resources of individuals' lifeworlds come to play a more important role in self-organized and flexible forms of work in the framework of indirect control, the "whole person" of the worker and his/her entire lifestyle become issues (see, for example, Badura, Schellschmidt, and Vetter 2004; Richter 2004; Kratzer 2003). As this happens, the traditionally limited responsibilities of the institutional actors involved in health and safety measures (company doctors, factory committees, health insurance companies) are increasingly placed in question. Both potentials and risks have to be seen in more complex constellations of factors, and new actors' constellations have to be created in which responsibilities are divided up differently (see Zukunftsfähige Arbeitsforschung 2005).

- *Thirdly*, employees, who continue to be "organized" by others but who are also autonomous actors within the work process, become "their own experts" – initially only in relation to the carrying out of work, but in the longer term also in relation to the way they look after their own health (see for example Kersting, Funk-Müldner, and Sonntag 2005). Under conditions of indirect control, employees have to be brought into internal or external company affairs as actors to a greater extent than in the past. This means that individual interests become a central starting point for collective measures and approaches to organization. This creates even more difficulties. Individuals do not "simply" have an interest in their own health – they have a number of interests which may conflict with one another. It is quite possible for the desire for professional fulfilment, expectations of one's work colleagues, and the demands one makes of one's own actions at work, which are based on professional norms and ideas about what constitutes a "good performance", to conflict with an interest in the long-term safeguarding of one's own health and capacity to perform. The relevant point here is that these contradictions appear *in the person* him/herself. They are not just dissolved into the diametrically opposed interests of enterprises (which want to get as much as possible out of their workers) and employees (who want to put as little strain as possible on their own resources). The example one comes across most frequently is that of employees who clock off and then go back to work.[6] This shows very clearly what kind of difficulties arise if individual interests are taken as the point of reference: personnel departments and bodies representing workers' interests are faced with the paradox that is both *in* employees' interests and *against* their interests to observe legal regulations or collective agreements. On the other hand, employees have an interest in their work, but on the other hand they also have an interest in preserving their own health and wellbeing, or in the compatibility of their work with the demands and needs of their lifeworld (see Kratzer 2003).
- *Fourthly*, forms of indirect control are a component of process-oriented enterprise structures which place a high value on permanent change. This means that organizational problems and the conditions of organization are also being permanently transformed. Just as enterprise structures and work increasingly have to be understood as processes, so too do approaches to organization need to take account, in a process-oriented way, of preventive health and safety measures in the context of indirect control (see Sonntag 2005).

---

6 This is evidently a widespread practice, as we found in our interviews with personnel managers and factory committee members in the framework of the PARGEMA project.

This means that the tasks of "participatory health management" cannot only consist of a transfer of existing conceptions of participation to health and safety measures within companies. If this were done, there would be a danger of "transferring" the misunderstandings and contradictions of these conceptions at the same time. To put it another way: one would then be confronted with the same problems and obstacles that arise when attempts are made to implement "ideal" forms of innovative work policy and participatory management. Going beyond this would mean, above all, developing and supporting ways of formulating these issues and processing them, that is to say creating institutions, actors' constellations, and processes within which the contradictions and conflicts of new forms of control can be articulated and dealt with.

References

(Verbund) Zukunftsfähige Arbeitsforschung (Hrsg.) (2005): Zukunftsfähige Arbeitsforschung – Arbeit neu denken, erforschen, gestalten; Veröffentlichung des Projektträgers Innovative Arbeitsgestaltung, Bonn/Dresden.

Ahlers, E. / Brussig, M. (2004): Gesundheitsbelastung und Prävention am Arbeitsplatz – WSI-Betriebsrätebefragung 2004, in: WSI-Mitteilungen 11/2004, S. 617-624.

Altmann, N. / Deiß, M. / Döhl, V. / Sauer, D. (1986): Ein "Neuer Rationalisierungstyp" – Neue Anforderungen an die Industriesoziologie. In: Soziale Welt, Heft 2/3, 37. Jg., S. 191-206.

Badura, B. / Schellschmidt, H. / Vetter, C. (Hrsg.) (2004): Fehlzeiten-Report 2003 – Wettbewerbsfaktor Work-Life-Balance, Berlin.

BARMER Gesundheitsreport 2007, Wuppertal.

Beiroth, A. (2005): Gefährdungsbeurteilung in der Forschung und Entwicklung eines High-Tech-Unternehmens: Belastungen und Anforderungen in der Projektarbeit. Diplomarbeit, Albert-Ludwigs-Universität Freiburg.

Bollinger, H. (2001): Neue Formen der Arbeit – neue Formen des Gesundheitsschutzes: Das Beispiel Projektarbeit. In: WSI Mitteilungen, Heft 3, S. 685-691.

Brödner, P. (2002): Flexibilität, Arbeitsbelastung und nachhaltige Arbeitsgestaltung. In: P. Brödner / M. Knuth (Hrsg.): Nachhaltige Arbeitsgestaltung. Trendreports zur Entwicklung und Nutzung von Humanressourcen. München, S. 489-541.

Döhl, V. / Sauer, D.: Einführung. In: ISF-München u.a. (Hrsg.) (1997): Jahrbuch Sozialwissenschaftliche Technikberichterstattung 1996 – Schwerpunkt: Reorganisation, Berlin 1997, S. 9-18.

Dörre, K. (2001): Partizipation im Arbeitsprozess- Alternative oder Ergänzung zur Mitbestimmung? In: Industrielle Beziehungen, 8. Jg., Heft 4, 2001, S. 379-407.

Dörre, K. (2002): Kampf und Beteiligung. Arbeit, Partizipation und industrielle Beziehungen im flexiblen Kapitalismus. Eine Studie aus dem Soziologischen Forschungsinstitut Göttingen (SOFI), Wiesbaden.

Dörre, K. / Röttger, B. (Hrsg.) (2003): Das neue Marktregime. Konturen eines nachfordistischen Produktionsmodells, Hamburg.

Fuchs, T. (2006): Was ist gute Arbeit? Anforderungen aus der Sicht der Erwerbstätigen, Bremerhaven.

Gerlmaier, A. / Reick, C. / Kastner, M. (2003): Neue Formen selbstregulativ-flexibler Arbeit im IT-Bereich: Anforderungen, Ressourcenpotenziale und ihre Auswirkungen auf die Arbeits- und Lebensqualität, in: Kastner, M. (2003): Neue Selbständigkeit in Organisationen. Selbstbestimmung, Selbsttäuschung, Selbstausbeutung, Ergebnisbericht des NESTO-Projektes; München/Mering, S. 217-246.

Gerstlberger, W. / Blume, L. (2007): Determinanten betrieblicher Innovation: Partizipation von Beschäftigten als vernachlässigter Einflussfaktor, in: Industrielle Beziehungen, 14. Jg., Heft 3, 2007, S. 223-244

Gließmann, W. / Peters, K. (2001): Mehr Druck durch mehr Freiheit. Die neue Autonomie in der Arbeit und ihre paradoxen Folgen, Hamburg.

Greifenstein, Ralph / Jansen, Peter / Kißler, Leo (1993): Gemanagte Partizipation: Qualitätszirkel in der deutschen und der französischen Automobilindustrie. München, Mering: Hampp.

Groß, H. / Schwarz, M. (2006): Betriebs- und Arbeitszeiten 2005. Ergebnisse einer repräsentativen Betriebsbefragung, Dortmund.

Kamp, L. / Simon, N. (2005): Mitbestimmung als Faktor nachhaltiger Unternehmensentwicklung, in: WSI Mitteilungen, 58. Jg., Heft 8, 2005, S. 459-465.

Kern, H. / Schumann, M. (1984): Das Ende der Arbeitsteilung? – Rationalisierung in der industriellen Produktion, München.

Kersting, J.-M. / Funk-Müldner, K. / Sonntag, K. (2005): Das Projekt SERO: Veränderungen erfolgreich gestalten, in: GfA (Hrsg.): Personalmanagment und Arbeitsgestaltung, Dortmund, S. 81-84.

Kiel, U. / Kirner, E. (Hrsg.) (2002): Formen innovativer Arbeitsgestaltung in Unternehmen und öffentlichen Einrichtungen, München und Mering.

Kocyba, Hermann / Voswinkel, Stephan (2007): Krankheitsverleugnung: Betriebliche Gesundheitskulturen und neue Arbeitsformen. Frankfurt a. M.: Abschlussbericht für die Hans-Böckler-Stiftung.

Kratzer, N. (2003): Arbeitskraft in Entgrenzung. Grenzenlose Anforderungen, erweiterte Spielräume, begrenzte Ressourcen, Berlin.

Kratzer, N. / Sauer, D. (2005): Zeit, Leistung, Beschäftigung – Anforderungen an eine erweiterte Arbeits(zeit)politik. In: H. Seifert (Hrsg.): Flexible Zeiten in der Arbeitswelt, Campus Forschung, Frankfurt/New York, S. 244-259.

Krömmelbein, Silvia (2005): Kommunikation und abnehmende Rollendistanz. Zur Ambivalenz der aktiven Aneignung subjektivierter Arbeitswelten, in: AG SubArO (Hg.): Ökonomie der Subjektivität – Subjektivität der Ökonomie. Berlin: Sigma.

Kuhlmann, M. (2004): Modellwechsel? Die Entwicklung betrieblicher Arbeits- und Sozialstrukturen in der deutschen Automobilindustrie, Berlin.

Kurz, C. (1998): Repetitivarbeit – unbewältigt. Betriebliche und gesellschaftliche Entwicklungsperspektiven eines beharrlichen Arbeitstyps, Berlin.

Latniak, Erich / Gerlmaier, Anja (2006): Zwischen Innovation und alltäglichem Kleinkrieg: zur Belastungssituation von IT-Beschäftigten. Internet-Dokument. Gelsenkirchen: Inst. Arbeit und Technik. IAT-Report, Nr. 2006-04.

Lehndorff, S. (2003): The Long Good-By? Tarifvertragliche Arbeitszeitregulierung und gesellschaftlicher Arbeitszeitstandard. In: Industrielle Beziehungen, 10. Jg., Heft 2, S. 273-295.

Lenhardt, U. / Priester, K. (2005): Flexibilisierung – Intensivierung – Entgrenzung: Wandel der Arbeitsbedingungen und Gesundheit. In: WSI Mitteilungen, 58. Jg., Heft 9, 2005, S. 491-497.

Lenhardt, U. / Rosenbrock, R. (2006): Wegen Umbau geschlossen? Auswirkungen betrieblicher Reorganisation auf den Gesundheitsschutz, Berlin.

Lüders, E. / Pleiss, C. (1999): Werkzeuge gesundheitsgerechter Arbeitsgestaltung – Von der Analyse zur Praxis. In: Oesterreich, R. / Volpert, W. (Hrsg.): Psychologie gesundheitsgerech-ter Arbeitsbedingungen. Konzepte, Ergebnisse und Werkzeuge zur Arbeitsgestaltung, S. 217-266, Bern.

Mikl-Horke, G. (2000): Industrie- und Arbeitssoziologie, München und Wien.

Minssen, H. (1999): Von der Hierarchie zum Diskurs? – Die Zumutungen der Selbstregulation, München/Mering

Moldaschl, Manfred (2001): Herrschaft durch Autonomie – Dezentralisierung und widersprüchliche Arbeitsanforderungen. In: B. Lutz (Hrsg.): ENTWICKLUNGSPERSPEKTIVEN VON ARBEIT, Berlin, S. 132-164.

Naphtali, Fritz (1966): Wirtschaftsdemokratie. Frankfurt a. M.: EVA (orig. 1928)

Nordhause-Janz, J. / Pekruhl, U. (2000): Managementmethoden oder Zukunftskonzepte? – Zur Entwicklung von Arbeitsstrukturen und von Gruppenarbeit in Deutschland. In: J. Nordhause-Janz / U. Pekruhl. (Hrsg.): Arbeiten in neuen Strukturen? München/Mering, S. 13-68.

Oesterreich & Volpert, W. (Hrsg.) (1999): Psychologie gesundheitsgerechter Arbeitsbedingungen. Konzepte, Ergebnisse und Werkzeuge zur Arbeitsgestaltung, S. 217-266, Bern.

Pekruhl, U. (2001): Partizipatives Management. Konzepte und Kulturen, München/Mering.

Peters, K. / Sauer, D. (2005): Indirekte Steuerung – eine neue Herrschaftsform. Zur revolutionären Qualität des gegenwärtigen Umbruchprozesses, in: Wagner, H. (Hrsg.): ‚Rentier' ich mich noch?' Neue Steuerungskonzepte im Betrieb, Hamburg, S. 23-58.

Pohlmann, M. / Sauer, D. / Trautwein-Kalms, G. / Wagner, A. (Hrsg.) (2003): Dienstleistungsarbeit: Auf dem Boden der Tatsachen. Befunde aus Handel, Industrie, Medien und IT-Branche. Berlin: Sigma.

Pröll, U. / Gude, D. (2003): Gesundheitliche Auswirkungen flexibler Arbeitsformen, Schriftenreihe der Bundesanstalt für Arbeitsschutz und Arbeitsmedizin, Fb 986, Dortmund/Berlin/Dresden.

Richter, P. (2004): Gesundheitsförderung in Organisationen – arbeits- und organisationspsychologische Präventionsansätze, in: Wegge, J. / Schmidt, K.-H. / (Hrsg.): Förderung von Arbeitsmotivation und Gesundheit in Organisationen, Göttingen u.a., S. 197-214.

Sauer, D. (2005): Arbeit im Übergang. Zeitdiagnosen, Hamburg.

Sauer, Dieter / Boes, Andreas / Kratzer, Nick (2005): Reorganisation des Unternehmens. In: SOFI / IAB / ISF München / INIFES: Berichterstattung zur sozioökonomischen Entwicklung in Deutschland – Arbeit und Lebensweisen. Erster Bericht, VS Verlag für Sozialwissenschaften, Wiesbaden, S. 323-350.

Sauer, D. / Döhl, V. (1997): Die Auflösung des Unternehmens? – Entwicklungstendenzen der Unternehmensreorganisation in den 90er Jahren, in: IfS / INIFES / ISF / SOFI (Hg.): Jahrbuch sozialwissenschaftliche Technikberichterstattung '96 – Schwerpunkt: Reorganisation. Berlin: Sigma, S. 19-76

Schumann, M. (1998): Frißt die Shareholder-Value-Ökonomie die Modernisierung der Arbeit? In: H. Hirsch-Kreinsen / H. Wolf (Hrsg.): Arbeit, Gesellschaft, Kritik, Berlin, S. 19-30.

Schumann, M. (2003): Metamorphosen von Industriearbeit und Arbeiterbewusstsein. Kritische Industriesoziologie zwischen Taylorismusanalyse und Mitgestaltung innovativer Arbeitspolitik, Hamburg.

Schumann, M. / Baethge-Kinsky, V. / Kuhlmann, M. / Kurz, C. / Neumann, U. (1994): Trendreport Rationalisierung, Berlin.

Schumann, M. / Gerst, D. (1997): Produktionsarbeit – Bleiben die Entwicklungstrends stabil? In: Ifs / INIFES / ISF / SOFI (Hrsg.): Schwerpunkt: Reorganisation, S.131-167.

Sennett, R. (1998): Der flexible Mensch. Die Kultur des neuen Kapitalismus, Berlin.

Sonntag, K. (2005): Innovative Arbeitswissenschaft – Träger von Gesundheit und Leistung bei Veränderungen, in: Gesellschaft für Arbeitswissenschaft

(Hrsg.): Personalmanagement und Arbeitsgestaltung, Bericht zum 51. Kongreß der GfA im Frühjahr 2005, Dortmund, S. 15-21.

Springer, R. (1999): Rückkehr zum Taylorismus? Arbeitspolitik in der Automobil-Industrie am Scheideweg. Frankfurt a. M., New York: Campus.

Sydow, J. / Windeler, A. (Hrsg.) (1994): Management interorganisationeller Beziehungen, Opladen.

Ulich, E. (2005): Gesundheitsmanagment – Elemente einer Positionsbestimmung, in: Gesellschaft für Arbeitswissenschaft (Hrsg.): Personalmanagement und Arbeitsgestaltung, Bericht zum 51. Kongreß der GfA im Frühjahr 2005, Dortmund, S. 131-134.

Vilmar, Fritz (1973): Strategien der Demokratisierung. 2 Bde. Darmstadt, Neuwied

Wengel, J. / Lay, Gunter / Pekruhl, Ulrich / Maloca, S. (2002): Verbreitung innovativer Arbeitsgestaltung. Stand und Dynamik des Einsatzes im internationalen Vergleich, München und Mering.

The role of trade union representatives in the conduct of workplace relations

Sonia McKay

Introduction

Kerr et al (2002) argue that 'union influence in the workplace depends on paid facility time and concrete management support in the shape of good facilities'. However, workplace representatives in the UK have more limited legal rights than is the case for similar representatives in many other EU15 states and a decline in trade union membership and density in UK workplaces means that trade union representatives are now under increased pressure to limit the amount of time that they spend on trade union duties and activities. This has consequences for existing representatives, who perceive their trade union role as stressful and not valued, and also for potential future representatives who are deterred from becoming activists because they are aware of the difficulties which existing representatives experience in trying to combine their union duties with their own work responsibilities and also with their individual work/life balance.

Methodology

The data for this paper is based material from focus groups of workplace trade union activists carried out as part of the UK Labour Government's Review of Workplace Representatives' Facilities and Facility Time in 2006[1]. This involved three focus groups, facilitated by the Trades Union Congress (TUC) and conducted in three UK cities, Manchester, Newcastle and London with 30 existing active workplace trade union representatives representing 12 TUC unions. The focus groups were designed to explore representatives' experiences and attitudes to the current statutory arrangements. Participants came from a wide range of sectors, both public and private, and from small and medium, as well as large workplaces. Selection aimed to ensure that focus group participants were as representative as possible of workplace representatives in terms of their role, gender, ethnicity and age.

1 The authors were commissioned to undertake the research by the then UK Department for Trade and Industry (now BERR).

Employment law and trade union organisation

Until the 1970s there was no UK legislation that set out the rights of trade union representatives to time off to carry out their duties or which provided any rights to basic facilities. Unlike the situation in many other EU15 countries, UK workplace representatives were entirely reliant on their ability to win concessions from employers in respect of time off. This was commonly achieved though trade union recognition agreements that would include provisions on the amount of time off that representatives could claim from the employer and on the range of facilities that the employer would make available to these representatives. In 1968 the Donovan Commission noted that while it was the choice of management whether or not they dealt with workplace representatives, where managers 'had a choice of dealing with either full-time officers[3] or shop stewards, three-quarters of them choose shop stewards'. Workplace representatives were thus acknowledged as a key component of effective industrial relations. However, this did not mean that the exercise of their rights to time off and to facilities was conceded without contest. Employers not only would attempt to restrict entitlement as much as possible but also would withdraw entitlements during periods of conflict.

The absence of legislation providing time off rights for trade union representatives was not unusual in the UK context of the time, where little legislation regulated relationships between workers and employers. The majority of workplaces were covered by union recognition agreements and trade union strength, asserted through a large membership base, was considered sufficient to guarantee the exercise of rights to sufficient time off to perform trade union duties. Indeed the context was one of a general reluctance to consider the use of the law, primarily because, where the law had been used, the judges had generally interpreted it in a way to narrow trade union activities. This position was well summed up by Wedderburn, in his seminal book *The worker and the law* with the words 'British workers wanted 'no more of the law than that it should leave them alone'.

The election of the Wilson Labour Government in 1964 signalled a change in the government's attitude to employment law rights. Labour was keen to create greater worker mobility, to facilitate in the closure of old industries and the movement of workers to new industries. This resulted in a new law, the Redundancy Payments Act 1965, which compensated workers who lost their jobs through redundancy. The law had two outcomes: first it facilitated industrial reorganisation, by making it more attractive to individual workers to change jobs; second, it altered the focus of conflict over industrial reorganisation, by moving it from the location of the workplace to the courts. Trade unions began to construct *legal* arguments for compensation, as an alternative to industrial action to challenge job losses.

In 1971 the newly elected Conservative Government introduced a comprehensive law covering individual and collective workplace issues. Organised workers contested this law and following large-scale protests, including demonstrations and industrial action, the government called an election that it lost. Labour returned to office in 1974, repealing the Conservative law, and replacing it with new laws that would both guarantee individual and collective rights but which consequently would start a process of the incorporation of trade unions within the legal system.

The law on the right to time off

In 1975, the arrangements on time off rights, which had been established through collective agreements, acquired legal support through the introduction of the Employment Protection Act 1975. The Act gave trade union representatives, in workplaces where there was a recognised trade union, the statutory right to paid time off during working hours, to carry out their trade union duties and activities and to participate in trade union training. The law has been amended and in its current form is to be found in section 168 of the Trade Union and Labour Relations (Consolidation) Act 1992. This states:

(1) An employer shall permit an employee of his who is a union official of an independent trade union recognised by the employer to take time off during his working hours for the carrying out any duties of his, as such an official, concerned with
  (a) negotiations with the employer related to or connected with matters falling within section 178(2) (collective bargaining) in relation to which the trade union is recognised, or
  (b) the performance on behalf of the employees of the employer of functions related to or connected with matters falling within that provision which the employer has agreed may be so performed by a trade union.

(2) He shall also permit such an employee to take time off during his working hours for the purpose of undergoing training in aspects of industrial relations
  (a) relevant to carrying out such duties as are mentioned in subsection (1), and
  (b) approved by the Trades Union Congress or by the independent trade union of which he is an official

Thus lay officials of recognised trade unions, including workplace representatives, have the right to time off with pay to carry out their trade union duties. The law does not set out any requirements regarding the number of representatives the employer must accommodate nor does it provide a statutory minimum number of paid hours/days for workplace representatives to perform their functions. Furthermore, the right to time off is restricted to those workplaces where the trade union is formally recognised by the employer and additionally only covers those trade union duties for which there is specific collective agreement. Trade union duties are defined as activities in relation to: terms and conditions, recruitment, suspension, dismissal, work allocation, discipline, union membership, time off facilities and procedures.

However, both the right to time off for trade union duties and for training are restricted by a test of 'reasonableness' and thus constrained by the overall needs of the business. This means that in practice employers may place limits on the number of representatives who can exercise the right to time off at any one time. However, given that under UK law such agreements are not legally enforceable, concessions can always be withdrawn at any stage. Furthermore these agreements require the existence of workplace representatives who are capable of challenging employer power. Deacon and Morris (2005:809) note that the restrictive nature of the legal right means that generally locally agreed arrangements on time off are more generous than the law requires. Bercusson (2002), in contrast, noted that representatives in the UK generally have more limited rights than is the case for representatives in many other EU15 states, where rights are more precisely defined, with representative structures established by legislation or by generally applicable collective agreements.

In addition to the rights to time off, employers who recognise trade unions will usually also offer facilities to employee representatives to enable them to carry out their duties. Although not set out in the statute, the Acas Code of Practice (para 38) states that employers 'should consider making available to officials the facilities necessary for them to perform their duties efficiently and communicate effectively with their members, other lay officials and full time officers.'

While the Conservative government of 1979 to 1997 narrowed workers' rights in a whole range of areas, the rights to time off for trade union duties remained untouched, in the first ten years of the government. However, in 1989, the government did narrow the circumstances where rights to time off could be claimed to those strictly related to collective bargaining, rather than to wider industrial relations issues. This meant that employers could refuse time off for any activities beyond the workplace.

However, soon after the government was obliged to extend the rights to time off to workplace representatives in unrecognised workplaces, as a consequence of EU directives on acquired rights, on the establishment of European works councils and on collective dismissals. Following the election of New Labour in

1997, Union Learning Representatives were promoted through a Union Learning Fund (ULF) set up by the government in 1998, with the stated aim of promoting activity by trade unions in support of the objective of creating a learning society, trade unions were able to build a network of over 18,000 trained Union Learning Representatives, whose role has been to encourage union members to engage and re-engage with learning, largely in the workplace. Thus a key legislative development of significance for union activism was the introduction, in the Employment Act 2002, of statutory rights to time-off for Union Learning Representatives (ULRs). Research suggests that union learning has generated a new layer of union activists and these are often more diverse in terms of gender, race and age than existing representatives (Wood and Moore, 2005).

Two other categories of union representative – equality and environmental representatives – have recently emerged, but as yet there are no specific statutory entitlements covering their activities. In relation to the former, the Women and Work Commission in 2005 had proposed a system of trade union equality representatives who would provide 'a lens of equality across workplace practices, raise issues related to equality and diversity, tackle discrimination, resolve conflict and seek solutions with management alongside other union colleagues' (WWC, 2005). This proposal received concrete support from the government through the Union Modernisation Fund. However, despite a 2006 TUC Congress resolution for equality representatives to be put on a statutory footing, with rights to time off and training, similar to those for trade union workplace representatives, the government has refused this demand (Labour Research, 2008).

The scope of the rights and how they can be exercised have been established through key legal rulings, the most important of which are described below.

Key legal cases on time off rights

Where cases have reached the UK courts they have generally been as a result of the employer setting a narrow definition of the range of activities covered by the time off rights or where the employer denies that there is a right at all. An example is the case of London Ambulance Service v Charlton [1992] ICR 773 (EAT) where workplace representatives in the health service were refused time off by their employer to attend preparatory/co-ordinating meetings of the trade union side. The employer argued that these did not come within the definition of trade union duties. The court, however, ruled against the employer by holding that where meetings are called 'for the genuine purpose of officials discussing their approach to forthcoming negotiations or their consideration as a co-ordinating body of negotiations which have or will take place in other bodies' there was a legal right to time off.

An example of where an employer successfully argued that there was no right to time off is the case of Luce v London Borough of Bexley [1990] IRLR 422. There a teacher representative had been denied time off by his employer to attend a lobby of Parliament organised by his union to protest about an Education Reform Bill. The employment appeal tribunal (EAT) ruled that the lobby was not capable of being a trade union activity and was therefore not covered by the time off rights.

But the real difficulty, which workers have in enforcing the law, is to do with the fact that all employers' actions in response to requests for time off are measured by whether or not the response is reasonable. This means that it is difficult for a representative to know precisely when time off can be claimed and when it cannot. In Diamond v Park Lane College UKEAT/0249/05/LA, Ms Diamond, a workplace representative, lectured for 20 hours a week and was also paid 10 hours' preparation time. She requested and was given twelve days' off with pay, to attend a TUC course, but on condition that this was all set against her preparation time. The employment appeal tribunal held that there was no rule that would prevent what the employer had proposed provided it was a 'reasonable' response by the employer.

The amount of pay to which representatives are entitled has also been the subject of legal rulings. In the case of Hairsine v Kingston-Upon-Hull City Council [1992] ILRL 211 Mr Hairsine, a pool attendant and workplace representative, was given permission to attend trade union training on 12 consecutive Thursdays. However, because he worked shifts, there were days when he would have been rostered to work hours outside those on the course and his employers argued that if he did not work those hours he would not be paid. Mr Hairsine lost his claim at the appeal tribunal, which held that the employer was reasonable in refusing to pay for the hours, which Mr Hairsine did not work.

The practice of union representation

Kelly, in his articulation of mobilisation theory, argues that collective organisation 'is heavily dependent upon the actions of small numbers of leaders or activists' (1998: 44). He suggests 'they' are key in 'framing' injustices, in promoting a shared identity amongst workers, in persuading workers of the benefits of collectivism and in defending collective action in the face of employer opposition. Similarly, Moore's (2004) study of mobilisation and counter-mobilisation in the statutory recognition process confirms that the absence of union activists in the workplace makes it virtually impossible for the union to win recognition ballots,

Sanchez (2007), in his study of Spanish temporary workers, finds that the actual performance of local union representatives is critical to the participation and involvement of atypical workers. Kilkauer (2004), looking at the German automobile sector, similarly finds that trade union shop floor representation is of crucial importance for works councils, industrial democracy and trade unions in German industrial relations. Additionally, Moore and Read (2007) have shown that the absence of key activists in small firms, along with the specific nature of social relations in such workplaces, meant that attempts to organise collectively were unsuccessful or that existing organisation either collapsed or represented a hollow shell. Activists are thus not only critical in generating union organisation and recognition, but also in sustaining organisation (Terry and Edwards, 1988).

Although it is possible to debate the definition and attributes of an activist and the nature of activism and whether it can include anyone who holds a union branch or workplace representative position, this paper explores the barriers to activism, in other words what prevents individuals from becoming workplace representatives or existing activists from being effective. These can be related to wider trends identified as undermining voluntarism and active democratic participation in society. For example White (2004) has argued that the increased importance of market activity and the intensification of work 'crowds out the time and energy needed to develop, maintain and exercise the capacities of competent, democratic citizenship' and that this ultimately undermines the quality of democratic life. Further, with labour market restructuring comes a decline of industrial cultures embedded in localities across Europe and a 'fragmentation' of social identities based upon class, culture and community. This is manifest in unstable and precarious conditions (Beck, 2000), with flexible contracts of work, irregular working hours, and discontinuity in working lives (Sennett, 1998). Thus economic restructuring in the last 20 years has removed many of the supports for collective organisation and representation within the workplace and union involvement in wider society.

In line with the decline in union membership and with the increase in workplaces without union representation in the UK, there has been a reduction in the number of workplace trade union representatives. Over the past ten years the overall numbers of UK trade union activists have fallen and there are also fewer activists in workplaces where there is trade union representation. WERS2004 data (Kersley et al., 2005) records a decline in union workplace representation; members had access to a lay representative at their own workplace in less than half (45 per cent) of recognised workplaces in 2004, compared with more than half (55 per cent) in 1998. Charlwood and Terry (2007) draw upon the WERS2004 data to indicate that the fall in workplace representation 'might suggest a degree of organisational weakness in workplace union structures and a degree of dependence on employer support and goodwill to maintain union presence'. They conclude that any effective system of representation requires the organisational cohesion and strength that has traditionally been provided by trade unions. As Kilkauer, in his study of General Motors in Germany insists, the success of workers' representation through a highly regulated works council system, is 'strongly dependent on a strong union movement at shopfloor level'. However, without the necessary institutional support to activists in carrying out their representative functions such a movement cannot be sustained.

The changed context of representation

The implications of increased international competition, structural change and the reassertion of managerial prerogatives in reshaping workplace employment relations and interest representation have been well documented (Cully et al., 1999; Heery et al., 2003; Terry, 1995). Yet the challenge of these developments for workplace union activism has been less well explored. Upchurch et al (2002) recognise the increasing pressure on the time of stewards due to employers' intensification of work as well as the greater range of substantive and other issues needing to be dealt with. The UK government's 2006 review of facilities and facility time for workplace representatives addressed whether new methods of working at the modern workplace seriously affect the ability of workplace representatives to function well; and whether the effectiveness and efficiency of workplace representatives can be enhanced in order to optimise the net benefits they bring to employees, employers and society more generally. This review assessed whether representatives had sufficient access to facilities and facility time to enable them to carry out their functions efficiently and effectively, bearing in mind the needs and resources of modern workplaces. It also assessed whether there was a need to clarify or simplify the relevant statutory rights governing facilities and facility time, and whether there was adequate practical guidance provided to help parties apply those entitlements at the workplace. The review noted that union representatives are relatively old, on average aged 46 and that women, though an increasing proportion of the total, are under-represented.

The focus group research illuminated the changed context for union activism. The majority of participants were long-standing representatives of ten years or more and able to reflect upon change. Overwhelmingly they reported that organisational change had an impact on their roles and workloads. There were specific issues arising from the reform of the public service sector; for example structural changes in the National Health Service and education; the privatisation of the rail sector (and subsequent negotiation of new company level agreements); and the introduction of performance management and targets. In the private sector the takeover or merger of companies generated new challenges for union representatives. Outsourcing was identified as a major issue for public sector unions, but also in the private sector – one representative working for a contractor reported that this meant that increasingly management could shift the responsibility for issues like health and safety.

Both public and private sector representatives talked about the increase in the number of procedures that they had to be familiar with and the intensification of management systems, (for example, sickness absence) and the greater use of 'capability dismissals'. At the same time managements were using new monitoring and control systems to support individual appraisal, targets and payment processes.

A key area, where the focus group representatives did not feel adequately equipped, was in dealing with their members' stress and wider emotional and mental health problems, which they perceived had increased through organisational change. One representative reported that there were cases that representatives dealt with where members get distressed, and sometimes where members appear suicidal. She suggested that representatives did not have the skills to deal with the personal side of cases, which often demand a counselling role. Another representative concurred that representatives are often 'social workers', but they are not equipped to deal with stress and there was a need to refer members to trained counsellors. In relation to this, participants acknowledged the stress experienced by the representatives themselves, which it was felt was often not recognised; 'unions do not look after their own very well'.

Most of the participants took on multiple roles, as workplace representatives, health and safety representatives and, in a number of cases, as Union Learning Representatives. It appeared that the longer representatives had been in post the more likely they were to combine a number of roles and that those with full-time facility time tended to cover a range of responsibilities. One workplace representative felt he was a 'jack of all trades, but master of none'. As another representative put it:

'It has been a case of you take on one role and you end up finding that you've got three or four. So you might start being health and safety, you know, but you end up looking at union learning and being the union learning rep and then you, all of a sudden, find yourself representing someone in a grievance, because there's no one else to take that on board and invariably you end up swamped, that's the experience that I seem to have at the moment.'

WERS2004 shows that 79 per cent of union reps spent time on terms and conditions; 73 per cent on individual disputes; 69 per cent on selection, development and staffing issues and 68 per cent on welfare issues (Kersley et al., 2006). For the vast majority of the focus group participants their union work was dominated by individual representation and casework. A representative from the Public and Commercial Services trade union (PCS), working in a call centre, reported that very high levels of staff turnover meant that she was continuously involved in disciplinaries, with individual cases 'coming out of our ears'.

Individual casework was accompanied by collective representation; workplace representatives were also engaged in discussions with management about issues affecting the workplace, in particular organisational change. Issues mentioned included the introduction of new sickness procedures, consultation on restructuring, changes to the staff handbook and, in the case of a representative at an airport, discussions on heightened security arrangements. Only one representative mentioned involvement in bargaining over pay or terms and conditions, although this may reflect the sectoral distribution of the representatives (there was a predominance of public sector representatives) or the role of full-time officers in negotiations.

The focus group research confirmed that many workplace representatives had difficulties in securing paid time-off for union duties. The main barrier was the issue of staff cover and the pressures that time-off places upon work teams and work colleagues. Recent workforce reductions were seen to increase pressures on staff and in the public sector the introduction of performance targets and indicators intensified this. As one participant put it, 'time spent on union duties is considered time lost'. One representative said she could take time off as and when needed, but that she 'capped herself' because of the pressure of her personal workload and deadlines. There were specific difficulties for shift workers, who often had to give up their own time to represent or deal with workers on other shifts. Continuing workforce reductions together with the widespread use of performance targets and indicators meant that local managers and line supervisors were reluctant to agree to time off, where this would have an impact on their overall productivity. The fact that the law has a 'reasonableness' test allowed managers to assert that their right to manage superseded the right of employee representatives to time off. Representatives also felt that while employers might grant time off for duties that were very directly relevant to the specifics of the workplace, they were less willing to do so for activities that were perceived as being outside the employer's core interests, including rights to time off for trade union training. Although participants generally got time off for formal representation and meetings with managers, many reported that they did not get time to talk to members about union or workplace issues. The privatisation of public services had also resulted in employers restricting time off rights. Employers were reluctant to grant time off to represent members who had been outsourced to other employers under contracting out arrangements, and privatisation and outsourcing had presented particular challenges for union representation and organisation.

There was variation in the number of members each representative was responsible for, but representatives increasingly had responsibility for representing larger groups of workers, spread throughout diverse locations. Increasingly varied working patterns and arrangements made communication with members difficult and were seen as undermining union organisation. This picture is supported by Kerr et al., (2002) earlier study of representatives in what was then the largest UK trade union, UNISON. This found that UNISON representatives on average had responsibility for 32 members and that up to a quarter of representatives had no paid release time, while a further 18 per cent received only an hour a week.

The pressures faced by activists in terms of time also meant that representatives did not take up the opportunity for activist training, which was crucial for their development. As one focus group participant, who worked in a public sector workplace where there had been job cuts, put it:

'I've had stage one [training], but it's been a case of the training is available, certainly if I want to go on training I could, but I think because the section has shrunk so much, I just feel that I can't do that, I feel guilty taking a day off. But if I say I really need this training, they will be fine about it, but I just wonder what they say behind your back? So it's basically a guilt thing that I don't take it up, but it is available if I wanted to do it, I just basically do the basics, that I have to and learn most of it on the job, by speaking to the other reps'.

In some cases representatives felt pressure from colleagues that made them reluctant to pursue training. Participants said that attendance on union courses was often perceived by work colleagues as a 'good blag' or 'off on a jolly', particularly when courses were away from home; it was reported that members said they 'couldn't see the benefit'. One participant said that she had produced leaflets for members outlining what she had learned on courses in order to demonstrate what she was doing when she was out of the workplace.

WERS2004 shows that senior union representatives at recognised workplaces spend an average 12.5 hours a week on their union duties, most is taken during working time, although the Government's review acknowledges that a significant amount is taken in the representative's own time. Across the focus groups it was clear that the vast majority of participants spent a substantial amount of their own time, outside work, undertaking union activities. In one group four participants agreed that they spent on average ten hours a week of unpaid time. All participants reported that members expected them to be constantly available, including outside of work, and they themselves felt they had to be accessible at all times. Many shared the experience of being contacted in the evenings and weekends. In terms of work-life balance there was an absolute assumption by all participants that union activity had an impact upon this, but there was little discussion on it as it appeared to be taken for granted, or seen as a 'given'. One representative from a top UK supermarket reported:

'Personally, my husband has banned anyone from using the home phone because when I'm at home, I'm at home. But then if I'm not on the phone then I'm on the computer trying to research whatever it is I'm doing. Or emailing people because we haven't got that access at work and my mobile is always going. Sometimes they'll call me over the weekend. I've been on the nightshift; I've dropped everything and gone in first thing in the morning, even though I'm going off to do something. I'm in the store at six o'clock in the morning if they've had an issue go on overnight. And it's just... quality time rather than work life balance. It has an impact on quality time.'

One further concern was in relation to their own career or professional development. There was an almost universal view that trade union activity had a negative impact on workers' career progression and that trade union representatives were more at risk, for example from selection for dismissal in the event of redundancies, despite the fact that the law is supposed to give them protection from victimisation. These findings resonate with those of Kerr et al (2002), where respondents stated that the reason why members were not taking up representative positions was because the jobs involved too much responsibility and might damage career prospects.

The vast majority of focus group participants displayed high levels of commitment to trade unionism. This suggests that the levels of work outside working hours necessary to sustain their role as workplace representatives may discourage those with less commitment, or who could not or would not be prepared to accept disruptions to their work-life balance. The difficulties representatives faced in performing their duties effectively, along with high workloads, were seen as a deterrent to the generation of new representatives, as articulated by this focus group participant:

'The problem is, you're obviously an extremely dedicated person to do this, but it's scandalous really, how can we bring new people in? Because new people, you know, don't have the depth of experience and dedication that you have and neither could you expect them to. We have just no hope of bringing people on.'

There was a consensus that it was extremely difficult to encourage new representatives, mainly because likely candidates could see the pressures which representatives experienced, and that this meant existing activists had to take on more roles, with implications for their effectiveness, but also the time available for training. As another participant commented:

'A lot of members turn around and say that they wouldn't do a representative's job for all the money in the world, because they just won't put up with the hassle that you get from either side, because you are caught in the middle.'

It is likely that the experience of UK representatives resonates across Europe, even in those countries traditionally perceived as supportive of trade unionism. A Swedish survey notes the problems faced by workplace activists: 'shop stewards generally experience a situation characterized by inherent conflict and wide-ranging tasks, resulting in high demands on their skills and in role overload' (Pilemalm et al., 2002).

It is not just the intensification of work that has undermined union workplace activity; the shift in the political climate and strengthening of managerial prerogative also appears to have had an impact. Bryson and Willman (2006) have used WERs data from 1980 to 2004 to show that although there is little evidence of large scale withdrawal of employer recognition or facilities, managerial support for trade unions in terms of check-off[2], management recommendation of membership or a closed shop, and having an on-site union representative has declined since 1984. Management endorsement of union membership in workplaces with more than 25 employees declined dramatically from 34 to 21% between 1990 and 1998, with the decline most marked in the private sector. In addition the probability of lay representation in unionised workplaces fell by 17% between 1984 and 2004. A number of the activists engaged in the focus group research identified a reduction in the legitimacy of the union in the workplace and placed this in the context of wider political changes. They felt strongly that their work as union representatives was not valued in the workplace and that this reflected the wider weakness of trade unions in the law and society. There was a widely held view that managers did not understand or appreciate the role union representatives played in the organisation or their entitlement to time-off to undertake their duties.

Many focus group participants saw this weakness as reflected in the ignorance or lack of understanding shown by line managers who were often unaware of the content of union agreements or of contractual or legal rights, and they believed the consequences could be poor relations between managers and unions. A number of representatives acknowledged distinctions between immediate supervisors who were seen as hostile to the union and more senior management who were perceived as supportive. Management and union interpretations of what was 'reasonable' in terms of time-off did not generally coincide. Yet the problem was also seen in political terms. As already noted, the difficulties representatives

2 'Checkoff' is the name given to the system under which the employer deducts members' union subscriptions directly from their salaries and then forwards these to the trade union.

faced in performing their duties effectively, along with high workloads, were seen as a deterrent to the generation of new representatives. In discussing the issues that might discourage new representatives a number reflected on their weak bargaining power and expressed a view that unless union activity was recognised as benefiting organisations and as legitimate, it would be impossible to encourage new representatives, thereby reinforcing pressures on existing representatives. One representative asserted, 'the government should be less scared about stating the impact unions can have on working lives'. A number of participants argued that it was necessary to repeal the 'anti-trade union laws' on the basis that legislative intervention had eroded the status of trade unions in the workplace and that repeal would confirm trade union legitimacy.

Some of the participants favoured a change to the law that would bring their rights more into line with those in France or Italy, with fixed entitlements to time off and with less employer influence on when the rights should be exercised. However, this view was not unanimously held, with other representatives, from workplaces where industrial relations were perceived as positive, willing to rely on existing arrangements. These were seen as giving them the flexibility which they required and which they feared they might lose if time off rights were strictly prescribed by law. In contrast those in workplaces where organisation was weaker or where the trade union was less well established were more disposed towards the setting of legal minima.

Conclusion

In the event, the UK government decided against making any statutory changes to workplace representatives' time off rights, relying instead upon a voluntary response from employers. It accepted that some workplace representatives faced problems in balancing their normal work duties with their representative functions, but proposed non-regulatory measures only. These include a strengthening the Acas Code of Practice outlining the time and resources that employers grant union representatives to do their jobs. It also proposed measures to make it easier to access electronic information and guidance on workplace representatives' rights and supported the production of a joint statement with the TUC and employer organisations, stating the positive role played by union representatives. It is questionable how far this can reverse persistent management opposition or at best neutrality to unions. The review opposed the extension of workplace rights to new types of representatives and the TUC expressed disappointment that the Government has not used the review to give environmental and equality representatives the right to paid time off 'so that unions can do more to make the UK's workplaces greener and free from discrimination'.

The government's response has done little to address changes brought about by restructuring and the intensification of work in the past decades, which the focus groups suggest has had a substantial impact upon the ability of workplace representatives to fulfil their roles. It has not tackled the shift in political power towards employers and away from workers. Indeed the Labour government has done little to support the collective role of unions in the workplace. Instead Government support for unions is largely based upon individual representation, for example the provision of a right for a worker to be accompanied by a representative of their choice in disciplinary or grievance procedures. Brown and Oxenbridge (2005) have identified the 'steady and continuing growth' of statutory individual rights since the 1970s as changing the role of unions to one where they have become upholders of an increasing number of statutory individual employment rights in the workplace. This has contributed greatly to the workload of representatives, which is dominated by individual casework, whilst the intensification of work and increase in workplace stress demands that they are often dealing with members' emotional and mental health problems, for which they do not feel equipped. This focus upon individual grievances may narrow the scope of the union agenda, whilst managerial pressures may encourage representatives to be more cautious and to focus upon workplace issues, rather than wider more political activity.

Whether the emergence of union learning representatives, with similar rights to workplace representatives, can help reverse these trends and encourage and assist in the development of a new generation of workplace representatives, is as yet uncertain. What is clear is that, without a new generation of workplace representatives, employers will have a free hand in imposing workplace change and in driving back the gains achieved by past workplace activism.

References

Beck, U. (1992): Risk Society: Towards a New Modernity (Original edition: Risikogesellschaft. Auf dem Weg in eine andere Moderne, Frankfurt a.M. 1986: Suhrkamp), London: Sage.

Bercusson, B. (2002): 'The European Social Model Comes to Britain', Industrial Law Journal, 31:3 (September 2002) p. 209-244.

BERR (2007): Workplace representatives – a review of their facilities and facility time, November 2007.

Brown, W. / Oxenbridge, S. (2005): 'Trade Unions and Collective Bargaining: Law and the Future of Collectivism' in Deakin, S. and Wilkinson, F. (Eds), The Law of the Labour Market: Industrialization, Employment, and Legal Evolution, Oxford: Oxford Monographs on Labour Law.

Charlwood, A. / Terry, M. (2007): '21st century models of employee representation: structures, processes and outcomes', Industrial Relations Journal, 38:4, pp. 320-337.

Collins, H. / Ewing, K.D. / McColgan, A. (2005): Labour law – texts and materials, 2nd ed. Hart Publishing.

Cully, M. / Woodland, S. / O'Reilly, A. / Dix, G. (1999): Britain at Work. London: Routledge.

Deacon, S. / Morris, G. (2005): Labour Law, 4th ed. Hart Publishing.

Forrester, K. (2004): 'The quiet revolution? trade union learning and renewal strategies. Research Notes', Work, Employment and Society, 18, 2: 413-420.

Heery, E. / Healy, G. / Taylor, P. (2004): Representation at Work: Themes and Issues' in (eds.) G. Healy, E. Heery, P. Taylor and W. Brown, The Future of Worker Representation, Basingstoke: Palgrave Macmillan, 1-36.

Kelly, J. (1998): Rethinking Industrial Relations: Mobilization, Collectivism and Long Waves, Routledge: London.

Kerr, A. / Perks, L. / Waddington, J. (2002): The characteristics, role and activities of UNISON stewards, UNISON.

Kersley, B. / Alpin, C. / Forth, J. / Bryson, A. / Bewley, H. / Dix, G. / Oxenbridge, S. (2006): Inside the workplace: Findings from the 2004 Workplace Employment Relations Survey, London: Department of Trade and Industry.

Kilkauer, T. (2004): 'Trade union shopfloor representation in Germany', Industrial Relations Journal, 35:1, pp. 1-18.

Kolins Givan, R. (2007): 'Side by side we battle onward? Representing workers in contemporary America, British Journal of Industrial Relations, 45:4, pp. 829-855.

Labour Research (2008): 'The race is on to get equal' Labour Research, 97:3 pp. 18-21, March 2008.

Moore, S. (2004): 'Union mobilization and employer counter-mobilization in the statutory recognition process' in Kelly, J. and Willman, P. (Eds) Union organization and Activity, London: Routledge.

Moore, S. / Read, I. (2006): 'Employee representation, voice and unionisation in small and medium-sized enterprises in the UK', Human Resource Management Journal 16(4), November 2006.

Moore, S. / Jefferys, S. (2007): 'The impact of employee representation upon workplace industrial relations outcomes" Department of Trade and Industry, United Kingdom, Employment Relations Research Series.

Murakami, T. (1999): 'Works councils and teamwrok in a German car plant', Employee Relations 21:1 1999, pp. 26-44.

Pilemalm, S. / Hallberg, N. / Timpka, T. (2001): 'How Do Shop Stewards Perceive Their Situation and Tasks? Preconditions for Support of Union Work'. Economic and Industrial Democracy 22 (4): 569-599.

Roche, W. (2007): 'Social partnership and workplace regimes in Ireland, Industrial Relations Journal, 38:3, pp. 188-209.

Sennet, R. (1998): The Corrosion of Character. The Personal Consequences of Work in the New Capitalism, New York: Norton.

Terry, M. (1995): 'Employee Representation: Shop Stewards and the New Legal Framework' in Edwards, P (ed.) Industrial Relations – Theory & Practice. Oxford: Blackwell.

Terry, M. / Edwards, P.K. (eds.) (1988): Shopfloor Politics and Job Controls: the Post-War Engineering Industry, Basil Blackwell, Oxford

Upchurch, M. / Danford, A. / Richardson, M. (2002): 'Research Note: Profiles of union workplace representatives: evidence from three unions in South West England', Industrial Relations Journal, 33 (2) 127-140.

White, S. (2004): 'Markets, time and citizenship', Renewal: A Journal of Labour Politics, 12: 3.

Willman, P. / Bryson, A. (2006): 'Accounting for collective action: resource acquisition and mobilization in British unions', CEP Discussion Paper, 768.

Women and Work Commission (2005) A: fair deal for women in the workplace.

Work organisation, workers' participation and the role of EU legislation in Italy

Volker Telljohann

1. Introduction

In the 1990s also in Italy the connection between new technologies, work organisation, productivity, innovation and employment entailed new strategies of human resource management (HRM) including new forms of direct employee involvement. Due to the increased complexity of the internal corporate processes, the hierarchical forms of leadership manifest strong limits. Thus, employee involvement is increasingly seen as a resource within the scope of organisational innovation processes and, as a consequence, more and more companies are trying to implement participative practices with the aim of improving their competitiveness on the international markets.

In general, the new HRM strategies are based on forms of direct employee involvement which imply contradictory impacts on traditional forms of representative participation. A major challenge thus regards the need for an integration and coordination of new forms of direct participation with the industrial relations system in general and with forms of representative participation in particular.

1.1 The diffusion of participative experiences in the context of organisational change

The Italian industrial relations are characterised by an almost non-existent institutionalisation of participation rights. In the absence of legislation, the experiences of worker participation or their representatives in regard to the decisions relating to the organisation of work appear in the form of direct participation or in the form of representative participation.

As in Italy the most significant experiences in the field of representative participation are based on agreements between the social partners, we can speak of a negotiated road to participation. After the early experiences of introduction of the right to information in the mid-1970s, in the second half of the 1980s there was a qualitative leap forward represented by the introduction of participation bodies and procedures through company-level bargaining. The most significant experiences promoting the introduction of participation mechanisms were the agreements signed by State holdings such as IRI and ENI as well as by the household appliances producer Electrolux-Zanussi. These agreements provided for the inception of specific joint committees for the management of the issues of common interest (Telljohann 2008).

Subsequently, various highly differentiated participative experiences were developed in that they answered the specific needs of the relevant companies. In the most advanced cases there have also been experiences of co-design of organisational innovations (Garibaldo 1988 and 1990). The lack of an institutionalisation of the participative rights, and the differentiated approaches of the various companies to participation, meant that the Italian situation in terms of participation resulted to be particularly limited and fragmented.

Direct participation and work organisation

Since the 1990s there has also been a growing discussion on the importance of experiences of direct participation in the context of organisational change. Numerous research works underline that in respect to the choices of the actors in the participative processes, the involvement of the workers themselves is fundamental for guaranteeing the use of their skills and their creativity, which, in turn, is indispensable for an effective implementation of organisational innovation (Brödner 2000). In the second half of the 1990s, the EPOC report (European Foundation for the Improvement of Living and Working conditions 1999) examined the different experiences of direct participation in the Member States of the European Union. From the conclusions it emerged that:

- direct participation has a greater likelihood of being introduced in companies inside which complex and non-manual tasks are performed and in companies with teamwork, highly skilled labour force and in-house training;
- economic and qualitative performance rises as direct participation rises;
- employment cuts are likelier in the workplaces without direct participation rather than in the companies that contemplate it.

In regard to the Italian situation it has been highlighted that if in regard to group consultation Italy is situated more or less in the average, as much cannot be said for the delegating of responsibilities to the workers (both at individual and at group level). Overall, the results seem to indicate that the diffusion of experiences of a participative nature is rather weak. Instead, when we are faced with the involvement of the workers it generally does not come about in the initial phase of the design of new organisational models, but on the basis of a model already defined by the management. Another important consideration concerns the fact that in the cases in which there is worker involvement in the organisational change, it seems that the unions remain excluded (Fondazione Istituto per il Lavoro 2000).

The problems that arise when the union is excluded from the processes of organisational innovation are highlighted in the third annual report of the Fondazione Istituto per il Lavoro (2003). An important thematic aspect of the report concerned the diffusion and the quality of the practices that could be classified as forms of direct participation. Empirical research has been performed through case studies distributed in the national territory in the economic sectors of the automobile sub-supply industry, the building industry, the software industry, the banking and insurance sector and the public utilities. In nearly all the cases analysed in which there was a direct worker involvement these forms of direct participation are experienced by the workers' representatives as a threat and in some cases lead to open conflicts. Unilateral decisions for the introduction of forms of direct participation can undermine the relations of trust between the actors and as a consequence, the direct participation experience nearly always remains scarcely effective. These cases indeed make evident the need to choose an integrated approach between forms of direct and representative participation. In the event of a lack of coordination between the two forms of participation, the forms of direct participation that in theory find their justification are mostly cases destined to failure. As a whole, the results appear to indicate that the diffusion of successful experiences of direct participation is rather weak.

Representative participation and work organisation

In Italy there has always been a preference to aim at bargaining for the defining of the criteria and the forms of participation. In the absence of a legislative regulation of participation, till 2007, the year of the transposition of the EC Directive on information and consultation into Italian law, the tripartite agreement signed on 23 July 1993 represented the only institutionalised basis for promoting experiences of participation. In particular, the social pact provided for the following possibilities of participation:

a) economic participation through wage increases linked to the trend in productivity, the quality of the product and the profitability of the company. The wage increases should be correlated to the results achieved in the realisation of the programmes, agreed between the parties. On the basis of this formulation, agreed programmes could be hypothesised concerning the processes of organisational innovation with a consequent positive impact on the labour productivity and/or the product quality which on its part ought to create leeway for wage increases;

b) the information and consultation procedures with regard to the social effects connected with the corporate transformation, such as technological and organisational innovations as well as processes of restructuring that affect the conditions of safety, work and employment, also in relation to the law on equal opportunities.

To these possibilities is added the participation within the scope of the bilateral commissions that in general is defined through collective bargaining (Lugli and Tugnoli 1999). Increasingly, discussions at company level take place in such joint committees, which formally are intended to prepare the groundwork for collective bargaining by providing technical support. Generally speaking these committees are made up half of management and half of union representatives. Members may be permanent or elected on an ad hoc basis depending on the issues to be discussed. The principal aim of these joint committees is to encourage a non-confrontational exchange between the two sides, in the process stimulating cooperation aimed at solving organisational problems (Fulton 2007). That means that the role of these joint committees tends to be limited to resolving specific problems rather than examining broader strategic issues. In general, these commissions deal with questions concerning working conditions in the company and they are limited to a consultative function; they hardly ever play a decision-making role.

As regards the possibilities of participation laid down in the social pact, it can be concluded that they represent a rather weak and insufficient basis. On the one hand, as regards the economic participation there is only a generic reference to the chance that the social partners jointly develop programmes to establish mechanisms for the definition of wage increases at company level; on the other hand, as regards the participation within the scope of restructuring processes, the social pact of 1993 lays down a role for the unitary workplace union structures only with regard to the "management of the social effects connected to the company transformations, such as the technological and organisational innovations, and the restructuring processes", and thus not an involvement ex ante, but only ex post.

Considering that these are the only possibilities envisaged by the 1993 social pact that allow for the promotion of participation experiences at the company level, we must conclude that at least till 2007 in Italy we were faced with a low level of institutionalisation of the rights to participation. The possibilities for participation have proven, from the standpoint of timeliness, certainty and incisiveness, to be wholly inadequate such that in practice the experiences of participation within the scope of organisational innovation processes have remained very limited.

In its conclusions the third annual report of the Fondazione Istituto per il Lavoro (2003) states, in fact, that no important experiences of bargaining and/or representative participation have been found in terms of work organisation. In the best of cases there were well-structured experiences of industrial relations within the scope of which the union bodies act on the basis of a consolidated presence. But it seems that in no case a relatively strong position of the union bodies has led to an innovative practice of industrial relations based on experiences of bargaining and representative participation characterised by the development of autonomous projects of organisational innovation by the union. Even in the scope of direct participation the experiences carried out in the cases analysed are quite disappointing, both from the point of view of their efficacy and from the point of view of the integration between direct participation and representative participation.

In 2006 the Industrial Association of Lombardy, Assolombarda (2006), published a report on trends in relation to the introduction of new forms of work organisation in the area of Milan. Although the survey is not representative of the country as a whole it provides interesting information on the spread of new forms of work organisation and on the ways they were introduced. According to the report companies largely adopt unilateral action by management when it comes to the introduction of new forms of work organisation. With regard to the introduction of job rotation and job enlargement also forms of direct involvement were found. The involvement of trade union representatives is much less frequent. That means that in general the introduction of new forms of work organisation is not an issue of company-level industrial relations.

Workers' participation in the context of a single-channel system of interest representation

When organisational innovation becomes a topic of industrial relations in the company there is a further problem concerning employee involvement. In the Italian single-channel system of interest representation the underlying problem is that trade unions regard the members of the unitary workplace union structures as protagonists even of the participatory processes. This approach can lead in practice to an overload of the interest representation structures at the company level, since the role of participation is added to their functions of interest representation, company bargaining, and proselytism (Carrieri 1995: 50). Furthermore, when it comes to participating in work organisation issues, certain very specific competencies are required, which the unitary workplace union structures do not always possess. From this point of view, there is a risk of undermining the effectiveness of the participation bodies (Telljohann 2008). It is also obvious that unless the unions have the necessary skills their scope for action with regard to managerial strategies will be limited. The contribution of the workers' representatives concerning management proposals for solving problems that the management itself has identified will be mainly reactive. It is unlikely that the representatives of the unitary workplace union structures (Rappresentanze Sindacali Unitarie – RSU), will play a proactive role in terms of problem solving or even problem setting, that is to say, the development of autonomous proposals for identifying and solving problems.

The allocation of the participation function can be based on the criteria of *membership* and *competence*. As already mentioned, in Italy the unions generally choose the membership criterion in order to guarantee control – the necessary political reliability. Indeed, it is difficult to imagine that the unions present in a company decide, on the basis of the competence criterion, to delegate the participatory function to workers who are experts in a subject that the respective joint committees deal with. Another indicator that seems to confirm the extent to which competence is regarded as a necessity of lesser importance is that external experts are rarely called in in the course of the joint bodies' activities (Lugli and Tugnoli 1999). This model of union policy in the participation context can be considered characteristic of a single-channel representation system, in which the union exercises a function with emphasis on control. Participation is liable to be politicised not only by the unions but also by management, which seems more interested in political coverage by the union bodies of projects for organisational change than in a genuine contribution by the workers' representatives. There could thus be some scepticism as to how useful it is in terms of effectiveness for unions to politicise participation bodies by choosing the membership criterion.

Politicising participation means that important resources such as the knowledge and creativity of the employees themselves often are not used in participatory experiences. It thus constitutes a concrete obstacle to the involvement of employees in innovation processes.

1.2 The failure of the negotiated road to participation

As a whole, the bargaining of processes of organisational change and the involvement of the workers must be considered below the expectations and therefore a clue in terms of the as yet insufficient spread of a participation culture. This problem is posed both in quantitative and in qualitative terms. The reasons that have triggered the modest diffusion of significant participation experiences are also to be sought in the tradition of the industrial relations system that in the past was characterised by an elevated level of conflict and, as a consequence, by a particularly critical attitude towards the participation models practiced in other countries. Starting from the second half of the 1980s the social partners have tended to start to overcome the conflictual mindset in favour of a more cooperative strategy. Contemporaneously, the unions have developed a new attitude vis-à-vis participation: at the start of the 1990s the CGIL launched a strategy for co-determination. The CISL shared the information and consultation practices without, however, wanting to achieve actual co-determination. The strategic objective of the CISL is instead the promotion of employee share ownership schemes. Obviously this divergence in the union policy with regard to participation makes it objectively more difficult to extend the positive experiences of participation in regard to the processes of organisational change and achieve results that are also quantitatively significant (Telljohann 2008). Since the beginning of the decade joint strategies in the field of worker participation have also been undermined by a more general crisis of unity of action between the CGIL, on the one hand, and the CISL and the UIL, on the other hand.

It can be concluded that up until today in the Italian context participative experiences within the scope of organisational innovation processes have hardly been widespread. There are various reasons that can explain why in Italy participatory approaches to organisational change are so infrequent. If we investigate the causes of the insufficient spread of participation experiences in the processes of organisational innovation we have to highlight the fact that historically the characteristics of the industrial relations system and the orientations of the social partners determined a context that is so little inclined to allowing participation experiences in the scope of organisational change.

Seeing that even the negotiated road to participation was not able to give satisfactory results there seems to be a need for a more incisive regulation, that is to say for a legislation more capable of promoting participation in the processes of organisational innovation. The limitation of the 1993 tripartite agreement instead lies in the fact that it only indirectly provides an incentive to participation. The rather unsatisfactory participatory experiences of the past suggest the need for an institutionalisation of the rights providing a clear definition of the concept of participation including aspects such as the timeliness of the involvement and the rights to develop autonomous proposals, to training, to resources and to the possibility to turn to outside experts.

Another challenge is of a political nature and concerns the union strategies. As has been shown above, in regard to the issue of participation very different orientations can be observed. While one part of the union is oriented towards models of employee share ownership, the other part instead is aiming at promoting industrial democracy. As a consequence, apart from some isolated cases, there is no significant advancement in the field of participation. It would thus be necessary to have a process of harmonisation of the union strategies.

Apart from the divergent orientations of the various unions there is also the problem that the companies are aiming increasingly at forms of direct involvement of the workers thereby avoiding coordination between the different forms of participation. In order to guarantee an effective integration also on the part of the union it would thus be auspicious to open the traditional systems of representative participation in order to attempt to overcome the limitations of the single-channel representation system.

There is thus the need to innovate the traditional system of interest representation by developing new hypotheses capable of clarifying the relationship between direct participation and representative participation. Clarity as regards the respective competencies and the interconnections between the different levels seems to be indispensable as otherwise the experiences of participation risk failure.

Due to the voluntaristic tradition in Italian industrial relations and the divergent orientations of the various trade unions all attempts to institutionalise participation rights that have come up within the national context have failed so far. That also means that the European Council directives might prove to be the real driver for innovation and institutionalisation of participation rights in the Italian context.

2. The impact of the Europeanisation of industrial relations on workers' participation

It has been shown above that the Italian industrial relations system is traditionally characterised by a relative absence of participatory instruments. The use of participatory approaches to resolve individual and collective problems of the employment relationship through cooperation has never been significant. The limited importance of participatory experiences can be put down to the socio-economic imbalances, the high degree of socio-political conflict and polarisation, and the strongly class-based and bargaining-oriented nature of the Italian trade union tradition.

The wider information and consultation rights that in the meantime have been established also in Italy are mainly the result of the transposition of European Council directives and European framework agreements signed in the context of the European social dialogue. The European regulatory regime comprises a number of directives aimed at promoting the engagement and participation of workers and their representatives, through enterprise representation, in decision-making in the enterprise.

Initially, information and consultation rights were introduced only for crisis situations and restructuring processes. The regulatory framework was then extended to the transnational dimension of multi-national enterprises with the adoption of the EC directive on European Works Councils (EWCs) in 1994 which was recasted in 2008. In 2001 the project for the creation of the European company statute was made conditional on arrangements for the involvement of workers and their representatives in the company's decision-making mechanisms. With regard to workers' involvement in the context of organisational change the most relevant European regulatory initiative is represented by Council Directive 2002/14 which established a general framework for information and consultation of employees.

The adoption of this directive is justified by the partial inefficacy of the juridical frameworks in countries such as Italy with regard to the involvement of workers at the company or plant level. The objective of the directive consists, amongst other things, in the intensification of the social dialogue to foster the anticipation of risks, develop the flexibility of work organisation, ease the access of workers to training and promote the involvement of workers in the company running and in the determination of its future. The aim is to promote and intensify the information and the consultations on the situation and the evolution of employment, in particular when it appears that the employment within the scope of the company could be threatened. The directive also states that the information and consultation processes must occur in good time to guarantee the success of the processes of company adaptation to the globalisation. Another merit of the directive lies in the accurate definition of the concepts of 'information' and 'consultation'.

Furthermore, it is specified that the information must occur according to appropriate methods and contents, susceptible to allowing the employees' representatives to conduct an adequate study and, where necessary, prepare for consultation. Also for the consultation the choice of the moment, the methods and the contents must be appropriate. The employees' representatives have a right to meet the employer and have a motivated answer to any opinions they may put forward. The consultation should moreover take place in order to find an agreement on the decisions that in any case depend on the management's power to run the company.

It can be concluded that in Italy the establishment of wider information and consultation rights by law is mainly due to the transposition of European directives.

The adoption of the EC Directive within the Italian context

Although the deadline for the implementation of the EC Directive 2002/14 was March 2005 the transposition into Italian law by Legislative Decree has taken place only in March 2007. The delay was attributed to the need to respect autonomous bilateral dialogue between the social partners. As in Italy the directive's implementation had an impact on important matters regulated by collective bargaining the social partner organisations reached an agreement on the approach to implementation only in November 2006 (Carley and Hall 2008).

In Italy in general the implementation of EC Directives is based on proposals developed by the Italian social partners. The rationale of this method of regulation of labour issues is that the development of joint proposals representing an outcome of collective bargaining is considered more flexible and can provide solutions supported by employers and employees and, consequently, is more effective. Since collective bargaining has no erga omnes effect, any agreement reached between employers' associations and trade unions cannot be considered binding by the legislator. However, de facto, the legislator usually takes into account the social partners' joint position in the implementation of the directives. Also in the case of the implementation of EC directive 2002/14 the legislative decree is based on the joint opinion of social partners. That means that the social partner organisations have strongly influenced the implementation process.

According to the legislative decree unitary workplace union structures are entitled to information and consultation rights in undertakings with at least 50 employees. The definition of the practical arrangements is left to collective bargaining. Through the implementation of the EC Directive information and consultation rights have been introduced for the first time in Italian industrial relations in a generalised and legally binding way.

In the general legal framework provided by the decree it is laid down that information and consultation shall concern

- the recent and probable developments of the undertaking's activities and economic situation,
- the situation, structure and probable development of employment within the undertaking and, where there is a threat to employment, the anticipatory measures envisaged, as well as
- decisions likely to entail substantial changes in work organisation or in contractual relations.

According to article 2 of Legislative Decree no. 25/2007, information means the transmission of data by the employer to the employee representatives in order to enable them to acquaint themselves with the subject matter and to examine it.

Legislative Decree 25/2007 also lays down that information shall be given appropriately concerning timeliness and content, in order to enable the employees' representatives to conduct an adequate study and, where necessary, prepare for consultation.

According to article 2 of Legislative Decree no. 25/2007 consultation means the exchange of views and the establishment of dialogue between the employee representatives and the employer. The legislative decree also provides that consultation shall take place

a) while ensuring that the timing, method and content are appropriate;
b) between relevant levels of management and interest representation, depending on the subject under discussion;
c) on the basis of information supplied by the employer and the opinion which the RSU is entitled to formulate;
d) in such a way as to enable the employee representatives to meet the employer and obtain a response, and the reason for that response, to any opinion they might formulate; and
e) with a view to reaching an agreement on decisions within the scope of the employer's powers.

With regard to information and consultation processes the practical arrangements are defined by collective bargaining according to the provisions of art. 4 of the legislative decree. This is another example of interaction between the law and collective bargaining. The fact that the legislative decree allows and even stimulates collective bargaining to implement its provisions also implies a certain continuity of the negotiated road to participation. The important difference compared to the past consists in the fact that the new legislation provides for a framework of clearly defined and enforceable rights on the basis of which collective bargaining processes take place in order to define the concrete modalities of implementation and application in the respective sectors.

The transposition of the directive into Italian law should also ensure conditions of effectiveness and enforcement of the rights to information and consultation. The directive obliges the Member States to guarantee the efficacy of the EU rights through the issuing of "effective, proportional and dissuasive" sanctions. In the Italian case the non-compliance with information and consultation obligations by the employer incurs sanctions ranging from a minimum of € 3,000 to a maximum of € 18,000.

It can be concluded that the legislative decree no. 25/2007 has contributed to a certain extent to closing the gap of institutionalisation of employee rights guaranteeing for the first time the generalisation of information and consultation rights. Providing a clear definition of the scope and of the concepts of information and consultation including also aspects such as the timeliness of the involvement and the right to develop autonomous proposals, the implementation of the directive entailed an important extension and specification of information and consultation rights. That means that the legislative decree no. 25/2007 represents a major change in Italian industrial relations.

3. Effective participation as a future challenge for the Italian industrial relations system

The Italian scenario in terms of participation was traditionally not just characterised by an almost non-existent institutionalisation of participation rights but also by results and trends that are little encouraging as regards the few concrete experiences that took place in the past. It could be argued that the Italian experiences of participation represent some missed opportunities. In this regard, the most significant cases are the IRI protocol, the ENI protocol, the tripartite agreement of 1993 and, lastly, the Electrolux-Zanussi model. The social partners have never fully used the slim margin that the 1993 tripartite agreement offers in terms of participation; instead the IRI protocol and above all the Electrolux-Zanussi model have not withstood the various forms of contradictions they were exposed to from the outset. Besides, it is worth underlining that although these two experiences have always been considered advanced cases to be taken as a model, they have never taken a leading role; they have substantially remained advanced cases, but isolated ones. We can thus sum up that negotiated forms of participation have produced disappointing results from the quantitative standpoint and hardly stable from the qualitative standpoint.

In front of such a poorly promising balance, the implementation of the EC directives in the field of information and consultation takes on a certain relevance as regards the rights to participation at the national level. The EU norms in terms of the rights of workers to information and consultation in the companies located in the European Union above all contained in the three directives 94/45/EC, 2001/86/EC and 2002/14/EC represent a chance for a modernisation of the participation instruments in Italy.

The most important contribution could come from the directive 2002/14/EC that establishes a general framework of rights relating to the information and consultation of the workers in the European Union and that provides for the application of these rights to all the undertakings with at least 50 employees. As regards the impact of this directive on industrial relations, it can be argued that the methods and principles that characterise the EU norms can contribute to the recognition of the role of the workers and of their company-level structures of interest representation also within the scope of the processes of organisational change and restructuring. Compared with the traditional Italian juridical framework, it can be stated that the European legislation has led to an improvement in the national norms on the subject. The transposition of the directive into Italian law has contributed to more certainty and to the generalisation of information and consultation rights.

The fact that the application of the legislative decree is imposed upon undertakings with at least 50 workers implies a significant impact for Italy given the country's productive structure. The transposition of the directive will in any case contribute to improving the quality of the rights. If in the 1993 tripartite agreement an involvement guaranteed only in regard to the management of the social effects of restructuring processes and technological and organisational change, the EU norms provide for information and consultation processes well in advance in order to anticipate and prevent the risks linked to the processes of change. Furthermore, the legislative decree allows the employees' representatives to prepare opinions and hypotheses alternative to those of the management. It is interesting to note that these provisions represented also the key achievements of the most advanced company-level level agreements signed in the past at ENI, IRI and Electrolux-Zanussi which, however, remained isolated and temporary experiences. That means that the legislative decree could take on an important role in reviving the union strategy on the subject of participation within the scope of organisational innovation processes. The question is, however, whether trade unions will be able to overcome divisions and to develop joint strategies at company level.

It can be summarised that due to the history of voluntaristic industrial relations there has been a major impact of the directive on Italian industrial relations also from a legal point of view. The legislative decree no. 25/2007 has given legal force to information and consultation rights that in the past were regulated exclusively through collective agreements and at the same time it has extended these rights. It has, however, to be pointed out that the legislative decree has to be implemented through industry-level collective agreements. The collective agreement for the retail and services sector signed in 2008 and the one for the chemical and pharmaceutical industry signed in 2009 were the first ones having taken up the legislative decree. The fact that the major part of industry-level collective agreements does not yet include the provisions of the legislative decree prefigures a lengthy and complex phase of implementation (Muratore 2008).

The complexity of the implementation process might also be due to the fact that trade unions will have to respond to the precise definitions of the concepts of information and consultation. In theory, the definitions proposed by the legislative decree would imply the opportunity for trade unions to shift from reactive to more proactive strategies. Such a shift would first of all imply the need for the necessary competencies and resources on the side of the trade unions. The even more important challenge would, however, regard the need for a cultural change of the Italian trade unions that in the past in general stuck to defensive and reactive strategies as they considered organisational change a task of the management.

4. Open challenges

As important as certain and enforceable rights may be, there are still other factors that influence the development of processes of participation in the context of organisational innovation. The results of the participation also depend on the knowledge made available to the workers and their representatives. There is therefore also a material dimension to participation represented by the availability of resources dedicated to processes of training and research. Seeing that the incisiveness of the processes of participation also depend on the competencies, a serious approach to participation should be based on guarantees for all the actors involved as concerns the chances of access to the existing knowledge, as well as the production of new knowledge through research. In regard to the problem of providing the employees' representatives with the necessary competencies in order to guarantee an effective participation the EC directive 94/45/CE on European Works Councils was the first one to contain an interesting point to reflect upon. In the subsidiary requirements there is the right of the EWC to be able to seek assistance from experts of its choice, in so far as this is necessary for it to carry out its tasks. The costs, in the event of the use of an expert, are borne by the company. Such a provision is of crucial importance in order to guarantee the efficacy of information and consultation rights and it would thus also be useful in the national context.

On the basis of the analysis of the Italian representation and participation system, it also seems to be important that future innovations aim to develop a hypothesis for integrating and coordinating the various forms of representative and direct participation in order to overcome the traditional limitations of participative experiences. Innovative approaches would have to recognise the role of collective bargaining in defining employees' participation rights as well as the scope and general framework of that participation in organisational innovation processes. On the other hand direct employee participation should take place on the basis of a broad definition of participation aimed at drawing on employees' skills with regard to both problem setting and problem solving in the context of organisational change.

If participation is to be an effective instrument it would seem to be essential to develop approaches that guarantee that workers' skills are used to better advantage. Furthermore, it has to guaranteed that the workers can be involved without excluding the company-level structure of interest representation.

The opportunity to use workers' skills has various advantages for the representation bodies operating at company level. Worker involvement can help to reduce the gap with regard to the competencies so that the company-level structures of interest representation are enabled to deal with new issues. At the same time a division of labour is fostered that can help to reduce the workload of the representation bodies. Another advantage is that the representation bodies can improve their own legitimisation through employee involvement.

Efforts to modernise the Italian system must thus take account of the specificities of the Italian industrial relations system that consist in the negotiated road to participation, on the one hand, and in the single-channel system of interest representation, on the other. A first proposal for promoting experiences of employee involvement in innovation processes could be to introduce mixed working groups composed of members of the unitary workplace union structures and professionals such as highly qualified employees or engineers.

Bibliography

Appelbaum, E. / Bailey, T. / Berg, P. / Kalleberg, A.L. (2000): Manufacturing advantage. Why high-performance work systems pay off, Ithaca: Cornell University Press.

Assolombarda (2006): La modernizzazione del lavoro nelle imprese milanesi, research report, Milan.

Baglioni, G. (2000): 'La partecipazione nel tempo della globalizzazione', L'impresa al plurale. Quaderni della partecipazione, 5, 13-43.

Becker, K. / Brinkmann, U. / Engel, T. (2008): „„Hybride" Beteiligung im Betrieb? – Sachkundige Beschäftige in der Betriebsratsarbeit', WSI-Mitteilungen, 6, 305-311.

Bion, W.R. (1961): 'Experiences in groups', Human Relations, Vols. I-IV, 1948-1951, London: Tavistock.

Brödner, P. (2000): 'Organisational Learning? Beyond Continuous Improvement', Paper presented at the 3rd International Conference (Euro) CINet CI 2000: from Improvement to Innovation, Aalborg, 18-19 September 2000.

Brödner, P. / Latniak. E. (2004): 'Innovation strategies, work organisation and competitiveness – experiences in EU Member States', in F. Garibaldo / V. Telljohann (eds.) Globalisation, Company Strategies and Quality of Working Life in Europe, Frankfurt: Peter Lang, 53-86.

Carley, M. / Hall, M. (2008): Impact of the information and consultation directive on industrial relations, Dublin: European Foundation for the Improvement of Living and Working Conditions, http://www.eurofound.europa.eu/eiro/studies/tn0710029s/tn0710029s.htm [Accessed 1.6.2009]

Carrieri, M. (1995): L'incerta rappresentanza. Sindacati e consenso negli anni '90: dal monopolio confederale alle rappresentanze sindacali unitarie, Bologna: Il Mulino.

Carrieri, M. (1998): 'Zanussi: dal modello al sistema', L'impresa al plurale. Quaderni della partecipazione, 1, 95-102.

Della Torre, E. (2006): 'Increasing use of new work practices in companies', Dublin: European Foundation for the Improvement of Living and Working Conditions, http://www.eiro.eurofound.eu.int/2006/10/articles/it0610039i.html [Accessed 01.06.2009]

European Foundation for the Improvement of Living and Working Conditions (1999): Employment through flexibility: Squaring the circle? Findings from the EPOC Survey, Luxembourg: Office for Official Publications of the European Communities.

Fondazione Istituto per il Lavoro (1998): Technical notes on the search conference and their re-elaboration by IpL, http://www.fipl.it/docs/altro/protocollo_operativo_01_en.pdf[Accessed 01.06.2009]

Fondazione Istituto per il Lavoro (ed.) (2000): Sviluppo, lavoro, competitività in Emilia Romagna. Primo rapporto annuale dell'Istituto per il Lavoro, Milan: Franco Angeli.

Fondazione Istituto per il Lavoro (ed.) (2003): Globalizzazione dell'economia, strategie di impresa e qualità della vita lavorativa, Milan: Franco Angeli.

Fulton, L. (2007): Worker representation in Europe. Brussels, Labour Research Department and ETUI-REHS.

Garibaldo, F. (1988): 'Problemi di politica rivendicativa: la natura dei rapporti cooperativi fra i lavoratori rispetto alla struttura dell'impresa. Esperienze e problemi di progettazione organizzativa nei metalmeccanici bolognesi', in O. Marchisio (ed.), Frammenti di innovazione, Milan: Franco Angeli, 13-42.

Garibaldo, F. (1990): 'Dai casi ai contratti: iter ed output negoziale', in O. Marchisio (ed.) Frammenti di sindacato: dai casi ai contratti, Milan: Franco Angeli, 26-41.

Garibaldo, F. / Rebecchi, E. (2004): 'Some reflections on the epistemological fundaments of an Italian action-research experience', AI & Society, 18, 1, 44-67.

Garibaldo, F. / Sbordone, F. (2001): 'Un'esperienza di partecipazione nel settore sanitario', L'impresa al plurale – Quaderni della partecipazione, 7-8, 391-396.

Garibaldo, F. / Sbordone, F. / Telljohann, V. (2000): 'Forme della divisione del lavoro e i processi di cambiamento del lavoro e delle sue modalità organizzative', in Fondazione Istituto per il Lavoro (ed.) Sviluppo, lavoro e competitività in Emilia Romagna. Primo rapporto annuale dell'Istituto per il Lavoro, Milan: Franco Angeli, 285-321.

Garibaldo, F. / Telljohann, V. (eds.) (2004): Globalisation, Company Strategies and Quality of Working Life in Europe, Frankfurt: Peter Lang.

Kratzer, N. / Dunkel, W. / Menz, W. (2009): 'Neue Managementmethoden – neue Belastungsformen?', in Gesellschaft für Arbeitswissenschaft e.V.; Schriftltg. Martin Schütte (ed.) Arbeit, Beschäftigungsfähigkeit und Produktivität im 21. Jahrhundert. Bericht zum 55. Kongress der Gesellschaft für Arbeitswissenschaft, 4.-6. März 2009, Dortmund: GfA-Press.

Lay, G. / Shapira, P. / Wengel, J. (eds.) (1999): Innovation in production. The adoption and impacts of new manufacturing concepts, Würzburg: Physica-Verlag.

Lugli, L. / Tugnoli, S. (1999): 'La partecipazione dimezzata: cambiamento organizzativo e coinvolgimento dei lavoratori, una sintesi problematica', in IRES Emilia-Romagna (ed.) Secondo rapporto sulla contrattazione in Emilia-Romagna: 1994-1997. Un'indagine sull'esperienza della contrattazione aziendale dopo il 23 luglio 1993, Collana IRES, 22, Milan: Franco Angeli.

Muratore, L. (2008): 'Italy: The impact of the information and consultation Directive' Dublin: European Foundation for the Improvement of Living and Working Conditions, http://www.eurofound.europa.eu/eiro/studies/tn0710029s/ it0710029q.htm [Accessed 01.06.2009]

Pini, P. (ed.) (2002): Innovazioni organizzative, risorse umane e relazioni industriali. Un'indagine sulle imprese dell'industria alimentare dell'Emilia-Romagna, Milan: Franco Angeli.

Sauer, D. (2005): Arbeit im Übergang. Zeitdiagnosen, Hamburg: VSA Verlag.

Telljohann, V. (2003): 'Strategie di impresa, relazioni industriali e modelli di partecipazione', in Fondazione Istituto per il Lavoro (ed.), La globalizzazione dell'economia, strategie di impresa e qualità della vita lavorativa, Milan: Franco Angeli, 496-497.

Telljohann, V. (2008): 'Structural changes and new forms of social regulation in 'Third Italy' – the case of the Emilia-Romagna Region', in: K. Bluhm / R. Schmidt (eds.) Change in SMEs. Towards a new European Capitalism? Basingstoke: Palgrave Macmillan, 203-227.

Wengel, J. / Wallmeier, W. (1999): 'Worker Participation and Process Innovations', in G. Lay, P. Shapira, J. Wengel (eds.), Innovation in Production. The adoption and impacts of new manufacturing concepts, Würzburg: Physica-Verlag, 65-78.

Managers and management: The impact of Western Foreign Direct Investment in the new EU Member States

Jochen Tholen

Introduction

Among other things, foreign companies provide not only capital, technology, organisation and market strategies to the host country of their direct investments, but also the underlying notions of management style, management concepts, human resource policy, etc. To what extent these notions are realisable in practice or whether other notions prevail is one of the cognitive objectives of an research project by the University of Bremen (Institute Labour and Economy), from which the partial findings are now being presented[1].

These partial findings have been compiled through the evaluation of studies, so-called "grey literature", but above all through over 50 expert discussions on the supra-operational level with representatives of employers' associations, trade unionists and representatives from responsible ministries in Germany, as well as on the European level, in Poland, the Czech Republic and Slovakia.

Nine business enterprises (seven of them from Germany, one Swiss and one German/French enterprise) from the metal & electrical industry (including automobile construction), the food processing industry, and the chemical and energy industry in the differing configuration are the second empirical sources for our argumentation.

In the following we will initially summarise the empirical findings, and thereafter we will attempt to provide an – also theoretically conducted – elucidation of management actions and management perception in the CEE subsidiaries of the West European parent enterprises.

---

1 Jochen Tholen,Ludovit Czíria, Eike Hemmer, Wieslawa Kozek, Zdenka Mansfeldová: *Labour Relations in Central Europe: The Impact of Multinationals' Money,* Ashgate, Aldershot/UK 2007. The empirical work has been carried out between 2002 and 2005, sponsored by the Hans-Böckler Foundation and the Otto Brenner Foundation.

1. Staffing of top positions in the Central & East European subsidiaries and the subsequently related notions and concepts

With respect to foreign direct investments (FDI), we asked to what extent the implementation of a different management concept occurred, how considerable is the local management's leeway vis-à-vis the corporate group management, and how the local management is comprised.

1.1. The notions of managers from the western parent enterprises in the initial developmental phase of the Central & East European subsidiaries

First of all, foreign managers bring a different kind of thinking and action into the CEE countries. Of course, the question refers to what extent this has also prevailed.

In essence, there was no management concept in the CEE countries at the beginning of the transformation period[2]. As far as that is concerned, the parent companies attempted to completely change the management side (Int1)[3], which also led to resistance in the initial period, however (Int2).

In addition, there was also a somewhat unfortunate dispatching policy of the western (German) parent enterprise: According to the statements from representatives of the employers' associations from the metal, chemicals and foodprocessing industry, it is disadvantageous for the CEE subsidiaries of West European parent enterprises that there is a rapid rotation process for managers in major West European enterprises. The managers are transferred after a maximum of four years in Germany or in other West European countries (and a bit longer in foreign countries). At any rate, as a German, Swiss or French manager (indeed, usually as a plant manager in the beginning) this is too brief to build up a bond of trust with regard to the workforce and the representation of interests in the CEE subsidiaries.

On top of that is the fact that the major German enterprises have initiated an intensified process of detachment in recent years. These detached corporate elements and the transformation into legally unaffiliated firms are now managed above all by younger managers from the parent enterprise, who have acquired their pertinent merits abroad (especially in the USA). In general, it is considered that only the manager who has experience abroad climbs the career ladder. Thus

2 Regarding the concept of management in planned economy business enterprises see Eberwein, Tholen 1997, pp. 46.

3 A list of quoted interviews will be found at the end of this article.

said: These young managers (ca. 6 years experience abroad) then return as an "Americanised German", and then become plant managers in a CEE subsidiary. Of course, the consequences are not very nice, since these managers no longer recognise the solution-oriented German management culture.

Moreover, in the past it was not always the best managers who were sent by the German parent enterprises to their CEE subsidiaries. The philosophy of the German enterprise is that the best managers have been sent into the immediate core areas for enlargement of profitability and productivity. The personnel realm is *not* among the immediate core areas. As a result, those whom the executive board considered as expendable were sent to the CEE subsidiaries – with the exception of greenfield investments, however.

In view of these difficulties and the impediments with regard to optimal staffing of management positions in the CEE subsidiaries, it is quite astounding that a truly successful business management was able to emerge in most cases.

1.2. The notions and methods of the Central & East European managers in the second developmental phase of FDI

In general, there is a "historic" succession of staffing with regard to the management positions in the development of the FDI subsidiaries (Int3), which also had an influence on the autonomy of the FDI business enterprises vis-à-vis the parent enterprise and the application of management styles:

A very close connection of the subsidiaries to the parent enterprises – in terms of personnel as well as leeway – followed in the start phase of the FDI. The managing director came from the parent enterprise (in the beginning he also had better contacts with the banks, which was supposed to have changed later (Int4); the subordinate was predominantly comprised of locals.

After the parent enterprises brought along their own management style in the first phase at the beginning of the 1990's ("A one-to-one transfer of western management style to the CEE subsidiaries followed" (Int5)) and their CEE subsidiaries hardly had any autonomy, this changed in procedural terms – intertwined with the altered personnel composition of the management crew for the subsidiaries (Int6).

As a result, the leeway of the local business operation was enlarged, but with differentiations. Locals took over as managing directors (however, quite often a representative of the parent enterprise remained as deputy plant manager, but he was not always on hand in the subsidiary). Then local specialists were very frequently utilised as personnel managers, because they were more familiar with the local circumstances, language, mentality, etc. Then in this second phase the technical boards of directors were also comprised of locals, whereas the financial boards of directors quite often remained in the hands of representatives from the parent enterprises. These local specialists are to a great extent trained by the investing parent enterprise in the fields of technology and labour organisation in order to accompany the modernisation process from brownfield investments.

On the whole, it can be maintained that the personnel composition of the management personnel for the FDI subsidiaries gradually changed, and thus also the autonomy vis-à-vis the parent companies. Of course, the dominance of the structures in the parent companies is also emphasised here by our respondents. "There are clear instructions from the West, since in earlier times there was no specific management culture in the CEE countries" (Int7). Nevertheless, a hybridisation process seems to be taking place here (Doerrenbaecher et al 2000), in which elements of the management culture prevailing in the company are adapted to the conditions of the recipient country of the FDI. "A process of reciprocal learning is important with regard to the organisation of management. The success of the cooperation is contingent on the people keeping their nose to the grindstone. Here the western style is attractive for CEE countries employees. It differs in a positive sense from the old command style" (Int8). This assessment is also partially shared by trade unionists in the CEE countries. "If the parent enterprise appoints a German manager (example: VW/Skoda), the German industrial culture comes to the Czech Republic. And that is a good thing. If the parent enterprise appoints a local manager, he turns out to be the worst capitalist, because these are converted communists" (Int9).

This means that as a result of the increasing recruitment of local managers, a successful management style did not necessarily arrive on the scene in the FDI subsidiaries:

Due to the absolute dearth of suitable management personnel in the CEE countries in the beginning of the transformation period, many of the old cadres were retrained and partially even "involuntarily" recruited for staff departments in the FDI business operations. In the beginning this caused quite a few irritations, and not just because these now retrained cadres had retained their traditional qualifications of "deception and muddling about" (as many EU enterprises had feared in the beginning), but because they now believed as 'converts' – popularly spoken – that they must profile themselves through "rigid appearance as manager capitalists" (Int10). But in the meantime this not only refers to the old cadre, but also partially to the new, young managers from the CEEC, who – in exaggerated demarcation from the planned economy times – seek their role models in the "radical nature" of certain (liberal) market concepts (Domanski 2001), and who "really want to show this to the parent company" (Int11).

Even Mendius & Deiss point out in their studies in the Bavarian/Czech border region that if Czech managers are utilised by the foreign parent enterprise as business or plant managers in Czech locations, these individuals have a tendency towards a particularly uncompromising behaviour vis-à-vis the workforce. This then results in the fact that numerous violations of labour law and collective agreement regulations as well as industrial safety requirements are complained about (Deiss 2003, 43).

Collectively these are not isolated cases, but empirically quite evident, as the responses from the representative of the Polish trade union Solidarnosc ("Polish managers are much more rigid than foreign managers") and the representative of the Czech metal workers' trade union KOVO indicate:

"For instance, the foreign managers are much more sensitive than the Czech managers vis-à-vis the public opinion through the media. As far as that is concerned, they also treat their employees much better than local managers. ... The traditional Czech business culture was not particularly favourable for FDI. It was characterised by

- an unsteady business environment
- unsteady industrial relations
- the dishonesty of the Czech managers
- i.e., all things that were customers in the communist society when it was valid to grab as much personal leeway as possible.

This has continued to this day: While local Czech enterprises prefer to invest their corporate surpluses in speculative funds instead of reinvesting in their own enterprise (this is why KOVO is engaged in a dispute with the Czech government, so that the speculative funds should be taxed as high as possible in order to increase the self-financing ratio of the business enterprise), the (large) FDI enterprises reinvest their surpluses in their own CEE subsidiaries."

The Czech added that on the whole, "the large FDI enterprises have corrected the 'wild' East – with the exception of the chain stores".

In a survey of 167 managers in 7 CEE countries, Edwards (2003) ascertained that in principle the managers in these countries are structurally overburdened (in comparison with EU-15 managers), since they

a) have been continuously confronted with transformation problems, which are actually a unique historic event, and
b) had to solve quite normal capitalistic problems at the same time.

We would like to add that the local managers

c) must come to terms with their own personal past and that of their home countries, since they – differently than the Western managers, and irrespective of their age and their professional positions up to 1989/90 – grew up in "loser societies".

2. The autonomy of the FDI subsidiaries vis-à-vis their parent enterprises

2.1. *The profit expectations of parent enterprises with respect to their FDI subsidiaries*

The profit expectations of the investing business enterprises are also among the immediate questions pertaining to the autonomy of the FDI subsidiaries. Is an *immediate* profit expected from the CEE subsidiaries, or is the strategic development (market development, etc.) in the foreground, i.e. will losses be tolerated in the first years?

First of all, the answer to these questions depends on the *objective of the FDI*: "First of all, losses are also planned-in with regard to the strategic objective of market development" (Int12). However, profits are also expected here after a certain period of time, on the average after 2 years.

Representatives of the BDI and IG Metall concurrently reported that as a rule the CEE subsidiaries (and not merely the greenfield investments) generate a relative profit very quickly, because the CEE subsidiaries frequently yield higher returns than the parent enterprises (however, the latter still bundle the back office functions in the head office, which always adjusts the average returns downwardly) as a result of job reduction (with brownfield investments), the utilisation of more modern technologies and organisation.

Moreover, profit expectations from business enterprises are very often also *sector-specific* with regard to their CEE subsidiaries. In accordance with the almost identical statements from our interview partners, it can be said of the following industries (which are not completely listed here, but which cover the industries on which we attach special empirical importance) that

- *no immediate* profit expectations exist: energy industry, pharmaceutical industry, steel industry, and metal processing with the focus on the automobile industry. Typical for these industries are the partially very high investment sums, which make an immediate "return of investment" impossible right from the beginning;
- *immediate* profit expectations exist: tyre industry, retail trade (supermarkets), information technologies (mere transfer and not development) and financial investments.

Furthermore, the *size of the business enterprise* naturally also plays a role. As a rule of thumb, it can also apply here that large business enterprises do not entertain any exaggerated profit expectations on account of their strategic alignment and very high investment sums in the initial years. On the other hand, small-scale enterprises in particular must generate immediate profits, namely because their equity position is much too short to be able to cover long-term losses. This compulsion is also strengthened through the behaviour of the banks: In anticipation of Basel 2, to grant only "safe" credits – to the disadvantage of the soliciting SMEs.

Small enterprises are just not able to undertake a diversified/mixed calculation as is the case with regard to the major investors ("expensive German motors and cheap Czech sheet metal result in a diversified/mixed calculation for VW/Skoda, in order to improve the position on the world market" (Int13).

However, one thing should be referred to at this point: Even if no immediate profit expectations exist on the part of the parent enterprise in many FDI, the pressure remains on the employees in the CEE subsidiaries, the same as with regard to investments which must immediately work with a profit (Int14).

2.2. *Management models and human resource policy*

In the further expansion phase of their FDI, the (large) business enterprises from the EU-15 were not able to export their own management models. For instance, Frosta in Poland adapted their entire marketing model to the Polish conditions, and after two years there was a Polish works management there (Int15).

However, this autonomy of the local management vis-à-vis the parent enterprise is limited at the moment (short-term) insofar as wage negotiations and settlements are concerned. The specifications of the parent enterprise still dominate here (Int16) – since the often observed alliances of the local management with the representations of interest in the CEE subsidiaries also provide little help.

But these procedural changes of management concepts and also the recruitment policy of local managerial personnel in the CEE subsidiaries are not CEE-specific. Apart from the desire of many parent enterprises "just not wanting to take over any old cadre without scrutiny", and thus also to preclude planned economy elements (including individuals) in their CEE subsidiaries right from the beginning, the representative of the European trade union of Mine, Chemical and Energy Workers (EMCEF) can certainly be concurred with: "There is no difference vis-à-vis the EU-15. If the result tallies, then the local management everywhere have a certain degree of leeway".

But, as (nearly) everywhere, these statements must also be put into perspective, namely

a) *With respect to the type of production*

If the subsidiaries merely represent an "extended workbench", the autonomy of the subsidiary is very marginal.

On the other hand, if the FDI expands a specific product range, the autonomy is relatively large (example Siemens). In this case, the parent enterprise makes a fundamental strategic decision with regard to the FDI, and thus defines the basic conditions. Under this "umbrella" the subsidiaries then have a considerable degree of autonomy – "but only if everything's hunky-dory" (so said the representatives of the German employers association "Gesamtmetall" and the German trade union "IG Metall" unanimously).

b) With respect to the size of the investing business enterprise

The FDI of the small enterprises are thoroughly characterised by the parent company, provided that the SMEs assert to a much greater extent their own management notions and corporate culture in their CEE subsidiaries.

But also large-scale enterprises from the EU-15 (and first and foremost here from Germany) not only brought along their technology and organisation, but also attempted in the first phase – also in matters of industrial relations and corporate culture – to initially assert the notions of the parent enterprise. However, in a second phase they gradually adapted to the conditions of the host country and the respective region. The recognition of the significance of mentality issues for corporate policy was and is linked as a result.

One can only concur with Galgóczi (2003) in his argumentation (which is first of all only empirically restricted to Hungary), and expand this argument to the relationships in the new Central & East European EU member states – that the multinational concerns had a positive influence on the corporate culture in the respective host countries with their FDI in the CEE countries. In particular, the human resource policy has a considerable influence on the corporate culture and thus also on the industrial relations of the CEE subsidiaries. According to Galgóczi in a concluding evaluation, the most significant function of such a creative HR strategy is the evolution of the business enterprise into a "learning organisation" based on the principles of social dialogue and the respect of the interest of the other respective actor.

c) With respect to the corporate-specific strategy of the individual business enterprise

Irrespective of the size of the business enterprise and other factors, the autonomy of the FDI subsidiaries vis-à-vis their parent enterprises also depends on the respective corporate culture and the strategic alignment of the investment, which can be very different from company to company.

The studies by Doerr and Kessel (1999) have provided good examples for this: A new product concept was developed by VW/Skoda on account of strong pressure on the part of the Czech partner; accordingly, this also comprised a different management concept. A new factory was built by Audi in Gyoer/Hungary within the framework of the internal corporate group combine. This did not mean that the factory management board in Gyoer adopted the Audi concept on a one to one basis, but the management policy in Gyoer had to be oriented to a stronger extent on the "European management style" (see Doerre 1997 for more details pertaining to this term), because with the Hungarian FDI Audi pursued a globalisation/Europeanization strategy which – other than with regard to VW/Skoda – integrates the individual factories into *one* production combine.

On top of that is the fact that business enterprises – even in the same size class and within one industry – prefer different models of hierarchy and centralisation. For instance, the head offices at VW, General Electrics and Philipps are very powerful, and "let nothing escape from their hands" (Int17), whereas Siemens, for instance, pursues a more decentralised approach.

d) With regard to the country of origin of the FDI

The perceptions of the representatives from the CEE countries are interesting, since they have better possibilities of comparison with regard to the differentiations among western management styles.

This is how a representative of the Slovakian trade union KOZ presents a ranking of foreign management concepts with regard to their (practiced) interpretation of social dialogue in their respective CEE subsidiaries: Accordingly, the investors from the EU-15 solicit a dialogue with the trade unions, American FDI enterprises entirely disregard any dialogue whatsoever, and FDI enterprises from South Korea even implement their traditionally dismissive attitude vis-à-vis trade unions in their Slovakian subsidiaries. A representative of the Polish Chamber of Industry and Commerce adds that in the FDI from major American business enterprises in Poland "the people are supposed to function like little cogs in the wheel, and all important decisions are made in the head offices".

Also Galgóczi (2003) adds that the uncompromising transfer of management cultures from the countries of origin would be typical for Asian FDI enterprises. Americans prefer effectiveness first and foremost, and the corresponding corporate culture transports this objective. The most important thing for them would be the "corporate identity" and the loyalty of the employee vis-à-vis the company. Particularly German firms had an innovative interpretation of corporate culture (Galgóczi differentiates between an *adaptive* behaviour pattern oriented towards the circumstances of the FDI host country and an *innovative* approach preferential to the corporate culture of the country of origin), which then procedurally becomes an adaptive behaviour, however. German parent enterprises do not normally force their model on their CEE subsidiaries; they rather prefer more flexible structures.

But there are also differentiations within the EU-15 management "models": For instance, French and Dutch FDI models would rely more on local specialists than the German model (Int18).

And FDI from Romance (EU-15) countries would have had much greater difficulties building up dialogue structures with the CEE trade unions within their subsidiaries than German and Scandinavian investors, because in their countries of origin there already was a culture of codetermination (Int19).

When asked about the model function of American and EU-15 management concepts for the CEE countries, the representative of the EU Commission (GD Employment and Social Affairs) thought that the (west) European "model" (see Doerre 1997 with regard to conceptuality) would be dominant in the future EU member states.

2.3. "Solution-Oriented Corporate Centralisation" with regard to the arrangement of HRM and industrial relations

The answers from our respondents indicate that technology, organisation of labour and partially also management concepts may not always be transferred on a one to one basis, but have been nevertheless transferred to a distinctive extent from the (mostly) German parent enterprises to their CEE subsidiaries.

This appears somewhat differently with regard to the industrial relations and HRM on the operational/corporate level. Certainly our empirical findings reveal that there is a general tendency in the CEE countries towards establishment of a culture of negotiation solutions as the main method for regulation of industrial relations (see also Gradev 2001, 16), and that the German investors also prefer this solution-oriented method. However, our study also corroborates the results of the studies from Kluge & Voss, who ascertained a "selective transfer" for the industrial relations overall (Kluge, Voss 2003, 67), and from Doerrenbaecher (2003, 167). Even German companies make codetermination an element of a cross-border corporate culture and identity, and only achieve on a limited basis their positive experiences with the cooperative management model.

In their transfer of industrial relations and HRM, German companies particularly avoid legally established agreements for regulation of this "solution orientation".

This "reluctant" commitment of German companies regarding general transfer of their experiences in German industrial relations to the CEE subsidiary enterprises is also expressed in the fact that as a rule, no efforts have been made in the Greenfield investments to establish (juridically secured) institutions of workforce representation – despite the subsequently related difficulties through the absence of a corresponding negotiation partner on the part of the employees.

Under these general determinations, there is no general model for the arrangement of industrial relations and HRM in their CEE subsidiaries that would be identifiable on account of their specific strategies obtained from German parent enterprises in the manufacturing industry (we explicitly preclude business services and the retail trade here). Of course there are nuances between the branches of the individual companies (such as between the chemical, energy, automobile and steel sector). Furthermore, the size of the parent enterprises may play a role; as a rule, medium-size and large-scale companies in Germany feature a works council (which could then theoretically exert influence), whereas in small companies this is often not the case. Investment reasons (market developments or reasons of cost) now and then have a certain influence on the arrangement of industrial relations and HRM.

But on the whole, all of these independent variables do not construe any general explanatory model in the sense implied above. For instance, the existence of a works council in the German parent enterprise does not automatically signify the possibility, the will – or even the attempt – to establish representations of interest in the CEE subsidiary enterprises with respect to greenfield investments. Yet another example for this is the very different attitude of German works councils towards the integration of CEE interest representatives in the European Works Council (if available) before 1 May 2004 (accession of the eight CEE countries into the EU). And in this overall context it must be asked to what extent the works councils in the German parent enterprises are even included in the investment decisions in their respective company, and whether subsequently secured conclusions allow the influence possibilities of the representations of interest with regard to the set-up and structure of representations of interest in the CEE countries.

As the recipient countries of the investments, the (quite different) CEE countries do not offer any explanatory model for different country strategies among the West European and here espec. German parent enterprises with regard to the arrangement of industrial relations and HRM in the subsidiary enterprises. In general, it is determinable that the companies observe the respective laws, which are of course different from country to country. But apart from this general determination there are no indications that historical, social, political and economical differences in the CEE countries lead to a country-specific, different strategy of the parent enterprises with regard to the organisation of the industrial relations and HR policies for their subsidiaries.

This all indicates that it particularly depends on the strategies of the *individual* parent enterprises (theoretically including the position and the policy of the works council), independent from industrial-sector affiliation, share of the wage costs in the total cost of the product, company size, etc. We call this a "corporate-centred approach" for explanation of the corporate policy[4] with regard to the development of industrial relations in their CEE subsidiary enterprises – which also includes the history of the business enterprise, the corporate culture, the size, the subjective behaviour of the acting corporate protagonists, etc.

However, this "corporate approach" is characterised by the "solution-oriented" imprint. As far as that is concerned, with the notion of "*solution-oriented corporate centralisation*" we offer an explanation for a potential transfer model of industrial relations and HRM through German parent enterprises to their CEE subsidiaries.

The "German production model" is not transferred in its entirety, but the basic assumptions of this model (negotiation and dialogue on different levels with different radii of action) are also reflected – albeit with many variations – in the industrial relations of the CEE subsidiary enterprises.

2.4. Path dependency of management concepts and management behavioural patterns

The following typification of the nine corporate cases occurs under the restriction that these types are never to be found in pure culture, that in addition to the mentioned main features there are still numerous other – but less dominant – influences, and overlaps between these types are often perceivable. But nevertheless, this form of typification has its purpose wherever sharp-edged contours become visible.

For this, we refer to the above, already theoretically substantiated categories regarding the various possibilities of "cross-border model transfer" from multinational companies (Doerrenbaecher 2003)[5], whereby we add an additional Type 3:

- Type 1: Predominant characterisation through the HRM concepts in the parent enterprise/country of origin of the investments – unilateral path dependency
- Type 2: Predominant characterisation through the HRM in the target country of the investments/handed-down HRM with Brownfield investments and

4 In his Hungarian case study pertaining to the effects of German direct investments on the Hungarian subsidiaries, Doerrenbaecher (2003) ascertains a "strong heterogeneity in the internationalisation of business enterprises" (167).

5 In the application of the conceptualities of the path dependencies we relate primarily to the real conditions of the respective parent enterprises/subsidiaries, which are naturally embedded in the respective national "models" of industrial relations.

laws/visions of the CEE social actors in the resp. companies – unilateral path dependency

- Type 3: Characterisation through conditions in the country of origin *and* the target country of the investments – mixed HRM policies
- Type 4: Substantial influences through third countries/organisation – Europeanisation
- Type 5: The rootless enterprise – "footloose" company

Table: Division of the companies into the five types

	Unilateral path dependency/ country of origin investment	**Unilateral path dependency/ target country investment**	**Mixture of industrial relations in the target country and country of origin**	**Third-country influences/EU**	**Footloose Companies**
Volkswagen AG	X				
Robert Bosch GmbH			X		
Siemens AG			X		
RWE AG			X		
Nestlé SA					X
Dr. August Oetker KG		X			
Continental AG			X		
Aventis SA (Sanofi Aventis SA after 20 August 2004)				X	
Henkel KgaA			X		

The trend is clear. The mixture of HRM policies from the country of origin and the target country of the direct investments predominates (Type No. 3). Type 1 (unilateral path dependency/country of origin), Type 2 (unilateral path dependency/target country), Type 4 (third-country influences/Europeanisation) and Type 5 (footloose companies) constitute the exceptions:

The VW AG on the one hand (Type 1: dominance of the country of origin in the arrangement of CEE HRM), the Dr. August Oetker KG (dominance of the target country as Type 2), the French-German Aventis SA as a "prototype" for third-country influences (here: EU/Type 4) and the (Swiss) Nestlé SA as representative of Type 5 (bound neither to the country of origin nor the host country nor a third country) represent the minorities. One can describe them as the "mavericks" in the "normal division" of companies with regard to the influence on the HRM, management´s behaviour and attitude in their CEE subsidiary enterprises/plants[6].

In the aggregate, the hybridisation thesis[7] is thereby also corroborated through the study encompassing the three CEE countries (Poland, Czech Republic and Slovakia) at issue.

At the same time, this "hybridisation of HRM" – as a mainstream type of influence from West European/German parent enterprises on HRM policies of their CEE subsidiaries in their *not precisely* determinable borders, contours and contents – also presents substantial definition and arrangement possibilities for protagonists taking action.

3. The typology of "in-patriat" managers in the transition from the planned economy to the market economy

As we have learnt from above, foreign (western) mother companies more and more replaced ex-patriats by in-patriats, at least in specified positions (mostly HR managers). But what kind of manages western companies met initially in the transformation societies to recruit in-patriats? How the old cadres (not only in terms of age) from the communist times did "convert" from a planned into a market economy – with the exception of the very young people, whose first career steps started only in the beginning of the 1990s after the velvet revolution?

There is a connection between the development of the market society, the degree of privatisation and specific types of "in patriat" managers, which we have initially developed in the example of Russia, and which – in accordance with our adaptations and judgement – could also be adapted to the CEE countries as a (theoretical) explanatory model for the changing behaviour patterns of managers (Eberwein, Tholen 1997, pp 209):

6 However, what is conspicuous – even if not able to be generalised on account of the negligible number of cases – is that among the "mavericks", the non-German companies (Aventis SA and Nestlé SA) are assigned to the types with international or non nationally-determined path dependencies, whereas German companies attempt to transfer either the HRM from their country of origin – or more or less attempt to entirely adapt the conditions in the target country of the investments.

7 Doerrenbaecher (2000 and 2003) tested this thesis in only one CEE country (Hungary), though on a broader branch dispersion.

Diagram: Typology of management in transformation societies

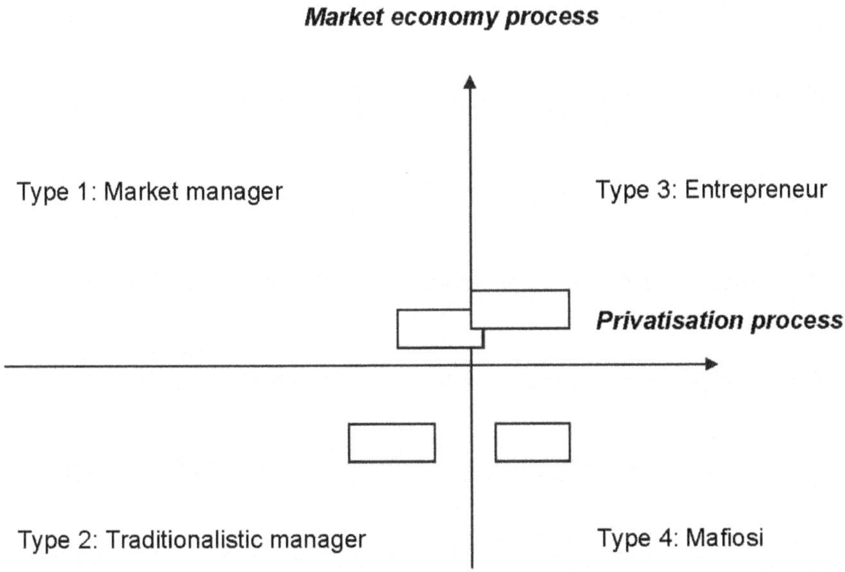

© University of Bremen-IAW

The abscissa of our coordinate system symbolise the degree of privatisation, whereas the ordinates symbolise the development of the market economy.

The *market manager (Type 1)* encompasses those managers created through the societal and economical transformation, usually from larger industrial enterprises, which are fundamentally ready and willing to adapt to the market economy instead of the planned economy. While doing so, their perception of market economy is inseparably linked with a more or less expanded operational or supra-operational social policy. At the same time, this type of manager only appears in a limited fashion or with specific notions of privatisation. This attitude regarding privatisation prompted us to position our Type 1 partially on the left (negative) side of the privatisation axis, and also partially on the right side.

As far as the perception of the market economy is concerned, all managers of this type are positioned on the positive side of the corresponding axis. As an economical regulatory mechanism, they prefer the market economy vis-à-vis the planned economy, i.e. in particular: They advocate the independence of the business enterprise, especially their activity at their own risk and for their own account. This also implies that they anticipate and call for the business enterprise to assert itself on the market in competition with others.

In empirical terms they partially stem from the old class of production directors. Thus said, with the market managers this fundamentally concerns reform-oriented managers, who actually reject the introduction of Manchester-liberal capitalism, as they appeared quite early and openly against the state-controlled planned economy.

And so they differ from their former colleagues (Type 2: traditionalistic manager), who had secured high positions in the new privatised business enterprises, exclusively in the interest of their personal enrichment and political position of power, and thus ultimately had a destructive effect in terms of the society and the economy.

Finally, a series of "lateral newcomers" also fall under the market manager type. These are highly-intelligent, creative people – often scientists and at that time in opposition to the communist regimes in the CEEC – who partially with considerable success established new business enterprises or newly managed and restructured old business enterprises. During the upheaval phase they developed new, previously unknown qualifications and competencies. For instance, those Solidarnosc members who became managers after 1989 and who replaced the old, reform-unwilling production directors (Type 2: traditionalistic manager) are also empirical.

In contrast to the market manager, the type of managers compiled under *traditionalistic manager (Type 2)* not only reject privatisation, but also the introduction of the market economy. Therefore they are depicted in the rectangle in the left lower quadrant of our diagram, i.e. on the negative side of our two axes. They deliberately adhered to the political and economical traditions as long as this was possible in the transition phase. In empirical terms, this type is nearly extinct in the future EU member countries, at most in the mining industry and perhaps partially in the steel industry.

And now we come to the *Entrepreneur (Type 3)* in our diagram. This type is not to be exclusively equated with the owner-entrepreneur, but is also found in the ranks of salaried managers. He is to be positioned in the right upper field of our diagram, since he is an advocate of the market economy as well as a wide-ranging privatisation. The entrepreneur is not only found in the trade and service sector (and here in the SMEs), but often also in industrial operations. He is the type who converted from the planned economy to the market economy, or is otherwise the young manager. Both characterisations have a (socio-) political conception of the market economy, which approximates neo-liberal or even Manchester-capitalistic ideas.

We have somewhat spectacularly called the fourth type *Mafiosi*. Much like the Entrepreneur type, the Mafiosi are interested in private profits. In contrast to the Entrepreneurs, they resort to criminal methods. The Mafiosi originate from the "traditional criminal" milieu as well as from the state bureaucracy – i.e. also that environment after the fall of communism. In our diagram the Mafiosi type is positioned on the positive side of the privatisation axis, since the privatisation of profits is the fundamental prerequisite for their personal enrichment. At first glance, the classification of the Mafiosi in the negative area of the market economy axis may seem surprising. But we think that the Mafiosi are no expression of market economy thinking and action, but that they have particularly made the malfunction of the market a prerequisite. From that point of view their economic role is more like that of a robber baron or highwayman than that of the market economy entrepreneur. Of course, the Mafiosi may not have any interest in a return to the former central administrative economy, but also not in the establishment of an intact market economy system with its specific structural standards. Because in such a system the black market, corruption and other illegal business activities – from which the Mafiosi sucks his nectar – may not be precluded, but is merely a peripheral phenomenon. But unfortunately these phenomena are to be found all too frequently in the new EU member countries, as the EU progress report from November 2003 made very clear with its references to the widespread corruption (European Commission 2003a).

Of course there are devolutions among the four types, and in empirical terms these types are never to be found in "pure culture" – besides, this is merely a typology as defined by Max Weber. But all of these elements are certainly to be found among the managers in the CEEC.

Indeed, this typology, which also emerged in the consideration of the past 14 years (and as far as that goes, a third axis – namely the time axis – would have had to proceed at right angles to the two other axes; but this would make the presentation too complex), clearly illustrates the major difficulties of the transformation process that is certainly coming to its (official) conclusion in many CEEC. The traditionalist and the Mafiosi *were* and *are* not suitable – due to aforementioned reasons – as champions of such a transformation. This role and function *could* and *can* only be realised by the market managers and the entrepreneurs. But these types are in and of themselves very complex, and above all so differentiated that no consistent thinking and action structure concomitant with a social group of entrepreneurs and managers could (still) emerge here. What seems important to us in this connection is that the Entrepreneur *alone* may not be perceived as a guarantor of a market economy and social democracy, as this is frequently done particularly by certain groupings in the west. On the contrary and in our opinion, particularly that type designated as Market Manager also assumes a decisive role in the configuration of the new EU member countries.

Such a typology of management in the transition from planned economy to market economy does not evolve in a vacuum, but is contingent on a variety of economical, political, social, but also cultural factors; and at the same time management actions and management behavioural patterns influence these factors in a complex process (see also our third "co-contrived" time axis above).

4. Summary

The autonomy of the CEE subsidiaries vis-à-vis the western parent enterprises is increasing step by step – even with some differences, which result from the objectives of the investment (market or cost reasons), the type of product, the subsequently resulting diversity of the corporate cultures, the size of the parent enterprise as well as of the subsidiary etc.

This was accompanied by an augmented recruitment of local managers (in-patriats) in their different shapes (see chapter 3). Local personnel have been/are quite frequently taken on particularly as personnel managers, since they are more familiar with the local circumstances, the national industrial law, language, mentality, etc. The personnel sector in a company is rooted deeper in the local context than any other sector. Under this aspect, this position in management forms the bridge to the representatives (if existent) in the subsidiary. Both roles are thus staffed with local personnel and also have an overriding importance as intermediaries. However, this increasing replacement of Western European managerial personnel (ex-patriats) through locals (in-patriats) does not necessarily signify an improvement of solution-oriented cooperative willingness, since partially old (cadres still accustomed to the communist era) and/or young junior staff have been recruited, who – in exaggerated demarcation to communist times – seek their role models in the "radicalism" of certain market concepts.

On the other hand, western management (in our cases most German companies) generally behaved respectfully in the CEE subsidiaries, which is not only attributable to a longstanding, proven dialogue culture with the inclusion of collective bodies of representatives in the western, esp. German parent enterprises, but can also be substantiated through the respect vis-à-vis the existing technical and engineering competencies of the Central & Eastern Europeans, as well as consideration – particularly on the part of the managers from the parent enterprises in the west – arising from the war history. These reasons had an effect to the extent that an authoritarian manner on the part of western management could be relegated to the closets in the CEE subsidiaries.

Considerable differences between the management styles of various western countries are described at the same time. Although not a main object of our case studies, it can be deduced from the literature and our expert interviews on the supra-company level that Asian companies/managers most easily and consistently pursue a model transfer of corporate culture and (authoritarian) management style, and

French managers in Central & Eastern Europe behave in a much more authoritarian manner (“*le patron*”) than Germans, who perceive themselves as more committed to a cooperative corporate culture and industrial relations.

The company’s image, especially with regard to brand name producers, additionally plays a very important role in the arrangement of industrial relations through the managers. Independent of the respective company size, these western companies are very interested in a positive image – first of all in the region of the subsidiary, and moreover in the country on the whole – which is also depicted through the workforces, their representatives and through the media, etc. Thus, not only the products, not only the quantifiable working conditions (such as wages, working hours, etc.) play a role, but also the quality of the industrial relations. As soon as this image is damaged through an excessively authoritarian attitude on the part of the local management or also through mere politically-motivated action from representatives and any subsequently related disputes in the public realm, the foreign headquarters intervenes. Here lies a major difference in contrast to the domestic-owned companies in Central & Eastern Europe.

Large as well as small companies from the EU-15 (and first and foremost here from Germany) not only brought their technology and organisation with them, but they also attempted to assert the visions of the parent enterprise in matters of industrial relations, HRM and corporate culture in an initial phase of investment. But in a second phase they gradually adapted to the conditions of the host country and the respective region, and they also continued to expand these aspects in accordance with their own visions: Company collective agreements (and not the supra-company collective bargaining still dominating in Germany), human resource management (i.e. direct relations between plant management and workforces without intermediaries) as an additional pillar of industrial relations, and “works councils” without union involvement are all elements of the CEE industrial relations which did not have to be forced on the western/German management, but were certainly also enthusiastically adopted.

List of quoted interviews

Int1 European Trade Union Institute ETUI
Int2 Polish Solidarnosc trade union
Int3 Bundesverband der Deutschen Industrie [Federal Association of German Industry] BDI
Int4 Czech labour ministry
Int5 Gesamtmetall [German Employers’ Association for the Metal and Electrical Industry]

Int6 European Federation of Commercial Enterprises UNICE
Int7 European metal workers trade union EMF
Int8 Bundesverband der Deutschen Industrie [Federal Association of German Industry] BDI
Int9 Czech metal workers' trade union KOVO
Int10 European trade union for food processing industry EFFAT
Int11 German trade union for the metal sector IG Metall
Int12 German employers' association Nahrung und Genuß ["Food & Consumption"]
Int13 Czech metal workers' trade union KOVO
Int14 German trade union for the metal sector IG Metall
Int15 Federation of German Food and Drink Industries BVE
Int16 German trade union for the metal sector IG Metall
Int17 European metal workers trade union EMF
Int18 IG Bergbau-Chemie-Energie [German industrial trade union for the mining, chemical & energy industries]
Int19 European trade union for food processing industry EFFAT

References

Altvater, Elmar/Mahnkopf, Birgit (1996): Grenzen der Globalisierung. Oekonomie, Oekologie und Politik in der Weltgesellschaft, Publishing House Westfaelisches Dampfboot, Muenster

Deiss, Manfred (2003): Ausgewaehlte Ergebnisse aus der Empirie und Zwischenfazit des Projektes "Risiken und Chancen der EU-Osterweiterung für die ArbeitnehmerInnen am Beispiel der ostbayerisch/tschechischen Grenzregion", in: ISF Munich: Forschungsprojekt "Risiken und Chancen der EU-Osterweiterung für die Arbeitnehmer am Beispiel der ostbayerisch/tschechischen Grenzregion", Dokumentation zum 2. Arbeitsgespraech am 2./3. April 2003 in Regensburg, www.isf-muenchen.de/pdf/284_dokumentation2_030624.pdf

Doerr, Gerlinde/ Kessel, Tanja (1999): Restructuring Via Internationalization. The Auto Industry's Direct Investment Project in Eastern Central Europe, in: Series from the Department of Labour Regulation, research emphasis Technology, Labour & Environment at the Berlin Science Centre, Berlin, May 1999

Doerre, Klaus (1997): Globalisierung – eine strategische Option. Internationalisierung von Unternehmen und industrielle Beziehungen in der Bundesrepublik, in: *Industrielle Beziehungen* [Industrial Relations], Volume 4, Issue 4, Munic and Mering, 265-290

Doerrenbaecher, Christoph (2003): Grenzueberschreitende Modelltransfer in multinationalen Unternehmen. Heimat-, Gast- und Drittlandeffekte am Beispiel deutscher Investitionen in Ungarn, in: Ch. Doerrenbaecher (Ed): Modelltransfer in multinationalen Unternehmen. Strategien und Probleme grenzüberschreitender Konzernintegration, Publishing House edition sigma, Berlin 2003, 151-171

Doerrenbaecher, Christoph / Fichter, Michael / Neumann, László / Toth, András/ Wortmann, Michael (2000): Transformation and foreign direct investment: Observations on path dependency, hybridisation and model transfer at the enterprise level, in: Transfer (2)/ 2000, Brussels, 434-449

Domanski, Boleslaw (2001): Poland: Labour and the Relocation of Manufacturing from the EU: in: Grigor Gradev (ed.): CEE countries in the EU companies' strategies of industrial restructuring and relocation, EGI, Brussels, 21-50

Eberwein, Wilhelm / Tholen, Jochen (1997): Market or Mafia. Russian managers on the difficult road towards an open society, Ashgate Publ., Aldershot/UK 1997

Edwards, Vincent (2003): Organisational leadership in transforming economies: leadership management and national culture in selected countries of Central and Eastern Europe, in: Journal for East European Management Studies, Vol. 8, No. 4, 2003, Rainer Hampp Publishing, 415-429

European Commission (2003a): Comprehensive Monitoring Report on Poland's, Slovakia's, Czech Repblic's preparations for membership, Brussels, 05.11.2003

Galgóczi, Béla (2003): Passing from low-road to high road competition strategies in CEE countries with a view to working relations, in: IPL (Istituto per il Lavoro): Prospettive delle condizioni sociali e ruolo lavoro nella società italiana ed europea, Bologna, June 2003

Gradev, Grigor (2001): EU Companies in Eastern Europe: Strategic Choices and Labour Effects, in Grigor Gradev (ed.): CEE countries in the EU companies' strategies of industrial restructuring and relocation, EGI, Brussels, 1-20

Hofstede, Geert (1980): Culture's Consequences: International Work-related Values; Sage, London

Hofstede, Geert (1991): Cultures and Organisations: Software of the Mind, McGraw-Hill

Kluge, Norbert / Voss, Eckhard (2003): Managementstile und Arbeitnehmerbeteiligung bei auslaendischen Unternehmen in Polen, Tschechien und Ungarn, in: WSI-Mitteilungen, 1/2003, Duesseldorf, 66 contd.

Sachs, Jeffrey (1993): Poland's Jump to the Market Economy, Cambridge, Mass.

Stark, David (1994): Path Dependency and Privatization Strategies in East Central Europe, in: East European Politics and Societies, Vol. 8, No. 1; Winter

Stark, David / Bruszt, Lazlo (1998): Post-socialist Pathways, Transforming Politics and Property in East Central Europe, Cambridge

The role of Industrial Relations and HRM in direct participation practice in Spain

María C. Gonzalez

Introduction

Despite a recent abundance of practitioner-oriented books on how to implement workers' direct participation at firm-level, our knowledge of workers' direct participation practice in Spain is very scant. This can be partly attributed to the way the sphere of work is studied in Spain. There remains little academic integration between industrial relations, often conceptualised mainly as a political-juridical construct, and the management of labour in the workplace. HRM research within Spanish academia has tended to follow American trends; it focuses mostly on HR strategic fit and its links with organisational performance and to a lesser extent on best practice determinants, alongside a certain interest in knowledge management. The much more critical analytical strand prominent in the UK, which analyses the politics and context of HRM (Martinez Lucio 2007) is much less present in the field in Spain. That which exists is generally connected to sociology of work and informed by qualitative research (key examples in the area of workers' participation are Blyton and Martinez Lucio 1995; Ortiz 1998; Gutierrez 1998; Juan Albalate 2005).

Spain also lacks a tradition of large-scale workplace surveys of industrial relations. Accordingly, there is a paucity of survey data capable of showing the relationships among different HR policies and practices, and between these and industrial relations variables. These gaps include, but are not limited to, the issue of worker participation. The reference cross-sectional workplace data for workers' direct participation thus remains that of the influential comparative EPOC (1997) study which showed Spain to be unique in exhibiting a negative relationship between worker representatives' involvement in negotiations and the existence of direct participation. This finding is important for our theorisation of participation; it is unsatisfactory to somehow treat Spain as an 'exception' without reaching a practically adequate response to the question as to why Spain fails to follow normal patterns of correlation.

The advancement of participation is seen as contributing to higher productivity, more innovation and hence better economic performance, as well as to improving job quality, to the point that along with social dialogue direct participation is considered one of the dimensions of quality of work in the European Employment

Strategy. It is therefore also of practical significance to achieve a better understanding of the relationship between direct and representative participation. To do this, it is necessary to establish the conditions which make relatively high degrees of direct participation more or less likely, taking into account the nature, and internal variability, of both workplace-level institutions and of management beliefs and practices.

This chapter reflects on the characteristics of the institutional industrial relations framework of direct participation and the traits of Spanish HRM in two distinct sections. It also reports our findings regarding the extension of direct participation and the impact of IR and HRM on it, resulting from the analysis of a representative survey carried out in 1999 among Spanish managers of workplaces with at least twenty-five workers in the industry, services and construction sectors (cf Gonzalez 2008 for more technical detail).

Institutional IR framework of direct participation

The most important aspect of regulation regarding direct participation in Spain is that the adoption of direct participation practices in Spain is considered a work organisation decision, and in Spanish labour law the employer prerogative in work organisation matters is protected. This has been reflected in policy: governmental and social partners' action on issues relating to work organisation modernisation have mostly been in the spirit of reinforcing the autonomy of the actors by extending employers' legal capacity to change the duties of workers while fostering collective bargaining on the topic (QUIT 1999).

Yet, it is also important to note that the attitude of Spanish employers and unions towards direct participation has been found to be remarkably defensive in comparative European studies (Regini 1993; Regalia 1996), with both parties perceiving it as a threat to their prerogatives. Such attitudes make direct participation itself or collective bargaining on the topic, in principle, quite unlikely. They also explain why promotion of a more participative organisation of work has not been present in the agenda of the government or the social partners (QUIT 1999), with recent governmental policy on improving the quality of working life focusing most prominently on the promotion of contractual stability, health and safety and gender equality.

The absence in Spain of governmental legal or best-practice guidelines in this area – unlike France and the UK respectively – follows the spirit of respect for social actors' autonomy. However, since Spain also lacks a tradition of workplace direct participation and Spanish unions have a low level of interest in work organisation matters – unlike the Nordic countries –, regulatory abstention does not contribute to diminishing social actors' suspicions of direct participation.

To understand the defensive attitude of Spanish actors it is important to consider that, compared with other countries, the introduction of direct participation in Spain has to be framed with a background of a young system of representative participation at the workplace. Thus, governmental and unions' concerns around workers' participation focused on strengthening the role of weak unions through legal regulation of workers' representatives information and consultation rights, while leaving to the autonomy of the parties the contents of bargaining. Yet, the Spanish workplace, and particularly work organisation in its widest sense, has traditionally been the realm of managers (Blyton and Martinez Lucio 1995), and any further extension of workers' participation, whether direct or indirect, immediately threatens managerial prerogative. This is more so if it means opening a new issue – as could be direct participation – to collective bargaining, which will increase the power of trade unions (Blyton and Martinez Lucio 1995). At the same time, Spanish trade unions can be suspicious of managerial initiatives on direct participation fearing their functions as representatives may be weakened. Thus, for every Spanish actor, the uncertainties of direct participation outcomes are greater than those regarding economic impact abundant in the literature: it may affect the national institutional pact over the always contested ground of labour relations at firm level.

More recently the transposition in November 2007 of the 2002 European Directive on informing and consulting employees -which could have opened the door for more direct participation- reinforced the traditional approach to participation. While the Workers' Statute was changed to include workers' explicit right to information and consultation, the works councils' rights were expanded to some new issues, and collective bargaining called to decide on the modalities by which the rights of information and consultation of works councils will be exercised (CES 2008).

The Spanish system of representative participation at firm-level is peculiar because the works council – or workers′ delegates in smaller firms (between 6 and 49 workers) – can legally sign collective agreements affecting all workers and call a strike; these are unique legal features of works councils in the European context. Table 1 below describes, among other features, the legal rights of participation of elected workers' representatives. Please note that representation is mandated by law upon workers' request and therefore that not all workplaces/firms that could have workers' representatives do have them. In our study, for instance, nearly seventeen per cent of workplaces did not have elected workers' representatives. Also, the regulation of workers' representative participation is not applicable to firms with less than six workers.

Table 1: Main features of the Spanish system of elected workers' representatives at workplace/firm level

Workers appoint Board members	No
Works councils mandated by Law	Yes, on workers' request
Statutory threshold for workers' representation and initiative for formation of a works council	6 to 30 workers: 1 delegate 31 to 49 workers: 3 delegates Works council: o 50 to 100 workers: 5 delegates o 101 to 250 workers: 9 delegates o 251 to 500 workers: 13 o 501 to 750 workers: 17 o 751 to 1.000 workers: 21 o More than 1.000: 2 more for each other thousand workers or fraction, with a maximum of 75 delegates
Procedure for election	Universal suffrage every 4 years among all workers of the workplace or firm that have been employed for at least one month
Works councils/workers' delegates information entitlement	Financial affairs, employment contracts and absenteeism, gender equality situation and plans for equality, disciplinary actions, production, health & safety and general plans
Works councils/workers' delegates consultation entitlement	Hours of work, workforce restructuring, work organisation changes, training plans, work monitoring, incentive systems, dismissals, productivity, health & safety and social activities
Works councils/workers' delegates decision-making powers	Company or workplace collective agreements and right to call a strike
Coverage	Applicable to 306,778 undertakings and 72% of the workforce in 2003[a]. More than 260,000 representatives in 2003[a].
Practice / significance	– Key for company bargaining. Effectiveness depends on quality of relations between unions. In 2007 company agreements affect to 11% of the workforce[b]. – Workplace elections determine trade unions' representativeness for collective bargaining at levels above the firm. Total coverage of collective bargaining estimated in 2007:80-90% workforce[b].

Sources: Gonzalez (2008); (a) White (2003); (b) CES (2008)

As in other EU countries Spanish works councillors or workers' delegates tend to be trade union members but they do not have to be. It is only the majority of the works council rather than of trade unions delegates – even if they often overlap in practice – that may sign a firm-level collective agreement affecting all workers Although some alternatives are allowed (i.e. the trade union representatives negotiating directly as such) under certain conditions, these other channels are very limited in powers and little used in practice.

Thus, the unitary representation principle is adhered to at firm/workplace level in Spain (Knudsen 1995). Above the firm, it is the 'representative trade unions' that can conduct bargaining, and representativeness status above the firm is also defined by the works council/workers' delegates seats held (see below). In that sense the Spanish system of representation is dual *by bargaining level*. An important result of this legal regulation is that a fierce union competition for works councils' seats is one of the defining features of Spanish IR.

Yet, the Spanish system of participation is often misinterpreted in comparative analysis. A competition for workplace influence between works councils and unions is often reported as typical (cf. Van der Meer 1996: 329; Gill and Krieger 2000: 128) when in fact it is the competition between unions for works councils' seats that informs their bargaining position and politics at firm-level. Thus, it is often the case that the union holding the majority of the works council seats signs a collective agreement (applicable to all employees) while the union holding fewer seats opposes it and may even call for a strike in protest. If the minority union is successful in mobilising workers' discontent with the agreement this tactic often achieves a reversal of seats at the next works council election. It is also not rare that the trade union that holds the majority of the works council behaves as the only valid interlocutor with management. Thus, the effectiveness of works councils depends substantially on the relations between the unions present in them. Such union competition for representation at the works councils and the micro-politics of works councils functioning are neglected in most representations of the Spanish system of workers' participation.

Workplace elections for works councillors (or workers' delegates in smaller firms) are of utmost importance for Spanish trade unions because their status as 'most representative trade union' depends on holding a sufficient proportion of workplace workers' representatives (either 10% nationally or 15% in an Autonomous Community), and in any case a minimum of 1,500 workplace workers' representatives. The status of most representative trade union – obtained typically by CCOO and UGT among other smaller unions – is then 'irradiated' to their affiliated unions. This status is necessary by law to first, negotiate collective agreements of 'general efficacy' (i.e. *erga omnes*) at various levels above the firm; second, to be present in public bodies; and third, for national-level negotiation with representative employers' organisations of collective agreements and to be consulted by the government on economic and social policy. In other words, workplace elections hold the key for representation at meso and national level where the unions can exert a wider influence.

Regarding company/workplace collective agreements it is of particular importance to consider that finding collective bargaining at the firm-level or below in the Spanish context means finding decentralisation of collective bargaining, which is relatively unusual. It should also be noted that presence of workers' representatives does not necessarily mean presence of collective bargaining or even compliance with the law in terms of information and consultation. For instance, in our sample of workplaces with at least 25 workers there had been no exchange with workers' elected representatives during the previous year in 13 per cent of the workplaces where there was at least one worker delegate (Gonzalez 2008).

The application of the *erga omnes* principle to collective bargaining means that most Spanish workers' wages and working time has been determined at a level above the firm. Thus, the firms that have collective bargaining respond to one of two patterns: they are either large firms that, rather than apply higher-level agreements, regulate all labour matters through a firm collective agreement (*convenio colectivo de empresa*), or they are firms that apply national or sectoral agreements on pay and working time but they are in need of regulating other matters locally and thus enter negotiation with the workers' representatives (*pacto de empresa*); the former cases have their own all-encompassing collective agreements while the latter cases are representative of articulation of collective bargaining. In our sample of workplaces with at least 25 employees, some 30 per cent of cases affirmed to negotiate wages or working time and thus can be thought likely to be in the first group (Gonzalez 2008).

In either context there is a likelihood of discussion of work conditions and work organisation matters such as the introduction of direct participation since it will be a matter for consultation (see Table 1). However, where the 'hard' matters of pay and working time are taken out of the negotiation spectrum by a collective agreement above the firm, working conditions and work organisation aspects are more likely to receive more attention by unions, while in large firms unions' attention can be largely deflected to 'hard' matters. Further, workers' representatives in firms with all-regulating collective agreements are the most likely to feel indirect participation threatened by direct participation, in case it may affect somehow their power of negotiating on the 'hard' matters (Ortiz 1998). This may explain EPOC's (1997) finding of a negative association between having a collective agreement and direct participation. The larger size threshold considered, as well as the disproportionate presence of foreign MNCs in the Spanish EPOC sample (24%), that are more likely to have an all-regulating collective agreement, makes possible that in EPOC's sample firms with *convenio colectivo de empresa* were over-represented.

Having said that, it is also possible that, as Ortiz (1998: 295) pointed out, workers' representatives may be using employers' initiatives in the area of direct participation to instil new life to representation by engaging further with work organisation issues in large establishments (see also Blyton and Martinez Lucio 1995). In other words, direct participation, a realm of managers in pertaining to work organisation, if negotiated upon to ease its introduction will have the effect of enriching and widening the contents of collective bargaining.

Next we analyse the extension of direct participation in Spain and the effect of indirect participation on direct participation practice. The list of direct participation practices considered in our study (Gonzalez 2008) was as follows: 'Information' practices were: systematic use of the management chain, regular newsletters, team briefings such as group/management meetings, section/department meetings and, individual performance discussion meetings. 'Consultation' practices were: attitude surveys, suggestion schemes, and regular meetings with the workforce. 'Participation' practices were: quality circles, joint committees on specific issues (e.g. health & safety), other formal problem-solving groups and formal teamwork. The classification followed that of Tüselmann et *al.* (2003).

In our study, only 9 per cent of the sample had no scheme of direct participation. Of those workplaces that had at least one scheme, a quarter of them had only one scheme, while nearly another quarter of them had 6 or more schemes. The average number of schemes adopted in our sample was 3.2; this is similar to the average found in a Spanish study of manufacturing plants (Bayo and Merino 2004).

By types, information-based schemes were the most extended (71 per cent of workplaces had at least one) while consultation-based were the least (39 per cent of the workplaces had at least one). Regarding specific schemes, the presence of formal teamwork for workers in the largest occupational group in 55 per cent of the workplaces made it the most popular direct participation mechanism; although only in 9 per cent of the sample did teamwork apply to at least 80 per cent of the relevant workers. Conversely, employee surveys were the least adopted schemes, being present in only 7 per cent of the sample.

Direct participation's extension in Spain in 1999 was thus low but not necessarily as low as presented in the influential comparative study carried out by EPOC (1997). In that sense, this study confirms the more positive view of the 1999 Spanish Working Conditions Survey (WCS) to employers (see Table 2 below). In fact, the results of our study appear somewhat more positive regarding the extension of direct participation than those of the 1999 WCS.

Table 2: Extension of different forms of direct participation: comparison of present study with 1999 Spanish Working Conditions Survey, % of workplaces

Type of scheme	**Present study**[a]	**EPOC**[b]	**1999 WCS**[c]
Suggestion schemes and similar[1]	39.3	20	31.6
Participation in decision-making relative to the job occupied by the worker[2]	44	30-40	51.8
Improvement, development, quality groups[3]	33.6	23	27.7
Autonomous or semi-autonomous teamwork	-	10	10.3
Formal teamwork	55.1	-	-
Formal teamwork for at least 80 per cent of the largest occupational group	9.3	-	-

1 For the present study is used as proxy having suggestion schemes, employee surveys and/or regular meetings with the workforce; for EPOC, arms-length individual consultation.

2 For the present study is used as proxy having individual performance discussion meetings, group meetings with management, and/or section/department meetings; for EPOC, face-to-face individual consultation and individual delegation figures are presented.

3 For the present study is used as proxy having quality circles, joint committees on specific issues and/or formal problem-solving groups; for EPOC, permanent group consultation.

Sources: (a) Gonzalez (2008); (b) EPOC (1997); (c) CIS (1999)

While our results for presence of formal teamwork may seem high they find correspondence in other studies. The percentage of workers in autonomous work teams in a study of Spanish manufacturing plants in the late 1990s (Bayo and Huerta 2002) has been reported to be 17% of manual workers on average and the median for teamwork in our study corresponds to the 1-19% bracket. From the same data Bayo and Merino (2002) report 47 per cent of the plants as having autonomous teamwork and 39 per cent as having development groups; these figures are much closer to ours than to those of the EPOC and Working Conditions surveys.

In order to analyse the determinants of direct participation practice, following Tüselmann *et al.* (2003) a composite index where an information practice carried a score of 1, a consultation practice a score of 2, and a participation practice a score of 3, was built to reflect the qualitatively differential strength of the various practices. Then, workplaces were divided into those with above average levels of direct participation and those with average or below average levels of direct participation.

To assess the quality of indirect participation, instead of having or not a collective agreement (which excludes information and consultation processes) our study considered the number of subject matters as well as the types of exchange over each. In other words, it was considered that workplaces without collective bargaining (i.e. negotiation) but offering at least information on one issue have more indirect participation than a workplace where workers' representatives are never met by management; it is also considered that a workplace that negotiates with workers representatives over five matters has more indirect participation than one negotiating over two, and so on and so forth. This is a finer measurement of the quality of indirect participation than just the presence or absence of collective agreement or workers' representatives (EPOC 1997).

The analysis of indirect participation in terms of the level of involvement of workers' representatives in the regulation of labour matters as a proxy for workers' representatives' influence and thus, for collective workers' voice, finds evidence of a significant positive association between indirect participation and direct participation practice emphasis in Spain (Gonzalez 2008). In other words, the more workers' representatives are informed, consulted or negotiated with, the more likely is a workplace to emphasise direct participation practice as well. Despite the likelihood of finding a less positive attitude towards direct participation among workers' representatives in large firms as described above, the positive association of indirect participation with direct participation was found to be independent of workplace size, and larger workplaces were more likely to have a greater emphasis on direct participation (Gonzalez 2008).

This may be interpreted as supporting case studies' findings of Spanish unions perceiving several advantages for themselves and workers in direct participation and of being active in its introduction. For instance, direct channels of communication between workers and managers can relieve workers' representatives of the pressure of handling matters like individual workplace grievances, a function of little interest to Spanish unions; they also perceived advantages for workers in the areas of information, promotion, job autonomy and health and safety (Ortiz 1998; 2002).

This result also renders support for theses on complementarity between both voice channels and the existence of low-road and high-road approaches towards participation in different workplaces (cf Dundon et *al.* 2006; Gallie et *al.* 1998). Some evidence of this from case study research in Spain can be found in Juan Albalete's (2005) study of participation at the introduction of new technology. He found that overall workers' participation was greater where there were workers' representatives present than were they were absent.

In summary, the regulation and dynamics of industrial relations in Spain make a high extension of direct participation in this country unlikely as a result of social actors' fear of seeing their respective prerogatives undermined. It is however found that the more extensive representative participation is in a workplace the more likely it is the workplace to have above average levels of direct participation. In other words, the more extensive the collective voice the more extensive the individual voice. This indicates that in the Spanish institutional context outlined above the voluntaristic approach to direct participation emphasising the autonomy of bargaining of the parties may be being fruitful.

Labour management traditions, practices and values

There is very little that is 'known fact' about contemporary Spanish labour management, its characterisation is patchy and under-researched. Regarding large firms we know that comparatively, the HRM function in Spain in the 1990s was quite centralised and that the HR director's influence on boards of directors was quite high, although half of them did not have a decisive role in deciding on HR strategy (García and del Val 1996). The logic of this strange pattern of partial power among so many HR directors is that one of the main competitive strategies of Spanish companies has traditionally been keeping labour costs down (Prieto 1991). When the HR strategy is *the* competitive strategy – or at least a very large part of it – the HR director effectiveness at implementing it is crucial. This should lead to further study of the influence of labour management traditions and strategies on HRM practices and innovation but this is largely absent in comparative studies of Spanish HRM.

On the contrary, the dominant comparative characterisation is that labour management in this country is constrained by oppositional – if not very powerful – trade unions and, mostly, by a restrictive labour legislation (e.g. Gooderham et *al.* 1999; Brewster 2007), which leave management to focus on administration rather than on innovation. As just shown, the administrative focus of Spanish HRM is partly a result of corporate governance structure and the prominence of minimising labour costs in competitive strategy. Also, in fact, neither are Spanish trade unions as oppositional (Guillen 2005), nor is the legislation as restrictive as they are mostly depicted. Regarding the latter, it need only be mentioned that given the strong legal protection of the employer prerogative on work organisation matters, innovation in this area is the employer's remit.

Despite their prerogative, Spanish employers are not particularly innovative in work organisation out of the neo-Taylorist comfort zone. In the European Working Conditions Survey (EWCS) 2000 for EU-15 countries, Spanish employees report having to do monotonous tasks to a much greater extent than their European counterparts (60 per cent vs. a European average of 40 per cent). The data also show above average levels of a pace of work depending on numerical production targets, automatic speed of machine and direct control of the boss, and below European average levels of jobs involving complex tasks and of learning new things. Spanish workers also report above average levels of task interruptions due to bad organization of work, requests and machinery or equipment working badly. Further, there is no evidence of recent change. An analysis of the EWCS 2005 data for the EU-27 shows that Spanish workers are significantly less likely to have a job involving complex non-monotonous tasks, with a high level of autonomy and/or involving problem-solving and learning (Burchell et *al.* 2007). In no other European country do the odds of having a simplified job appear so consistent.

Contrary to expectations however, our study found that it is precisely workplaces where the largest occupational group has jobs that can be defined as simplified – where new workers need only days or weeks to do their jobs as well as their colleagues – that are the over-performers in terms of direct participation practice (Gonzalez 2008). This supports a view of direct participation being used predominantly to counteract the negative effects of rationalisation on flexibility and satisfaction (Walton 1985), and is consistent with an observed expansion of neo-Taylorism in Spain by combining an increased rationalisation with task-rotation and problem-solving groups (Martín Artiles 1999). The main question that arises from this finding is why workplaces with more complex jobs are not adopting direct participation.

García and del Val (1996) offer a different explanation for the lack of innovation in Spanish HRM and for the low competitiveness of Spanish firms: managers' lack of interest in integrating workers and an essential distrust of them. They found that, compared with German managers, very few Spanish managers valued positively workers' self-regulation, teamwork, self-realisation through work and ability to configure the job. Spanish managers also rated workers' values poorly: only around 40 per cent of the firms said their workers had negotiating ability, were productivity-oriented, were flexible and motivated, and only around 27 per cent valued favourably workers on factors such as disposition to change, innovative suggestions, ability to delegate and mobility.

Regarding practice, their study also shows that only around 45 per cent of firms had a policy concerning specific training, labour integration and labour motivation. The study pointed to a general worry of Spanish HR managers about the lack of an adequate policy of HRM in 60-70 per cent of the firms studied in what was considered as a transition period in labour management. There was ample agreement (more than 90 per cent of the HR managers) on the changes needed: great relevance ought to be given in the future to training, motivation, remuneration by results, promotion by ability and development of communication with employees as the basis of HR policies in Spanish firms.

On the basis of these managers views it seems reasonable to think first, that their hands were to some extent tied by a pre-ordained labour strategy of containing labour costs and second, that if they were to use direct participation practices they would support them with other HR policies. In this sense it has to be taken into account that the introduction of direct participation practices may lead to greater labour costs directly – the costs of administering the schemes – and indirectly – they could lead to wage increases if they implied a redefinition of job categories, which can easily be the case with teamwork. However, and consistent with the traditional emphasis on labour cost reduction of Spanish firms, one report on new forms of work organisation does associate direct participation with restructuring processes featuring redundancies and dehierarchisation (QUIT 1999).

Following EPOC's (1997) study of HR activity, to measure the degree of change the persons interviewed in our study were asked to specify how many HR initiatives had been taken in the last five years from a list that included: working time reduction, staff reduction, delayering, job rotation, flexible timetable, annualised hours, training courses for new employees and training courses for established employees. In Table 3 below, it can be seen that workplaces with above average levels of direct participation are a lot more active in adopting HR change than those with average or below average levels of direct participation. However, HR change was not found to be a significant determinant of direct participation practice, once other variables were considered.

Similarly HR practices that could be supportive of direct participation practice such as sophisticated procedures for selection (proxied by the number of selection methods) and variable pay (proxied by having or not a group-based incentive) were not found to be significant predictors of direct participation practice once other variables are considered. Thus, HR activity and policy variables appear as a whole of little significance to explain direct participation in Spain in 1999 – though their consideration improves the fit of the model and affects the significance of some of the control variables (differences in technological change and being owned or not by another firm become non significant).

*Table 3: Low and high levels of HR change in workplaces with and without direct participation**

Workplaces with *above average levels* of direct participation		**Workplaces with *average or below* levels of direct participation**	
Low level of HR change (%)	**High level of HR change (%)**	**Low level of HR change (%)**	**High level of HR change (%)**
18	38.5	44	8.8

* *Low level of HR change: no change or only one. High level: four or more changes.*
Source: Gonzalez (2008)

Regarding the possible influence of managers' attitudes to labour on direct participation practice, our study focused on values towards workers and towards unions building on the items developed in other research (Godard 1997; Guest and Peccei 1998; WERS 1998). The persons interviewed were asked to express their agreement with fifteen items referred to the workers and their participation and with twenty-eight items referred to business, regional and national levels of union action relevant in the Spanish context. Through factor analysis four factors were identified from this data (see Table 4) explaining 68.5 per cent of the total variance (Kaiser-Meyer-Oklin value of .84).

The factor called *unions restrictive* reflects a laissez-affaire viewpoint: union power as a restriction to economic activity at micro, meso and macro level. The factor called *unions conflictive* reflects a view of trade unions as heralds of conflict at the firm-level and is a proxy for unitarism towards unions. The factor called *unions social actor* reflects a social-partnership view: trade unions as social actors at micro and macro levels can make a valuable contribution. The factor called *organisational culture* shows a strong cultural trait, an emphasis on identity of values and family-like co-operation and on individual's participation, and an implicit denial of conflict. The positive correlation found between this factor and those reflecting views on unions as a restriction and conflict-mongers as well as the negative correlation with an acceptance of unions' role as social actors point that this factor reflects a unitarist form of collectivism. Paternalism has a long tradition in Spain and the factor could well reflect remnants of those values and attitudes towards the workforce in the aspiration to a 'family-like' co-operation; yet this aspiration is not connected to a feeling of obligation in terms of stability of employment since the item that reflected it was dropped.

Table 4. Descriptive statistics for factors of managerial values on unions

Factor **Items** (Value range: 1 = totally disagree; 5 = totally agree)	**Cronbach's alpha**	**Variance explained**	**Mean (S.D.)**
Factor 1: Unions conflictive	0.79	37.4%	2.83 (.91)
Firms should do everything possible to avoid unions' presence			
Unions are unnecessary if management treats its workers properly			
In small and medium sized firms, trade unions' presence makes no sense			
Factor 2: Organisational culture	0.76	14.9%	3.61 (.60)
Our workers identify totally with the firm values			
The firm benefits from a general atmosphere of trust and co-operation			
Our workers' ideas are usually put to use			
We try to promote a family-like atmosphere			
We would rather consult directly with employees than unions			
Factor 3: Unions restrictive	0 .83	8.6%	3.33 (.83)
Unions have more power in Asturias than in the rest of the country			
Unions too often place unnecessary restrictions on management			
Unions have too much power in Spain			
Asturian trade unions are among the main problems of the region			
Factor 3: Unions social actor	0.77	7.6%	2.88 (.82)
Unions help find ways to improve business performance			
Unions have contributed towards political stability in this country			
Unions contribute more to the maintenance of industrial peace than is often thought			

Source: Gonzalez (2008)

Taking a score above 3.5 to express agreement, it was found that most respondents showed agreement with the values represented by the organisational culture factor (66 per cent of the sample). In other words, the majority of Spanish managers do hold the unitarist values with paternalistic overtones, emphasising the importance of employees' commitment in respect to the employment relationship characteristic of the HRM paradigm (Guillen 1994).

With our chosen cutting point for agreement, most managers did not show agreement with the values expressed by the variables related to views on unions (unions as restrictive, unions as conflictive and unions as social actors), this study's proxies for views of unions as generally too powerful, as competing for workers' loyalty at the workplace and therefore to be avoided, and as valuable socio-economic partners, although disagreement was strongest with the variable expressing positive views of unions (disagreement with values of union as social actors was present in 81 per cent of the sample). In other words, unions are not perceived to contribute positively as political economy actors at the societal or workplace level; yet at the same time unions are not feared in terms of their overall curtailing power at any level, and should not be avoided at firm level. The institutionalist or neo-corporatist ideology that the union social actor variable reflects is thus the least extended among Spanish managers; however, neither the neo-liberal ideology reflected by the union restrictive variable, nor the 'non-unionism with unions' expected to derive from the HRM paradigm's adaptation to the Spanish context are espoused by a majority of managers. Such a mix of values points to a constitutionalist approach to trade unions based on union tolerance or acceptance akin to the one proposed by Purcell (1987) for workplace management styles, closer to adversarial than to cooperative relations.

In summary, in Spain, a majority of the managers in the sample can be categorised as holding unitarist values in respect to the workers at the workplace but the view of unions is mixed and cannot easily be categorised as either pluralist or unitarist, at best it can be seen as tolerant.

Regarding the connection between managers' values and direct participation, it is interesting to note that there was no significant association between holding the organisational culture views and direct participation practice, if the sign of association was positive as expected. In other words, a view of the employment relationship in which employee commitment and identification with the firm are core values is not determining direct participation practice. It is not possible to know if this manifests that the traditional Spanish managers' distrust of workers overpowers the unitarist rhetoric, if there is no connection between values and practice because our analysis focused on formal practices only or if values translation into practice is limited by other variables such as financial constraints.

The results regarding values on unions connection with direct participation practice were even more interesting in that the signs of association were consistent with the presence of high-road vs. low-road approaches to participation: the variables *unions restrictive* and *unions conflictive* were negatively associated with direct participation, and the variable *unions social actor* positively associated with direct participation. However, only the negative association of *unions conflictive* with direct participation was initially statistically significant, and it ceased to be significant once other variables were considered. The most important implication of these findings is that no evidence is found of direct participation being intended to substitute for indirect participation at the Spanish workplace. If that were the case we would expect to have found the opposite signs of association between values towards unions and direct participation practice.

Finally, our finding that employment size and competitive strategy (more specifically, not competing mostly on the basis of price) are significantly and positively associated with direct participation means that some other workplace-context variables are more important in explaining patterns of participation than the labour management practices and values analysed (Gonzalez 2008). It also means that direct participation may be a strategic HR policy area, and that its expansion is severely limited by the cost-centred administrative HR tradition and the predominant competitive focus on minimising labour costs. These, paired with – and maybe even rooted in – a tradition of authoritarian hierarchical and distrustful relations with workers, are likely to make high-commitment practices in general appear like unnecessarily expensive risky social experiments to most employers.

The inability of many Spanish employers to conceive that efficiency can be improved by other means than containing labour costs (Figuera 1999) seems however insufficient to explain why workplaces with workers occupying less standardised jobs -and therefore likely to be more skilled- have less instead of more direct participation. It could be that these workplaces have informal mechanisms for participation and/or that the necessity of keeping managerial prerogatives clear is felt more strongly in such labour settings.

Conclusions

Comparative characterisations of the Spanish system of IR and of HRM have so far failed to grasp some important characteristics that affect the dynamics subjacent to the process of workers' participation. Despite the importance commonly given to the weight of legislation in analysing Spanish IR and HRM, a very important legal feature such as the managerial prerogative in work organisation matters is most often ignored. When this variable is considered, explanations of the low level of innovation in HR practices in terms of a restrictive legal framework are found wanting. This is even more the case in workplaces where workers do not have elected representatives, commonly expected to curtail managers' initiatives on labour management. Similarly, it has been shown how the system of indirect participation is often misunderstood and, subsequently, often analysed by variables thought to be functional equivalents across Europe but inadequate, at least for the Spanish context.

It is proposed that some traditional features of Spanish labour management – a generalised distrust of workers and an emphasis on keeping labour costs down – help to explain both the comparatively low levels of direct participation and the unusual pattern of adoption found regarding work organisation. Contrary to expectations and most recent theoretical approaches to direct participation based on developing the 'knowledge economy', we found that workplaces with simplified jobs were the Spanish over-performers in terms of direct participation practice, pointing to the use of direct participation being greater in Spain in neo-Taylorist workplaces. While the logic of using direct participation in these workplaces is apparent, the puzzle of why other workplaces do not respond to theory had to be explained by resorting to the labour management tradition variables mentioned above.

Besides the type of work organisation, our study finds another industrial relations variable to be an important explanatory variable of direct participation practice in Spain: the quality of representative participation. The finding that workplaces with richer indirect participation also have a greater emphasis on direct participation points to a virtuous participatory link stemming from indirect participation. While the dynamics and regulation of the IR system are found to limit the expansion of direct participation in Spain, the voluntaristic approach to direct participation is working to some extent in fostering it.

Further, it was found that the HR practices and managers' values supportive of participation studied were not significant explanatory variables of direct participation practice, while organisational characteristics such as employment size and competitive strategy were. Regarding values it is possible that the study of a different set of values – perhaps more connected to quality of working life – may have rendered different results. However, our analysis proved of interest in picking up the persistence of some traditional paternalist values among Spanish managers paired with a fairly neutral stance towards unions. Regarding the non-significant impact of HR policies it must be taken into account that our analysis was carried out on the basis of 1999 data and that the 1990s were considered a period of transition in labour management by HR managers themselves (García and del Val 1996). Still, the type of main competitive strategy may be considered a proxy for HR strategy. It has been argued that labour cost competition is the dominant competitive strategy and that this has informed the dominant HR strategy in Spain. Finding that workplaces not competing mainly on the basis of price have more direct participation may indicate a lower emphasis on keeping labour costs down and thus a deviation from the archetypical HR strategy. The fact that the HR practices analysed did not pick up the possible influence of HR strategy on direct participation as the competitive strategy did could reflect that direct participation is in itself an HR policy thought more strategic than others where used.

Thus, the workplace industrial relations practices (work organisation and the quality of indirect participation), and HR strategy (proxied by competitive strategy) are found to explain direct participation practices in Spain at the end of the 1990s. It seems reasonable to think that these variables will continue to have an impact today. Yet, it would be of interest to research whether non-Taylorist workplaces have changed their approach to direct participation or still stand, deaf to the arguments of the better labour productivity of a knowledge economy, as representatives of traditional Spanish HRM.

Acknowledgements

This research was partly funded by the British Economic and Social Research Council (Award number: R00429634328). Rodolfo Gutierrez' comments greatly improved this chapter.

References

Bayo-Moriones, A. / Huerta-Arribas, E. (2002): 'The adoption of production incentives in Spain', British Journal of Industrial Relations, 40, 4: 709-724.

Bayo-Moriones, A. / Merino-Díaz de Cerio, J. (2002): 'Las prácticas de recursos humanos de alto compromiso: un estudio de los factores que influyen sobre su adopción en la industria española', Cuadernos de Economía y Dirección de la Empresa, 12: 227-246.

Bayo-Moriones, A. / Merino-Díaz de Cerio, J. (2004): 'Employee involvement: its interaction with advanced manufacturing technologies, quality management and inter-firm collaboration', Human Factors and Ergonomics in Manufacturing, 14, 2: 117-134.

Blyton, P. / Martinez Lucio, M. (1995): 'Industrial relations and the management of flexibility: factors shaping developments in Spain and the United Kingdom', International Journal of Human Resource Management, 6, 2: 271-291.

Brewster, C. (2007): 'Comparative HRM: European views and perspectives', International Journal of Human Resource Management, 18, 5: 769-787.

Burchell, B. / Fagan, C. / O'Brien, C. / Smith, M. (2007): Working Conditions in the European Union: the gender perspective, Luxembourg: Office for Official Publications of the European Communities.

CES, Consejo Económico y Social, CES (2008): Memoria sobre la Situación Socioeconómica y Laboral 2007, Madrid: CES.

CIS, Centro de Investigaciones Sociológicas (1999): Encuesta Nacional de Condiciones de Trabajo (Empresas), Estudio N° 2368/1, Septiembre-Diciembre 1999, Madrid: CIS.

Dundon, T. / Curran, D. / Ryan, P. / Maloney, M. (2006): 'Conceptualising the dynamics of employee information and consultation: evidence from the Republic of Ireland', Industrial Relations Journal, 37, 5: 492-512.

EPOC (1997): New Forms of Work Organisation. Can Europe Realize its Potential?, Dublin: European Foundation for the Improvement of Living and Working Conditions.
Figuera, J.R. (1999): 'La introducción de innovaciones en la organización de las empresas españolas', Economía Industrial, 330: 19-30.
Gallie, D. / White, M. / Cheng, Y. / Tomlinson, M. (1998): Restructuring the Employment Relationship, Oxford: Clarendon Press.
García Echevarría, S. / del Val Núñez, M.T. (1996): Los recursos humanos en la empresa española, Madrid: Díaz de Santos.
Gill, C. / Krieger, H. (2000): 'Recent survey evidence on participation in Europe: towards a European model?', European Journal of Industrial Relations, 6, 1: 109-132.
Godard, J. (1997): 'Whither strategic choice: do managerial IR ideologies matter?', Industrial Relations, 36, 2: 206-228.
Gonzalez Menendez, M.C. (2008): The Determinants of Workers' Direct Participation in Spain, PhD Thesis, Manchester: Manchester Metropolitan University.
Gooderham, P.N. / Nordhaug, O. / Ringdal, K. (1999): 'Institutional and rational determinants of organizational practices: human resource management in European firms', Administrative Science Quarterly, 44: 507-531.
Guest, D. / Peccei, R. (1998): The Partnership Company: Benchmarks for the Future. The Report of the IPA Survey, London: Involvement and Participation Association.
Guillen, M. (1994): Models of Management. Work, Authority and Organization in a Comparative Perspective, Chicago: The University of Chicago Press.
Guillen, M. (2005): The Rise of Spanish Multinationals: European Business in the Global Economy, Cambridge: Cambridge University Press.
Gutierrez, R. (1998): 'Individualismo y colectivismo en la gestión de los recursos humanos: un estudio de casos de empresas', Revista Asturiana de Economía, 12: 87-112.
Juan Albalate, J. (2005): 'La ideología de los actores en la participación en la tecnología en quince empresas del sector "auxiliar" del automóvil de Cataluña', Papers: Revista de Sociologia, 77: 43-77.
Knudsen, H. (1995): Employee Participation in Europe, London: Sage.
Martín Artiles, A. (1999): 'Organización del trabajo y nuevas formas de gestión laboral', in: F. Miguélez Lobo and C. Prieto Rodríguez (eds.): Las relaciones de empleo en España, Madrid: Siglo XXI, 79-100.
Martinez Lucio, M. (2007): '¿Neoliberalismo y neoconservadurismo interrumpido? El porqué de la existencia de una tradición crítica en las escuelas de dirección de empresas británicas', in: Fernández Rodríguez, C-J. (ed.): Estudios Sociales de la Organización: El Giro Postmoderno, Madrid: Siglo XXI.

Ortiz, L. (1998): 'Union response to teamwork: the case of Opel Spain', Industrial Relations Journal, 29, 1: 42-57.
Ortiz, L. (2002): 'The resilience of a company-level system of industrial relations: union responses to teamwork in Renault´s Spanish subsidiary', European Journal of Industrial Relations, 8, 3, 277-299.
Purcell, J. (1987): 'Mapping management styles in employment relations', Journal of Management Studies, 24, 5: 533-48.
QUIT (1999): 'Partnership for a new organisation of work (involving in particular the replacement of hierarchical and rigid structures by more innovative and flexible structures based on high skill, high trust and increased involvement of employees)', European Industrial Relations Observatory On-line, (www.eurofound.europa.eu/eiro/1999/03/word/es9903205s.doc at 15/11/2008)
Regalia, I. (1996): 'How the social partners view direct participation: a comparative study of 15 European countries', European Journal of Industrial Relations, 2, 2: 211-234.
Regini, M. (1993): 'Human resource management and industrial relations in European companies', International Journal of Human Resource Management, 4, 3: 555-568.
Tüselmann H-J. / McDonald, F. / Heise, A. (2003): 'Employee relations in German multinationals in an Anglo-Saxon setting: toward a Germanic version of the Anglo-Saxon approach?', European Journal of Industrial Relations 9, 3: 327–349.
Van der Meer, M. (1996): 'Aspiring corporatism? Industrial relations in Spain', in: J. Van Ruysseveldt and J. Visser (eds.): Industrial Relations in Europe. Traditions and Transitions, London: Sage, 310-336.
Walton, R. (1985): 'From "Control" to "Commitment" in the workplace', Harvard Business Review, 63, 2: 77-84.
WERS, Workplace Employee Relations Survey (1998): Main Survey Questionnaires – Part A: Management Questionnaire, Version 1.1., June.
White, R.M. (2003): 'Works councils and other workplace employee representation and participation structures: Spain', European Industrial Relations Observatory On-line, ES0309203T,www.eurofound.europa.eu/eiro/2003/09/tfeature/es0309 203t.htm

New forms of interest organisation: the state of the art

Mirella Baglioni

Foreword

Employees' participation takes place in different forms. Direct representation usually occurs in high performing work organisation, while representative participation is embedded into institutional or contractual arrangements. The continuous changes of work organisation, with their impact on the labour markets, are progressively questioning the legitimacy of socio-economic institutions of representation. The study of new forms of interest organisation, in its broad implications, should thus benefit of different analytical approaches. The required box of tools includes the following approaches:

- The socio-political approach as it allows focusing on how to represent the unrepresented (employees).
- The sociological approach as it allows exploring the social identities on ground of the concepts of inclusion/exclusion.
- The socio-economic approach that focuses on labour market analysis and socio economic regulation.
- The managerial approach that insists on the HRM in high performing organisations

In order to elaborate some initial answers to research questions as the emergence of new identities in our economies and on their influence on the traditional forms of interest organizations this review of the state of the art, although mainly based on articles published by the journals specialised on IR, HRM and organisation studies, benefits of the larger multidisciplinary debate about the new union strategies of interest organising and the spontaneous organisation of workers interests.

As sporadic organisations have no impact on the macro socio-economic regulation, IR scholars have not paid the due attention to the **societal implications of the new identities.** There is however a striking difference between the American and the European research sensitivity as American literature is increasingly committed to this field of research.

The European debate on the new forms of interest organisations is to a large extent shaped by the contributions of study and research on **the unions' crisis** and unions' revitalization opportunities. In spite of the existing differences between the crisis of British unionism and the decline of the continental unions, the contributions of study and research are shaped on the same common background, the twenty century's model of socio – economic regulation built on union growth and legitimacy. This model, being deeply embedded in EU old continental member states, is not replaced, but increasingly complemented by new forms of interest organisation. (Grumbrell-McCormick and Hyman, 2006).

The concern about the crisis of trade union membership, being, however, a concern about the existing model of interest composition, should increasingly lead to develop the field of research on new form of interest organisation.

Important questions remain somehow in the shadow of the specialized literature. They can be summarized in the followings:

- Are new forms of associations and interest representation emerging?
- Who is or will replace union representation at the macro, meso and micro level?
- Is the present crisis leading to a revitalisation of the pluralism in our societies?

The European debate on the new forms of interest organisations is to a large extent shaped by the If union crisis is leaving space for new socio-economic identities, how do these identities emerge and stabilize within the socio-economic arena? Are unions trying to incorporate these new identities? Where do these new identities arise? Are they emerging at the level of production sites or at the level of the local communities? How do these levels interact with each other?

1. Work segmentation: the need for enlarging the scope of union representation

The increasing complexity of the employment representation is a consequence of the many competitive pressures that force the process of work segmentation. Distinctive features can be used to define work experiences: the status of permanent employment as opposed to contingent work; the status of core workers as opposed to peripheral, the employment in the mother company or in the subsidiary; the employment in high value production vs. the employment in traditional services. In addition the subjective profile of the employees further differentiate their expectations and interests: working women and young employees exhibit specific values and expectations about wages, working conditions, career prospects that can hardly be recomposed by a comprehensive strategy of interest representation.

As a consequence of work segmentation, interest representation is now-a-days becoming more dispersed among different actors and different kinds of action.

The organisation of peripheral workforce can rarely rely on the limited or non existent bargaining strength of such groups: success requires the mobilization of broader local/community alliances on the basis of a more encompassing agenda (Hyman, 1997: 321).

While peripheral workers often coincide with the last comers into the labour market as is often the case of immigrants, contingent workers can either be employees with fixed term contracts or autonomous employees. Their propensity to join unions is very low, but unions are increasingly trying to represent them. Italian unions have created specific associations for representing and assisting contingent workers. Leonardi, (2008) remarks that unions are increasingly active in negotiating enterprise level contracts for atypical employees.

Depending on the quality and character of these workers, we can recognize attempts by unions (and allies) of extending basic rights to those contingent workers who occupy peripheral positions in the labour market (e.g. immigrants, Fine, 2006), trends of creating favourable conditions for unionising contingent workers in particular professions (Heery et al., 2004)) which is also a way of controlling competition in a particular labour market, like the self-employed free-lances in the UK. By analysing this particular labour market, the authors discover that there is a distinctive form of free lance unionism in the UK which aims at organising and representing workers in the external labour market where they seek work and develop a mobile career.

The increasing complexity of work identities is in fact enlarging the scope for union interest representation. The need of individualized representation of interests is particularly felt by high – profile employees and is thus leading unions to formulate plans of market –oriented incentives towards specific targets of worker interests. (Bjorkman, 2006). Unions are facing, on one hand, the need of providing unprotected employment with some form of basic rights and this perception is contributing to enlarge the scope of their action towards social rights and assume the identity of social movement unionism.

The need to regulate working conditions is, on the other hand, forcing unions to enter into managerial strategies in order to reverse management's unilateral approach to rewarding individuals and work teams and unilaterally fixing their working conditions. The prospects of unions' success in complementing HRM through a negotiated process are the object of debate among those researchers who analyse American and the European labour relations.

2. The social union movement: in search of justice for unprotected workers

Hymans' article in the British Journal (1997) provides a comprehensive analysis of employee interest representation. Within the summary of the four main areas that unions should incorporate into their agenda, the author includes both traditional and new forms of interest organisation: a)the traditional core agenda of bread and butter leading to collective bargaining on wages and working conditions; b) the agenda relating to procedure, status and opportunities; c) the agenda focusing on the role of the state in enacting social wages, legislation concerning labour and trade union and the regulation of the labour market; d) the agenda of civil rights that addresses the environment, the sphere of consumption, the institutions and facilities of local communities. Leaving apart the bread and butter agenda (traditional content of union action), interest representation is increasingly dependent upon union influence on socio economic regulation and also upon the union ability to extend the scope of workers protection towards social and civic rights. Social movement unionism is equally developing its non bargaining function on macro items such as environment, health and safety and on basic rights to benefit unprotected workers. By using a wide range of organisational structures and funding sources and by activating occasional alliances with the local communities this can be regarded as a way of enlarging the scope of democracy.

The analysis of movement unionism is mainly developed in contributions by American scholars. The need of justice for unprotected workers is leading American scholars to increasingly analyse the experiences of occasional interests organisations – non bargaining actors – and their ability to influence employment conditions.

Kolins Givan's (2007) analysis of the dilemmas of workers representation focuses on the responses given by unions and non bargaining actors to workers interests consisting of bargaining needs and other needs. The forms and the number of interest organisation are uncertain as a number of loose associations are acting in the social field.

As collective bargaining in the United States declines, diverse forms of worker representation are proliferating. Strategic dilemmas of representation are central to the diverse organizations and coalitions representing disparate aspects of workers' interests. Unions continue to bargain collectively, while forming alliances with other groups and providing an array of services to their members. Other organizations and loose associations represent specific aspects of workers' interests and advocate on their behalf while stopping short of collective bargaining. .. The non bargaining actors are key strategic allies for unions. While these organizations do not take on collective bargaining they are sometimes better positioned to represent other key needs and interests of workers. The legal-political and mutual insurance needs of workers are sometimes well met by these emergent groups. However these organizations do not and can not provide the advantages of collective bargaining (Kolins Givan, 2007: 829).

In fact the occasional coalitions between formal and loose organizations often finalise their action in defence of employment and happen to pave the way for its regulation. The scarce incidence of the emerging organisations of interests on the employment conditions is contested by the optimism of other scholars (Turner et al. 2001) who regard the positive influence of occasional interest organizations for union revitalization particularly when successful coalitions at the local level contribute to union recognition and bargaining rights (Erickson et al. 2002; Greer et al. 2007).

Piore and Safford (2006) suggest that civil rights organizations when making specific claims for employment-based rights are in fact performing an important substitute function for unions in contributing to improved standards of working conditions in the labour market. Their analysis suggests that a new regime of employment rights is emerging.

The authors assert that legal rights are filling the gap left by the declining coverage of collective bargaining. According to the authors "the old system of IR has been replaced not by market, but by an employment rights regime in which the rules of the workplaces are imposed by law, judicial opinions and administrative rulings, supplemented by mechanisms at the enterprise level that are responsive to the law, but also are susceptible to employee pressures both individual and collective. The emergence of this regime is the product of a shift in the axes of social and political mobilization from mobilization around economic identities rooted into the society outside the workplace: sex, race, ethnicity, age, disability and sexual orientation. The shift in the axes of mobilization in turn reflects the collapse of the underlying model of social and economic organization upon which collective bargaining regime was built and more fundamentally a shift in our understanding of the nature of industrial society and its direction of evolution in history." (299)

2.1. The new rights regime

The analysis of Piore and Safford on the new rights regime can be usefully complemented by Safford (2005).This contribution deserves special attention as it develops a very original socio-economics analysis, based on new identities shaped by the process of social mobilization, mainly at local level, and compares this experience with the development of union mobilization, growth and legitimacy.

The author first focuses on the origins of new rights, a response to new ways of mobilization. In fact, in Safford's view, the more recent legislation have been originated as a response to black civil movement, much of which involved extra electoral politics, demonstration and riots.

The process of mobilization at the state or local level has produced the new living wages, but also has developed new social identities that have appeared within the production sites. "Identity groups of this kind have emerged within many enterprises and most professional associations pressing for rights and benefits at this level in much the same way as union pressed for employment benefits historically".

The diffusion of the benefits like domestic-partner benefits spread from one enterprise to another in part through grassroots organization of gay and lesbian employees.

The focus on groups that generate claims under employment rights regime is mainly developed by American researchers. Alternative organizations and movements have emerged in the USA in order to fill the gap of interest representation caused by union decline.

The analysis on social mobilization (Kurz, 2002; Fine, 2006) points attention to the networks that are filling the gap of union interest representation. The contribution of Hecksher and Carré (2006) provides a positive evaluation of networks perspective and potentialities in mobilizing new identities. Nevertheless the authors also underline the weakness of the networks, the lack of stable communication channels and the need to better finalize their scope.

The attention on the socio and political processes generated by the segmentation of interests and by declining class identities is also developed by Osterman's research (2006) on *Community organizing and employee representation.* Central to this contribution is the role of local networks of interests in developing democracy, but also in defining social justice. The author's research focuses on the IAF (Industrial Areas Foundation) modes of operating. A close analysis of the network of organization in the Southwest allows Osterman to assess the prospects of growth and the limitations of these experiences and to locate their role with respect to trade unions scope and organizational models. Looking at the organisation identity the author suggests that the IAF enjoy better stability than other associations. In fact, as they affiliate churches and public schools, they are organisations of organisations and do not have to rely on the individual choices of joining (or leaving) the association. The focus of their action is on community interest representation. The community's interest identification is consequent to their main action, i.e. leadership development and training.

Community interests do often overlap, but not coincide, with the typical union domain, i.e. labour market. Osterman's research describes how these networks operated when emergences arose within the community: the case of Levi Strauss closing a plant where 1000 employees worked was dealt with by forming a job training committee, then identifying a project that could support a training experiment ant obtain job commitments from the business community. Another main issue was the living wage: IAF worked in order to raise the legal minimum wage and by this contribute to changing the character of the local economy (low cost production).The opening of health clinics is also an initiative proposed by local networks in Nebraska to assist with occupational injuries, a constant problem of the packaging industry. According to the author, the success of the IAF strategies is mainly due to this form of organisation (networks) and he suggests the need for reversing the organizational model of trade unions and saving people's energies.

The strength of IAF is that they are based in the community, not in the workplace, that they are broad-based; that they place a great deal of weight on leadership development and finally that they are deeply involved in labour market issues.

The author's conclusion is that, given the IAF ability of representing employees, trade unions learn from this experience and establish stronger relationships and coalition with low-income communities.

Fine's article of 2007 analyses the potential benefits of the Worker Centres to union interest representation. This sociological and labour centred research is increasingly focusing on the ways of supporting the interests of low waged workers. Workers centres, community based and community –led organizations engage in combination of service, advocacy, and organizing to provide support to low-wage workers'.

Many low-wage immigrant workers in the United States today function within industries in which there have been few or no unions through which they can speak and act to affect improvements. Into this breach, new modes of organization have emerged. The worker centre is one of the most promising of these emergent institutions. These centres are community-based mediating institutions that provide support to communities of low-wageworkers and pursue their mission through a combination of service delivery (including legal representation to recover unpaid wages), advocacy (including lobbying for new laws and working with government agencies to improve enforcement) and organizing (building organisations of workers to take action on their own behalf for economic and political change) (2006: 336).

The author focuses on cooperation taking place between worker centres and trade unions. This starts with the ALF-CIO commitment to a closer cooperation with the National Day Laborer Organizing Network (NLDLON) in order to enforce immigrant workers rights at the level of workplace and to support immigrant reforms that include legalization and a pathway to citizenship.

Worker centres have social movement orientation and organize around both economic and socio-political rights. They combine elements of different types of organizations: either the organisational model of political parties or the immigrant civic organizations; either the social movement groups or union model; either feminist consciousness-raising organizations or producer co-operatives.

Union organisation is, on the contrary, based on the assumption of stable membership as a consequence of monopoly of representation. This leads to develop a focus of union action on the workplace "one-firm-at-a-time", but also to increase a bureaucratic organisation for controlling collective resources and making strategic choices.

Fine remarks on the difficulties of matching the different organisational logics of unions and work centres "despite a common interest in organizing low-wages workers union and worker centres struggle along the three dimensions of ideology, structure and culture".

From the point of view of structure unions should consider which form of membership they could offer to low wage workers. This should lead to consider alternative forms of membership but also revising their ideologies and cultural legacy which are deeply rooted in industrial development and industrial worker identities.

Coalition building within territory is analysed by Regalia (2006). The book debates the role played by unions in facilitating technological adaptation of employees by specifically tailored training programs and services at the local level. This research focuses on the negotiated adjustments at the local level. Local employment experimentation has attracted the interests of many researchers who have investigated the role of the institutions in enhancing technological adjustment and economic development. The concentration of small and medium sized firms within a restricted local area has stimulated the creation of mixed (private/public) networks in order to deal with employment adjustments and training needs. The cases investigated allow the researchers to identify on the employers' side the need for flexibility and high commitment, while on the unions' side an increasing attention to the specific nature of non standard worker interests and the willingness to develop innovative representational models. Despite changing attitudes, the modes of regulating workers representation are neither changing nor supporting trends towards work flexibility.

3. Interest representation in the workplaces

Interest organisation in global enterprises is increasingly internalised within enterprise management or by services enterprises or consultancy agencies. According to Heery and Frege (2006) editorial to a BJIR special issue on interest organisation the decline of trade unions is provoking a research interest towards those institutions which, by campaigning, advocacy, advisory and service-providing, discharge some of the functions of unions, often for a particular segment of the workforce or an identity group.

Moreover in the HRM literature there is an implicit model of the firm as a strategic actor that can project and perform a comprehensive model of regulation that transcends the market. However, the enterprise-based model of employment regulation – according to the authors' suggestion – according to Freege and Henry – is, to a great extent, shaped by the advisors like management consultants and employment agencies and business organizations that formulate standard of good practices and CSR should be analysed. Together with the management consultants, pressure groups, like consumer organisations, can influence the enterprise-based model.

The enterprise – centred perspective usually concentrates on HRM modes of dealings with the interests of medium/high profile positions and suggests that their representation is to some extent defined by the consultancy services that operate in support of the managerial strategic choices. Particular attention has been paid to the modes of direct interest representation of employee groups within high commitment HRM. The direct line between management and workers seems to exclude the presence of outside advocates of the workforce and, by consequence excludes any kind of trade union assistance and service.

While social movement unionism can contribute to reaffirm, in coalition with occasional interest groups workers' basic rights, the prospects of union cooperation with work groups and management in order to regulate working conditions are very poor. Hyman (1997) expresses a deep scepticism about the possibilities of combining union representation with high commitment human resources policies and reconciling the individual /groups interests within their agenda.

Gospel and Willman (2003), on the contrary, affirm on ground of their research that that there can be a mutual reinforcement of direct and representative forms of participation.

Looking at the American HRM experience Paula Voss (1997) in her comments on Hyman's article points to the fact that unions by engaging themselves in high commitment workplaces can positive influence the managerial scheme.

Managerial attitudes towards worker participation into work organization are discussed by Gollan, Poutsma and Veersma (2006) in their editorial to the *IR* special issues. Their analysis of organizational participation also deals with interest representation within the managerial high commitment or high involvement approach. The authors suggest that organizational participation can lead to two different outcomes as far as interest representation is concerned. On the one hand, direct participation excludes union intermediation. In fact the managerial option for participation arrangements is excluding trade union involvement in organisational decision making in view of keeping strategic choices within the organisation.

On the other hand, a number of analyses have demonstrated that direct participation does not necessarily exclude other forms of interest representation. Indeed direct and representative participation mutually reinforce each other.

The debate on work organisation and interest representation is also developed on ground of the Commission *Green Paper for a new organisation at work* (1997). Social partnership between unions and company management is taking different forms in different IR systems. The book by Huzzard et al. (2004) provides a very extensive interpretation of union participation into work organisation. The analysis of a pharmaceutical enterprise conducted by Huzzard et al. (2004) pointed to the adjustment of union traditional collective bargaining strategy in order to better represent the different interests of the workforce. It cites specifically rewarding technicians and researchers as separate from the production workforce, so the union was able to enlarge the scope of negotiation into some strategic choices, to better represent the expectations of the skilled and professionals and to consolidate its presence in the company. A number of similar experiences can be more frequently observed during the phases of privatisation of formerly public enterprises.

Interesting experiments have been conducted in the privatised sectors in UK (Gregory, 2004).

The British literature is increasingly concentrating on the non union firm. Research questions can be summarised in the followings:

- How is interest representation taking place without unions?
- How is employee voice expressed?
- What role can employees' councils/ forums and other forms of interest consultation really play? Can these representation bodies formulate autonomous strategies and guarantee the interest of the workforce?

Many contributions proceed from the critical analysis of the data supplied by WERS (the Workplace Employment Relations Survey). Charlwood and Terry's (2007) article is based on WERS, 2004 (Kersley et al.2006). According to this survey in the majority of British workplaces there is no employee access to any form of indirect representation, union or non-union (83% private sector and 20% public sector: p. 324). The existing bodies of employee representation are quite differentiated. Charlwood and Terry underline that a plurality of representative forms is emerging in British IR. They identify the union, non union, and hybrid typologies and evaluate their impact on interest representation. The outcomes of these forms of representation are very poor. The best outcomes (lower wage dispersion and higher productivity) seem to arise when union and non union representation co-exist side-by-side.

On the ground of these results Charlwood and Terry affirm that any effective system of representation requires the organisational cohesion and strength that have traditionally been provided by trade unions. The conclusion of the authors is that union presence is still a prerequisite for effective representation, while pure non union forms serve neither employee nor employer interests.

New models of interest representation are also being increasingly investigated after the ICE regulation has come into force (2004)

A number of analyses share Charlwood and Terry scepticism about direct participation.

Gospel and Willman (2003) provide evidence that suggests that there can be a mutual reinforcement of direct and representative forms of participation. By considering the efficacy of direct participation in productivity improvements Bryson, Charlwood and Forth (2006) remark on the positive relationship between productivity and management responsiveness, but note that this outcome only occurs when unions are present in the workplaces.

Specific comments on the way participation has developed after the ICE regulation are provided by Hall (2006) who criticises the poor improvements of workplace arrangements due to both union and managerial reluctance to subscribe to formal arrangements.

Employees councils (EC) acting as substitutes for union representation have been analysed in Caroline Lloyd's article (2001). The author focuses on an aerospace plant where the unionisation rate, before the de- recognition, was high. The experience of an EC as substitute actor is not completely satisfactory for both sides and the conclusion is that there are signals of a renewed interest in union support. Moreover Terry (1999) and Golan (1999) provide evidence about ECs and conclude that these bodies have serious problems related to the limited commitment by managers to providing information, to the absence of sanctions in case of non consultation and to marginalisation of the EC in case of difficulties faced by the companies.

Gollan's research (2006, 2007) addresses organizational experiences with non union representation and union voice arrangements. In his book (2007) the author, while offering a comprehensive overview of this practice in the UK, also locates this within an international context. The case studies presented examine various arrangements concerning the interest representation process. The analysis deals with two main questions: a) are non-union systems of representation an acceptable alternative to union-based systems? b) Do non union systems of representation complement more traditional forms of union representation?

The role of union and non union forms of representation face managerial arrangements on work organisation is also examined in relation to the role that the new institutions of information and consultation could play in this game. According to Gollan's (2006) the existence of a mechanism – union or non union – for communication between management and employees at the workplace does not guarantee an effective representation of employee interests. While it is true that trade unions' voice could be more effective than the voice expressed by non-union representatives, the crucial points are the legitimacy and effectiveness of trade unions in representing employees' interests and the perception of their representative role by the workforce. Lacking effective legitimacy, unions will be supplanted under the prevision of the new European Directive on Information and Consultation.

A closer perspective to the new scenario of interest representation after the Information and Consultation Directive (ICE) implementation is presented by Whittal and Tuckman (2008). Their contribution analyses two cases of employees' forum in the finance sector. The authors underline that the ICE are first a management construct and, as such, they are regarded as a means for high commitment practices. The evaluation of this forum is measured, using the Hyman's (1997) three indicators of representative ness: autonomy/legitimacy/ efficacy of the newly instituted bodies. Though the two cases under investigation display different features, the authors express criticism about these forms of interest representation as they are driven by management, as they serve management purpose and can not progress in autonomously defining their objectives.

Interest representation in the new EU member states can also be analysed in relation to the ICE. As Meardi (2008) explains the legislation is opening the possibility of statutory works councils in countries where they were not foreseen. These representative bodies could progressively enter into new forms of work regulation, either management led or participative.

The article on the Baltic States by Woolfson et al. focuses (2008) on workers interest representation in relation to health and safety at work. After underling the high degree individualism by workers that leaves work organisation in management hands, the authors debate the possibility that a new scenario of shortages in the labour market will possibly facilitate employee voice in these countries. Many uncertainties remain as far as whether this scenario could lead to collective or trade union empowerment or to an increased individualism.

The dilemma of organising unorganised workers is also analysed for the British context by Pollert's research. The identity of unorganized workers, their individual and collective needs and their representation have been analysed by Pollert (2008). The research aim is to understand how unorganized workers with problems at work can react: if formally or informally, if individually or collectively. This research also investigates how far low-paid, non-unionised workers benefit from institutions of management-worker consultation and grievance and discipline handling (based on survey respondents' awareness of these bodies at their workplace. The research also investigates non-unionised workers' experience of seeking redress for workplace problems with the UK charity, the Citizens Advice Bureau (CAB). The research is based on a rich database provided by the Unrepresented Worker Survey (URWS) of 501 non-unionised, low paid workers with problems at work and on a qualitative investigation of the workers with employment problems who approach the CAB.

Pollert's analysis reveals a number of interesting features:

- The unrepresented workers do not only display "individualized interests", but also collective identity.

- The unrepresented workers use their (individual/collective) voice in the response to work problems.
- The voice is often used (by the individual/collective workers) in order to informally resolve matters with management. Only a minority of workers uses the formal complaints procedure.
- Either collectively or individually, partly depending on their jobs, workers express their voice.
- The degree of conclusion and satisfactory outcome to their attempts to use voice to resolve problems is very low.

This research also investigates union attitudes. Unrepresented workers are not against the unions, but the status of non unionised prevents workers from approaching union representatives for help in grievances even if their workplace is covered by a collective bargaining agreement. The institutional support for unrepresented workers is weak and ineffective. In particular the CAB (Citizen Advice Bureau), being a charity institution, is under-funded and under-resourced. A large number of employees, deprived of their basic rights, may gain support from the CAB, but this form of representation is often hard to reach and the results poor.

This research demonstrates that British unions should better consider how to fill the divide between represented and unrepresented workers, but herein, as in the case of USA, unions should make some strategic choices in order to include new members.

4. Reforming union strategies

4.1. .Individualised services

The restructuring process and the changes in the workforce composition that took place all over the eighties have increasingly questioned trade union representative ness (Terry, 1994).

This trend is having on impact on unions, but also on societal cohesion. The decreasing identification of collective interest is leading to a deficit of solidarity (Zoll, 2002)

The different pressure for flexibilisation have changed not only the "constituencies" of unions but also the market and bargaining power of groups within the workplace and the interests that these constituencies.

The individualization of worker interests and also the emerging identity of group interests already outlined by Terry is further explored in more recent analysis dealing with the dilemma of interest representation.

A response to the union crisis of representation consists in increasing the services provided to union members. The scope of this strategy is to stimulate new members to join the unions. Incentives like discounts, insurance and consulting have been projected in order to capture young employees, white collars and high educated people. Among the others this strategy has been developed by: Ver.DI in Germany, by SIF in Sweden and by FNV in the Netherlands.

The Swedish case is analysed in Bjorkman's article (2006) which explores union attractiveness to highly educated employees. The focus of the article is on the strategies adopted by the Swedish white collar union (SIF) in order to better satisfy individual needs of his potential constituency. This strategy consists in targeting individuals and specific member groups in view of supplying them with a service portfolio.
The individualised services provision model has been planned as follows:

- Problem-solving has been combined with services aimed at being delivered before acute problems occur, such as career planning activities, thus indicating a switch from a reactive to a proactive service mode.
- The design of the new services indicates a shift in the trade union role from reliever –taking care of the members' problems – to enabler- providing the member with the tools of self action.
- New services are seldom dependent on local union representatives as they are mainly provided on Internet by Sif staff. (321)

The orientation to the services is posing problems to the union survival. First of all by opting for market efficacy, unions lose their democratic structure. According to the author "the modernisation of a trade union implies the dilemma of maintaining service efficiency at the same time as nurturing democratic processes. Moreover "if active participation in trade union work is substituted by individual consumption of trade union services, the union influence at workplace level may be swept away".. The combination of individual needs should not sacrifice collective services and member participation in trade union work.

The Dutch case consists of career development services (Sprengler and Van Klaveren, 2004): the Union Confederation (FNV) set up a career service project to support members in their orientation in the labour market. Most expertise in this project is provided by skilled union members, many from new members categories (women, high skilled, services workers).Using the expertise which is 'at hand' in the union itself is one of the means to rebuild union into learning organisations.

4.2. Women inclusion

An equal balance between male and female union members seems to be, first of all, a problem of the organisations themselves. In fact a great effort has been made by the British unions in order to include women within their headquarters (unions' constitutions that often require such a balance).

In a special issue of IRJ in July 2006, the editorial suggests, among the other developments, the increasing significance of women both numerically and as activists challenging traditional union forms. Women are numerically vital to trade union survival and revival. Briskin and Sayce et al. (2006) provide a range of insights into the gendered nature of trade unions.

More than one article suggest that industrial relations research should develop a gendered approach (Danieli, 2006) in order to overcome male hegemony .Empirical studies relate to discrimination in pay and jobs

Dickens (2006) links the item of gender and labour law to the problem of justice at work and particularly to the program of the labour government since 1997.

Thornley (2006) provides an analysis of public sector employment conditions with a special focus on women at work. She also analyses the role of UNISON in reducing unequal and low pay. The relatively new institution of Unison (1993) allows focusing on the union strategy mainly built on equal pay. "The emergent twin –track approach evidenced most notably by UNISON to the problem of unequal pay and low pay combines traditional solidaristic collective bargaining with gender-centred litigation, negotiation, education and public and political campaigning, and this has helped push the issues of unequal and low pay in the public sector to centre stage"(356)

The successful case of a small union in involving women activism is reported by Sayce et al. (2006). The argument is that a relatively new and small organisation is more reactive to the organisation of gender interests and that the leadership of women help changing traditional strategies.

Tomlinson's research(2005) on full- and part-time women workers provides evidence that their attitude toward unions are similar, but their experience of trade unions depend on their work life balance and on the change from full to part-time work. By linking analysis to the life experience of women, the author suggests an interpretation of the lower propensity of part-timers to unionise.

Kirton (2005) explores the influence of women joining and participating in unions. The article provides an analysis of the factors affecting the women's choices to join unions. The gendered experience has important consequences for their participation.

Concluding remark

The state of the art of new forms of interest organisation shows a polarisation of research interest between American and British scholars. Socio-political implications of unrepresented employment are largely developed by American scholars, while British researchers concentrate on the analysis of workplaces in order to monitor the process of de-unionisation and the perspectives of direct participation.

Despite the many changes occurred in European labour markets, labour relations studies still pay little attention to social identities and to social cohesion. Individual profiles, the gender identity and the marginalised segments of the labour market are scarcely represented by the actors of IR, but their needs should be investigated in order to compensate for the democratic deficit of capitalist societies. New forms of communications like the Internet could help monitoring employee demands and create networks that could contribute to strategic choices for traditional unions.

Bibliography

BERR (Department of Business, Enterprise and Regulatory Reform), 2006, The Information and Consultation of Employees Regulations 2004 DTI Guidance (January 2006) available at http://www.berr.gov.uk/employment/employment-legislation/ice/index.html

Bjorkman, H. (2006): Targeting individuals and specific groups of employees: an emerging trade union challenge, Transfer 2006/12(3): 315-332.

Bronferbrenner K. / Friedman, S. / Hurd, R.W. / Oswald, R.A. / Seeber, R.L. (eds.), Organising to win, Ithaca, Cornell University Press.

Brown, W. / Deakin, S. / Hudson, M. / Pratton, C. / Ryan, P. (1998): The individualisation of employment contracts in Britain, DTI Research Paper, June.

Bryson, A. / Charlwood, A. / Forth, J. (2006): Worker voice, managerial response and labour productivity: an empirical investigation, IRJ, 2006/37 (5):438-455

Charlwood A. / Terry, M. (2007): 21st –century models of employee representation: structures, processes and outcomes, IRJ 2007/38(4), 320-337.

Colling, T. / Dickens, L. (2001): Gender, equality and trade unions: a new basis for mobilisation, in M Noon and E. Ogboona (eds.) Equality, diversity and disadvantage in employment Basingstoke, Macmillan

Dickens, L. (2006): Relegulation for gender equality : from either/or to both, IRJ 2006/37/4:299-309

Dufour, C. / Hege, A. (2002): L'Europe syndicale: la représentation des salariés en France, Allemagne, Grande Bretagne et Italie, Bruxelles, P.I.E.-Peter Lang

Erickson, C.L. / Fish, C.L. /Milkman, R. / Mitchell, D.J.B. / Wong, K. (2002): Justice for janitors in Los Angeles: lessons from three rounds of negotiations, BJIR, 2002/40(543-567

Fine, J. (2006): Worker Centers: organizing workers at the edge of the dream, Ithaca, NY: ILR Press/Cornell University Press.

Fine, J. (2007): A Marriage made in heaven? Mismatches and misunderstandings between workers centres and unions, BJIR 45(2): 335-360.

Gollan, P.J. (2006): Editorial: consultation and non –union employee representation, IRJ, 2006/ 37(5):428-437.

Gollan, P. / Poutsm, E. / Veersma, U. (2006): New roads in organizational participation? Industrial Relations 2006/45(4): 499-512

Gollan, P.J. (2007): Employee representation in non-union firms, London, Sage

Gospel, H. / William, P. (2003): The coming of workplace information sharing and consultation: What it means for employee representation in Britain, Perspectives on Work, 7, 1: 38-39.

Greer, I. / Byrd, B. / Fleron, J.L. (2007): Two paths to the light road : the dynamics of coalition building in Seattle and Buffalo in Turner, L. and D.B. Cornfield (eds.), Labour in the new urban battleground. Local solidarity in a global economy. Ithaca, New York, Cornell U.P.:11-128.

Grumbrell-McCormick, R. / Hyman, R. (2006): Embedded collectivism? Workplace representation in France and Germany, IRJ/ 37(5): 437-491

Hall, M. (2006): A cool response to the ICE regulations? Employer and trade union approaches to the new legal framework for information and consultation, IRJ 2006/37(5):456-472

Healy, G. / Hansen, L.L. / Ledwith, S. (2006): Editorial: still uncovering gender in industrial relations, IRJ 2006/37(4): 290-298.

Heery, E. (2002): Partnership versus organising: alternative futures for British trade unionism, IRJ 2002/33(1), 20-35.

Heery, E. / Conley, H. / Delbridge, R. / Steward, P. (2004): Beyond the enterprise: trade union representation of freelances in the UK, Human resource Management Journal, 2004/14(2): 20-35.

Heery, E. / Frege, C. (2006): New actors in Industrial relations,. BJIR 2006/44 (4): 601-604.

Herkscher, C. / Carré, F. (2006): Strength in networks: employment rights organizations and the problem of coordination, BJIR/44(4): 605-628.

Huzzard, T. / Gregory, D. / Scott, R. (ed.) (2004), Strategic Unionism and partnership. Boxing or Dancing, London Palgrave Macmillan: 343-350

Hyman, R. (1994): Changing trade union identities and strategies, in Hyman R and A. Ferner, New frontiers in European industrial relations, Oxford, Blackwell: 108-139.

Hyman, R. (1997): The future of employee representation, BJIR, 35(3), 309-36.
Kersley, B. / Alpin, C. / Forth, J. / Bryson, A. / Bewley, H. / Dix, G. / Oxembridge, S. (2006): Inside the workplace, London Routledge.
Kirton, G. (2005): The influences on women joining and participating in unions, IRJ. 2005/36(5):386-401.
Kolins Givan, R. (2007): Side by side we battle onward? Representing workers in contemporary America, BJIR 2007/45(4):829-855.
Kurz, S. (2002): Workplace justice: organizing multy-identity movements, Minneapolis, MN/London, University of Minnesota Press.
Leonardi, S. (2008): Union organisation of employees in atypical and precarious work in Italy, paper presented at the Conference on EU workplace participation, Rome, September 24-26 2008.
Lloyd C. (2001): What do employee councils do? The impact of non union forms of representation on trade union organisation, IRJ 2001/32(4): 313-327.
Meardi, G. (2007): More voice after more exit ? Unstable industrial relations in Central eastern Europe, IRJ 2007/38(6): 503-523.
Meardi, G. / Strohmer, S. / Traxler, F. (2008): Ligths and shadows of direct participation in foreign companies in the Czech Republic, paper presented at the Conference on EU workplace participation, Rome, September 24-26 2008.
Munroe, A. (1999): Women, work and trade unions, Aldershot, Ashgate.
Osterman, P. (2006): Community organizing and Employee representation, BJIR /44(4): 629-650.
Oxembridge, S. / Brown, W. (2002): The two faces of partnership? An assessment of Partnership and co-operative employer/trade union relationships, Employee Relations, 2002/24(3):262-276.
Piore, M.J. / Safford, S. (2006): Changing regimes of workplace governance, shifting axes of social mobilisation and the challenge to industrial relations theory, Industrial Relations, 45 (3): 299-325
Pollert, A. (2008): The Non-unionised Worker and Workplace Problems: Forms of Individual and Collective Voice at Work paper presented at the Conference on EU workplace participation, Rome, September 24-26 2008.
Regalia, I. (ed.) (2005): Regulating new forms of employment- local experiments and social innovation in Europe, London and New York/ Routledge.
Saundry, R. / Stuard, M. / Antcliff, V. (2007): Broadcasting discontent-freelancers, trade unions and the Internet, New Technology, Work and Employment, 2007/22:2, 178-191
Upchurch, M. / Richardson, M. / Tailby S. / Danford A. / Steward, P. (2006): Employee representation and partnership in the non-union sector: a paradox of intention? HRMJ, 2006/16 (4): 393-410.

Safford, S. (2005): Rethinking Voice and Power: national civil rights organizations and their role in contemporary American industrial relations, Paper presented at the BJIR Conference on new actors in industrial relations, LSE September 2005.
Saundry, R. / Stuard, M. / Antcliff, V. (2007): Broadcasting discontent-freelancers, trade unions and the Internet, New Technology, Work and Employment, 2007/22:2, 178-191
Sprengler, W. / Van Klaveren, M. (2004): Employability and career services: a Dutch example of combining collective and individual, Dancing and Boxing in Union strategies, in Huzzard (cit): 343-350.
Terry, M. (1993): Workplace unionism: redefining structures and objectives, in R. Hyman and A. Ferner (eds.), New frontiers in European Industrial Relations, Oxford Blackwell, pp. 192-216.
Terry, M. (1999): Systems of collective employee representation in non-union firms in the UK, IRJ, 1999/30 (1): 16-30.
Tomlinson, J. (2005): Women's attitudes towards trade unions in the UK: a consideration of the distinction between full- and part-time workers, IRJ 2005/36(5)402-418.
Thornley, C. (2006): Unequal and low pay in the public sector. IRJ 2006/37 (4): 344-358
Turner, L. et al. (eds.): Rekindling the Movement: Labor's Quest for Relevance in the 21st Century Ithaca: Cornell University Press/ILR Press, 2001.
Voss, Paula (1997): Discussion on Hyman BJIR 1997/35(3): 332-336
Voss, K. / Sherman, R. (2000): Breaking the iron law of oligarchy: union revitalization in the American labor movement, American Journal of Sociology, 2000/106: 106-49
Witthatl, M. / Tuckman, A. (2008): Giving Employees a Voice? Lessons from the New Employee Forums in the UK, paper presented at the Conference on EU workplace participation, Rome, September 24-26 2008
Wood, S. (2008): Job characteristics, employee voice and well-being in Britain, IRJ 2008/39(2): 153-168
Woolfson, C. / Calite, D. / Kallaste, E. (2008): Employee voice and working environment in post communist New Member states: an empirical analysis of Estonia, Latvia and Lithuania., IRJ 2008/39: 314-334.
Zoll, R. (2003): La solidarietà. Eguaglianza e differenza. Bologna, Mulino

Lights and shadows of employee participation in the new EU member states

Guglielmo Meardi

Introduction

The post-Soviet bloc new member states of the European Union differ from most of the old member states for the weaker 'embeddedness' of their employee participation structures, and for the relative weakness of organised labour. This allows employers to often choose their preferred form of employee participation, including direct participation, and affects the possibility of transferring participation mechanisms from western Europe.

The access to the European Union introduced three important changes. First, EU legislation on Information and Consultation of Employees was introduced, opening the possibility of statutory works councils in countries where these were not foreseen. Second, employees of multinational companies were included into the European Works Councils, where these existed or could be created. Third, more indirectly, the increase in economic and industrial integration within the single market, and larger flows of foreign direct investment, increase the scope for the transfer, direct or adapted, of participation mechanisms from western Europe, including direct participation. If developments occurred on all these three dimensions, we could assist to the development of a 'European', multiple-pillar model of participation in the new EU member states (NMS) (Gill and Krieger 2000).

This chapter discusses the current developments on these three processes of change, reviewing the issues and discussing in particular research evidence on multinationals' practices in the Czech Republic.

Recent developments in employee participation in the new EU member states

Implementation of the European Directive on Information and Consultation

The EU Information & Consultation Directive (2002/14/EC) was expected to affect the new post-communist member states more than the old ones, as in the majority of them (the exceptions being Hungary and Slovenia) trade unions were the only channel of employee representation, which might now be replaced by a dual channel. However, such transfer has not occurred, at least not in a way that makes the NMS more similar to the German model (Rogers and Streeck 1995).

Promoters of the transfer of the dual channel into the NMS (e.g. Tholen 2007) may be neglecting that works councils have historically been an effective channel for employee voice only in countries where they have been preceded and supported by a strong labour movement like in Germany. In countries where union penetration is low, works councils have mostly been manipulative tools in employers' hands (Freeman and Medoff, 1984). The actual relationship between works councils and trade unions is more problematic, and while being generally one of complementarity (Brewster *et al.*, 2007), the actual dynamics depend on the specific and changing contexts and legislations. Even in Germany, strains on the relation between works councils and trade unions have recently appeared, with the CDU reform proposal of a collective bargaining role for the works councils, and with instances of 'yellow' trade unions infiltration in works councils of companies such as Siemens and Lidl. In post-communist countries (including in East Germany, where works councils undermine unions more often than in West Germany), the context is rather negative, as private employers are already reluctant to negotiate with trade unions and the weakness or inexistence of multi-employer collective bargaining means that trade unions could be deemed redundant if they lost their workplace role. Even in the 'best case' Hungary, where the dual system had been introduced 'endogenously' in the 1990s, works councils failed to play the expected role wherever unions were absent.

While the Directive was officially meant to set a minimum floor of rights for employees in the EU, as it happened with other elements of the social *acquis (Meardi 2007)*, several NMS governments have been quick at exploiting the opportunity to undermine, rather than reinforce, employee prerogatives. Governments' initial proposals tried to replace the single channel with a dual-channel system in which the establishment of a works council could have easily made the unions disposable. The specific proposed laws allowing works councils to replace the prerogatives of existing unions were particularly dangerous, as they would have opened an avenue for union-avoidance techniques and 'yellow', or at least ineffective, works councils. Although other possible transpositions introducing works councils *while* strengthening unions were available, for instance along the Italian *Rappresentanze Sindacali Unitarie* or the South African Workplace Forums examples, both guaranteeing union presence in the works councils, this option was not considered. Union-threatening legislative proposals were pushed by governments in Poland, Czech Republic (this country had started the legislation process well before EU accession), Slovakia and Estonia. Only after strong union opposition (which in the case of Estonia, where the proposed law restricted the prerogatives of trade unions, also required the solidarity intervention of international unions) were such proposals amended and replaced by 'residual' works councils systems, which give priority to unions as employee representatives in workplaces (Carley and Hall 2008). Only Bulgaria and Estonia introduced a dual channel that guarantees union presence but still raises some union concerns.

The legal framework has since been changed in some countries by interventions from the Constitutional Courts, reintroducing threats for trade unions. In the Czech Republic, in March 2008 the Constitutional Court decided that a works council can be established at an employer's business and can also operate alongside a trade union, which raised preoccupation from the trade unions. In Poland, in July 2008 the Constitutional Court took a similar decision. Thereby, a dual channel has been introduced by the back door. In the short term, experts expect no major change (trade unions are likely to keep their dominance of the already established works councils), but for the future the option for non-union representation and the undermining of independent employee organisation is now open: if German trade unions struggle to fend off 'yellow' rivals and conservative reforms, the task will be even more difficult for their weaker counterparts in the NMS. However, not all Courts decisions have been in this direction. An earlier Polish ruling increased the scope of information and consultation rights, which initial legislation had established in a very vague form.

The implementation of the new I&C bodies seems to be proceeding slowly. In the Baltic states, it is reported that employees lack the assertiveness and information to take action demanding I&C rights, and the lack of participation and voice has been documented on the Health and Safety issue (Woolfson et al. 2008). In Slovakia and Poland few companies have introduced innovations (Gładoch 2008). In Poland, according to data from the State Labour Inspectorate, about 2,000 I&C bodies (out of at least 17,000 companies covered by the legislation, i.e. with over 50 employees) have been constituted, but 90% of them are simply ratifications of previously existing union bodies. Moreover, the remaining 10% appear to be weaker and less active than union bodies (Surdykowska 2008). The expectation that works councils would not be an effective tool for employee voice in the NMS seems therefore confirmed.

The extension of European Works Councils

The process of enlarging the European Works Councils (EWC) to employees from the NMS had started voluntarily in many companies before EU accession, raising some expectations of side-effects for employee participation (Meardi 2004). Notably, the degree of information obtained by NMS representatives could have allowed them to strengthen their local bargaining position.

However, in the last few years, in spite of the enlargement that increases the number of companies covered by the EWC Directive, the process of creation of new EWC has significantly slowed down. Only a handful of EWC have been created in companies based in the NMS. The practice in the EWCs including NMS representatives is varied (Voss 2006), but importantly the 'pro-active' EWCs, affecting industrial relations transnationally and locally, appear to be from the same few companies that had enlarged the EWC before 2004. There are some cases of productive cross-border co-operation among trade unions within the EWCs (Fichter and Meardi 2008, Meardi et al. 2009a, Fetzer 2008, Gajewska 2008), but in most cases resources and networks are too weak to lead to active solidarity.

Indirect effects from foreign investors

Apart from the statutory EWC, foreign investors may transfer or introduce other practices, or cultures, of employee participation. The evidence is however limited. Research in the automotive sector has showed that strategies from foreign investors in this field are pragmatic and imprecise, so that, for instance, it is difficult to distinguish German from US approaches (Tholen 2007, Meardi et al. 2009b.) Other researchers have detected some positive effects of continental (especially German) investors (Bluhm 2007, Krzywdziński 2008), but concentrated in some large MNCs with specific corporate governance or industrial relations. Kahancová (2007), on the basis of an in-depth case study across the region, argued that MNCs in the region have the power to make the most of national difference, and may therefore be ready to exploit weaker employee prerogatives.

Expectations that western European investors might have transferred a culture of participation and social dialogue proved to be naïve. A graphic tale of the resulting confusion, among NMS employee representatives, about MNC's intentions has been published in a Polish union magazine:

> 'In our company there are no trade unions. The owner is an Austrian firm, that is from a country where there is a long tradition of social dialogue. Hence the feeling that works councils' prerogatives and competences should be well known to the employer. In conformity to the law, the employer organized the elections and the first meeting of the council. After that we heard: 'we have organized you, the rest depends on you, we'll wait for the effects of your activity'. We asked ourselves what's this council for at all, because the employees imagine that we are some sort of social affairs commission, while the employer treats us as – even if they don't say so openly – rather an opponent, not as a consultant and partner. Basically we appear as a body that threatens complaints. We can't fulfil the expectations of either side, because in practice we have no powers that would allow us to do it.' Anna Lewandowska, Works Council of TU Compensa SA. (Dołowska 2007)

Other effects might be expected from companies from other countries than western continental Europe. Anglo-American companies have their own industrial relations and HRM specificities that are sometimes exported abroad (Almond and Ferner 2006). Specifically, Anglo-American companies, with no statutory works councils at home, have been pioneering on forms of direct participation. Research on British-based multinationals confirms the frequency of direct participation practices in foreign subsidiaries, and that when combined with absence of unions of works councils (as may be expected in Central Eastern Europe), these translate in strongly management-led employment relations (Wood and Fenton-O'Creevy 2005).

Additional insights to the understanding of MNCs influence come from economic geography's contribution to industrial relations (Herod et al. 2003). Multinationals' network vary by geographic spread, and this affects production and employment strategies. Therefore, MNCs in the NMS will have different effects depending on how far their other locations are. One can expect US or Japanese foreign investment into the region to be, due to the geographic distance and the EU barrier, dominated by large companies, motivated mostly by market-access, and therefore involve with little or no relocation pressure, and little or no direct control, but intensive procedural control. Companies from closer countries with no tariff barriers, such as Germany or France, are more likely to be motivated by efficiency consideration can by contrast be tempted by relocations strategies and a direct pressure on labour conditions. Finally, companies from contiguous regions, such as from the Austrian borders, are able not only to relocate, but to completely restructure their production across the border, so that some core activities are kept in Austria and all labour intensive ones are transferred to facilities in the neighbouring countries a few kilometres away. This process reminds the *maquiladora* phenomenon of the Mexico-US borders, and combines strict direct integration (the managers can be the same individuals for plants on both sides of the border) with deep segregation of activities so that different and incomparable working conditions are introduced on the two sides. This geographic insight may help explain why German and especially Austrian companies may actually have indirect participation mechanisms less frequently than their, theoretically less union-friendly, Japanese or American competitors.

Case studies from the Czech Republic

The Czech Republic is an interesting case for the study of developments in employee participation. Among the post-Soviet bloc EU member states, it is the economically most advanced, but with a particular hostility to collective forms of participation, in spite of macro-level corporatist practices. In 2004, on its website the Czech Agency for Foreign Investment even mentioned explicitly as one of the country's attractions the fact of having the fastest decline in union membership (it currently does so only implicitly). Its geographic position in the centre of Europe and close to the core markets of Germany and Austria makes it also particularly subject to cross-border influences. Therefore, it provides a relevant test bed for the development of the different forms of employee participation mentioned in the previous section.

This section presents early findings from research on Anglo-American, Austrian and German investors in the finance and automotive sectors.[1] The research looks at both sector and country-of-origin effects in the field of employee participation. The twelve case studies allow a comparison between the rather well-known automotive components sector and the finance sector, where international restructuring is of major importance but attention to cross-border industrial relations effects has been rarer (Arrowsmith and Marginson 2006), as well as a comparison between Austria, Germany and UK/US in terms of country of origin. The research involved interviews with managers and employee representatives in the Czech sites and in the German. Austrian or British headquarters or subsidiaries, and was carried out in 2007-08. The automotive sector companies are all component-makers, while the finance companies come from the banking, insurance and personal credit sub-sectors.

As a first general finding, none of the foreign investors appears to have had a clear strategy on industrial relations transfer, nor to have chosen the Czech Republic because of its industrial relations features. This seems to confirm the sceptical view of 'regime shopping' by multinational companies (Traxler and Woitech 2000) rather than the more alarmist one (Cooke and Noble 1998). This section will focus on the Anglo-American cases only.

Employee participation in Anglo-American subsidiaries

The Anglo-American manufacturing case studies are distinctive in two respects. First, in this case employee information and participation rights appear actually stronger in the Czech Republic than in the British sites: even if the British factories are strongly unionised, their relations with management are purely of collective bargaining on wages and working conditions, with very little information on work organisation or on restructuring. The Czech unions, by contrast, even if

1 The research project 'Market Efficiency and Employee Participation Rights' is funded by the Austrian Federal Ministry for Science and Research, directed by Prof. Franz Traxler of the University of Vienna, and benefits from the co-operation of Sonja Strohmer and Manfred Krenn.

heirs of the communist-time ones, have developed strong participation activities, without however becoming deferential: at US-CAR there have been strike threats in the past, even if not actual strikes, and at UK-CAR they appear better informed and more active than in the British plant. Secondly, the companies have a declared preference for direct participation over indirect, especially through individual interviews and job satisfaction surveys. The same direct participation methods reveal however limitations and a social demand for more information, which at US-CAR has translated in broader scope for trade unions. High turnover and difficult retention work in the same way, forcing the employers to develop communication and participation further, and with the trade union organising own interviews with leaving employees, which then inspire union requests in negotiations. The EWCs are not particularly strong, though, reflecting relatively little power and capabilities from the western employee representatives. In both companies, an ironic fact is that while western managers resist the EWC and see it as an impediment and a cost, the Czech managers see an advantage in it: the Czech representatives, by being informed of the high job insecurity in the West, due to restructuring and relocations, might come to appreciate more their own conditions. In a situation of overall weak trade union power, the information effect of the EWC could therefore have a 'backfiring' moderating impact on eastern representatives, instead of motivating them to raise social standards towards western levels.

In the finance sector Anglo-American companies, the preference for direct participation is even clearer. Both companies are hardly unionised in the West. US-BAN explicitly rejects trade unions as a 'third, external part' distorting the direct unitaristic relationship between employer and employees, and only accepts them when imposed by the law or by inherited conditions. Its 3,000 Czech employees have no form of collective representation besides the statutory elected representative in the supervisory board, who is a manager. Interestingly, this elected representative tells to be asked by employees to demand higher salaries, and therefore to play a collective bargaining role, which apparently, to a small extent, he does play. The situation may change: in line with the general trend of unionisation in the Czech banking sector, at the time the research was being concluded a union organising effort was taking place. UK-FIN introduced a works-council like 'Employee Forum' in most of its European operations. Interestingly, this was first experimented in Poland and then introduced back in the UK and in other countries including the Czech Republic. In spite of the big importance given to these bodies, their actual working is questionable: in the UK, it had been completely restructured after little time and was not meeting at the time of the research; in the Czech Republic, its mandate had expired two years earlier, all representatives had long left the company, and no new elections had been yet organised because management prioritised the conduction of an employee survey, a more important direct communication tool. As a simple consequence of the weakness of independent employee representation, in these two cases there are no EWCs, nor any other form of cross-border networking among employee representatives. UK-FIN's management is aware of the possibility of a EWC in the future, but employee representatives are too focussed on their national situation to be interested in it. Although in these companies there is very little internal competition as the markets are distinct and the services are provided in loco, some areas of the American company (Research & Development, Information Technologies) are affected by relocations, and more back-office operations are threatened to relocation to even lower-labour cost countries than the Czech Republic, notably Romania and Bulgaria.

Table 1: Forms of employee participation in Czech subsidiaries of Anglo-American MNCs

Company	**Indirect participation**	**Direct participation**	**Transnational participation**
UK-CAR Car parts (Tier 1) 600 employees Brownfield	Trade union: 55% unionisation, 1 FT rep	Satisfaction survey & feedback Works meetings	Active EWC
US-CAR Car parts (Tier 1) 700 employees Brownfield	Trade union: 40% unionization Time-off provision for union reps.	Employee survey & feedback Works meetings	Active EWC
US-BAN Bank 3000 employees Brownfield	None [apart from employee representative in supervisory board]	Employee survey & feedback Works meeting Appraisal interviews Open doors	No EWC No cross-border union contacts
UK-FIN Personal credit 500 employees Greenfield	Non-statutory Employee Forum [but not re-elected for the last 3 years]	Engagement survey Open doors	No EWC No cross-border union contacts

Discussion and conclusion

If regulatory changes (Information & Consultation Directive, EWCs) seem to have had little or no impact on employee participation, the situation in the workplaces is far from immobile. The overall picture of the four Czech case studies presented (Table 1) shows that the legislation on works councils linked to the EU Directive on Information and Consultation of Employees has had virtually no impact in these companies. Employee participation depends either on pre-existing union presence (in manufacturing brownfield sites), or on informal and employer-led solutions. Where unions exist, they are not particularly strong but they know how to play their role: Czech union reps actually emerge as better informed and more active than their British counterparts. The EWCs, where they exist, have little impact as these companies do not have strong cross-border union networks. Most investors have a pragmatic approach to employee representatives, with the exception of the explicit anti-unionism of US-BAN.

The direct influences from Anglo-American patterns are more visible on direct participation or management-led indirect participation. UK-FIN had introduced a voluntary Employee Forum, although its limitations are apparent in the fact that it has not met in the last three years. More actively used are forms of individual participation, especially surveys and related feedback meetings.

Although the Czech operations of these companies are overall successful, the prevalence of direct participation does not seem to have avoided a 'representation gap' and a demand for collective services in the workplaces, in a situation similar to that of the USA (Freeman and al. 2007). The employee representative in the supervisory board of US-BAN is asked to play a collective bargaining role, although this is not part of its role. At US-BAN, an attempt at creating a trade union occurred (the outcome is still unknown), and at US-CAR employee surveys revealed dissatisfaction with the existing degree of information. Employee demands for more participation might not matter to management, if they were not combined with high and often increasing levels of turn-over. Retention is a major preoccupation for all employers researched, reflecting the tight Czech labour market. Managers report that direct participation solutions are a part of their retention strategies: if they appear to be insufficient, more experimentation may follow.

The Czech Republic, like the rest of the NMS, appears to have only started its expected laboratory role, and it is still early to say whether it will entail a downwards or upwards development in employee participation rights. Their work environment is as rich of tensions as anywhere else.

References

Almond, P. / Ferner, A. (eds.) (2006): American Multinationals in Europe: Managing Employment Relations Across National Borders. Oxford: Oxford University Press.

Arrowsmith, J. / Marginson, P. (2006): 'The European Cross-border Dimension to Collective Bargaining in Multinational Companies', European Journal of Industrial Relations, 12, 3: 245-266

Bluhm, K. (2007): Experimentierfeld Ostmitteleuropa? Deutsche Unternehmen in Polen und der Tschechischen Republik. Wiesbaden: Vs Verlag.

Brewster, C. / Wood, G., et al. (2007): 'Are Works Councils and Joint Consultative Committees a Threat to Trade Unions? A Comparative Analysis.' Economic and Industrial Democracy, 28, 1: 49-77.

Carley, M. / Hall, M. (2008): Impact of the information and consultation directive on industrial relations. Dublin: European Foundation for the Improvement of Working and Living Conditions.

Cooke, W. / Noble, D. (1998): 'Industrial Relations Systems and US Foreign Direct Investment Abroad.' British Journal of Industrial Relations, 36, 4: 581-609.

Dołowska, A. (2007): 'Droga przez mękę' Tygodnik Solidarność, 22.

Fetzer, T. (2008): 'European Works Councils as Risk Communities: The Case of General Motors', European Journal of Industrial Relations, 14, 3: 289-308

Fichter, M. / Meardi, G. (2008): 'Production Relocation. Impacts on Home, Host and Cross-border Industrial Relations.' In M. Blas-Lopéz and M. Moreau (eds.) Restructuring In The New EU Member States: Social Dialogue, Firms Relocation And Social Treatment Of Restructuring. Frankfurt/M: Peter Lang, 135-156.

Freeman, R.B. / Boxall, P. / Haynes, P. (2007): What Workers Say: Employee Voice in the Anglo-American Workplace. Ithaca: ILR Press.

Gajewska, K. (2008): 'The Emergence of a European Labour Protest Movement', European Journal of Industrial Relations, 14, 1, 104-121.

Gill, C. / Krieger, H. (2000): 'Recent Survey Evidence on Participation in Europe: Towards a European Model?', European Journal of Industrial Relations, 6, 1, 109-132.

Gładoch, M. (2008): 'Meandry partycypacji pracowniczej w Polsce', Dialog, 2, 59-64.

Herod, A. / Peck, J. / Wills, J. (2003): 'Geography and Industrial Relations.' In P. Ackers and A. Wilkinson (eds.) Understanding Work and Employment, Oxford, Oxford University Press, 176-192.

Kahancová, M. (2007): Making the Most of Diversity. Social Interaction and Variation in Employment Practices in a Multinational Company. Amsterdam: Amsterdam University Press.

Krzywdziński, M. (2008): 'Work models under strain of offshoring. East-West competition in the European car industry', Paper presented at the GERPISA International Colloquium, June 18-20, Turin.

Meardi, G. (2004): 'Short Circuits in Multinational Plants. The Extension of European Works Councils to Poland', European Journal of Industrial Relations, 10:2, 161-78.

Meardi, G. (2007): 'More Voice after more Exit? Unstable Industrial Relations in Central Eastern Europe', Industrial Relations Journal, 38, 6, 503-23.

Meardi, G. / Marginson, P. / Fichter, M. / Frybes, M. / Stanojević M. / Tóth, A. (2009a): 'The Complexity of Relocation and the Diversity of Union Responses', European Journal of Industrial Relations, 15, 1, 27-47.

Meardi, G. / Marginson, P. / Fichter, M. / Frybes, M. / Stanojević, M. / Tóth, A. (2009b): 'Varieties of Multinationals. Adapting Employment Practices in Central Eastern European Sites', Industrial Relations (forthcoming)

Rogers, J. / Streeck, W. (eds.) (1995): Works Councils. Consultation, Representation, and Cooperation in Industrial Relations. Chicago: Chicago University Press.

Tholen, J. (2007): Labour Relations in Central Europe. The Impact of Multinationals' Money. Aldershot: Ashgate.

Traxler, F. / Woitech, B. (2000): 'Transnational Investment and National Labour Market Regimes: A Case of "Regime Shopping"?' European Journal of Industrial Relations, 6, 2: 141-159.

Surdykowska, B. (2008): 'Prześwietlanie rad pracowniczych', Dialog. Pismo Dialogu Społecznego, 2.

Voss, E. (2006): The experience of European Works Councils in new EU Member States. Dublin: European Foundation for the Improvement of Working and Living Conditions.

Wood, S.J. / Fenton-O'Creevy, M.P. (2005): 'Direct Involvement, Representation and Employee Voice in UK Multinationals in Europe', European Journal of Industrial Relations, 11, 1: 27-50.

Woolfson, C. / Ceite, D. / Kallaste, E. (2008): 'Employee 'voice' and working environment in post-communist New Member States: an empirical analysis of Estonia, Latvia and Lithuania', Industrial Relations Journal, 39, 4, 314-334.

The non-unionised worker and workplace problems: Forms of individual and collective voice at work

Anna Pollert

Introduction

The issue of worker participation at the workplace can be framed in terms of employee 'voice' at work. 'Voice' can be explored in terms of participation in managing the employment relationship, including the regulation of conflict. This is a traditional collective role for trade unions, but within increasingly individualised employment relations in Britain, 'voice' at the individual level is little understood. How far can individual exercise voice at work and how it is used in resolving grievances? Based on both quantitative and qualitative research,[1] this paper examines forms of representation, both individual and collective, among non-unionised workers who attempt to resolve problems at work. Part 1 presents findings from a survey conducted in 2004 of 501 low-paid, non-unionised workers who had experienced problems at work in the previous three years – the Unrepresented Worker Survey (URWS). Worker participation is examined in terms of types of response to individual grievances and whether such 'voice' is heard by the employer in terms of outcomes. Participation is also addressed at the institutional level, in terms of management-worker consultation and grievance-handling mechanisms and their relationship, if any, with the occurrence and resolution of problems. The survey concludes with an exploration of collective experience and representation as further dimensions of actual or potential worker participation and voice: the extent to which individual grievances are shared and acted upon collectively, the types of informal group action taken and workers' experience of and views on trade unions.

Part 2 provides in-depth insights into how fifty workers who sought support for workplace problems with the charity, the Citizens Advice Bureau (CAB) experienced their attempts to exercise voice to resolve their grievances.

1 *The Unorganised Worker, Routes to Support, Views on Representation* funded by the ESRC. Thanks to Dr. Surhan Cam (research fellow), Dr. Andy Charlwood for statistical analysis, to Citizens Advice for help with the CAB research and the workers who gave up their time in talking to the research interviewers.

The Background: Non-unionism and worker representation in Britain

UK union density continues to decline: in 2007 28.0 per cent of employees were union members, down from 28.3 per cent in 2006. In the private sector, membership fell by to just 16.1 per cent (Mercer and Notley, 2008: 3). Collective bargaining coverage has plummeted from a peak of 85 per cent of employees in the mid-1970s (Milner, 1995: 85), to around 30 per cent and in the private sector, which comprises 80 per cent of employment (Labour Market Trends 2006), only 20.00 per cent (Mercer and Notley, 2008: 41). The decline in unionisation and union recognition is especially marked in small workplaces with less than 25 employees (Kersley et al., 2006: 119, Brown and Nash, 2008: 94).

In the UK, if a worker is not a union member, he or she cannot approach a union representative for help with an individual grievance, even if their workplace is covered by a collective bargaining agreement. In the latter circumstances, the non-unionised benefit from the pay and working conditions negotiated for all, becoming so-called 'free-riders'. However, collective agreements have declined to almost the same level as union membership and have 'been transformed from being public goods supporting much organised labour, to being private goods confined to union members' (Brown and Nash, 2008: 95). 'Free-riding' has thus declined: in 1998, 25.7 per cent of non-union members worked in workplaces covered by collective bargaining or a pay review body, but in 2004 this was only 16.9 per cent (Pollert and Li 2006). However, even this minority among the non-unionised cannot seek union help for *individual* support for problems and new members usually require a minimum membership period before they can seek it.

While collective disputes are 'the lowest on record stretching back to 1930' (116 in 2005, DTI, 2006: 5), individual disputes have been rising, as is partly demonstrated by the rise in Employment Tribunal (ET) applications from 40,000 in 1980 to 130,000 in 2001 and 132,577 in 2006/07. However ET applications only reflect the minority of problems for which legal redress is sought. The 2001 British Worker Representation and Participation (BWRP) survey found 38 per cent of respondents had problems at work (Gospel and Willman, 2003: 157) and the 2004 URWS found that 49 per cent of workers contacted for the survey (including the unionised and those earning above the median who were then excluded from the sample) had experienced at least one of ten potential problems in the previous three years (Pollert and Charlwood 2008: 12) – slightly more than the 42 per cent who had experienced a problem at work in the previous five years (Casebourne et al., 2006: 98). And an increase in problems is suggested by a rise in calls from employees or workers to the Advisory, Conciliation and Arbitration Service helpline from 34 to 55 per cent of the total between 2002 and 2004 (ACAS 2004: 52).

In spite of this evidence on the scale of individual disputes, most research focuses on ET applications and there is little empirical evidence on non-unionised workers' experience of grievances at the workplace. The UK government asserts that, apart from a minority of 'vulnerable' workers, for most, that 'the climate of industrial relations in Britain is sound' and 'the vast majority of employers give their staff the rights to which they are entitled' (DTI, 2006, 5, 25, 30). Another theory is that where grievances exist, workers without collective 'voice' use the alternative form of response, which is to 'exit' their job (Hirschman, 1970). The evidence provided by the URWS shows that neither of these conjectures is correct: the primarily individualised British workplace is not, in general, harmonious, but unorganised workers with problems at work do not just exit, but try to exercise voice in trying to resolve them.

The first part of this paper presents evidence on 'voice' among the non-unionised as a response to workplace grievances, with analysis of the relationship with institutional mechanisms for worker participation. The second half focuses on the CAB as an increasingly important form of individual worker representation for the non-unionised. This summarises key findings from a qualitative study of the types of problems which prompted workers to seek help with the CAB, the process of attempted resolution and views on both the CAB and trade unions as forms of representation.

Part 1: The Unrepresented Worker Survey

The URWS was a regionally representative telephone survey of 501 workers who had experienced any of ten problems within the previous three years, who were not represented by a union and whose hourly pay was below the median at the time of their problems (for research methods, see Pollert and Charlwood, 2008: 71).

The sample of low paid workers without union representation with problems showed a sectoral spread similar to the low paid and non-unionised in the wider labour force (82 per cent were in the private sector, 18 per cent in the public sector, Pollert and Charlwood 2008: 80). However, women were 61 per cent of the sample (their over-representation partly reflecting women's preponderance among the low paid in the labour force as well as other surveys of lower paid workers with problems at work [Russell and Eyers, 2002: 1]), as were minority ethnic workers (8.8 per cent), those in small workplaces with fewer than 25 workers (42 per cent), and those with less than one year's service (48 per cent – arguably reflecting the insecurity created by the UK's one year qualifying period for coverage by statutory unfair dismissal rights). The majority (58 per cent) had never belonged to a union 34 per cent had been members at some time and 6 per cent were union members but without union recognition at work.

Types of Problems, Existence of Consultation Procedures and Responses

The survey explored both problems experienced and what workers did about them. Ten areas were examined: pay, job security, job opportunities, discrimination, taking time off, working hours, workload, health and safety, job description/contract and work relations in terms of stress and bullying. Key findings were that *pay* problems were the most frequent (dominated either by a concern that pay was less than what others in the same type of job earned, or being incorrectly paid), followed by *work relations* (chiefly stress or a sense of management 'taking advantage or bullying'), *workload, working hours, job security, contracts* and other problems (Table 1).

Did the existence of any type of worker representation system make any difference to the occurrence of problems? An average 60 per cent of all respondents had an employee representation/management consultation forum, 73 per cent in workplaces of over 500 employees, but only 54 per cent in workplaces with below 25 workers and 67 per cent in the public sector compared with 56 per cent in the private sector. An average 62 per cent also reported that their workplace had a disciplinary procedure[2]. We found that workers who reported regular meetings with management at their workplace were less likely to report problems with pay, job security, discrimination, taking time off or working hours (Table 1). We do not know how, if at all, these mechanisms were used, but their presence appears significant.

---

2 For the presence of consultation procedures, the URWS asked respondents: 'In the workplace where you had the problems, could/can staff or their representatives meet regularly with management to discuss workplace issues?' For disciplinary procedures it asked, 'In the workplace where you were/are having problems, if a problem came up between you and your employer, are there set rules for how they should be dealt with? (Prompt if necessary: for example, the making of a written statement or warning, or a formal meeting). Although the question on 'employee representation' in the URWS was not identical to that in the 2004 Workplace Employment Relations Survey (WERS), the findings suggest a similar pattern. WERS 2004 found that 40 per cent of employees in workplaces of 10-24 employees had an arrangement compared with 92 per cent of those in workplaces with above 500 workers, and 61 per cent in the private sector compared with 98 per cent in the public (Kersley et al. 2006: 133).

Table 1: All Problems and Comparison of Percentage of Respondents with each Problem in Workplaces with and without Information and Consultation Procedures

	All problems in 1 Job (average)	*Regular meetings to discuss workplace issues*	*No regular meetings to discuss workplace issues*
Pay related problem	36.1	32.8	42.5**
Job security problem	24.8	20.7	31.2***
Opportunities problem	20.4	19.4	23.1
Discrimination problem	15.2	11.4	19.4**
Problem with taking time off	21.8	17.7	27.4**
Problem with working hours	25.3	20.1	35.0***
Workload problems	28.5	27.4	31.2
Health and safety problem	21.8	19.4	26.9
Contract/ job description problem	22.8	20.7	26.9
Work relations problem	34.3	33.1	37.6

** statistically significant at the 10% level or better*
*** statistically significant at the 5% level or better*
**** statistically significant at the 1% level or better*
Results rounded to one decimal place

The most striking finding of the URWS was that the main response to problems was to exercise individual voice: 86 per cent took action to resolve their problems, leaving only a minority (14 per cent) doing nothing. The majority tried to resolve matters informally with management, 69 per cent with immediate managers and 47 per cent with senior managers. However, just 12 per cent used the formal complaints procedure. Few resorted to external organisations, such as trade unions and the CAB and just 2 per cent made an Employment Tribunal application (Table 2). A surprising finding, to be further explored below, is the 24 per cent who took group action.

Clearly, in a labour market in which fear of job loss is pervasive, workers try to resolve problems and keep their job. Indeed, the URWS found that the majority of respondents (58 per cent) were still in the job with the problems when interviewed and among the 42 per cent who had left, the same high percentage had taken action to try resolve their problems. Further, most workers attempted several actions – with an average of 2.2 actions.

Table 2: What actions did respondents take?

	All Actions	
Type of Action	*Percentage of respondents (base: whole sample)*	*Percentage of those who took action (base: all who took action)*
Informal approach to line manager	69.3	80.8
Informal approach to senior manager	42.7	49.9
Joined together with other workers	24.2	28.2
Used formal complaints procedure	11.6	13.5
Went to Citizen's Advice Bureau	9.2	10.7
Sought help from friends or family	8.0	9.3
Sought help from a trade union	6.0	7.0
Approach to co-workers responsible for the problem	5.2	6.1
Began Employment Tribunal Proceedings	2.4	2.8

Results rounded to one decimal place.

Informal Collective Action: Joining with other workers.

Given debates about the individualisation of UK employment relations (Brown et al., 1998, 2000), a question relevant to the future of worker participation is the extent to which individual 'voice' becomes collective. The URWS questionnaire ensured that 'collective action' was not confined to simply discussing problems. It asked about 'Joining with others in your workplace who share your concerns to get together as a group to pursue your claims'. Over a quarter (28 per cent) of those who took action reported taking informal collective action.

Collective action was significantly more likely among workers in the Transport, Storage and Communication industries and in Health and Social Work. The more problems a respondent had experienced, the more likely they were to have taken informal collective action. Mobilisation theory (Kelly, 1998) points to the importance of group identities in determining whether or not they will act collectively when they experience a problem or grievance. For example, working in a team might predispose to forming group identity and taking informal collective action. Teamwork did predict taking informal collective action. Interestingly, lower paid respondents were more likely to take informal collective action than the highest earning quartile in our sample. Part-time workers and respondents on temporary and fixed term contracts were less likely to take informal collective action, possibly reflecting the effects on group communication and solidarity of fragmentation of working-time, as well as insecurity. However, when respondents were asked about the main action taken, group action was reported to have this importance by only 8 per cent of actors, which indicates it was attempted by many but pursued by only a third of these.

The URWS explored the area of collective identity further. As Kelly points out, 'the absence of collective organisation in a particular workplace in and of itself tells us nothing about the degree of collective interest definition amongst the workforce' (1998: 26). The survey, in addition to investigating concrete responses to problems, later investigated whether individuals felt their own grievances were shared by others – an enquiry into collective consciousness. It then proceeded to ask who among 'collective identifiers' attempted informal group action and what forms it took.

Collective identity was high: 75 per cent of the sample felt that their problems were shared by others in their workplace and 75 per cent of these answered positively when asked 'Did you discuss these issues or concerns with these other people or did you do anything together to try to resolve them?' Thus, 55.8 per cent of the sample had taken some form of collective action when asked in this form – over twice the first result of 24 per cent when asked about group action the first time. As a methodological observation, this shows how subtle differences in timing and form of questions can influence responses.

By far the most important action was joint discussion about what to do. It could be that in the first questioning of 'actions', workers discounted this as 'action'. In addition, almost a fifth went as a group to see their manager and 13 per cent arranged a group meeting to discuss what they could do (Table 3).

Table 3: Types of joint action.

Type of action	*Percentage of those who took collective action*
Informal discussions with other workers	78.6
Group meeting	12.9
Went as a group to managers	18.9

Joined a union as a group	2.1
Stopped work as a group	0.7
Wrote a letter of complaint as a group	2.1
Resigned or accepted redundancy as a group	1.8

While these more organised activities are minorities, such spontaneous self-organisation is considerable, considering that these workers were not unionised. However, no work stoppages or other forms of protest were recorded, indicating that while a surprisingly high percentage attempt group action, have collective identification of problems, and attempt collective solutions, leadership and further organisation to challenge power relations is lacking.

Outcome to All Actions

The URWS demonstrated that, in spite of the high level of problem-solving activity by workers, 47 per cent of those who tried to solve their difficulties had *no conclusion with their employer*. Thus, for nearly half, 'voice' was unheeded by management. Of the 38 per cent with an outcome (12 per cent had ongoing negotiations at the time of the survey), only half were satisfied, with a quarter neutral and a quarter dissatisfied. This left only 19 per cent of those who took action and 16 per cent of the sample with a satisfactory outcome to individual problem resolution.

A series of regression analyses were used to investigate first, the relationship between *any conclusion* and type of problem, type of action and individual, job and workplace characteristics and second, between *satisfactory resolution* and type of problem, type of action and individual, job and workplace characteristics. Pay problems and problems concerning work relations were more likely to reach a conclusion and a satisfactory resolution than other problems, but problems that respondents perceived to be violations of their employment rights were *less* likely to be satisfactorily resolved. This suggests that more severe problems are even less likely than average to reach a conclusion. Taking informal collective action was more likely than other responses to result in a conclusion to the problem, but not in a satisfactory resolution. Qualitative research is needed to probe this interesting result, but it does suggest that group action is more likely to trigger a response than individual action, which can be ignored, but without further organisation and deployment of power, is no more likely to achieve a satisfactory response for workers than individual actions. Clerical and administrative occupations were less likely to get satisfactory resolutions. Union status and former union experience had no impact on a respondent's probability of getting a satisfactory resolution, although former union members were more likely to report a conclusion.

Interestingly, when workplaces had mechanisms for regular consultation and communication between employees and management, problems were more likely to reach a conclusion, and to be resolved satisfactorily. However, respondents who had a formal grievance procedure were not significantly more likely to get a conclusion or a satisfactory resolution than those who worked in a workplace without such a procedure (Table 4).

Table 4: Outcomes by the presence of workplace grievance procedures and consultation

	Consultation Procedure		*Grievance Procedure*	
	% Yes	*% No*	*% Yes*	*% No*
Respondents who took action (base 429)				
No outcome	59	67.3*	63.2	60.6
Any outcome	41	32.7*	36.8	39.4
Respondents who took action (base 429)				
No outcome/unsatisfactory outcome	77.3	88***	80.7	82.5
Satisfactory outcome	22.7	12***	19.3	17.5
Respondents with an outcome (base 162)				
Unsatisfactory outcome	43.1	62.8**	46.4	54.1
Satisfactory outcome	56.9	37.3**	53.6	45.9

* *statistically significant at the 10 per cent level*
** *statistically significant at the 5 per cent level*
*** *statistically significant at the 1 per cent level*

While the URWS showed that 'voice' and 'exit' are not alternatives, since the same percentage (86 per cent) of those who had left their 'problem' job (42 per cent of the sample) as of those who remained had taken action, it does show that *successful* voice – that is, action with a positive outcome – is associated with lower quit rates. Respondents who had not quit were almost twice as likely as those who had quit to have had a satisfactory resolution to their problems (20 per cent compared with 12 per cent) – a difference that was statistically significant at the one per cent level. Put another way, 29 per cent of those who had achieved a satisfactory resolution had quit, compared to 44 per cent of those who had not reached a satisfactory resolution. This result was robust to the addition of controls for individual, job and workplace characteristics, as well as variables for the type of problem and the type of action taken. Therefore we can say with a degree of confidence that effective voice that results in workers resolving problems to their own satisfaction results in lower quit rates. It is noticeable that the majority of our respondents seem to lack such effective voice – a finding which suggests the government's assumptions of healthy industrial relations means unchallenged managerial power.

Attitudes to trade unions

A further issue pertinent to the future of worker participation in and influence on the workplace is views among the non-unionised on unions.[3]

A first line of enquiry was why over half the sample had never joined a union. The URWS sample comprised 58 per cent never having been union members, and 34 per cent who had been members at some time. This is comparable to the 48 per cent of British workers who had never been trade union members in 2001, and the 20-25 per cent who had previously been union members across the period 1983-2001 (Bryson and Gomez 2005). Ethnic minority workers, workers aged below 40 years old, those employed in small workplaces and in the private sector in the URWS were more likely to have never been union members.

'Never members' were asked why they had never joined a union (Table 5).

Most reported that their workplace had not had a union and/or they did not feel they needed one. Interestingly, no respondents cited 'preferring to talk to management themselves' or 'preferring to use other channels of communication' as reasons for not being union members, which recalls Gospel and Willman's (2003: 158) observation of a general preference among the non-unionised for collective representation on most issues (even though this tendency is lower than among the unionised).

Table 5: Reasons for never having joined a trade union.

	Percentage of never members
Never worked in a union workplace	33.6
Union membership might cause trouble with employer	1.4
Never 'felt the need'	27.1

3 This topic was raised after respondents were asked whether they would take the same actions again to solve their problem if they were in the same position again. Over half (56 per cent) said that they would, but 39 per cent said they would not, with a further 5 per cent not knowing.

'I don't know much about unions'	13.7
'Unions are too weak to make a difference'	2.1
Don't like the workplace union	1.4
Unions too pro-management interests	0.3
Unions too militant	1.0

Base: 292. Multiple responses were possible, column total does not sum to 100 per cent because not all respondents answered the question

A second interesting issue is why former members left union membership. Existing evidence suggests that the main reason is that they left union jobs for jobs where unions were not recognised (Charlwood, 2005). The URWS offers a broader choice of reasons for leaving membership (Table 6).

Table 6: Reasons for having left union membership

Reasons.	*Percentage of former members.*
Present employer does not recognize unions	24.2
Joining a union may cause trouble with employer	3.4
Trade unions are too weak	0.7
The union I was a member of did little or nothing to help me	4.7
I don't need a union in my present job	10.7
Not currently employed	5.4
Too expensive/ poor value	3.4
No one has encouraged me to join	2.7

Base: 149, multiple responses were possible, column total does not sum to 100 percent because not all respondents answered the question

Lack of union presence/recognition in the workplace or leaving employment were the major reasons for leaving union membership, corroborating the findings of Charlwood (2005), although a significant proportion of respondents felt that they did not need a union in the job they had at the time they experienced a problem, or felt that there was no point in union membership because unions had done little to help them in the past or that union membership was too expensive or poor value for money.

What were the general attitudes of respondents towards trade unions? Previous research (e.g. Charlwood 2002, Kochan 1979) found that general attitudes towards unions and specific beliefs about union efficacy are both predictors of willingness to join a union. The URWS asked a number of questions about general attitudes towards unions (Table 7).

Table 7: General attitudes towards trade unions, percent.

	Disagree strongly	*Disagree*	*Neither*	*Agree*	*Agree strongly*	*Mean*	*n*
1. Unions make a real difference to workers	4.0	13.7	9.2	51.4	21.8	3.73	469
2. Unions are too weak to make a difference to workers at work	18.4	42.8	10.7	18.2	9.9	2.58	467
3. If I have problem at work, I prefer dealing with management myself than have a union represent me	6.8	16.6	8.1	43.9	24.5	3.63	469
4. I don't like unions in general	23.6	51.6	9.53	10.5	4.7	2.21	465
5. Unions are concerned with employers interests rather than workers	22.3	49.4	8.9	14.3	5.2	2.31	462
6. Unions tend to be militant	12.6	47.4	8.9	14.3	5.2	2.31	562
7. I don't like the existing union(s) at my workplaces	12.8	39.7	25	13.7	8.8	2.66	204

Factor analysis reveals that respondents are narrowly pro-union[4]. Looking at the responses to individual items of the scale, respondents generally agree that unions make a difference to workers, do not agree that unions are too weak or that unions are too concerned with employers' interests or that they tend to be militant. However, respondents generally preferred to deal with management themselves if they had a problem at work. Thus, while being generally well disposed towards unions, a significant proportion of respondents did not see them as being particularly relevant to the circumstances of their problem. Yet when asked whether they thought that a union would have helped them with their problem, 52.5 per cent thought so, 37.2 percent thought not, with 10.3 per cent being undecided. There are thus contradictions in consciousness.

4 This is based on the finding that the first six statements are correlated with an underlying union attitudes latent variable (with an eigenvalue of 1.247), so can be combined into a single scale (with a scale reliability coefficient of 0.63). The mean of this scale is 2.57, indicating that, on average respondents are narrowly pro-union in their general attitudes).

There was a predictable relationship between general and specific views: respondents were more likely to think a union could have helped solve their problem if they had broadly positive attitudes towards unions. A series of regression analyses were used to investigate the relationship between beliefs about union efficacy and the nature of the problem, individual, and workplace characteristics. Interestingly, if respondents felt that their problem was a violation of their rights they were more likely to believe a union would have helped. However, it is not possible to identify whether this is because experiencing a rights violation makes people more likely to think that a union could help with their problem, or that those who are more likely to perceive union efficacy are also are more likely to perceive that their rights have been violated.

Respondents were less likely to perceive union efficacy if their problem related to workload, if they were aged over 40 and if they worked in Public Administration. In terms of age, an important finding is that *younger workers* – noted for their higher level of *never-membership* – were more likely than older ones to believe being a union member would have helped them. This finding is in line with the work of Gomez, Gunderson and Meltz (2001) and Charlwood (2002), who found that younger workers in Canada and Britain respectively were more likely to desire unionisation despite lower levels of union membership.

There have been several studies of desire for unionisation among non-union workers in Britain. Charlwood (2002, 2003) found that between 40 and 50 per cent of non-union workers would join a union if one were available to them. The URWS also examined desire for unionisation in the context of experiencing problems. Specifically, it asked if the respondents' experience of a problem made them want to join a union. While 6 per cent were unsure, 40 percent of respondents said that they would like to join a union, a figure in line with the results reported by Charlwood (2002, 2003) for the workforce as a whole. The literature on desire for unionisation among unorganised workers highlights the difference between *general* or *abstract* positive views, from a concrete decision to join a union (Bryson, 2003: 5). The URWS confirms that fewer workers actually said that they wanted to join than stated that a union would have helped. There is, nevertheless, a large overlap.

Again, a series of regression analyses were used to investigate the relationship between willingness to unionise and the nature of the problem, individual, job and workplace characteristics. Respondents were more likely to want to unionise if they had formerly been a union member, believed that a union would have helped them to deal with their problem and had generally positive attitudes towards unions. Again, those who felt that their problem represented a breach of their rights were also more likely to be willing to unionise: 48 per cent of those who thought so would join a union compared with 30 per cent of those who did not. Once again, we are not able to identify the direction of causality between these two variables. Respondents were less likely to want to unionise if their problem related to pay or if they worked in a predominantly female workplace.

Belief in whether a union might help a problem and willingness to join one might also be related to the existence of voice mechanisms at the workplace. We found that significantly fewer respondents among those with some form of consultation procedure felt that a union would have helped them with their problem than among those who did not have one. Similarly, significantly fewer workers said they would join a union as a result of their problems if they had a consultation procedure than if they did not have one (Table 8).

Table 8: Impact of workplace consultation procedures on attitudes towards unions

	Perceived union efficacy		
	No %	Yes %	Row Total
Workplace without consultation	30.9	69.1	100
Workplace with consultation	48.0	52.0	100
N	404	Pearson Chi Squared statistic	11.406***
		Wants to join union	
Workplace without consultation	46.5	53.5	100
Workplace with consultation	63.3	36.7	100
N	424	Pearson Chi Squared statistic	11.398***

**** = statistically significant at the 0.01 per cent level or better*
Results rounded to one decimal place

Without further detail about the nature of such consultative mechanisms, interpretation is tentative, but the evidence suggests that the existence of some form of voice avenues in the workplace reduces the perception of union efficacy and desire for union membership. Previous research has also found that those in workplaces with only works councils as voice mechanisms are unlikely to think a union would make them better off. Although the BWRS asked attitudinal questions without the context of concrete problems examined in the URWS, it found that 40 per cent of workers who only had works councils thought they would be 'better off' with just a works council, but only 2 per cent thought they would be better off with only a union, and only 24 per cent thought they would be better off with both a works council and a union. Non-unionised workers were equally likely to think a works council on its own or a works council and a union would improve their workplace (Gospel and Willman, 2003: 159).

Interestingly, the existence of grievance procedures was also significantly associated with a lower incidence of belief in union efficacy, although not with a desire to join a union (Table 9). This suggests that grievance procedures also provide some form of voice which reduces desire for collective union voice for solving grievances, but not a desire for general collective voice in terms of joining a union.

Table 9: Impact of workplace grievance procedures on attitudes towards unions

	Perceived union efficacy		
	No %	Yes %	Row Total
Workplace without grievance procedure	30.6	69.4	100
Workplace with grievance procedure	47.0	53.0	100
N	397	Pearson Chi Squared statistic	10.299***
	Wants to join union		
Workplace without grievance procedure	54.7	45.3	100
Workplace with grievance procedure	59.1	40.9	100
N	419	Pearson Chi Squared statistic	0.777

**** = statistically significant at the 0.01 per cent level or better*
Results rounded to one decimal place

A further line of enquiry is why 54 per cent of workers did *not* want to unionise. Broadly, just under a fifth gave no reason, one fifth cited a reason suggesting they felt their grievance was outside the scope of union help and under one sixth suggested outright hostility to trade unions, with the remainder of respondents citing a variety of different reasons.

These views on unions had little predictive power in terms of what respondents did about their problems: just 7 per cent of those who took action reported that they had sought help from a union to try to solve their problem (Table 2). This finding is explicable in terms of the likelihood that most respondents lacked knowledge about unions at the time they experienced the problem, while the URWS made them think about unions as a potential solution to their problems. Indeed, the union-related questions could be defined as 'consciousness-raising'

A further finding was that there was no relationship between taking informal collective action and positive attitudes towards trade unions. This suggests that grass-roots workplaces collectivism is not connected with awareness of or positive attitudes towards trade unions – a difference which underlines the 2001 BWRS finding of a preference among the non-unionised for fellow workers to unions for collective representation (Gospel and Willman, 2003: 158).

While the URWS provides important statistical findings on 'voice' among the low paid non-unionised with problems at work, it cannot convey the texture of experience. The following offers an insight among a particular sample of workers who sought external help for their problems with the CAB.

Part 2: The unorganised worker and the CAB

The work of the CAB

Citizens Advice is a generalist, volunteer-led service providing free advice on a range of issues, including employment problems, across England, Wales and Northern Ireland.[5] However, the majority of CAB do not have advisers with more than a general knowledge of employment rights (Citizens Advice 2007). In 2006/2007 144 out of 433 bureaux had an adviser with specific knowledge of employment law (paid and/or voluntary) – just 33 per cent. The general approach of the CAB – a 'new industrial relations actor' in the context of union decline – is to 'empower' clients by providing information, help in writing letters and referring them to experts (Abbott, 1998).

As a charity, the CAB has always been under-resourced (Citron 1989, Richard 1989, Pollert 2005, 2007a: 124, Genn 1999: 76, 89). In recent research for the TUC Commission on Vulnerable Employment (CoVE), 70 per cent of CAB advisers felt they had too few or far to few advisers, around two thirds had experienced financial cuts in real terms in the previous three years and for 81 per cent, time spent on fund-raising had increased or greatly increased over the same period (Pollert et al. 2008: 39-51). Despite government declaration of support for 'vulnerable' workers, its funding to Citizens Advice headquarters – the provider of legal information and training to bureaux – was cut by 10 per cent in 2006/07, forcing a £4 million (20 per cent) savings programme to reduce annual expenditure. Citizens Advice (2006: 4) felt this would 'inevitably have an impact on the levels of service'. Meanwhile, increasingly complex state contracts for free 'legal-aid' drove many solicitors away from free employment advice (Pollert 2005: 225, 2007a: 121) and the CAB refers most needing more specialised employment advice to 'no-win, no fee' lawyers, the system extended from personal injury to other areas of law since 1998, allegedly to extend 'access to justice' for those confident of winning their case. But while no fees are charged if a case is lost, a higher fee than 'normal' is charged if it is won (Lord Chancellor's Department, 1998: 24). Now, however, growing concerns about the quality of the conditional

5 Further details at http://www.citizensadvice.org.uk/index/aboutus/factsheets.htm.

fees arrangements have prompted the government to commission a major review of its operation (Ministry of Justice, 2008).

CAB Clients and Problems experienced

The research project contacted 30 bureau managers in three English regions in 2004-05, requesting them to distribute to clients with employment problems an invitation to participate in the project, together with a return envelope for their telephone contact details. Fifty respondents (35 women and 15 men) were interviewed, 20 from London and the South East, 17 from the Midlands and 13 from the North, with 28 of these summarised here (Appendix, Table 10). The telephone interviews were tape-recorded and interviews anonymised.

The URWS found that relatively few respondents sought external assistance – 9 per cent approached the CAB, although this rose to 15-20 per cent for problems with pay, dismissal, redundancy, discrimination and working hours (Pollert and Charlwood, 2008: 46). Nevertheless, the CAB is sought by between 48 and 32 per cent of those seeking external advice on employment problems (Genn, 1999: 91, Meager et al., 2002: 185).

Interviews with CAB clients revealed the prevalence of bullying – one of the major 'work relations' problems identified in the URWS. Additionally, respondents had been dismissed, or were being threatened with dismissal, a finding which supports the CoVE research, which found that CAB and Law Centre clients' most common problem was in dismissal, although this was followed by pay and working time (Pollert et al. 2008: 90).

The employment characteristics of the CAB clients interviewed were also similar to those reported in the CoVE research: most were low paid, non-unionised, but with full-time, permanent employment – reflecting the dominance of full-time work in the labour force (Pollert et. al. 2008: 106). Certain sectors dominated: hospitality (public houses, hotels and restaurants), care-homes, cleaning and security companies, retail, hairdressing and small factories (Citizens Advice 1997, 2000). These are also identified as frequent in ET applications and Minimum Wage regulation breaches (DTI 2006: 25). However, the clients with longer and more complex problems were concentrated in large organisations in both the public and private sectors, including multinational companies with Human Resource (HR) departments.

Problems experienced (summarised in Appendix, Table 10, details Pollert 2007b) occurred in overlapping clusters of summary dismissal, prolonged bullying and victimisation, unpaid wages, no paid holidays, sexual and racial discrimination, dismissal during sickness, unlawful contract change, dismissal during takeover and forced redundancy and resignation.

Although some began ET applications, most settled before a hearing and only two people received more than a few hundred pounds in compensation. Although half the respondents were satisfied with CAB help, this includes those who were grateful for support but lost their jobs, suffered indignity and ended with paltry or no financial settlement (Table 10). The narratives of problems were complex and expressed worker isolation, powerlessness and vulnerability to unfair treatment, while attempted individual resolution to grievances by an external agency, such as the CAB, was weak. This is partly because of the limitations in the applicability of many statutory employment rights, particularly protection from unfair dismissal, to employees (and not all workers) and to those with over a year's service. Employers could, for example, legally sack workers approaching one year's service, which applied to several of those interviewed. However, a further reason lies in the problems in enforcing legal rights, such as the Working Time Regulations and anti-discrimination law, without the expertise and experience for full, impartial investigation and cross-examination. The CAB was usually only able to obtain minimal settlement, if any, for what were usually complex grievances.

In dismissal cases, lack of proof meant that employers who often fabricated charges of misdemeanour (especially theft), could not be challenged, and hence unfairness difficult or impossible to prove. In many cases, the employer also paid below the minimum wage, but this was rarely the issue that drove the person to the CAB. Sacking workers for asking for minimal rights, which is illegal, were frequent abuses. Victimisation was often complex, but it was usually only final dismissal which was challenged as unfair by most CAB – primarily on procedural grounds, since procedural legal breaches (at the time of research, not following the statutory dismissal procedures, see e.g. Hepple and Morris, 2002) were simpler to challenge than more complex illegal practices. Thus, the poor remedies achieved were sometimes due to lack of resources and professional expertise, but fundamentally to the intrinsic weakness of external, remedial support which cannot 'shadow' a problem as it unfolds in the workplace. Such a role can best be performed with expert, professional legal representation with full (and costly) investigation and cross-examination, and/or with worker workplace representation, with enforcement backed by the threat of collective sanctions on the employer.

More protracted problems arose in small workplaces but also in large companies. Employers frequently prolonged and disguised malpractice with more subtle processes, such as changing contracts, pseudo-appraisal and untenable performance targets, forced resignation, re-engagement, intimidating meetings, falsifying records and losing employees' correspondence, including sick-notes (Pollert 2007b). Most large employers had legal representation, and in addition to manoeuvres to evade challenge, used court cost threats to intimidate both workers and their representatives (Citizens Advice, 2004). Workers in large organisations had the additional difficulty of attributing responsibility for the problem. When higher-level HR managers became involved, they initially appeared to uphold 'good practice', but ended supporting managerial subordinates. Employment agency or sub-contracted workers, as well as their representatives, were caught by agency/sub-contractors and their clients giving contradictory messages to workers and shifting responsibility for the problem between each other. In one case, an agency's end user sacked a worker (although it had no right to do so, since it was not the employer), while the agency instructed the worker to report to work. Sometimes workers suffered adverse consequences of transfer of undertakings to new contractors, by being illegally dismissed or suffering pay cuts. These complex problems were very difficult to challenge for generalist CAB advisers.

These respondents testified to the complex web of employment problems experienced, the weakness of individual voice with external help and a crisis in access to justice for the vulnerable workers (Pleasence et al. 2004: 105).

CAB clients' views on Trade Union representation

The URWS finding that 52 per cent of the sample felt that a union would have helped resolve their problems and 40 per cent would join one as a result of their experience (Pollert and Charlwood, 2008: 55) was largely reflected in the CAB interviews: 53 per cent favoured unions, or felt they would help their problem, but 47 per cent felt unions could not help. Of the latter, seven were ignorant about or indifferent towards unions, three were too frightened to contemplate joining, two were disillusioned with union behaviour and one was anti-union. As with the URWS, there was little hostility to trade unions. Of the fifteen who felt a union would help and/or would join one, most were from the Midlands or North of England, regions with stronger union traditions than the South. Many of these mentioned a family or local union tradition or previous union membership. These findings support theories of union-joining propensity being associated with job dissatisfaction or problems at work *and* ideological factors associated with locality, family and social networks (Charlwood 2003: 54, Kochan 1979,

Charlwood, 2002: 469-471). Nevertheless, four in the pro-union group came from London – not typically associated with union traditions – including two from hard-to-organise sectors. Yet many of those who favoured unions were ignorant of how they could join, and those with union traditions had never heard of legislation of the 1999 Employment Relations Act for statutory union recognition procedures. The CAB findings endorse those of the URWS that most workers leave unions, or do not join them, because there is no union presence at work, and a general sense of ignorance among the non-unionised about the existence and purpose of trade unions.

Conclusions

The URWS showed that, when faced with grievances at work, most unorganised workers attempt to resolve them. This is primarily through individual, informal representation to managers, with little use made of formal grievance procedures and low resort to help beyond the workplace. A further area highlighted by the URWS is that of the relationship between the experience of individual grievances and collective identity and mobilisation (Kelly, 1998). This advances the substantial body of literature which demonstrates that most workers join unions for support with their problems (Waddington and Whitston, 1997: 518, Bryson, 2003: 6) and develops an exploration of grass-roots collectivity which is separated from views on trade unionism. The importance of this to understanding more fully different dimensions of worker voice is suggested by the BWRP survey, which found that, despite the de-collectivisation of industrial relations, most workers preferred to deal with problems collectively, but the non-unionised preferred to be represented by fellow workers, rather than by trade unions (Gospel and Willman, 2003: 157).

The URWS found that, despite the individualisation of the employment relationship, collective labour continued to foment informal collective identity and action. These findings challenge the widespread perception that workers have become individualistic and atomised. However, they also show that when workers do attempt to organise collectively to tackle problems they face, the form of collective action is usually limited, with little evidence that workers are able to move from collective voice to develop and deploy collective strategies and power to challenge management. The evidence also suggests that in itself, informal collective action is unlikely to be a precursor to unionisation, because workers who took informal collective action were no more or less likely to want to unionise than those who did not.

The existence of some form of consultation between workers and their representatives and management was low within the sample – a finding in itself about the workplace characteristics of the low paid, unorganised with problems at work. Where it did exist, there was a positive association with lower incidence of problems with pay, job security, discrimination, taking time off and working hours, although not with the major problems of stress and bullying. Further research is needed into the types and operations of these consultative arrangements among the unorganised and the reasons for such a relationship with problems. The URWS also found a positive relationship between consultation bodies and there being outcomes to problems, as well as satisfactory resolution and a negative association with belief in union efficacy and desire for unionisation.

Despite workers' efforts to resolve grievances within the workplace, resolution is very poor: almost half of those who took action had no conclusion at all. While only 16 per cent of the sample had a satisfactory resolution, it is notable that those who had left their job were half as likely to have had a satisfactory outcome as those who remained in it. Thus, although the findings prompt a recasting of the theory of 'voice' and 'exit' as alternative forms of response to grievances (Hirschman, 1970), successful voice is associated with lower likelihood of exit. Collective action was more likely to result in conclusions, but not in satisfactory ones – an intriguing finding which may suggest that group voice elicits management response, but not necessarily in workers' favour.

The URWS showed that only a minority of unorganised workers with workplace grievances approach a CAB, and these tend to be those with more extreme problems, particularly in pay, dismissal, redundancy, discrimination and working hours. The study of workers who used the CAB found that resolution to problems was poor. This was partly due to limitations in employment rights which left some workers outside legal protection, but also due to the under-resourcing and lack of expertise of CAB advisers. Some CAB support did provide redress and greater resources and professional expertise would go a long way to improve the service. However, worker representation supported by collective mobilisation would go further in raising employment standards and preventing abuse than individual external representation on its own. Indeed, recent debates about union renewal have pointed to the need to organise beyond the workplace and gain the participation of 'communities'. UK initiatives such as 'London Citizens', 'Living Wage Campaign' have proved that these can be successful (London Citizens website).

Both studies showed positive attitudes towards unions and half of the URWS and the CAB sample felt a union could have helped them. However, only 6 per cent of the URWS sample actually approached a union for help, while most of the CAB sample had little idea of how to approach a union. If more unorganised workers were to approach unions, unions need to renew their strategies to include and organise the unorganised, as some unions are now attempting, although this will tax both the resources and traditional cultures of the UK trade union movement (Bryson and Willman, 2006, Colling, 2006). If unions are to be able to help this type of worker, they have much to do in terms of raising awareness so that more workers approach them for help.

References

Abbott, B. (1998): 'The emergence of a new industrial relations actor – the role of the Citizens' Advice Bureaux?' Industrial Relations Journal, 29 (4): 257-269).

Acas (2004): Annual Report and Resource Accounts, 2003/04, London: Advisory, Conciliation and Arbitration Services.

Brown, W. / Deakin, S. / Hudson, M. / Pratten, C. / Ryan, P. (1998): 'The Individualisation of Employment Contracts in Britain', DTI Employment Relations Research Series, No. 4, London: Department of Trade and Industry.

Brown, W. / Deakin, S. / Nash, D. / Oxenbridge, S. (2000): 'The Employment Contract: From Collective Procedures to Individual Rights', British Journal of Industrial Relation, 38 (4) 611-629.

Brown, W. / Nash, D. (2008): 'What has been happening to collective bargaining under New Labour? Interpreting WERS 2004.' Industrial Relations Journal, 39: 91–103.

Bryson, A. (2003): Employee Desire for Unionisation in Britain and Its Implications for Union Organising, PSI Research Discussion Paper 12, London: Policy Studies Institute.

Bryson, A. / Gomez, R. (2005): 'Why Have Workers Stopped Joining Unions?: Accounting for the Rise in Never-Membership in Britain', British Journal of Industrial Relations, 43:1, 67-92.

Bryson, A. / Willman, P. (2006): Accounting for collective action: resource acquisition and mobilisation in British Unions, Centre for Economic Performance Discussion Paper 798, London: Centre for Economic Performance.

Casebourne, J. / Regan, J. / Neathey, F. / Tuohy, S. (Institute of Employment Studies) (2006): Employment Rights at Work – Survey of Employees 2005, DTI Employment Relations Research Series No. 51, London: Department of Trade and Industry.

Charlwood, A. (2002): 'Why Do Non-Union Employees Want to Unionize?' British Journal of Industrial Relations 40(3): 463-92.

Charlwood, A. (2003): 'Willingness to Unionize Amongst Non-Union Workers' in Howard Gospel and Stephen Wood (eds.) Representing Workers: Trade Union Membership and Recognition in Britain, London: Routledge, pp. 51-71.

Charlwood, A. (2005): The Anatomy of Union Membership Decline in Great Britain 1980-1998, Unpublished PhD thesis, University of London.
Citizens Advice (1997): Flexibility abused. A CAB evidence report on employment conditions and the labour market, London: Citizens' Advice.
Citizens Advice (2000): Wish you were here. A CAB evidence report on the paid holiday provisions of the Working Time Regulations 1998, London: Citizens' Advice.
Citizens Advice (2004): 'Employment Tribunals: the intimidatory use of costs threats by employers' legal representatives', March CAB Evidence, London: Citizens Advice Bureau.
Citizens Advice (2006): Citizens Advice Annual Report, 2005/2006, London: Citizens Advice.
Citizens Advice (2007): 2006/07 Citizens Advice Bureau Information Survey London: Citizens Advice.
Citron, J. (1989): The Citizens Advice Bureaux, for the Community, by the Community (London: Pluto Press).
Colling, T. (2006): 'What Space for Union on the Floor of Rights? Trade Unions and the Enforcement of Statutory Individual Employment Rights', Industrial Law Journal, 34 (2), 140-160.
DTI (2006): Success at Work: Protecting Vulnerable Workers, Supporting Good Employers. A policy statement for this Parliament, March, London: Department of Trade and Industry.
Genn, H. (1999): Paths to Justice: what people do and think about going to the law, Oxford and Portland, Oregon: Hart Publishing.
Gomez, R. / Gunderson, M. / Meltz, N. (2001): From Play Stations to Workstations: Youth Preferences for Unionisation in Canada, Centre for Economic Performance Discussion Paper 512, London: Centre for Economic Performance.
Gospel, H. / Willman, P. (2003): 'Dilemmas in worker representation' in H. Gospel and S. Wood (eds.), Representing Workers: the Future of Trade Unions in Britain', London: Routledge.
Mercer, S. / Notley, R. (2008): Trade Union Membership 2007, London: Department of Trade and Industry, Office for National Statistics.
Hepple, B. / Morris, G. (2002): 'The Employment Act 2002 and the Crisis of Individual Employment Rights', Industrial Law Journal, 31: 245-269.
Hirschman, A. (1970): Exit, Voice and Loyalty: Responses to Decline in Firms, Organisations and States. Cambridge: Harvard University Press.
Kelly, J. (1998): Rethinking Industrial Relations: Mobilization, Collectivism and Long Waves, London: Routledge.

Kersley, B. / Alpin, C. / Forth, J. / Bryson, A. / Bewley, H. / Dix, G. / Oxenbridge, S. (2006): Inside the Workplace: Findings from the 2004 Workplace Employment Relations Survey, DTI, ESRC, Acas, PSI, London: Routledge.

Kochan, T.A. (1979): 'How American workers view labor unions', Monthly Labor Review, 104 (4): 23-31.

Labour Market Trends (2006): Public and private sector employment, Table S29, December 2006, Labour Market Trends, Office for National Statistics.

London Citizens website http://www.londoncitizens.org.uk/campaigns.html.

Lord Chancellor's Department (1998): White Paper, Modernising Justice: the Government's plans for reforming legal services and the courts, Cm 4155 www.open.gov.uk/lcd.

Meager, N. / Tyers, C. / Perryman, S. / Rick, J. / Willison, R. (2002): Awareness, knowledge and exercise of individual employment rights' Employment Relations Research Series, No. 15, London: Department of Trade and Industry.

Milner, S. (1995): 'The Coverage of Collective Pay-setting Institutions in Britain' British Journal of Industrial Relations, 33 (1) 69-92.

Ministry of Justice (2008): No win, no fee under scrutiny 25 June 2008 http://www.justice.gov.uk/news/newsrelease250608a.htm.

Pleasence, P. / Buck, A. / Balmer, N. / O'Grady, A. / Genn, H. / Smith, M. (2004): Causes of Action: Civil Law and Social Justice, Legal Services Commission, London: TSO.

Pollert, A. (2005): 'The Unorganised Worker: The Decline in Collectivism and New Hurdles to Individual Employment Rights', Industrial Law Journal, 34 (3) 217-237.

Pollert, A. (2007a): 'Individual Employment Rights: 'Paper Tigers, fierce in appearance but missing in Tooth and Claw'', Vol. 28: 1 February 2007 Economic and Industrial Democracy, 110-139.

Pollert, A. (2007b): The Unorganised Vulnerable Worker: the Weakness of External Remedy and the Case for Union Organising, Liverpool: Institute for Employment Rights.

Pollert, A. / Charlwood, A. (2008): The Unrepresented Worker Survey 2004: Who experiences problems at work, what problems do they experience, what do they do about them and what happens as a result? The Unorganized Worker: Problems at Work, Routes to Support and Views on Representation, Working Paper 11, University of the West of England, Bristol Business School, Centre for Employment Studies Research, http://www.uwe.ac.uk/bbs/research/cesr/esrc/WP11.pdf

Pollert, A. / Danford, A. / Tailby, S. / Wilton, N. / Warren, S. (2008): Survey of Employment Rights Advisers from Citizens Advice Bureaux and Law Centres, TUC, Commission on Vulnerable Employment, London: Trades Union Congress.

Pollert, A. / Li, Y. (2006): The Unorganised Employee in WERS 2004: Socio-demographic attributes, workplace characteristics and job experience unpublished draft, Employment Relations Research Series, London: Department of Business, Enterprise and Regulatory Reform.
Richard, J. (1989): 50 Years of the CAB, (London: Citizens Advice Bureaux).
Russell, C. / Eyers, D. (2002): Clutching at Straws, Rights at Work, Briefing Paper No. 53, West Midlands Employment and Low Pay Unit.
Waddington, J. / Whitston, C. (1997): 'Why do People Join Unions in a Period of Membership Decline?', British Journal of Industrial Relations, 35 (4) 515-547).

Appendix

Table 10: Summary of Experiences and Views of 28 Low paid, Unorganized Workers who sought help with CAB, 2004-2005.

	Pseudonym	Age	Region and/or town and date	Workplace or Occupation	Type of Problem
1	Tina	18	November 2004, Norfolk	Hairdresser	Wrongful dismissal
2	Christine	20s	November 2004, Norfolk	Holiday camp	Pregnancy dismissal
3	Marge	53	December 2004, Greater London	Labour club	Automatic unfair dismissal (procedural grounds).
4	Becky	20s	May 2004, Stoke on Trent, 3Midlands	Shop	Pregnancy dismissal
5	Tony	24	December 2004, the North East	Animal shelter charity	Unfair dismissal and bullying
6	Iqbal	31	November 2004, Wolverhampton, West Midlands	Garment factory	Dismissal after asking for paid holidays
7	Bill	30	November 2004, Scarborough the North East.	Small firm (lorry driver)	Unfair dismissal for asking for rights
8	Jacque	20s	November 2003, in Dudley, the Midlands	Security company	Unpaid wages
9	Graham	20s	May 2005 London	Security company	Unpaid wages
10	Tom	28	October 2004, Staffordshire, the Midlands	Building company	Unfair dismissal or redundancy (no warning)
11	Sheila	40s	December 2004, the Midlands	Pub, general worker	Dismissal, no reason
12	Jane	40s	December, 2004, the Midlands	Pub barmaid	Dismissal, no reason
13	Pat	25	December 2004, Leeds, the North	Pub Training manager	Harassment, potential constructive dismissal
14	Penny	33	December 2004, Worcestershire, the Midlands	Motorway service station, Fast-Food Team Leader	Harassment, potential constructive dismissal
15	Alpay	40w	December, 2004, Newcastle, the North.	Large hotel chain	Racial discrimination
16	Lawrence	40s	December 2003, London	Hotel restaurant	Racial discrimination
17	Jasmine	34	May 2005, London	Large hairdressing chain	Bullying while ill, potential constructive dismissal
18	Chitra	56	December, 2004, London	Multinational recruitment company	Bullying, unfair dismissal, multiple discrimination?
19	Moira (not in narrative, unionized)	40s	December, 2004, London	Major Airline	Harassment and victimization
20	Jane	59	December, 2004, London.,	University	Potential constructive dismissal

Table 10: Summary of Experiences and Views of 28 Low paid, Unorganized Workers who sought help with CAB, 2004-2005 – Fortsetzung.

Resolution to Problem	CAB Access	Opinion of CAB	View of Unions	Wider Views and Civic Engagement
Settlement: unpaid wages and holiday pay	Good (already sacked)	Very good	Ignorant (I)	Interested in knowing about rights (E)
Settlement: £200 (hoped for £500-£1,000).	Good	Good but stressed	Not discussed (I)	No views, depression (O)
Unknown	Good (already sacked)	Good	Agreed with unions; felt did not apply to cleaners (Y)	Disillusioned with Labour Party (D)
Settlement unpaid wages and holiday pay	Difficult	Good	Might join if knew of one (Y)	Isolated – only friends and family. Angry (O)
Constructive dismissal case not pursued.	Poor and Discon-tinuous	Poor	Very keen but ignorant (Y)	Wanted employer inves-tigated (E)
Settlement: £350	Difficult	Poor	Frightened in small firm (F)	No discussion (O)
ET ruled in favour, £1000 with friend in legal firm.	Difficult	Respected CAB but found service poor.	Frightened in small firm (F)	Disappointed with Acas conciliation (D)
Successful ET claim, but not enforced	Good	Good.	Ignorant (I)	Never voted. In elec-tions, isolated. (O)
None	Poor	Poor (but so was solicitor)	No views (I)	Cynical about law (D)
£700 from National Insurance funds	Good	Good, but failed to get £1000	Very keen but ignorant (Y)	Doesn't vote. Depression and anger (O)
None	Good	Good	No view (I)s	No views (O)
Settlement amount gagged	Fair	Poor	No view (I)	No views (O)
ET application withdrawn, no settlement	Good	Poor	In favour (Y)	Did not vote, but wanted to challenge abuse. (ER)
Nothing	Fair	Poor	Sceptical for her problem (S).	No views (O)
ET application; £100 in settlement	Good	Good	Ignorant (I)	No views (O).
'Satisfactory' but would not disclose	Went to Law Centre for ET form	Had paid solicitor	In favour (Y)	No views (O)
No compensation	Difficult	Fair, but found Acas advice most helpful	Joined GMB after problem in new salon job (Y)	No views (O)
No outcome after more than a year	Good	Poor, changed to soli-citor (not confident)	Frightened (F)	No views, depression (O)
Union compromise	n.a	n.a.	Member (Y)	Sense of injustice (E)
Redundancy package	Fair	Very poor	Sceptical. (S))	Sceptical about unions and politics (D)

Union organisation of employees in atypical and precarious work in Italy

Salvo Leonardi

1. At present trade unionism is everywhere challenged by the deep transformations that over the past decades have seriously undermined the material and cultural basis of that world of labour on which it had traditionally drawn its social and political force.

In the last twenty-five years trade unions have been suffering a wide and consistent reduction of their social representativeness. Practically all the principal organisations appear to be in serious difficulty in intercepting the new typologies of employment relationships; in interpreting their new identity profiles; the expectations for representation and voice that emerge at both an individual and collective level.

An important indicator measuring the actual strength of trade unions, even though not the only one, is usually represented by membership, gauged by the level of unionisation within the active labour force. National union density rates, as recorded in the last two decades by international statistics and comparative studies, have spared no model whatsoever, impacting unions with highly diverse backgrounds in terms of history, culture, organisational model and institutional context. After having record highs at the end of the 70s, with peaks of around 40-50%, unionisation rate in Western countries have fallen constantly quite everywhere[1].

The only remarkable exception is represented by those few Nordic countries where trade unions enjoy the institutional prerogative of managing the unemployment insurance funds – the so-called "Ghent system" – in force in Belgium, Sweden, Denmark and Finland. These four countries have the world's highest union

1 It has fallen to 28% in the United Kingdom, to around 20% in the Netherlands; to 18% in Germany, 16% in Spain; to 8% in France (Eiro, 2006; Visser, 2006; Cecchi and Visser, 2005; Frege and Kelly, 2004; Boeri, Calmfors et alii, 2001; Scruggs and Lange, 2002; Ebbinghaus and Visser, 2000; Blascke, 2000; ILO, 1998). The situation is altogether critical in the new member states – with the only positive exceptions of Slovenia and Slovakia (Dimitrova et Vilrockx, 2005; Casale, 2007) – and also of South Korea, the US and of Japan, where union density rates range between 11-18%, or in Australia or New Zealand, were the decline has been very severe during the last twenty-five years. As in the case of Austria or Ireland, where the union density is still relatively higher – in both cases around 35% – but with a serious fall if compared with the early 80s, when it was more than 20 points higher.

density[2] and are the only ones in the world of industrialised democracies to have resisted declining unionisation.

Italy maintains a comparatively medium-high rate of unionisation, estimated at around 33% of the active subordinate workers population (Feltrin, 2005). With 12 million members, retired included (but excluding autonomous and professional unions), Italy is by far the first in Europe with regard to the overall number of trade union members. CGIL alone has around 5.600.000 members (2007), which is an all-time high, making it the third largest trade union confederation in Europe, behind the German DGB and the British TUC.

Year	CGIL	CISL	UIL	Total
1980	4.599.050	3.059.845	1.346.900	9.005.795
1990	5.150.376	3.508.391	1.148.758	10.144.525
1998	5.231.360	3.847.388	1.603.940	10.682.688
2007	5.604741	4.427.037	2.060.909	**12.092.687**

Yet notwithstanding these figures, it should be nevertheless observed that while trade unions confederations have increased overall membership:

- ⇨ they have lost, since 1980, 30% of their members among the active workers,
- ⇨ that the 33% rate of unionisation is the lowest in the past 35 years,
- ⇨ that nearly 50% of the overall membership are retired workers[3].

The decline has been probably slower and more gradual than elsewhere, showing in the last five years an encouraging counter tendency also among the active working population. A significant contribution has come from migrant workers. Their number is increasing year after year. Nowadays, unionised migrant workers amount to nearly 700,000, more or less 10% of the overall active work force affiliated to trade unions.

---

2 See Western, 1997; Scruggs, 2002; Kjellberg, Jokivuoiri, Vandaele, 2006; Leonardi, 2006; Coulet, 2008.

3 They are almost 3 million in CGIL alone. In Italy they are organised separately, but still within their confederation, from the sector unions where they were members before they retired. One of the reasons of such a peculiar capability in representing and recruiting the retired workers depends on the good performances in supplying services and stipulating social agreements with the local authorities. More than 1000 agreements have been signed at the local level only in the last year. See Carrieri M. and Leonardi S., *Il sindacalismo dei pensionati: il valore di una "anomalia"*, in CGIL-SPI, "Fare benessere", Edizioni LiberEtà, 2007.

2. The reasons for such an erosion, or decline, are global and of different kinds. In this venue, I will mention just a few:

1) the gradual shift from industrial to post-industrial employment, and the demise of those sectors union settlements had been traditionally much stronger (mines, steel, shipyards, automotives). The crisis of the most unionised sectors/branches has not been sufficiently compensated by the weak unionisation of some new expanding branches and wage-earners (private services, ICT, distribution, knowledge workers). Also the pubic sector – which in the last decades had partially compensated the loss in the traditional blue collars and manufacturing branches[4] – is now under strain due to the ongoing privatisation and outsourcing of many public services, the reduction of the welfare state, a broader reliance on precarious workers.
2) Furthermore, through subcontracting and externalisation, companies have reduced the average size of the establishments and plants, with an expansion of SMEs, where it has been traditionally more difficult for unions to assert themselves. In all the national systems, laws and/or collective agreements define a special threshold, linked to the average number of employees, below which certain workers rights or unions prerogatives are not equally applied and protected as when that threshold is crossed. The absence of a works council at the workplace implies a lack or a weakness of all these tools, with ensuing worst pay, longer working hours, dangerous health and safety conditions, less opportunities for vocational training and career.
3) The traditional juridical partition – between self-employed and dependent workers – is now being eroded by the new forms of work organisation and by the legal qualification of the jurisprudence. In this regard, the trends are of two kinds: a) the growth of atypical and substandard jobs (fixed-term, agency temporary workers, job on call, etc.), characterised by a weaker regime of rights and protections both at an individual and collective levels; b) the growth of new forms of self-employment, that which we call "semi-dependent work", *arbeitnehmerähnlichePerson,* "legally autonomous but economically dependent" (Supiot, 1999). These new self-employed workers fall outside the rights and protections granted by labour law. Today almost 50% of the EU workforce is made by this broad "grey zone" of substandard and atypical workers. New ambiguous borders now separate the "insiders"

4 Union density, in the public sector, is generally esteemed to be quite higher than in the private sectors: around 10% in the average of most of the European countries. See EIRO, *Industrial relations in the public sector*, Dublin, 2007. This is the case in Italy. In CGIL, the unions federation of the civil servants (*FP – Funzione Pubblica*) overstepped in the last years the number of members of the metal workers federation (*FIOM*).

from the "outsiders" of the labour law and welfare state that have been constructed during the last century.

These trends heavily impact union membership. The thesis is simple: the spread of employment relationships that are too flexible produces conditions of legal instability and psychological subjection/fear that are totally unfavourable for the individual choice of becoming union members. Without members there are no workers' representatives and, consequently, no workplace collective bargaining. It is a vicious circle that destabilise trade union authority in our contemporary societies.

4) Last but not least, we notice a deep and broad cultural change, depending on a trend towards a "de-traditionalization of the social links", the individualisation of the styles of life (Giddens, 1990; Beck & Beck–Gernsheim, 2002; Bauman, 2001; 2006), the death of the old ideologies and the crisis of the traditional cultures of solidarity, typical of the history of international unionism.

The experience of risk and injustice at work is increasingly individualised in the common perception (Beck, 1986; Dubet, 2006) and, cause of this, de-politicized.

The younger and highly skilled workers, many women, and knowledge workers all seem to be little attracted to the traditional forms of trade union representation, showing expectations, approaches and individual strategies that differ significantly from the typical social prototype of the old union members and militants.

We refer to these changes as the passage "from Fordism to post-Fordism" (Linhart et Moutet; 2005; Kumar, 1995; Gorz, 1992; Coriat, 1991; Harvey, 1990; Dore, 1990; Murray, 1989; Lash and Urry, 1987).

Unions have to cope with this new kind of scenario: more and more SMEs companies, in the service sector, with skilled white collar workers, many of which female, with atypical or subcontract employment relationships, new cultural attitudes and expectation in terms of representations and voice. From a trade union viewpoint, all these elements impose a radical turnaround of attitudes and approaches in order to maintain and possibly reach all those employees who still suffer inequalities, precariousness, exploitation. Unions suffer because a growing number of workers have a bit lesser need for them, whereas another portion need them greatly but fail in the attempt to access them (Accornero, 1997).

3. European trade unions are facing a very serious crisis of identity and strategy. Probably the worst for a long time. They need to re-orientate their approaches and policies in order to increase membership; to extend represenativeness to the new work typologies; to give voice to all those employees who still suffer inequalities, precariousness, exploitation, alienation. There's a future for trade unions, indeed. But a deep restyling and organisational change is definitively required (Waddington and Hoffman, 2001; Carrieri, 2003; Phelan, 2007; Veron, 2006; Klosterboer, 2007; Hyman, 2007).

In these years, Italian trade unions have shown deep commitment in searching new ways to respond to the global challenges faced by the new labour world.

But before we proceed any further, it is useful to recall some of the distinguishing traits of Italian trade unionism: a pluralism of organisations that goes back to the beginning of the cold war period (1948-1950), but with a substantial unity of action among CGIL, CISL and UIL, the three largest confederations; confederate primacy over a network of 12-15 medium-sized industry-wide federations; a strong membership of retired workers; the significant role played by "horizontal" and territorial/local structures; a single-channel system of workplace representations (RSU – *Rappresentanze Sindacali Unitarie*), elected by all the employees, regardless of membership; a strong capacity for mobilisation during industrial action and general strikes; an equally strong propensity for social negotiations, in terms tripartite talks and social pacts; one of the highest levels of abstention of law in the area of industrial relations (representation, strikes, collective bargaining), all regulated by tripartite agreements and not by the law (except that in the public sector).

Collective bargaining coverage in Italy is, on an average, rather high, estimated at around 80% of the entire employed workforce, without any administrative procedure of extension *erga omnes* to the national sector/branch agreements. Such a good result is guaranteed by more than 400 national sectoral/branch contracts, formally covering the entire workforce. It is a two-levels system, with a primacy of the national sector. The second level can be developed at company or, alternatively, at territorial level (constructions; hotels and tourism; artisans; agriculture). It is mostly focused on the additional pay and working hours. Most of the SMEs, which in Italy represent more than 90% of the enterprises, are excluded – *de facto* – by this second level of bargaining. It covers around 35% of the whole workforce; no more than 4% in the micro firms. That's why, unlike the other biggest confederations (CISL and UIL), the CGIL is rather sceptic about a shift in the focus of the collective bargaining system from the national to the company level; in fact two-thirds of the overall workforce – lacking representation at the workplace level – would remain excluded by better protection and treatment.

Italian trade unions have traditionally shown a considerable ability in mobilising general strikes or other forms of industrial action, which are weakly regulated by legislation[5]. This does not imply that Italian trade unions continue to

5 Remarkable, in this light, was the mobilisation in 2002 to protest against the measures promoted by the centre-right government, for making easier the collective dismissals, when CGIL alone brought nearly three million people in the streets of Rome.

maintain a stance that is merely ideological and confrontational as far as industrial relations are concerned. Italy is in fact among those countries where there has been, starting from the 1990s, the "revival of neo-corporatism" amply described in related international literature[6]. Tripartite social agreements have been signed on practically all principal social issues (income policies; collective bargaining; workers representation at the workplace; pension systems; labour market; economic development and competitiveness), proving that they receive a high degree of recognition on the part of the political and institutional system (top-down) and among workers and pensioners (bottom-up).

Among the reasons that contribute to explaining the relative success of the Italian trade union, there is probably the ability to tackle efficaciously the central issues of labour and social citizenship and to create a democratic relationship with the base it represents at both a bargaining and political levels (Baccaro, 2003). In response to internal and external challenges, the Italian confederal unions have been engaged in organizational reforms aimed at increasing internal democracy and transparency. For instance collective bargaining and tripartite agreements are subject to approval on the part of all workers; each peak role into the organisation (members of secretary or directory board) are subjected to rotation, lasting no more than two continuous mandates in the same position: eight years in all. This was instrumental in re-legitimising the confederal unions' role as bargaining agents in the eyes of both the employers and the rank-and-file workers (Locke and Baccaro; 1999). The last good instance concerned the welfare protocol the government signed with social partners associations, in July 2007. A referendum was organised all over the country that saw the participation of some 5 million citizens, including workers, pensioners and unemployed; the favourable to the agreement were 82%.

The reinvigoration of the confederation is strictly correlated to the value of citizenship and bargaining at a territorial level, which also constitute a central node in the management of corporate conflict and the more complex model of life in society. Inspired by the old leader Bruno Trentin, since 1991 the programme of CGIL is focused on the key words of new *rights, solidarity and citizenship.*

---

6 See, among the others, Schmitter P. and Grote J., *Sisifo corporatista: passato, presente e futuro*, in "Stato e Mercato", n. 50/1997; Crouch C., *Non amato ma inevitabile il ritorno al neo-corporativismo*, in "Giornale di diritto del lavoro e delle relazioni industriali", n. 77/98; Fajertag G. and Pochet P. (Eds), *The role of* tripartite *concertation in the reform of the welfare state*, in "Transfer", 1/2: 64–81; 2000; Regini M., *Tripartite Concertation and Varieties of Capitalism*, in "European Journal of Industrial Relations, Vol. 9, No. 3, 251-263; 2003; EIRO, *Social partners and Social Security systems*, European Foundation for the Improvement of Living and Working Conditions, Dublin, 2007.

Since then, the programme focused on some fundamental politico-organisational principles: the concept of "a trade union of rights as opposed to corporatism" based on the confederative approach, defined as "general, united and voluntary" and based on democracy, pluralism and autonomy; the centrality of the work; the assumption of individual rights of social citizenship as a priority in CGIL's action. Highlighted to this end is the universal value of knowledge, information and training at an individual level.

At an organisational level, the strategic guideline of the confederation targets "the renewal of the trade union" where holding central stage is "the construction of a new solidarity between the parties that make up the working world". The objective is to open more and more the confederation and its policies to the new generations, defined as "the biggest challenge of our future", to the migrants, to the women, through an higher attention paid to the work balance conciliation[7]. Last but not least, at the Conference of organisation of May 2008, a crucial role has been recognised to the territorial level of organisation.

4. One of the most important and recent achievements of the Italian trade union movement concerns the specific organisation of the atypical workers (*lavoratori atipici*): a socially and juridical heterogeneous universe, composed by agency temporary workers and « semi-subordinate » workers. Fixed-term workers and part-time workers are instead affiliated to the traditional industry-wide federations.

After the last important reform of the labour market, realised by the centre-right government in 2003 (Act 30/2003), listed in Italy are more than 40 different types of employment relationships.

Italy is more or less in line with the EU average for what concerns some atypical kinds of work (part-time, fixed-term and temporary agency work). Instead, it is remarkably above the averages for what concerns self-employment and undeclared jobs.

The use of fixed-terms work (between 12% and 13%) is not very different from the EU15 average. The temporary agency work (now called "*lavoro in somministrazione*"), introduced into our legislation in 1997 (Act 196/1997) and amended in 2003, involves 574,000 workers (2007) and represents 1.2% of the overall workforce. Even less if we account them as full time equivalent (0.7%)[8].

---

7 According to the CGIL's Statute, each gender must be equally represented into the peak positions of the Confederation, in all the sectors and at all the levels. Because of this rule, women are the 50% in all the secretaries of this trade union.

8 IRES, *Dal lavoro interinale alla somministrazione: primo monitoraggio*, Collana dell'Osservatorio Centro Studi Ebitemp, Roma, 2006

Table 10: Country level data on fixed-term work, part-time work and self-employment

	Fixed-term work (% of total employees)		Part-time work (% of total employment)		Self-employed (% of total employment)	
	2000	**2005**	**2000**	**2005**	**2000**	**2005**
Belgium	9.1	8.9	18.9	22	17	16.2
Bulgaria	6.3 (2001)	6.4	3.2	2.1	-	-
Czech Republic	8.1	8.6	5.3	4.9	15	18
Denmark	9.7	9.8	21.3	22.1	6.6	6.3
Germany	12.7	14.2	19.4	24	10	11.2
Estonia	3	2.7	8.1	7.8	9	8.1
Greece	13.5	11.8	4.5	5	43.3	40.8
Spain	32.2	33.3	7.9	12.4	15.8	14.4
France	15.2	13.3	16.7	17.2	9.2	8.9
Ireland	5.9	3.7	16.4	16.8 (2004)	18.6	17
Italy	10.1	12.3	8.4	12.8	26.4	24.5
Cyprus	10.7	8.9	8.4	8.9	25.8	23.6
Latvia	6.7	8.4	11.3	8.3	14.9	11.6
Lithuania	4.4	5.5	10.2	7.1	20.1	16.9
Luxembourg	5.3	5.3	10.4	17.4	7.3	6.6
Hungary	7.1	7	3.5	4.1	15.1	13.8
Malta	4.1	4.5	6.8	9.6	11.8	11.7
Netherlands	13.7	15.5	41.5	46.1	14.2	13.7
Austria	8	9.1	16.3	21.1	20.5	19.9
Poland	5.8	25.7	10.5	10.8	37.7	28.8
Portugal	19.9	19.5	10.9	11.2	24.5	24.1
Romania	2.8	2.4	16.5	10.2	46.2	43.7
Slovenia	13.7	17.4	6.5	9	18	17.1
Slovak Republic	4.8	5	4.8	5	8.3	13
Finland	16.3	16.5	12.3	13.7	12.2	11.6
Sweden	15.8	16	19.5	24.7	5.4	4.8
UK	6.9	5.7	25.2	25.4	11.9	12.7

Source: Employment in Europe 2006, statistical annex

The law limits the use of temporary work to: a) types of work which are not normally done in the firm; b) the substitution of absent workers; c) cases defined by collective bargaining. Temporary work is forbidden: a) for unskilled workers; b) for replacing workers on strike; c) by firms which have resorted to collective dismissal in the last 12 months; d) in dangerous jobs and by firms not complying with health and safety legislation. Temporary workers have the same rights as employees of the firm-user; in particular, the pay treatment must not be inferior to that of employees of the firm-user. All the national sectoral collective agreements, in each sector/branch, fix limits and maximum percentage to the use of these kind of contracts in the user-companies. Usually between 8% and 15% of the total workforce. The largest majority of the agency temporary workers have a fixed-term employment relationship with their agencies;

70% work in the northern regions of the country and 52% in the industrial manufacturing sectors. Most of them are quite young (the average age is 31). The women are 45%; they are a bit older than the average, employed in the service sectors, more highly qualified than their male colleagues, who are largely employed in the manufacturing factories. An increasing number is covered by migrant workers: 23% of the all temporary workers[9].

In average, each "mission" in the company-user lasts for no more than 44 paid days. The monthly average pay is between 1000 and 1,500 euros, but with a relevant wage gender gap (70% of the women earn 1,000 euro per month). All the agency workers have weak income security for the periods of unemployment, when they're not working, whereas they have many good opportunities for continuous vocational training. The 4% of their global wage must be allocated by the agency to finance a national training fund, jointly managed by the most representative social partners organisations.

Self-employed workers represent 17% of the national employment rate (24%, if we also include the employers). A sub-specie of them is composed by the so called "coordinated and continuous assistants", a sort of "semi-subordinated workers", legally autonomous but economically dependent (Supiot, 1999). They are 1,500,000 and represent one of the real peculiarities of the Italian way to flexibility and precariousness (the other is represented by the huge share of unrecorded/undeclared employees), since – unlike all the other atypical jobs – this one is all but excluded by labour law protections[10]. Not all these new self-employees really need the traditional collective forms of representation. Most of them are in fact very high professionals and really self-employed in the traditional sense. Therefore, those who are really in need of collective forms of representation are estimated to be around 700,000. Around 80% have just only one single employer; contracts of 6-7 months per year; similar working time of their stable colleagues but with worst incomes (they earn 40-50% less than their stable subordinated colleagues with equal or similar skill profile), rights and professional opportunities (career, training, pensions perspectives).

Since the end of the 90s, the temporary agency workers and the semi-dependent assistants are organised and represented by their own unions, affiliated to the three main confederation. As far as we know it's a quite unique ex-

---

9 Ebitemp, *Il lavoro interinale nel 2007,* Osservatorio Nazionale, Collana dell'Osservatorio Centro Studi Ebitemp, Roma, maggio 2008; Altieri G., Dota F., Piersanti M., *Percorsi nel lavoro atipico: il caso dei lavoratori interinali*, IRES-FrancoAngeli, 2008.

10 At present, in the Italian legal system, the "co-ordinated and continuous assistants" are entitled only to the special labour litigation procedure applied to employees, but in all other aspects they fall outside labour law provisions.

perience in the scenario of international unionism[11]. Their names are NIdiL (*Nuove Identità del Lavoro*) for CGIL, ALAI (*Associazione Lavoratori Atipici e Interinali*) for CISL and CPO (*Comitati per l'Occupazione*) for UIL. These three organisation have different statutes within their confederations. In fact, whereas NIdiL is recognised as a proper *Federation*, in charge of representing agency workers and semi-subordinated self-employed, ALAI has a weaker status of *Association* within CISL, representing the agency workers only and not even the semi-dependent self-employed. Similarly to the CPO, which instead – as NIdiL-CGIL – is considered a federation of UIL. In CGIL the plan is to include also the unemployed members under the domain of NIdiL.

Unlike the workers of the other unions, the atypical workers share a juridical condition and not the employment in a specific productive sector or branch.

Most of these workers are young and highly educated; so they do represent the future of trade unionism of the 21st century. The CGIL is very aware of this fact, which has been emphasised during the last Congress, in 2006, and at the Conference of Organisation, last spring.

The number of members has been increasing gradually and constantly during the whole decade, remaining – nevertheless – below the potential area of recruitment.

In the case of NIDIL-CGIL, the number of members doubled in ten years, from 15,000 in 1998 to 32,800 in 2007. ALAI-CISL, in the same period, declared 27.698 members. The 2007 membership of CGIL by sector federations was the following:

SECTOR	**Total**
Funz.Pubblica (Public workers)	404.697
Fiom (Metal/ Engineering)	359.669
Fillea (Construction)	357.955
Filcams (Hotelling, Tourism, Dinstribution; Cleaning)	345.372
Flai (Food Industry and Agricolture)	287.786
Flc (School, University and other knowledge workers)	181.596
Filcem (Chemical and Energy)	162.530

11 About self-employed, atypical workers and trade unions studies and surveys are available also in other countries, as in the case of Susanne Pernicka (2006) for the Austrian experience, Andrew Nibby for the UK (2005), Francois Michon for France (2008), Heiner Dribbush (2008) or Karin Schulze Buschoff (2008) or Bernd Reissert (2008) for Germany. Some of their articles are available in English, some others in German, edited by the WZB discussion papers in 2005 or WSI Mittelilungen (2006). The EIRO Obesrver Bulletin has been focusing some of its *comparative supplement* to the non-permanent employment, unionism and industrial relations.

Filt (Transport)	147.225
Filtea (Textile And Clothing)	102.120
Slc (Media)	95.909
Fisac (Bank And Insurance)	87.962
Nidil (Atypical Workers)	**32.799**
Miste (Mixed)	30.196
Spi (Retired)	2.991.604
Unemployed	17.277

Out the 32.799 members of NIdiL, nearly 8.000 are temporary workers, whereas the largest majority is composed by 25.000 autonomous assistants (semi-dependent workers). The average level of education, among these members, is quite high; 45% have in fact a high school diploma and almost 40% an academic degree. Only 15% have an inferior secondary school diploma.

NIdIL is present in 80 territories. The most relevant activities of the atypical workers unions are collective bargaining, advice on legislation and contracts (also on-line); trade union education; research and studies.

For the trade unions, collective bargaining is traditionally the most typical tool of the workers collective representation and voice. But just in the case of the atypical workers unions there are in Italy a number of distinguishing traits. In fact, whereas the national industry-wide level represents the core of the Italian collective bargaining system, in the case of the atypical workers the core becomes the single company or unit level. With one remarkable exception: the national collective agreements negotiated and subscribed by the atypical workers unions with the most representative association of the temporary work agencies (*Assolavoro*). In July 2008, the second agreement was signed (the previous one was in 2002), covering 90% of Italian agency temporary employees; nearly 500,000.

According to the new collective agreement, temporary workers have the right to elect their own delegates at three different levels: national (for agencies with offices spread around the country), territorial (nominated in this case by the external unions), workplace. At this level, agency workers have the right to elect one delegate when the company-user hires more than 30 agency workers for more than 3 months. These delegates normally act beside the standard workers union representation (RSU) of the company-user.

It is worth mentioning the model of what in Italy we call "*bilateralità*" (Leonardi, 2005), the joint management – by the main social partners associations – of parts of the welfare schemes and vocational training. This is the case of the agency temporary workers, where the law and the collective agreements oblige the agencies to finance the jointly managed funds with a sum amounting to 4%

of total salary expenditure; 3.8% for the vocational training fund (it's only 0.30% for the standard workers) and 0.2% for the micro-credit assistance to the workers who will require an aid for paying the house rent or personal ICT.

The continuous vocational training for the agency workers can be considered a good practice. It is managed by a joint fund called *Formatemp*. Nearly 100,000 workers have been involved in some project of training, with initiatives especially focused on single target groups, as the migrant workers, or important issues, as the health & safety policies at the workplace level.

One of the biggest problems faced by Italian atypical workers is the very poor income protection for the periods between one job and another. The shortage of a fair and inclusive system of social protections in case of unemployment increases the sense of precariousness felt by Italian atypical workers with respect to most of their colleagues in other European countries (Accornero, 2006). Though unemployment insurance is foreseen by the legislation, for agency temporary workers it is related only to the number of the days worked during the previous year. It is the equivalent of 35% of the last income whereas the "ordinary treatment of unemployment" is 60% for standard workers.

Following a request by trade unions, social partners are considering a different share of the 4% allocated from the wages, giving a bit less to training and a bit more to income security. According to the tripartite social agreement of July 2007, new economic resources and benefits will be directed to improve either active labour policies or income protections for the unemployment periods.

The new national agreement has introduced several new important norms regarding the stabilisation of the agency workers hired with a fixed-term contracts by their agencies. In case they have been working in user-companies for 42 months, summing-up all the single missions for the same agency, they will be hired by the agency with an open-end contract. This change implies that, for the periods in which the worker is not hired by any user-company, he/she will receive an indemnity of availability of € 700 per month. In case such a situation should protract for too long, the worker can be fired by the agency, receiving € 700 euro per month for a duration of six months (seven if the worker is over 50). 60% of this indemnity will be paid by the agency and 40% by the bilateral fund (called *Ebitemp*), which is managed by the social parties' organisations. With such a measure of social protection, the social partners of this branch have interestingly surrogated the weakness of other forms of unemployment insurance for this kind of atypical workers.

Welfare and territorial collective bargaining constitute, for CGIL, the best way to cope with the challenges of the post-Fordist de-centralisation and fragmentation out of the old big factories of the previous era; a "golden age" also for the international trade unions movement.

At the company or single unit level, negotiations mostly concern the self-employed assistants. Until now the atypical workers unions have signed nearly 130 company-level collective agreements, covering around 120,000 assistants in the public sector (especially local administrations), in the no profit sector and in the private service sector (in particular: call centres; polls institutes).

The aim is to strengthen the territorial level of collective bargaining and local welfare, in order to cover the micro- and small-sized companies, otherwise excluded by any form of collective representation and negotiation.

In some cases (public sector; call centres), atypical workers unions share the negotiating recognition with the unions of the stable employees of those branches. We call it "bargaining co-promotion". It is ruled by bilateral agreements between the trade unions federations. The objective is to pay the collaborators no less than their equivalent stable colleagues (according to the principle "equal pay for equal work").

Which are the contents of these collective agreements? They normally aim to give a minimum platform of rights, either individual or collective. In the former case the items concern the work tasks and organisation; the pay (amount/criteria); duration of the contract; the absence/leave for sickness or maternity; training. The collective rights concern the possibility to gain a basic number of unions freedoms and rights, such as the right to organise assemblies or elect own employee reps.

NIdiL has been very active in asking, and obtaining, the stabilisation of 20,000 precarious workers, especially in call centres.

As for the other individual forms of representation and services, they belong to a well known and successful experience of legal assistance provided to employees, out of the workplace, at the local level, with specialised offices and more and more qualified experts and unions advisers (website; mailing list; magazine/news).

Notwithstanding these interesting and useful activities, the role – as well as the very future – of unions like NIDIL are questioned by other influential sectors of the trade union organisation. Especially those who act in situations where there is a big and increasing number of atypical jobs. The metal/engineering sector for what concerns agency temporary workers, and the public and the knowledge workers sector for what concerns the coordinated and continuous assistants.

The metal workers and the public sectors unions – the two biggest sector federations – do not sympathize much with this new entity of the employees representation. Not only because, understandably, they feel threatened in their monopolistic representation, but also because they postulate that the workers representation must achieve the unity of the workers of a single site/company, against the fragmentation according to the legal nature of the employment relationship.

According to these unions, the workers have to be organised and represented where they work and not where they are formally employed.

Furthermore, for what concerns the semi-dependent assistants, a number of unions (as well as some scholars) believe that their collective representations risk to imply a recognition also from the unions of what instead they consider an abuse of the labour law legislation; a tricky manner to elude and escape from it. The debate is open and the outcomes not predictable.

5. What is it that atypical workers demand from unions? Which policies? According a survey of 2005, realised by IRES[12], atypical workers demand more job security and more income security. This fact requires new policies. It is absolutely vital for unions to renew and update their ability to broaden their social representativeness to include the new realities of the labour market. The unity within the labour world can be achieved today by recognising either what is similar and what is different from a condition to another. The era of the standardisation of the union representation is behind us and so is the era of the standardisation of the production system.

At a more general political level, new laws have to halt and turnaround the trend leading to precariousness of these years. It is no easy task in a Europe dominated by centre-right governments, but we cannot renounce this objective. A whole generation risks compromising their right to a decent present as workers and a decent future as pensioners.

These reforms must aim to two purposes, currently much debated among Italian labour lawyers and within the unions and political forces. An approach emphasizes more on the need for a new model of welfare system. It is a huge issue. But I would like to recall the proposal of Alain Supiot and his European high level group in 1999, according to which we should build up a gradual system of legal protections. The model of the concentric circles: basic social rights for all citizens (anti-discrimination rights; health and safety; basic unemployment insurance; good job services), regardless of their legal status, further rights and protections for the workers of SMEs, high employment legal strictness for the workers of the larger companies. In this approach, a "grey zone" between autonomy and subordination is still admitted but better protected than today. This is the position of the Democratic Party. Another approach insists more on the need for a new concept of subordination, updated to the new models of productions, where the socio-economical conditions of the employees are taken in consideration, as well their

12 Altieri, Dota, Piersanti (2008).

functional participation within the employers' project[13]. The traditional dualism autonomy / subordination of the civil codes must be reinstated and the grey zone in the middle (semi-dependent workers; autonomous assistants; etc.) has to be removed, eliminating all abuse (a typical example of abuse: the workers of the call centres or tele-workers, erroneously considered self-employees in several countries only because they are formally not subjected to some of the old traditional forms of subjection at the employer's workplace). In other words, the ongoing "escape from labour law" must be stopped. This is the position held by CGIL and of the radical left.

To this end, parts of the recent EU Green Paper about flexicurity "*Modernising labour law to meet the challenges of the 21st century*"[14]– which was rejected by the Italian unions – could be received. But not when it recommends to make dismissals easier, but where it recommends to improve the active labour market policies, life-long learning, better income security and a better social dialogue among the social partners.

Bibliography

Accornero, A. (1997): Era il secolo del Lavoro, Bologna, Il Mulino.

Accornero, A. (2006): San Precario prega per noi, Rizzoli.

Altieri, G. / Dota, F. / Piersanti, M. (2008): Percorsi nel lavoro atipico: il caso dei lavoratori interinali, IRES-FrancoAngeli.

Baglioni, G. (2008): L'accerchiamento. Perché si riduce la tutela sindacale tradizionale; Il Mulino.

Baglioni, G. / Crouch, C. (eds.), (1991): European industrial relation: The challenge of flexibility, London, Sage.

Bauman, Z. (2001): The Individualized Society, Cambridge Polity.

Bauman, Z. (2006): Liquid Times: Living in an Age of Uncertainty, Cambridge Polity.

13 In Germany, for example, an autonomous assistant (*arbeitnehmerähnlichePerson)* is partially treated as a dependent colleague of him/her when more than 50% of his/her income is depending just on one single employer. No matter how he/she is legally defined.

14 European Commission, *Green Paper: Modernising labour law to meet the challenges of the 21st century*; Brussels, 22.11.2006, COM (2006) 708 final http://ec.europa.eu/employment_social/labour_law/docs/2006/green_paper_en.pdf.; European Council, *Towards Common Principles of Flexicurity. Draft Council Conclusions,* Brussels, 23 November 2007.

Beck, U. (1986): Risikogesellschaft. Auf dem Weg in eine andere Moderne, Suhrkamp, Frankfurt aM,.
Beck, U. / Beck-Gernsheim, E. (2002): Individualization. Institutionalized Individualism and its Social and Political. Consequences. London, Sage.
Buschoff, K.S. (2008): Absicherung und Interessenvertretung von Solo-Selbstständigen im Fünf-Ländervergleich, paper, "Atypische Beschäftigung und Prekarität im europäischen Vergleich", in www.boeckler.de/85_91174.html, Berlin, 19. Juni.
Blaschke, S. (2000): Union density and European Integration: Diverging Convergence, in "European Journal of Industrial Relations", n. 2/.
Boeri, T. / Calmfors, L. et al. (2001): The Role of Unions in the Twenty-first Century, Oxford University Press.
Bouquin, S. / Leonardi, S. et al. (2007): Can Europe's Trade Unions represent and organise workers in SMEs ? in "Trasnfer", n. 1.
Casale, G. (2007): Diritto del lavoro e relazioni industriali nell'Europa che cresce, Ediesse.
Carrieri, M. (2003): Sindacato in bilico. Ricette contro il declino, Donzelli, Rome.
Carrieri, M. (2007): L'altalena della concertazione, Donzelli,.
Carrieri, M. / Leonardi, S. (2007): Il sindacato dei pensionati: il valore di una "anomalia", in CGIL-SPI, "Fare Benessere", LiberEtà,.
Cecchi, D. / Visser, J. (2005): Pattern persistence in European. Trade union density
CES-Businesseurope-CEEP (2007): Key challanges facing European Labour market, Brussel.
Coriat, B.: Penser à l'envers, Paris, Christian Bourgois.
Coulet, C. (2008): Une chute rapide du taux de syndiclaisation induite par la riforme de l'assurance chomage, in "Revue de l'IRES", n. 112, may
Dimitrova, D. / Vilrockx, J. (eds.), (2005): Trade Union Strategies in Central and Eastern Europe. Toward Decent Work, ILO, Budapest.
Dribbusch, H. (2008): Organising Agency Workers: recent approaches in Germany, Paper, TURI network conference, Brussels, 14 October.
Ebbinghaus, B. / Visser, J. (2000): The Societies of Europe. Trade Unions in Western Europe since 1945, Mac Millan,.
Ebitemp (2008): Il lavoro interinale nel 2007, Osservatorio Nazionale, Collana dell'Osservatorio Centro Studi Ebitemp, Roma, maggio.
EIRO (2004): Trade Union Membership, 1993-2003, European Foundation for the Improvement of Living and Working Conditions Dublin, Dublin.
EIRO (2007): Industrial relations in the public sector, European Foundation for the Improvement of Living and Working Conditions Dublin, Dublin.

EIRO (2007): Social partners and Social Security systems, European Foundation for the Improvement of Living and Working Conditions, Dublin.
European Commission (2007): Employment in Europe 2006, Bruxelles.
European Commission (2007): Industrial Relations in Europe 2006, Bruxelles.
European Commission (2006): Green Paper: Modernising labour law to meet the challenges of the 21st century; Brussels, 22.11.2006, COM 708
Fajertag, G. / Pochet, P. (eds.) (2000): The role of tripartite concertation in the reform of the welfare state, in "Transfer", 1/2: 64–81.
Feltrin, P. (2000): La sindacalizzazione in Italia (1986-2004): Edizioni Lavoro.
Frege, C. / Kelly, J. (2004): Varieties of Unionism. Strategies for Union revitalisation in a Global Economy, Oxford Press.
Giddens, A. (1990): The Consequences of Modernity, Cambridge Polity Press.
Gorz, A. (2004): Metamorphoses du travail, Gallimard Folio.
Grote, J. / Schmitter, P. (1997): Sisifo corporatista: passato, presente e futuro, in "Stato e Mercato", n. 50.
Harvey, D. (1990): The condition of Postmodernity, Basil Blackwell,
Hyman, R. (2001): Understanding European Trade Unionism: Between Market, Class and Society; Sage.
Hyman, R. (2007): How Can Trade Unions Act Strategically?, Transfer 13(2),
ILO (1998): Le travail dans le Monde, Geneve.
IRES (2006): Dal lavoro interinale alla somminstrazione: primo monitoraggio, Collana dell'Osservatorio Centro Studi Ebitemp, Roma.
Kelly, J. (1998): Mobilization, Collectivism and Industrial Relations, Emerald.
Kjellberg, Jokivuoiri, Vandaele (2006): Special focus on the Ghent system, in "Transfer", n. 12.
Kloosterboer, D. (2007): Innovative Trade Unions Strategies, FNV, Utrecht, Mai.
Kumar, K. (1995): From Post-Industrial to Post-Modern Society. New Theories of the Contemporary World,.
Lange, P. / Scruggs, L. (2002): Where have all the members gone?, in "Journal of Politics", 64.
Leonardi, S. (2005): Bilateralità e servizi. Quale ruolo per il sindacato. Ediesse, Roma.
Leonardi, S. (2006): Gewerkschaften und wohlfahrtsstaat: Das Gent-system, in "WSI Mitteilungen", March.
Leonardi, S. (2008): Le syndicat de demain. La nouvelle composition de classe et l'organisation des travaillers, in « Le syndacalisme au défi du 21 siècle », Editions Syllapse,.
Linhart, D. / Moutet, A. (eds.) (2005): Le travail nous est compté, La Decouverte.

Locke, R. / Baccaro, L. (1999): The Resurgence of the Italian Unions? in Martin A. and Ross G., "The Brave New World of European Labor", Berghahn Books.
Michon, F. (2008): French Unions and Temporary Agency Work, paper, Berlin, "Atypische Beschäftigung und Prekarität im europäischen Vergleich", in www.boeckler.de/85 _91174.html
Murray, R. (1989): Fordism and Post-Fordism, in Hall and Jacques, New Times, Lawrence and Wishart,
Nibby, A. (2005): Opening the doors wide to the self-employed. How trade unions are recruiting and organising self-employed workers as members. UNI, in www.andrewbibby.com.
Pernicka, S. (2006): Organising the Self-Employed, in "European Journal of Industrial Relations", n. 12.
Phelan, C. (eds.) (2007): Trade union revitalisation. Trends and prospects in 34 countries, Peter Lang.
Regini, M. (2003): Tripartite Concertation and Varieties of Capitalism, in "European Journal of Industrial Relations, Vol. 9, No. 3, 251-263.
Reissert, B. (2008): Regulierung atypischer Beschäftigung – Impulse aus dem europäischen Vergleich für die deutsche Debatte? Paper, Berlin, "Atypische Beschäftigung und Prekarität im europäischen Vergleich", in www.boeckler.de/85_91174.html.
Scruggs, L. (2002): The Ghent system and union membership in Europe, 1970-1996, in "Political Research Quarterly", n. 55.
Supiot, A. (1999): Au de là de l'emploi, Flammarion.
Vernon, G. (2006): Does Density Matter? The Significance of Comparative. Historical Variation in Unionization, in "European Journal of Industrial Relations", SAGE, Volume 12.
Visser, J. (2006): Union membership statistics in 24 countries, in "Monthly Labor Review".
Waddington, J. / Hoffman, R. (eds.), (2001): Trade Unions in Europe. Facing Challenges and Searching For Solutions, Etui, Bruxelles.
Western, B. (1997): Between Class and Market: Postwar Unionisation in the Capitalist Democracies, Princeton Univeristy Press.
WSI Mitteilungen (2006): Schwerpunktheft. Atypiche Beschaftingung – sozialvertraglich oder prekar?, n. 5.

Giving employees a voice? Lessons from the new employee forums in the UK

Alan Tuckman, Michael Whittall

1. Introduction

Employee representation in Britain was until recently seen almost exclusively in terms of trade union channels of collective bargaining. However, in the last decade or so there has been an increased awareness of other forms of workplace representation. On the one hand this is the result of a decline in trade union membership in Britain, on the other this decline has been mirrored by an increase in the deployment of alternative non-collective forms of employee relations such as the individualisation of pay and conditions particularly in the private sector. Intertwined with this are initiatives, mainly through EU Directives, giving employee's rights to information and consultation over major issues.

The purpose of this paper is to examine such alternative forms of employee representation, in this case two employee forums set up in anticipation of the 2002 Information and Consultation Directive (ICE). We aim to consider whether they might be, at least potentially, a means of advancing employee voice and representation within the workplace in the absence of trade unions. The purpose of such an exercise is well founded if one considers that the emergence of employee forums have been in response to a management led agenda (Hall, 2006). We argue that management have seen employee forums as a means of avoiding trade union recognition, a means of retaining an individualisation of employment, as well as sustaining a paternalistic style of management.

Hence, management usually determines the consultation parameters (Hall, 2006) and because of this we may therefore forgiven for asking questions about the autonomy of forums and their delegates from management (Butler, 2005; Gollan, 2007; Lloyd, 2001; Terry, 1999). For example, while "trench warfare" represents the root metaphor of traditional UK industrial relations (Dunn, 1990), this current departure seems rooted in the idea of an essential harmony between labour and capital, i.e. divisions no longer exist. However, we argue, the establishment of employee forums can represent the emergence of a collective voice. This is because managements' myopia potentially opens a Pandora's Box out of which employee discontent and perceived injustice can appear.

The paper seeks to explore the development and actions of two forums as organs of employee voice and representation. Both cases are from the finance sector and draw on interviews with employee representatives and other actors associated with the forums. In analysing the development of these forums we use Hyman's (1997) framework designed to understand the changing landscape employee representation in the UK. In this Hyman has distinguished between the autonomy, legitimacy, and efficacy of employee representation, a distinction we claim which is ideally formulated to understand the role of such forums. Both these forums have been established by local management relatively recently in part to comply with ICE regulation. One may be considered to have gained some autonomy and effectiveness, while the other though remaining constrained by managements' continued domination exemplifies how employee representatives are beginning to articulate an independent strategy and voice.

The paper first elaborates on Hymans' analysis of employee representation, then examines the cases studies – referred to here as Isar AG and Interbank to maintain anonymity. While in the case of Interbank the forum has established an independent identity and a degree of autonomy the officers of the forum at Isar AG have increasingly attempted to challenge management. While in both cases we may see limitations to these as voice mechanisms our examination does not preclude such bodies adopting a more independent stance in the future.

2. Framework for the analysis of employee representation

In 1997 Blair's 'New' Labour Government was replacing the Conservatives with the promise of opting into EU employment regulation and the possibility of a reversal of trade union fortunes in Britain. In this context Hyman (1997) published a predictive future of employee representation in what he termed Britain-in-Europe. The analysis rests heavily on the UK tradition of a single channel of representation but recognises the likelihood of some move towards a 'Europeanization' with the emergence of a dual system incorporating some form of direct representation, similar to a Continental works council. At the time there was some talk of the establishment of works councils in the UK, something which might complement or support the revitalisation of trade unions, or act as a barrier to their revival. In the paper Hyman (1997) conceptualises 'interest representation' in terms of autonomy, legitimacy and efficacy of the employee representatives and representative system. Autonomy, the independence from the employer, has proved the main concern with the new representative forums which have been established in Britain (Butler, 2005; Terry, 1999; Gollan, 2007) and, as we shall see, has also been important in shaping the development of our case study forums. A central issue with forums is whether they are the articulation of a coherent employee voice independent of management – who invariably bankroll such bodies – or a voice for management in conformance with regulation and an attempt to incorporate employees and dissipate any minor conflict. A common comment, echoed early in the development of one of our cases, is that they spend all their time discussing trivia rather than the major strategic direction of the company which EU policy suggests.

Legitimacy of representation, the 'precondition of the representivity of representatives', is 'gained and sustained by a record of delivering the goods' (Hyman, 1997 p310). Thus the employee representatives may gain legitimacy by the process of election but must sustain it amongst their electorate – the employees who they represent – through their activities and achievements in office. In this sense the legitimacy of representatives is also based on their efficacy, their effectiveness in office. Efficacy a "'self evident' concept but also complex and multifaceted" (p 311) is conceptualised by Hyman in terms of the ability to acquire relevant information (intelligence), formulate policies coherently and dynamically (strategically), and to implement them appropriately. However, it assumes a position independent of, and in opposition to, that of management, so much so that there is a possible linkage to a process of interest mobilisation (Kelly, 1998). In this context, there may be an assumption of common interest. This may be a mobilisation in favour of management interest rather than of employee interest challenging management. It may be, as Hyman argues, that:

> All three elements of interest representation are commonly viewed as subject to recent challenges which are likely to persist and perhaps intensify in the future. Changed management policies (strategies?) threaten the autonomy of representative institutions from the employer. More diversified patterns of employee interests intensify the problems of filtering and aggregating constituents' expectations. This in turn contributes to a legitimation gap, as does the difficulty of satisfying these expectations in a harsher environment. Delivering results in hard times appears to require enhanced organizational capacity when representative institutions (trade unions, certainly) are in general forced to juggle with depleted resources. Devising new pathways to effective intelligence, strategy and competence may be crucial in their future. (Hyman, 1997, 311)

Thus to examine the efficacy of employee representation we are required not to just look at the autonomy of representatives, that they are an authentic and independent representative voice, but also their ability mobilise and to act independently. That is that they are not purely a filter for information passed between employees and managers but are also able to explore, analyse and judge this information and act on it. However, in examining the efficacy of such a relationship we need to explore – as Hyman suggests – the levels at which such a consultation occurs, the structure of the relationship as well as of the employee representative system, the process of representation – to what extent is it an informed and meaningful interchange – and who sets the agenda of the exchange and how.

3. Case Studies

a) Isar AG

Isar AG is a subsidiary of a major German multinational involved in financial services. Based at two sites in London, one in the financial district and the other in Canary Wharf, the UK subsidiary has gone through major changes in recent years following expansion in the 1990s and recession after the stock market crash in 2001. Initially, Isar AG consisted of a small office of around 20 employees. At the time of the research it had a combined workforce of well over 500 workers. Expansion reflects the company's policy of developing its global portfolio able to adapt to new high risk market conditions. A central aspect of Isar AG's commitment to change involves developing a new working environment, one which is 'a little bit more dynamic, a business focussed organisation' according to the UK HR manager. Such dynamism is designed to replace what was seen as a 'civil servant' mentality that had prevailed in the company.

To facilitate such change an employment strategy consisting of four factors has been implemented. The first concerns an employment drive focussed on hiring young ambitious graduates. Next, parts of the UK subsidiary were moved to a state of the art office complex in the City of London. This modern open-plan working environment is not only designed to create synergies between the different business units, but also communicate that a new regime is in place. The third involves a higher degree centralisation, the German headquarters increasingly overseeing the day-to-day running of the UK subsidiary. And the final change involved setting up an Employee Forum.

Initiated by the UK personnel department in 2006 the UK HR manager had to fend off stiff opposition from both central and local management over the establishment of the Forum. The HR, though, was able to make a strong case for such a body:

> There were two drivers behind the thinking of the Staff Group; one was legislation (information and consultation directive)... it was felt that a pre-emptive approach would be better. By not waiting until employees called for such a Forum, management would be in a position to determine how such a body should work – ultimately its remit. Secondly it was felt that such a forum would be a good means of getting employees' "feedback".

The last point, 'employees' feedback', was of specific importance to the HR department. Conscious that the UK subsidiary had gone through and was still going through a major period of change, HR felt the Employee Forum would be a good instrument to manage such change. As is implicit in such a stance, this newly founded body was brought into life first and foremost to assist management rather than offer employees the chance to have their views heard. As will be demonstrated below, the fact that this was very much a management led exercise had far reaching consequences for the independence, legitimacy and efficacy of the Isar AG Employee Forum.

Though the Forum provided employees the chance to raise issues for the very first time, the issues that employees were allowed to address at the Employee Forum were strictly controlled by management. The constitution, drawn-up together with an external law firm, excluded consideration of anything relating to terms and conditions of employment:

> [T]he key parameters were set by me and the MD before discussions took place within the Forum. It was agreed that the Forum would not discuss individual pay or pay related issues, benefits, salary reviews, pensions, redundancies that affect less than 20% of staff, individual staff grievances and individual staff disciplinary matters.

The constitution's restrictive nature was not welcomed by employee delegates to the Employee Forum. The inability to discuss salary related issues resulted in delegates christening the forum "paper tiger".

b) Interbank

Internet bank was established by a traditional insurance company as part of diversification following the deregulation of the financial markets and at the time of the e-boom of the late 1990s. Separated formally from its parent, like Isar AG it is far removed from the 'traditional' image and practices of the finance sector. The main operation of the new company was housed more than one hundred miles north of the financial centre.

The early years of Interbank were very turbulent. There the start-up itself; and the attempt at stock exchange floatation were punctuated by the bursting of the e-boom bubble. The decade since establishment has been one of instability.

Overall Interbank employs about two thousand two hundred employees with about fifteen hundred of them at the contact centre. Employees tend to be relatively young with an average age in the mid-20s. Most have taken employment at Interbank as their first job after graduation from higher education with some working part-time while studying. Employee discontent was principally expressed through the exit of attrition – with turnover rate usually around twenty but sometimes reaching forty percent – although voice was also occasionally mobilised over conditions. A trade union, recognised at other sites owned by the parent company, attempted to gain recognition at Interbank, protesting about limitations on breaks at the contact centre.

The initial impetus for establishing the Interbank Peoples Forum (IPF) came from the CEO and management, this a means of avoiding union recognition and anticipating compliance with the ICE regulation whose details were, at the time, still unknown. Originally confined to bi-monthly fireside chats with the CEO, officers have increasingly seen their role as more substantive in building relationships with managers across the organisational hierarchy, articulating the interests of Interbank employees and supporting a network of external organisations to gain and maintain support and information.

4. Autonomy

a) Isar AG

In terms of autonomy huge question marks hang over Isar AG's Employee Forum. As indicated above, the setting up of the forum was first and foremost a management led exercise, a pre-emptive move to control what the forum could discuss, who sat on the forum and what information could be reported back to the workforce. For example, although management supported an election process in choosing delegates to sit on the forum, three of the eventual six delegates indicated that either their line manager or the CEO had approached them to put their name forward for election. Nevertheless, as will become apparent below, managements' attempt to load the Forum with likeminded individuals was only partly a success. Of those managerial sponsored delegates only one was perceived to have remained an important ally; a manager interviewed referring to the individual in question 'as my favourite delegate'.

Another major management concern involved issues prohibited from the Forum's agenda. This relates to managements' main fear that the Forum could become a platform for collective bargaining. The constitution ensured that so-called "salary related" issues were not part of the Forum's remit. Employment terms and conditions remained within the scope of what line managers agreed with individuals. As the following respondent suggests, employee delegates are far from happy about the restrictive nature of the Forum:

> I personally wanted benefits there, and the company said "anything that is salaried related would be out". Because they can put a price on all the benefits they said "that was salary related." So we do have a constitution but every time we seem to raise something we either get "that is to do with office services, that is noting to do with this forum or that is salary related, that costs money and is out of our scope".

Another factor which highlights the Forum's lack of independence concerns the restrictions placed on delegates' ability to report back to the workforce. Specifically the HR department's blatant censorship of the Forum's newsletter:

> We put together a newsletter which gets heavily edited, watered down. If we raise things and we get a "no" from the company that tends to get edited out of the newsletter. Only the real positive things tend to make the newsletter which I think is wrong. I don't think the newsletter gives a balanced view of what actually happened and I think that is the general opinion and not just the people on the Forum. We are an intelligent company and the people can see through it, they see that it is a load of tosh.

Recently, though, the newsletter has been produced with very little management interference. As the following employee respondent indicates, though, this ironically has more to do with employee representatives becoming acquainted with management's censorship guidelines than management becoming more lenient towards the newsletter's content:

> I now think we know who our audience is and the audience is not just the staff. We have to consider HR as well .... They (HR) do put a bit of slant on it, which does not always reflect the true outcome.

Management's fear of ICE Directive saw it reluctantly establish and employee forum, a forum which was tolerated because management had a decisive say in how it functioned. However, as the proceeding sections demonstrate, pre-emptive approaches are no guarantee that employee delegates are willing to comply with the guidelines set down management.

b) Interbank

Initially as a means of excluding the trade union, a member of the HR Department at Interbank was given the task of establishing an employee forum. They based this on the EWC model and constitution established by Interbank's parent company. At first this allowed for elected officers from different levels and departments within Interbank to meet about six times a year with the CEO for what were described as 'fireside chats'. Some elected representatives on the IPF became discontented with the limited role the body was playing; concerned as they said with 'sausages in the canteen' they pushed for a more significant voice in shaping the strategy and policy of the bank. This seemed to come in the role the IPF played, if often ambiguous, in the attempt at union recognition. Two influential IPF officers, members of a trade union, blocked recognition but pushed for an expanded role for the forum. These two officers were given secondment to explore how they could develop the Forum's role, successfully pushing for the election of three full time officers, an autonomous budget, and an elected forum of twelve representatives. Representatives were to be drawn from the main and two smaller sites of Interbank and sections of the workforce including management. At least formally the forum remains jointly chaired by the CEO and an employee representative, one of the full time officers, who takes on the day to day responsibility of the Forum. As the employee chair explained:

I've been called the (IPF) manager but I'm not, I'm the employee chair of the EPF. The forum is still jointly chaired by myself and … the chief exec but, in reality, as he says "You do it all" and that's something that's evolved since 2002 and the advent of the full-time reps. He knows now that I do it full time and I get on with it. He trusts me to get on with it and when I meet with him on a regular basis he just says 'how's it going?"

Following the abortive trade union recognition campaign the two seconded employee representatives set about reforming the IPF. This included replacing the constitution with a 'commitments document', giving the IPF the mission to "represent the voice of all (Interbank) People to make working life great and help drive superior business results". Its objectives were presented as:

- To increase the level of employee involvement in changes and business initiatives which affect employees using effective consultation
- To build and maintain effective relationships within all departments of (Interbank) through consultation
- To represent independently and without prejudice the interests of (Interbank) People both collectively and individually

The overall intention of the move from a constitution to a set of commitments was to make it less like a trade union body, avoiding formal agreements as well as a constitution. Also the full time IPF officers report to the HR Department but, they claim, this is no more than a formality. Like at Isar AG this may be because officers have learnt, or in this case may share, the same parameters of acceptability as corporate managers. In this they espoused an essential harmonious view of relations in the workplace so that, while they rejected the trade union approaches, they found certain aspects of 'partnership' appealing.

Very sensitive of the accusation that they were not autonomous of management the IPF set out to establish its own identity. Importantly, also, the changes in the IPF also meant an effective expansion in its role to what they characterised as moving to 'playing it big'. Additional to the established quarterly information and consultation meetings with the CEO the IPF moved to 'involvement at all levels' establishing relations with as wide a range of managers within the company as possible. The idea of this was to allow a level of intelligence on any issues that may be arising and consultation at as early a stage as possible. It also began establishing relationships with outside bodies through which it could gain support, the provision of training and expertise that might be expected of a trade union.

5. Legitimacy

a) Isar AG

Quite clearly the lack of autonomy employee representatives enjoy can be a threat to their legitimacy. Certainly, delegates to the Isar AG forum were more than conscious of this potential problem. In particular they were aware that the issues the workforce was interested in, terms and conditions, were formally excluded from the Forum's agenda. Delegates, however, felt a strong sense of responsibility to the people they not only represented, but equally felt representative of. There was a strong commitment not just to appear a 'voice box to collate information about queries, questions and concerns'. Such concerns had the effect that Employee Forum delegates were very committed to demonstrating to the workforce that they were not the extended arm the HRM department.

Although management had gone to great lengths to control the agenda, this did not deter employee representatives from raising salary related issues at Forum meetings. When interviewed employee respondents demonstrated, to the annoyance of management at times, a strong commitment to representing the workforce. Delegates were quite subtle and strategic in the way they raised issues. A procedure was followed which involved delegates posing questions irrespective of the agenda's restrictive guidelines they felt management might wish know about, issues that the workforce had raised. In this sense the delegation was able to place itself in a positive light, a conduit through which the workforce could enter into consultation with management.

One issue that has been raised on many occasions concerns maternity leave:

> Therefore, we put it (maternity leave) forward at the Employee Forum and we said "Yes we are aware that we cannot raise it but we think you should be aware that it is being raised." Therefore, it is down to them (management) what they do with it, it is not something that we sit and discuss and say "This is what people are asking for." From my point of view if something is raised, if people have come to us and asked us to put something forward we should do that. Whether we are allowed to actually sit down and talk about it is another matter, but at least we have raised it and then we can go back to that person and say "look we have raised it in the Employee Forum, it is actually something we are not allowed to discuss ourselves but HR are now aware of it."

Raising unconstitutional issues and ensuring that issues discussed at meetings are correctly documented is a means of demonstrating to the workforce, but equally to the HR department that the delegates are not “management lackeys”:

> There are points we have raised and we say “look can we just minute it, that we did actually raise it? If you are not going to do anything about it that is down to you but make sure that it is in the minutes. That we brought it up.” So we are doing our part of the deal if you like.

Faced by a management team not always co-operative, Forum delegates, who after all are conscious that they cannot hide away in the confines of a delegate office like their German counterparts, have to return to the shop floor and work alongside their colleagues. For this reason Forum delegates are required to demonstrate their legitimate right to represent the workforce. As will be indicated below, delegates’ insistence that they are not “management lackeys” helps steer management into a cul-de-sac, one in which management potentially faces a legitimacy crisis of its own if the workforce should question the value of the Forum.

b) Interbank

One of the reasons that the IPF initiated its transformation was because of accusations coming from many members of the workforce as well as the trade unions that it was ‘managements’ poodle’. It was also concerned that the consultations it was engaged in mainly, like other non-union consultative bodies (Dundon and Rollinson 2004; Gollan 2007), concerned trivial issues. Increasingly they sought to present an independent identity, one which involved their own logo sported in sweatshirt, a banner, and more substantively, presenting themselves for consultation and as party to involvement with the company at all levels. The promotion of this independent identity involved the production of a video with the IPF presenting itself as both useful to management but also as, in the words of one employee who is featured in the video, ‘like having our own little union’. Given that the IPF, unlike a trade union, is not dependent on recruitment of employees this exercise must be seen as part of an attempt to establish legitimacy amongst both management and employees.

While bargaining appears not to be an aspiration of the forum officers, bargaining of any sort would appear alien to the Interbank culture. Interbank people engage in frequent ‘conversations’ rather than get involved in anything which might be considered conflictual or confrontational. There are, however, consultations with management on all issues which may involve Interbank employees. However, Forum officers also represent employees in grievances and take up individual cases which often involve pay levels or the result of reviews. To gain visibility IPF officers hold monthly 'awareness days' on each of the sites in which they are available to hear any grievances or to discuss problems with any employees who may approach them. These are also used as an informal hustings for candidates at IPF elections. The IPF have become involved in all the areas where consultation may be expected in a traditional workplace and are the direct concern within ICE regulations. Recently they had consulted over TUPE (transfer of undertakings) and over redundancies resulting from rationalisation.

6. Efficacy

a) Isar AG

The efficacy of Isar AG delegates was severely hampered by problems associated with autonomy and legitimacy discussed above, and hence necessitated a high degree of skill in formulating and promoting policies supported by the workforce but opposed by management. As Hyman (1997: 311) notes, the question of efficacy needs 'to be viewed as relative to what is potentially attainable'. Undoubtedly, there were numerous factors which hampered the efficacy of Employee Forum delegates. First and foremost there was the issue of time. Delegates complained that they were often required to undertake Employee Forum duties, i.e. preparing for meetings, liaising with the workforce and other delegates in their own time (usually dinner-break). According to chair of the Employee Forum, who is also the HR manager, 'Delegates are given what the company refers to as a reasonable amount of time to fulfil their Forum duties'. However, by not clearly defining what amounts to "reasonable" allows line managers' to abuse their position of power by not respecting delegates' rights to undertake Forum duties. One respondent noted:

> I imagine the time in the constitution is okay. It is whether we actually get it, whether our managers, whether our workload reflects this time, that we actually get this time.

When faced by such opposition, though, respondents were not reluctant to point out that management had favoured the establishment of the Forum. Generally delegates complained that they were not allocated enough time for Forum business.

Time alone, though, was not the only issue which had a potentially negative bearing on the efficacy of employee delegates. The other concerned skill sets. All respondents indicated, that excluding the one day they had spent with a lawyer to discuss the constitution, they had received no training to support them in tasks on the Forum. Nevertheless, delegates have been quite adroit in addressing their skills deficit. Undoubtedly, their cause has been furthered by their own accumulation of often tacit skills and experience. With the exception of one delegate all were former graduates with considerable experience in the industry. Hence, as a group they could draw on a considerable pool of knowledge. In addition, they had access to a network of contacts in the financial sector. Combined, these two factors helped the delegates to often outflank management, providing them with the ability to draw-up well thought through proposed changes to company policy. An example, involved recent changes to the salary review that management had implemented without consulting the workforce. But, as the following respondent notes, such a move not only undermined the value of the Forum but also failed to consider that delegates could recognise such underhand management manoeuvres. As one of the Forum representatives explained:

This is what we do. This is our job to load things monthly. It is how premiums work … They did all this (salary review) without any consultation and they should have loaded it with around 4% to take into account changes in interest rates. This is what we do and they sometimes think they can get away with these things and they don't realise that we are actually quite intelligent people.

Certainly, contacts that delegates have at other companies prove an excellent source of information. It represents a key factor that contributes to their efficacy. This quite clearly proved to be case when management agreed to undertake a benchmarking exercise in connection to maternity leave. Management argued that its existing maternity leave policy (one that complies with statutory maternity regulations) was in line with the entitlements of employees at other companies. Delegates, however, refused to accept this and undertook their own benchmarking exercise. In fact this suggested that Isar AG's policy was inferior to what employees were entitled to at other companies:

(Management) respond by saying they have listened to us and that they have reviewed it (maternity leave) in the past and that they are in line with the market – end of story. This is often challenged – the Forum members want to see the benchmarking the company has done – but the company refuses to share this information. Like I said we work in employee benefits and we know lots of other people in other companies and people will do their own benchmarking. There was an even an article in the Guardian which graded companies and the general benefits were there and if you placed us into those benefits we would have been right at the bottom. So we said "you say we are line with the market but everything we see says that we are not. Prove it to us!"

b) Interbank

One immediate contrast between Isar AG and Interbank forums appears the issue of time for officers. As we have seen IPF has three full time officers whose time is fully funded by the company. The other eight or nine Employee Forum delegates receive time to perform their duties agreed with their line manager and can vary dependent on demands. It is an arrangement that appears not to have been problematic. The time allocation was the result of the 'playing it big' initiated two years after the forum was founded. To a large extent this put the Forum into the hands of the employees, managements' role becoming more notional, giving them both time and control over a budget. Importantly the independent budget has allowed the reps to undergo a range of training. As the employee chair explained:

> One of the beauties about … having your own budget is the fact that I can decide, we can decide and when, how and who actually does the – does the training. And – and who it's for, so it's not HR thinking we'll do this training for you.

The existence of three full time officers, the employee chair and 'A' and 'V', also means that IPF consultation has expanded dramatically beyond the original bimonthly meetings with the CEO. Again, as the employee chair relates:

> one of the advantages of us having three full time people about is that each one of us has different relationships. … So we've got, we've got (A) and (V) both meeting the head of banking once a month. So we've got two of our reps meeting the head of banking on a monthly basis. … I'm meeting banking products director once a month. I've got meetings with – I'll meet the chief exec personally once a month. We've got (A) meeting the chief information officer, head of technology, once a month. You've got all sorts. There – so those sorts of things at the top are going on. Then we've got well, people leaders. We've got meetings with them fortnightly. I'll meet with the head of borrowing every fortnight. So we've got – it's just so regular. It's so regular with no – no particular agenda, just what's going on, what you'd like to tell me, what – what you want from me, how can I help you?

The changes have not just meant an expansion in information and consultation but also into what may be considered more traditional, even trade union, areas of activity. IPF delegates act as health and safety reps, and at least the full time officers take on a caseload in individual discipline and grievances. What might best characterise their approach is that essentially they would see their role as not an advocate of the individual or collective employees but one of creating harmony and consent within the employment relationship.

7. Discussion

The emergence of new employee representative forums at Isar AG and Interbank are symbolic of quite wide-raging changes sweeping through British industrial relations. The establishment of such employee representative bodies is, as at Isar AG and at Interbank, often a management initiative to comply with ICE regulations that also helps to exclude trade union involvement. Conscious that UK and European law had opened new representative avenues for employees, management within both our case studies adopted a pre-emptive strategy and drew-up a constitution which ensured them ultimate control over the supposed representative forum.

In both cases, however, Forum delegates were opposed to playing the role of mere extras, when presented with roles that appeared rigidly scripted by management they increasingly gained confidence and skill to improvise and develop alternative scenarios. Even where employee delegates were hand-picked by management the individuals in question could distance themselves from their initial benefactor. This expressed itself in a general opposition on the part of employee reps to being treated as nothing more than the extended arm of the HR department. Although representatives accepted they had an important communication role to play between management and the workforce, these representatives felt such a role had to include a degree of participation which allowed them to influence company policy.

The very establishment of an employee representation body for consultation – however tokenistic – seemed to create a conduit for employee grievances and concerns. Managements' customising project was clearly not the unmitigated success it was intended to be and, as in other studies of non-union employee representation (Butler 2005; Terry 1999; Gollan 2007), autonomy proved to be a contentious issue. In the case of the Interbank Forum the process of distancing from management had been symbolised by 'playing it big', which was also represented a distancing from traditional employee representation. Symbolically this could be seen in the IPF moving from the constitution they had written for them by management, to a commitments document in part because they felt the constitution resembled the bureaucratic rule they associated with trade unions. This move had been precipitated by some representatives' concern that they were only dealing with trivia issues, a concern that had also emerged – although at an earlier stage – amongst the reps at Isar AG. The desire to distance themselves from management also involved the question of legitimacy, in particular the workforce's view of the representatives' position within the Forum. At one level this concerned not appearing more than a "management poodle". It also involved, though, representatives acknowledging that they had an ethical duty to their constituents. Moreover, reps noted, that the workforce had a right to a collective voice which could only be realised if the Forum attained its independence of management.

Combined, these factors ensured that delegates were committed to moving the goalposts initially set down by management. In the case of Interbank the Forum has gone from being a "sausages in the canteen" structure to one which now possesses three fulltime officers and is consulted by management on a wide-range of issues. This developmental process mirrors many of the current research findings on

EWCs. Researchers demonstrating that even though such bodies often have limited rights to start with this does not have to deter employee representatives from broadening its initial management remit (Lecher et al., 2001; Whittall, 2003; Kotthoff, 2006). Our cases have been limited to non-union workplaces in the insurance and finance sector. Our conclusion may have been different if we had considered the introduction of forums in already unionised workplaces where they may stifle a more traditional union voice. However these cases may hold lessons about where no collective voice exists, which could be highly important now that the economic bubble has burst which threatens to throw this sector into crisis and by doing so creating increased tension in the employment relationship. Our two case studies indicate that the establishment of collective employee representation, however dependent it is initially on management, may open a 'Pandora's box'. Delegates of the forum, while maybe adopting management's agenda, can use the forum to extend employee involvement and voice. While, the forums are themselves limited in their autonomy by the very dependence on management patronage for their resources they may prove a platform for the establishment of a more independent voice for employees.

References

BERR (Department of Business, Enterprise and Regulatory Reform) (2006): The Information and Consultation of Employees Regulations 2004 DTI Guidance (January 2006) available at http://www.berr.gov.uk/employment/ employment-legislation/ice/index.html

Butler, P. (2005): Non-union employee representation: exploring the efficacy of the voice process. Employee Relations, 27(3): 272-283.

DTI (2007): Workplace representatives: a review of their facilities and facility time. London: Department of Trade and Industry (BERR).

Dundon, T. / Rollinson, D. (2007): Employment Relations in Non-Union Firms London, Routledge

Dunn, S. (1990): Root Metaphor in the Old and New Industrial Relations. British Journal of Industrial Relations, 28(1).

Gall, G. (2005): Union organising in the "new economy" in Britain. Employee Relations, 27(2): 208-225.

Gollan, P.J. (2007): Employee Representation in Non-Union Firms. London, Thousand Oaks, New Delhi: Sage.

Hall, M. (2006): A cool response to the ICE Regulations? Employer and trade union approaches to the new legal framework for information and consultation. Industrial Relations Journal, 37(5): 456-472.

Hyman, R. (1997): The Future of Employee Representation. British Journal of Industrial Relations, 35(3): 309-336.

Kelly, J. (1998): Rethinking Industrial Relations: Mobilization, Collectivism and Long Waves. London and New York: Routledge and LSE.

Kersley, B. / Alpin, C. / Forth, J. / Bryson, A. / Bewley, H. / Dix, G. / Oxenbridge, S. (2006): Inside the Workplace: Findings of the 2004 Workplace Employment Relations Survey. London and New York: Routledge.

Lloyd, C. (2001): What Do Employee Councils Do? The Impact of Non-Union Forms of Representation on Trade Union Organisation. Industrial Relations Journal, 32(4): 313-327.

Mercer, S. / Notley, R. (2008): Trade Union Membership 2007. London: Department for Business Enterprise & Regulatory Reform.

Rogers, J. / Streeck, W. (1995): The Study of Works Councils: Concepts and Problems. In Rogers, J. and Streeck, W. (eds.), Works Councils: Consultation, Representation and Cooperation in Industrial Relations: 3-26. Chicago and London: The University of Chicago Press.

Terry, M. (1999): Systems of collective employee representation in non-union firms in the UK. Industrial Relations Journal, 30(1): 16-30.

Whittall, M. (2003): European Works Councils – A Path to European Industrial Relations? The Case of BMW and Rover. PhD, Nottingham Trent, Nottingham.

II. Strategies of improving organizational performance through workplace participation

Strategies of improving organizational performance through workplace participation – Report from Stream II

Paul Oehlke

1. Introduction into the presentation of selected results

The *European Workplace Participation Forum* offered a mosaic of topics in the field of worker participation concerning general trends and specific challenges, in particular, its changing role and function with regard to working conditions and competitiveness. In this broad context, the *second stream* dealt with quite heterogeneous organizational strategies of improving performance. In view of the interdependence of the diverse action and research fields of workplace participation, parts of the individual lectures overlapped within and between the workshops. Therefore, their contents shall be not summed up strictly in line with the course of the programme.

Already the variety of speakers confined to the northern and western, less to the southern and not at all to the eastern states in Europe, reveals a north-south and a west-east divide concerning the *strategies of improving organizational performance through workplace participation.* It is no accident that this selection demonstrates that participative approaches, their contents, objectives and effects also depend on the respective systems of industrial relations, regional and national research activities which are interrelated with the economic and political development on macro-level. After the *introduction into the presentation of selected results* (1) this paper continues with a short analysis of *context-dependent changes* (2) transforming participation from a *constitutional issue of society* to a more or less *strategic management approach* which might gain a renewed political significance in the present crisis period. The short presentation of the political determinants of the development of European participation objectives lays the ground for the main part presenting *the development of organisational strategies* (3) with respect to cost-reducing profit maximization undermining participation rights (3.1), to keeping up participation opportunities through industrial relations systems (3.2) and to diverse support structures fostering high road participation processes (3.3). In connection with these aspects there is a short summary of selected *features of some regional and national programme activities* (4). Finally, I will give some *conclusions for further research activities* (5).

2. Context-dependent changes of the objectives of participation

The new organizational forms of worker participation including their rejection have been decisively influenced by the *changing macro-level context* which should not be neglected when analyzing, promoting and evaluating the concepts, developments and results of participation strategies. Though regrettable, it is a nearly two decades-long fact, that various participation studies have laid their focus merely on defining and classifying the qualitative stages of participation and on measuring and evaluating their quantitative dissemination or taking part in private and public consulting often taking not sufficient care for the rapidly changing economic and political background. But, the quite heterogeneous state of the art in different European countries demands to take far more into account the relationship of company and management strategies with economic and political developments – an urgent need that has been thoroughly elaborated in the contribution of *Volker Telljohann* and been taken up systematically by *Tuomo Alasoini* and his colleagues referring to former studies of *Frieder Naschold* (1993) which were initiated by the thorough evaluation of the Swedish *Leadership, Organisation and Codetermination Programme* (LOM).

The concept of participation was originally deeply rooted in strategies of industrial democracy which tried to *transfer objectives and procedures of political democracy into the economy* since the 19th century (Abendroth 1972). Especially during the revolutionary period after First World War and after the defeat of German National Socialism and Fascism in Italy both of them supported by influential economic powers there were strong endeavours all over Europe first of all to break and later on to balance the dominance of big business by introducing three elements of structural change more or less interconnected with each other: *democratic regulation of the economy on the basis of a broad public sector and an institutionalized participation of workers on company level* reaching from involvement in social aspects of work until co-determination in economic decisions. Under this constitutional umbrella, there were launched in many European countries during the middle of the 1970ies public activities for improving working conditions of employees and performance of companies alike. The *concept of participation as integral part of social dialogue* though mainly within the realm of thriving public activities embraced diverse subjects of decent, humane and good work: such as safety, health and well-being; enriching contents of work tasks, work processes and work design; extending communication, cooperation and competence at work. The broad range of participation issues – but less of improving employment contracts, wage structures and working time reserved to collective bargaining – did already comply with new economic challenges of saturated markets which demanded more product variety, change and quality stimulating flexible process and product innovations.

The crisis of hitherto successful Fordistic mass production modes with their Tayloristic division of work increased the need for organizational change from hierarchically divided to horizontally integrated forms which led to the *implementation of semi-autonomous work groups with complex work tasks* paving the way to a new evaluation of work. On the road to a knowledge-intensive economy relying more and more on the competence of staff, new concepts of human capital or resource management flourished. They try to convert individual tacit knowledge within its local social context into streamlined codified knowledge suited to the objectives of profit-making organizations to get competitive advantage. Thus, the trend to an *individualization of work* implied *modern direct forms of participation* which substituted more and more the traditional forms of representation parallel to a systematic weakening of the unions while publicly being denounced as bureaucratic, outmoded and unfashionable. Accordingly, in *Germany*'s *labour research programmes based on representative participation structures* the originally social-oriented emphasis was transformed from employee- to employer-related objectives of improving innovation, productivity and competitiveness which replaced gradually the design of workplaces, processes and technologies according to human needs through objectives of empowerment, employability and entrepreneurship of employees parallel in tacit correspondence to similar European labour market acitivites (Oehlke 2001).

But, the transformation of the comprehensive participation approach with regard to new knowledge-driven demands from an integral element of industrial democracy to managerial human resource policies got a specific coinage through the stepwise changing socio-economic framework since the 1970ies. National economic policies, in particular, demand regulation by financial interventions lost their effectiveness with *the termination of the gold standard, fixed rates of exchange and the liberalization of international capital transactions* which pushed forward global competition. Based on political decisions in the Anglo-Saxon world, the door was opened for *neoliberal policies* which got a final break-through on the European continent with the collapse of the Soviet Union. They smoothed the way to a gradual transformation from mainly humane to economic objectives, from industrial relations to human resource management, from social welfare to liberal competitive policies, from industrial development strategies to pure money-making for shareholders exclusively. In accordance with a finance-oriented *colonizing of life worlds* (*Jürgen Habermas*), there is to be acknowledged a statistically well proven polarization between a minority of people on the top becoming extremely richer and a growing minority on the bottom living in poverty (Bourdieu 1993) while the majority of the middle classes experience the spreading of insecurity with slower growing, stagnating or even shrinking income.

This down- and backward spirals of working and living standards, however, have been strongly supported in many European apart from Scandinavian countries by a range of political interventions under the label of promoting competitive performance growth through rising societal inequality and extended dumping strategies. Already a decade ago, a *high-level expert group of the EU* warned of *negative forms of harmonization through the erosion of tax, wage and social standards* (Commission européenne 1998, 53-55). Parallel to the weakening of the systems of industrial relations design units in companies, public labour research centers and national programmes for improving the quality of work have been reduced or even closed down with some hopeful exceptions in Norway and Finland, Ireland and Belgium. In general, however, protagonists did fight a *Sisyphus contest* from the very beginning (Hertog 1992; Andreasen et al. 1995). Even on European level they could not cope with the dominant trend by marketing again and again *the high road of participation driving innovative performance* through elaborated papers, official communications and collections of good practice examples all over Europe (Brödner et al. 1998, European Work and Technology Consortium 1998). Even more or less advanced forms of direct employee participation under the tutelage of management were rather marginally diffused in Europe except in the Nordic countries (European Foundation 1997, Brödner/Latniak 2003). Thus it is no wonder that the Green paper on *Partnership for a new organisation of work* (Europäische Kommission 1997) was openly rejected by influential groups of employers and their federations as well as checkmated through the Commissions' market and economic policies, e. g. concerning the *Services directive* which may function as a stimulator for social dumping.

At present, the deep crisis of finance-oriented market policies reveals to be the offspring of growing disproportions of wealth accumulation being responsible for a *lacking demand of the majority of customers not compensated by luxury consumption of the upper layers of society combined with shrinking public and private investments* straightly leading into overheated financial speculations and, *with a time-lag,* an economic recession (Perez 2002). In contradiction to the neoliberal prayers all the years before, political classes, however, seem to have learnt to pour financial stabilizers into the economy reminding the non-interventionist failures during the world economic crisis from the Black Friday 1929 onwards. But, there is still looming the danger in Europe of governments helping primarily big business and financial capital being to a great extent responsible for the crisis by their finance-driven accumulation policies. Whether the *urgent need for regulating financial markets, strengthening the public sector and increasing infrastructural investments* will be sufficiently fulfilled, depends mainly on the configuration of social forces, in particular, *a progressive alliance between the organizations of the labour market* which are willing to overcome the backlashes for innovative change. Dependent on participation and cooperation of all competent stakeholders social and economic progress will be accomplished by an *activated society embedded in a structured interplay between strong labour organisations, courageous state interventions and responsible capital groups* – a long-time ignored, if not suppressed lesson which has to be learnt again (OECD 1988).

In the present situation, a public promotion of further participative approaches through social pacts including programmes for the high road of improving working conditions and innovative competencies in companies would make much sense on social as well as on economic grounds. Thus, *a comprehensive participation approach ensuring high road production systems in a knowledge-intensive society with better and more jobs* may realize the failing Lisbon agenda which has been reduced to the dead end of pursuing the *European Commission's mantra of competitiveness in deregulated markets* (Alhadeff, Hugendubel 2005) – a neoliberal obsession which has been criticized by the present nobel prizewinner *Paul Krugman* already in 1994. There is an urgent need to put more emphasis on innovative work and organisational renewal that will contribute to a dynamic knowledge society with increasing employment opportunities thereby fostering likewise stable growth and social cohesion. But, this means to replace the market prerogatives through political objectives, profit maximization through social welfare, plutocracy through democracy.

3. Development of organisational strategies and the quality of participation

In the present situation of financial market crises, heralding heavy economic slumps in almost all highly developed countries and their industrial branches, there are still to be found quite different management approaches to participation according to national and regional distinctions and differences between private and public sectors. They are ranging from a persistence of purely cost-reducing strategies during the last two decades undermining participative approaches (3.1) via keeping up participation opportunities in industrial relations systems (3.2) until the existence of diverse support structures fostering high road participation processes to the advantage of employees' well-being and companies' performance (3.3). The objectives of the Participation Forum prevented most speakers referring to the rather big, in many countries prevailing stream of purely profit maximizing strategies on the expense of participation. Therefore, it shall be mentioned here.

3.1 Cost-reducing profit maximization undermines participation rights

Increasing returns for shareholders and top management in the short run doubled by financial innovations as private equity companies, hedge-funds and derivatives have become dominant beliefs in the financial and economic world since the 1990ies making long-term firm policies to dependent and neglected variables combined with damages for the workforce experiencing worsening employment contracts and working conditions. This does often happen to the *disadvantage of companies' innovative capacities by outsourcing and offshoring even strategic units* for research and development. The pure announcement of streamlining companies today less to formerly so-called core competencies, but of filleting them more to highly profitable branches with laying off workers, make the stock market prices jump up promising the shareholders increased dividends and management additional bonuses, with the side-effect of a loss of influence for the employees' representatives on company and union levels.

The restructuring of companies and workplaces around the globe shifts the already asymmetric balance between capital and labour to the detriment of social and democratic standards, in particular of industrial relations and above all trade unions generally getting disregard and even disdain in the media. Thus, the living and working conditions of the workforce still kept in jobs begins to deteriorate not to speak of the staff set on the dole. Under this persistent danger the employees and their unions are forced to accept the results of *concession bargaining* as there are reductions of wage levels, extensions of working times and speeding up of work processes. Regarding such negative framework for representing the interests of the employees in modern *casino capitalism* headlines in journals as Newsweek (2004) state the general perspective of *Labor Pains. Working Harder For Less Pay? Welcome to the New World Economy*!

In accordance with short-sighted management strategies aiming at short-term profit growth in favour of shareholder value expectations and bonuses, the public rules regulating employment and working conditions including working time have been successively deregulated creating a state of generalized insecurity and a growth of precarious employment. The results are well documented on national as well as on European levels: longer daily, yearly and life working times, higher strain and stress at work with increasing mental diseases and a general decay of qualification, training and competence standards. Accordingly, *public policies have intensified the rat race to the bottom and indirectly promoted the reemergence of company strategies of primarily and purely reducing labour costs.* Thereby, the already gained industrial experience and scientific knowledge on the design of work and technology according to human needs have been spoilt and blocked, moreover, the innovative high road work systems built on developing internal functional flexibility. Instead of developing the skills of their employees and knowledge transfer from the older to the younger staff many companies choose the low road of relying on numeric external flexibility thanks to deregulated labour markets.

There is much evidence for these trends in Germany. Contrary to the metal employers' propositions 15 years ago to match global competition by motivated and qualified employees through forms of organizational renewal *a regressive participation approach* has been propagated by their regional chairman in South-West Germany since a few years. The main proposals rely on strengthening the managerial control functions at the expense of the autonomy of work, standardizing work tasks for an increased work speed and reducing the surplus of qualifications by introducing more simple and cheaper labour (Gryglewski 2007). The statements of this high-ranking representative of industry justified euphemistically as incremental innovations for matching global competition pressures stimulated a controversial debate with strong criticism from the side of metal workers' union and labour researchers. They qualified these arguments as *backward orientations closing the doors for a sustainable future of employees and employers in German metal industries* which are demanded to continuously developing their competence for innovating processes and products to keep up their competitive edge.

The cost-oriented reduction of participation opportunities opens the way backwards to semi-tayloristic forms of work which might be successful in the short run to keep market shares especially in sectors of mass production although such downgrading work and labour policies cannot avoid *the trap of less cyclical than structural overproduction* in relation to the forced shrinkage of demand. By the way, the now highly controversial financial support by the governments of the triade USA, Japan and Germany for the crisis-prone motor industry in particular will deepen this dilemma already in the medium term. And, the way out of a competitive dead end will be locked without promoting radical product innovations and supporting infrastructures. They should be arranged to open up new markets and employment opportunities in areas of social and ecological needs, e.g. for integrated, thereby service-oriented mobility systems (Bullinger 1998) which may further future-enabling development paths of declining private and increasing public elements.

3.2 Keeping up participation opportunities through industrial relations systems

Trends to undermining participation opportunities indicate the growing need for their stronger anchorage in intact or revived systems of industrial relations. But, their development depends on the concrete power relationships between capital and labour which differ from country to country in the European Union. Although a general loss of unions' organizational strength except in the Nordic countries is to be stated since the 1990ies, there have been developed new strategic concepts in some countries as Belgium, Finland, Ireland and Norway relying on an extended social dialogue partly also on regional level (Fricke, Totterdill 2004). In Germany, the metal workers' union (IGM) have launched new initiatives under the labels of *good work* and *better than cheaper* aiming at mobilizing industrial workers and a wider public for neglected objectives of humanization of work and urging employers and their associations to seize all opportunities for quality products which may open up new future-oriented markets. Taking the offensive the IGM tries to overcome the downward spirals of purely cost-reducing production models implying at least in the longer run increased burdens for all stakeholders particularly the workers.

Contrary to such negative options of the still dominant business strategies laying the focus on rising profitability in Germany there is to be found in some companies and regions especially in Northern Europe a positive correlation between integral union and management strategies combining the demands of improving work quality with companies' innovation competence. The experience from many good practice examples is veryfied though cautiously by conclusions of *Davide Antonioli* and his colleagues from the *University of Ferrara* who compared two Italian local production systems while investigating the interdependence of innovation, industrial relations and working conditions. Their empirical analysis of representative data of small and medium-sized enterprises in the region *Emilia Romagna* confirms the results of former studies that the well-being of workers and innovative capacities at workplaces are fostered by a grown milieu of cooperative industrial relations. They can function as *fertile humus* for an innovation-oriented growth. Likewise questionnaires of *Erko Martins* from the *German University of Rostock* document that an organizational culture of qualified participation will have positive effects on employees' work attitudes and management's behaviour.

These perceptions are indirectly backed by a Dutch case study of *Jan Ekke Wigboldus and his colleagues* which, with the help of a theoretical model, indicates that work councils do not only effect employees' and management's attitudes but give also additional information to managerial decision-making processes thus influencing organizational performance. Accordingly, *Annette Van den Berg and her colleagues* analyzed *managerial perceptions of works councils' effectiveness in the Netherlands* referring to German studies on the acceptance of German works councils from the point of managers' view. Their econometric study uses a nation-wide dataset including all branches of the private sector. In general, the data confirm that management perceives works councils in a *functionalist perspective* whether they are apt to increase efficiency and innovativeness. The positive effects are increasing with the existence of collective labour agreements and of a qualified workforce with two exceptions that process innovations lead to lay-offs and that management tries to substitute works councils by giving individual workers more influence. Negative outcomes of such *divide et impera* policies are generally connected with a weakening of the system of industrial relations which, in addition, will be fragmented through transnational outsourcing.

From the unions' point of view capital transfer strategies might be countered by an intense trans-national cooperation of works councils and their unions' headquarters as practised, though still reluctantly, in metal industry, here especially in reorganisation projects by developing alternative solutions. A partial success story was demonstrated by *Ralf Nieman,* acting works council of a big steel factory of a multinational company supported by the scientific advisor *Wilfried Kruse*. Both of them indicated two important aspects of participation which are often neglected in rather abstract scientific discussions. Works councils are used to make the *experience that participation opportunities have to be bargained often very hardly with management* in periods of organisational adaptation to competition challenges, particularly with regard to safeguarding the interests of employees concerning job security and qualification opportunities, pay levels and structures, gender issues and working time. Moreover, works councils have often to cope with nearly unavoidable backlashes in processes of acquisitions and mergers, outsourcing and offshoring when *decisions of remote headquarters* are outmaneuvering well bargained social plans, budgets for skill enhancement and timetables with the local management which, in the best case, may be rebargained but to minor deals for the employees.

In view of encroaching new forms of corporate financing with their primary aim of short-term profits for investors and shareholders, *Peter Wilke* discussed *good corporate governance* corresponding with an obligatory involvement of employees in European Union member states. He argued that participation rights in supervisory or management boards should function in the interest of making employees a *citizen in the workplace*. Moreover, through increasing the commitment of the workforce and quality of work processes, as numerous studies emphasize, the innovative capacity and productivity growth of companies could be improved alongside with their long-term performance and competitiveness. In addition, the debate on *corporate social responsibility* indicates a growing awareness of social and environmental impacts of corporate governance which includes a stakeholder approach in contradiction to the negative effects of shareholder capitalism endangering democracy in Europe. Such dangers speak strongly in favour of further developing participation and codetermination rights for example with regard to the *European Works Councils* which are positively correlated with good governance practices as measured by various sustainability indices.

All the more the unions are challenged to gain a *proactive role* together with employees in developing innovative alternatives in the context of renewed social dialogues. *But, there are traditional barriers on all sides to an allover organizational empowerment and modernization of industrial relations:* managers being keen to preserve their traditional prerogatives, full-time officials having climbed up the union's hierarchical ladder and many employees not trusting their tacit competence, sometimes remaining in a state of learnt helplessness. Inherited organizational blockades produce a state of inertia which is often legitimized by an abstract radicalism against the atrocities of the other side not taking adequately into consideration structural frameworks of liberalized markets. Such attitudes of personalizing context dependencies poison the climate for innovative solutions which, however, have to be fought for in change arenas of the industrial relations system. That demands the development of self-conscious codetermination and co-management practices *from a position of strength of employees and their representatives based on acquiring organizational, technological and workplace design competence* for improving the quality of working life and work processes as integral prerequisites of company performance.

3.3 Diverse support structures fostering high road participation processes

The institutional deregulation is going hand in hand with spreading applications of market principles governing production units and work processes. In the utmost consequence, every worker shall be directly faced with the volatile demands of dynamic, even financial markets he or she cannot control at all. Thus, there may be a growing ambivalence turning greater self-determination at work through more responsibilities, process autonomy and direct participation as ingredients of qualitative, creative and innovative performance, in particular, a precondition of successful knowledge management in high-involvement work systems, to greater self-exploitation through extension of working time, intensification of work and less time for acquiring skills. Generally increasing physical and mental pressures related to the diffusion of high performance work systems with forms of direct participation have been documented by international studies (Docherty et al. 2002). Such evidence indicates the need to take into account the other side of the coin: forms of representative participation rooted in the industrial relations system. The advantages of such a combination, while only marginally realized in Italy, have been analyzed by *Volker Telljohann* in his basic paper on *direct and representative participation in the context of organizational innovation processes.*

Being likewise aware that the adoption of new flexible work arrangements including increased employee involvement may also lead to more stress and job intensity, *Elise Ramstad* developed the mutual gains perspective of *promoting company performance and the quality of working life simultaneously*, which, however, requires *a supportive development process and an adequate institutional framework*. Thus, *collaborative industrial relations in coordinated market economies* – here, in the case of the Finnish Workplace Development programme (Alasoini et al. 2005) – do contribute effectively to sustainable workplace practices. *Elise Ramstad* referred to a collection of studies in the Finish metal industry and USA steel industry which show a positive correlation between a bundle of coherent workplace practices as job security and higher wages, active training and responsible teamwork with commitment, competitiveness and product development. Corresponding with own data from 409 projects gained by self-assessment methods of the competent parties, performance and innovation-oriented approaches based on high involvement of employees start with their affecting the planning and implementation of change processes which, more and more knowledge-intensive, demand increasingly external networking.

Accordingly, the risk of corporate underperformance without support structures was highlighted by *Romain Chevallet* on the basis of a study of *95 investment projects* in French SMEs which verified a common experience in other European countries. There is still to be found a centralized technical project culture without relying on the tacit knowledge of employees' operational practices. Besides a brief training organized by the equipment provider there is a general lack of user involvement which is more or less limited to organizational adjustments. Here, regional players in charge of financing and implementing investment grant systems may help through guides like cardboard models, layout plans, logic diagrams and skill benchmarks. This conclusion is backed by qualitative change projects in Denmark. *Palle Banke* outlined his substantial experience on innovative cost-saving for companies in his contribution on *setting the scene for employee participation in design and implementation of new production technology*. He demonstrated convincingly how to overcome the barriers towards innovation deriving from traditional expert-led thinking around design, development and implementation of new technology often producing suboptimal results. By offering a fair platform for employees to participate the operators are given a voice by creative methods which are built on elements of forum theatre, change videos, photo safaris and scanning interviews to improve the utilisation of competencies in the whole organisation. By involving the future users from the very beginning in the work performed by managers, architects, engineers, machine suppliers and consultants, the operators become important stakeholders in the whole process architecture of change saving costs and paving the way for incremental innovations.

The difficulties of empowering individuals to overcome traditional organizational barriers were discussed by *Rosemary Exton* referring to her experience throughout an English county as a Programme Lead of the *Improving Working Lives (IWL) initiative.* She discovered *residual deep structures of hierarchical management* with bureaucratic demarcations and cultures of conformity and compliance as forms of social domination and traps of hybrid regulation under the flexibility imperative including partnership and networking. In face of still resisting forces to change the interviews of IWL leads made apparent that *creative employees may exploit inconsistent objectives and even construct an entrepreneurial identity* challenging subversively the fortifications of the status quo. Identity research suggests, however, that sustainability demands *codified participation in discursive practices* with senior management, genuine staff involvement and evident workforce benefits. Correspondingly, there is to be acknowledged *an interaction of individual identity construction and supportive regulatory structures* at all stages of the innovation chain which are conducive for the emergence of entrepreneurial behaviour. The research-backed experience delivered by Rosemary Exton indicated the social determinants of fragile behaviour patterns of dependent wage-earners who are tied in frozen hierarchies whether in public services or in private industries without being able to rely on any private property of companies' assets as a certain background for genuine entrepreneurship.

In view of the European Commissions' insisting on a framework of employment quality which demands new forms of corporate employees' financial participation as means to reach a better distribution of wealth and positive effects on productivity *Patricia Nieto Rojas* discussed *financial participation in Spain* between salary compensation as reality and employee co-responsibility in corporate decisions as development opportunity for a new corporate governance policy. Employees would become co-owners and would have influence not only as stakeholders but also as shareholders who should have access to corporate organs thus stimulating the entrepreneurial spirit of business-like attitudes. But, *Patricia* indicated that without *sufficient legislative support*, the bulk of Spanish companies does not practice any financial participation schemes which, in the case of some relevant companies, for example by stock options and shares are confined to instruments of human resource management in order to inciting employees' individual or group performance and to retaining the most qualified employees as sources of organizational flexibility and productivity growth. For the sake of global competitiveness, the more *collaborative evolution of companies' power relationships* might also be used to promote long-term investment policies and stakeholder approaches.

4. Features of regional and national participation programmes

Most of the studies referred to show that there is a growing need for a wider institutional framework which extends public and private interactions to create more work quality, innovative competence and productivity increases. They are altogether integral elements to match the demands of a dynamic knowledge society for *continuous high-involvement innovation and progressive knowledge-sharing* what has been outlined in detail in the respective paper and other reports of *Peter Totterdill.* Crucial points are that these qualitative performance factors depend on the scope of an active intra-firm involvement of employees and inter-firm co-operation between manufacturers and their clients often demanding professional expertise in a regional or national, sometimes even international context of consultants, research institutes and training facilities. Though there is ample empirical evidence in favour for such combined and interactive approaches, the findings from European-wide surveys and case studies demonstrate that organisations following such a determined *high road innovation strategy* are still relatively thin on the ground in Europe. This state of the art demands to launch or to stock up work-oriented innovation activities on a tripartite basis of labour, capital and state embedded in a wider political framework (Totterdill et al. 2002; Oehlke et al. 2007).

But, the present situation of national programmes which support workplace research and development in Europe is still fragmented and unevenly developed among EU member states. Most of these activities except those in Northern countries have been rather modest in terms of their financial budgets, particularly compared to technology R&D programmes. This state of the art is confirmed by *Tuomo Alasoini* who presented a *comparative analysis of nine national and regional approaches* in the context of a still running network of national programmes in order to develop complementary, synergetic and coordinated research activities for a European productivity strategy based on work-oriented innovations (Work-In-Net). The *Work-In-Net-benchmark study* shows that the policy context of workplace development strategies varies widely being an established area of public policy in only a few countries so far. Except of the well established communication channels in Nordic regions, cross-border learning is still quite difficult because of only fragmented and unreliable information and its context- as well as system-dependent nature which needs the acquisition of thorough knowledge. There is a growing need for establishing multi-national interactive forums that provide common conceptual tools for making the experience of different countries more understandable before taking promising transfer perspectives in further consideration.

Swedish work structuring projects played already a role in the continuous chain of national programmes in Germany presented by *Claudio Zettel.* In the initial period, the organizational models in plants of the car manufacturers Saab and Volvo got strong notice in the programme on *Humanization of Work* from 1974. It took up further research and design areas during the 1980s which received a new umbrella through the *Work and Technology* programme from 1989 onwards. On the basis of a *comprehensive understanding of innovation* already developed in 1984 and afterwards adapted to new societal demands, the *Federal Ministry of Education and Research* launched in 2001 a five-year Framework Concept *Innovative Development of Work – The Future of Work* renewed by the still running programme *Working – Learning – Developing Competence – Innovation competence in a new world of work.* Both programmes intend to cope with challenges caused by demographic, technological and organizational changes for employees and companies. They shall be tackled by enlarged project networks e. g. on innovation cultures, electronic learning devices and organizational models of ageing workforces. But, the formerly broad participation approach functioning as an upward learning spiral has been reduced concerning firstly the introduction of enriched participation procedures in change projects according to the Works Constitution Act, secondly the autonomous transfer projects of the social partners enabling unions' representatives to develop proactively alternative design solutions and thirdly the various advisory panels with equal representation of unions and employers on the level of focus points as interactive arenas of joint discussions, learning and problem-solving. *Volker Klotz* explained such shortcomings from a financial point of view when pointing to the unmasking fact of work research policies covering only 0, 2% of the competent ministry's budget.

Though rather small the national activities influenced some federal states in Germany like North Rhine-Westphalia and the Free Hanseatic City of Bremen to run their own programmes co-financed by the European Social Fund (Oehlke 2007). In 1985, the most populated Federal State of *North Rhine-Westphalia* with around 17 million inhabitants started a programme on *Social Design of Technology* followed in 1994 by a more development-oriented activity which placed more emphasis on work organization, group work and employees' competencies. Six years later the meanwhile integrated *Ministry of Economy and Labour* launched a more pragmatic *Work-Oriented Modernization* strategy which was presented by *Friedhelm Keuken.* The so-called "*potential consulting*" projects are carried out through the steps of analysing the recent situation, creating a mid-term vision, planning the realization und turning the ideas into practice. This is done by a process-oriented approach based on informational transparency and participation of employees to improve workflows and employees' qualifications, productivity and innovation, access to new markets and sales' increases. For the promotion of regional effects there has been activated a network of 120 local agencies for economic development and social labour market policies as well as 2.300 consulting companies specialized on supporting change processes. According to this broad approach including different stakeholders the funding offers covering half of the expenses have been taken up by meanwhile more than 10.000 SMEs distinguishing by an average employment increase of 1.5% from 2000 until 2006 in contrast to the then declining employment on federal level.

In contrast to the long-term activities of the meanwhile regionalized French agency for the improvement of working conditions *ANACT* as well as the regional and national German programmes, not to forget the plethora of Nordic activities since the 1960ies in Norway, Sweden and, later on, Finland in the middle of the 1990ies there are two hopeful newcomers in Ireland and Flanders in the 21st century. The activities in both countries rely on industrial experience for an increasing need of broadening the concepts of innovation policy from technological to social innovation built on stronger cooperation between capital and labour. In Flanders, the new consensual atmosphere between the social partners was embodied in the *Pact of Vilvoorde* of 2001 linking the quality-of-work issue to the goal of increasing employability including the elderly and still unemployed. This pact contained a long-term socio-economic vision inducing the ambitious target to improve the quality of working life and entrepreneurial performance through better organization of work. Thus, the *Flemish* government started a work organization development programme in 2006 entitled as the *Flanders Synergy programme* co-financed through the *European Social Fund Agency of Flanders*. As such, it was a rather small and short 18 month programme with 12 selected pilot projects. But, according to *Paul Berckmanns* it signified an important breakthrough in policy thinking which resulted in follow-up activities on *Social Innovation* with increased financial resources for 16 projects approved in March 2008. Finally, organizational innovation has been accepted as a legitimate target of policy intervention and an integral part of the regional government's global innovation strategy.

5. Conclusions for further research and development topics

In spite of the divergent research approaches and results, there is a common denominator that *high road approaches need a wider social and institutional framework* even for enlightened management strategies which will be further developed with the help of diverse programme activities. They have to be built more explicitly as already in the past on forms of tripartite cooperation which take care for genuine participation and cooperation within and between companies including a broad range of social stakeholders and infrastructures, especially in the area of research and development. The combined efforts of developing innovative solutions for an increased company performance and improving quality of work for the workers shall be promoted by *organizational empowerment structures* which combine human resource approaches of management with participation opportunities of the works council based on collective bargaining and legislative acts.

In addition to an effective institutionalization, a balanced social dialogue demands for the parties of the labour market, especially the unions to open up opportunities for qualifying themselves what seems to be widely forgotten today. *A constant competence accumulation for employees, works councils and full-time officials creates the conditions for transforming participation from a formal right into a substantial practice of intervening in change processes and of balancing partially the asymmetry between labour and capital which derives from the predominance of the market principle* (Volker Telljohann). Social infrastructures and legal regulations for a power-related and competence-based participation integrating direct and representative forms are the keys for discussing design alternatives and implementing the best solutions for innovative high roads of sustainable development (Brödner et al. 1998). They have increasingly to take up matters of public interest with regard to social and ecological needs.

On the contrary, the conclusion of an *endemic neglect of social infrastructures, preconditions and objectives* can be drawn in view of several methodological approaches, strategic concepts and research results presented in the *European Workplace Participation Forum.* It gave an insight into a landscape of participation research being not spared from the temptations of neoliberal postmodernism. There has to be acknowledged a still *lacking action research* dealing with ambiguous situations on company and societal levels. Questionnaires on opinions and attitudes of managers and employees are related sometimes only to managers and not cross-checked by employees and their works councils or vice versa. Furthermore, the specific regional and national context and its fundamental changes in the course of time effecting substantially the beliefs and strategies of the social partners were partly out of the horizon of methodological approaches. Such a *regressive state of participation research* might be caused by the indirect effects of the neoliberal traps of the *pensée unique* (Pierre Bourdieu). It sacrifices categorically society and history in favour of an immutability of market principles and egoistic behaviour of man which in reality are deducted from lasting effects of specific social structures and their power relationships.

On the contrary, there is a strong need of *historically conscious, context-oriented and prospective basic research* dealing with the development, present state und new challenges with regard to the interrelations between management strategies and industrial relations, social regulations and the promotion of innovation competence. Thus, micro-level research should refer to macro-level developments, particularly with respect to techno-economic paradigms, their up-and-down stages and corresponding liberal market or interventionist public policies (Freeman 1992, Perez 2002). This includes also the courage for controversial debates about the opportunities of reversing the dominant trend from long-term stakeholder strategies to short-term shareholder value policies in order to strengthen again the elements of innovation potential in companies and supporting infrastructures. *Research tasks in the tradition of humane and innovative development perspectives have to be linked with social interests and forces to find ways and means for coping successfully with the erosion of the institutional context of formerly coordinated market economies in order to empowering again the system of industrial relations and participation rights of employees for generating sustainable change.* After more than two decades of decay and destruction, the reemergence of social infrastructures for workplace development in private companies, societal organizations and public institutions has to be set again on the agenda in European countries and the European Union. Coping effectively with the presented challenges of the neoliberal breakdown of market fundamentalism helps to improve the opportunities for mutual learning within and between companies, regions and nations, especially to lay the ground for concepts and methodologies to implement high roads with *corporate social responsibility (CRS)* objectives in a European social development model (European Commission 2001).

The overall message, that decent, humane and innovative work replacing through participative forms of cooperation managerial hierarchies and authoritarian decision-making does pay for both industrial sides, should be propagated offensively by participation protagonists. They are demanded to referring to the unambiguous results of labour and social research as well as to the strategic setting that *all stakeholders have to design the future together* and thereby are forced less to compete and more to cooperate with each other to find the best sustainable solutions (Rouilleaut, Rochefort 2005). Concerning the present crisis-prone framework conditions there are now to be put on the agenda again basic tasks linking more or less all streams of the Forum though they were not explicitly dealt with by all workshops and speakers:

- Firstly, there is the general task of all participation efforts that improving company performance should be reconciled with a good quality of working life including extended participation opportunities and, more explicitly, co-operative actors working together in dialogue-fostering arenas of finding creative solutions should push ahead good company performance on the basis of good work.

- Secondly, there is the political task blurred during the past twenty years that participative forms should not only be granted by a more or less enlightened management but, moreover, should be rooted in public regulations by collective bargaining as well as national laws as Works Constitution and Co-determination Acts and respectively European directives.
- Thirdly, there is the present task, in particular concerning the crisis of financial and industrial markets that there should be a renewal of innovative regional, national and European workplace development programmes launched on a tripartite basis embedded in coordinated market policies which turn the competitive edge from financial accumulation objectives to social and ecological needs.

Literature

Abendroth, W. (1972): A Short History of the European Working Class. New York: Monthly Review Press

Alasoini, T. / Ramstad, E. / Rouhiainen, N. (2005): The Finnish Workplace Development Programm as an expanding activity. Results, challenges, opportunities. Reports 47. Helsinki

Alhadeff, G. / Hugendubel, K. (2005): What future for a social Europe. In: EPC (European Policy Centre): The Nordic model: A recipe for success? EPC Working Paper No20, 101-108

Andreasen, L.E. / Coriat B. / Hertog, F. d. / Kaplinsky, R. (1995): Europe's Next Step: Organisational Innovation, Competition and Employment. Ilford: Frank Cass

Bourdieu, P. et al. (1993): La misère du monde. Paris

Brödner, P. / Garibaldo, F. / Oehlke, P. / Pekruhl, U. (1998): Work Organisation and Employment. The Crucial Role of Innovation Strategies. Projektbericht 1998-05. Gelsenkirchen

Brödner, P. / Latniak, E. (2003): Sources of Innovation and Competitiveness. National Programmes Supporting the Development of Work Organisation. Concepts and Transformation 8 (2), 179-211

Bullinger, H.-J. (ed.) (1998): Service 2000plus. A future report on services in Germany. Stuttgart

Commission européenne (1997): Construire la société européenne de l'information pout tous. Rapport final du groupe d'experts de haut niveau. Luxembourg

Docherty, P. / Forslin, J. / Shani, A.R. (2002): Creating Sustainable Work Systems. Emerging perspectives and practice. London

European Commission (2001): Green Paper: Promoting a European framework for Corporate Social Responsibility. Brussels, COM(2001) 366 final
Europäische Kommission (1997): Grünbuch: Eine neue Arbeitsorganisation im Geiste der Partnerschaft. KOM(97)128 final. Luxemburg
European Foundation for the Improvement of Living and Working Conditions (1997): New Forms of Work Organisation. Can Europe realize its potential? Dublin
European Work and Technology Consortium (1998): Work Organisation, Competitiveness, Employment. The European Approach. Brussels.
Freeman, C. (1992): The Economics on Hope. Essays on Technical Change, Economic Growth and the Environment. London
Fricke, W. / Totterdill, P. (2004): Action Research in Workplace Innovation and Regional Development. Amsterdam
Gryglewski, S. (2007): Sicherung von Produktionsarbeit in Deutschland. Reformbedarf der arbeitsorganisatorischen Leitbilder (Protection of production work in Germany. Needs for reform oft the models of work organisation). In: Zeitschrift für Arbeitswissenschaft (Journal for Industrial Science) 1/2007, 47-53
Hertog, F. d. (1992): Technology, Work and Organisation: A New Research Field for Concerted Action in Europe? MERIT Maastricht Economic Research Institute on Innovation and Technology
Krugman, P. (1994): Competitiveness. A Dangerous Obsession. In: Foreign Affairs 3/4, 28-44
Naschold, F. (1993): Organization Development: National programmes in the context of international competition. In: Naschold, F. / Cole, R. E. / Gustavsen, B. / Beinum, H. v.: Constructing the New Industrial Society. Maastricht – Stockholm, 3-119
Newsweek (2004): Cover Story: Labor Pains. Working Harder For Less Pay? Welcome to the New World Economy. August 23, 34-44
OECD (1988): The New Technologies in the 1990ies. A Socio-Economic Strategy. Report of a Group of Experts on the Social Aspects of New Technologies. Paris
Oehlke, P. (2001): The development of labour process policies in the Federal Republic of Germany. In: Concepts and Transformation No 2, 109-140
Oehlke, P. (2007): La promotion publique des innovations sociales dans les enterprises privées – trois cas d'intervention dans un programme regional allemande. Intervenir en entreprise: pratiques actuelles. Sous la direction de Julien Pelletier. ANACT, 57-69

Oehlke, P. / Riegler, C. / Wuppermann, D. / Zettel, C. (2007): Why High Road of Innovation? Work-Oriented Innovation Strategies in Europe. Work-In-Net Background Paper (http://www.workinnet.org/10.html

Perez, C. (2002): Technical Revolutions and Financial Capital. The Dynamics of Bubbles and Golden Ages. Cheltenham 2002

Rouilleault, H. / Rochefort, T. (2005): Changer le travail … oui mais ensemble. ANACT

Totterdill, P. / Dhondt, S. / Milsome, S. (2002): Partners at Work? A Report to European Policy Makers and Social Partners. Nottingham: The Work Institute (Available at www.ukwon.net)

Role of workplace practices and supporting development process and institutional condition in the promotion of performance and quality of working life

Elise Ramstad

1. Introduction

In recent years researchers and policy makers have paid considerable attention to the significance of workplace practices in boosting productivity and competitiveness of companies. It has been argued that in order to improve national competitiveness, there is a need to develop, in addition to new technology, also workplace practices. New products and services can be created and implemented more rapidly, when the organization is being developed simultaneously. Research has also been able to show that workplace practices can have direct effect on performance at workplace. However, the impact of these practices on quality of working life (QWL) has been two-fold. In the mutual gains perspective (Kalmi / Kauhanen, 2008) the effects of workplace practices are seen mainly positive to the employees, while the representatives of critical perspective (e.g. Ramsay et al., 2000) argue that the adoption of workplace practices can lead to decreased well-being among employees such as increased stress and job intensity.

This article makes a contribution to the debate on the effects of workplace practices on performance and QWL, and adds some new empirical findings. We still have limited understanding of the role of workplace practices, measurement of outcomes and the link between workplace practices and outcomes. The aim in the paper is to answer the question; how can workplaces be developed in a way that improves simultaneously performance and QWL. Based on the earlier organization and management literature, our basic assumption is that a successful adoption of workplace practices cannot be predicted on the basis of the adopted workplace practices alone, but in addition it requires a supportive development process and institutional condition.

The following chapters introduce the ongoing discussion in the literature and the conceptual framework on the effects of workplace practices, the mechanisms by which workplace practices affect and the role of development process and institutional condition. In the empirical part the research question, methodology and the data will be presented. The empirical data consists of the results of 1,113 self-assessments by management, employees and experts of 409 development projects implemented at workplaces as a part of the Finnish Workplace Development

Programme (1996-2005). After presenting the results and conclusions the limitations of the study and future challenges will be discussed.

2. What are sustainable workplace practices?

On the basis of earlier organizational and management research and the many development projects carried out at workplaces, it is possible to list various workplace practices related to management, organization and labour resources. The number of practices used in the studies has typically varied from three to twenty. The practices usually refer to flexible work arrangements, employee involvement, participation or the whole workplace culture. The overarching purpose of workplace practices is to contribute to organizational effectiveness through the development of an integrated range of policies which can enhance QWL and encourage high commitment and high performance with employees. A variety of names have been used for these practices, such as Human Resource Management (HRM) practices, High Performance Work Practices (HPWS), High-commitment Management Practices or Participative Workplace Practices. This shows that the practices do not have a single definition shared by researchers, but the volume and content of the practices often varies from one study to another.

While the traditional workplace or organizational development focused mainly on group and interpersonal level issues, the object of development today has become more wide-ranged and systemically complex. This is partly because of the shorter life span of products and more information-intensive and increasingly networked production and operations. Besides the traditional problems at work such as physically demands, monotony and pace, and opportunities to influence and develop skills, new problems are emerging that are related to the challenges of continuous learning, knowledge management and creation of innovations. This has resulted development activity that focuses more on the comprehensive development of work organization. Over the past 50 to 60 years, the object has expanded from traditional shop-floor work locations or work units to entire workplace organizations, production systems, or even business networks or regional innovation systems (Alasoini / Ramstad, 2007). According to Schienstock (1999) characteristics for the *new organizational logics* is the functional integration of processes, discursive coordination, increased organizational reflexivity, use of ICT, the dismantling of vertical integration, and the systematic globalization of production processes.

In this work the interest lies on Sustainable Workplace Practices (SWP) that can promote simultaneously performance and the quality of working life. Unlike earlier studies, *sustainable perspective* here means that the issue is not only how to make best use of human resources, but also how to create and manage successful organizations in a way that promotes the well-being of the workforce. In order to main high performance, there is a need to create favourable conditions to QWL – and the other way round (Ramstad, 2008). It can be difficult to maintain good productivity growth without a favourable development in QWL in the long run – and the other way around. The performance of firms that apply workplace practices systematically may enable them to improve QWL, pay employees higher wages and rewards for improved skills, provide more training and promotion opportunities, and lay off fewer people during economic downturns. Assuming that firms act in this way, workplace development may yield positive benefits to individuals, organizations, and more broadly the economic and social system. These workplace practices can include a grand scale of organization and management actions, such as reforms in the structure, processes or boundaries of a work organization. Examples of typical targets can include e.g. self-management teams and flattering hierarchies, networking, flexible working methods, diversifying personnel skills and job rotation, business practices based on trust and participation. An example from Finland is the collection of studies (2002) edited by Tuomi and Vanhala on companies in the metal industry and metal product retailing. The findings showed that the scope of teamwork, good opportunities for staff training and development, good organization of work operations, support for human resources, support from supervisors a low incidence of conflict and uncertainty at work and high psychological and physical demands of work had a positive correlation with the success of companies, and staff well-being.

The earlier HRM studies can be criticized by the fact that in these the practices that are investigated by different researchers, are often selective and inconsistent (Wood and Albanese, 1995). This article do not restrict to some specific practices, while it is thought that the practices and the system of practices are context and workplace specific. It is very difficult determine some general level "good practices", while the development needs to be raised from the individual workplaces. In the empirical part of the study development targets and their relationships in the development projects funded by the Finnish Workplace Development Programme will be studied.

3. Effects of workplace practices on performance and QWL

There are relatively few studies which have examined the simultaneous improvement in performance and QWL as the result of changes in workplace practices. The interest has typically been on performance alone or an attempt has been made to explain performance through certain QWL related factors. The earlier empirical studies have been able to show a link between certain practices and performance (Appelbaum et al. 2000; Cappelli 1996; Huselid 1995), but the effects of workplace practices on QWL have been uncertain and partially contradictory. The representatives of mutual gains perspective (Kalmi / Kauhanen, 2008) sees that workplace practices can benefit employees and improve QWL, while the critics question the positive impact of these practices on QWL.

The studies have reported positive contributions from workplace practices on job influence (Kalmi / Kauhanen, 2008), skills (Felstead / Ashton, 2000), wages (Kalmi / Kauhanen, 2008; Appelbaum et al., 2000; Cappelli, 1996), organizational commitment (Ogilvie, 1986), satisfaction at work (Appelbaum et al., 2000; Patterson et al., 1997), diminished turnover (Huselid, 1995) and sick leave (EPOC Research Group, 1997), while critics argue that workplace practices can lead to higher levels of job intensity and mental strain and work related exhaustion (e.g. Godard, 2004; Kumar, 2000; Lloyd / Payne, 2004). The same practices might in some cases also both improve and detract from QWL. For instance, Antila and Ylöstalo (2002) found in their study on proactive and traditional companies that proactive work based on influence opportunities and greater responsibility can be "tough and enjoyable" at one and the same time.

The study by Guest (2000) showed that the results of development activities depend part who on who you ask. It seems that the question concerns particularly employees, and how they react to the adoption of workplace practices. That is why it is particularly important to study the views of employees. In this study I'll focus, in addition to the views of management and experts used during the process, also the opinions of employees. The starting point is that implementation of workplace practices can be mutually beneficial when both management and employees estimate that performance and QWL have improved simultaneously (Ramstad, 2007, 112). In this way performance growth does not come at the expense of employee well-being. The work and operations needs to be agreeable also from the employee's point of view, as this is a key factor in how well staff cope at work, to make the work more productive, stay at work and to carry on longer at their work.

4. The mechanisms by which workplace practices affect the outcomes

There exist various theoretical frames of reference in organizational and management research on the mechanisms of how workplace practices effect performance and QWL. The link between the practices and their outcomes has been explained, for instance with the universalistic, contingency and configurational mechanism (e.g. Delery / Doty 1996; Pettigrew / Whittington, 2003). The universalistic mechanism is based on the idea that it is possible to identify some general principles and practices linked to positive effects. For instance, Pfeffer (1994) and Osterman (1994) identified a number of "best practices" which resulted in higher productivity in US organizations. It is thought that these principles and practices can also be transferred and applied to other workplaces. Such individual practices include teamwork, delegation of responsibility, employee skills, organizational structure and active training.

The contingency and configurational viewpoints differ from the universal approach in that they do not incorporate any general practices and principles. In the contingency model, what is important is that practices concur with the demands of corporate strategy and the operating environment. In the contingency approach, HRM practices should vary from one workplace to another, depending on their strategy. The configurational model is broader in that it stresses not only compatibility between a company's internal practices and external demands but also mutual compatibility between these practices. Using the compatibility basis, more or less unique entities are formulated from declared strategies and HRM practices.

Though all the above mechanisms have their own distinctive features and empirical grounds, they all seem to involve *broader application of workplace practices*. Several empirical studies have been published which show that the volume of practices, i.e. comprehensive development, has a positive impact on performance. The study by Ichniowski et al. (1997) on the steel industry in the USA showed that innovative HRM practices such as payment by result, systematic labour recruitment criteria, teamwork, job rotation, job security arrangements and active training and information provision, when applied throughout, were clearly linked with a higher utilization rate and higher-quality products than in the comparison group. On the other hand, the use of individual practices showed no clear link with performance. Similarly, the study by Cully et al. (2004) on private-sector workplaces in the UK showed that the use of several high-commitment management practices improved the working climate according to both management and staff. The recent study by Kalmi and Kauhanen (2008) showed that the adoption of several workplace practices (four or over four practices) were associated with increased job satisfaction, increased job security, higher wage, lower stress, and higher job satisfaction than in the case where only one or two practices are adopted. They analysed the effects of workplace practices on employees' (N=4 104) based on the Quality of Work Life Survey carried out by Statistics Finland in 2003. However, there exist also critical views on the use of several workplace practices. Godard (2004) has suggested that the amount of workplace practices can have decreasing "returns to scale". All in all, most of the empirical studies suggest that introducing a bundle of workplace practices is usually more effective than single practices. The workplace practices should be introduced as a coherent, complementary system.

5. Impact of development process and institutional framework on the spread of practices

The above-mentioned models are useful in increasing our understanding of impact mechanisms concerning workplace practices and their effect on performance and QWL. They make a good starting point but are not enough to bring about successful change in the workplace. New practices are not simply absorbed by the workplace community, but need a development process to help them to take root and spread into everyday working life. It is argued that the development process, i.e. how practices are introduced and implemented, plays an important role in disseminating practices and ensuring a successful result. The earlier HRM studies have usually failed to take into account how the practices were introduced, e.g. how employees contributed to their creation, whether the practices were planned jointly by the various parties involved. However, the nature of the development process can be critical in determining how broadly practices finds acceptance and how much commitment there is to them in the workplace.

Godard (2004) differentiates between two ways of implementing workplace practices. The *intensification approach* is based on increased workload and cost reductions, while the *involvement approach* is based on high involvement of employees. Further, he argues that the choice between intensification and involvement may depend on the institutional framework. Concerning our analysis, where the aim is to understand how both performance and QWL can be improved, it is rather easy to reject the intensification approach that clearly decreases the well-being at work. Instead a development approach that is based on participation is of importance. It is argued that the employees need to be able to affect both the planning and implementation of workplace practices and comment on "what" to develop and "how" the practices should be adopted. Further, Salminen et al. (2000) studied development projects carried out in Finland and their most typical success factors. Researchers found (Salminen et al. 2000, 35-44) that typical features of successful projects include a clear need for change, commitment by the management, staff motivation and commitment, good planning and organization, and staff skills and experience.

Such research based on conventional literature on organizations and management typically underlines internal interaction at the workplace in the change process, whereas more recent innovation research (e.g. Hargadon, 2003; Chesbrough, 2006) takes a broader view on development work. It is based on the idea of open innovation, where in addition to internal participation the external networking is emphasized. This is because the use of external knowledge such as external experts (universities, consultancies, educational institutes) and customers during the development process can broaden the view of development work and in this way affect the quality (e.g. what workplace practices are being introduced), legitimation and dissemination of workplace practices. In this study, it is suggested that an *innovation-oriented development approach,* consisting of both internal (management and employees) and external participation (external experts, other workplaces), could contribute to positive outcomes both in performance and QWL.

At macro level, the more recent discussion suggests that the results from workplace practices may also depend on the broader *institutional conditions* in a country. According to Godard (2004), in co-ordinated market economies (e.g. Sweden and Germany) workplace innovations are more likely implemented in a way which benefits also the employees when compared to liberal market economies. It is characteristics to the co-ordinated market that there is a collective coordination of the labour market which in turn supports co-operative and high-trust management and employee relations that are important prerequisites for innovation-promoting activities at workplaces (Lorenz / Valeyre, 2006). Our data is from Finland, where the industrial relations system provides a supportive institutional environment for workplace practices. The Finnish labour is highly unionized (about 70-80 per cent), there exists laws that support collaboration between management and employees (e.g. the Act on Co-Operation within Undertakings) and general agreements between central organizations of employees and employers have been signed for that purpose, too. That is why, it is suggested that there is collaboration also in the workplace level between management and employees that predict positive outcomes. It is assumed that when debate and interaction are boosted inside the workplace and with outside bodies, this will promote and accelerate the adoption and creation of new practices, and further a mode of operation that develops workplace functioning in a way that concurrently promotes performance and QWL.

6. Methodology and material of the study

The aim of this article is to examine which workplace practices within a development process and institutional condition result in a concurrent improvement in performance and QWL, and in what way. However, the approach is not limited solely to successful changes, as it is also important to learn from 'unsuccessful' projects and make comparisons between them. In the article, this comparison is mainly made between two extremes, i.e. the 'best' and 'poorest' groups. Unlike earlier studies, the statistical research starts with performance and QWL and traces back the workplaces and the characteristics of development process. The method used is comparative analysis. The objective is to discover whether the groups differ with regard to their a) workplace practices and b) how these practices are put into effect, that is, their development process.

The article uses empirical material to examine the effects of various practices and development processes on performance and QWL. The material was compiled in 1996-2005 within the Workplace Development Programme. The FWDP was launched in 1996 by the Government of Prime Minister Lipponen. The lead actor has been the Ministry of Labor who financed and coordinated the programme whilst managing it on a joint basis with the social partners. Since 2008 the programme has been coordinated by the Finnish Funding Agency for Technology and Innovation Tekes. The programme's main focus area has been to provide financial expert support to development projects at Finnish workplaces and to improve their modes of operation in a way that they develop both their performance and QWL. In addition to funding projects, the FWDP distributes information on organizational development and enhances organizational development expertise in Finland. The Author is familiar with the data, while being involved in planning the questionnaires, collecting the data and done several analyses and reports on it during the years.

The analyses utilize self-assessment data and a background information questionnaire from development projects supported by the programme. Workplaces of all sizes and in all sectors were able to apply for support for their development projects. All development projects in the programme have to be workplace initiated which means that development targets need to become from the work organizations themselves. Most typical targets of the projects have been the promotion of new working practices (such as team working and multi-skilling), work processes, management systems, networking, the work environment (especially for older workers), staff skills and equal opportunities. The maximum level of expert support for development projects has been FIM 400 000 (about EUR 67 000), which was normally not to cover more than half of the computed project costs.

The self-assessments were collected at the end of each project, from both management and staff and also from experts used in the project concerned. The primary purpose of the self-assessment is to produce information about the effects of the projects and to support the constant development of the programme. Self-assessment gives information about how well the objectives set for the projects have been realized, what the effects of projects have been, how successful projects are perceived to have been, how the various parties involved have influenced the implementation of a project, and what funding and other support from the programme has meant for project implementation (Ramstad, 2005a; 2005b). The material comprises a total of 1,113 responses from 409 workplace development projects. The response rate is a high 81%. The replies from the various groups are almost equally divided (management N = 379, staff N = 361 and experts N = 373). Approximately one third of the answers reflect the views of more than one person. In particular staff representatives have tended to answer the survey as a group. The branch distribution of the development projects was the following: the private sector 47 per cent (industry and service sector), the public sector 41 per cent (municipal sector and state) and other sectors (e.g. NGOs) 12 per cent.

The form of background information has been used to judge how well the project's objectives (practices) were met. A form comprising a ready list of some twenty workplace practices was used for every project, and was filled in by representatives of the Workplace Development Programme project team when each project began.

7. Results

This section first defines the criteria used to measure performance and QWL. Thereafter, the findings are examined largely by comparing two extreme groups of projects: 1) those in which performance and QWL both improved simultaneously, and 2) projects in which the impact on both performance and QWL was poorest, as assessed by management and staff. In addition, a study is made of links between these groups and the number of practices, links between practices, and the groups' links with the development process.

7.1 Breakdown of development projects based on their impact on performance and QWL

How concepts are defined plays a crucial role in measuring impact on performance and QWL. In the article, factor analysis was utilized to formulate the measurement criteria (Table 1). In the self-assessment questionnaire, respondents were asked five multiple-choice questions to establish how the project had affected productivity and QWL factors (1 = definitely deteriorated – 5 = definitely improved). The first factor comprised elements measuring performance: a) productivity of work, b) quality of goods and services, c) quality of operations, d) flexible customer service, e) smooth running of operations. Overall, the coefficient of reliability, i.e. the Cronbach alpha, was as high as .815. Similarly, the *Quality of working life* indicator comprised the following variables: a) cooperation between management and staff, b) team-like working processes, c) social relations, d) mental well-being and e) development of vocational skills. Here, the Cronbach alpha was .777. The factors were loaded in a similar manner in the tests on different personnel groupings and in different sectors.

Table 1: Rotated factor matrix of performance and quality of working life variables (rotation method: Varimax, Maximum Likelihood).

	Factors	
	1	2
Impact of project on:	Performance	Quality of working life
Work productivity	.607	.204
Quality of goods or services	.756	.179
Quality of operations	.605	.191
Flexible customer service	.637	.203
Smoothness of operations	.560	.256
Team-like working methods	.217	.533
Cooperation between management and staff	.208	.548
Social relations in the workplace	.132	.777
Development of vocational skills	.311	.361
Mental well-being	.221	.599

In the analysis, the projects were divided into three groups, according to the results. The first group included projects showing concurrent improvements in performance and QWL. Those projects in which management and staff gave positive assessments for both factors, i.e. the 'best', were allocated to this group. The criterion was that distinct improvements had to have taken place in both performance and QWL, i.e. the results had to be at least as high as 3.5 (on a scale of 1 to 5). There were 152 of these projects in all. The other group comprised projects in which both management and staff assessed the impact as poor, or even worse than before, for both factors (< 3.5), i.e. the 'poorest' projects. There were 31 such projects. The third group comprised all the remaining projects, in which only either performance or QWL had improved, or in which management and staff assessed the results differently ('middle' group).

7.2 Characteristics of the groups and links between practices

The averages for performance and QWL in the three groups differed to a statistically significant degree (Table 2). In the 'best' group, the average for both performance and QWL was higher than in the other two groups. There was a positive correlation between performance and QWL showing that they are related to each other. The correlation was higher in the 'best' group (correlation coefficient r = .452***) than in the ‘poorest’ group (r=.325**). The next analysis concerned the link between number of objectives and impacts in the three groups. The findings indicated that the number of objectives set to the projects was somewhat higher in projects showing improvements in both performance and QWL. The difference compared with the other groups was statistically significant. This result supports the earlier studies that have stressed the volume of practices and comprehensive development predicts better results (e.g. Ichniowski et al., 1997; Cully et al., 1999); Guest et al., 2006).

Table 2: Means of performance, QWL and number of objectives in the three groups (Anova).

	Performance	QWL	No. of objectives
I Best	4.04	4.17	4.00
II Poorest	3.50	3.59	3.65
III Middle	3.80	3.86	3.63
F	82.654***	89.006***	15.009***

A more detailed analysis was then made of the breakdown of practices in to the ‘best’ and ‘poorest’ groups. This only applied to the projects in the second period of the programme (N=226 projects), as the objectives were grouped slightly differently in the first period. Table 3 lists the objectives stated 1) more frequently and 2) equally frequently for the two extreme groups. The findings show which development targets are related to both performance and QWL. The practices linked with improvements in both outcomes in the ‘best’ group were teamwork, leadership, working capacity and coping, pay, development for ageing workers, quality work, customer service and matters related to external networking. There were fewer objectives in the ‘poorest’ group, and the objectives there were more frequently development of working processes, organizational structure and smooth functioning of the workplace community, together with environmental issues. The findings derive from a means test (t-test) between the groups.

Table 3: Breakdown of practices in the development projects to promote performance and quality of working life in the ‘best’ and ‘weaker’ groups’.

	I Best (N=85 projects) Improved both performance and QWL	II Poorest (N=15 projects) Poorest impact on performance and QWL
Objectives more frequently (Sig.= ***<.001,	Teamwork*** Strategic leadership* Human Resource Management*	Working processes*** Organizational structure* Smooth functioning of work

**<.050, *<.10)	Working capacity and coping*** Pay* Development related to ageing workers** External networking*** Customer service** Quality systems*	community*** Environmental issues***
Objectives equally frequently	Working methods Working climate Working hours Multiskilling Development skills Remote work Equality Developing the mode of operation required by new technology	Working methods Working climate Working hours Multiskilling Development skills Remote work Equality Developing the mode of operation required by new technology

Next, the relationships between practices were studied using factor and correlation analysis. Factor analysis did not yield any clear results, while correlation analysis indicated links between certain objectives. However, most of the objectives did not correlate with any others, and were 'independent' practices, the most pronounced being 1) remote work, 2) equality, 3) organizational structure, 4) teamwork, 5) developing the mode of operation required by new technology, 6) smooth functioning of the work community and 7) quality systems. The practices that did correlate were 1) management (strategic leadership and HRM r=.310), 2) boosting of skills (multiskilling and development skills) (r=.210), 3) networking (external networking and customer service) (r=.293). Some practices correlated with several others but did not form clear units. The following are some examples of these and of the correlations between practices. Working processes correlated with working methods (r=.159), multiskilling (r=.108), and environmental (r=.162) and quality systems (r=.129). Development related to ageing workers correlated with multiskilling and working hours (r=.193). Pay correlated with working hours (r=216) and teamwork (r=.196). Working processes and methods correlated with each other (r=.178). Working methods correlated with climate (r=.204).

7.3 Link between implementation and concurrent improvement in performance and QWL

The nature of development process and institutional conditions were examined using six dimensions: 1) participation of employees, management and experts during the planning and implementation stage, 2) internal collaboration (between management and employees), 3) external networking with other expert organizations and projects, 4) initiation of the project (who was the initiator of the development project), 5) project management skills (ability to keep timetable, costs and achieve goals) and 6) contribution of experts (satisfaction with used experts and their training and development methods). The analysis continued to use two extreme groups ('best' and 'poorest') formed from the overall material (N=409 projects). The analysis method used was the means test (t-test), except in the case of 'initiators'. The main findings are shown in Table 4.

The findings indicate clear differences between the two extreme groups in the development process. In both groups the initiator was usually the top management, followed by middle or shop-floor management, experts and personnel representatives. By contrast, the personnel themselves only acted as initiator in the 'best' group. The findings for participation show that participation by management, employees and experts in project planning and implementation was stronger in the group which improved both performance and QWL. They also indicate that there was more internal collaboration in the 'best' group while the project was taking place and greater satisfaction with the experts used and methods adopted, the objectives were achieved better, the project kept to timetable, and external networking was more active than in the comparison group. No statistical differences were found between the groups vis-à-vis keeping the cost estimate.

Table 4: Differences in implementation of development projects between the groups ranked 'best' (N=152) and 'poor' (N=31) for performance and QWL.

	I Best (N=152 projects) Best impact on both performance and QWL	II Poorest (N=31 projects) Poorest impact on performance and QWL
Initiators	Mainly top management (55%), but also middle management, personnel representative, personnel and expert.	Mainly top management (57%), but also middle management, personnel representative, expert – never the personnel.
Participation in planning and implementation	Strongest participation by top management**, personnel** and experts*.	Participation by the different parties poorer than average.
Internal collaboration	Internal collaboration mainly between management and personnel**, management and experts**, and personnel and experts***.	Less than average collaboration between the different parties.

Networking	More interaction with other workplaces*** and experts**.	Little contact outside the workplace.
Project skills	Project objectives*** achieved better, kept to timetable*** better.	Project objectives and timetabling more poorly achieved, but cost estimate kept to as well as in 'best' group.
Experts	Greater satisfaction with research, training and development methods*** used by experts.	Action and methods of experts not felt to be so successful.

*(Sig. = ***<.001, **<.050, *<.10)*

8. Conclusions

This article has examined concurrent improvements in performance and the quality of working life achieved by means of a development process and institutional framework supporting workplace practices and their application. The results indicate that performance and QWL can be improved concurrently, and using the same workplace practices. So, there is no need to execute separate projects for improving one or the other. The results are consistent with the earlier study by Appelbaum et al. (2000) who have also been able to show the direct impact of workplace practices on positive outcomes in performance and in some QWL factors.

Secondly, the systemic application of workplace practices is positively related to simultaneous improvement, even though it was not possible to separate any clear clustering between the various practices that could be generalized. Rather, it seems that combinations vary from workplace to workplace depending on their specific needs and past development. The results are supported the earlier studies (e.g. Appelbaum, 2000; Kalmi / Kauhanen, 2008) which show that applying several workplaces practices is usually more effective than single practices. The projects in which performance and QWL improved concurrently developed a variety of practices, such as teamwork, leadership, working capacity and coping, incentive system, customer service, quality systems, external networking and practices related to ageing workers. Hence, in the future it would be interesting to study deeper how does the interrelationship work between the practices with qualitative data.

The results suggest that the key is to generate a synergistic effect that depends on the fit between the various workplace practices. It is the combination of practices that make difference when these operate in a complementary way. For example, the application of teamwork does not necessarily improve productivity, if it is not supported with a related management and incentive systems. Virkkunen at al. (2007)

speak of the importance of developing the whole operating concept in which the workplace is examined as a functional system. This is because the various parts of the functional system may operate at different times during the historical process, causing disturbances and coordination problems. However, this is not to suggest a "one best way", because complex combination of workplace practices also has to be well adapted to the technology in a given workplace and its network. In general, it is important not to limit development work too narrowly, but to look for development needs elsewhere in the organization, too.

Concerning the development process: broad participation, collaborative orientation and good project management skills predicted best the positive outcomes. A broad development coalition, including both internal and external participation, enables more critical and reflexive approach towards the practices and development methods in question. The internal collaboration refers particularly to the constructive labour-management cooperation, while the external collaboration with other organizations, such us customers, consultants and researchers enables to broaden and diversify our knowledge base. This way the quality and the acceptance and commitment to the practices can be improved. The result is supported both by the high-involvement literature (e.g. Godard, 2004) and more recent innovation research (e.g. Hargadon, 2003; Chesbrough, 2006), while the first one is concerned with the internal participation and the second one with the external participation as a source for innovative practices. This study shows that these both approaches, which is called here for innovation-oriented development approach, are needed in order to promote sustainable workplace practices. It has been suggested (Ramstad, 2008) that in the future there is a need for more intensive discussion between organizational development and innovation literature that can open up new ideas and approaches to the comprehensive and innovation-oriented development of workplaces.

Finally, there are some elements of uncertainty among the results that should be pointed out to the reader. Firstly, the analytical findings have not at this stage been examined separately for the different sectors of business and industry, so we cannot be completely sure that there are no differences between them. Secondly, the findings are based on the subjective opinions of the participants. However, a study by Wall et al. (2004) indicates that subjective and objective judgements of workplace performance capacity correlate positively and thus largely measure the same thing. The reliability of the self-assessment method is also increased by the fact that responses were obtained from most of the parties involved. Thirdly, the data has been gathered by the development programme that has financially supported the development of the workplaces. This might have effect to assessments of the respondents positively. However, it has been estimated by an international evaluation group (Arnkil et al., 2003) that the results of self-assessment are highly valid. The group studied the results of the projects after two and a half years later and found that compared with the self-assessment results reported earlier (Ramstad, 2001); the assessments were highly accurate and surprisingly similar and also gave a good picture of the longer-term effects of the projects. This finding supports the longitudinal reliability of the self-assessment system.

References

Alasoini, T. / Ramstad, E. (2007): Yhteiskuntapolitiikan rooli ja mahdollisuudet työelämän kehittämisessä, in E. Ramstad / T. Alasoini (eds.) Työelämän tutkimusavusteinen kehittäminen Suomessa. Lähestymistapoja, menetelmiä, kokemuksia, tulevaisuuden haasteita. [Research-assisted Development in Finland.] Ministry of Labor. Reports of Workplace Development Programme 53, 431-449.

Antila, J. / Ylöstalo, P. (2002): Proaktiivinen toimintatapa. Yritysten ja palkansaajien yhteinen etu? Labour policy studies 239. Helsinki. Ministry of Labour.

Appelbaum, E. / Bailey, T. / Berg, P. / Kalleberg, A.L. (2000): Manufacturing advantage: Why high-performance work systems pay off. Ithica, NY: ILR Press.

Arnkil, R. / Rissanen, P. / Pitkänen, S. / Piirainen, T. / Koski, P. / Berg, P. / Vartiainen, M. / Gustavsen, B. / Ekman Philips, M. / Finne, H. / Riegler, C. (eds.): The Finnish Workplace Development Programme. A small giant? Evaluation report. Ministry of Labour: Helsinki.

Cappelli, P. (1996): Technology and Skill Requirements: Implications for Establishment Wage Structures. Special Issue. New England Economic Review, 139-54.

Chesbrough, H. (2002): Open Innovation. The New Imperative for Creating and Profiting from Technology. Boston – Massachusetts: Harvard Business School Press.

Cully, M. / Woodland, S. / O'Reilly, A. / Dix, G. (1999): Britain at Work; As Depicted by the 1988 Workplace Employee Relations Survey. London: Routledge.

Delery, J.E. / Doty, D.H. (1996): Modes of Theorizing in Strategic Human Resource Management: Tests of Universalistic, Contingency and Configurational Performance Predictions. Academy of Management Journal, 39(4), pp. 802-835.

EPOC Research Group (1997): New Forms of Work Organization. Can Europe Realise its Potential? European Foundation for the Living and Working Conditions. Dublin.

Felstead, A. / Ashton D.N. (2000): Tracing The Link: Organisational Structures and Skill Formation, Human Resource Management Journal, 10(3), pp. 5-21.

Godard, J. (2004): A Critical Assessment of the High-Performance Paradigm. British Journal of Industrial Relations, 42 (2), pp. 349-378.

Guest, D. (2006): High-Performance Working. HRM and Performance. In S. Porter / M. Cambell (ed.) Skills and Economic Performance. London: Sector Skills Development Agency, pp. 173-195.

Guest, D. (2000): Human Resource Management, Employee Well-being and Organizational Performance. Paper presented at the CIPD Professional Standards Conference, 11. July.

Hargadon, A.B. (2003): How Breakthroughs Happen. The Surprising Truth about How Companies Innovate. Cambridge, MA: Harvard Business School Press.

Huselid, M. (1995): The Impact of Human Resource Management on Turnover, Productivity, and Corporate Financial Performance. Academy of Management Journal, 38, pp. 635-60.

Ichniowski, C. / Shaw, K. / Prennushi, G. (1997): The Effects of Human Resource Management Practices on Productivity. American Economic Review, 87, pp. 291-313.

Kalmi, P. / Kauhanen, A. (2008): Workplace Innovations and Employee Outcomes: Evidence from Finland, Industrial Relations 47(3): pp. 430-459.

Kumar, V. / Simon, A. / Kimberley, N. (2000): Strategic Capabilities which lead to Management Consulting Success in Australia, Management Decision 38(1), pp. 24-35.

Lloyd, C. / Payne, J. (2004) Just Another Bandwagon? A Critical Look at the Role of the High Performance Workplace as Vehicle for the UK High Skills Project. SKOPE Research Paper 49. Warwick Business School. Coventry.

Lorenz, E. / Valeyre, A. (2006): Organizational Forms and Innovative Performance: A Comparison of the EU-15', pp. 140-160 in E., Lorenz and B.-Å. Lundvall (eds.) How Europe's Economies Learn: Coordinating Competing Models. Oxford: Oxford University Press.

Osterman, P. (1994): How Common is Workplace Transformation and Who Adopts it?, Industrial & Labor Relations Review, 47(2), pp. 173-88.

Patterson, M.G. / West, M.A. / Lawthorn, R. / Nickells, S. (1997): The Impact of People Management Practices on Business Performance, People Management, 22, London: IPD.

Pettigrew, A. / Whittington, R. (2003): Complementarities in Action: Organizational Change and Performance in BP and Unilever 1985-2002. In A. Pettigrew, R. Whittington, L. Melin, C. Sanchez-Runde, F. Van Den Bosch, W. Ruigrok, T. Numagami (eds.) Innovative Forms of Organizing, Sage Publications, London, 173-207.

Pfeffer, J. (1994): Competitive Advantage through People. Boston, MA: Harvard Business School Press.
Ramsay, H. /Scholarios, D. /Harley, B. (2000): Employees and High-Performance Work Systems: Testing inside the black box, British Journal of Industrial Relations 38(4): 501-31.
Ramstad, E. (2008): Innovation Generating Model – Simultaneous Development of Work Organization and Knowledge Infrastructure. Experimenting in the Field of Organizational Development. Dissertation of Helsinki University of Technology. Reports of Finnish Workplace Development Programme 65. Helsinki: Tekes.
Ramstad, E. (2007): Unresolved couple? The Relationship between Performance and Quality of Working Life and the Role of Development Approach. In J. Pelletier (ed.) Intervention Practices in Firms. Anact. Lyon, pp. 93-107.
Ramstad, E. (2005a): Self-assessment Results of the TYKE Programme's Development Projects (1996-2003) in Examination. In T. Alasoini, E. Ramstad / N. Rouhiainen (eds.) The Finnish Workplace Development Programme as an Expanding Activity. Results, Challenges, Opportunities. Ministry of Labor. Reports of Finnish Workplace Development Programme 40. Helsinki, pp. 71-109.
Ramstad, E. (2005b): Simultaneous Improvement in Performance and Quality of Working Life, in T. Alasoini, E. Ramstad / N. Rouhiainen (eds.) The Finnish Workplace Development Programme as an Expanding Activity: Results, Challenges, Opportunities. Ministry of Labor. Reports of Finnish Workplace Development Programme 40. Helsinki, pp. 110-135.
Salminen, A. / Rintala, K. / Korpi-Filppula, M. (2000): Kehittämisen jyvät ja akanat: tutkimus suomalaisten yritysten kehittämishankkeista. Helsinki University of Technology. Industrial Management and Work and Organizational Psychology. Working Paper No 23. Espoo.
Schienstock, G. (1999): From Direct Technology Policy towards Conditions-Enabling Innovation Policy. In G. Schienstock / O. Kuusi (eds.), Transformation towards a Learning Society. Challenge for the Finnish Innovation System. Helsinki: Sitra, pp. 420-441.
Tuomi, K. / Vanhala, S. (eds.) (2002): Yrityksen toiminta, menestyminen ja henkilöstön hyvinvointi: seurantatutkimus metalliteollisuudessa ja vähittäiskaupan alalla. Helsinki School of Economics and Business Administration. Publications B-40. Helsinki.
Wall, T. / Michie, J. / Patterson, M. / Wood, S.J. / Sheehan, M. / Clegg, C.W. / West, M. (2004): On the Validity of Subjective Measures of Company Performance. Personnel Psychology 57(1), pp. 95-118.

Virkkunen, J. / Engeström, Y. / Miettinen, R. (2007): Sosiaalihuollon kehittämistoiminnan tulevaisuus. Ministry of Social Affairs and Health reports 2007:49. Helsinki.

Wood, S. / Albanese, M. (1995): Can We Speak of High Commitment Management on the Shop Floor? Journal of Management Studies 32(2), pp. 235- 247.

Participation and organizational performance

Jan Kees Looise, Nicole Torka, Jan Ekke Wigboldus

1. Introduction

The connection between worker participation and organizational performance is an under-researched area. Last decade the relation between HRM and company performance has been extensively studied. However, within this stream of research, compared to other aspects of HRM, not much attention has been given to the role of worker participation, especially in its indirect and institutional forms. This is somewhat surprising given the fact that authors like Rogers and Streeck (1995) state that one of the aims of these forms of participation lies in performance upgrading and the relatively little research conducted has shown a positive effect of indirect participation on firm performance. This article adds to the understanding of the connection between worker participation – in both its direct as well as its indirect forms – and organizational performance. Our frame of reference in this article is the Dutch one. However, we think that our line of thought is also applicable to other contexts.

With respect to worker participation a distinction can be made between direct participation on the one hand and indirect or representative participation on the other. Direct participation can be defined as "opportunities which management provide, or initiatives to which they lend their support, at workplace level for consultation with and/or delegation of responsibilities and authority for decisions making to their subordinates either as individuals or as groups relating to the immediate work tasks, work organization and/or working conditions" (Geary / Sisson, 1994). Examples of forms of direct participation are: individual participation or delegation, group information and consultation via quality circles, autonomous teams, job consultation and financial participation through profit sharing and/or employee share ownership. In contrast to direct participation, indirect participation can be defined as opportunities that management mandatory – according to law or collective agreement – has to offer to representatives of employees at organizational level for consultation and authority for decision making regarding the organization as a whole or large parts of the organization, especially when it effects the position of the employees in broad sense. Examples of forms of indirect participation are: works councils and worker representatives in supervisory boards in countries like Germany and the Netherlands, union representatives at company level (shop stewards) in the Scandinavian and Anglo-Saxon countries and forms of worker-ownership including worker-cooperatives and union enterprises.

This article is organized as follows. At the end of this article, we present an integrative model that can be guiding for future research on the participation-performance link and policymaking in this field. This model is based on two streams of research we are actually performing. The first is about the connection between direct participation and employee outcomes like commitment and in line with that organizational performance. We will present a short overview of this research line in paragraph 2. The other regards the connection between representative participation – especially works councils in the Dutch context – and organizational performance. This research line will be summarized in paragraph 3. The combination of both research lines leads to the integrated model that we present in paragraph 4.

2. Direct participation and organizational performance

Given its background as a voluntary provided opportunity by management, direct participation can be seen an HRM-practice. Despite the overwhelming amount of research to the performance effects of HRM-policies and practices, only very limited research has been done to the contribution of this practice to the performance of the organization. And in the research that has been done more accent is given to the presence of direct participation and not so much to the quality of direct participation (Cox et al., 2006; Purcell / Georgiadis, 2006), while one may expect that quality is more decisive for employee attitudes and behavior and in line with that for organizational performance.

Scholars have been put much effort into studying the relationship between HRM and performance. Several authors present models aiming to illustrate this relationship (e.g., Beer et al., 1984; Fombrun et al., 1984; Guest, 1997; Paauwe / Richardson, 1997). All models share the following line of thought: There is a relationship between organizations strategy, the choice for a certain HRM approach (or system) and consequences. For example, when choosing for quality as a strategy to foster competitive advantage, this target has to be aligned within the various HR practices. Concerning the consequences, one has to distinguish between employee and organization outcomes. Employee outcomes refer to the effects of HRM on employee attitudes (e.g. satisfaction, commitment) and behavior (e.g. absenteeism, turnover) and these influence organization outcomes. The latter refer to objective (e.g. profit, return on investment; productivity, growth) as well as to subjective performance outcomes (e.g., quality of products and services, client satisfaction, innovativeness). Currently, several authors (e.g., Paauwe,

2004; Addison / Teixeira, 2006; Forth / McNabb, 2008) emphasize that the current approach of organizational performance is too narrow. In most research, the focus is on financial performance. They advice to 'operate' a multidimensional performance perspective including additional objective (e.g., employment growth) as well as subjective performance measures (e.g. employee health and safety, societal and professional performance).

Based on these general notions about the connection between HRM and performance we come to the following relationships between direct participation and organizational performance (see figure 1).

Figure 1: The relationship between direct participation and organizational performance

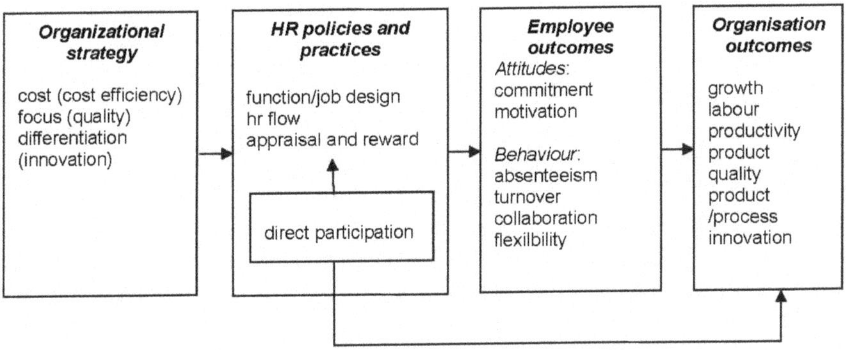

As we can see in figure 1, the position of direct participation in HR policies and practices is a rather prominent one. In the first place, via direct participation employees can influence organizations performance directly. Employees can give suggestions that lead to more efficient processes or to better product quality. By doing so, employees can contribute to higher labor productivity and more product and process innovation (e.g. De Leede, 1997). In the second place direct participation can indirectly contribute to organization outcomes, via employee outcomes like commitment, motivation, collaboration, flexibility, reduced absenteeism and turnover. Research shows that direct participation influences employee outcomes like organizational commitment and reduced turnover and performance outcomes like improved productivity and product quality (Doucouliagos, 1995; Dundon et al., 2004). Therefore, we are convinced that participation deserves an, at least, equal place compared to other HRM-practices in connection to organizational performance. Several authors assume that direct participation should even have a special status within research on performance: direct participation presumes *listening* to employee needs and only when meeting their needs desired outcomes will be gained (e.g. Gollan, 2003; Torka et al., 2007). In other words, managerial responsiveness to worker voice may lead to superior performance (Bryson, 2004, Bryson et al., 2006). Last but not least, direct participation can also influence other aspects of HRM, e.g. when employees have voice in the way these practices are applied. Beer et al. (1984) support this central position with the following arguments: "If employees are major stakeholders in the enterprise, then it is critical that managers design and administer various mechanisms for employee influence" and "employee influence in its broadest sense is a central perspective in the formulation of all human resource management policies". This last role of – both direct and indirect – participation is mostly forgotten.

In the chain from HR-practices to organization performance, employee outcomes like commitment and motivation seem to play a decisive role. Especially affective organizational commitment can be seen as a good predictor of employee behavior in terms of (reduced) absenteeism and turnover and (higher) collaboration and flexibility and in line with that organization performance. Direct participation on its turn is an important contributor to affective commitment. However, Cox et al. (2006) state that more emphasis needs to be on the perception of direct participation. Therefore, it can be argued that getting insight into the absence or presence or the *amount* of participation opportunities (see for example Forde, Slater / Spencer, 2006) seem less important than the *quality* of the given opportunities as perceived by the employees. Folger and Konovsky (1989) and Greenberg (1990) included in their studies two constructs two measure perceptions of pay: satisfaction and justice. Therefore, we can assume that satisfaction as well as perceived fairness can also shed light on the perceived quality of participation. Several studies show that justice perceptions are strong predictors of job satisfaction and organizational commitment (e.g. Colquitt et al., 2001). More specific, managerial strategies absent of fairness seem to undermine productivity (Kick et al., 2006). Finally, concerning the quality, research has also shown that participation is often in serious need of improvement. The role of managers (including direct supervisors), the quality of participation policies and practices, job and workforce characteristics are still under-considered (e.g. Bryson et al., 2006; Cunningham / Hyman, 1999; Torka et al., 2008).

3. Indirect participation and organizational performance

We can observe a growing interest in involving representative firm-level participation (e.g., unions, partnerships, work councils and other forms of joint consultation) in performance research. To explain this, we revert to German evidence. The reason for research on the consequences of representative participation for companies seems to be inspired from an economical-political point of view, that is: The discussion on the competitive position of European economies. In Germany, the system of firm-level representative participation was under debate, questioning if the two institutes within the firm (the 'betriebliche Mitbestimmung' on company issues and the 'Aufsichtsrat' on concern issues) hamper German competitiveness ('Standort Deutschland'). After all, in 2006, the so-called 'Commission Biedenkopf', concluded that a revision of the system seems inappropriate since research could not reveal a relationship with poor company performance. Contrarily, research shows that the German mandatory work councils may improve firm performance and more specific productivity (Addison et al., 2000; Addison et al., 2003; Frick / Möller, 2002). Also research in other countries shows a positive relationship between (the presence of) representative participation in firms and performance. Addison's (2005), Rose and Woolley's (1992), Sengupta's (2008) research highlights the relevance of unions for firm performance and high performance work systems. Kleiner and Lee (1997) conducted research in large South Korean firms. They conclude that effective works councils are associated with higher levels of employee satisfaction and higher productivity.

To date, scholars are not very explicit in the way(s) representative participation can influence performance. However, Dutch research on work council effectiveness can be helpful in developing an understanding on how representative participation can contribute to performance. Based on the study of Van het Kaar and Looise (1999) to the position of Dutch works councils (see table 1), we come to a three-channel model of possible works council contribution to performance, namely: one direct channel and two indirect channels.

The direct channel stands for the direct contribution of works councils to performance effects in terms of, for example, improving the efficiency, profitability and innovativeness. Studying the table we can learn that only a limited number of managing directors and works council members agree with such a direct contribution. The first indirect channel stands for a contribution of works councils to organizational performance via employee attitudes and behaviour, like a larger amount of acceptance, better representation of employee interests and reduction of power differences. According to the table this channel receives a lot of support from managing directors and works council members. The second indirect channel stands for a contribution of works councils via management attitudes and behaviour. Examples of these are better and more careful decision making. The table shows that also this channel receives a lot of support from both respondent groups. Although the questions in the table were not deliberately developed to understand the contribution of the works council to organizational performance – they were developed to measure some effects of works councils –, they offer the chance to understand the channels by which representative forms of participation can influence organizational performance (for more information, see Wigboldus et al., 2008).

Table 1: Works council effects based on perceptions of managing directors and works council members (Van het Kaar and Looise, 1999)

Effects	**Management**	**Works councillors**
(Direct)	%	%
Enhancing efficiency	9	26
Enhancing profitability	4	10
Enhancing innovation	12	24
(Indirect 1)		
Improved acceptance among employees	64	43
Improved representation of employees' interests	55	78
Reduction of power differences	28	27
(Indirect 2)		
Improvement of decision making quality	38	52
More careful decision making	65	67
Faster decision making	3	11

(percentages of managing directors (N=450) and works council members (N= 380) that agree with this effect)

The relationships discussed can be presented as follows (see figure 2).

This model shows that performance effects can be created by indirect forms of participation both directly and indirectly. Representative participation bodies like works councils in the Netherlands and Germany can make suggestions for performance improvement or can influence decisions by management which directly lead to better performance outcomes. These bodies can also influence employee attitudes and behaviour which on their turn will lead to better organizational outcomes. And last but not least these bodies can influence the organizational system (i.e., governance, goals/strategy, structure and culture), policies and practices for the management of human resources and via these or direct performance. Also in the case of indirect participation it is important to note that the quality of participation is decisive got its results. The quality determines the real power these institutes can have on performance and this power may exceeds even minimum rights as given by (country-specific) regulations. Representative participation quality depends on managers' attitudes towards such institutions as well as the expertise and skills of representative participation agents. We can even assume that the latter might direct the former, but research on this relationship lacks. Moreover, we suggest that not only the quality of this form of participation seems to be a function of managers as well as agents: both are also responsible for the quality of direct participation. Concerning the latter, they may guide and support direct supervisors – those who receive employees direct voice frequently – in dealing with direct participation.

Figur 2: The relationship between indirect participation and organizational performance

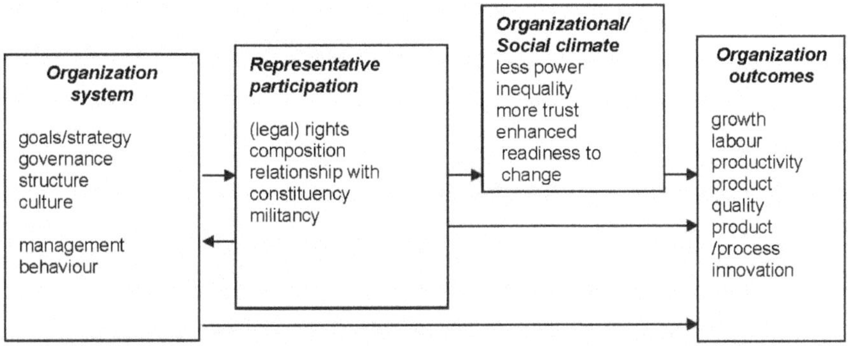

What in general has been neglected until now is the possible impact of representative participation on the firm's organizational or social climate, that is: a shared perception at the firm level. Climate is a critical mediating construct in exploring, for at least, the relationships between aggregated HRM (systems) and performance (Bowen / Ostroff, 2004: 205). Thus, HRM determines the strength of the climate and via the climate performance. In a strong climate organizational members show conformity or congruence concerning organizational values (e.g. cost effectiveness, quality, innovativeness) and act according to these values. Ostroff, Shin and Kinicki (2005: 596) refer to Quinn's (1988) value dimensions: The first contrasts stability and control with flexibility and change, the second an internal focus (well-being and development of employees) versus an external focus (well-being of the organization). Therefore, representative participation can be seen as an explicit attempt to create and integrate mutual benefits of managers' and employees – organizational and employee well-being – leading to a strong climate and via this performance. Research shows that participative organizational climates are perceived as more effective in terms of trust than authoritarian climates (Farris / Senner / Butterfield, 1973) and trust influences labor-management relations (Taylor, 1989), enhanced readiness to change (Lawler, 1992) and negotiation (Bazerman, 1994).

Concerning the latter, the assumption of a reversed effect of trust seems also appropriate: trust – as a consequence of a strong climate – may influence the quality of representative participation.

4. Inter-relatedness of direct and indirect participation and organizational performance

The aim of this article is to show the inter-relatedness of direct and indirect participation and organizational performance. The inter-relatedness between – both direct and indirect – participation and organizational performance has hardly been studied. This is somewhat surprising given the positive effects that have been assumed by several authors like Strauss's (1998) who stated that institutionalized indirect participation is inevitable for successful direct participation. And also given the positive relationships between indirect and direct participation that have been found in research. For example, Kleiner and Lee (1997) found for South Korean firms that both work councils and unions enhance direct participation on several key personnel practices and Poutsma et al (2006) found substantial effects of country-specific institutions on direct participation in European firms. So, what is the explanation for the lack of research that includes the three central topics of this article: indirect participation, direct participation and organizational performance? We assume two reasons: (1) including both forms of participation may is more complicated than focusing on the impact of one form and (2) research on the influence of the distinct forms of participation on performance is still limited. However, we assume that a study of the connection between participation and organization performance is only meaningful when we combine both forms. Figure 3 shows this combination.

Figure 3 not only shows the combination of figures 1 and 2 but also the mutual connections. This model also shows that both indirect and direct participation have their own roles and functions within organizations and that there is no need for fear of taking over (part of) these roles or functions by the one or the other. The role and function of representative participation cannot be taken over by direct participation and the other way around. A second important aspect is the role of indirect participation with respect to HRM and direct participation. Indirect participation is not (only) a HRM-practice: indirect participation is also a 'co-designer' of HRM policies and practices. Representative committees discuss and co-decide on HRM topics such as benefits, job design and employee health. In that sense, indirect participation channels and influences HRM policies and practices such as those related to direct forms of participation. Members of these indirect bodies should be more aware of these options and also use these to strengthen direct participation in their organizations. A third important point is the combination of social climate and employee outcomes, especially commitment. While social climate refers to collective experiences, employee consequences such as commitment and satisfaction refer to the impact of participation on individuals perception. However, research shows that collective and individual experiences are interrelated (Carr et al., 2003) and have a positive impact upon performance (Katz et al., 1985).

Figure 3: An integrated model for HRM, participation and organization performance

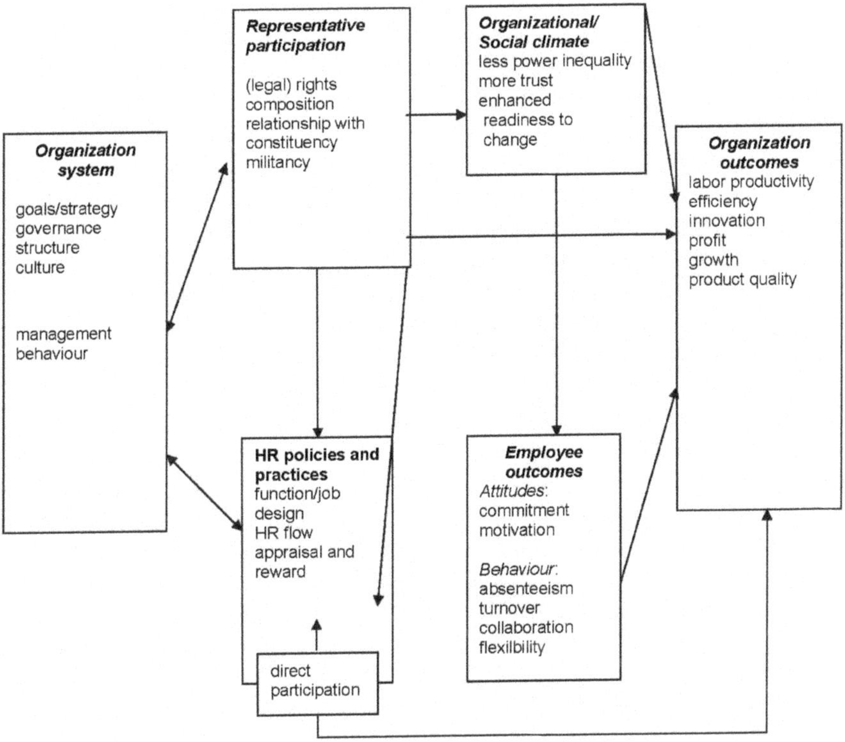

5. Conclusion

Representative participation seems to influence direct participation (e.g. Kleiner / Lee, 1997; Poutsma et al., 2006) as do managers' expertise and skills to implement participation initiatives in a way that they meet employees' interest in satisfying and fair opportunities to raise voice *and* decide on HRM issues important to them. This also points once again on the significance of direct supervisors' attitudes and behaviors and top-managers capability to direct those. Concerning fairness, compared to relevant others, not only participation as an 'outcome' (distributive justice) is important, but also the process of participation (procedural justice). The inclusion of both relevant variables – role of the managers', and especially direct supervisor, and justice – is still relatively rare in research on participation in general and research on the participation-performance link. Concerning the latter, a comparable conclusion can be made for the role of the social climate, employee outcomes (attitudes and behavior), the possible routes in the participation-performance chain and broader operationalizations of performance.

Theoretical and empirical insights support our idea that research on indirect participation deserves scholars and practitioners devotion when aiming for answers on how to improve not only organizational, but also employee and, as an ultimate goal, societal well-being: All outcomes that fit to an enlarged definition of performance. Our insights, based on the work of colleagues, can enhance the position of representative participation in 'real organizational life'. On the organization level, for managers' this knowledge can be beneficial for the design of HRM as well as their attitudes and behavior towards representative participation. HR managers and consultants may profit from this knowledge when advising top-management and, finally, the agents of representative participation may 'exploit' these ideas for choices on contents as well as intervention strategies.

Last, but not least, we suggest that also on a societal level a grasp of participation and its effects might help in future decision-making on representative participation. In the Netherlands, debates on the value and *Zeitgeist fit* of representative firm-level participation blaze up frequently. In this debate, opponents of the current system mention cost arguments as well as the assumed so-called progressing individualization that leads to less interest and importance of indirect participation. Research and theory so far, can take the wind out of their attitudinal sails.

Literature

Addison, J.T. / Siebert, S. / Wagner, J. / Wei, X. (2000): Worker participation and firm performance: Evidence from Germany and Britain. British Journal of Industrial Relations, 38, 7-48.

Addison, J.T. / Schnabel, C. / Wagner, J. (2003): The course of research into the economic consequences of German works councils. British Journal of Industrial Relations, 42, 255-282.

Addison, J.T. (2005): The determinants of firm performance: unions, works councils, and employee involvement/ high performance work practices. Scottish Journal of Political Economy, 52, 406-450.

Addison, J.T. / Teixeira, P. (2006): The effect of work councils on employment change. Industrial Relations, 45, 1-25.

Bazerman, M.H. (1994): Judgment in management decision making. New York: Wiley.

Beer, M. / Spector, B. / Lawrence, P.R. / Quinn Mills, D. / Walton, R.E. (1984): Managing Human Assets. New York: The Free Press

Bowen, D.E. / Ostroff, C. (2004): Understanding HRM-firm performance linkages: the role of the "strength" of the HRM system. Academy of Management Review, 29, 203-221.

Bryson, A. (2004): Managerial responsiveness to union and nonunion worker voice in Britain. Industrial Relations, 43, 213-241.

Bryson, A. / Charlwood, A. / Forth, J. (2006): Worker voice, Managerial Response and Labour Productivity. An Empirical Investigation. Industrial Relations Journal, 37: 438-455.

Carr, J.Z. / Schmidt, A.M. / Ford, J.K. / DeShon, R.P. (2003): Climate perceptions matter: A meta-analytic path analysis relating molar climate, cognitive and affective states, and individual level work outcomes. Journal of Applied Psychology, 88, 605-619.

Colquitt, J.A. / Conlon, D.E. / Wesson, M.J. / Porter, C.O. / Ng, K.Y. (2001): Justice at the millennium: A meta-analytic review of 25 years of organizational justice research. Journal of Applied Psychology, 86, 425-445.

Cox, A. / Zagelmeyer, S. / Marchington, M. (2006): Embedding employee involvement and participation at work. Human Resource Management Journal, 16, 250-267.

Cunningham, I. / Hyman, J. (1999): The poverty of empowerment? A critical case study. Personnel Review, 28, 192-207.

De Leede, J. (1997): Innoveren van onderop; over de bijdrage van taakgroepen aan product- en procesvernieuwing. Deventer: Kluwer Bedrijfsinformatie.

Doucouliagos, R. (1995): Worker participation and productivity in labor-managed and participatory capitalist firms: A meta-analysis. Industrial and Labor Relations Review, 49, 58-77.

Dundon, T.A. / Wilkinson, A. / Marchington, M. / Ackers, P. (2004): The meanings and purpose of employee voice. International Journal of Human Resource Management, 15, 1149-1170.

Farris, G.F / Senner, E.E. / Butterfield, D.A. (1973): Trust, culture and organizational behaviour. Industrial Relations, 12, 144-157.

Folger, R. / Konovsky, M.A. (1989): Effects of procedural and distributive justice on reactions to pay raise decisions. Academy of Management Journal, 32, 115-130.

Fombrun, C.J. / Tichy, N.M. / Devanna, M.A. (1984): Strategic Human Resource Management. New York: Wiley.

Forde, C. / Slater, G. / Spencer, D.A. (2006): Fearing the worst? Threat, participation and workplace productivity. Economic and Industrial Democracy, 27, 369-398.

Forth, J. / McNabb, R. (2008): Workplace performance: A comparison of subjective and objective measures in the 2004 Workplace Employment Relations Survey. Industrial Relations Journal, 39, 104-123.

Frick, B. / Möller, I. (2002): Mandated Works Councils and Firm Performance: Labor Productivity and Personnel Turnover in German Establishments. Working Paper.

Geary, J. / Sisson, K. (1994): Conceptualising Direct Participation in Organisational Change – The EPOC Project. Luxembourg: Office for Official Publicatons of the European Community

Gollan, P.J. (2003): All talk but no voice: Employee voice at the Eurotunnel call centre. Economic and Industrial Democracy, 24, 509-541.

Greenberg, J. (1990): Organizational justice: Yesterday, Today and tomorrow. Journal of Management 16, 399-432.

Guest, D.E. (1997): Human Resource Management and Performance: A Review and Research Agenda, International Journal of Human Resource Management, 8, 263-276.

Katz, H.C. / Kochan, T.A. / Weber, M.R. (1985): Assessing the effects of industrial relations systems and efforts to improve the quality of working life and organizational effectiveness. Academy of Management Journal, 28, 509-526.

Kick, E.L. / Fraser, J.C. / Davis, B.L. (2006): Performance management, managerial citizenship and worker commitment: A study on the United States postal service with some global implications. Economic and Industrial Democracy, 27: 137-172.

Kleiner, M.M. / Lee, Y.-M. (1997): Work councils and unionization: Lessons from South Korea. Industrial Relations, 36: 1-16.

Lawler, E.E. (1992): The ultimate advantage: Creating the high-involvement organization. San Francisco: Jossey-Bass.

Ostroff, C. / Shin, Y. / Kinicki, A.J. (2005): Multiple perspectives of congruence: relationships between value congruence and employee attitudes. Journal of Organizational Behavior, 26, 591-623.

Paauwe, J. (2004): HRM and Performance. Achieving Long Term Viability. Oxford, Oxford University Press.

Paauwe, J. / Richardson, R.R. (1997): Introduction: Special Issue on HRM and Performance, International Journal of Human Resource Management, 8, 257-362

Poutsma, E. / Ligthart, P.E.M. / Veersma, U. (2006): The diffusion of calculative and collaborative HRM practices in European firms. Industrial Relations, 45, 513-546.

Purcell, J. / Georgiadis, K. (2006): Why should employers bother with worker voice? In: R. Freeman, P. Boxall / P. Haynes (eds.), What workers say: Employment voice in the Anglo-American World. Ithaca, NY: Cornell University Press.

Quinn, R.E. (1988): A spatial model of effectiveness criteria: toward a competing values approach to organizational analysis. Management Science, 29, 363-377.

Rogers, J. / Streeck, W. (1995): Work councils: Consultations, representations, and cooperation in Industrial Relations. Chicago, IL: University of Chicago Press.

Rose, E. / Woolley, T. (1992): Shifting sands? Trade unions and productivity at Rover cars. Industrial Relations Journal, 23, 257-267.

Sengupta, S. (2008): The impact of employee-share-ownership schemes on performance in unionised and non-unionised workplaces. Industrial Relations Journal, 39, 170-190.

Strauss, G. (1998): An Overview (pp. 8-39). In Heller, F., Pusic, E., Strauss, G. and Wilpert, B. (eds.) Organizational Participation: Myth and Reality. Oxford: Oxford University Press.

Taylor, R.G. (1989): The role of trust in labor-management relations. Organization Development Journal, 7, 85-89.

Torka, N. / Riemsdijk, M. van / Looise, J.C. (2007): Werkgeversbetrokkenheid. Tijdschrift voor Arbeidsvraagstukken, 23, 45-59.

Torka, N. / Woerkom, M. van / Looise, J.C. (2008): Direct Employee Involvement Quality (DEIQ). Creativity and Innovation Management, 17, 147-154.

Van het Kaar, R. / Looise, J.C. (1999): De volwassen OR. Groei en grenzen van de Nederlandse ondernemingsraad. Alphen aan den Rijn: Samson.

Good corporate governance and the function of obligatory employees' involvement: the concept of a sustainable company

Norbert Kluge, Sigurt Vitols, Peter Wilke

Introduction

Highly developed industrial relations are regarded as one of the core mechanisms for realising the Lisbon strategy. Statutory employees' participation at all levels, with the inclusion of trade unions, serves as a basis for this. The legally guaranteed space for employees' participation helps to strengthen both European democracy and the European economy, and may hold an answer for the crisis of 'unbridled' global capitalism.

However, rules for obligatory employee' involvement normally are not seen in the context of corporate governance. The current debate on Europe corporate governance seems to touch only the transparency and structure of the relationship between managers and shareholders. However, in many EU member states and in European legislation (on European Companies – SE – and on European Cooperative Societies – SCE –) provisions for employee involvement are common and include representation in company boardrooms. This has historical roots and is perceived as mechanism for embedding business in society. In this view, worker participation functions in the interests of both achieving long-term competitiveness of companies and strengthening participatory democracy:

- Participation rights make the employee a "citizen in the workplace" in European firms – that is their *democratic function.*
- From the point of view of management, these rights facilitate agreements with employees' representatives and their trade unions on managing and shaping change in companies in a socially acceptable way, and they foster employee acceptance of the decisions made by the company – that is their *economic function.*

Today, the question of how to organize effective supervision of management decisions has received fresh prominence through new concepts and forms of corporate financing, for example through large hedge funds or private equity, whose primary aim is to achieve short-term profits for investors rather than to promote the long-term performance of a company. Overall, the company financing environment has become more aggressive. Moreover, in Europe the intensity of the restructuring process has increased enormously. The primary victims are the employees of companies that have been relocated or stripped of assets. These developments have raised the question of the responsibility, legitimacy and social role of companies: Do they only generate a cash machine for their shareholders or do they have also a social function to be considered as an objective of management? The voluntary approach to Corporate Social Responsibility (CSR) leaves doubts about the ability of a neo-liberal system to address social needs properly and it is not likely to repair the lack of legitimacy.

The discussion on the character of the evolving European system of corporate governance is still open. At issue is the fundamental choice between two different conceptions of the firm: the shareholder model, where the purpose of the firm is to maximise value in the interest of the shareholders, and a more stakeholder-orientated model, where the firm also has responsibility to a broader range of stakeholders. An alternative European model still is missing. There is a need to start a broader debate on a new 'leading model' for the 21. century.

We will argue in this paper that statutory employees' involvement could serve as one proper tool for shaping the new challenges to the benefit of employees but also to the benefit to the society as its whole. Employee representation at board level linked to the other levels of interest representation by works councils or trade union bodies in the company may serve as a proper framework in which social groups other than shareholders are able to organise and determine their interests in the company.

Empirical evidence from numerous studies suggests that there is no serious economic argument against obligatory involvement of employee representation due to disadvantages for business performance because of limiting and delaying necessary management decisions. This paper presents those findings with the aim of underling the increasing economic importance of creating employee commitment, which is also beneficial for global competitiveness, at least for European companies.

Obligatory employees' board-level representation – present and functioning in the corporate systems of a number of EU member states

Looking back to the origin of the European Union after the Second World War there is historically a continuous thread running from the European Coal and Steel Community that supports employee participation in general and board-level employee representation within systems of corporate governance in particular. Accordingly, it is no surprise to consider obligatory presence of employee representatives as a reality in the guidance of companies in many EU member states. The obligatory presence of employee representatives in the boardroom contributes to another style of managing a company according to the different backgrounds of national industrial relation systems. And it is not possible to reduce employee' board level representation to the issue of dealing with the social consequences of management decisions or simply providing information and consultation rights.

Figure 1: Board-level participation rights in 30 countries applying the European Company (SE) legislation

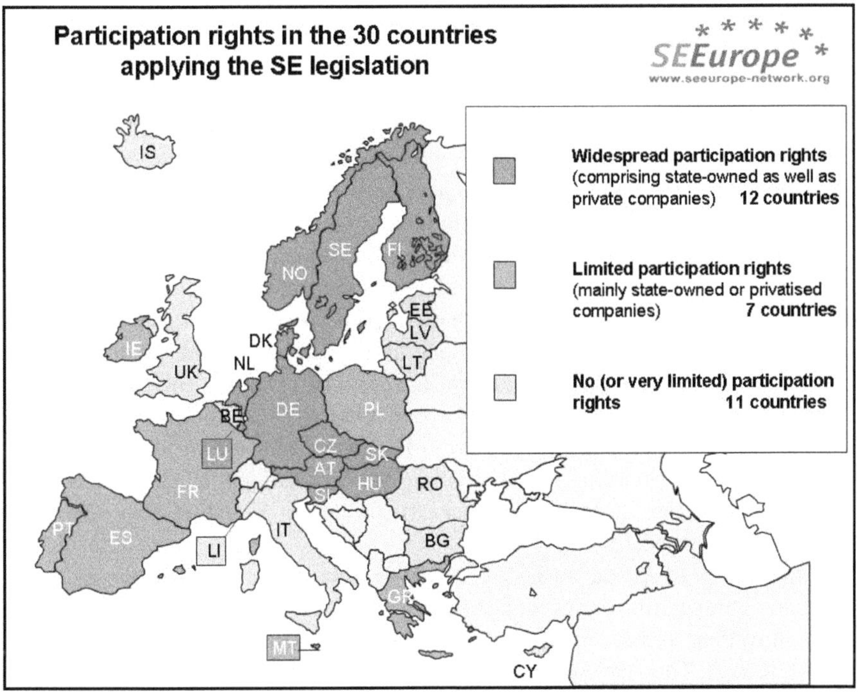

Similar provisions on the statutory representation of employees can be found in 18 out of the EU-27 member states and in Norway. In 12 states employees' board-level representation is a part of the national corporate governance system.[1]

1 In 11 EU member states (or 12 when including Norway), employees can have their interests represented in the administrative bodies of the enterprise in all sectors, in both private and state-owned companies. In the Nordic countries, Austria, Germany, Luxembourg and the Netherlands, as well as central and east European countries (the Slovak and Czech Republics, Slovenia and Hungary) employee participation rights have emerged at national level and are a stable component of national 'economic culture'. In seven EU member states, employee representation on administrative bodies is foreseen only in

It is also a fact that in most European countries – irrespective of the basic legal company structure – employees' representatives have seats and voting rights on one or other of the company's top administrative organs and are also involved in a supervisory capacity. In Europe, the two-tier management model with a management board and a supervisory board is by no means a thing of the past. Indeed, the two-tier system exists in the majority of the new Member States. The law stipulates the two-tier system in ten Member States and the single-tier system in 11 EU countries, and allows companies to choose between the two models in the remaining four. In European Companies (SEs), where the legal structure is established voluntarily, it is generally possible to choose freely between the systems that exist in the country where the company is domiciled.

In the United Kingdom and the United States, there is a historical move in best practice and corporate governance codes towards separation of the Chief Executive Officer (CEO) and top supervisory (board chair) roles to different people, which suggests a growing preference for the two-tier system.

However, so far any attempt to establish a European standard of worker participation in large companies (i.e. with more than 500 employees) throughout Europe have failed. There have been a number of initiatives intended to establish a European standard of worker participation in large companies – without much success because of the differences between systems . Consequently, the solution achieved by the rules on employees' participation in the European Company Statute (Societas Europeae – SE) has no European standard on the matter: they constitute the safeguarding of pre-existing rights at national level in the context of a transformation into a cross-border structure of an SE rather than a uniform new European standard.

Given the wide spread presence of employee representatives in the top organs of companies they must – under changed environment conditions of financial capitalism – show their further importance by conducting a "double accounting" (doppelte Buchführung): They have to give evidence that their presence serves as the better social model of a corporation which is being, at the same time, more successful in economic terms, too. In this respect, it is worth to investigate whether one can find some economic proof that obligatory employees' board-level representation also contributes positively to the economic performance of companies.

---

certain sectors (like public savings banks in Spain) or for state-owned and privatised enterprises (in France and Poland), or only in state-owned enterprises (Greece, Ireland, Malta and Portugal). Employees' participation at this level is therefore not generally perceived as an element of national labour relations. In the Nordic countries, the law provides seats on the one-tier administrative board (board of directors) which not only supervises the enterprise's strategic decisions but may also take such decisions.

The economic effects of obligatory employee involvement – empirical evidence

The question on the economic effects of obligatory employee involvement has no clear theoretical answer. The positive view stresses the increased quality of labour input available to the firm through greater job satisfaction, commitment and so on through the improved efficiency of operations, e.g. through valuable suggestions for improving company operations. The negative view focuses on increased costs and rent-seeking strategies by labour: restricting the optimal reduction of labour during downturns, blocking the use of more efficient technologies, or trying to increase the share of value added appropriated by labour at the expense of investors.

If we go beyond the more ideological arguments we still see some uncertainty. On the one hand a broad social consensus acknowledges the fact that the greatest advantage of codetermination is its contribution to maintaining social harmony and high productivity through partnership-based working relations. On the other hand studies which examine the effect of employee participation on the operational side of companies generally indicate only that there are no negative consequences of employee participation for the owners and there exist positive effects on innovativeness and productivity improvements. But there is no clear correlation between employee involvement and economic performance.

At this point it must be said that comparison between European countries of the intensity of participation and so also the quality of supervision provided by employees' participation is difficult. Both the degree and the range of participation are extremely variable. The effectiveness of employees' participation in the different systems depends partly on the general significance of the administrative organ in national company law. On what exactly can the administrative organ take decisions, and to what extent is there a list of issues which requires its agreement? Only in Austria is such a list prescribed in law. While in some countries interest representation of the employees' side on the supervisory board (in Germany and Austria) or on the board of directors or the management board (in Sweden and Denmark) is laid down in special laws, the relevant foundations in other countries are to be found in commercial law. This applies, for example, to the Czech Republic. It is clear that in such cases employees' participation on the highest level enterprise organs (board level) is understood less as a direct form of interest representation.

There are numerous studies which emphasise that managers see economic benefits from seeking social harmony with their employees. The German example can be used as a basis for assessing how strong company employee participation is reflected economically through Works Councils.

In general one can identify different possible ways how worker participation can influence the performance o companies .[2] The literature identifies four main possible areas where performance might be affected by the presence of worker participation upon:

- impact on the behaviour of employees themselves – variables like job satisfaction and commitment, level of labour turnover, and willingness to invest in firm-specific skills would measure this impact. The argument here is that participation affects the quality, quantity, and cost of labour input into the 'production function' of the firm;
- impact on company operations (understood as the combining of factors of production into goods or services) – here productivity is the typical measurement of operational efficiency within the firm, but innovation is also important;
- impact on the financial performance of the firm – typically measured in terms of profits or the division of value added between capital and labour; and
- impact on the stock market performance of the firm, measured by share price performance or share valuation.

Typical approaches to measure the impact performance include labour variables, operational variables and financial participation variables. Studies have used either employees' or managers' subjective evaluations of the impact of participation (e.g. very positive, somewhat positive, neutral, somewhat negative, very negative, etc.) or have tried to get 'hard' quantitative data on these variables. Supporters of hard data argue that subjective evaluations are not reliable or may be even misleading ('cheap talk'), whereas supporters of subjective data argue that too many factors influence short-term financial performance to allow meaningful econometric tests.

Kluge and Vitols (2008) suggest as an additional approach using the country as the main unit of analysis, rather than the company, and look at the relationship between the strength of worker participation (WP) at board level and economic performance.[3] To test this approach one can divide up the 25 countries in the EU-25 into two groups according to the strength of rights to worker representa-

2 This subsection draws heavily on Wigboldus' excellent paper. See also Freeman and Lazear, which has become something of a classic regarding the economic effects of works councils; and Addison et al., who survey the 'state of the art' in terms of studies on Germany.

3 Kluge and Vitols (2008): The European Company: A Pilot for Integrating Shareholder Value into Stakeholder-Orientated European Societies? Andreas Nikopoulos, Michael Gold and Norbert Kluge (eds.): The European Company Statute: A New Approach to Corporate Governance. London: Peter Lang (i.E.).

tion in company boards. The group with strong rights, in which rights for worker participation at the board level exist for most large private sector companies, include the following eleven countries: Austria, Czech Republic, Denmark, Finland, Germany, Hungary, Luxembourg, Netherlands, Slovak Republic, Slovenia, and Sweden. The group with limited rights, which apply to worker board representation in only public sector companies, or rights to attendance but no voting rights, or no formal rights, include the following fourteen countries: Belgium, Cyprus, Estonia, France, Greece, Ireland, Italy, Latvia, Lithuania, Malta, Poland, Portugal, Spain, and the UK.

The table shows the average scores of the two groups of countries along a broad range of indicators of 'national performance'. The difference between the averages is quite striking. With the exception of economic growth, the group of countries with strong worker participation board rights scored consistently and significantly better than the group with limited or no rights.

Other recent studies on the impact of worker participation at the plant level (through works councils) are provided by Addison and Jirjahn based on the improvement of the data on works councils as well as the econometric methodology used. Its findings suggest that the current generation of studies show an overall positive impact of works councils on company performance in particular productivity is significantly higher in plants with works councils than in plants without one.

One can conclude from this studies that worker participation at the board level do not lead to reduced company performance, and thus do not have negative welfare effects for shareholders and creditors . However, it is not possible from the given data to argue that strong participation rights 'caused' superior economic performance in the first group of countries. Nevertheless, this provides interesting evidence that strong participation rights on company boards do not stand in contradiction to strong national performance. It may taken a s granted that the traditional European management and control systems, and in particular those with a separate tier of supervision in the shape of a supervisory board or administrative board (dual-tier system), function just as well as the supposedly more effective single-tier management systems that originate from the Anglo-Saxon world (Maher and Andersson, 1999).

Table 1: Comparison of European national economic performance.

Performance Variable (weighted averages)	Group I: EU Countries with Strong Codetermination	Group II: EU Countries with Weak/No Codetermination
Unemployment rate (2004), as % of labour force	8.0	8.2
Trade balance (goods), as % of GDP (annual average, for the 5 years 1999–2003)	3.9	-2.0
Current account balance, as % of GDP (annual average, for the 5 years 1999–2003)	1.0	-0.8
Labour productivity per hour (2003)	101.0	95.3
BCI (Business Competitiveness Index)[4]	6.8	19.9
R&D expenses, as % of GDP, ca. 2000	2.4	1.6
Strike rate (days per 1000 employees), annual average 2000–2002	9.7	104.8
Gini coefficient	0.259	0.321
GDP real growth (annual average, for the 5 years 1999–2004)	1.6	2.4

Sources: EUROSTAT, World Competitiveness Report, OECD, EIRO Online

Employee representation as pro-active driver towards corporate social responsibility and sustainability?

If we come back to the initial idea of the paper to use the legitimation crisis of the shareholder oriented approach for introducing a more stakeholder oriented model which tries to foster sustainable companies, we are looking for indications whether employee representation is playing a role in progressing social issues in

4 The latest *Global Competitiveness Report 2006–2007*, released by the World Economic Forum on 26 September 2006, shows five European countries with obligatory employees' board representation within the Top Ten (Finland, Sweden, Denmark, Germany and the Netherlands). The United Kingdom is the only European exception. According to the World Economic Forum, over 11,000 business leaders were polled for this report in a record 125 economies worldwide. The rankings are drawn from a combination of publicly available hard data and the results of the Executive Opinion Survey, a comprehensive annual survey conducted by the World Economic Forum, together with its network (further information see http://www.weforum.org/en/initiatives/gcp/Global%20 Competitiveness% 20Report/index.htm).

company decision making. In recent years there has been an increasing emphasis on the public's interest in company governance and practices. In addition to the corporate governance structures and practices of companies, environmental and social impact of corporations has also been receiving increasing attention and demands for regulation. The concern with these practices has variously been labelled CSR (Corporate Social Responsibility).

Part of a CSR policy is how stakeholders in the company, particularly employees, should be involved in company decision-making. In practice also European works councils are an important place for discussing CSR issues. The European Commission acknowledges in several communications the constructive role of European Works Councils in cross-border restructuring as well as in developing best practices on corporate social responsibility (CSR), which, going beyond legal requirements, are part of the obligations of pro-active corporate management[5].

In order to ascertain the rank of EWCs as one of the "good governance" practices, Vitols (2008) did a correlation analysis between different sustainability indexes (as an indicator for good governance) and the presence of an EWC. Each of the 390 companies among the STOXX 600 that is eligible to have an EWC was assigned a variable for inclusion or exclusion in three existing sustainability indexes.[6]

The result is that the presence of a EWC at a company is strongly correlated with that company's inclusion in the various sustainability indexes. This correlation is the strongest in the case of the Ethibel excellence index (correlation of 0.38) and weakest in the case of the FTSE4Good index (0.20), with the Dow Jones Sustainability Index being in between (0.30).

This analysis shows that the presence of a EWC is strongly correlated with other good governance practices, as measured by the leading sustainability indexes.

Even if positive results/effects cannot always be traced back to employee participation, it can nevertheless be demonstrated that employee representation is clearly supposed to take over a more pro-active role in promoting other goals of corporate management than only creating benefits for shareholders. Although, in particular, EWCs are not legally mandated to deal with subjects on sustainability and corporate social responsibility, in practice, they are concerning with them as these topics are relevant within their turn of everydays work.

---

5 COM(2005)120 final and COM(2006)136 final.

6 Sustain – Dow Jones sustainability index (see www.sustainability-index.com/ for a description), ethibel – Ethibel excellence index (see www.ethibel.org for a description) ftse4g – FTSE Group "for good" index (for a description see www.ftse.com/Indices/FTSE4Good_Index_Series/index.jsp).

Prospective outlook: corporate governance reform in Europe towards the sustainable European Company

In the world of financial capitalism an obligatory voice for labour in management control and decision-making sometimes seems like a unrealistic idea without future prospects. Due to the globalisation of capital and the increasing importance of institutional investors, some experts have suggested that the stakeholder model is out of date and that Europe must adopt the shareholder model to be competitive.

However, we think that obligatory board-level employees' participation is often a 'forgotten resource' . Its historical thread comprises both policy statements and legal measures, more recently illustrated by the adoption of the European Company Statute in 2001. Underpinning this approach is the assumption that employee participation is a prerequisite of ensuring 'high road' production systems throughout the EU . This includes the necessity of highly committed employees with their companies, in particular, by the highly qualified employees. They will not provide their knowledge entirely to one company if they see no potential for the future development of this company. Consequently, owners and companies are well-advised to allow them influence on decision making. This includes the idea to provide them with representation in the boardroom, as Osterloh/Frey (2006) suggest. Today such an approach fits well with the recent objectives of European policies. Strong and obligatory employee involvement based on European law can be seen to be in accordance with the main objectives of the 'Lisbon Agenda'. This proposes combining economic performance with social (and environmental) objectives in favour of a 'high road' of production and services carried out by a high qualified workforce, which should characterize the European way of being competitive in a global economy.

Recent developments in Germany and the Scandinavian countries and also the Netherlands, where elements of the shareholder model are being successfully integrated into existing stakeholder systems, prove that there are alternatives to shareholder capitalism. It is possible to describe a new system of 'a sustainable European Company' or, in more conventional terms, 'negotiated shareholder value' that appears to fulfil the key demand of institutional investors for greater transparency and helps to avoid excessive short-terminism..

For the time being, the idea of a 'sustainable company' is not much more than a concept to be discussed. It can be characterized by the following advantages:

- for employees: providing training, well-paid and satisfying jobs, with the maximum possible employment security;
- for the environment: using resources in ways that do not contribute to the further deterioration of the environment;

- for customers: providing reliable, high quality products;
- for creditors/bondholders: providing interest payments at low risk;
- for stockholders: providing high transparency and a financial return commensurate with the risks of shareholding.

To meet these challenges, companies need to develop policies which are sustainable in three respects: (i) with regard to human resources, (ii) with regard to the environment, and (iii) with regard to financial policy (patient capital).

Part of the policy of a sustainable company in the field of human resources includes statutory employee participation at all levels. Industrial relations with statutory employee participation and with the inclusion of the trade unions serve as a good basis for combating the notion that only share ownership can make a good citizen out of a European citizen. It is the legally guaranteed space for employee participation that helps make European democracy and the European economy strong. The citizens of Europe must be convinced of the seriousness of political intentions to enable them to influence their working life in the course of social and economic transformation. It is against the common understanding of freedom and democracy to simply deliver them up to market forces.

If the key factor for lasting economic success in the future is the ability to continually adjust to new market conditions through innovation and process modernization, it will only work in companies that have a corporate culture which actively encourages employees to prepare for and implement innovation strategies and which challenges and encourages innovation in the way how decision-making and practical work are organized.

The time seems ripe for a new model for the era which will succeed shareholder capitalism. Participation will play a path-breaking role in this. But the trade unions cannot go back to the ideas and instruments of 'industrial democracy', the model of the 1970s and 1980s. Circumstances have changed: financial markets know no boundaries, and extremely demanding and enormously wealthy international investors and powerful multinational companies influence public life more than ever, including people's working lives. European policy would be well advised to establish a counterforce if the idea of the European social model is not to continue to lose ground.

Literature

Bedrac, Janja (2006): What makes a good company? Employee representation in European company law: reflections and legal provisions. Brussels: ETUI report 94

Benchmarking Working Europe 2006 (2006): hrsg. Von Europäischen Gewerkschaftsbund und Europäischem Gewerkschaftsinstitut, Brussels

EU-Commission (2003): Modernising Company Law and Enhancing Corporate Governance in the European Union – A Plan to Move Forward, Brussels: Communication from the Commission COM 2003 (284),. http://europa.eu.int/eur-lex/en/com/cnc/2003/com2003_0284en01.pdf.

EU-Commission (2004): Facing the challenge. The Lisbon strategy for growth and employment, Luxembourg: Office for Official Publications of the European Communities

European Foundation for the Improvement of Living and Working Conditions (2005): Financial Participation in the EU: A benchmarking study of Slovenia

EU-Kommission (2005): Sozialpolitische Agenda 2005-2010, Brussels: KOM (2005) 33 endgültig: http://europa.eu.int/comm/employment_social/social_policy_agenda/spa_de.pdf

Europäischer Gewerkschaftsbund, EGB (2006): Corporate Governance auf europäischer Ebene. Entschließung vom 14.3.2006. www.etuc.org

Frick, Bernd (2005): 'Kontrolle und Performance der mitbestimmten Unternehmung: Rechtsökonomische Überlegungen und empirische Befunde', Kölner Zeitschrift für Soziologie und Sozialpsychologie, Sonderband "Vom Manager- zum Finanzweltkapitalismus" Global Competitveness Report 2004 (2004), Davos: World Economic Forum.

Fulton, Lionel (2007): The forgotten resource: Corporate governance and employee board-level representation. The situation in France, the Netherlands, Sweden and the UK. Düsseldorf: Hans-Böckler-Stiftung, edition 190

Höpner, Michael (2003): Wer beherrscht die Unternehmen? Shareholder Value, Managerherrschaft und Mitbestimmung in Deutschland., Frankfurt a.M.: Campus.

Hopt, Klaus J. et al. (2004): European Corporate Governance in company law and codes, Report prepared for the European Corporate Governance Conference of October, 18th, The Hague, The Netherlands. C:\B-EUCG\Den Hague_CG_Final Report_0105.doc.

Möller, Iris (2001): Institut für Arbeitsmarkt- und Berufsforschung (IAB): Produktivitätswirkung von Mitarbeiterbeteiligung, empirische Analysen mit Daten des IAB-Betriebspanels. In: H.-G. Guski-Schneider (Hrsg.)

Jürgens, Ulrich / Inge Lippert (2005): Kommunikation und Wissen im Aufsichtsrat, Berlin: Wissenschaftszentrum Berlin in Kooperation mit der ULA.

Kluge, Norbert (2004): Employees' Involvement in Europe – A Still Unfinished Jigsaw. In: Henning Jorgensen, Mette Baerentsen and John Monks (eds.): European Trade Union Yearbook 2003/2004, ETUI: Brussels, pp. 115-136

Kluge, Norbert (2004): 'Handle with care. How economic civil rights in Europe are taking shape', Mitbestimmung, 8 (engl. edition), 8-13.

Kluge, Norbert / Vitols, Sigurt (2008): The European Company: A Pilot for Integrating Shareholder Value into Stakeholder-Orientated European Societies? Andreas Nikopoulos, Michael Gold and Norbert Kluge (eds.): The European Company Statute: A New Approach to Corporate Governance. London: Peter Lang (i.E.)

Kluge, Norbert / Stollt, Michael (Hrsg.) (2006): Die Europäische Aktiengesellschaft (SE) – Perspektiven für eine europäische Unternehmensmitbestimmung. Brüssel: Social Development Agency, ETUI, Otto-Brenner-Stiftung, Hans-Böckler-Stiftung

Lannoo, Karel / Khachaturyan, Arman (2004): 'Reform of Corporate Governance in the EU', European Business Organization Law Review (EBOR), 5: 1, 37.

Martins, Erko / Pundt, Alexander / Nerdinger, Friedemann W. (2005): Mitarbeiterbeteiligung und Unternehmenskultur. Zum Konzept der Beteiligungsorientierung in Organisationen. Arbeitspapier Nr. 1 aus dem Projekt TiM, Universität Rostock

Maul, Silja / Lanfermann, Georg (2004): 'Europäische Corporate Governance – Stand der Entwicklungen', Betriebs-Berater, 59 (35), 1861-1868.

Nagels, Karlheinz / Sorge, Arndt (1977): Industrielle Demokratie in Europa, Frankfurt am Main: Campus Verlag.

Osterloh, Margit / Frey, Bruno S. (2006): Shareholders Should Welcome Knowledge Workers as Directors. Zurich: University of Zurich (Available at SSRN: http://ssrn.com/abstract=900344).

Rose, Caspar / Kvist, Hans Kurt (2004): Employee directors – What is their say?, Copenhagen: Copenhagen Business School.

Taylor, Robert (2004): 'Taking responsibilities in an SE`- a new challenge for employees from different cultural and political backgrounds', in Hans-Boeckler-Foundation, European Trade Union Institute (ed.) The European Company – prospects for board-level representation, Brussels and Düsseldorf: ETUI, 40-49.

Vitols, Sigurt (2008): European Works Councils: An Assessment of their welfare impact. ETUI report, Brussels: European Trade Union Institute (i.E.)

Vitols, Sigurt (2005): 'Changes in Germany`s bank-based financial system: implications for corporate governance', G. Jackson and A. Moerkes, guest editors, Corporate Governance: An International Review. Special Issue on Germany and Japan, 13 (2),

Vitols, Sigurt (2005a): Prospects for trade unions in the evolving European system of corporate governance. Brussels: ETUI report 92

Voss, Eckhard / Wilke, Peter / Maack, Klaus (2003): 'Mitarbeiter am Unternehmen beteiligen'. Wiesbaden
Weiss, Manfred (2003): 'Arbeitnehmermitwirkung in Europa', Neue Zeitschrift für Arbeitsrecht, 20: 177-232

Employee financial participation in Spain

Patricia Nieto Rojas

I. Introduction. Financial participation of employees in the European Union

With the conviction that the competitiveness of European companies demands a framework of employment quality which promotes the creation of value for their workers, European administrations insist on the need to support new forms of corporate employee participation. In this context, COM (2002) 364, within a framework for employee financial participation, refers to the potential of this type of participation in attaining the objectives established at the Lisbon Summit, that is, to ensure that by 2010 the European economy is "the most innovative knowledge-economy of the world." The European Union (EU) also maintains that its employees' financial participation must be considered as an optimal means of reaching a better distribution of wealth, taking into account the positive effects on the productivity and motivation of the implied workers, and therefore it urges the Member States to promote its development by adopting the following measures: a) creation of networks that facilitate the exchange of information between the interested parties; b) sensitization of social interlocutors, and c) promotion of a favorable fiscal framework for the adoption of these formulas

However, there are still significant differences in the development of these mechanisms among the different member states. On one hand, the countries with a long history of promoting these systems, especially France, have developed a complex normative that recognizes new forms of employee corporate participation (EUROFOUND, 2007: 10-20). On the other hand, in Spain employee financial participation has not been a target for relevant legislative pronouncements in labor or in private law, despite the fact that Article 129.2 of the Spanish Constitution rules that public administrations should promote different forms of employee corporate participation and facilitate employees' access to productive means of ownership.

The reduced legislative attention that these formulas have received in the Spanish model has been pointed out in all the communitarian reports. For example, a study coordinated by Professor E. POUSTSMA in 2001 concludes with worrisome data: 84% of the Spanish companies surveyed did not have any financial participation policies. Of the rest, only 6% had implanted a component of profit participation as opposed to 8% that had supported this type of ownership participation. As a recent report elaborated by the EUROFOUND shows, this tendency persists in Spain, whereas share ownership shows a considerably lower incidence – around half of all other countries (EUROFOUND, 2007: 26), unlike what happens in Ireland and France, which show the highest degree of share ownership even after other variables are controlled for: the odds ratio of participating financially in these countries is three times higher than in the rest.

Despite the above, it is true that in recent years we have observed the emergence of certain polices that facilitate employee financial participation in Spain's most relevant companies, basically by developing benefits linked to the companies' performance or by employee participation policies such as free or discounted shares, bonds that can be upgraded into stock option plans or warrants. The objective of this presentation is to analyze the reasons that determine this renewed interest, its development, and especially what its function is; that is, if these mechanisms can be considered exclusively new compensation formulas or whether, on the contrary, their appearance may respond to a broad objective, such as the incorporation of a new way of managing human resources, which is more integral and oriented to corporate social responsibility.

The growing importance of human capital to guarantee corporate competitiveness has facilitated, in a more general context, the development of increasingly intense forms of cooperation between a company and its employees. Among these policies, we must talk about the mechanisms that financially link the employees with the company for which they work. Once the communitarian theses have been surpassed, the employees' financial participation appears as a sort of voluntary collaboration that does not respond to the logic of the abandonment of the established economic system where the employee becomes an owner of production means, thus subverting the established order, but rather to criteria nearer to efficient human resources management (MERCADER, J.R., 1996: 210).

Ever since 1984 when WEITZMAN presented his share economy model, it has been demonstrated that the implantation of financial participation policies is a measure whose development is recommendable for economic reasons since it can play an excellent role in the attainment of microeconomic objectives, basically through its incentives in the productivity of employees, especially in the mechanisms that link workers' wages with company benefits (ROBINSON, A; WILSON, 2006: 44). We cannot ignore the fact that one of the main challenges companies face is the so-called "agency problem" which can be concisely defined as the difficulty in motivating an agent (employee) to act in the name of someone else (company), knowing that their retribution is going to be totally disconnected from the obtained results. With the aim of diminishing these negative effects, following the notion that if "the agents (workers) behave in agreement with the desire of the interested party, it is necessary for them to reach an agreement that makes them take some responsibility for the result of their activities and, therefore, to support a greater risk than if that need did not exist." (MCCONELLL, C; BRUE, S; MACPHERSON, D. 2007: 211).

Production changes and the overcoming of a model of industrial economy where egalitarian wage structures prevailed have given way to models that value the individual's contribution to the organization. Today, monetary compensation is structured as a management tool with a strategic function; therefore, companies must devise policies that act as an incentive to enter or remain in a certain company. Historically, salary structures were designed to serve the entire organization regardless of each worker's contribution to the company. But this model is no longer valid in today's labor market where corporate competitiveness is directly related to the creation of value by employees. Egalitarian systems have been relegated to workers with less negotiation power who cannot agree on individualized wage policies. With the aim of obtaining and retaining the best employees, companies can establish two strategies in the design of their payroll policies (PÉREZ INFANTE, J, 2003: 70):

a) To establish efficiency wages, that is, to pay higher than the market's standard wages and therefore offer salaries with a rent component that surpass the minimum wage.
b) To introduce variable incentives that link workers' salaries with the companies' benefits, reaching certain goals or reaching a determined level of profits. Among these new compensation policies we find:
    1. Systems linked to the attainment of corporate goals that can be granted directly, conditional on the attainment of positive results, or on the fulfillment of collective objectives (gain sharing). This last formula is calculated based on a group's performance level, and the incentive is distributed among its members independent of their individual performance, as it is only granted when the group surpasses a predetermined goal.
    2. The other large block of compensation formulas which facilitates financial participation are those that allow an integration of the employees in a company's capital by means of: a) distributing stock options among the company's employees, which may be free or available at a reduced cost; b) granting bonds that can be upgraded into stock options, which can be defined as a negotiable value represented by a title or annotation which gives its owner the possibility of being a shareholder; c) conceding the option to exercise those options, which can be defined as a financial agreement by which a company recognizes its employees' right to buy its own stock options at a fixed cost and within a time frame which is normally established at the time the offer is made.

The implantation of these initiatives also facilitates greater compensation flexibility as long as employees link part of their salaries to the results obtained when the system they are using is a distribution of benefits or enables cash salaries to be replaced with salaries in which the employees are paid with stock options or shares of the company. Moreover, these methods may help to mould attitudes towards the company and its profits; performance-related pay and reward systems, together with control over results and goals (measured to company profits, productivity and so on) make up a central core of instruments of economic control within the new managerial thinking (EDLING, C; SANDBERG, A., 2003: 159).

II. Spanish framework. Objetives and development

Once we have identified the main tendencies of employees' economic participation, it should be asked what the real extent of these policies or formulas is in Spain. As already noted, the development of these mechanisms is still at an early stage and, accordingly, their presence in collective bargaining is not very generalized. However, we must point out that the *Acuerdo Interconfederal para la Negociación Colectiva* –a pact made by the unions and most representative chambers of commerce with the aim of defining the directives, recommendations, and criteria that are to be observed in collective bargaining negotiated in any sector or branch of activity – recommends that collective agreements define the compensation structure and, where appropriate, drive the implantation of mechanisms of financial participation. With this in mind, the definition of variable concepts should take into account the following: criteria of objectivity and clarity to be considered when implementing them; the delimitation of variable compensation percentages versus total compensation; the employee representatives' right to access to information and to participation in the company, and the realities specific to each company or productive sector.

This thesis is also maintained in the criteria for collective bargaining approved by the unions. For instance, *Comisiones Obreras* considers it a high priority to include clauses that link workers' compensation with the results obtained, understanding that "companies which year after year accumulate profuse benefits must pave the way to return policies, where part of the benefits generated go back to the workers to increase their spending power." This position contrasts with the one maintained in the criteria of collective negotiation approved by the principle Spanish employers' association, CEOE, which makes no reference to this matter.

Regardless of the programmatic declaration on the inclusion of financial participation formulas found in the *Acuerdo Interconfederal para la Negociación*

Colectiva, these systems are still an exception in Spanish business practice. One of the reasons for this divergence is that the implementation of these systems is normally initiated unilaterally by the company and not as the result of a collective agreement. Nevertheless, some compensation agreements are now incorporating formulas such as the ones described above. Such is the case of the Group EROSKI in which a three-part employee participation model is anticipated: capital, results, and management. The cooperative tradition of this company explains the origin of this patrimonial integration. This experience, implemented in 1998 and unprecedented in Spain, transfers the will of its employees as owners of the company to an anonymous society. On the other hand, and especially notable, is the DANONE agreement which includes a pact on profit participation to make the employees participate in the company's direction. This is based on the following premise: "when wealth and prosperity are created within the company, it is right and desirable that the personnel who have contributed to them annually receive part of the generated wealth growth."

Finally, the most significant experience of employee patrimonial integration in Spanish companies took place when INDITEX joined the stock market, a moment in which a process of distribution of free shares among its employees was promoted. This release facilitated the integration in the shared capital of around 20,000 workers and represented 0.7% of the company's capital. The only criterion used in the distribution was the number of years of employment with the group, so that all the employees who were active on December 31, 2000 and would be so four months prior to entering the stock market received 50 options per year served, with a maximum of 1000. In other companies, such as the case of OERLIKON, the right of their employees to buy stock options is conventionally granted after the first year that employees work in the company.

As can be seen, all of the above experiences relate to mid-sized and large companies, with good labor conditions and whose human resources strategy is based on the integration of the employees in the companies' actions. We must not forget that with this type of financial participation structure, the aim is to interest the employees in the company's direction. Companies seek to motivate their employees with the same formulas used with their shareholders: the greater the profits a company obtains, the greater its employees' compensation will be, especially when this occurs through stock options, which enable the creation of a longer and more solid link between the company and the employee, who becomes part of the corporate dynamic just like any other stockholder.

This analysis was guided by the proposition that financial participation and other HRM measures have a reciprocal relationship. If employees are to accept performance-enhancing initiatives from management, such as performance appraisals, it can be argued that they should receive a pay-off from any improvements in performance that might result. The analysis of the data on financial participation of employees in the European Union coordinated by EUROFOUND shows that, indeed, employee training and performance appraisal schemes are associated with the presence of share ownership schemes. This supports the notion that companies try to protect human capital development through the combined use of training, appraisal and share ownership schemes. The results also show that there is a correlation between profit sharing schemes and individual performance-related pay measures (EUROFOUND, 2007: 10). These methods could be regarded as ways of securing workers` commitment to the company's overall goals, and could therefore be viewed as part of the attempt to gain ideological control. According to this hypothesis, schemes of financial participation function better where these are combined with institutions of employee participation in decision making and, that employee share-ownership plans (ESOPs), in particular are most likely to flourish in a participatory environment.

In the same way, these mechanisms have a valuable function in the selection of determined employees and are a key instrument to retain the most qualified employees. Companies seek to retain qualified employees in order to eliminate high turnaround costs, and this is one reason why the promotion of these formulas can be decisive. This function is very clear in stock option plans, the exercise of which is conditional on the preset term to the point that an employee will not be able to leave the company if he/she wants to exercise his or her option.

However, in Spain the real incidence of these formulas, still in the establishment and consolidation phase, is limited: the number of affected companies is reduced; the fact that employee stock option ownership is so small in big companies does not allow them to have a direct influence on the company's direction; and the inexistence of an adequate policy for stockholding employees unlike, for instance, in France's legal system, have obscured the advantages linked to these participative structures (ALFARO, J. 1995: 135). Following this thesis, the economic integration of employees has been used more for the fulfillment of other aims more related to social stability than to real promotion of the participation of employees in the corporate structure. Thus, these mechanisms have made the following possible:

a) Guarantee of social peace: It has been demonstrated that companies which implement policies of financial participation display lower levels of social conflict and fewer strikes (VAQUERIZO. A, 2004: 515).
b) As a management tool with the aim of making employees a more receptive group that will adapt to organizational changes, following the logic that if they financially participate in the company, they must be more flexible in terms of the changes that may arise (VELASCO SAN PEDRO, L, 1999: 44).

c) Finally, if the formula adopted is the granting of stock options, this mechanism can serve to reduce a stock option excess or to "park options in friendly hands." Employees' traditional resistance to changes can be a useful tool for securing a high number of stock options that will not be used in mergers, public offers or other similar operations

However, we cannot admit a reductionist interpretation of the employees' financial participation that unconditionally establishes the convenience or inconvenience of these mechanisms. These formulas must be understood in a more general evolutionary process of a company's power relationships; this way, in contrast to the traditional select relationship based on conflict, we must now try to promote integrative aspects for the sake of the corporate competitiveness that a globalized economy demands. The existence of opposing interests between employees and entrepreneurs is intended to be diminished. In the new socio-labor model, the ideas of collaboration and cooperation gain terrain over previous notions of conflict, antagonism, and confrontation.

This new work organization, where productivity is elevated as a central value of the system, is a challenge for the unions, since many of these instruments are implemented directly by the company with no prior agreement or consultation with the employees' representatives. It is true that the increase of these schemes does not suppose a significant displacement of the indirect participation mechanisms as long as these new formulas coexist, without too many difficulties, with collective mechanisms of employee representation. Nevertheless, the unions are in a complex situation. Their role, if not completely accessory, may be reduced, as long as the strategies of employees' financial participation are not a collective result but a unilateral decision of the company. Human resources' homogeneity is one of the principal challenges the unions face now that corporate decisions are linked to a global context (BAYLOS, A. 2005: 242).

Thus, in large companies which have developed financial participation mechanisms, this decision has not been decided based on one specific country, nor is it the result of national legislation or a particular collective agreement, but rather is the corporation's response to a multinational compensation strategy. Such is the case of MICROSOFT, whose employee shareholding participation plans have been widely studied as a paradigm of employee loyalty techniques. This company considers as its zone of influence regions that surpass national limits and, consequently, include several countries; this reflects the fact that the most important management decisions are located in the group's direction, not in the national branches.

III. Corporate governance policy framework

At this point, we must evaluate to what extent these participatory initiatives respond to their own logic. That is, whether they are the result of a new, less hierarchic, more democratic concept of the company where employees financially integrate themselves in the company as a response to a socio-corporate responsibility policy; or whether, on the contrary, they merely form a new group of compensation formulas which are more flexible and better adapted to a company's economic situation. The interest in corporate governance policy within the logic of voluntary integration of the social and environmental aspects of its commercial operations and their relationship with its interlocutors on the part of the companies has undergone significant growth in the last two decades. But these policies should also be seen as a way to make our societies more competitive and better prepared to face the challenges of globalization. With regard to our study, employees' financial integration in the company for which they work, whether by participating in its profits or by means of stock options, appears in the "Green Paper – Promoting a European framework for Corporate Social Responsibility", COM(2001) 366, as a practice that facilitates the hiring and retention of key employees.

Although the EC´s interest in CSR remains high for state intervention, there is no consensus over the future shaping of a mandatory law in this space. Spanish legislation covers many issues such as working conditions, health and safety, equality, that many people could consider implicit or minum CSR. In addition, the Spanish Government has created the State Council on Corporate Social Responsibility as a collegiate, advisory and consultative body at the service of the Government, of a quadripartite and joint nature, in charge of strengthening and promoting Corporate Social Responsibility policies [RD 221/2008].

The objectives of the Council shall be as follows: a) to constitute a forum for debate on Corporate Social Responsibility between the most representative Employers' and Trade Union Organisations, Public Administrations and other organisations and institutions with an acknowledged representative role in the field of Corporate Social Responsibility, in order that it may serve as a framework of reference for the development of Corporate Social Responsibility in Spain: b) to promote initiatives regarding Corporate Social Responsibility and in the context of its advisory and consultative functions, to propose measures in this regard to the Government, paying special attention to the unique characteristics of SMEs.

A considerable number of European companies include CSR-related initiatives in their corporate mission. The implementation and strategic integration of CSR by enterprises should be further improved and the role of employees, their representatives and their trade unions in the development and implementation of CSR practices should be further enhanced.

Employee financial participation can also play an important role in the creation of corporate value through improvements in terms of employee effectiveness, commitment, and flexibility. Accordingly, the internal dimension of corporate commitment is seen in the consideration of the employees as stakeholders whose financial integration not only fulfills an economic objective, but also responds to an ethical objective of the company with and for its employees. This concept of business management which integrates not only the shareholders but also applies to other stakeholders (clients, providers, employees) results in a strategic direction with dimensions that go beyond economic results and include social and environmental aspects, trying to balance all the interests involved in the company –as in a coalition– even while admitting that these interests may at times be opposed (LANDA, J. P., 2006: 28).

This pluralistic model of the company comes from the idea that it is not only the shareholders who support risks; employees also participate in a company's overall situation and we have analyzed the possibility of introducing the stakeholder model in firms that promotes the development of more intense formulas for employees' corporate integration, such as giving stakeholders decision-making rights. Productivity growth and management effectiveness demand the implementation of participation mechanisms for all risk takers and all who contribute specific resources for these goals.

The corporate governance framework should recognise the rights of stakeholders established by law or through mutual agreements and encourage active co-operation between corporations and stakeholders in creating wealth, jobs, and the sustainability of financially sound enterprises (OECD, 2004: 21). This point of view contrasts with the classic theory of property rights, obviously against sharing the profit among the employees since, in pure business logic, it starts from the base that the social interest in corporations must be represented by the shareholders' interest, and that the value creation must consequently be focused towards these and not towards other stakeholders. In adittion, in the capitalist firms irrespective of size or ownership structure, the formal decision-making rights lie with the owners or shareholders (JANSSON, E. 2005: 1).

The need to create value for the shareholder requires, therefore, a calculation of the financial results not by their intrinsic value but by the remuneration the shareholders hope to receive. This option has far-reaching consequences in labor relations. Since they lack the power of intervention in shareholders' decisions, employees will not be able to participate in matters that affect them directly. For this reason, any strategy that aims to facilitate greater cooperation in the company's decision making process must start with its integration in the corporate structure (MORIN, M.L, 2005: 11).

While it is true that the financial integration of employees makes a long-term investment policy possible, as opposed to market investors who are focused on short-term results, it is not so easy to affirm that employees' financial participation is in fact an advancement in the recognition of mechanisms that facilitate greater cooperation of employees and management. The corporate motivations to articulate these formulas respond to diverse goals from obtaining a more cohesive group to improving productivity or propitiating a compensation strategy linked to the company's real situation. The new needs imposed by the market and the transformations in labor relations systems are factors which must be considered when analyzing the evolution of these financial participation mechanisms. Today, companies need an ample margin of flexibility for their immediate adaptation to changes, and their competitiveness will clearly be influenced by their capacity to create value for the people who comprise them. In this context, the design of a compensation policy is clearly a differentiating corporate element. Compensation has gone from being a tool of financial return to being a management tool. From this perspective, new compensation formulas directed towards linking a productive agent with the owner of the production have appeared.

Therefore, the implementation of these mechanisms fulfills two basic functions. First of all, it links employee wages to the results obtained, allowing a greater adjustment between the company's real situation and employee compensation. Second, it allows the integration of the different interests existing in an organization to fortify this collaboration and increase its implementation. Consequently, financial participation should not be seen as a gift from the company. It is the employees' financial entailment with their company that contributes to increased productivity, thus, the other shareholders also benefit from this agreement.

IV. Conclusions.

One conclusion we can infer from the capacity of these formulas to propitiate greater participation of employees in corporate management is that this power is still not significant in Spanish companies. These mechanisms are usually introduced as a tool of variable contribution which plays a major role in attracting and retaining talent, and not so much for these formulas' potential to generate an attitude of employee co-responsibility in corporate decisions. Among the reasons that may explain this divergence are: a) the reduced number of shares owned by employees, and b) the nonexistence of specific participation mechanisms to grant shareholding employees access to corporate organisms. The employees' financial integration in companies does not respond to the logic of the established economic system by which employees become owners of mass productions. Its emergence responds to criteria closer to efficient human resource management.

Another factor that explains its reduced development in Spain is the insufficient legislative support for these formulas. In 2002, the Socialist Parliamentary Group presented a law proposing to regulate employees' right to information, counseling, and corporate participation; Article 10 established the right to participate in a company's financial profits, materialization of which was linked to the attainment of general goals set in a participation agreement. However, this initiative was not approved in the end and has not been reintroduced in the two successive legislatures under the Socialist Group Government.

VI. References

AAVV (2001): Models of employee participation in a changing global environment. Diversity and interaction. Hampshire: Ashgate.

Baylos Grau, A. (2005): Códigos de conducta y buenas prácticas de las empresas en materia laboral. El problema de su exigibilidad jurídica. En. AAVV. LILLO, E (Dir.). Aspectos económicos de la jurisdicción social. Madrid: CGPJ; Generalitat Valenciana.

EUROFOUND (2007): Financial participation of employees in European Union: Much ado about nothing? Luxembourg, Office for Official Publications of the European Communities.

– (2005): Employee financial participation in the European Union Luxembourg, Office for Official Publications of the European Communities.

EUROPEAN COMMISSION (2002): On a framework for the promotion of employee financial participation, COM (2002) 364 final, Brussels.

– (2001): Promoting a European framework for corporate social responsibility, COM (2001) 366 final, Brussels.

Jansson, E. (2005): "The Stakeholder Model: The Influence of the Ownership and Governance Structures", Journal of Business Ethic, nº 56, vol. 1. pp. 1-13.

Gold, M. (ed.) (2003): New frontiers of democratic participation at work. Hampshire: Ashgate.

Landa Zapiraín, J.P. (coord.) (2004): Nuevas formas de participación de los trabajadores y gobierno de la empresa. Albacete: Bomarzo.

Mcconelll, C. / Brue, S. / MacPherson, D. (2007): Economía Laboral, Madrid: McGraw-Hill.

Mercader Uguina, J.R. (1996): Modernas tendencias en la ordenación salarial. Navarra: Aranzadi.

Morin, M.L. (2005): El derecho del trabajo ante los nuevos modos de organización de la empresa. En. Revista Internacional del trabajo, vol. 124, 2005, n° 1, pp. 5-30.

Pérez Infante, J.I. (2003): La estructura de la negociación colectiva y los salarios en España. En. Revista Ministerio de Trabajo y Asuntos Sociales, n ° 46, pp. 41-97.

Poustma, E. / Kaarsemaker, E. (2006): The Fit of Employee Ownership with Other Human Resource Management Practices: Theoretical and Empirical Suggestions Regarding the Existence of an Ownership High-Performance Work System, Economic and Industrial Democracy, Vol. 27(4), pp. 669–685.

Poustma, E. (2001): Recent trends in employee financial participation in the European Union, Luxemburg: Eurofound.

Robinson, A. / Wilson, N. (2006): Employee financial participation and productivity: an empirical reappraisal. British Journal of Industrial Relations, Vol. 44 (1), March 2006, pp. 33-50.

Vaquerizo Alonso, A. (2003): Asistencia financiera para la adquisición de acciones propias. Madrid: Civitas; UAM.

Velasco San Pedro, L. (1999): La adquisición de acciones propias: problemas de política jurídica y tendencias legistlativas, Revista de Derecho de Sociedades, n° 11.

Weitzman, M. (1984): The share economy. Conquering stagflation. Harvard: Harvard University Press.

Workplace quality as a "contested ground": comments on the ambivalence of workplace participation today

Wilfried Kruse

The talks and above all the discussion at the Workplace Participation Forum in Rome (October 2008)[1] covered a wide range of reflection on the state and status of direct employee participation in the labour process. The focus was above all on its risks and opportunities under new economic and social conditions, which can be characterised by catch phrases such as globalisation, European knowledge community, "post-Fordist regulation", casualisation, etc. However, the economic crisis that was beginning to loom on the horizon was not yet an issue in autumn 2008.

The general approach and the thread were to be the subjective perspective of the workforce towards direct participation in the labour process. The assumption of an "ambivalence" in workplace participation was above all related to this particular element – a complex mixture of opportunities and risks that is the result of direct participation for the workforce under the available conditions. Ambivalence presupposes that, to a greater or lesser extent, workplace participation may involve opportunities and gains as well as risks and losses, but that this conflict cannot be resolved one-sidedly in one direction. The purpose of this introduction is to present an outline and to combine the articles and debates into an up-to-date "profile" of the ambivalence that characterises direct workplace participation in the labour process. In doing so, we are also making use of our research and practical experience as consultants.

Productivity – workplace participation and ordinary life

The example of Arcelor Mittal[2] in Bremen shows very clearly that as long as the labour process is at a certain technical and organisational level, the imperative of an increase in productivity puts the issue of workplace participation on the agenda and that, under certain conditions, this imperative provides a certain leeway and creative margin that can be occupied by the representatives of the workforce. Yet as soon as the strengthening of direct workplace participation during a period of crisis is to be extended beyond that phase, into the ordinary life of the company, we can

1 Reference to workshop.
2 Reference to article by Niemann.

frequently see its ambivalent character, particularly against the background of changed expectations of the workforce towards, let us say, "sustainable conditions within their general sphere of life" – something which others might call a positive work-life balance. Ongoing commitment to workplace participation affects one's organisation of life, as it undermines the separation of working time and non-working time, a distinction that was asserted in "Taylorism" and which was subsequently developed as "social progress". Moreover, it involves tougher performance standards in the workplace itself.[3]

The position of the worker in the labour process: the core issue of labour models

If we assume that the European Union comprises a variety of different socio-cultural labour models, then we need to ask where we can find the differences and similarities between them. The core of labour models – and this is the thesis here – is the specific social background to the relationship between the work-force and their work, in other words the extent and quality of the workers' separation from or participation in the structuring of their work as well as the immediate and further contextual conditions (use, utilisation, etc.) of this structuring.

It is these different manifestations of the relationship between the workforce and their work which have been at the focus of intervention – albeit primarily through indirect means – in European labour policies since the nineties. Whereas these policies have acquired European dimensions with regard to occupational health and safety, their core focus – a secure right of the workforce to exert an influence on the specific structuring of their work, i.e. workplace participation, co-determination and ownership – has remained rather weak, particularly in the definition of standards, despite numerous declarations (such as the Green Book and slogans about more and better workplaces). However, this should hardly come as a surprise, as it concerns in many ways the basic core issue of who should rule, be in charge and have authority. Correspondingly, any cultural and moral values of work that refer to dignified labour and not to the performance of a duty towards society are largely invisible to the public eye.

Work structuring as the key element

Seen from a social perspective, work structuring is the key element of work organisation. Its focus is on the task at hand and on the activity-specific combination of the various tasks that are involved in a process of manufacturing goods or

3 See also article by Paul-Kohlhoff on this issue.

performing services. At the same time, it goes without saying that any task or work organisation has a certain structure already. This is why any talk about desirable work structuring of the future necessarily involves the use of qualifying adjectives (such as "innovative work structuring" or "participative work structuring"). The significance of "external" working conditions, wage issues and social welfare issues, which once figured so prominently on traditional negotiation agendas, obstructed the view to the fact that labour has always been a hotly contested central ground. The Taylorist standardisation and routinisation of labour requirements and the resulting level of accuracy and depth in the horizontal and vertical compartmentalisation and division of labour must be seen as the massive structuring of this contested ground. The increasing lack of productivity in narrowly managed Taylorist work structuring shows the true extent of the contest. Today's emphasis on soft competencies such as a responsible attitude, an ability to cooperate, etc. signal the "battle for the minds" of the workforce.

It should not come as a surprise that labour has again become such a hotly contested central ground. This is fundamentally due to its dual character, i.e. on the one hand, its productivity and value-creating side, and, on the other, the plain fact – which is often distorted by a simplified understanding in purely economic terms – that a human resource and thus job content cannot be separated from the person, thus making it an important part of their personality and everyday activities in the widest possible sense. So there is always a lot at stake. If we imagine a given work structure as a comprise that has always worked reasonably well and is based on certain working methods and lifestyles (ranging from routines for coping with certain tasks to the management of resources and finance), then we begin to understand that any change to existing structures is bound to pose risks while perhaps also offering opportunities.

Change vs. stability

We can assume that any impending changes primarily cause fear and anxiety – perhaps of a rather diffuse kind – rather than arousing hope. Such expectations, which are based on experience and on lifestyle, must not be disregarded as external conditions of work structuring. In fact, they are fundamental structural elements.

An enquiry into the conditions of successful innovation in work structuring cannot ignore the respective interests of the various protagonists at a given enterprise. The production of goods and performance of services presupposes a well-functioning combination of different "production factors"; when it comes to concrete action, this means a social arrangement between those representing the purpose of the enterprise – i.e. to make a profit in the case of a private company – and those who are in paid employment. Strictly speaking, this always involves a general and a specific social compromise between different opposing interests in the quest for the biggest common denominator.

The different pursuits of interests and the resulting risks of mutual obstruction lead to the development of power structures and patterns of domination within an enterprise that are intended to safeguard the ongoing achievement of the corporate objective. In this social system, which is characterised and dominated by corporate power structures, the individual paid employee usually has very few resources that might enable them to assert or safeguard their interests. The institutionalised representation of interests must therefore be understood as empowerment and thus a way of giving these paid employees more weight in the formation of compromises. It follows that any existing corporate social system in its specific form and thus also any existing work organisation is an expression of that social compromise and thus a social arrangement, whatever the constellation of authority and influence, i.e. even if the employees have very little or no institutional weight in a given enterprise.

Upward revaluation and weakening at the same time?

A given work organisation and its conditions are therefore some kind of "texture" that tells us about the social conditions within the enterprise. Whatever work organisation is in place, it is the result of a bargaining process, regardless of whether and to what extent this process has been institutionalised and takes place "consciously". Obviously, the degree of institutionalisation and awareness of the negotiation process are important factors for the quality of the result. The ongoing modernisation of products and services therefore continually comes up against such fixed social arrangements. The currently noticeable weakening of the institutionalised representation of interests can therefore hardly be seen as improving the conditions for innovative work structures

If there is even a fraction of realism in the European notion that the strong competitive edge of the European economic and social area is based on the knowledge society, then we must assume that at least some production and service clusters have unparalleled "careers": after all, it is through responsible cooperation with other skilled employees that a skilled employee becomes the pivotal point of this new model of competition. If, under a given corporate strategy, the factor of "skilled labour" is upwardly revaluated, then this should lead to far-reaching changes in the industrial conditions at that enterprise. Opposition mainly appears to be directed against the *implicit democratising tendencies* of the new business model of competition.

Under-use of workplace participation

We can conclude that labour itself – quite apart from any plans for social reform – becomes an import structuring target for modernisation within an enterprise, and work structuring thus becomes relevant to labour policies. After all, it would involve using the innovative potential of the entire workforce with all their experience and production expertise – activated, supported and enhanced through process-specific further training – and therefore seeing the workforce as a productive force. Their development would make it necessary *to dismantle hierarchic structures* – a process which is, however, eyed with suspicion due to the supposed or actual imponderables of *control*. It is therefore one of the most important dilemmas of innovation.

A comparison of case studies of the direct participation of employees in medium-sized companies in the metal and chemical industries in Germany[4] has shown that workplace participation is seen as "under-used" both by the management and by employees' representatives, even though it is believed to be reasonable or even necessary by all sides. We see this "under-use" as the result of "compact social obstacle structures" which indicate inequality in the power and dialogue structure at a given enterprise.

Any improvement in the use of direct participation both for the affected workforce and the company can therefore only succeed under some kind of "dual strategy": on the one hand, through the simple improvement of workplace participation structures – "beyond the limits of naïvety" – recognising, in particular, that participation has a powerful effect on the traditional relationship between performance and counter-performance, and, on the other hand, through the recognition of corporate democratic structures as a condition for the further development of productivity. Both perspectives involve the relevant interest groups of employers and employees, the trade unions and industrial relations. Finally, a number of proposals are discussed how workplace participation might productively develop "beyond the limits of naïvety".

Workplace quality and participation: potentially central platform after the onset of a new era?

This is where the much quoted onset of a new era – an era of deregulation and re-regulation after the Fordist era – has a central platform on the shop floor. At the

4 Susanne Felger, Wilfried Kruse, Angela Paul-Kohlhoff, Silke Senft (2003): Partizipative Arbeitsorganisation; Beteiligung jenseits von Naivität, Münster.

same time, however, the shop floor is understood as something that also includes the extension of the value creation process, where workplace quality is a potentially controversial area. In this context workplace participation is both the means and the end, i.e. the means to ensure and safeguard the quality of a workplace, but also one of its essential components, understood as participation "beyond the limits of naïvety".

The onset of a new post-Fordist era was immensely significant because it did not appear on the horizon until southern enlargement of the EU in the latter half of the eighties and was already fully in progress during its eastern enlargement. EU accession in the eighties and in 2004 were important landmarks in the convergence processes of national and European working cultures.

In this general picture the threats to existing social safeguards and to the existing representation of interests were exacerbated by a further powerful undermining force – the trend towards individualisation. We are often given the impression that "globalisation" and "individualisation" are two sides of the same coin known as "marketisation". Yet we must also remember that individualisation in the sense of the creative power of autonomous personalities has always been one of the basic utopian ideas of the trade union movement, a utopian concept that is increasingly becoming a social and personal "necessity", albeit usually as part of paid employment, so that individualisation itself becomes subject to intensive marketisation.

It is due to the developmental dynamics of the capitalist economy at the turn of the millennium that these two processes – which mutually impact and reinforce each other – are mainly felt to be threats to outmoded trade union policies and to the organisations that carry them, thus influencing their potential roles in affecting the emerging new cultures of paid employment. A new balance therefore needs to be achieved in the relationship between confident individualism and conscious participation in a collective endeavour. But how could this balance be created, what are its continuing threats and what are the effects of those threats?

Does workplace participation form part of a "good workplace" that people would like to see?

Can it be assumed that the upward revaluation of skilled labour – which occurs in connection with and as a result of a general rise in the level of education – has also changed patterns of cultural expectations among the workforce? What is today's understanding of a "good workplace"? A report from Italy[5] shows that job satisfaction and thus motivation are closely associated with aspects such as a

5 Title of the talk.

wide range of requirements, scope for decisions, responsibilities and recognition. It is easy enough to see that these are indeed important dimensions in the quality of a workplace.

Workplace quality and local labour policies

Another article from Italy suggests that this clear connection between workplace quality (i.e. "a good workplace") and productivity should continue to be looked at in the future, even if the focus of attention at the regional or local level should shift towards supporting the productive potential of labour as a locational factor and policy[6]. However, if it is true that the (partial yet strategically significant) upward revaluation of workplace quality does not stop the ambivalence of workplace participation but – on the contrary – intensifies it even further, then it is vitally important at every level how its opportunities and risks are safeguarded by an institutional representation of interests and by a strong role of the trade unions.

Some conclusions

On the one hand, everything indicates that under the further development of the European competition model there will be a further upward revaluation of people's skills and competencies in terms of our knowledge society. *On the other hand,* there is no reduction in insecurity concerning employment prospects, but this insecurity seems to increase.

There are always two aspects which are equally important from the individual worker's point of view: Firstly, whenever and as long as a person is in employment, the relevant working conditions need to be optimised, partly with a view to using and developing one's own skills in a specific job and partly to prevent those skills from being used to no more than a limited extent or even falling behind the level that has already been achieved, while at the same time having to make a living with the income that is earned (for oneself and/or a family), as well as satisfying one's needs, achieving a reasonable balance and fulfilling one's aspirations as much as possible.

Secondly, in view of the uncertainties and insecurities of the future, it is important for an individual to make certain provisions, e.g. to put two successive periods of employment – which may be interrupted by unemployment or further education – into a succession that reflects one's own personal improvement while at the same

6 Title of the article.

time carrying as much as possible forward into the future, both in material and non-material terms. The latter concerns a person's future security, an aspects we call "backpacking behaviour". Although these two sides of an individual's interest in the *personal outcome* of labour policies and employment do not always harmonise, they nevertheless mean that increasing significance is attached to the existing or potential significance of *workplace participation* for the individual, as they form part of a person's – albeit inconsistent – self-realisation at work and serve as a means of protection and structuring through the joint representation of workers' interests.

It was one of the bitter experiences of the radical changes in the sixties that, under capitalist conditions, direct workplace participation is marked by a fundamental ambivalence which cannot be resolved in the direction of workers' autonomy. Neither is it likely that the ambivalence of workplace participation can be resolved by devolving all the relevant functions onto the management. After all, if employee participation is no more than a faked tool, then it does not in essence lead to the wide-ranging know-how of the workforce which the management would want to see as a mobilising factor. We can therefore expect both sides to take a view of workplace participation which, based on our research, we have described as being "beyond the limits of naïvety"

For the time being, however, this is no more than a general statement of the situation at the beginning of turbulent changes.

Drawing from the collected insights, experiences and debates in Rome, we can summarise the following *expectations*:

In a number of important segments of the European economy the significance of direct workplace participation will increase in order to boost productivity. At the same time, however, we will also see the multiplication and exacerbation of its ambivalence, particularly because social conditions – which also include the workforce – will be marked by a rise in tensions. On the one hand, employees will be increasingly forced to take the role of "workforce entrepreneurs". Yet on the other hand, they will increasingly feel that, although this is a prerequisite for getting on well at work, it is by no means a "guarantee".

The least we would expect from direct workplace participation under today's conditions is a *reduction in the risk of devaluation* for the workforce.

What it might potentially achieve is something we could then see along a continuum of individual and collective utilisation opportunities. It would always be linked to the strengthening of self-confident personalities who see the safeguarding of their individual interests and needs as being ultimately tied to collective solidarity, yet without losing their identity "lock, stock and barrel".

Innovation, industrial relations and working conditions – Evidence from two Italian local production systems

Davide Antonioli, Massimiliano Mazzanti, Paolo Pini

1. Introduction

In the present work we intend to complement the widespread literature that investigates the effects of innovation on firms' economic outcomes, providing some evidence on the effects of innovation activities on working conditions.

The subject is not new, but is under-researched. The economics and sociology literatures have investigated the detrimental effects generated by the adoption of a Fordist-Taylorist production organization on the workers well being, in the second half of the past century: "the reduction of the skill content of work task and an ever-finer division of labor, it was argued, were designed to allow an intensification of work through the weakening workforce's capacity of resistance, more precise measurement of tasks activities and a tighter linking of financial incentives to output" (Gallie, 2005, p. 352). More recently, the increasing diffusion of so called High Performance Work Practices (HPWP henceforth) and the contraction of the traditional Fordist-Taylorist organization of production have spurred a renewed interest in the consequences of 'new' forms of production organization for workers' conditions. A widespread endorsement of the HPWP benefits on workers emerged during the '90s, especially in the US context: wider discretion, greater opportunity for using their skills thorough job redesign, decreased level of control by management and greater worker involvement in decision-making processes were perceived as aspects that increased workers' well being (Handel, Levine, 2004). However, some scholars (Gallie, 2005; Green, 2004; Brenner, Fairris, Ruser, 2004; Askenazy, Caroli, 2006) have highlighted that there are costs to workers associated with organizational changes: intensification of the working activity, reduction in working dead-times, psychological and physical pressures. About this issue, the evidence that in several OECD countries work intensity increased during the '90s has been consolidated[1] (Green, 2004).

In addition to organizational changes there are innovation activities that may influence jobs and the way job tasks are managed, which may have an impact on

1 See also the works of the symposium of the Eastern Economic Journal (2004).

workers' well being, including diffusion of information and communication technology (ICT), technological[2] innovations and training activities.

Coupled with the potential effects of these innovation activities on the working conditions we also analyze the way cooperative aspects of industrial relations are related to the changes in workers' well being. Unions are clearly concerned about the welfare of their members, but management may be less sensitive to workers' interests and more focused on workers' efforts. Thus, the presence of cooperative relations between management and union delegates may help to resolve in a non-conflictual way, the partially divergent objectives of the two parties.

The empirical work is grounded on the above considerations. Two Local Production Systems (LPS henceforth) are analyzed, through the utilization of different sources of information. The data collected are very similar for the two LPSs although they do not perfectly match. The first LPS is that of Reggio Emilia (RE henceforth) for which we use a unique data set of 192 manufacturing firms located in the RE province. The second LPS is that of Modena (MO henceforth), for which we have information on 176 manufacturing firms. Both the surveys provide a wide range and in depth information on several aspect of firms activities, ranging from innovation activities (organizational, technological and ICT activities) to industrial relations climate at firm level. To our knowledge, very few empirical works on small and medium sized enterprises (SME) can rely on such a set of information.

The paper is structured as follows. Section 2 reviews the existing literature in order to contextualize the present work. Section 3 outlines RE and MO LPSs in addition to data description and methodological issues. Section 4 provides the results of the analysis and section 5 concludes.

2. Related Literature

The linkages between the introduction of HPWP and increased productivity have been widely analysed by several scholars (Black, Lynch, 2001; Caroli, Van Reenen, 2001; Janod, Saint-Martin, 2004; Huselid, 1995; Huselid, Becker, 1996; Cappelli, Neumark, 2001; Ichniowski, Shaw, Prennushi, 1997; Ichniowski, 1990; Zwick, 2004; Antonioli, Mazzanti, Pini, 2007; Leoni, 2008). However, such relationships represent only one side of the coin when the impact of HPWP on firm's constituen-

2 In this paper the term technological innovation encompasses product and process innovations, both incremental and radical, quality control innovation, formal Research and Development (R&D) division, resources and employees involved in R&D activities, collaborations with other firms on R&D (Tab.A.2 in Appendix).

cies is taken into account. The other is related to the impact of reorganization on workers' well being. Notwithstanding its importance, the latter issue is rather under-researched[3].

As a matter of fact the diffusion of HPWP spurred a lively literature about their effect on different firms outcomes, but the field of research is still pervaded by a substantial terminological blurriness as it has been highlighted by several scholars (Belanger et al., 2002; Butler et al., 2004). As put forward by Wood (1999), the two main conceptualizations that emerged during the 80s stressed the accent on the presumed capacity of "new work practices" to induce a high level of workforce commitment: *high commitment model* (HCM) and *high involvement management* (HIM). The interesting point to be stressed is the subject of the two definitions of the early phase of "new work practices" diffusion: employees and employees involvement. The priority given to gains in economic performances, in the definition(s) of 'new work practices' (HPWP), emerged during the 90s and it has pervaded the literature, both theoretical and empirical, since now.

The conceptual framework of this work is drawn from the literature that aims at disentangling the effects of innovation activities, with a particular focus on organizational change, on working conditions. It also takes account of the nexus between cooperative industrial relations and working conditions, which can be thought of as being complementary to the literature on the effects of innovation activities (Antonioli, Mazzanti, Pini, 2009), because the institutional framework can be considered and important variable in the determination of the HPWP effect on worker's well being (Kalmi, Kauhanen, 2008; Godard, 2004)

In the attempt of providing a brief systematization of the existing literature (see also Ramsay, Scholarios, Harley, 2000 for a review) we can follow Vidal reasoning (Vidal, 2007) when he puts forward that despite the advocates of the HPWP (lean production practices in Vidal original framework) recognize benefits for workers subsequently to the adoption of such practices, the changes in the production systems do not necessarily imply high level of workers involvement in decision making or problem solving. In fact, the detractors of the HPWP list a series of potential detrimental effects on workers conditions. In this view (*intensification thesis*) the management introduces changes in the organizational environment to strengthen control over workers' efforts and to intensify the pace of work. Self-managing teams are seen as instruments that substitute the hierarchical control with the peers control. Worker participation is perceived as a method for co-opting workers into a managerial perspective in order to preserve hierarchical authority without bureaucratic control (Vidal, 2007). The work intensification

3 Most of this work is focused on the relation between changes in organizational practices and workers' wages (Black, Lynch, Krivelyova, 2004; Handel, Gittleman, 2004; Forth, Milward, 2004).

that several economies have experienced during the 90s and in more recent years (Green, McIntosh, 2001; Green, 2004; Askenazy, 2004; Fairris, 2004) can be also understood as a result of HPWP diffusion.

Parallel to the critical view exposed above a more positive position maintains that the adoption of HPWP has a positive impact on workers' well being (*empowerment thesis*) through a multiplicity of channels (Handel, Levine, 2004; Askenazy, Caroli 2006). In this perspective both management and workers gain from the introduction of organizational changes: the former obtain higher levels of productivity; the latter receive economic benefits (e.g. higher wages), enjoy higher levels of job satisfaction, are better trained, more motivated and capable of implementing and using their skills. The advocates of HPWP are used to stress the accent on the role of complementarities between such practices. A wide endorsement about the positive impact of bundles of practices on firm performances (see Lynch, 2007 for recent evidence), rather than single practices adoption leads to expect the same when the outcome variables are measures of working conditions. Although, it is not necessarily true that the introduction of HPWP implies high level of workers involvement, the adoption of bundles of HPWP may reflect the management willingness to deeply reconsider the production and labour organization structures in a way that may also alter the hierarchical roles and the power equilibria between the firms constituencies.

The equilibria between the firm constituencies represent a key point to understand whether or not the implementation of organizational changes affect the workers well being. If high commitment workplace practices are seen as instruments to align management and workers' objectives, spurring a more intense direct dialogue between the parties, the role of a cooperative and participative industrial relations climate in influencing the workers well being cannot be neglected too. Participatory industrial relations may be legitimately thought of as complementary aspects of innovation activities in influencing working conditions[4] and not only firm economic performance (Menezes Filho, Van Reenen, 2003; Metcalf, 2003). In fact, unions are clearly concerned about the well being of their members, but management may be less sensible towards workers' well being and more focused on workers' efforts. Thus, the presence of unions in the workplace, their recognition by and, more importantly, their cooperative relations with management, and the specific strategic orientation of the latter, may contribute to non-conflictual resolution of the partially divergent objectives of

4 Within this line of empirical research the issue of reverse causality emerges (Renaud, 2002): the good quality of the dialogue between union delegates and management spurs workers well being, because management is more receptive to the union voice and consequently to the workers' needs, or instead, better quality working conditions promote less adversarial industrial relations?

the two parties. It is worth remarking that such a reasoning holds if industrial relations are not poor, but driven by union/management cooperation[5]. In fact, it may be argued that within a cooperative environment unions are able to influence management decisions on innovation implementation, leading to the choice of configurations that produce high efficiency coupled with positive or at least not detrimental impact on workers' conditions.

In addition to and interrelated with organizational changes and workers representation we also have to enumerate other innovation activities, which revolve around training policies, technological changes and ICT adoption, that are potential sources of changes in working conditions. In particular, the increasing diffusion of ICT (Brynjolfsson, Hitt, 2000; Bresnahan, Brynjolfsson, Hitt, 2002) has been identified as a cause of stress among workers because of the possibility they provide to management to monitor and control workers more intensively (Green, 2004). In synthesis, the skills upgrades necessitated by the increased degree of worker autonomy implied by the introduction of HPWP, the introduction of ICT that can be used by the management to intensify the pace of work and control over workers, the shifting of responsibility from management to shop floor levels, are all elements that potentially cause psychological and physical stress. However, ICT and other innovation activities may alter the working environment in positive ways as well. The possibility provided by the ICT of improving information sharing may help to spread information about best safety practices, for example, and provide workers with greater degrees of autonomy in their jobs. The same reasoning may hold for innovation in processes or quality control. On the one hand, their introduction can increase mental strain for workers and reduce safety because the 'ever' changing production environment reduces the possibility of setting and learning safety procedures; on the other hand, the focus on quality, and especially in the processes implemented, can be thought of as improving occupational safety (Askenazy, Caroli, 2006). Within the last set of innovation activities the training ones are the less ambiguous innovation aspects, which potentially influence workers well being: the better trained the employees the better should be their working conditions[6].

---

5 We can also argue that unions may be conservative (and likely operating in a poor industrial relations environment); hence, they may be prone to adopt behaviours that hinder the introduction of innovations, both technological and organizational, independently by the interest of their members. Some empirical studies have pointed out that unions may exert a hindering effect on R&D expenditure and on profitability (Menezes-Filho, Ulph, Van Reenen, 1998; Betts, Odgers and Wilson, 2001).

6 For example, it can hardly be argued that training in safety and security issues does not positively affect workers well being.

3. Empirical framework and methodology

Two Northern Italy provinces in Emilia-Romagna, Reggio Emilia and Modena, are the geographical locations of the manufacturing firms analysed in the present work. The two LPS share some common features both in terms of industrial system structures and of institutional settings.

Both the LPSs are characterized by a predominant presence of Small and Medium Enterprises (SME)[7] as we can see by the population distributions in tables A1a and A1b in Appendix. A second characteristic of the RE and MO LPSs, which is linked to the prevalence of SME, is the existence of districts (Brusco, 1982; Brusco, Cainelli, Forni, Franchi, Malusardi, Righetti, 1997): non-electrical machinery and equipment and ceramic tiles for RE; ceramic tiles, wood processing machinery and biomedical for MO. The presence of districts that are usually constituted by networks of small firms and the institutional settings characterized by a strong social cohesion and by a traditional deep rooted unionism make the two LPSs paradigmatic versions of the so called '*Emilian model*' (Amin, 1999; Brusco, 1982). The latter, indeed, is characterized by a well marked entrepreneurship spirit and an equally strong, deep-rooted unionism that coexists with a productive apparatus characterized by the presence of a district-like production systems[8].

The empirical analysis is conducted using two unique datasets. The first data source is a firm level survey conducted on the manufacturing firms located in RE[9]. The criteria we adopted for the identification of the population of 376 firms were: (a) firms with at least 20 employees[10]; (b) firms belonging to manufacturing sectors according to the ISTAT ATECO 2002[11] classification; (c) presence of union delegates to be interviewed. The data for 2004 were provided by union

---

7 According to the European Commission (Official Journal of the European Union, L 124, May 2003) a SME is defined as a firm with less than 250 employees. Table A.1 shows that in our local production system about 85% of the firms with union representatives are below this threshold.

8 We especially refer to the role of CGIL, the left wing union. For an overview of the union history and the linkages with political parties we refer the interested reader to Baglioni (1998).

9 Several official sources were used to construct the firm population of RE: Reggio Emilia Chamber of Commerce, Istat Census, Aida data bank, "Impero" data bank, balance sheets data bank of the Reggio Emilia "Camera del Lavoro Territoriale". For reasons of homogeneity and information availability the population refers to the year 2001.

10 Five size classes in terms of employees were constructed for RE: 20-49, 50-99, 100-249, 250-499, more than 499. Four size classes for MO: 50-99, 100-249, 250-499 and more than 499.

11 The sectors are: food, textiles, wood, chemicals, non-metallic mineral products, machinery, other industries. The ISTAT ATECO classification coincides with the NACE Rev1.1 and thus with ISIC Rev3.1.

delegates, through face-to-face interviews. On the basis of a representative sample (250 firms) of the 376 firms with union delegates the interviews led to 192 respondents, which constituted 51% of firms with union representatives.

The second survey has been conducted on manufacturing firms located in MO province. The criteria for the identification of the population slightly differ from those used on RE firms. In fact, only the firms with at least 50 employees were used to select those having union representatives to be interviewed: 246 firms is the firm population identified in MO LPS. The manufacturing sectors were still determined on the basis of the two digit ISTAT ATECO 2002 classification and the number of firms for which we have information is 176[12].

As we can see in tables A.1a and A.1b only some minor distortions of the two samples of interviewed firms, with respect to the populations, emerge. A version of the Cochran Test (Cochran, 1977) for sample distortions shows acceptable results[13].

Both the two surveys are unique sources of information about firms' structural characteristics, workforce composition, innovation activities, working conditions and industrial relations. Although the questionnaires administered were not identical and although the samples are constructed on slightly different criteria it is still possible, in the econometric exercise, to formulate some comparisons on the main issue of the present work: the relationship between innovation activities, industrial relations and working conditions.

The empirical model is based on the following regression function:

(1) Working Condition (WC_EMP; WC_SAFE) = β_{0i} + β_{1i}[structural variables] + β_{2i}[innovation activities] + β_{3i}[industrial relations] + ε_i

where the dependent variable is defined according to two specifications: WC_EMP and WC_SAFE[14]. The index WC_EMP concerns the trend in working conditions more akin to job content and potentially explains *job empowerment*: the higher (lower) the index, the higher (lower) is the intensity of job enrichment and empowerment. The index WC_SAFE was constructed using the variables *stress* and *safety/security:* the higher (lower) the value of the index the

12 For MO database we gratefully acknowledge the work of IRES-ER. A special thank goes to Loris Lugli and Stefano Tugnoli for providing us the database which we worked on. We further refer the interested reader to the report by Lugli and Tugnoli 'Innovazione e Qualità del Lavoro a Modena' www.er.cgil.it/ireser.nsf/Documenti.

13 For details of the data see Antonioli, Delsoldato, Mazzanti, Pini (2007) and Lugli, Tugnoli (2008).

14 Because WC_SAFE assumes only few values in the interval 1-3 we have rescaled the variable using integers on a range going from 1 to 5 and using ordered probit regressions in the estimation phase.

higher (lower) the *safety/security* level and the lower (higher) the level of *stress*[15]. Hence, the higher (lower) the index WC_SAFE the better (worse) is the trend in working conditions in terms of *stress* and *safety/security* (see Tab. A.2 in Appendix for a detailed description of variables construction).

The separate utilization of the two dependent variables is aimed at verifying the impact of the innovation and industrial relations variables on different items enclosed in the concept of working conditions: using WC_EMP we investigate the relations between changes in job empowerment, innovation and industrial relations; using WC_SAFE we aim at verifying the existence of relations between 'critical' aspects of the working conditions, which can be considered as proxies for psychological and physical strain, innovation and industrial relations.

It is important to note that there may be a lack of simultaneity between the dependent variables and the innovation variables, which derives from how the question was framed: "*... subsequently to the introduction of changes by the management, how did the working conditions change?*" for both the questionnaires. The generic term 'changes' without other specifications, in the context of the questionnaires, refers to changes in innovation areas (technology, organization, training and ICT).

Among the covariates we can distinguish: the structural variables, which capture as much as possible the firm specific heterogeneity in our cross sectional environment; innovation indexes and cooperative aspects of the industrial relations system, mainly capturing union delegates/management relations. It is worth stressing the accent on the fact that innovation activities are thought to encompass several spheres. In fact, the administered questionnaire allowed collecting information not only on product and process innovations (with a wealth of information on R&D activities), but also on organizational changes, training activities and ICT adoption (see Tab. A.2 in Appendix for a detailed description of the explanatory variables).

The richness of the data reduces to some extent the likelihood of relevant variables being omitted.

The information at our disposal allow us finding answers to the following main research questions:

15 The respondents to the questionnaire (union representatives) were asked to indicate the trend for ten items (effort, security and job stability, employees competences, information disposable to the employees, autonomy in accomplish the job tasks, influence over the managerial decisions, monetary incentives, non-monetary incentives, stress, safety/security) concerning the working conditions on a scale from 1 (decreased) to 3 (increased). Only for the stress item the number 1 means increased and 3 decreased, so that the higher is WC_SAFE the better is for workers.

1. Is there an indication of a different impact of techno-organizational changes on working conditions for the two LPSs?
2. Is the impact of organizational changes univocal in the two LPSs?
3. Are the industrial relations differently linked to working conditions in the two LPSs?

The expected signs of the factors potentially influencing workers' conditions are reported in table 1:

Table 1: Hypothesized signs of influencing variables on the working conditions for both the LPSs

Influencing factors	**WC_EMP**	**WC_SAFE**
Hypothesized causality directions: *Innovations → Working Conditions*		
Technological innovation	(+,-)	(+,-)
Organizational innovation	(+,-)	(+,-)
Training	(+)	(+)
ICT	(+,-)	(+,-)
Hypothesized relations[16]: *Industrial relations ←→ Working Conditions*		
Cooperative Industrial relations	(+)	(+)

4. Results of the econometric analysis

The results of the econometric exercises are reported in tables 2a.1, 2a.2, 2b.1 and 2b.2[17].

First, it should be stressed that because of the importance of organizational changes in influencing working conditions, we estimate both a specification with only the synthetic index of organizational innovation (INNO_ORG) and a specification with the disaggregated variables used to construct INNO_ORG. The same has been done with the industrial relations index (IND_REL). Second, we have settled up different specifications for each synthetic innovation index because of

16 When we take into consideration the linkages between working conditions and industrial relations we do not have the potential causality direction implied by the question posed to the respondents. Thus, we can strictly refer to correlations rather than to weak causality relations.

17 Because the aim of the empirical analysis is not to calculate elasticities we avoid presenting the coefficients, rather we adopt a more qualitative way of results displaying.

their quite high bivariate correlations[18] (tables 2a.1 and 2b.1). Third, we have also run regressions with multiplicative interaction terms between innovation indexes and the industrial relations one, in order to verify whether the interactions of industrial relations and innovations reinforce the impact of the latter on working conditions (tables 2a.2 and 2b.2). Finally, we have chosen to drop those firms having less than 50 employees for the RE system, in order to make the comparison with MO results more direct[19].

Starting from table 2a.1 where the dependent variable is represented by WC_EMP we note a positive and significant impact of the innovation activities on WC_EMP for both the LPSs, with only some specificities. When we disaggregate the synthetic index INNO_ORG, using its components in the estimation, we notice that the sign of the synthetic index is mainly driven by the two components that capture changes in production and labour organization (ORG_PROD and ORG_LAB). This means that workers empowerment is spurred by such typologies of organizational changes, in accordance with the advocates of HPWP implementation. The same strong and positive relations emerge when the index capturing the intensity of good quality (cooperative) industrial relations at firm level is considered. Again when we disaggregate the index in its components we find that the sign of the synthetic index is driven by specific components that can be considered the less formal aspects of good quality industrial relations: the index capturing the management attitude to inform, consult or negotiate with union representatives on several items (REL_ITEMS) and the index providing the union representative perception of the industrial relations trend over time (INDREL_TREND). The result does not come unexpected (Antonioli, MAzzanti, Pini, Tortia, 2004; Antonioli, Pini 2004), but despite the proximity of the two LPSs an interesting difference concerning the role of good quality industrial relations on working conditions emerges. For RE firms the variable REL_ITEMS is strongly significant, while it is not for MO firms. We may argue that due to historical and idiosyncratic conditions, local unions in RE have a stronger power than the MO ones. Such power translates into the capacity to make the union voice listened within the firm. At the same time it is possible that RE firms' managements are more inclined to discuss union instances. This finding support a literature that recognizes in the institutional setting a factor influencing the sign of the impact of organizational changes implementation on working conditions (Godard, 2004).

18 Correlation coefficients are not reported but they are available upon request.

19 We also run regressions using all the 192 firms for RE. The results slightly differ from those obtained here using a restricted sample of firms with at least 50 employees.

Table 2a.1: Results of the econometric exercise with WC_EMP as dependent variable (OLS)

Dependent variable WC_EMP	RE							MO						
	1	2	3	4	5	6	7	1	2	3	4	5	6	7
	Structural Variables							*Structural Variables*						
SECTOR DUMMIES	Yes	Yes	Yes	Yes	Yes	Yes	Yes	Yes	Yes	Yes	Yes	Yes	Yes	Yes
SIZE DUMMIES	Yes	Yes	Yes	Yes	Yes	Yes	Yes	Yes	Yes	Yes	Yes	Yes	Yes	Yes
Other Controls^	Yes	Yes	Yes	Yes	Yes	Yes	Yes	Yes	Yes	Yes	Yes	Yes	Yes	Yes
	Organizational Innovation							*Organizational Innovation*						
INNO_ORG	***							**						
ORG_LAB		*							**					
ORG_PROD		**							***					
REW		n.s.							*					
	Industrial Relations							*Industrial Relations*						
INDREL			***							**	n.s.			
BTC				n.s.							n.s.			
BARG				n.s.							n.s.			
REL_ITEMS				***							n.s.			
INDREL_TREND				**							***			
	Innovation Activities							*Innovation Activities*						
INNO_TRAIN					***							***		
INNO_TECH						***							n.s.	
INNO_ICT							***							**
R^2	0.26	0.34	0.25	0.28	0.29	0.24	0.28	0.16	0.28	0.16	0.18	0.23	0.12	0.15
F test prob.	0.00	0.00	0.00	0.00	0.00	0.00	0.00	0.00	0.00	0.00	0.00	0.00	0.00	0.00
N	134	134	134	134	134	134	134	176	176	176	176	176	176	176
VIF	1.55	1.35	1.25	1.19	1.50	1.58	1.82	1.9	1.46	2.08	1.99	1.93	1.97	1.94

Notes: only the level of significance of the coefficients and their signs, when negative, are reported (10% *, 5%**, 1%***); the coefficients are not reported for brevity but full results are available upon request; n.s. means not significant; empty cells mean the variable is not included in the specification; regressions have been conducted with standard errors robust to heteroskedasticity; VIF is the Variance Inflation Factor and it represent a 'test' to recognize the existence of multicollinearity when the threshold of 10 is exceeded.

^Among Other Controls we have a Performance index (PERF); Delocalization Dummy (DELOC); Group Dummy (GROUP); Dummies capturing the strategic orientation of the firm (TQ_STR; VA_STR; CP_STR; BR_ST); International turnover (INT_TURN); Indexes capturing labour contract flexibility (LCF; CONV_LCF).

In order to verify the importance of industrial relations we construct several multiplicative interaction terms between the synthetic industrial relations index and the innovation ones. As expected, the relations between the interaction terms and WC_EMP (table 2a.2) are reinforced versions of those obtained without interactions. As a relevant example the INNO_TECH variable, which is not significant for MO firms, when it is interacted with the industrial relations index turns out to be significant. This result represents supporting evidence to the idea that good quality industrial relations are a complementary element to innovation[1].

Table 2a.2: Results of the econometric exercise with WC_EMP as dependent variable with interaction terms (OLS)

Dependent variable	RE				MO			
WC_EMP	1	2	3	4	1	2	3	4
	Structural Variables				*Structural Variables*			
SECTOR DUMMIES	Yes	Yes	Yes	Yes	Yes	Yes	Yes	Yes
SIZE DUMMIES	Yes	Yes	Yes	Yes	Yes	Yes	Yes	Yes
Other Controls^	Yes	Yes	Yes	Yes	Yes	Yes	Yes	Yes
	Interaction Terms				*Interaction Terms*			
INNO_ORG* INDREL	***				***			
INNO_TRAIN* INDREL		***				***		
INNO_TECH* INDREL			***				**	
INNO_ICT* INDREL				***				***
R^2	0.27	0.31	0.28	0.30	0.18	0.25	0.14	0.18
F test prob.	0.00	0.00	0.00	0.00	0.00	0.00	0.00	0.00
N	134	134	134	134	176	176	176	176
VIF	1.12	1.66	1.98	1.25	2.11	2.14	2.17	2.10

Notes: only the level of significance of the coefficients and their signs, when negative, are reported (10% *, 5%**, 1%***); the coefficients are not reported for brevity but full results are available upon request; n.s. means not significant; empty cells mean the variable is not included in the specification; regressions have been conducted with standard errors robust to heteroskedasticity; VIF is the Variance Inflation Factor and it represent a 'test' to recognize the existence of multicollinearity when the threshold of 10 is exceeded. ^Among Other Controls we have a Performance index (PERF); Delocalization Dummy (DELOC); Group Dummy (GROUP); Dummies capturing the strategic orientation of the firm (TQ_STR; VA_STR; CP_STR; BR_ST); International turnover (INT_TURN); Indexes capturing labour contract flexibility (LCF; CONV_LCF).

1 In our previous researches we have found that industrial relations exert an indirect role on labour productivity, spurring innovation activities: Antonioli, Mazzanti, Pini (2007).

If the results are quite clear cut when we consider the index of empowerment as expression of working condition changes subsequent to innovations introduction, the same cannot be said when the index capturing the trend in workers stress and in safety/security is used as dependent variable of our regressions (tables 2b.1 and 2b.2).

Looking at the results reported in table 2b.1 we notice that only the training index is significant and positive for the firms belonging to both local production systems. This result does not come unexpected since a better trained workforce is likely to better know and implement safety/security norms[2]. The other innovation indexes do not increase the probability of having high values of the dependent variable, that is a positive trend in the aspects enclosed in the dependent. However, when the INNO_ORG variable is disaggregated we find that for RE the changes in production organization likely spur better working conditions while the presence and intensity of diffusion of reward schemes is negatively related with the dependent variable. The latter result may be interpreted as a consequence of the intensification in working pace due to the linkages between the reward system and performance indicators. Things are slightly different for MO context. Here we have a negative sign associated to ORG_LAB variable, while positive is the association of the dependent with ORG_PROD and REW. The absence of significance of the synthetic index of organizational changes is given by the fact that the negative sign associated to ORG_LAB seems to be strong enough to offset the positive impact of changes in production organization and of reward mechanisms presence. The result of the ORG_LAB variable is in line with the recent, critical literature on the relations between organizational changes and working conditions (Green, 2004; Brenner, Fairris, Ruser, 2004; Askenazy, Caroli, 2006). Although those organizational changes clustered in ORG_LAB variable are usually interpreted as ameliorative elements of the job content, the results we obtained underlines the possibility that the workers are subject to higher level of stress when changes in labour organization are introduced. The only variable which is constantly significant, in the specifications in which it is included, is the index of cooperative industrial relations, which shows the same results obtained with WC_EMP index as dependent variable when disaggregated.

2 We also cannot forget that part of training activities on safety/security norms is compulsory.

Table 2b.1: *Results of the econometric exercise with WC_SAFE as dependent variable^ (Ordered Probit)*

Dependent variable WC_SAFE	RE							MO						
	1	2	3	4	5	6	7	1	2	3	4	5	6	7
	Structural Variables							*Structural Variables*						
SECTOR DUMMIES	Yes	Yes	Yes	Yes	Yes	Yes	Yes	Yes	Yes	Yes	Yes	Yes	Yes	Yes
SIZE DUMMIES	Yes	Yes	Yes	Yes	Yes	Yes	Yes	Yes	Yes	Yes	Yes	Yes	Yes	Yes
Other Controls^	Yes	Yes	Yes	Yes	Yes	Yes	Yes	Yes	Yes	Yes	Yes	Yes	Yes	Yes
	Organizational Innovation							*Organizational Innovation*						
INNO_ORG	n.s.							n.s.						
ORG_LAB		n.s.							**(-)					
ORG_PROD		*							***					
REW		**(-)							**					
	Industrial Relations							*Industrial Relations*						
INDREL			***							*				
BTC				n.s.							n.s.			
BARG				n.s.							n.s.			
REL_ITEMS				**							n.s.			
INDREL_TREND				***							***			
	Innovation Activities							*Innovation Activities*						
INNO_TRAIN					***							*		
INNO_TECH						n.s.							n.s.	
INNO_ICT							n.s.							n.s.
Cut1	***(-)	***(-)	***(-)	*	***(-)	***(-)	***(-)	n.s.	n.s.	*	***	n.s.	n.s.	n.s.
Cut2	***(-)	***(-)	n.s.	n.s.	**(-)	***(-)	**(-)	***	***	***	***	***	***	***
Cut3	n.s.	n.s.	**	***	n.s.	n.s.	n.s.	***	***	***	***	***	***	***
Cut4.	n.s.	n.s.	***	***	n.s.	n.s.	n.s.	***	***	***	***	***	***	***
Pseudo R^2	0.11	0.14	0.11	0.12	0.13	0.11	0.11	0.08	0.12	0.08	0.13	0.08	0.08	0.07
Prob. Wald Chi2	0.00	0.00	0.00	0.00	0.00	0.00	0.00	0.00	0.00	0.00	0.00	0.00	0.00	0.00
N	134	134	134	134	134	134	134	176	176	176	176	176	176	176

Notes: only the level of significance of the coefficients and their signs, when negative, are reported (10% *, 5%**, 1%***); the coefficients are not reported for brevity but full results are available upon request; n.s. means not significant; empty cells mean the variable is not included in the specification; regressions have been conducted with standard errors robust to heteroskedasticity; VIF is the Variance Inflation Factor and it represent a 'test' to recognize the existence of multicollinearity when the threshold of 10 is exceeded. ^Among Other Controls we have a Performance index (PERF); Delocalization Dummy (DELOC); Group Dummy (GROUP); Dummies capturing the strategic orientation of the firm (TQ_STR; VA_STR; CP_STR; BR_ST); International turnover (INT_TURN); Indexes capturing labour contract flexibility (LCF; CONV_LCF).

As far as we consider the innovation indexes interacted with the industrial relations synthetic index (INDREL) we do not have a robust evidence supporting the hypothesis of a synergic nature between innovations and cooperative industrial relations. Nevertheless, we may say that at least for RE context interacting innovations in ICT with cooperative industrial relations leads to a significant relations with the dependent variable, significant relations that the ICT innovation index does not show when it is not interacted with INDREL. The same result does not hold for MO LPS, underlying again the role of context/firm specific conditions in determining the effectiveness of innovation and industrial relations linkages on working conditions.

Table 2b.2: Results of the econometric exercise with WC_SAFE as dependent variable with interaction terms (Ordered Probit)

Dependent variable WC_EMP	RE 1	RE 2	RE 3	RE 4	MO 1	MO 2	MO 3	MO 4
	Structural Variables				*Structural Variables*			
SECTOR DUMMIES	Yes	Yes	Yes	Yes	Yes	Yes	Yes	Yes
SIZE DUMMIES	Yes	Yes	Yes	Yes	Yes	Yes	Yes	Yes
Other Controls^	Yes	Yes	Yes	Yes	Yes	Yes	Yes	Yes
	Interaction Terms				*Interaction Terms*			
INNO_ORG* INDREL	n.s.				n.s.			
INNO_TRAIN* INDREL		***				**		
INNO_TECH* INDREL			n.s.				n.s.	
INNO_ICT* INDREL				*				n.s.
Cut1	***(-)	***(-)	***(-)	***(-)	n.s.	n.s.	n.s.	***
Cut2	**(-)	**(-)	**(-)	*(-)	***	***	***	***
Cut3	n.s.	n.s.	n.s.	n.s.	***	***	***	n.s.
Cut4.	**	***	***	***	***	***	***	n.s.
Pseudo R^2	0.11	0.14	0.12	0.12	0.08	0.09	0.08	0.08
Prob. Wald Chi2	0.00	0.00	0.00	0.00	0.00	0.00	0.00	0.00
N	134	134	134	134	176	176	176	176

Notes: only the level of significance of the coefficients and their signs, when negative, are reported (10% *, 5%**, 1%***); the coefficients are not reported for brevity but full results are available upon request; n.s. means not significant; empty cells mean the variable is not included in the specification; regressions have been conducted with standard errors robust to heteroskedasticity; VIF is the Variance Inflation Factor and it represent a 'test' to recognize the existence of multicollinearity when the threshold of 10 is exceeded.
^Among Other Controls we have a Performance index (PERF); Delocalization Dummy (DELOC); Group Dummy (GROUP); Dummies capturing the strategic orientation of the firm (TQ_STR; VA_STR; CP_STR; BR_ST); International turnover (INT_TURN); Indexes capturing labour contract flexibility (LCF; CONV_LCF).

A qualitative synthesis of the main results is reported in table 3, which provide insights helping in punctually answer to the main research questions.

At first we have put in evidence that some differences in the impact of techno-organizational changes on working conditions exist between the two LPSs (see italics in table 3). This means that idiosyncratic, context specific factors affect the relations between working conditions and explanatory variables in the two LPSs. The contiguity and the substantial homogeneous social environment of the two LPSs do not avoid the emergence of specificities in the results, although for the strong majority of the specifications we have similar signs for the coefficients related to the explanatory variables.

Table 3: Synthesis of the results.

	WC_EMP		*WC_SAFE*	
Influencing factors	**RE**	**MO**	**RE**	**MO**
Organizational Innovation …	Positive and significant	Positive and significant	Not significant	Not significant
… Changes in Labour Organization	Positive and significant	Positive and significant	*Not significant*	*Negative and significant*
… Changes in Production Organization	Positive and significant	Positive and significant	Positive and significant	Positive and significant
… Reward System	*Not significant*	*Positive but weakly signifi-cant*	*Negative and significant*	*Positive and significant*
Cooperative Industrial relations	Positive and significant	Positive and significant	Positive and significant	Positive and significant
… Union/Management relations	*Positive and significant*	*Not significant*	*Positive and significant*	*Not significant*
… trend in industrial relations	Positive and significant	Positive and significant	Positive and significant	Positive and significant
… BTC	Not significant	Not significant	Not significant	Not significant
…bargaining	Not significant	Not significant	Not significant	Not significant
Training	Positive and significant	Positive and significant	Positive and significant	Positive but weakly significant
Technological innovation	*Positive and significant*	*Not significant*	Not significant	Not significant
ICT	Positive and significant	Positive and significant	Not significant	Not significant

Second, the focus on the organizational changes has furthermore stressed that the impact of specific organizational aspects affects the working conditions indexes differently for the two LPSs. In addition, the index synthesizing the trend in safety/security and workers' stress (WC_SAFE) shows, for MO LPS, a negative relation with changes concerning labour organization. This evidence partially support the *intensification thesis*.

Finally, the industrial relations variables are always positively related to both the indexes of working conditions and for the two LPSs as well. Furthermore, the results of the interaction terms induce to hypothesize the existence of complementarities between innovations and industrial relations on working conditions.

5. Conclusions

The intensification of work in Europe during the '90s and the simultaneous diffusion of ICT and organizational changes have raised concerns about the effects of innovations on workers' well being. In fact, the outcome of innovation activities is not confined only to the firm, it also affects the workers. Similarly, the effect of cooperative relationships between union delegates and management cannot be thought to be neutral in terms of the quality of work. The main hypothesis underlying the present work is that techno-organizational changes and the industrial relations climate are both factors that influence workers' well being.

Our empirical results support the hypothesis that working conditions are an outcome of techno-organizational changes, irrespectively of the context specific factors as the results for the two LPS suggest. There are certainly some peculiarities in the relationships estimated for the local contexts, but as a whole we may say that both techno-organizational innovations and industrial relations are factors that positively influence working conditions. This homogeneity in the relations is especially found when we consider, as dependent variable, those aspects more closely related to the definition of job empowerment. When we look at the other aspects of the job, namely stress and safety/security issues, we may highlight only the positive impact of training activities, among the innovation variables. At the same time cooperative industrial relations preserve their capacity of positively influencing also the specific items stress and safety/security.

Finally, the rather different results for the two indexes of working conditions highlight the importance in the empirical analysis of considering specific aspects of workers' conditions as outcomes of innovation and industrial relations. Indeed, the definition of workers' well being encompasses several components and dimensions, and calls for further empirical evidence.

Appendix

Table A.1a: Firms percentage distribution in RE: firms population and interviewed firms.

RE Population with UR (376)						
	Size classes 31.12.2004					
Sectors	20-49	50-99	100-249	250-499	>499	Total
Food	1.6	1.3	1.9	0.3	0.5	5.6
Other Industries	1.6	0.3	0.0	0.0	0.3	2.1
Chemical	4.5	1.9	2.4	0.0	0.3	9.0
Wood	1.1	1.3	1.1	1.1	0.0	4.5
Machineries	23.1	16.5	12.2	3.5	2.4	57.7
Non-metallic mineral	3.7	4.3	4.5	2.6	1.9	17.0
Textile	1.1	1.6	0.5	0.8	0.0	3.9
Total	36.7	27.1	22.6	8.2	5.3	100
RE Interviewed Units (192)						
	Size classes 31.12.2004					
Sectors	20-49	50-99	100-249	250-499	>499	Total
Food	1.6	2.1	3.1	0.5	0.5	7.8
Other Industries	2.1	0.0	0.0	0.0	0.5	2.6
Chemical	4.7	1.6	3.1	0.0	0.5	9.9
Wood	1.0	1.0	1.6	1.6	0.0	5.2
Machineries	15.1	13.5	14.0	3.6	3.6	50.0
Non-metallic mineral	4.7	3.1	5.2	4.1	2.1	19.2
Textile	1.0	2.1	1.0	1.0	0.0	5.2
Total	30.2	23.4	28.1	10.9	7.3	100

Cochran Test *Margin of error* θ *	*Interviewed firms vs.* *Population with RSU*
$\theta = \sqrt{\frac{N}{(N-1)n} - \frac{1}{N-1}}$	**0.05**

* Margin of error θ "usually" tolerated: 0.05. Restrictive test for small population: the smaller is N, the lesser the distance between N and n has to be in order to generate an acceptable θ.

Table A.1b: Firms percentage distribution in MO: firms population and interviewed firms.

MO Population with RSU (246)					
	Size classes 31.12.2006				
Sectors	50-99	100-249	250-499	>499	Total
Food	3.7	6.5	0.0	0.8	11.0
Other Industries	0	0	0	0	0
Chemical	3.3	4.9	1.6	0.4	10.2
Wood	2.8	2.4	0.8	0.4	6.5
Machineries	24.8	14.6	5.7	2.0	47.2
Non-metallic mineral	4.9	10.2	2.8	2.8	20.7
Textile	2.4	1.6	0.4	0.0	4.5
Total	41.9	40.2	11.4	6.5	100
MO Interviewed Units (176)					
	Size classes 31.12.2006				
Sectors	50-99	100-249	250-499	>499	Total
Food	3.4	5.1	1.7	0.6	10.8
Other Industries	0	0	0	0	0
Chemical	6.3	2.3	0.6	0.6	9.7
Wood	2.3	4.0	0.6	0.0	6.8
Machineries	18.2	15.3	4.0	3.4	40.9
Non-metallic mineral	9.1	12.5	2.3	0.6	24.4
Textile	6.3	0.6	0.6	0.0	7.4
Total	45.5	39.8	9.7	5.1	100

Cochran Test Margin of error θ *	*Interviewed firms vs. Population with RSU*
$\theta = \sqrt{\frac{N}{(N-1)n} - \frac{1}{N-1}}$	**0.04**

Source Lugli and Tugnoli (2008)

* Margin of error θ "usually" tolerated: 0.05. Restrictive test for small population: the smaller is N, the lesser the distance between N and n has to be in order to generate an acceptable θ.

Table A.2: Descriptive statistics

Variables	Description	RE (192 obs) Min	Max	Mean	MO (176 obs) Min	Max	Mean
	Dependent Variables						
	Working Conditions						
WC_EMP	Index capturing the trend of 8 job items (effort, security and job stability, employees competences, information disposable to the employees, autonomy in accomplish the job tasks, influence over the managerial decisions, monetary incentives, non-monetary incentives) on a scale from 1 to 3 (decreased, stable, increased)	1	3	2.04	1	3	1.97
WC_SAFE	Index capturing the trend of two job items, safety/security and stress, on a scale from 1 to 3 (decreased, stable, increased). Codified as an ordered variable from 1 to 5.	1	5	2.48	1	5	2.31
	Controls and Explanatory Variables						
	Structural Variables						
Sectors Dummies (Food, Other Industries, Chemical, Wood, Machineries, Non-metallic minerals)	Binary variables (0,1)	0	1	/	0	1	/
Size Dummies (20-49, 50-99, 100-249, 250-499, >499 for RE; and 50-99, 100-249, 250-499, >499 for MO)	Binary variables (0,1)	0	1	/	0	1	/
Firm Typology Dummies (private firm, industrial group, cooperative firm, cooperative group; private firm/group, cooperative firm/group)	Binary variables (0,1)	0	1	/	0	1	/
Percent of International Turnover (**INT_TURN**)	Percentage of turnover made on international markets. Rescaled on interval (0-1)	0	0.9	0.42	0	1	0.40
Delocalization (d) (**DELOC**)	Binary variable (0,1)	0	1	0.17	0	1	0.41
Cost-Price Strategy (d) (**CP_STR**)	Binary variable (0,1)	0	1	0.62	0	1	0.50
Technology-Quality Strategy (d) (**TQ_STR**)	Binary variable (0,1)	0	1	0.87	0	1	0.78
Brand Strategy (d) (**BR_STR**)	Binary variable (0,1)	0	1	0.3	0	1	0.40

		RE (192 obs)			MO (176 obs)		
Variables	*Description*	*Min*	*Max*	*Mean*	*Min*	*Max*	*Mean*
Variety Strategy (d) **(VA_STR)**	Binary variable (0,1)	0	1	0.45	0	1	0.32
Performance Indicators from questionnaire (**PERF**): Productivity, Revenue, Profit, Investment	Indexes: each type of performance is ranked on a -5 (worse than the preceding year)+5 (better then the preceding year) scale	-5	5	/	-5	5	/
Labor Contract Flexibility (**LCF**)*	Index: captures the characteristics of the contractual flexibility (number of contracts, typology of contracts, trend of the flexible contracts diffusion etc…). Interval (0-1).	0	1.2	0.66	0	1.5	0.85
Conversion of Flexible Labor Contracts in Long-lasting Ones **(CONV_LCF)**	Index: percentage of workers who are hired permanently after the flexible contract expires. Rescaled on interval (0-1).	0	1	0.39	0	1	0.39
	Training						
INNO_TRAIN.... (interval 0-1)	Composite index capturing the intensity in training activities Mean of the following indexes:	0	0.97	0.31	0	0.95	0.43
....Training Coverage	Index: percentage of employees involved in training programmes (0 nobody; 1=1-24%; 2=25-49%; 3=50-74%; 4=75-100%)	1	4	2.08	1	4	2.37
Training Modalities	Index: modalities of training (side-by-side training with structured programmes, internal and external to the firm programmes). Interval (0-1).	0	0.76	0.33	0	1	0.40
Training Advantages	Index: advantages for employees involved in training activities Interval (0-1).	0	1	0.39	0	0.8	0.35
Index of Training Competencies	Index: based on the whole competencies the training programmes aim to develop. Interval (0-1).	0	1	0.41	0	1	0.36
	Technological Innovation						
INNO_TECH.... (interval 0-1)*	Composite index capturing the intensity in technological innovations Mean of the following indexes:	0	1	0.39	0	1	0.53
....Process Innovation (d)	Binary variable (0,1)	0	1	0.49	0	1	0.70
Product Innovation (d)	Binary variable (0,1)	0	1	0.55	0	1	0.74
Quality Control Innovation (d)	Binary variable (0,1)	0	1	0.61	0	1	0.64
Radical Innovation (d)	Binary variable (0,1)	0	1	0.27	0	1	0.38
Incremental Innovation (d)	Binary variable (0,1)	0	1	0.61	0	1	0.76

		RE (192 obs)			*MO (176 obs)*		
Variables	*Description*	*Min*	*Max*	*Mean*	*Min*	*Max*	*Mean*
R&D activities	Index: it synthesizes the information about innovation input (formal R&D division, R&D activities, resources and employees involved in R&D activities, collaborations with other firms on R&D for Reggio Emilia; formal R&D division and collaborations with other firms on R&D for Modena). Interval (0-1).	0	1	0.49	0	1	0.66
	Organizational Innovation						
INNO_ORG….. (interval 0-1)	Composite index capturing the intensity in organizational innovations Mean of the following indexes:	0.05	0.62	0.24	0	0.56	0.23
……Organizational practices in production (**ORG_PROD**)	Index: Changes in organizational practices in production (quality circles, team working, just in time, total quality management). Interval (0-1).	0	0.8	0.19	0	0.75	0.16
Organizational practices in labor services (**ORG_LAB**)	Index: Changes in organizational practices in labour services (job rotation, delegation, continuous training, etc…). Interval (0-1).	0	0.83	0.26	0	0.81	0.25
Reward System (**REW**)	Index: Individual and collective reward in 2004. Interval (0-1).	0	1	0.4	0	1	0.33
Out-sourcing (**OUT**)	Index: intensity of out-sourcing in ancillary activities, production support activities and production activities. Interval (0-4).	0	3.53	1.16	0	3.78	1.33
In-sourcing (**INS**)	Index: intensity of in-sourcing in ancillary activities, production support activities and production activities. Interval (0-4).	0	2.53	0.29	0	3.88	0.38
Relations with Client and Suppliers (**REL_SUPPCLI**)	Index: relations with clients and/or suppliers on furniture, assistance, changing technological equipment, exchange of technical and commercial knowledge/information etc…. Interval (0-1).	0	0.78	0.25	0	0.66	0.21
	ICT						
INNO_ICT… (interval 0-1)	Composite index capturing the intensity in ICT adoption Mean of the following indexes:	0.08	1	0.64	0	1	0.62
….ICT in Production	Index: introduction of ICT in production. Interval (0-1).	0	1	0.57	0	1	0.51
ICT in Communication	Index: introduction of ICT for communication purposes. Interval (0-1).	0	1	0.82	0	1	0.88
ICT in Management-Integration	Index: introduction of systems that use ICT such as EDI, Electronic Data Interchange, EDI (Electronic Data Interchange); MRP (Material Requirements Planning) etc… Interval (0-1).	0	1	0.52	0	1	0.48

		RE (192 obs)			MO (176 obs)		
Variables	*Description*	*Min*	*Max*	*Mean*	*Min*	*Max*	*Mean*
	Industrial Relations						
IND_REL (0-1)	Synthetic index of good quality industrial relations	0.16	0.76	0.39	0.14	0.93	0.54
Firm Level Bargaining (d) (**BARG**)	Binary variable (0,1): 1 if a second level formal agreement has been signed in 2004	0	1	0.68	0	1	0.90
Bilateral Technical Commissions (d) (**BTC**)	Binary variable (0,1): 1 if a BTC exists	0	1	0.32	0	1	0.11
Trend in Industrial Relations (**INDREL_TREND**)	Index: trend of the industrial relations compared to the preceding year (worsened, stable, improved). Interval (1-3)	1	3	2.03	1	3	1.97
Management/Union Interaction on Issues **(REL_ITEMS)**	Index: interaction between management and union representatives (no interaction, information, consultation, negotiation) on several items (e.g. production, quality, employment, working hours, etc…). Interval (1-4)	1	3.43	1.92	1	3.56	1.95

Notes: "(d)" stands for a binary variable (dummy);

* The two synthetic indexes for RE and MO slightly differ because we do not have at our disposal the same set of raw data. The RE index is based on a more complex set of information.

Ackowledgments

The authors thank the participants at the Third European Congress of the Work & Labour Network, Rome, 24-26 September 2008 for useful comments and suggestions. We also acknowledge with thanks IRES Emilia Romagna for the provision of the dataset for Modena local production system. Usual disclaimers apply.

References

Amin, A. (1999): The Emilian Model: Institutional Challenges, European Planning Studies, vol. 7, no. 4, pp. 389-406.

Antonioli, D. / Delsoldato, L. / Mazzanti, M. / Pini, P. (2007): Dinamiche innovative, relazioni industriali, performance nelle imprese manifatturiere. II^ Indagine sul sistema locale di Reggio Emilia, Milano, FrancoAngeli.

Antonioli, D. / Mazzanti, M. / Pini, P. (2007): Productivity, Innovation Strategies and Industrial Relations in SME. Empirical Evidence for a Local Manufacturing System in Northern Italy, Working Paper no. 21, DEIT, University of Ferrara, www.deit.economia.unife.it.

Antonioli, D. / Mazzanti, M. / Pini, P. (2009): Innovation, Working Conditions and Industrial Relations. Evidence for a Local Production System, Economic and Industrial Democracy, vol. 3, n. 2, forthcoming.

Antonioli, D. / Mazzanti, M. / Pini, P. / Tortia, E. (2004): Adoption of Techno-Organizational Innovations, and Industrial Relations in Manufacturing Firms: An Analysis for a Local Industrial System, Economia Politica, vol. XXI, no. 1, pp. 11-52.

Antonioli, D. / Pini, P. (2004): Dinamiche innovative e performance d'impresa: analisi cluster per un sistema industriale locale, Istituzioni e Sviluppo Economico, vol. 2, no. 1, pp. 65-104.

Askenazy, P. (2004): Shorter Work Times, Hours Flexibility, and Labour Intensification, Eastern Economic Journal, vol. 30, no. 4, pp. 603-614.

Askenazy P. / Caroli E. (2006): Innovative Work Practices, Information Technologies and Working Conditions: Evidence for France, Discussion Paper no. 2321, IZA, Bonn.

Baglioni, G. (1998): Il sistema delle relazioni industriali in Italia: caratteristiche ed evoluzione storica, in Cella G.P., Treu T. (eds.), Le nuove relazioni industriali. L'esperienza italiana nella prospettiva europea, Bologna, Il Mulino.

Bélanger, J. / Giles, A. / Murray G. (2002): Towards a New Production Model: Potentialities, Tensions and Contradictions, in Murray G., Bélanger J., Giles A., Lapointe A., Work and Employment Relations in the High-Performance Workplace, London, Continuum.

Betts, J. / Odgers, C. / Wilson, M. (2001): The Effects of Unions on Research and Development: An Empirical Analysis Using Multi-Year Data, Canadian Journal of Economics, vol. 34, no. 3, pp. 785-806.

Black, S. / Lynch, L. (2001): How to Compete: The Impact of Workplace Practices and Information Technology on Productivity, Review of Economics and Statistics, vol. 83, no. 3, pp. 434-445.

Black, S. / Lynch, L. / Krivelyova, A. (2004): How Workers Fare When Employers Innovate, Industrial Relations, vol. 43, no. 1, pp. 44-66.

Brenner, M. / Fairris, D. / Ruser, J. (2004): Flexible Work Practices and Occupational Safety and Health: Exploring the Relationship Between Cumulative Trauma Disorders and Workplace Transformation, Industrial Relations, vol. 43, no. 1, pp. 242-266.

Bresnahan, T.F. / Brynjolfsson, E. / Hitt, L.M. (2002): Information Technology, Workplace Organization, and the Demand for Skilled Labor: Firm-Level Evidence, Quarterly Journal of Economics, vol. 117, no. 1, pp. 339-376

Brusco, S. (1982): The Emilian Model: Productive Decentralization and Social Integration, Cambridge Journal of Economics, vol. 6, no. 2, pp. 167-184.

Brusco, S. / Cainelli, G. / Forni, F. / Franchi, M. / Malusardi, A. / Righetti, R. (1997): L'evoluzione dei distretti produttivi locali in Emilia-Romagna, in Cossentino F., Pyke F., Sengenberger W., (eds.), Le risposte locali e regionali alla pressione globale: il caso dell'Italia e dei suoi distretti industriali, Bologna, il Mulino.
Brynjolfsson, E. / Hitt, L. (2000): Beyond Computation: Information Technology, Organizational Transformation and Business Performance, Journal of Economic Perspectives, vol. 14, no. 4, pp. 23-48.
Butler, P. / Felstead, A. / Ashton, D. / Fuller, A. / Lee, T. / Unwin, L. / Walters, S. (2004): High Performance Management: A Literature Review, Learning as Work Research Paper, n. 1, june.
Cappelli, P. / Neumark, D. (2001): Do "High Performance" Work Practices Improve Establishment-Level Outcomes?, Industrial & Labor Relations Review, vol. 54, no. 4, pp. 737-775.
Caroli, E. / Van Reenen, J. (2001): Skill Biased Organizational Change? Evidence from a Panel of French and British Establishments, Quarterly Journal of Economics, vol. 16, no. 4, pp. 1449-1492.
Cella, G.P. / Treu, T. (eds.) (1998): Le nuove relazioni industriali. L'esperienza italiana nella prospettiva europea, Bologna, Il Mulino.
Cochran, W. (1977): Sampling Techniques, New York, John Wiley and Sons.
Fairris, D. (2004): Towards a Theory of Work Intensity, Eastern Economic Journal, vol. 30, no. 4, pp. 587-601.
Forth, J. / Milward, N. (2004): High-Involvement Management and Pay in Britain, Industrial Relations, vol. 43, no. 1, pp. 98-119.
Gallie, D. (2005): Work Pressure in Europe 1996-2001: Trends and Determinants, British Journal of Industrial Relations, vol. 43, no. 3, pp. 351-375.
Godard, J. (2004): A Critical Assessment of the High-Performance Paradigm, British Journal of Industrial Relations, vol. 42, n. 2, pp. 349-378.
Green, F. (2004): Why Has Work Effort Become More Intense?, Industrial Relations, vol. 43, no. 4, pp. 709-741.
Green, F. / McIntosh, S. (2001): The Intensification of Work in Europe, Labour Economics, vol. 8, no. 2, pp. 291-308.
Handel, M. / Gittleman, M. (2004): Is there a Wage Payoff to Innovative Work Practices?, Industrial Relations, vol. 43, no. 1, pp. 67-97.
Handel, M. / Levine, D. (2004): Editors' Introduction: the Effects of New Work Practices on Workers, Industrial Relations, vol. 43, no. 1, pp. 1-43.
Huselid, M. (1995): The Impact of Human Resources Management Practices on Turnover, Productivity and Corporate Financial Performance, Academy of Management Journal, vol. 38, no. 3, pp. 635-672.
Huselid, M.A. / Becker, B.E. (1996): Methodological Issues in Cross-Sectional and Panel Estimates of the Human Resource-Firm Performance Link, Industrial Relations, vol. 35, no. 3, pp. 400-422.

Ichniowski, C. (1990): Human Resource Management Systems and the Performance of U.S. Manufacturing Businesses, Working Paper no. 3449, NBER, Cambridge.

Ichniowski, C. / Shaw, K. / Prennushi, G. (1997): The Effects of Human Resource Management Practices on Productivity: A Case Study of Steel Finishing Line, American Economic Review, vol. 87, no. 3, pp. 291-313.

Janod, V. / Saint-Martin, A. (2004): Measuring the Impact of Work Reorganization on Firm Performance: Evidence from French Manufacturing, 1995-1999, Labour Economics, vol. 11, no. 6, pp. 785-798.

Kalmi, P. / Kauhanen, A. (2008): Workplace Innovation and Employee Outcomes: Evidence from Finland, Industrial Relations, vol. 47, n. 3, pp. 430-459.

Leoni, R. (ed.) (2008): Economia dell'innovazione. Disegni organizzativi, pratiche di gestione delle risorse umane e performance d'impresa, Milano, Franco-Angeli, forthcoming.

Lugli, Loris / Tugnoli, S. (2008): Innovazione e Qualità del Lavoro a Modena, IRES-ER, Materiali, Giugno 2008.

Lynch, L. (2007): The Adoption and Diffusion of Organizational Innovation: Evidence for the U.S. Economy, Discussion Paper no. 2819, IZA, Bonn.

Menezes-Filho, N. / Ulph, D. / Van Reenen, J. (1998): R&D and Unionism: Comparative Evidence from British Companies and Establishments, Industrial and Labour Relations Review, vol. 52, no. 1, pp. 45-63.

Menezes-Filho, N. / Van Reenen, J. (2003): Unions and Innovation: A Survey of the Theory and Empirical Evidence, in Addison J.T., Schnabel C. (2003): International Handbook of Trade Unions, Cheltenham, Edward Elgar.

Metcalf, D. (2003): Unions and productivity, financial performance and investment: international evidence, in Addison J.T., Schnabel C. (2003) (eds.), International Handbook of Trade Unions, Cheltenham, Edward Elgar, ch.6.

Ramsay, H. / Scholarios, D. / Harley, B. (2000): Employees and >High-Performance Systems: Testing Inside the Black Box, British Journal of Industrial Relations, vol. 38, n. 4, pp. 501-531.

Renaud, S. (2002): Rethinking the Union Membership/Job Satisfaction Relationship: Some Empirical Evidence in Canada, International Journal of Manpower, vol. 23, no. 2, pp. 137-150.

Vidal, M. (2007): Manufacturing Empowerment? 'Employee Involvement' in the Labour Process after Fordism, Socio-Economic Review, n.5, pp. 197-232.

Wood, S. (1999): Getting the Measure of the Transformed High Performance Organization, British Journal of Industrial Relations, vol. 37, no. 3, pp. 391-417.

Zwick, T. (2004): Employee Participation and Productivity, Labour Economics, vol. 11, no. 6, pp. 715-740.

Innovation and work quality. A field research.

Loris Lugli, Stefano Tugnoli

Objectives

The changes that are under way in the national and local production systems make the object of studies by scholars interested in micro-enterprise aspects, from at least three points of view: technological change, organization and industrial relations. In particular, as far as Italy is concerned, the debate focuses on the loss of competitiveness as against its main European competitors, especially in terms of a slower growth of productivity, which entails, on one hand, the shrinking of our export market share, and on the other hand, of real wages[1].

Both widely shared diagnoses and solutions have been suggested about the loss of competitiveness of the Italian industrial system and, in particular, of its slow growth of productivity. As far as the diagnosis is concerned, reference has been made to issues like the specialization of the Italian industrial system in mature goods and technologies, the small size of enterprises, external diseconomies due to the poor quality of infrastructures, etc., and last but not least the rigidity of the labour market; As far as the solutions are concerned, there is a wide consensus about the need to enhance the quality of infrastructure services, increase investments in research and development, raise the skilling level of labour force, reduce margins and increase work flexibility[2]. These solutions are undoubtedly grounded. Yet, there is now greater convergence in focusing not only on the so-called intangible factors, i.e. those resources that are not built in capital goods (e.g. machines), but especially on the way in which work is used[3]. The way in which the work resource is used encompasses all those organization solutions that foster learning processes, employee involvement and participation: these approaches enhance co-operation between employees, their *problem solving* attitude, the continuous reproduction and improvement of skills (*learning organization*), the reduction of intermediate hierarchies and a greater decision-making power for employees, continuous training etc. All these aspects refer to a theoretical

1 For a more comprehensive analysis of this issue please refer to: A. Accornero, N. Acocella and others, *Per un nuovo Patto sociale sulla produttività e crescita*, www.pattosociasle. altervista.org.

2 Ibidem.

3 Being convinced that: "machines, although sophisticated, cannot replace the knowledge, will and determination of those who use them." In, ibidem.

proposal of work organization leading to high labour involvement workplaces (*High Performance Work Organization*)[4].

These aspects call into question the role played by industrial relations as a way to support change, also to avoid a rhetoric of labour involvement that is exclusively addressed to work subordination and subject to unilateral decisions made by enterprises.

In addition to the importance attached to the intangible factors as competitiveness drivers, research has focused on the need that technological innovation and organization is implemented according to "clusters"[5]. In other words, for the innovative strategy to be effective in terms of enhancing the productivity of enterprises, without exclusively focusing on work pressure or the mere numerical flexibility, it should envisage a simultaneous technological and organizational change, supported by an industrial relations system that allows the use of labour force according to the HPWO theoretical approach.

The main hypothesis has been verified on the field, in compliance with the previous prerequisites in order to assess whether work conditions and quality, measured in terms of professional content, independent decision-making power, participation, access to training, etc., do match HR management styles, organization models, industrial relations and innovative trends high profile products and manufacturing processes. In particular, the accent will be laid upon the behaviour of enterprises oriented towards work quality enhancement, both at collective and individual level.

Secondly, it will be necessary to explore whether "virtuous circles" exist between work quality and technical and organizational innovations going hand in hand with the attainment of premium economic performance levels.

The field research has consequently focused on the collection of information in four different areas: first of all, the technical and organization change; secondly the themes of various forms of work flexibility, thirdly, the changes in work conditions following the changes in production and work organization, fourthly the recent evolution and features of industrial relations.

More specifically, the survey has highlighted the following items:

a) General features of enterprises, competitive strategies and economic results (size, trade name, product and markets, evolution of turnover and of other *performance* indicators, etc.);
b) Employment structure with reference to qualifications and gender; forms of labour flexibility and labour contracts;

---

4 The HPWO acronym is often used.
5 R. Leoni, "Il crollo della produttività in Italia", in, *Quaderni di rassegna sindacale,* n. 4. 2007.

c) training (beneficiaries, format, contents, frequency, bargaining/incentives for training, etc.);
d) product and process technological innovations ("radical" or incremental innovations, innovation sources, relationships with suppliers and customers, difficulties in the innovation process, relationships with institutions, research centres, etc.);
e) production and work organization changes (subcontracting policies, forms of participation in subcontracting networks; innovative organization practices: quality circles, group production, etc.; innovative organization practices related to work activities: task turnover, skill enhancement, greater independence in individual or group work, etc.);
f) adoption of information and communication technologies (ICT);
g) work conditions and their evolution (assessment of work changes in various ways: safety, intensity, independence, incentives, participation, etc.);
h) pace of evolution of industrial relations (level of trade unions' involvement in various aspects of the corporate strategy, contents of collective bargaining, formal, informal and individual bargaining, atmosphere of trade relations, etc.).

Methodology

Field research was carried out by IRES Emilia Romagna and by Camera del Lavoro Territoriale of Modena on a sample of enterprises in the manufacturing sector with more than 50 employees[6] in the province of Modena and in the large-scale retail trade. The methodology and the main objectives of the investigation have been discussed and shared at the profit committee level, after an in-depth discussion with the local and branch trade union secretaries of the province of Modena.

The main investigation tool – in addition to a set of preliminary interviews – was a questionnaire based on closed questions addressed to the unitary union

6 A similar methodological approach has been used as the one that was adopted in the province of Reggio Emilia in a survey that was carried out by prof. P.Pini and promoted by the Camera del Lavoro Territoriale of that province in 2004 and carried out in collaboration with CREIC (Centro di Ricerca sull'Economia dell'Innovazione e della Conoscenza – Research Centre on Innovation and Knowledge Economy) of the University of Ferrara. We decided to narrow the scope of action on local units with more than 50 employees unlike the survey that was carried out in the province of Reggio Emilia on companies with more than 20 employees, since we believed that, given the complexity of the questionnaire and the need to identify sufficiently well defined strategies by enterprises and structured industrial relations, the 50 employee threshold seemed to be a better choice also in the light of the representation difficulties experienced by micro enterprises.

representative bodies (URB). IRES researchers and union representatives supported interviewees in filling in the questionnaire during joint meetings. Before the administration of the questionnaire URB discussed the contents of questions with researchers and union representatives to better and fully understand them. Every union representative body, which usually was made up of more members, discussed before replying to each question and in many case further information was asked to the company management.

The information collected by URB can be subdivided into two groups: one referring to structural corporate information, to the economic performance and the corporate competitive and innovative strategies; in this case, union representative bodies referred to corporate sources[7]. In the second group, information concerned work organization, conditions and industrial relations; the information reported by URB is of course based on their perception, but it is anyway of utmost importance to outline an overview of work conditions from the trade union's point of view.

In compliance with the scope of the survey, the questionnaire was mainly intended to collect the information concerning URB perception about changes in the work conditions, and to deepen the industrial relations question following the organization and technological changes in enterprises.

The enterprises taken into account in the sample

Manufacturing companies with local units (LU) with more than 50 employees located in the province of Modena were taken into account in the sample. Furthermore, as already pointed out, a few local units in the large-scale retail trade, organized in the FILCAMS CGIL union branch, were taken into account. Because of reasons that will be illustrated later on, the sample is not sufficiently big to represent all the enterprises of the sector. Hence, the statistical significance of the sample refers only to manufacturing companies.[8] To compare this survey with other similar ones and with institutional sources, and also due to the limited number of enterprises that were interviewed in a few branches, they have been regrouped in the following traditional CGIL trade branches: all the local food processing enterprises have been regrouped in the food sector, excluding the

7 Of course, the cases where there was little collaboration by the corporate management, there has been a greater degree of subjective interpretation by URBs.

8 According to the ISTAT ATECO 2002 classification, the following sectors have been identified: food, textile, clothing, wood, paper, print, publishing, chemical, metal and mechanic sectors, in addition to other manufacturing activities. No LUs with more than 50 employees were recorded in the province of Modena.

agricultural sector, organized by the FLAI CGIL branch union; the biomedical enterprises have been regrouped in the chemical sector organized by the FIL-CEM CGIL branch union; the manufacturing enterprises have been regrouped in the wood, paper, print and publishing sector organized by the SLC CGIL branch union and by FILLEA CGIL in the wood sector, excluding the building sector; the metal and mechanical sector is represented by FIOM CGIL; the ceramic tile enterprises have been regrouped in the non metalliferous mineral sector represented by FILCEM CGIL; and finally the fashion enterprises have been regrouped in the textile-clothing sector represented by FILTEA CGIL.

Table 1 shows the distribution of local enterprises with more than 50 employees grouped by trade sector and size in the province of Modena according to the 2001 ISTAT census.

Table 1: Number of local manufacturing enterprises grouped by trade sector and number of employees based in the province of Modena.

	Company size				
	50-99	100-249	250-499	>500	total
trade sectors:	v.a (%)	v.a (%)	v.a (%)	v.a (%)	v.a (%)
food	19 (5,1)	19 (5,1)	2 (0,5)	1 (0,3)	41(11,1)
chemical	15 (4,0)	8 (2,2)	0 (0.0)	0 (0.0)	23 (6,2)
wood, paper, print and pub.	13 (3,5)	6 (2,2)	0 (0.0)	0 (0.0)	19 (5,7)
metal and mechanical	97 (26,1)	41 (11,1)	17 (4,6)	5 (1,3)	160 (43,1)
Non-metalliferous mineral	48 (12,9)	31 (8,4)	3 (1,3)	4 (1,1)	99 (26,7)
textile-clothing	21 (5,7)	5 (1,3)	1 (0,3)	0 (0,0)	27 (7,3)
total	213 (57,4)	112 (30,2)	36 (9,7)	10 (2,7)	371 (100,0)

Source: 2001 ISTAT census

As can be observed, two main manufacturing sectors are located in Modena, which account together for about 70% of industrial enterprises with more than 50 employees: i.e. the metal and mechanical sector with 43,1% of L.U. and the non metalliferous mineral (ceramic tile) sector with 26.7% of L.U..; the rest includes textile-clothing, food, chemical (Biomedical) and wood, paper, print and publishing enterprises.

Enterprises with less than 100 employees account for 57% of the total and with more than 500 employees only 2.7%.

For our study purposes the sample has been selected from the world of manufacturing enterprises with more than 50 employees with the presence of a unitary union representative body (URB). As above-mentioned, in our study we have decided to interview the unitary union representative body members, because we were particularly interested in the URB perception of the issues under study.

Table 2 shows the LU structure, with URBs grouped by sector and size in compliance with the above mentioned census data. In the province of Modena two LU out of three, with more than 50 employees, have an elected union representative body. The URB presence strongly depends on the size of the plant, since almost half of the LU with less than 100 employees has an elected URB, whereas almost all LU with more than 250 employees have chosen their representative body; hence, in most LU with an URB there is a an under-representation of smaller companies and an overrepresentation of larger sized companies: for instance, LU with less than 100 employees with an URB account for 41.9% as against 57.4% of the set of enterprises taken into account in the ISTAT census. From the sector point of view, in the world of LU with an URB there is an overrepresentation of the mechanical and chemical sectors, whereas there is an under-representation of the textile-clothing and non metalliferous mineral (ceramic tile) sectors.

In absolute terms, during the second quarter of 2007, the questionnaire was administered to 246 LU belonging to the manufacturing sector; to 7 local units with an URB belonging to the large-scale retail trade. Yet, this cannot be regarded as a representative sample of the sector because of the method used to build this data.

Table 2: The world of local manufacturing enterprises with an URB grouped by trade sector and number of employees based in the province of Modena

	Company size				
	50-99	100-249	250-499	>500	total
trade sectors:	v.a (%)	v.a (%)	v.a (%)	v.a (%)	v.a (%)
food	9 (3,7)	16 (6,5)	0 (0,0)	2 (0,8)	27 (11,0)
chemical	8 (3,3)	12 (4,9)	4 (1,6)	1 (0,4)	25 (10,2)
wood, paper, print and pub.	7 (2,8)	6 (2,4)	2 (0.8)	1 (0.4)	16 (5,7)
metal and mechanical	61 (24,8)	36 (14,6)	14 (5,7)	5 (2,0)	116 (47,2)
Non-metalliferous mineral	12 (4,9)	25 (10,2)	7 (2,8)	7 (2,8)	51 (20,7)
textile-clothing	6 (2,4)	4 (1,6)	1 (0,4)	0 (0,0)	11 (4,5)
total	103 (41,9)	99 (40,2)	28 (11,4)	16 (6,5)	246(100,0)

The administration of the questionnaire was carried out between the second and fourth quarter of 2007[9] with a supplementary investigation to better balance the sample, during the early months of 2008.

It should be pointed out that in spite of the difficulties that have been encountered, the questionnaire, which is made up of nine sections[10], has met our expec-

9 In addition to summer holidays other stops occurred during the survey due to important trade union deadlines throughout the year 2007.

tations in terms of timing, sample coverage rate and response rate. The questionnaires that have been returned account for 71.5% of the world of LU with an URB in the manufacturing sectors, in addition to 7 more questionnaires concerning the large-scale retail trade for a total of 183 LU, 176 out of which in the manufacturing sector[11]. In terms of the number of employees, the sample has concerned 31,878 employees out of a total of 50,362 employees.

Table 3 shows the structure of the manufacturing LU sample that have been interviewed and that have been grouped by size and trade sector. If we compare the structure of the sample with the ISTAT data, Table 1, and with the world of local manufacturing enterprises with an URB, Table 2, it clearly emerges that the structure of the sample that has been surveyed is closer to the ISTAT data than to the reference context[12] for the administration of the questionnaires. In other words, the sample that has been surveyed seems to be more statistically representative than the structure of the world of local manufacturing enterprises with more than 50 employees regardless of the presence of an URB.

Table 3: Sample of the local manufacturing enterprises with an URB grouped by trade sector and number of employees based in the province of Modena

	Company size				
	50-99	100-249	250-499	>500	total
trade sectors:	v.a (%)	v.a (%)	v.a (%)	v.a (%)	v.a (%)
food	9 (3,7)	16 (6,5)	0 (0,0)	2 (0,8)	27 (11,0)
chemical	8 (3,3)	12 (4,9)	4 (1,6)	1 (0,4)	25 (10,2)
wood, paper, print and pub.	7 (2,8)	6 (2,4)	2 (0.8)	1 (0.4)	16 (5,7)
metal and mechanical	61 (24,8)	36 (14,6)	14 (5,7)	5 (2,0)	116 (47,2)
Non-metalliferous mineral	12 (4,9)	25 (10,2)	7 (2,8)	7 (2,8)	51 (20,7)
textile-clothing	6 (2,4)	4 (1,6)	1 (0,4)	0 (0,0)	11 (4,5)
total	103 (41,9)	99 (40,2)	28 (11,4)	16 (6,5)	246(100,0)

10 The following sections have been identified: a) the Union Representation Body fact sheet; b) company information; c) flexible labour contracts and employment; d) training; e) technology and product innovations; f) corporate organization and labour changes; g) information and communication technologies (ICT); h) work conditions; i) trade relations and bargaining.

11 The sample of manufacturing enterprises that were interviewed accounted for 47% of all the ISTAT companies according to the 2001 census.

12 This is due to a delay in the collection of questionnaires in smaller local units and to a difficulty in the collection of questionnaires in the mechanical sector that balanced the overrepresentation of the sector between the local units and the URBs.

Hence, if we take the ISTAT universe into account, the greater gap between the sample and the reference context concerns the under-representation of LU with less than 100 employees and an overrepresentation of the immediately successive group of enterprises. From the sector point of view, the sample seems to be extremely balanced with slight deviations – +/-2% – from the ISTAT universe except for the chemical sector.

The response rate to individual questions has generally been very high just like the level of consistency of replies.

Main conclusions

The field investigation has confirmed that the most innovative and generally lager enterprises feature a change pattern characterized by both technological and organization innovation, and a high degree of implementation of information and communication technologies (ICT). Furthermore, training is always present and more structured in innovative contexts, thus becoming the true *driver* of change. It can therefore be observed that the most dynamic companies adopt more innovative "cluster" approaches.

Furthermore, the close link that results from the adoption of individual innovative strategies and the presence of higher performance seems to be corroborated by the fact that when more innovative "cluster" approaches are undertaken, more successful and competitive economic results are achieved.

It has also clearly emerged that the competitive strategies implemented by enterprises have an impact on the choice of innovative approaches and on the likelihood to achieve more successful economic results. As a matter of fact, the implementation of quality-oriented and high technology strategies is more likely to lead to customer satisfaction and it is fundamental in leading to high innovative standards in all the areas that have been taken into account (technology, organization, training, etc.), and to successful economic results. Whereas, instead of high road, if low-road competitive strategies, centred on low prices are implemented poor results are attained.

The main conclusion drawn by our investigation – which is often neglected by similar analyses – allows us to put in context the role of IR with reference to the ongoing changes in the manufacturing system and their impact on economic performance. The field research findings once again point out that the presence of a virtuous circle[13] between high IR profiles and the rate of technological (in-

---

13 Similar results were reached by the survey that had been carried out in Reggio Emilia in 2004, as already mentioned. see P. Pini (2007).

cluding ICT) and organization change, on the one hand, and of the presence of widespread and well structured training policies, on the other hand, may lead to a better employment and economic performance. IR play a fundamental role in supporting the implementation of innovative change and in achieving satisfactory competitive performance levels when they are designed as a factual participatory and involvement tool, rather than merely like a formal tool, at the disposal of trade unions and employees in decision-making in the area of HR management.

Of course the question of employee participation in view of a further development of industrial democracy is not covered by the scope of this analysis, since further institutional and regulatory aspects should be taken into account when analysing the role played by labour within enterprises.

Nevertheless, two critical points should be highlighted. First of all the widespread and merely numerical use of work flexibility "escaping" from URB control, also in contexts characterized by good industrial relations, and in companies with a high innovative profile, with the consequent exclusion of a large number of employees from continuous training opportunities. It is true that in the short term this does not lead to relevant problems in terms of available highly skilled human resources, but in the long run it might lead to a dearth of highly skilled human resources, since the retraining mechanisms are no longer put in place.

The second critical point, emerging from our research, is that the abovementioned virtuous circle does not always imply an improvement of work conditions, even when highly positive trade relations where matched by a high technological innovation. Form this point of view it has been proven that work pressure prevails on organization models that foster independence and skills enhancement.

We need to underline the absence, in the present debate, on the loss of competitiveness of our economy, of the regulatory role that might be played by industrial relations with reference to the introduction of innovations and support fostering the dissemination of an organization model that would be likely to enhance work.

"Hybrid Participation" – the missing link? The role of expert employees and support groups for the works councils in Germany

Karina Becker, Ulrich Brinkmann, Thomas Engel

1. Participation – a response to artistic and social critiques

2008 saw the anniversary of 1968 and has thrown up some interesting questions, one them asking why different social groups frequently fail to get into communication to each other though they are in at least general agreement on the critical view they take of capitalism. In their major review of "The Spirit of Capitalism" Luc Boltanski and Eve Chiapello (2005, abbreviated below as B+C) made an attempt to conceptualise this phenomenon, dividing the critiques into different types. It is common to all approaches in the types of critique that they are nourished by distinct "sources of indignation" concerning both the form and the content of capitalist society-building, which are then expressed in the corresponding theoretical and political terms. Thus the "artistic" (sometimes cited in English as "romantic") type of critique grows up around the pillars erected by the antiauthoritarians among the activists of 1968: especially the conceptual pillars of "oppression" and of "lack of authenticity". This type grows on the ideological soil, in which the bourgeoisie is accumulating capital on principles which require to "meticulous forethought, rational management of space and time, and a quasi-obsessive pursuit of production for production's sake" (B+C, p. 37ff.).

The other type, that of "social" critique, has its roots in the labour movement which itself grew up in socialist and Christian traditions seething with indignation at "the egoism of private interests in bourgeois society" and "the growing poverty of the popular classes in a society of unprecedented wealth" (B+C, p. 82).

These two types of criticism are not, by nature, compatible with each other; indeed, there are multifarious points of friction between them which tend to result in the inability of one side to speak to the other. Boltanski and Chiapello cite as an example the way social critique "rejects" artistic critique, accusing it of "immorality or moral neutrality, the individualism, and even the egoism or egotism of artists" (B+C, p. 38), while the artistic side is repelled by the social critique's interest in bourgeois economic ways of life and its acceptance of bureaucratically organised and planned systems, even though the movement had once started with a critical stance towards this.

This thought, applied to organisational aspects of a company, means that criticism will express itself "primarily in terms of a demand for security (as regards the social critique) and a demand for autonomy (as regards the artistic critique" (B+C, p. 171). And, in the end, if they are applied to questions of employee participation, the two types of logic can be roughly allocated to the features of co-determination on the one hand and of works-level direct participation on the other.

The latter variant, of direct participation, has actually been brought in for certain companies since the 1980s by consultants and managerial supporters of new management theories underlying lean production and human resource approaches (Dörre 2002). It also serves to fulfil the wish of many groups of employees for voluntary, temporarily involvement in projects concerning operations or their workplace. That wish is often viewed less than favourably by the established representatives of co-determination because they see a threat to their success, now stable but so hard fought for, or to their set up power positions. As a result mutual accusations are often at hand. From one set of critics to the works councils "representationalism (Stellvertreterpolitik) is behind the times"; and in response, the claim that those critics are "blind to the company's power structure".

A glance at history reveals that such mutual reproaches and misinterpreting need not be the case. Even Boltanski and Chiapello suggest that the common factors of indignation need not cancel each other out. It is the basic argument of this paper that the new forms of "hybrid participation" (Brinkmann and Speidel 2006) adopted into the IndRA with the latest legislative change in 2001 could function as a hinge between the two blocks, institutional co-determination and direct participation. Co-determination as a manifestation of the principles of the social type of critique aims to guarantee social and biographical security against threats to workers from market conditions and so to construct "stable intertemporal links" to "ensure people's continuity between their current condition and potential future conditions" (B+C, p. 171). Some of the relevant issues concerned are remuneration, working hours and occupational health; the procedures are conducted through formal democratic elections and the principles of representation. In contrast, the artistic type of critique goes all out for liberating the potential of humans for "autonomy, self-organisation and creativity" (B+C, p. 40). The intention is to arouse the employees for "running their own affairs", for developing "demands for autonomy and self-management" (B+C, p. 170), or for direct participation at the workplace. Such an approach opposes any form of "paternalism, authoritarianism, compulsory work schedules, prescribed tasks, the Taylorist separation between design and execution, and, more generally, the division of work" (B+C, p. 170).

Linking artistic and social types of criticism in the field of worker participation thus is a challenge of combining demands for autonomy with the means of established procedures in the institutional hierarchy of power and management, or, in other words, making room for direct participation without at the same time jeopardising sound, established standards. This principle can cover almost all work-related issues, from those of categorising workers to ensure fulfilment of central collective agreements (Eingruppierung), right through to the company-level agreements on working hours, and beyond that to legally required risk assessments.

The new instruments for participation (§ 80, 2 (3) und § 28a), included in the revised German IndRA, offer the possibility of managing the challenges in these and other fields through management by representatives of various interest groups and raising the level of direct participation. If the idea of combining social and artistic types of critique by applying specific models of participation can, indeed, take hold, these instruments of hybrid participation should be welcomed by the relevant actors on the company-level. In fact, there is evidence that this wind of change is already blowing. Below, empirical data is offered on the basis of the latest WSI survey of works councils in 2007; which, however, reveals certain difficulties, too.

Thus this text not only points out that there is a chance of responding to both the artistic and the social types of critique by means of hybrid participation where works councils still have a leading function, but moreover that it implies possibilities for a reinforcement of works councils.

In an additional aspect the paper deals with the relation between the processes of reorganisation and the degree of openness in companies towards forms of hybrid participation. Research in company reorganisation processes indicate that management strategies directed at market orientation (cost-cutting programmes, centre-building, decentralisation or the like) do encourage innovative ideas on participation, if the benefits of positive experience from earlier" modernisation alliances", which involved some participation, are transferred not only on the side of the management but also on the side of the workers' representatives (cf. Martens 1997, 443 ff.).

Lenhart and Rosenbrock (2006) take a specific example of how operations are organised in companies and show that restructuring also facilitates concessions in the direction of the more up-to-date, i.e. participative, practice in occupational safety and health. When the workers and their representatives at company level are more inclined to negotiate compromises, this opens up, for the restructuring process, not only potential means of participative decision and action, as policies likely to be favoured by the workers, but also improved practice in occupational safety and health, so that this is "at times better than in companies which have been 'spared' any such restructuring" (ibid, 123). Thus it is worth discussing whether workers' participation approaches, in which interest groups are represented, might well also benefit from any restructuring processes.

2. Two modes of participation envisaged in the IndRA

It is a mark of those forms of participation, initiated by works councils, that the workers involve themselves both creatively in forms of autonomy and direct participation, but also in the parts of company policy, which are a response to the social type of critique, the works council even serving as a catalyst for "direct" participation. From the point of view of the works council this approach can serve to strengthen their effectiveness and thus reduce the risk of the management's using participation in a one-sided way for its own purposes.

Both forms of participation presented in this paper are to be found in the IndRA as revised in 2001. § 80, section 2, sentence 3 of the Act lays down that the works councils can, to support their work, co-opt experts from the workforce. The idea contributed by the employers to the legislative process was principally that the works council should not start by making use of external experts under the IndRA but by first using "internal expertise". Effectively, the general duty of the employer to inform was thereby extended (§ 80, 2 (1)), and, correspondingly, the right of the works council to be informed.

Case law as given by the BAG (the German national industrial tribunal) in 1987 and 1992 had already put into words the idea of using experts from among the workers to help fulfil the duties of the works councils; since 2001 there has been full legal underpinning for this. The initiative lies with the works council, as does the right to decide on how and to what extent the internal experts chosen should be involved. That involvement may only be refused by management for reasons of "economic necessity" and for a certain short period (cf. Becker and Thomas, 2005; Becker, Kunz and Schneider, 2002; Brinkmann and Speidel, 2006; Gramm, 2005).

In § 28a there is a provision that works councils may transfer their tasks under the Act partly to working parties. The basic idea of this paragraph is similar to that relating to "expert employees", the use of internal sources of knowledge. Such working parties ("support groups"), however, are capable of even more than simply support the immediate tasks of the works council in a specific project. Support groups which have been given delegated rights can, for instance, make agreements on behalf of the group which are similar to company-level agreements. Unlike that of expert employees, who are subject to legal protection against discrimination or dismissal, the legal position of support groups co-opted under § 28a is not, it must be said, absolutely clear (cf. Hromadka and Maschmann, 2007; Busch, 2003). To give them the same level of protection as that secured in § 80, 2 (3) (company-wide) agreements must have been made with the employer in advance.

The freedom of movement ensured by the two legal instruments of participation is thus revealed as of different scope and extent for each. As a result they also differ in their practical applicability. From the union side, the disadvantages are seen as being that "internal rules of procedure" is lacking for the support groups and that members might be exposed to pressure.

The nationally representative WSI-survey[1] of works councils in German companies with a staff of over 20 people contained items dealing with forms of hybrid participation for the first time in 2007. The responses to these questions permit an overview of the methods and extent of use of expert employees and of support groups since the IndRA of 2001 made its legal provisions.

These special questions about hybrid participation, placed at the survey, are a matter of particular interest for the PARGEMA project[2]. Further interviews carried out in the PARGEMA project of the University of Jena's Institute of Sociology underline the quantitative findings.

3. Expert employees and support groups within the work of works councils

61% of the works councils surveyed were unfamiliar with either regulation; about a third of those questioned (28% for § 80, 2 (3) or 35% for § 28a) said they were aware of the relevant part of the Act. Of those "aware", 64% make use of the instrument allowing expert employees (§ 80, 2 (3)) and 39% allowing support groups (§ 28a) to help them with the work of the works council. When this is related to the entire sample, 18% and 14% of the actors in companies (with works councils and employing more than 20 people) are aware of the new participation options in the IndRA as revised in 2001 and have made use of them at least once in their actual work (cf. Fig. 1).

The first conclusion to be drawn is that knowledge and conscious use of the newly created participation instruments is relatively high seven years after the law came into force. The awareness that it is possible to set up support groups is higher, but there is significantly less inclination to make use of the option. In contrast, the possibility of co-opting employees as experts seems to be less well known, though the rate of use by those who know it is considerably higher.
The existence of these preferences can be construed as an indication of the practicability of the instruments; also as a (related) strategy used by works councils

1 WSI stands for the German name of the institute of economic and social science of the Hans-Böckler-Stiftung. The institute of that foundation deals with co-determination and research linked to the world of work. The annual survey explores different topics of the work of works councils, it´s interrogating about 2.000 people.

2 PARGEMA stands for the German name of the project, meaning participative occupational health management. It is funded by the Federal Education Ministry: see also www.pargema.de. This project is handled by 6 institutional partners, two of them are the University of Jena in cooperation with the WSI.

in their approach to delegating decision-making authority on certain issues to other employees. The arguments against support groups of this kind are the efforts of coordination procedures and concerns about the loss of decision-making freedom for the works councils. The arguments for using expert employees are, firstly, the possibility of smoother communication between individuals and, secondly, the supervision that is maintained over the whole decision-making sequence and project implementation. The council is still "in charge" (cf. Brinkmann et al. 2008, 133 – who cite this and other features of hybrid participation in relation to the power and freedom to negotiate vested in the works council).

Figure 1: Knowledge and Usage of Hybrid Participation

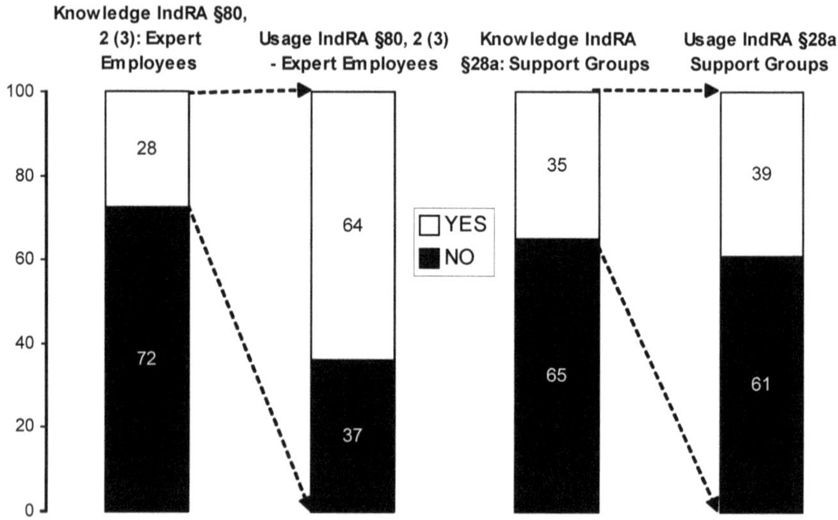

Share in %, Source: WSI-Survey of Works Councils 2007, own calculations)

As far as variations between East and West Germany or between different branches of industry are concerned, little difference is found on awareness and use of the two forms of participation, but the size of the company seems to make a considerable difference. In the majority of cases where a works council represents fewer than 200 employees, neither regulation is known. In companies with 20 to 49 employees (a category into which almost 60% of German companies fit) two thirds (65.7%) are aware of neither type of participation method under the IndRA. There is a significant increase in awareness and use as the size of the company increases.

Works councils for companies where the workers are mainly organised in smaller or medium-sized unions such as TRANSNET (railway), GEW (education) or IG BCE (chemical industrie, energy) show evidence of above average awareness of the new ordinances on these forms of participation. This is usually due to the detailed training given to members by these organisations. Works councils in companies with a higher degree of unionisation also tend to show better awareness and use of the two regulations. Unionisation is clearly a background factor in the extent to which the new forms of participation are applied.

It is interesting to note the actual ways, in which this takes place. Expert employees are primarily co-opted in situations requiring health and safety projects (61% of respondents who both know and use § 80, 2 (3)) and/or planning of work time (56%) and/or organisation of work (52%). In the case of support groups appointed under § 28a, the subjects are similar, though the order of importance given is slightly different (cf. Fig. 2).[3] It is also noticeable that there are many subjects and combinations of subjects which expert employees and support groups help with. These forms of participation are thus clearly suitable for assisting with a wide range of workplace policies.[4]

---

3 Processes implementing new agreements on wage assorting (like ERA) play a less significant but not irrelevant role in this specific connection (36%/38% of all mentions, with strong differences between the unions who mainly represent the employees of the companies, e.g. 59%/59% of all IG-Metall-companies. Background: ERA is one of the most important campaigns of the IG Metall in the recent years.)

For this item it was possible to mention more than one area and the possibility was frequently used. On average, three project subjects on which expert employees or support groups helped were named by all works councils which used one of the forms of participation with awareness of the legislative position. It is possible to interpret this as a sign of the many cross-functional subjects involved in projects (as when improvements are made to working time as part of a health and safety project); but also simply as a sign that both instruments are frequently used.

Figure 2: Subjects of Hybrid Participation

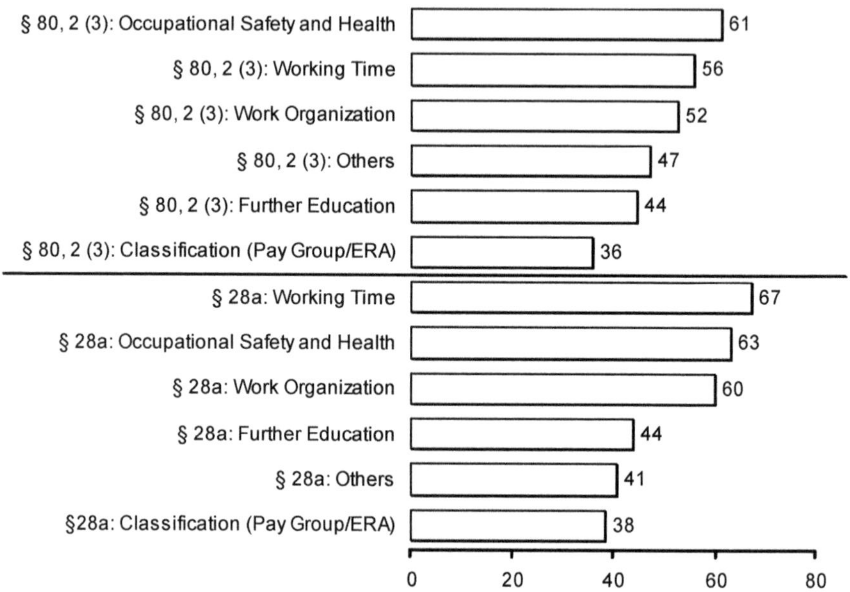

Share in %, Source: WSI-Survey of Works Councils 2007, own calculations

4. Contractual works agreements and conflicts with the management

There are a number of factors influencing the degree to which a participation project requires formalisation in the works: for example, the policy on communicative relations between management and works council (whether the culture is conflict-oriented or consensus-oriented – cf. Bosch, Ellguth and Schmidt et al. 1999), the experience already obtained in worker participation and participation-oriented skills resulting from it, but also the understanding that works councils have of their role (like e.g. as co-managers or as representatives). In a mechanical engineering company, which had already been successful in using the participation instrument § 80, 2 (3) with a contractual agreement on working hours two years before, the interaction of informal and formalised participation was evaluated as follows by the chair of the works council: "If there is no resistance to my co-opting colleagues to assist with my work, I don't need a contractual agreement. Right now we are granted plenty of scope and so there would be nothing to be gained by a formal agreement. Indeed, it would only end up restricting us. That is not to say that we might not one day have to make a formal contract. But, meanwhile, the motto is, 'Anything not forbidden is allowed'."

The new legislation has given works councils a legal base for a type of practice which had certainly been used previously. Workers' representatives have always, with more or less enthusiasm, sought participation by employees who, with their specific knowledge and as the experts in their own field, could provide information to support decisions which are part of the works councils' tasks. The question arises, however, whether this legalisation has led to a formalisation of participation – do the works councils now refer closely to the legal basis, for example by documenting the fact in the form of formal contractual agreements on the participation process with the management. This notwithstanding, it can be assumed that people are adopting "a wide range of practices in the use of the participation instrument" (Brinkmann and Speidel, 2006: p. 89): "Legally institutionalised conditions of a uniform nature do not necessarily bring with them uniform company practice" (ibid.). As shown before: Rules which have been reliably enacted can also reduce the necessity for formalised works agreements.

Indeed, the following survey result suggests just that. In 92% and 91% of companies which have had experience in using the expert employee and/or support group instruments, *no* works agreements were signed in association (cf. Fig.3) – the works councils can rely on the power of law (IndRA) in the background.

Figure 3: Works Agreement about Hybrid Participation

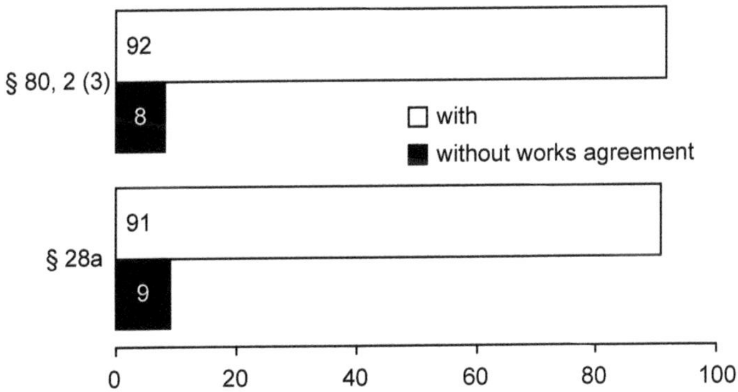

Share in %, Source: WSI-Survey of Works Councils 2007, own calculations

The picture of almost exclusively informal practice in using both forms of participation changes if only those companies are selected where this process was carried out in conflict with management concerning the use of the relevant participation option. Formal works agreements are more common in cases of conflict, the percentage of written works agreements for the cooption of expert employees rises from 8% to 14% in the case of companies with experience of conflict. And for support groups the figure is not 9% but 21%.

Thus it is also possible to read this inclination towards formal agreements as a safety mechanism for the employees vis à vis the management to ensure that the legitimacy of participation is actually respected in practice. The legal provision does, after all, as mentioned above, leave the management considerable scope for misuse if it is not comprehensively regulated by means of works agreements.

5. Reinforcing or weakening collective representation?

The revised IndRA was debated in the German Bundestag (Federal Parliament) in 2001. Among the controversial subjects were the two options discussed here as ways of giving employees more say in works organisation. One reason why the employers' representatives gave their assent at that stage was that an alternative was being provided to the previous legal position, in which works councils could take on (expensive) outside consultants to help them fulfil their duties.

The objections felt by the works councils and the union representatives concerned loss of negotiating freedom for people in the established representative structures. If there were to be new actors (like from the staff) appearing on the scene which had, to date, been so clearly set out as the stage for the conduct of industrial relations, there might be a risk of confusion and loss of solidarity among the workers.

The satisfaction expressed, and the intention to continue to use hybrid participation can be seen as indications whether these forms are tending to result in weakening or reinforcement of co-determination and collective representation. There is an assumption in the literature on industrial sociology that successful direct participation by employees is leading in the direction of reinforcement and that there are three areas being strengthened: the works councils which have initiated the participation; union work; and the fulfilment of staff expectations that their views will count in works policy (cf. Martens, 2002; Brinkmann et al., 2008).

The satisfaction expressed to the WSI survey of 2007 concerning the two forms of participation is, though not overwhelming, relatively high at 53% and 62% (cf. Fig. 4). The "marks" given as in school reports (1, excellent through to 5, poor) suggest likewise: 2.4 or 2.3. Actual dissatisfaction is expressed by only a very few respondents.

Intention to make use of the regulations in future can be taken as an indication of valued use and practicability of the instruments. Here it is interesting to note the divergence between the two variants. 70% of the respondents plan to use expert employees to support the works council in its duties in future, only 34% express the wish to speed up the formation of support groups (cf. Fig. 4). This is obviously the effect of the inadequacies in § 28a described above which are preventing effective use with stronger leadership from workers' representatives. The chairman of the works council in a mechanical engineering company explains the logic of preferring expert employees to support groups in this way: "If I need a support group, I can form it by co-opting several expert employees. I don't need the points in Paragraph 28 for that, and they aren't as good a protection for my people as the rule in Paragraph 80, 2 (3). Members of support groups always have to worry whether they are making a noose for themselves by getting involved. For expert employees, the access the management can have to them under the legislation is much clearer: the answer, during the period of the works council project, is 'none at all'."

Figure 4: Commitment to Hybrid Participation

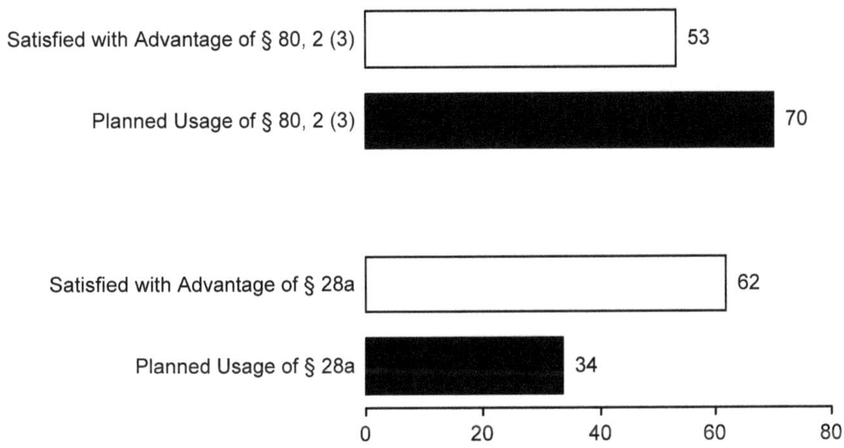

(Share in %, Source: WSI-Survey of Works Councils 2007, own calculations)

Experience gained in using the instrument of participation strongly affects the decision whether to declare oneself in favour of further use. This factor is strong in relation to § 80, 2 (3): for 84% of works councils which have already made use of expert employees, their further use is indubitable. However, only just over half (52%) of those who have obtained no experience with the instrument would say the same thing.

The variation is not so extreme in respect of using support groups under § 28a, but it does exist and, surprisingly, has an opposite implication. In this case, it is the respondents with no previous experience in relying on § 28a who say a little more frequently that they are planning to form a support group (36% as against an average of 33%).

Another surprising aspect of this finding, which is challenging to interpret, is that the satisfaction with the use of support groups comes out as greater than that with the co-opting of expert employees. Satisfaction with how such forms of participation have been applied may be recorded as high, but if the conditions for their use are difficult and the stumbling blocks in the way of the actual practice are dominant, then that will possibly have a negative effect on planning of further use. Or, in other words, with hindsight one knows more and can weigh a satisfactory result against the perceived investment of effort and the risks inherent in the procedure, so that one would prefer not to repeat the experience. It is, however, just those forms of participation which offer the employee less protection and security under the law that will have less chance of reuse.

With respect to expert employees, the results show more favourable experience of conflict on the subject with the management than of conflict with other employees. There is, at least, no evidence of avoidance of the option because of difficulties in convincing the management of its value. The decisive factor for both the success recorded and the future strategies on participation is, indeed, the fact that the employees view their experience of these forms of participation as having been positive.

It will be of relevance to discussions on whether they lead to weakening or reinforcement of collective representation that works councils are laying the foundations of greater acceptance for such representation by adopting these models of participation and, through the positive results, removing any staff doubts. It is when the participation is not ephemeral, "here today and gone tomorrow", that the role of the works council will be reinforced. Of the two instruments, however, each is not equally suitable for the direct and effective involvement of employees. While satisfaction with the results obtained from participation is high to very high in the majority of cases, the future use of the two regulations here investigated is predicted in very different terms. There is definitely a higher approval rating for approaches, in which individual employees are co-opted as experts in their field and then for formal support groups. The factors being weighed by the works councils in their cost-benefit analysis may well be the greater effort involved in setting up support groups and the gaps in the job security aspects revealed in § 28a as compared with § 80, 2 (3). Despite this, there is clearly no doubt of the effectiveness of hybrid participative strategies as here investigated; i.e., the specific features of the participation models examined have no influence on the strengthening or reinforcing character of hybrid participation.

6. Support organizing unions strategies?

Over the last 20 years, membership of trades unions in many OECD countries has dropped dramatically. In explanation, many factors can be cited and it is likely that analysis and discussion will continue in the coming years despite the fact that the drop recently seems to be levelling off. One of the main causes recurrently debated is the "traditional dominance of purely representative forms of participation" (Brinkmann et al., 2008: p. 129).

Dropping membership has, however, generated another fruitful subject of debate which names factors with a prospect of success for trade union organisation. The discussion has been conducted mainly in the English-speaking countries, but there are certain approaches in Germany, too, which are intended to contribute to policies, that may revive union involvement. Topics are whether collective representation policy can be newly configured to encourage greater identification with unions and their ideals and thus to attract new union members. This article now turns to the question of whether hybrid participation may extend beyond the reinforcement of the power in collective representation and be made use of to encourage trades union organisation.

At this point an example is presented of a company where expert employees have been systematically involved in two, now completed, projects after being co-opted under § 80, 2 (3) of the IndRA. The company's positive economic performance was helpful in the introduction of the hybrid participation, as was a change in management. The new CEO was open to participation from the moment he appeared, as this would provide him with a clearer picture of the operational situation. "The new one wants to profit from people's ideas because no-one is more knowledgeable about the specific work situation than the person who does the job. He is not hung up about using new methodology. It would have been *lèse-majesté* in the case of the previous one. The new one is also honest and trustworthy." (Thus speaks the chairman of the works council.)

The works council had previously been on the classic lines until IG-Metall union membership suffered setbacks at the end of the 90s. Poor results in elections to the works council, low turnout, and newly elected members from an opposing trade union (the "Christian Metals Union") with a closer relationship to the management had had an impact on the works council. The moment of truth came when a warning strike organised by IG-Metall clearly demonstrated that this union no longer had enough support among the staff.

The works council's policies needed to take another direction: "No longer in the direction of stubborn opposition to management and their policies, but of the really important subject, the staff". With a degree of self-criticism the chairman also records that "we hadn't really been involving people but had tended only to ask the questions we already knew the answers to." As he saw it, it was necessary to make the work of representation more transparent to the employees by a more consistent policy which offered participation, and to bring them closer to the unions by thus involving them in decision-making.

The works council had a positive experience of the use of hybrid participation by taking part in an initial project. Expert employees co-opted under § 80, 2 (3) of the IndRA contributed to the making of a works agreement on a completely new model of working hours. The decisive factor was that several employees were able to acquire participation skills by means of a training procedure. Other factors in the success of participative projects were, in the eyes of the works council, as follows: "conscientious planning and preparation", high input of time in the initial stages, works council relieved of effort in the middle stages and generally improved results. The work on the project had the desired outcome, a new works agreement, and a very positive evaluation after three years of the new timetable, measured by survey at the end of that period. With the new system, the status of the subcommittee (Vertrauensleuteausschuss) of the IG-Metall union improved because of the project, as the subcommittee members also took part.

The second project had to do with health and safety. Here the experience and skills built up in the earlier participation were of benefit. In contrast with the previous project, for which it was felt necessary to set up a works agreement in advance, the use of the participation instrument proceeded in the second case quite informally. Accordingly, it would seem that the crucial factor is the possibility at any stage of calling on the legal provisions, and "that the mere existence of the legal underpinning was frequently enough to enable participation processes to begin among staff where these were in previous years refused from the management side" (Brinkmann et al., 2008: p. 131).

In the course of the health and safety project, the various opportunities of participation found a warm welcome among the staff. One of them said: "Finally you're asking us! Obviously, it is we who are the first to know where the risks in the works are to be found and what could be done about them." The survey response is another indication of the degree of success, for it came out at almost two thirds.

For the works council (according to the chair) there was always a "parallel aim" of attracting potential new members by means of the activities under both projects. The main strategy was to tackle subjects which would improve workplace quality, the subject of the IG-Metall campaign known as "Gute Arbeit" (Deecent Work) (cf. Pickshaus and Urban, 2004). The fact that the alternative union (Christliche Metallgewerkschaft) could not increase its numbers and will (the chairman is sure) lose seats in the next election for the works council, is primarily due to the strategic change of direction in the work of collective representation. It is thus possible to see hybrid participation not only as a good thing in itself but also as an opportunity to pursue union organisation by judicious, strategic choice of content. It is also plainly a matter not only of quantitative but also of qualitative considerations if such a course is to be accompanied by successful unionisation. The case here described serves to illustrate that it has been possible to bring staff closer to ideas and programmes of unionisation.

7. Hybrid participation in the context of restructuring

In the light of the reconciliation between artistic and social critiques mentioned at the beginning of this paper, it is interesting to consider the relationship between corporate restructuring and participation. Companies, or at least their owners and managers, must, namely, find a reliable route to reorganisation and are here the central actors, in whom the decision-making power is vested. A number of strategies present themselves, either more or less promising in their nature: one type is to promote and legitimate the decisions or ask for understanding of the reasoning; frequently, management chooses to dress up reorganisations as due to the force of circumstances. Martens (1997: p. 443 ff.) suspects that there is a strong inclination towards new patterns of participation on the part of the collective representatives when their co-determination has been pushed into the defensive by corporate reorganisation or rationalisation. This may be read as an indication of yet further need to legitimate restructuring decisions by associating them with some independent investigation on the part of the workers themselves, and development of adaptive or practical strategies. Does the survey, indeed, give any indications in support of this suspicion as far as hybrid participation is concerned?

Workers representatives from companies where any such measures as reorganisation, secondment or outsourcing took place in any part of the company between 2005 and 2007 show significantly higher awareness (51%) of at least one of the two regulations than do works councils from companies not thus affected (36% – cf. Fig.5). Likewise, significant differences are observable to a similar degree in the use of the two models of participation. Here there is great variation, depending on which instrument is in question. 74% of reorganising companies use expert employees and 50% use support groups while the figures for the other companies are 56% and 35% respectively. (A test using simulated replication was carried out to assess the effect of company size, This was not negligible but makes no major difference to these findings.)

Figure 5: Hybrid Participation and Restructuring

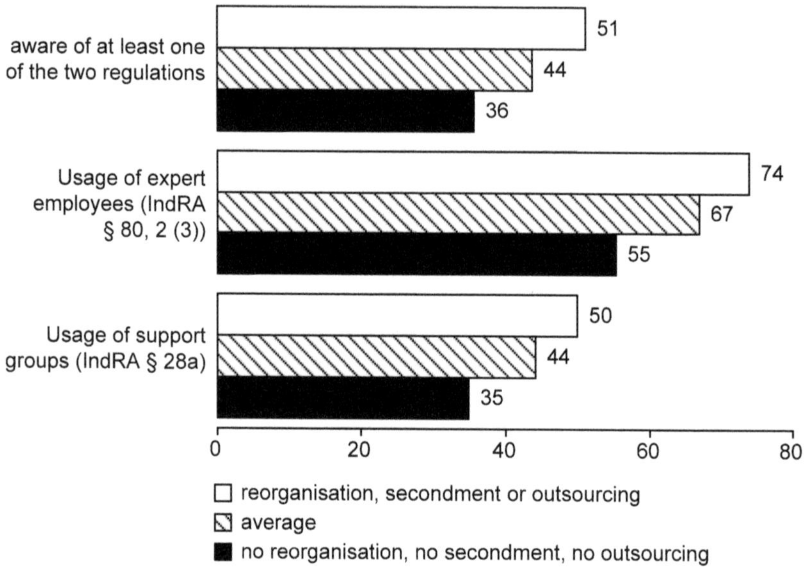

Percentage of respondents, Source: WSI-Survey of Works Councils 2007, authors'own calculations

8. Summary

Boltanski and Chiapello (2005) give an analysis of how employers in the traditional corporate system attempted to interpret the protest associated with 1968 as a "social" critique and to offer appropriate concessions in response. The yearning of employees for autonomy, a form of "artistic" critique, was repulsed, for it was neither compressible into the corseted norms of the hegemony nor susceptible of realisation within the institutional regulatory framework of the day.

Today, it often seems that the tables have been turned. There are many and various (voluntary) forms of participation on offer which have achieved recognition at company level and in society, and yet there are many variants from the social type of critique that fail to fit with the modern spirit of capitalism. It must, however, be admitted that such metamorphoses are clearly an expression of historical power constellations and as such may change again.

The forms of hybrid participation presented are a now proven means, supported by experience, to date, of linking the central notions of the two types of critique, social and artistic. If they are put into effective practice, they are an opportunity to put individual and collective participation on a sound footing for the long term, to bring back onto the agenda the issues from the social sphere (such as health and safety at work) and, at the same time, to give a new force to co-determination, even to win new union members. All in all the findings suggest that hybrid participation could become the missing link between direct participation and institutionalised co-determination to reduce the ambivalent character of participation. It will, nonetheless, be necessary to prove in practice whether, for new departures planned on a participative basis, taking the bandwagon fuelled by the artistic critique, the critique from the social side can really be brought aboard at the same time.

9. Bibliography

Becker, Iris / Kunz, Olaf / Wolfgang Schneider (2002): Die betriebliche Auskunftsperson nach § 80 Abs. 2 Satz 3 BetrVG. In: Arbeitsrecht im Betrieb (9/2002): p. 537-541

Becker, Iris / Thomas, Angelika (2005): Hilfe für den Betriebsrat. Wie sachkundige Arbeitnehmer sinnvoll in die Arbeit des Betriebsrats einbezogen werden können. In: Arbeitsrecht im Betrieb (4/2005): p. 209-213

Becker, Karina / Brinkmann, Ulrich / Engel, Thomas (2007): Die Haut auf dem Markte. Betrieblicher Gesundheitsschutz im Marktkapitalismus. In: PROKLA. Zeitschrift für kritische Sozialwissenschaft Heft 148 (37. Jg., Nr. 3): p. 383-401

Brinkmann, Ulrich / Choi, Hae Lin / Detje, Richard / Dörre, Klaus / Holst, Hajo / Karakayali, Serhat / Neis, Matthias / Schmalstieg, Catharina (2008): Strategic Unionism: Aus der Krise zur Erneuerung? Umrisse eines Forschungsprogramms – Wiesbaden

Brinkmann, Ulrich / Speidel, Frederic (2006): Hybride Beteiligungsformen am Beispiel 'sachkundiger Arbeitnehmer'. In: WSI-Mitteilungen 59 (2): 86-91

Boltanski, Luc / Chiapello, Eve (2005): The New Spirit of Capitalism – London/New York

Bosch, Aida / Ellguth, Peter / Schmidt, Rudi / Trinczek, Rainer (1999): Betriebliches Interessenhandeln. Band 1: Zur politischen Kultur der Austauschbeziehungen zwischen Management und Betriebsrat in der westdeutschen Industrie. Opladen

Brinkmann, Ulrich (2003): Die Verschiebung von Marktgrenzen und die kalte Entmachtung der WissensarbeiterInnen. In: Klaus Schönberger/Stefanie Springer (Hg.): Subjektivierte Arbeit – Frankfurt a.M., New York: p. 63-94

Brinkmann, Ulrich / Choi, Hae Lin / Detje, Richard / Dörre, Klaus / Holst, Hajo / Karakayali, Serhat / Neis, Matthias / Schmalstieg, Catharina (2008): Strategic Unionism: Aus der Krise zur Erneuerung? Umrisse eines Forschungsprogramms. Wiesbaden

Brinkmann, Ulrich / Speidel, Frederic (2006): Hybride Beteiligungsformen am Beispiel 'sachkundiger Arbeitnehmer'. In: WSI-Mitteilungen 59 (2): p. 86-91

Busch, Martin (2003): Arbeitsgruppen und Gruppenarbeit im Betriebsverfassungsgesetz. Berlin

Dörre, Klaus (2002): Kampf um Beteiligung. Arbeit, Partizipation und Industrielle Beziehungen im flexiblen Kapitalismus. Wiesbaden

Gramm, Rolf (2005): Betriebliche Auskunftspersonen. Experten in eigener Sache. In: Mitbestimmung (11/2005): p. 54-57

Hromadka, Wolfgang / Maschmann, Frank (2007): Arbeitsrecht Band 2. Kollektivarbeitsrecht und Arbeitsstreitigkeiten. Berlin, Heidelberg, New York

Lenhardt, Uwe / Rosenbrock, Rolf (2006): Wegen Umbau geschlossen. Auswirkungen betrieblicher Reorganisation auf den Gesundheitsschutz. Berlin

Martens, Helmut (1997): Betriebliche Beteiligungskulturen bei konzernweiten Modernisierungskonzepten im Arbeits- und Gesundheitsschutz. In: Arbeit 6 (4): p. 429-449

Martens, Helmut (2002): Die Zukunft der Mitbestimmung beginnt wieder neu. Bilanz und Perspektiven der Mitbestimmung im Lichte von Grundlagen- und Auftragsforschung, Beratung und Forschungstransfer in den 1990ern. Münster u.a.

Pickshaus, Klaus / Urban, Hans-Jürgen (2004): "Gute Arbeit" – eine arbeits- und gesundheitspolitische Initiative der IG Metall. In: Arbeit 13 (Heft 3/2004): p. 220-228

Direct participation as a way to safeguard a plant? The example of a German steel company

Ralf Niemann

In this article I would like to focus quite specifically on the "ambivalence of direct participation of employees". I will report on the experiences we have been and still are gaining at ArcelorMittal Bremen, formerly Stahlwerke Bremen. Starting with an existential crisis of the plant in 2002, "direct participation" became for us an important and regular activity of the workforce. Together with other factors, it brought about a fundamental change in the general perception of the steel industry as merely a "hard slog". Before presenting a brief outline of this development, I would like to provide some information of the plant and its industrial relations.

ArcelorMittal Bremen is an integrated smelting plant for the production of flat steel. It is located in Bremen in northern Germany, not far from the coast and along the lower reaches of the river Wesel. With its output of 3.5m metric tonnes of crude steel (2007) and a workforce of 3,750 (2008), it is one of three big companies in a region that has become economically rather more fragile over the last few years.

Background: traditional industrial relations are facing new challenges

Industrial relations at ArcelorMittal Bremen are marked by a special form of codetermination that generally characterises the German coal and steel industry. After the Second World War the two core sectors in German industry at the time, coal and steel, established a far-reaching degree of participation in business decisions on the part of employees. Two features, in particular, form an important part of this model: (1) Supervisory boards comprise equal numbers of shareholders and employees. To ensure that decisions can be made despite a deadlock, a neutral third party has to be agreed by both sides. (2) The Board of Management must have a so-called Director of Labour Relations who is primarily responsible for HR issues. This Board member cannot be appointed against the majority of votes of employees' representatives on the Supervisory Board. *In effect,* this means that employees' candidates are usually appointed to this post.

On the employees' side, the Supervisory Board comprises not only representatives directly from the shop floor, but also external trade union functionaries. A Director of Labour Relations therefore always has an obvious trade union background, which rather complicates his or her role as a regular Board member. One special feature in industrial relations and in this collaboration between "capital" and "labour" is that all 25 members of the works council are fully released from their normal work duties. Moreover, all 25 are members of the German metal-workers' union. The general level of trade union membership is nearly 60 per cent. The basic structure of the metal-workers' union hinges on shop stewards.

The plant was founded in 1957. In 1992, after a relatively quiet period, it met with a major existential threat to its very existence. After massive industrial action, which has since become quite legendary, the plant was eventually saved, partly through intervention from local government. In 1993 the plant was acquired by the Belgian Sidmar Group, which formed part of the Arbed Group. By entering into a wider group with transnational operations, a hitherto unbroken chain reaction was set off, so that the Bremen plant became part of increasingly bigger corporate entities: in 2002, together with Sidmar/Arbed, it joined Arcelor, and in 2006 Arcelor itself entered the new globally operating ArcelorMittal Group, dominated by Lakshmi Mittal.

Representing the interests of the workforce at the plant continued to be a "managerial" responsibility of works councils until well into the 1990s. This representational role, coupled with a political understanding of its function, continued to characterise its activities for many years. However, when the plant was taken over by Arbed – and later and more dramatically by Arcelor and then ArcelorMittal – the general framework for the representation of interests changed drastically. One central reason is that, unlike in the past, today's shareholders have no organically grown loyalty towards individual plants and thus no sense of responsibility for the region where a plant is located. Instead, they view each business primarily in terms of its contribution to the group as a whole, under a rigorous *benchmarking* scheme.

However, this new situation makes it impossible to rely on old and outmoded strategies in the representation of interests, as we can now see an increasing significance of the European and indeed wider international level. The works council of a plant such as Bremen needs to develop new strategic approaches in its representation of interests and has to do so under considerable difficulties. One of these approaches can be seen in the endeavour of the works council to broaden representation so as to include the direct participation of the workforce, *empowering* each individual and indeed the workforce as a whole.

The starting point for this approach was the critical situation of the plant within the Arcelor context in 2002.

2002: a threat to the plant

I have been a member of the works council for six years. Until then I used to be employed by the HR department. When I first joined the works council, I was immediately confronted with this situation. Based on my previous professional experience, I took an active part in the development of tools and processes that were subsequently used in the FIT project. Based on various agreements, FIT had been set up jointly by the management and the works council in response to the new threat and turned out to be a success. Under FIT all works councils members were directly involved in any of the HR decisions that became necessary. This gave me some good insights into the reactions of my colleagues to the existential threat and also to the countermeasures that were taken to avert this threat.

The critical starting point for the FIT process in 2002 was the wide gap between the Bremen plant and other flat steel producers in the group in matters of productivity and costs. This negative benchmark posed a direct threat to the existence of the plant, so that virtually the only way to adopt a suitable "survival strategy" within the group was to ensure the combination of immediate and substantial cost reductions and an increase in productivity . The management felt that this challenge could only present a viable opportunity if it was not obstructed by the works council and the workforce, but if it had their support. Success was unthinkable without the expertise of the workforce and their many years of experience in matters of reasonable cost savings and improvements. The uncertain survival of the plant and the threat to people's jobs put the works council of the steel plant under considerable pressure to deliver.

The FIT pact

After intensive discussions the works council eventually decided to conclude a "pact" that would lead to a jointly supported FIT process, although it specified a range of far-reaching conditions, requiring the consent of the workforce, their cooperation and the need for active input.

What was it about?

(1) It was not accepted that job cuts should become a decisive savings parameter. Instead the works council insisted on an overall cost evaluation.
(2) Technical and organisational rationalisation proposals were assessed and implemented under quality criteria that were closely associated with questions of "good workmanship". To achieve this objective, the works council had set up seven special criteria, interpreting the FIT process from an employees' perspective.
(3) To define measures and to explore their effectiveness and any potentially unintended effects, the entire production and service process was divided into smaller subprocesses. This was the level at which the direct participation of the workforce came into play, as the selection, evaluation and implementa-

tion of rationalisation activities required a close-meshed system of participation and codetermination. This system was gradually refined throughout the FIT process to the point where the works council was effectively granted a veto on certain measures. As the entire situation was marked by uncertainty for the workforce, one important psychological asset was the security of the procedure, guaranteed by the works council.

(4) The management instructed McKinsey to design and implement the entire process, while the works council also appointed its own consultant.

(5) A number of binding company agreements were concluded which collectively specified all the important aspects of the FIT project and, in particular, all the various options of staff changes, resulting from the FIT project.

(6) The works council demanded from the very beginning that the management should renounce the option of operational redundancies under FIT. Although the management refused to give their formal consent to this principle, a number of HR policy tools were agreed and implemented between the management and the works council, which meant *in effect* that not a single job was cut for operational reasons. The management were aware that the works council would equate any job cuts with the de-facto cancellation of the FIT pact.

Successful collaboration, yet neither without conflict nor with any permanent security

So what was the eventual outcome? The original aim had been to achieve a reduction of EUR 130m p. a. and to reduce the workforce by 1,700. Yet the proposals put forward by the workforce led to the overfulfilment of the savings volume without the full implementation of job cuts. Of the plant's former 4,800 employees, 1,160 left the company, including 820 who had taken subsidised early retirement. Another 340 either accepted a golden handshake or used the services of a transfer company that had been specially set up for this purpose, a company which prepared them for the external labour market and found employment for them. Of those who stayed, however, many had to accept a change to a different job. To make it easier for them, an internal HR pool was set up, acting as an in-house agency and helping with the formation of suitable skills. Up to 450 persons were employed under this scheme at times. By now this institution has become firmly established in the company as some kind of permanent "HR buffer".

Cooperation "at eye level" under the FIT project did not mean that it was without conflict. On the contrary, it was an ongoing "bargaining" process that was full of conflict. However, it proceeded under jointly agreed rules of procedure and on the understanding that only joint solutions would eventually be sustainable.

Nevertheless, the level and density of involvement in management decisions could no longer be maintained towards the end of the FIT project when it became obvious that the objectives would be achieved. At this point the management gradually lost interest in ensuring consensus at all cost. In particular, it became noticeable that the role of the workforce – as seen by the management – was to be reduced to a traditional codetermination hierarchy again: in other words it was to focus more on social than business issues. What was even more difficult was to apply the resulting quality of participation to the time "after FIT".

The time "after FIT" was seen by both sides as some kind of a "state of emergency" – a view that was above all reflected in two endeavours to apply the quality of participation to everyday life on the shop floor: First of all, there was the introduction of TPM, a rigorous fault avoidance project that was rolled out across all work routines, while, secondly, lengthy negotiations were started on a plant agreement about participation – negotiations which are still in progress today.

"Continuous improvement" and the ambivalence of participation

TPM follows a Japanese concept of continuous improvement and can only be successful if it has the full support and dedication of the workforce. However, unlike FIT, TPM was not borne out of an existential crisis and thus an emergency, as seen by the management, so that the participation philosophy of FIT was not applied to TPM in any way. Instead, the works council were compelled to negotiate rules of conduct, levels of participation and above all quite a few highly detailed qualifications, thus effectively re-negotiating the relationship between direct participation of the workforce and the protective and proactive role of the works council, while trying somehow to make this relationship manageable in the face of TPM processes being multiplied.

Participation of employees: a difficult organisational development job for the works council

Looking at the two aspects of participation on the employees' side – i.e. direct participation of the workforce at the local level and the role of the works council – it was assumed that after FIT and after the plant's existential crisis the workforce would no longer be as much prepared to become actively involved and to participate in the decision-making process. However, this expectation was not confirmed. To some extent, TPM continues along the lines of FIT in that it puts the focus on the special competencies of the workforce as experts in improvement. For the workforce it means that employees are taken seriously and are recognised as partners in the in-house design of work routines and the working environment. At the same time, it opens up a corridor for extended skills building activities that continued to be sustainable during the 2008/2009 sales crisis.

What has become more difficult is the role of the works council at the local level, because employees now tend to be more confident and speak up for their own interests in matters of work organisation, work routines and their working environment. The works council is therefore faced with the challenge of re-defining its protective and proactive roles in a way that is more dynamic and forward-looking. This strategic reorientation has by no means come to a conclusion.

The difficulty of the works council in finding its own "role" vis-à-vis direct participation of the workforce is partly due to numerous areas of tension that lie concealed behind a formally well endowed façade of participation. Such tensions also exist on the part of the workforce and cast rather an ambivalent light on participation.

While there was an emergency, under FIT, any ambivalence that was associated with direct participation was compensated by people's eagerness to maintain the plant and thus its jobs. After all, a third of all suggestions that were received centred around cost savings and were subsequently realised by the workforce themselves. At the same time, there was the concern at the back of people's minds – and indeed this was typical of direct participation – that any suggestions based on one's own direct rationalisation expertise might ultimately provide information that would make a person superfluous and thus lead to their own redundancy. Although such an effect was averted by the powerful role of the works council and the control it exercised, the fear itself nevertheless remained. What made it so attractive for an employee to be actively involved, both under FIT and later, was each person's recognition as an expert and an enhanced status through cooperation "at eye level". However, as participation became everyday normality, this also increased the regular requirements profile of a job, including elements such as responsibility, teamwork, work process expertise, etc.

When wider skills are required and employees are expected to work under greater pressure, these aspects may not be discussed very much, but they do soon become tangible at the local level. Inevitably, questions are raised concerning payment, working hours and time off and also questions about suitable teamwork rooms that need to be as close as possible to one's own workstation. After all, continuous improvement does accelerate change within a plant, thus causing insecurity which is quite often experienced as the opposite of the desired stability. In other words, the more participation becomes everyday normality, the more the works council effectively needs to ensure protection and must be proactive in counteracting the resulting risks and areas of ambivalence.

After lengthy negotiations the management and works council have set up a plant agreement that is now awaiting its conclusion and will act as a framework for employees' participation. It specifies three levels of direct participation which map (or should map) three decision-making complexes: "consultation", "having a say" and "involvement". "Consultation" means that employees are heard before a decision is taken; "having a say" means that whenever issues require decisions, they are discussed with the workforce; and "involvement" means that a decision cannot be taken without the consent of the workforce. The plant agreement expressly refrains from setting up a new system of participation at ArcelorMittal Bremen, but seeks to link all existing participation models and processes – for instance in TPM and in health & safety – to the same criteria and process safeguards, while also creating an effective network between them.

Outlook: turbulent times

In the middle of the decade and after the ArcelorMittal merger the success of FIT under the group's internal benchmarking system opened up the way for the Bremen facility to participate in the worldwide boom of the steel industry. It heralded some "golden years", as it were, during which the decision to add a second furnace also led to some far-reaching positive decisions in favour of the plant. However, at the end of 2008 the Bremen facility, too, was eventually overtaken by the massive sudden crisis in the steel industry and became subject to the acute crisis management of the ArcelorMittal leadership. The ArcelorMittal merger and the resulting dominance of Mittal in the group accelerated the centralisation of strategic decisions at the senior level of the group – a development that had already started at Arcelor. Partly due to a sophisticated data collection and processing system that continually provides the group management with the latest important key performance figures, local managers are rapidly losing their decision-making authorities. To safeguard employees' interests, this shift in decision-making powers must be countered by the expansion of joint national representational structures and above all the strategic use of the European level (i.e. European works council). Moreover, it must be done with an awareness that the group is already operating on a worldwide scale, with plants in a wide variety of countries and on different continents. This is why the Bremen works council has been trying for a while now to ensure that the experience gathered during and after FIT can be used in a joint European employees' policy at ArcelorMittal. This applies above all to the principle of contractually agreed process safeguards for innovations, including the entire complex of direct employees' participation.

Workplace innovation and development in Finland: Examining the workplace development programme TYKES

Tuomo Alasoini

Introduction

In recent years, Finland has gained a reputation as one of the most competitive countries in the world. Finland has also been regarded as an example of a country which has successfully integrated a technologically advanced information society and a socially responsible welfare state (Benner, 2003; Castells and Himanen, 2002). Finland's good reputation is highlighted particularly in studies of the innovation environment of companies. However, as the focus shifts from the innovation environment to the actual standards of national performance, Finland's position in relation to others tends to decline. In fact, Finland would appear to be suffering from some sort of gap in performance and living standards in relation to the innovation environment and all that has been done to improve it.

It is observations such as these, in combination with growing concern for the ageing population, which will alter Finland's demographic structure in the coming years, and compounded by recent news about transferring production to countries with cheaper labour costs, which have brought new flavours to debate in Finland. In this debate, views have been gaining ground which emphasize the need to boost the adoption of a broader view in innovation policy, with a better balance and interplay between technological and social innovation, in order to strengthen the country's competitiveness (Hämäläinen and Heiskala, 2007; Schienstock, 2004). For example, Finland's biggest R&D funding body Tekes – the Finnish Funding Agency for Technology and Innovation – is now increasingly taking also the promotion of non-technological business, service, managerial and organizational innovations on board (Tekes, 2008). A new guiding principle in the Finnish innovation policy debate is the notion of 'broad-based innovation policy', which is based on a systemic approach, which unleashes the potentials of innovative individuals and communities, which has a strong demand and user orientation, and which is global in its orientation.

From this broader view to innovation, the work, organizational and managerial practices adopted by companies have considerable significance for Finland's ability to succeed in globalized competition. Finnish companies find it increasingly difficult to compete with typical mass-produced products and services whose competitive edge is primarily derived from their price and low unit costs. Many recent examples indicate that a high quality of products or services, reliable deliveries and the expertise needed to provide them may not be enough in themselves to create a competitive edge for Finnish companies. It seems that the Finnish companies which have the best potential for success in globalized competition are those that are able to operate with speed and flexibility, that are capable of advanced tailoring, that are able to offer their clients integrated service packages, and that are able to continuously develop their products, services, operations and processes. The companies which compete through flexibility, quick response or customization, let alone innovativeness, are required to possess a greater variety of expertise than companies whose primary competitive advantage is, say, efficiency or quality. The new expertise is embodied in companies in the form of new work, organizational and managerial practices.

Finland will also be facing another particular challenge in the coming years in the form of a rapid ageing of the population, which is expected to cause a fall in the supply of labour. The situation in Finland will change unfavourably, not just in absolute terms, but also in relation to most other developed industrialized countries. This threatens to undermine the prospects of economic growth and, consequently, the potential for developing the welfare state, and at the same time, it will also lead to a weakening of Finland's international competitiveness.

For the above reasons it ought to be possible to boost productivity growth in Finland in order to preserve economic growth and the preconditions for a welfare state. As indicated above, productivity growth will depend to an increasing extent on innovations in the future. However, innovation-driven productivity growth is not in itself an optimal adaptation mechanism in a new situation; instead, the innovation-driven productivity growth should be sustainable in the sense that it provides simultaneous support for the other key factor in economic growth – workforce numbers – by encouraging people to stay on at work for longer. The challenge of the future lies in finding a way to integrate favourable productivity growth based on innovations with improvements in the quality of working life (QWL) on a broad front. In this paper, this is referred to as *the challenge of qualitatively sustainable productivity growth*, and in order to take up this challenge, Finland will need a policy approach which places equal emphasis on technological and social innovations.

At the core of this type of approach lies what is referred to here as *the expanded triple helix model* (Alasoini et al., 2005; Ramstad, 2008). It is application of the traditional triple helix model, which refers to the view that the most effective way of generating new innovative solutions is based on learning arising from cooperation between companies, universities and policy-makers, but it involves more parties and more interaction relationships. The parties have different competencies, but from the point of producing new knowledge they are considered equals as 'innovation clusters'.

The concept of parties to expanded triple helix cooperation is broad in the sense that, in addition to companies, it comprises public and non-governmental organizations. The challenge of qualitatively sustainable productivity growth in Finland does not apply solely to the private sector, but also to public service provision. The concept of parties to cooperation is also broad in the sense that, in addition to universities and research institutes, it also comprises units whose operations focus on development. Workplace innovations, with the exception of certain relatively simple business management techniques, are context-dependent, and the knowledge required for their successful application is difficult to translate into an explicit, codified form. Of course, product and process technology solutions typically have to be customized for local conditions too, but the specifications required for such customization can be determined much more unambiguously than those involved in work, organizational and managerial practices. The promotion of workplace innovations emphasizes also the importance of consultants and local educational institutes, which can commit to long-term cooperation with businesses and which can communicate effectively with them on the basis of shared tacit knowledge. Finally, the concept of parties to cooperation is also broad in the sense that it includes the social partners alongside the public authorities. In countries with highly institutionalized industrial relations such as Finland, collective agreements signed by the labour market organizations are tantamount to legislation in terms of their coverage and how binding they are. In such cases, the social partners can with justification be considered as policy-makers on a par with government. Confrontational industrial relations and a lack of institutionalized procedures can be substantial barriers to the promotion of workplace innovations (Figure 1).

This paper examines the Finnish Workplace Development Programme TYKES (1996-2009) as a response to the challenge of qualitatively sustainable productivity growth. The paper starts with a look at the background of the programme. This is followed by an overview on the policy rationale, goals, content, organization and advance of the programme. The paper ends with a summary of special characteristics of the Finnish approach to workplace innovation and development and future challenges.

Figure 1: The Expanded Triple Helix Model

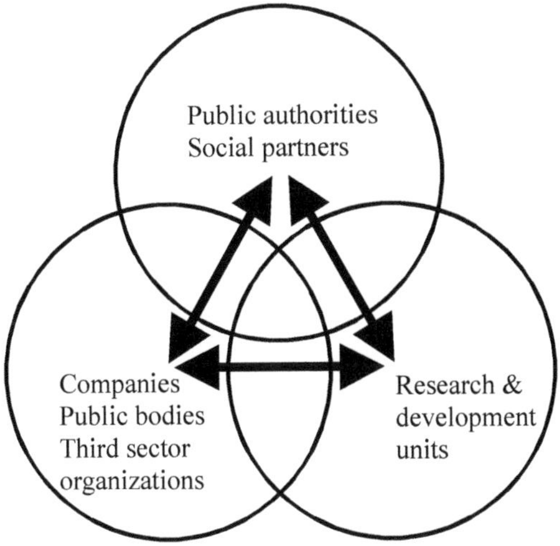

Launch of the Workplace Development Programme

Workplace innovation and development entered the policy agenda in Finland as subjects in their own right only in the 1980s and 1990s, i.e. later than in the other Nordic countries where many activities were launched by the government and the social partners already in the 1960s and 1970s. This laggard position of Finland owes to many factors.

Firstly, there were no serious recruitment problems in Finnish industry, nor did working conditions become the focus of employee dissatisfaction to the same extent as in many other industrialized countries. Many Finnish workers in the 1970s still had a rural background and thus also previous experience of heavy work in farming or forestry. Finland actually had very little mass production with extremely highly fragmented and fast-paced production line work of the kind that was the focus of worker dissatisfaction in other countries. Secondly, a technological bias was characteristic of Finnish management methods, and productivity improvements were mainly pursued through the introduction of new flexible production technologies, rather than new forms of work organization. Social and leadership skills played little part in the training of engineers. The trade unions also focused mainly on traditional distribution issues. Thirdly, workplace industrial relations in Finland in the 1970s were characterized by tension due to the collision between authoritarian and technology-based management methods and the growing power of the trade union movement and subsequent improvements in the workers' bargaining position. This atmosphere of distrust was further aggravated by internal political struggles within the trade union movement. Low-trust industrial relations, together with a high level of unofficial strikes throughout the 1970s, did nothing to encourage labour-management cooperation in workplace development. And finally, at the time Finland did not have a strong, sociologically-oriented tradition of working-life research which might have prompted general debate on workplace development issues. Discussion on QWL in Finland in the 1970s was mainly confined to occupational health and safety.

A severe recession that hit Finland in the early 1990s can be considered as an important watershed with regard to workplace innovation and development. Simultaneous collapse of the Soviet market and an economic depression in the European market had dramatic effects in Finland; numerous companies drifted into serious financial problems and went into bankruptcy and the unemployment rate skyrocketed from 3.2% (1990) to 16.6% (1994). The worst economic downfall during the post-war era, together with a reform in the system of collective bargaining that led to increased leeway for company-level bargaining, formed a fertile soil for workplace innovations.

Reforms in managerial and organizational doctrines and practices in Finnish companies would not have been possible without a sufficient supporting structure based on a close cooperation between the parties to expanded triple helix. A special feature in Finland in recent years is that, in addition to consultancy agencies, many university units, research institutes and other educational institutes have actively participated in development projects in workplaces. By the start of the 1990s, R&D on working life had acquired a relatively strong institutional and funding base in Finland. Over the past 20 years, that base has grown even more solid as a consequence to companies' increased interest in R&D cooperation with universities and consultants, science and education policy reforms, Finland's accession to the EU (1995) and workplace development programmes (Ramstad and Alasoini, 2006)

At the beginning of 1996, the Economic Council initiated the Workplace Development Programme (the TYKE programme) as part of the programme of Prime Minister Lipponen's Government. Initially, the programme which had been prepared by the Ministry of Labour and the labour market organizations together was set for four years, but it continued for another four years as part of the programme of the second Lipponen Government. The programme provided financial support for nearly 670 projects in 1996-2003; a total of 135,000 people in an estimated 1,600 Finnish workplaces took part in these projects. The clear majority of projects were *development projects* based on the needs of the workplaces concerned. In addition to these, the programme also supported shorter and smaller-scale *basic analyses* and more extensive *network projects*, which consisted of several companies (Alasoini et al., 2005).

Support from the programme focused on the work input of the experts used in the projects. The use of consultants accounted for about 45% of the funding granted by the programme, while experts from universities, government research institutes and polytechnics accounted for a total of 35%. In addition to these, developers from other educational institutes and from the workplaces themselves also took part in projects in the capacity of experts. The workplaces' own input into projects came chiefly in the form of the work input of their staff and, to some extent, participation in the funding of experts.

Workplaces of all sizes in all parts of Finland and in virtually all sectors participated in the TYKE programme. Workplaces in industry accounted for the highest percentage of the funding in both periods: 52% in 1996-1999 and 39% in 2000-2003. The percentage of funding accounted for by workplaces in the private service sector rose from 13% to 20%. The percentage of the local authority sector was just under 30% in both programme periods. Workplaces from the central government sector, the forestry and agriculture sector and the third sector also took part in the programme. A notable difference between the programme periods was the clear growth in the percentage of SMEs granted funding (companies with less than 250 employees) of all the funding granted for company development projects. The percentage grew from 46% to 68%.

At the beginning of 2004, the Ministry of Labour launched a new TYKES programme. TYKES was based on the programme of Prime Minister Vanhanen's Government, and was scheduled for the 2004-2009 period. The Ministry of Labour and the labour market organizations proposed a total budget for the programme of EUR 87 million, financed by the State. According to the proposal, this would permit programme support for some 1,000 development projects and participation by 250,000 employees (nearly 10% of the people employed in Finland). The content of TYKES was influenced by the results of the evaluation study of the TYKE programme which was implemented in 2002-2003 (Arnkil, 2004) and the new innovation policy doctrine, which emphasized the growing significance for national competitiveness of social innovations and of the interaction between them and technological innovations.

TYKES Policy Rationale in a Nutshell

Finns are strong supporters of a welfare state that guarantees them a comprehensive range of public or publicly supported services throughout their lives at a reasonable cost. The foundation of such a welfare state rests on continued economic growth.

Workplace innovation and development is related to the foundation of the welfare state in the following way:

The growth of income per head of the population is a function of the change in labour productivity and labour intensity. *Labour productivity* growth comes from investment in human capital, investment in new machinery, equipment and infrastructure, and technological development such as new products and modes of operation. For the future, the role of technological development as a booster of labour productivity growth will increase in developed industrialized countries such as Finland.

Change in *labour intensity*, in turn, is a function of the change in the share of employment in the total population and the change in hours worked per person employed. For the future, it is obvious that in a country such as Finland in which people increasingly value leisure time and family life it is more realistic to increase labour intensity by raising the share of employment in the total population than to increase the hours worked per person employed. Furthermore, in Finland it is more realistic to raise the share of employment in the total population by helping people cope and continue at work longer than to speed up the entry of the younger age groups to the labour market. There are two main reasons for that: Firstly, the older age groups are currently much bigger than the younger age groups. This means that it is easier to have an overall positive effect on economic growth through changes in the behaviour of the older groups in the labour market. Secondly, with the increasing knowledge intensity of the economy there is a pressure to lengthen rather than shorten the average time used for studies among the younger age groups, this making a quicker entry of the younger age groups to the labour market an unrealistic effort. Studies carried out in Finland clearly demonstrate that the key issue in helping people cope and continue at work longer is the improvement in QWL. For example, according to a survey by the Finnish Centre for Pensions (Tuominen et al., 2005), both management representatives and employees in an age group between 58 and 63 years considered working atmosphere, work environment, leadership and the possibility to have an influence at work as the four most important preconditions for continued work after the age of 63 years. The share of respondents who considered issues such as further training, possibilities for rehabilitation or financial incentives as important for continued work was remarkably smaller.

Following the line of argumentation presented above, measures which have an effect on both key factors contributing to economic growth – labour productivity (achieved mainly through technological development, such as new modes of operation) and labour intensity (achieved mainly through improvements in QWL) – are crucial. This problem setting also represents the point of departure for the TYKES programme. TYKES attempts to promote *workplace innovations*, which in the programme are considered as collaboratively achieved changes in a company's work, organizational or human resource management practices that lead to improved operative and human performance and that also support other types of innovation. The last part of the description is based on the view that different types of innovation at the company level are usually interwoven with each other, containing significant complementaries (Bresnahan et al., 2002; Laursen and Foss, 2003; Roberts, 2004). In the TYKES programme, improvements in labour productivity and QWL are not regarded in terms of a zero-sum game. On the contrary, problems in both of them are examined as shortcomings in the contemporary modes of workplace operation, which should be intervened with similar development methods. This also implies that the focus of development should be comprehensively on the workplace modes of operation, rather than in some narrowly-defined, stand-alone problem areas.

Is Finland Able to Cope with the Challenge of Qualitatively Sustainable Productivity Growth?

The size of the workforce in Finland can be predicted with a rather high degree of reliability and accuracy. According to long-term analyses of workforce trends, approximately one million people will leave the workforce between 2000 and 2015; that is the equivalent of nearly half the employed people in 2000. The size of the age group departing from the labour market began to exceed that entering the labour market in the middle of this decade. The size of the workforce available to the labour market will not, of course, depend mechanically on the size of the age groups entering and leaving. It is possible, however, to predict that the size of the workforce in Finland will in any case decline over the next 30 years. Here we have a fundamental, long-term turn (Figure 2).

Similar demographic trends are expected in the other developed industrialized countries. In Finland, however, the decrease in labour supply will be exceptionally large by international standards. The present dependency ratio (the ratio of 15-64 year-olds to the younger and older age groups), which is close to the EU average, will become considerably less favourable than the average rate for the EU countries during the next couple of decades. If Finland wishes to preserve economic growth on the average present level under these circumstances, this fall must be compensated for, in practice, by increasing the rate of labour productivity.

Figure 2: Changes in the Potential Labour Supply in Finland in 1945-2030 Based on Demographic Forecast (Ministry of Labour, 2003)

Accelerated growth in productivity is the key means for alleviating the problems arising from smaller labour inputs. Annual growth in labour productivity in Finland during the late 1980s and the first half of the 1990s was greater than that in the USA, Japan and the EU countries on average. Since the mid-1990s, and increasingly in the early 2000s, however, labour productivity growth in Finland slowed down and fell below the level found in the United States and Japan. The situation in Finland resembles that in Germany where the slowdown has been even greater. The Finnish growth figures also lag far behind Ireland, which has been the top performer among the EU-15 countries during the last 20 years (Table 1).

Table 1: Labour Productivity Growth in Selected Countries, 1987-2005, % (Van Ark, 2006)

	GDP per hour worked		
	1987-95	**1995-2005**	**of which 2000-05**
Finland	3.2	2.0	1.5
Germany	3.2	1.9	1.2
Ireland	4.0	4.3	3.0
EU-15	2.3	1.4	1.0
United States	1.1	2.4	2.6
Japan	2.8	2.0	1.9

A more detailed examination reveals that there prevail greatly different trends in different sectors of the Finnish economy. The high average annual growth figures in the electronics industry and telecommunications could not prevent the overall labour productivity growth turn into a decline since the mid-1990s. The development in labour productivity of many conventional sectors was sluggish at the same period of time. A long-term examination of the growth rate of labour productivity in Finland also reveals a clear downward trend since the 1970s in many key sectors of the economy (Forsman and Jalava, 2006). It is uncertain that the sectors, which served as the engine for favourable productivity growth in Finland in recent years, would serve the same purpose to the same extent in the future. Sustainable development in the long term will require favourable growth in productivity on a broader front and possibly the emergence of new engines for productivity growth.

However, in the long term, favourable productivity growth on a broad front alone will not be enough to ensure continued economic growth and, consequently, the conditions for a welfare state in Finland; productivity growth must also be qualitatively sustainable as described above. Examination of development trends of QWL in recent years shows that Finland's situation is ambivalent in a comparison with the EU: work organizations which offer employees opportunities for learning and development are more in number than the EU average, but the same is also true concerning work organizations which pose a risk to wellbeing at work (Dhondt et al., 2002). What makes Finland's situation a cause for concern, however, is the ageing of the population and the economic dependency ratio which is becoming more unfavourable. In order to make it possible to compensate for the demographic threats to Finland's competitiveness through a high QWL (and by supporting employees in staying on at work), the percentage of work organizations which produce effects for learning and wellbeing simultaneously would have to be on the top level internationally in the coming years. However, the research results (e.g. Lehto and Sutela, 2005; Ylöstalo and Jukka, 2008) do not indicate that the trend in recent years has been in this direction (Table 2).

Table 2: Development Features in QWL in Finland over the Past Few Years

Opportunities for development and training at work	Positive change 1977-2003 No clear change since 2003
Opportunities for exerting an influence at work (excluding pace of work)	Positive change 1977-1997 No clear change, but signs of slight negative trend 1997-2007
Opportunities for exerting an influence at work (pace of work)	Positive change 1977-1990 Negative change 1990-2007
Physical strain of work	No change 1977-2003
Psychological strain of work	Negative change 1977-1990 No change 1990-2007
Internal cooperation and trust in the work community	Negative change 1984-1997 No change 1997-2007

The challenge of qualitatively sustainable productivity growth does not apply just to companies in Finland, but also very definitely to the public sector. The challenge will particularly face there the provision of health care and social welfare services, which in Finland are largely provided by the local authorities. The need for new employees in this sector in the next years is particularly urgent, but the sector's potential for competing for labour with economic incentives alone are weak and boosting productivity without major reforms in managerial and work organizational practices is limited. Something which further adds to the challenge in this sector is the fact that there are numerous problems in QWL (e.g. heavy strain of work and little influence on the contents of tasks and the pace of work), as demonstrated by various studies.

Goals of the Programme

The goals of the programme can be structured in the following four levels. Table 3 shows also the main targets and indicators used by the programme at each level.

(1) The goal of the *public policy level* is to achieve qualitatively sustainable productivity growth in Finland. Here the degree of development of the innovation environment of workplaces will affect success. The degree of development of the innovation environment is indicated in particular by the diversity of expertise pos-

sessed by 'innovative centres' (for example R&D institutes, consultants, labour market organizations, public authorities and workplaces) and by the diversity of their cooperation. The vision of the programme is that by 2009 "Finland will have a network of expertise for work organization development which creates national competitive edge and which effectively promotes qualitatively sustainable productivity growth".

(2) The goals of the *programme level* reflect the goals of the public policy level. They are related to how the programme is able, via its own measures, to realize the TYKES vision. The goals concern the extent to which the programme's project and other operations generate qualitatively sustainable productivity growth and enhance the workplace innovation environment. The forms of the programme's project activity are (a) development projects and (b) basic analyses at workplaces, and (c) method development projects and (d) learning network projects (explained in more detail below).

(3) The aim of the *generative level* is to disseminate new work, organizational and managerial practices and development methods, models and tools created and tested in projects as sources of learning and inspiration (generative ideas) for other workplaces and stakeholder groups. This does not mean that other workplaces would in most cases adopt them as such, but rather that they would give rise to new ideas and encourage development activity. Success in turning new solutions as generative ideas requires information on the solutions to be disseminated outside the project and also that the solutions in questions have innovation value, relevance or that they are otherwise of interest for parties outside the project.

(4) The aim of the *workplace level* is to strengthen, via development projects, a mode of operation that will help workplaces to develop their operations in a manner supportive of qualitatively sustainable productivity growth. This will require enhancement of workplaces' development expertise, close cooperation between management and employees, and the ability to make skilful use of expert networks in support of development.

Table 3: Goals of the TYKES Programme

PUBLIC POLICY LEVEL **Qualitatively sustainable productivity growth in Finland** • labour productivity growth • changes in QWL • breadth of expertise and density of cooperation of workplace R&D institutions

PROGRAMME LEVEL **How can the programme and its measures promote qualitatively sustainable productivity growth in Finland and develop an innovation environment which supports it?** • number of projects and employees participating in projects • percentage of employees over 45 years, women and SME staff of participants in projects • number of employees participated in projects which show qualitatively sustainable productivity growth • percentage of funding of all project funding granted to experts from universities, government research institutes and polytechnics • number of polytechnics taking part in projects • number of workplace R&D units showing improvement in expertise and cooperation through participation in projects • number of doctoral dissertations and licentiate theses written in connection with projects
GENERATIVE LEVEL **How can the project results act as a source of learning and inspiration for other workplaces and the various stakeholder groups?** • coverage and usefulness of programme information channels as experienced by stakeholder groups • usefulness of programme information channels and mutual exchange of information between projects as experienced by participants (management, employees and experts) in projects
WORKPLACE LEVEL **How can the projects help reinforce a mode of operation which supports qualitatively sustainable productivity growth in the participating workplaces?** • changes in the work, organizational and managerial practices experienced by management and employee representatives • percentage of projects that generate improvements in performance-related and QWL-related issues as experience by management and employee representatives

Main Forms of Programme Activity

The programme has five main forms of activity. The following provides a short overview on each activity.

Workplace Development Projects

TYKES supports projects which develop the modes of operation of workplaces, aiming at simultaneous improvement in performance and QWL. Performance improvements may focus, for instance, on the productivity of work, the quality of products and services, the quality of operations, customer services or smoothness of operations. Improvements in QWL may focus, for instance, on employees' opportunities for development and exerting influence over their work, well-being at work, and cooperation and trust within the work community. Management and personnel must commit themselves to the project goals and to implementing the project together.

The majority of the projects are workplace development projects. The programme can also grant funding for basic analyses in preparation for development projects. Typically, it is the workplaces themselves that apply for funding. Programme funding focuses on the input of experts such as researchers and consultants for the projects.

Once a development project has ended, representatives of the management and personnel and the experts who worked on the project each produces a self-assessment of the project. This reflects their opinions on the effects, success and implementation method of the project, and the importance of the support received from the programme. Representatives of the management and personnel also evaluate the project's effect on work, organizational and managerial practices adopted by their workplace through a questionnaire at the beginning and the end of the project.

Method Development Projects

The purpose of method development projects is to promote qualitatively sustainable productivity growth in Finnish workplaces by producing new work, organizational and managerial practices and new development methods, models and tools. The emphasis in method development is on tangible methods, practices and solutions which are designed for an increasingly knowledge-intensive and networked economy, and which are widely applicable and suitable for dissemination. Projects are required to present a plan on how the results will be passed on for use by workplaces, educational institutes and consultants. The applicants for method development projects are typically universities, research institutes, polytechnics and other educational institutes.

Learning Network Projects

Learning networks represent a new, experimental form of project activity aimed at enhancing the ability of the programme to produce generative results. The learning networks in TYKES are joint learning forums of R&D units and workplaces. A number of researchers with common interests take part in the learning networks together with a number of workplaces, the development of whose operations is supported by cooperation with them. The networks may include other participants as well, for example consultancies and development agencies, labour market organizations or regional actors. The common development object uniting the participants may be only loosely defined at the outset of the project.

The purpose of the learning networks is to increase the developmental expertise of the participants, to create and experiment with new forms of development cooperation, and to generate new, innovative solutions for Finnish working life. In the forefront are networks that aim at the creation of new knowledge and expertise related to workplace innovation; that aim at learning at several different levels; that consist of a large number of expert organizations and work organizations of many different kinds; and that show obvious potential for development in terms of the network's structure and modes of operation, the benefits sought by its active participants, and its potential for expansion. Functions to be supported include setting up and coordinating the network, exchange of information in the network, small-scale development projects, international cooperation, improvement of development methods, and research, publications and post-graduate studies.

Dissemination of Information on Workplace Development

TYKES disseminates the information generated by the projects it supports. The programme's foremost target groups are workplaces, R&D units, consultants, labour market organizations and authorities. Key methods for disseminating information include publications, seminars and websites. Major networked development projects involving several parties and learning network projects can act as important means for disseminating information in their own right.

Reinforcing the Expertise on Workplace Development

TYKES strives to promote cooperation between workplaces and R&D units. The programme supports doctoral dissertations and licentiate theses written in connection with project activity. Promotion of 'the third task', i.e. the utilization of new knowledge and expertise, of universities and polytechnics is given a special attention.

TYKES takes part in international cooperation, especially at the EU level and in the Nordic countries. The programme represents Finland in the WORK-IN-NET (2004-2009) project within the ERA-NET scheme, which is funded out of the European Commission's Sixth Framework Programme for Research and Technological Development. TYKES is responsible for tasks related to benchmarking activities within the project.

Organization and Advance of the Programme

The programme has a *management group* of 14 members, made up of representatives of the Ministry of Employment and the Economy, the labour market and entrepreneurial organizations, and some other ministries and R&D funding bodies. The management group has set targets for the entire programme period. It also makes decisions on annual targets and operation plans and is responsible for evaluation of the programme. An external interim evaluation was commissioned by the management group in 2006-2007 (Arnkil, 2008), and a final evaluation will be carried out in 2009-2010. There is also an *expert group* which acts a preparatory body for the management group, an advisory *scientific forum of experts*, made up of experts from 31 R&D units, and a *network of regional contact persons*. Coordination of the programme is the responsibility of the programme's *project team* at Tekes.

The application period for the TYKES programme started in February 2004. By July 2008, the programme had received 1,375 project applications. The numbers of approved applications by type of project were as follows: development projects 735 (with 129,000 people taking part in the projects), basic analyses 118, method development projects 24 and learning network projects 17. The total number of approved projects by July 2008 accounted for 894, which is not far away from the original target of 1,000 projects. Expert support granted to the projects totalled about EUR 57 million, which is close to 90% of the total funding of the programme so far. According to a rough estimate, the financial contribution made by the workplaces themselves is twice as much as the support provided by the programme.

Table 4 shows the allocation of support granted to the projects by sector in the two TYKE programme periods and the TYKES period. During the first period, the largest sectoral grouping was clearly industry. The most clear-cut trend is the decline of the proportion of industry at the expense of private services. Owing to changes made in the classification, it is not possible to provide a full-length picture of major trends within the category of private services. New rising sub-sectors within private services during the last period include particularly business-related services (6.6%), welfare and health care services (5.3%), and societal and personal services (2.7%). Growth in the proportion of the private service sector is intertwined with a simultaneuous trend of a growing share of SMEs of all project funding. The share of SMEs of all funding granted to TYKES development projects and basic analyses for private enterprises is 75%, a figure far higher than in the two previous programme periods. Of all private enterprises participating in development projects in the TYKES programme period (about 1,800), about 90% are SMEs. Most of the smallest companies participate in the projects as networks, i.e. they join a joint project that is coordinated by an external expert such as a consultancy agency or a local educational institute or in some cases by their industrial association. Networks of small companies are usually made up on a regional or industry basis.

Table 4: Support by Sector in the Three Programme Periods, [%]

	1996-1999	**2000-2003**	**2004-2008 July**
Agriculture and forestry	0.5	0.9	1.6
Industry	52.0	39.1	35.4
of which metal and engineering and electronics	33.2	19.7	15.8
of which wood-processing	7.6	7.2	3.5
of which chemical	4.2	3.8	2.5
of which construction, installation and maintenance	4.1	2.3	3.8
Private services	12.6	19.8	27.7
of which hotels and restaurants	0.8	1.5	1.4
of which trade	3.2	3.7	5.4
of which transport and communications	3.5	4.0	4.0
of which finance and insurance	1.6	1.9	1.1
Local authorities	27.7	28.7	25.3
of which social and health care services	14.6	15.7	11.5
of which education and culture	3.9	3.7	5.0
of which technical services	1.7	2.3	1.4
Central government	4.3	5.4	2.7
Third sector	2.9	6.2	7.2
Total	100.0	100.0	100.0

The share of local authorities has maintained on a high level in all three programme periods. In Finland, the local authority sector has a wide responsibility for basic health, social welfare and education services where also serious problems with QWL can be found at present. Work organizations of almost half of the 416 municipalities that exist in Finland are participating in TYKES development projects.

Figure 3: Most Common Targets of TYKES Development Projects, %

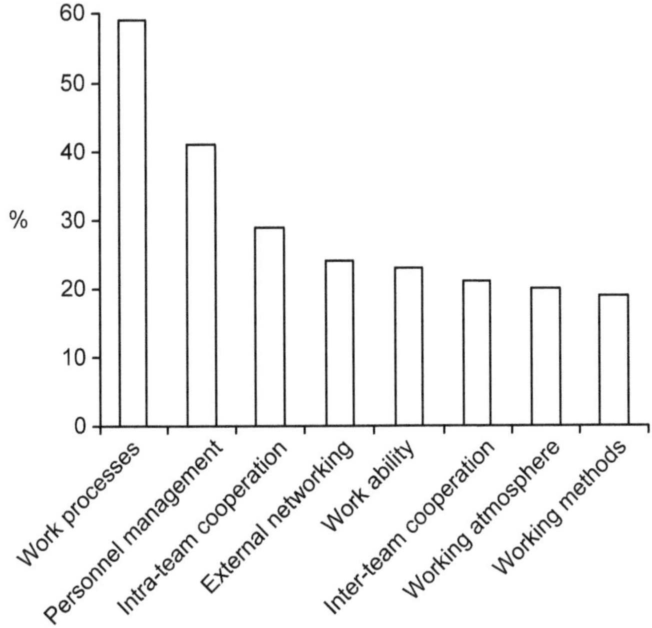

In terms of types of expertise used, the support granted to projects is distributed so that 52% is granted for hiring experts from consultancy agencies for projects. The total percentage of experts from universities, government research institutes and polytechnics comes to 33%. In development projects and basic analyses, the proportion of consultancy agencies is high, whereas in the more research-oriented method development projects and learning network projects most experts come from universities, research institutes and polytechnics. Most consultants that take part in the projects are self-employed or work in small Finnish consulting houses, which specialize in workplace development issues. The division of work between consultants and researchers is not so clear-cut in Finland as in many other countries, and in many cases consultants work together with researchers in close cooperation in the same projects. Furthermore, many consultants working in TYKES projects have a high-level educational background and may use similar development methods as researchers coming from universities.

The programme classifies development projects according to their targets. A project may have, and almost always has, more than one target. The most common targets are the development of work processes, personnel management and internal cooperation in teams (Figure 3).

The programme also gathers information on the different approaches, methods and tools used in support of development projects. In most cases, some analyses and mappings are carried out during the course of the projects at the starting phase or for the evaluation of project results. In about half of the projects, development groups are established with a view to implementing development activities in some special areas. Development methods used in at least every fifth project include also interviews, coaching, process consulting, team training, and process description and process flow analysis. All in all, the selection of methods used in the development project varies greatly according to the targets of the project, needs of the workplace in question and expertise of the consultants and researchers that take part in the projects.

Finnish Approach to Workplace Innovation and Development in Comparative Perspective

Workplace innovation and development entered the policy agenda in Finland later than in the other Nordic countries. Norway can be considered a pioneer, especially in the promotion of industrial democracy and sociotechnical forms of work organization, though the most famous examples of Nordic companies applying new forms of work organization are in fact found in Sweden. At the other extreme lies Finland. Finland could be described as a 'white spot' on the map of international debate on new forms of work organization in the 1970s and 1980s. Since the mid-1990s, the situation has changed radically, however, and workplace development has become increasingly integrated in the overall innovation policy framework.

As Gustavsen (2007) argues, policies and programmes never emerge of themselves; they always need actors who are able to build the frameworks integrating the various parties that are necessary for joint action. The content and form of workplace development has been most affected by who the central actors are, and how their mutual relationships are structured. The overall systems of regulation of working life in the Nordic countries differ from each other in many important aspects. In Finland, central government plays a more prominent role than in the other Nordic countries, while Denmark represents the other end of the spectrum. The labour market organizations, therefore, continue to show a stronger tendency in Finland than in the other Nordic countries to promote the development of working life 'through' central government in the form of labour legislation (instead of general and collective agreements between the social partners) and, as in the case of workplace development, government-funded programmes (instead of bipartite programmes, campaigns or other activities launched by the social partners).

The visible role played by central government is associated with another special character of the Finnish approach, namely the active involvement of public workplaces in development activities together with private companies. Many of the best-known action research projects in Finland have, in fact, been carried out in the local authority sector (Kalliola and Nakari, 1999; Lehtonen and Kalliola, 2008). The Finnish system of collective bargaining is one of the most centralized in Europe, and the local authority employers have played an important role as one of the key partners in the centralized incomes policy agreements that have been concluded in Finland during the last 40 years. Management systems and forms of work organization in the local authority sector have been a target of active renovation in recent years, as many municipalities are suffering from financial difficulties owing to ageing of the population, losses in the number of inhabitants and tax income, and rising costs of the welfare and health care sector. An additional underlying reason for the active involvement of the local authority sector in workplace development programmes in Finland is that both the employers' association and some of biggest trade unions have been active proponents of using (action) research as a means to help municipalities find innovative solutions to prevailing problems based on labour-management cooperation, instead of resorting solely to management-initiated cost-cutting measures.

A special feature of Nordic workplace development programmes in general seems to be the much closer cooperation between researchers and companies than in other European countries. This probably reflects the stronger role that action research, or, more broadly, research-supported development, plays in the Nordic countries (Aagaard Nielsen and Svensson, 2006; Gustavsen, 2007). In the other European countries, the dialectic between research and development is not as close-knit in workplace development, and development (often in the form of consultation) and research appear as largely separate activities, at least so far.

Facing Future Challenges

The challenge of qualitative sustainable productivity growth forms the basic policy rationale for the TYKES programme. It is quite clear that tackling with this challenge requires activities of many kinds in a variety of areas.

The main policy challenge with respect to the development of labour productivity is how to turn the long decline in the rate of productivity growth into an accelerating development, how to bring about favourable growth in productivity on a broad front of sectors and how to promote the emergence of new engines for productivity growth. The main policy challenge with respect to QWL, in turn, is how to have a positive impact on those aspects of working life that support employees in staying on at work. In practical terms, the percentage of workplaces that produce positive effects on learning opportunities and employee wellbeing simultaneously should be on the top level internationally in the coming years. Traditional indicators used in the Finnish working conditions surveys do not indicate that the trend in recent years has been in this direction (see Table 3).

In March 2008, responsibility for the TYKES programme was transferred from the Ministry of Labour to Tekes. This organizational rearrangement, together with a change in the act of Tekes, consolidated the promotion of workplace innovation as one of the permanent R&D areas within Tekes and brought also the improvement of QWL as a statutory task of Tekes. In autumn 2008, the Finnish Government decided on guidelines for a 'broad-based innovation policy', based on a proposal that was submitted by a high-level working group. According to the new strategy, workplace development should be closely integrated as part of innovation policy planning and implementation in the future, sufficient financial resources for the promotion of workplace innovation and development should be ensured and new methods for spreading workplace innovations should be extensively developed.

The Government's new policy approach forms a solid basis in reinforcing the national infrastructure for research and development on working life. The success of the new approach in confronting the challenge of qualitatively sustainable productivity will depend on the overall development of expanded triple helix cooperation. Success requires, above all, that the strong national consensus that has prevailed in Finland in workplace innovation and development so far will be sustained and new forms of joint actions between the parties to triple helix cooperation will be made possible.

References

Aagaard Nielsen, K. / Svensson, L. (eds.) (2006): Action and Interactive Research: Beyond Practice and Theory. Maastricht: Shaker Publishing.

Alasoini, T. / Ramstad, E. / Rouhiainen, N. (2005): The Finnish Workplace Development Programme as an Expanding Activity: Results, Challenges, Opportunities. Reports of the Finnish Workplace Development Programme 47. Helsinki: Ministry of Labour.

Arnkil, R. (2004): 'The Finnish Workplace Development Programme: A Small Giant?', Concepts and Transformation 9(3): 249-278.

Arnkil, R. (2008): 'In Search of Missing Links in Disseminating Good Practice – Experiences of a Work Reform Programme in Finland', International Journal of Action Research 4(1+2): 39-61.

Benner, M. (2003): 'The Scandinavian Challenge: The Future of Advanced Welfare States in the Knowledge Economy', Acta Sociologica 46(2): 132-149.

Bresnahan, T.F. / Brynjolfsson, E. / Hitt, L.M. (2002): 'Information Technology, Workplace Organization, and the Demand for Skilled Labor: Firm-level Evidence', Quarterly Journal of Economics 117(1): 339–376.

Castells, M. / Himanen, P. (2002): The Information Society and the Welfare State: The Finnish Model. Oxford: Oxford University Press.

Dhondt, S. / Kraan, K. / Van Sloten, G. (2002): Work Organisation, Technology and Working Conditions. Dublin: European Foundation for the Improvement of Living and Working Conditions.

Forsman, P. / Jalava, J. (2006): 'ICT's Contribution to Labour Productivity', Bank of Finland Bulletin 80(1): 85-89.

Gustavsen, B. (2007): 'Work Organization and the 'Scandinavian Model' ', Economic and Industrial Democracy 28(4): 650-671.

Hämäläinen, T. / Heiskala, R. (eds.) (2007): Social Innovations, Institutional Change and Economic Performance: Making Sense of Structural Adjustment Process in Industrial Sectors, Regions and Societies. Cheltenham: Edward Elgar.

Kalliola, S. / Nakari, R. (1999): Resources for Renewal: A Participatory Approach to the Modernization of Municipal Organizations in Finland. Amsterdam: John Benjamins.

Laursen, K. / Foss, N.J. (2003): 'New Human Resource Management Practices, Complementaries and the Impact on Innovation Performance', Cambridge Journal of Economics 27(2): 243–263.

Lehto, A.-M. / Sutela, H. (2005): Threats and Opportunities: Findings of Finnish Quality of Work Life Surveys 1977-2003. Helsinki: Statistics Finland.

Lehtonen, J. / Kalliola, S. (eds.) (2008): Dialogue in Working Life Research and Development in Finland. Frankfurt a/M: Peter Lang.

Ministry of Labour (2003): Preparing for the Labour Market Change Caused by the Baby Boom Generation. Publications of Labour Administration 320. Helsinki: Ministry of Labour.

Ramstad, E. (2008): Innovation Generating Model – Simultaneous Development of Work Organization and Knowledge Infrastructure. Reports of the Finnish Workplace Development Programme 65. Helsinki: Tekes.

Ramstad, E. / Alasoini, T. (2006): 'Interactive Research in Finland: Workplace Research from the 1940's to the Present Day', pp. 158-169, in K. Aagaard Nielsen and L. Svensson (eds.) Action and Interactive Research: Beyond Practice and Theory. Maastricht: Shaker Publishing.

Roberts, J. (2004): The Modern Firm: Organizational Design for Performance and Growth. Oxford: Oxford University Press.

Schienstock, G. (ed.) (2004): Embracing the Knowledge Society: The Dynamic Transformation of the Finnish Innovation system. Cheltenham: Edward Elgar.
Tekes (2008): People – Economy – Environment. Helsinki: Tekes.
Tuominen, E. / Takala, M. / Tuominen, K. (2005): Employers and the Flexible Retirement Age: Employer Views on the Finnish Pension Reform in 2005 and Older Employees' Continued Work. Working Papers 2005:3. Helsinki: Finnish Centre for Pensions.
Van Ark, B. (2006): Europe's Productivity Gap: Catching Up or Getting Stuck? Economics Program Working Paper Series #06-02. New York: Conference Board.
Ylöstalo, P. / Jukka, P. (2008): Työolobarometri: lokakuu 2007 [Finnish Working Life Barometer: October 2007]. Publications 16/2008. Helsinki: Ministry of Employment and the Economy.

"Quality of Working Life" on the agenda of Flemish regional policy

Paul Berckmans

1. Creating a favourable context

The last decade, several initiatives were initiated at the level of Flemish regional policy, creating a favourable context towards the issue of quality of working life.

1.1. "Pact of Vilvoorde": a global political view 2001-2010

In 2001, the Flemish government and the social partners gathered in 'The House of the Future' in Vilvoorde and signed an agreement that translated the European Lisbon agenda to the regional level of Flanders. This translation resulted in 21 goals covering all the socio-economic aspects of society. To measure the progress in reaching these goals in 2010, a framework of more than 80 quantitative indicators was developed. A 'progress report' will be published each year to allow evaluation of the evolution towards the goals[1].

One of the main goals is increasing the degree of employability. Although the unemployment rate in Flanders is very low, its employability rate of 65% is still 5% below the EU goal. The innovative aspect is linking the quality-of-work issue to this goal of increasing employability: "Increasing the quality of working life, of work organisation and of career perspectives should result in higher employability because working will be more attractive for all, including the elderly and the unemployed. The goal is a 'workability' rate that is substantially higher in 2010 than in 2001."[2]

To measure this 'workability' or quality-of-working life rate, the Flemish government and the social partners asked the Foundation Innovation & Work to develop a specific monitoring system and to organise three surveys in 2004, 2007 and 2010.

Another goal in the Pact of Vilvoorde also explicitly refers to innovation in work organisation as one element of an innovative society: "In 2010, Flanders

1 Het Pact van Vilvoorde in concrete cijfers. De opvolging van de 21 doelstellingen. 2007. Studiedienst van de Vlaamse Regering, Brussel, 2007, n.g.

2 Idem. p. 8

will be an innovative society. (…) The degree of implementation of innovative forms of work organisation and HR policies intended to develop and use competencies (among other things via networking) will be substantially increased."[3] The Foundation Innovation & Work was also asked to develop a monitoring instrument for this indicator.

The methodology and some results of both monitoring systems will be presented in chapter 2 of this paper.

1.2. "Pact 2020": designing Flanders' future

In January 2009, the Flemish government and the social partners renewed and updated their engagements made in the Pact of Vilvoorde. This resulted in the Pact 2020 in which 20 specific goals are formulated. Among these goals, the broadening of the concept of innovation beyond purely technological limits, a better quality of working life, and the stimulation of competence oriented organisations have a prominent place. This means that the monitoring of these goals by the Foundation Innovation & Work are guaranteed.

1.3. "Competence development": a key issue of the Flemish government

In 2006, Frank Vandenbroucke, at the time Flemish minister of work and training, launched the 'Competence Agenda', a coherent set of initiatives aimed at creating a culture of continuous development of competencies at different levels. On one hand, to improve the transition to the labour market within the educational system; on the other hand, to support all forms of vocational training (on the job learning, task enrichment, etc.) within companies.

To promote the idea of competence management, the social partners and the Social Economic Council of Flanders (SERV) set up a project to collect 101 good examples of competence management in all its various aspects. In fact, some 105 cases covering all aspects of the Flemish economy are described[4] and can be consulted on the Internet. Most of these cases illustrate the necessary link between competence management and organisational change.

---

3 Idem. p. 9

4 Inspirerende voorbeelden van competentiebeleid. Actie in het kader van de competentieagenda 2010. SERV, Brussel, 2009, 184p.

1.4. *"Broadening the concept of innovation policy"*

In the 1980's, Flemish innovation policy, like most innovation policies in Europe, focused on technological innovation. The DIRV campaign (Third Industrial Revolution in Flanders) was almost totally inspired by the push for technology[5]. Slowly, however, the concept of innovation policy is being broadened from purely technological product or process innovation to include a complementary social innovation aspect.

Based on several SERV advises and recommendations[6] and on a benchmark exercise performed by the Foundation Innovation & Work on several governmental programmes aiming at social innovation in the workplace (e.g. the Finnish TYKES programme, the Irish NCPP programme, the programmes in Germany)[7], the Flemish government set up a small ESF-financed programme (2006-2007) for 12 companies to experiment with organisational changes focusing on both a higher quality of working life and more sustainable productivity growth. The programme was continued this year (17 cases). In chapter 3 we will focus on this governmental programme.

2. Facts and figures on the quality of work in flanders

It is extremely important to collect facts and figures about the quality of working life on a representative scale, as objective as possible and on a regular base. The Flemish Workability monitor and the Indicator for Competence-oriented Companies both meets these scientific requirements.

2.1. *Monitoring the workability of the Flemish labour market*

2.2.1. *Some methodological aspects*

The workability monitor, developed by the Foundation Innovation & Work, is based on existing, validated instruments such as VBBA, SWING and ESWC.

5 The only exception was the creation, within the SERV, of STV Innovation & Work in 1984.

6 SERV Advies m.b.t. De verruiming van het steunbaar innovatietraject. Brussels, 2006

7 BAMPS Hadewych, BERCKMANS Paul: Overheidsbeleid ter stimulering van organisatie-innovatie in bedrijven: lessen uit het buitenland. SERV-STV Innovatie & Arbeid, Brussel, 2005, 155p

Several editions are planned, with two of them having been completed in 2004 and 2007, the following scheduled for 2010, 2013, 2017 and 2020.

In each case, a questionnaire is sent to a sample of 20,000 workers. The very high response rates of 60.6% (2004) and 53.3% (2007) enable us to offer a representative view of the quality of working life in the Flemish economy[8].

Since 2007, a similar questionnaire is sent to 6.000 self-employed persons (response rate in 2007 of 40%).

2.2.2. What is monitored?

The core of the questionnaire deals with 4 basic workability indicators and 6 risk indicators. The workability indicators are: job-related learning opportunities, work-life balance, work related stress, and well-being at work.

The 6 risk indicators are: workload, emotional load, skill variety, support from the supervisor, physical working conditions, and autonomy.

2.2.3. Some key results 2004-2007 (workability index for workers)

- The workability indicators

  A job is considered to be of good quality when there is no problematic score on any of the four workability indicators. In 2004, 52.3% of all jobs in the Flemish economy were of good quality. I.e.: there were sufficient learning opportunities, the work-life balance was OK, work related stress was under control, and there was positive well-being at work. In 2007, this global percentage increased to 54.1%. This is a statistical significant evolution.

  Figure 1 shows the distribution of jobs with zero problems or pressure points, with one problem or more.

8 All methodological details and all publications can be downloaded free from the website: www.serv.be/werkbaarwerk.

Figure 1: Workability rate Flemish labour market 2004-2007

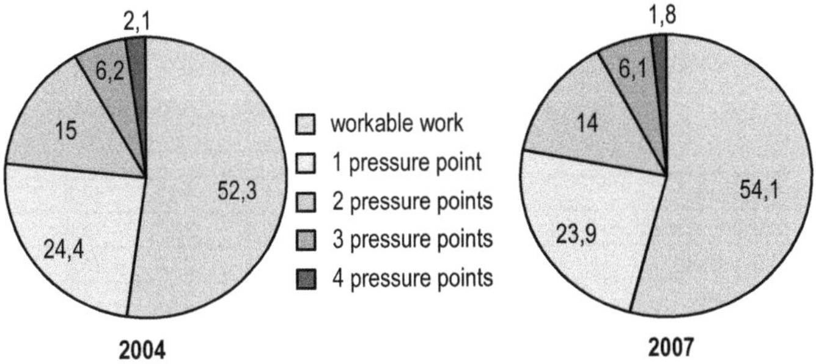

Source: De Sociaal-Economische Raad van Vlaanderen – SERV

More interesting is to look at the individual scores of each indicator, as shown in figure 2.

Figure 2: Workability indicators 2004-2007

workability	not problematic		problematic		acutely problematic	
	2004 %	2007 %	2004 %	2007 %	2004 %	2007 %
stress at work	71,1	71,2	28,9	28,8	10,2	9,7
well-being at work	81,3	81,9	18,7	18,1	8,0	7,9
learning opportunities	77,4	80,1	22,6	19,9	8,4	7,3
work-family balance	88,2	89,2	11,8	10,8	3,1	2,4

Source: De Sociaal-Economische Raad van Vlaanderen - SERV

Stress at work is by far the most problematic workability indicator: nearly 29% of all jobs have a problematic score, both in 2004 and 2007. Insufficient learning opportunities is the second problematic indicator although one can see that the globally higher workability rate is the result of a better score on this indicator and on the indicator of work-life balance.

- The risk indicators

Figure 3: Risk indicators 2004-2007

Risk indicators	not problematic		problematic		acutely problematic	
	2004 %	2007 %	2004 %	2007 %	2004 %	2007 %
workload	69,0	69,4	31,0	30,6	12,8	12,5
emotional load	79,5	79,3	20,5	20,7	4,0	4,3
skill variety	76,2	76,5	23,8	23,5	11,5	10,5
autonomy	79,2	79,8	20,8	20,2	7,3	7,5
social support	83,9	84,0	16,1	16,0	6,1	6,2
physical working conditons	87,9	86,3	12,1	13,7	4,5	5,3

Source: De Sociaal-Economische Raad van Vlaanderen - SERV

Figure 3 shows that the indicator workload had the lowest non-problematic score, both in 2004 and 2007 (69.0% and 69.4%), in other words: workload is the most problematic aspect with negative impact on the quality of work. For 12.5% of employees, the workload is even acutely problematic.

The less negative indicator is working conditions, although there is a statistically significant decrease in the non-problematic score from 87.9% in 2004 to 86.3% in 2007.

- Results for specific groups

All these indicators are available for different subpopulations in the labour market, so we can compare the workability and risk indicators by gender, age, type of contract, fulltime or part-time, profession, size of the company, and sector. Figures 4 and 5 gives examples of learning opportunities by job, and of the differences in workability in several industrial sectors.

It is clear that learning opportunities are directly and significantly linked to the type of job: about 50% of the unskilled blue-collar jobs have a lack of learning opportunities while this is only the case for about 6% of managerial staff functions.

Figure 4: Learning opportunities problematic by job

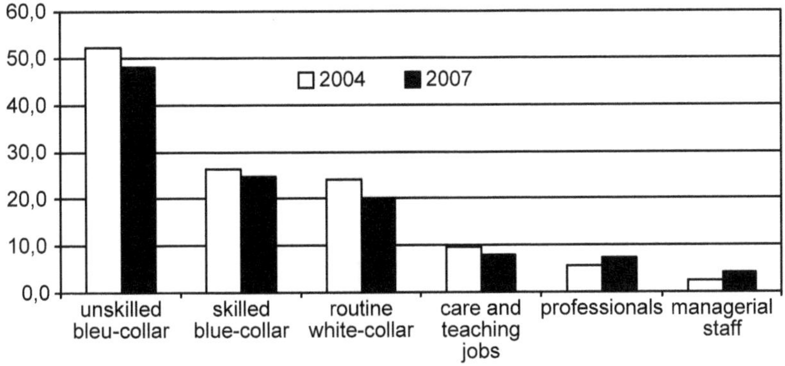

Source: De Sociaal-Economische Raad van Vlaanderen – SERV

Figure 5: No pressure points by sector (industry)

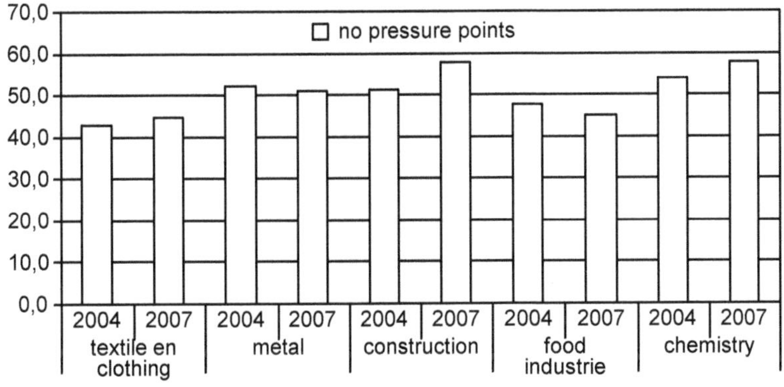

Source: De Sociaal-Economische Raad van Vlaanderen – SERV

There are significant workability differences between sectors: construction, chemistry and metal industry have a significant higher workability rate than textile and clothing and food industry, both in 2004 and 2007.

The workability monitor database is an enormously rich source for analysing the state of the quality of working life in Flanders, to gain a clear view of the evolution in time of specific parameters or indicators, and to help social partners and government set up sector-specific or group-specific action plans in order to obtain a higher quality of working life.

Figure 6: Effect results and workability (2004)

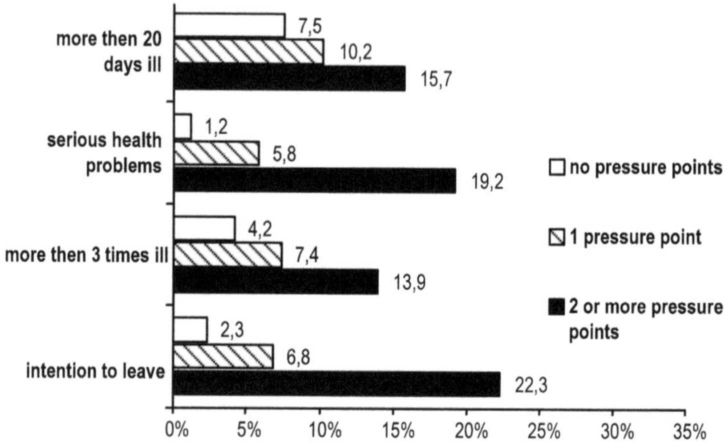

Source: De Sociaal-Economische Raad van Vlaanderen – SERV

The workability monitor also makes it possible to link certain aspects of workability with performance indicators. As is shown in figures 6 and 7, a higher workability rate results in significantly lower rates of absenteeism and illness, and in a much lower intention to leave the job.

When asked if people are capable to do their job until their legal date of retirement, it is clear that the workability of the job plays a determent role (figure 7).

Figure 7: Workabilty and feasable retirement

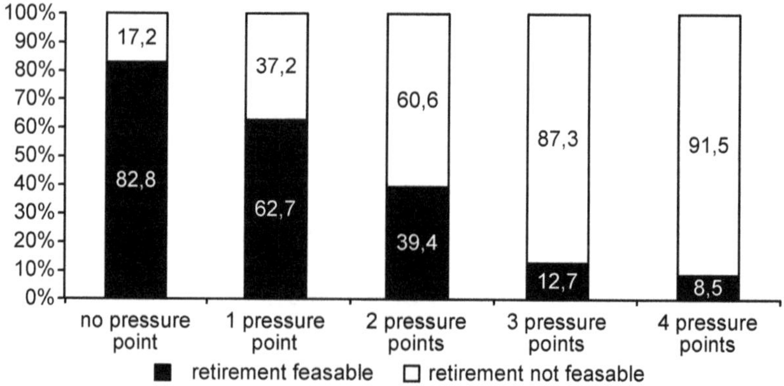

Source: De Sociaal-Economische Raad van Vlaanderen – SERV

2.2. *Monitoring competence-oriented companies*

2.2.1. *Some methodological aspects*

The Indicator of Competence Oriented companies (ICO) is based on the T(echnology)-O(rganisation)-A(rbeid) survey, developed by the Foundation Innovation & Work since 1998. It is a questionnaire administered by telephone to HR managers or CEOs (+/- 18 minutes), based on a representative sample of 2,000 companies in Flanders. The TOA screening was organised in 1998 (industry +10), 2001, 2004 and 2007. The high response rates (between 55% and 68%) allow us to obtain a 'helicopter view' (not an in-depth analysis) of trends concerning knowledge about and the implementation of innovative management concepts and new forms of work organisation.

Within the entire set of data, 13 criteria on developing and using competencies are assembled into the ICO. A company is evaluated as competence oriented if at least 7 of the criteria are put into practice.

2.2.2. *What is monitored by ICO?*

The 13 criteria are clustered in 4 groups.

The first cluster deals with 3 traditional aspects of competence development: (1) training is organised for at least 50% of the employees, (2) training is organised in the context of a training plan, (3) the concept of competence management is at least partially implemented.

The second cluster focuses on the use of competencies: (4) a formal evaluation system is implemented for at least 50% of the employees, (5) there is a formal platform where different aspects of the job can be discussed with the immediate manager for at least 50% of the employees, (6) a formal system of collecting suggestions is implemented and (7) management frequently makes an appeal to the employees concerning the company's innovation policy.

The third cluster deals with some specific characteristics of work organisation: (8) at least the work of 50% of the employees is teamwork, (9) the teams are responsible for the division of tasks within the team, (10) at least 50% of the employees are responsible for their work methods, (11) at least 50% of the employees are polyvalent.

Finally, the fourth cluster deals with external networking: (12) there is frequent collaboration with clients or suppliers, (13) clients, suppliers and knowledge services (such as universities or high schools) are frequently engaged in the innovation policy.

2.2.3. Some key results 2001-2007

- Figure 8 shows the global evolution of the ICO in the period 2001-2007. In 2001, 42.4% of companies in Flanders scored positively on a minimum 7 of the 14 criteria, so 42.4% were competence oriented. In 2004, the ICO score rose to 50.6%, a significant increase. However, in 2007, the ICO score fell back to the 2001 level.

Figure 8: Percentage of companies with a positive score on at least 7 of 13 criteria

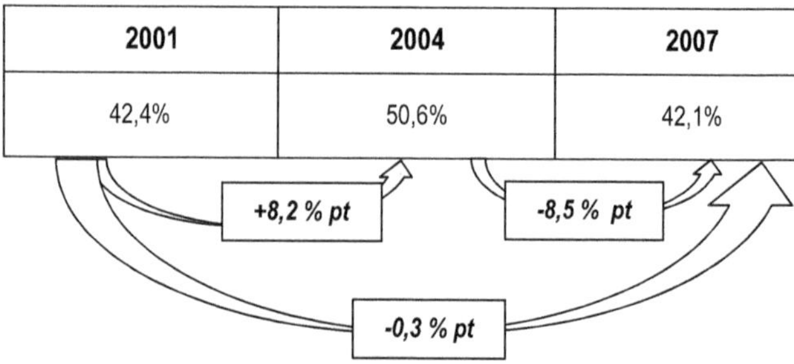

Indicator Competentiegerichte Ondernemingen

Source: stv Innovatie & Arbeid – SERV

- As figures 9 to 12 demonstrates, behind this global evolution lie many types of turbulence at the individual criteria level (the green upwards triangle indicates a significant increase of the score between 2001 and 2007, a red downwards triangle indicates a significant decrease).

Figure 9: Classics

Criterium	2007	*Verschil 2001-2007*
1. Training for at least 50% of employees	40,6%	=
2. Training plan exists	53,7%	▲
3. Competence Management at least partially impemented	30,7%	=

Indicator Competentiegerichte Ondernemingen

Source: stv Innovatie & Arbeid – SERV

Figure 10: Made appeal to competences

Criterium	**2007**	*Verschil 2001-2007*
4. Performance appraisel for at least 50% of employees	58,1%	▼
5. Work councils are implemented	59,1%	▲
6. Formalised follow-up of suggestions	54,2%	=
7. Employees are an important source of innovation	40,4%	▼

Indicator Competentiegerichte Ondernemingen

Source: stv Innovatie & Arbeid – SERV

Figure 11: Made appeal to competences

Criterium	**2007**	*Verschil 2001-2007*
8. Teamwork for at least 50% of employees	47,0%	▲
9. ... and work method and work division are delegated to the teams	43,8%	▲
10. At least 50% of the employees are responsible for their work method	55,1%	▲
11. At least 50% of the employees are polyvalent	41,0%	=

Indicator Competentiegerichte Ondernemingen

Source: stv Innovatie & Arbeid – SERV

Figure 12: External networking aimed at gaining competences

Criterium	**2007**	*Verschil 2001-2007*
12. Structural collaboration and electronic communication with suppliers or customers	72,5%	=
13. Suppliers, Customers and knowledge centers are used as sources of innovation	8,8%	▲

Indicator Competentiegerichte Ondernemingen

Source: stv Innovatie & Arbeid – SERV

- From a sectoral point of view, the ICO score is the highest in the social non-profit sector cluster. This result has remained constant over the years[9].
  Two main conclusions can be drawn to demonstrate the importance of this kind of quantitative monitoring: (1) there is no one best way for a company or an economy to be competence oriented; multiple strategies are possible; (2) it is very difficult to maintain a higher level of competence orientation in an organisation in the long run because of the constant attention required on several aspects together.

3. Broadening the concept of innovation policy

In this last chapter, we briefly refers to the international context, to focus on the specific Flemish situation.

3.1. International evolution

Of course, when seen in a European perspective, that which is actually happening in Flanders, namely placing the 'quality of working life' issue on the political agenda, is not new.

There is a long tradition in a number of European countries concerning programmes fostering organisational innovation on the work floor[10].

Actually, the well-known WORK-in-NET network consists of more than 20 partners in 13 European member states[11].

Also on a global European scale, the many years of experience of both the European Foundation for the Improvement of Living and Working Conditions[12], and the European Agency for Safety and Health at Work[13], in Dublin and Bilbao respectively, have been a continuous stimulation for putting quality of work on the national and regional agenda.

---

9 All results can be found on the SERV website: www.serv.be/stv

10 For a synthesis see: Totterdill Peter, Dhondt Steven, Milsome Sue: Partners at Work? A report to Europe's policy makers and social partners. Report of the H-Res Project, October 2002, 115 p.
And: Oehlke Paul, Riegler Claudius H., Wupperman Dietmar, Zettel Claudio: Why high road of innovation? Work-oriented innovation strategies in Europe. Work-in-Net Background Paper, December 2007, 32p.

11 See www.workinnet.org.

12 See www.eurofound.europa.eu.

13 See http://europe.osha.eu.int/info.

In june and September 2008, the European Economic and Social Council, more specifically the Labour Market Observatory, organised hearings on "sustainable productivity and quality of working life"[14]. Sustainable productivity is seen as an upward spiral in productivity based on the investment of profits in an increasingly motivated, healthy, skilled, responsible, creative and innovative workforce.

On a broader scale, in 2005 the OECD published a new version of the Oslo Manual that is the basis for several surveys imposed by the authorities, e.g. the Community Innovation Statistics (CIS). For the first time, the innovation concept is broadened to include organisational innovation: "Innovations in workplace organisation involve the implementation of new methods for distributing responsibilities and decision-making autonomy among employees (...)". Examples given include the establishment of formal or informal work teams, giving substantially more control and responsibility over work processes to the firm's workers, training programmes, etc.[15]

3.2. Evolution within the context of Flemish policy

3.2.1. Some specific regional initiatives

Of course, this international, global change towards the innovation concept has been discussed in Flanders but, as mentioned above, a number of specific initiatives accelerated their placement on the political agenda.

- In June 2005, the Foundation Innovation & Work published a report describing several governmental programmes abroad, focusing on or stimulating organisational innovation[16]. As a conclusion, 10 factors of a successful programme were derived from the good practices. In a brief benchmark, elements within the regional context that were positive or negative with respect to these factors were described.

  These 10 success factors were:
  - the need for a broad vision of innovation, including technological AND organisational aspects;

---

14 Sustainable productivity growth and quality of working life. Hearings of 12 june and 9 september 2008. Labor Market Observatory, Section for Employment, Social Affairs and Citizenship. EESC, Brussels, 2009, 36p.

15 See: OECD document DSTI/EAS/STP/NESTI(2005)2

16 Bamps Hadewych, Berckmans Paul: Overheidsbeleid ter stimulering van organisatie-innovatie in bedrijven: lessen uit het buitenland. SERV-STV Innovatie & Arbeid, Brussel, 2005, 155p

- the need for an open minded approach to organisational innovation: it may start directly from the focus on organisational change, or indirectly from e.g. competence management, or anti-stress strategies;
- the necessity of creating significant involvement on the part of all stakeholders: government, social partners, (social) researchers, academics, companies, consultants, ...;
- the necessity of building up large networks among all these stakeholders, without creating rivalry or the feeling that one stakeholder will control all the others;
- the necessity of a long-term perspective, independent of the relatively short perspective of a government;
- the need to find a balance between clear targets in the programme and flexibility in the implementation process;
- the use of a broad variety of instruments and tools to implement organisational innovation;
- great attention and a lot of energy must be put into the dissemination and valorisation of good (and bad) practices, so that the results of the programme are useful to a much larger group of companies than those directly involved;
- defining measurable targets is very helpful in monitoring the programme results;
- to have a real impact on a region's economy and welfare, the budget must be significantly high.

In fact, some of these criteria were taken seriously by the Flemish government in setting up the first small-scale regional governmental programme stimulating organisational innovation.

However, in 2008, a critical evaluation of this programme was drawn up by Alasoini TUOMO[17], coordinator of the Finnish TYKES Programme. It is very worthwhile taking his recommendations into account. We will return to his evaluation later.

- In February 2006, the Social Economic Council of Flanders (SERV) published an advise on broadening public finance opportunities for innovation policy in the economy. The social partners formulated it very clearly: "The Flemish social partners engage themselves, individually and collectively, to strengthen the innovation process in Flanders at the general, sectoral and entrepreneurial level. The need for technological innovation and innovation in

17 Tuomo, Alasoini; Ramstad, Elise; Hanhike, Tiina; Rouhiainen, Nuppu: Learning across boundaries. Workplace Development Strategies of Singapore, Flanders and Ireland in Comparison. Work-in-Net, Helsinki, 2008, 85p.

matters of work organisation and human capital is recognised. This recognition and engagement is the start of a new, enlarged vision of what innovation should be."[18]

This clear statement contributed to the creation of Flanders Synergy.

3.2.2. Flanders Synergy 2006-2007

- In 2006, the Flemish Minister of Work, Education and Training, Mr. Frank Vandenbroucke, took the initiative to create Flanders Synergy, a programme co-financed by the ESF and the 12 selected companies.

- A call for proposals was launched by ESF Flanders that specified the global goals and conditions of the programme. The global goal was to set up pilot programmes in which innovations in work organisation contributed both to a higher level of working life quality and to greater entrepreneurial performance. There was no strict guidance on how the pilot programmes had to be structured or organised; the company could choose to organise the process in a way that met most of their objectives. Only four general conditions were formulated:
  - The final goal of the pilot programme must be a higher degree of workability (a higher level of quality of the work) for the target group;
  - The pilot programmes must result in a structural, permanent change in the existing work organisation, and these changes must be situated at a collective level;
  - The pilot programmes must be organised with the involvement of all the stakeholders (management, workers,...);
  - If relevant, quantitative targets must be defined so that adjustments to the pilot programmes can be organised in a timely manner.

  The pilot programmes had to focus on one or more aspects of workability:
  - Reducing work-related stress;
  - Raising the motivational level of jobs, so that employees will be more engaged;
  - Raising the learning capacities of the jobs, so that competencies can be developed and used;
  - Focusing on a better work-life balance.

- A specific Task Force was created. The driving force behind this Task Force was Prof. Dr. Geert Van Hootegem of the University of Leuven (KULeuven)

18 Advies Visienota "De verruiming van het steunbaar innovatietraject". SERV, Brussel, 7 februari 2006, 15p.

and his team of scientific collaborators. All the major stakeholders were represented in this Task Force: the academic world, the government, the social partners, one consultant (Panta Rei) and the twelve pilot programmes. The Task Force had several goals: in the short term, to monitor and support the pilot programmes during the project; and to stimulate networking between all the stakeholders. To reach these goals, the Task Force organised 10 round table discussions during the period January 2007-April 2008. Five of these round table discussions were limited to the smaller public of the pilot programmes and their immediate stakeholders; the other five round table discussions were open to the broader public. In the long term, the Task Force was charged with disseminating and communicating the results of the pilot programmes to a broad public, and with setting up initiatives to raise awareness among the authorities.

- Of the 24 pilot proposals, 12 were selected; each received maximum financial support from the government of € 50,000, so the global financial input of the Flemish government was € 600,000. The pilot programmes cover a wide range of companies and organisations, and the focus on workability was very diverse, as can be seen in this table.

Table: Flanders Synergy, the 12 pilot programmes

Company	Core business activities	Name and development themes of the project
NV Deceuninck	PVC/vinyl window and door systems and building profiles for windows, doors, shutters, wall cladding, etc.	Proactive Health Policy: Development of a proactive health policy and its integration into the overall company policy
Roularta Media Group	Magazines, newspapers, radio and television programmes and the Internet	Integrated Newsrooms: Testing of innovative Integrated Newsroom concept in the event of merging together diverse production units
ArcelorMittal Gent	Maritime and integrated steel works	Knowledge Guarantee: Storing the experience-based knowledge of senior workers and organising its transfer to younger workers in a systematic way
Beschutte Werkplaats Klein-Brabant	Sheltered workplaces for disabled persons	Flow Line Perspective in Sheltered Workplaces: Improving the career perspectives of workers and decreasing the level of stress at work

Company	Core business activities	Name and development themes of the project
BnS Engineering	Multidisciplinary engineering office for industrial engineering projects	Optimatrix: Shift from a functional organisational structure to more self-managed, customer-driven units and decentralisation of responsibility
Robert Bosch Produktie NV	Car parts such as screen wipers, head lamp wiper engines, etc.	Evaluation-Based Learning on the Shop Floor: Creating a new operational model to improve opportunities for learning at work and having a positive effect on the working climate
TTL Camerlynck NV	Teeth technical laboratory	Teeth Grinding: Introducing self-managed teams capable of continuous learning
De Kringwinkel Midden West-Vlaanderen	Shop for recycled consumer products	Sustainable Work: Introducing a new form of work organisation with a view toward improving productivity and the quality of work
Deloitte	Audit and consulting agency	Towards Self-Guidance: Introducing self-guiding teams that improve work motivation, and opportunities for development and exerting influence at work
EADS Defence and Security Systems	Defence and security systems	EADS Becomes Main Supplier: Enhancing the knowledge base of workers and the innovativeness of the work community with a systematic knowledge management approach
De Oesterbank	Industrial sheltered workplaces for disabled persons	Buffer Atelier – Automation – Supporting Tools: Enhancing the labour market position and quality of work of the most vulnerable employees by means of reorganisation and ergonomic improvements
Philips Innovative Applications NV	Lighting applications	Self-Guidance 2008: Further development of the self-guidance of the already existing teams

- The results of the pilot projects, including some recommendations made by the Task Force to the Flemish government, are published in 3 volumes.[19] The pilot programmes have a very diverse focus, as do the results, e.g.:
  - The development of an e-learning tool;
  - Higher performance (new markets, new clients) and a higher degree of worker motivation;
  - More multitasking, more involvement through greater variation and motivation;
  - Higher level of team working;
  - Successful implementation of an anti-noise policy;
  - New organisational structure based on the optimal use of human capital (competence management);
  - Transformation from individual thinking to collective thinking;
  - Etc.

- In April 2008, Tuomo Alasoini and his collaborators made a benchmark exercise of the Flanders Synergy programme. The results of this benchmarking are very interesting and should be taken into account in further initiatives. Alasoini uses the six dimensions of a revised version of the Nashold (1994) model. The main results can be summarised as follows:
  - Policy context: the programme is embedded in the Pact of Vilvoorde, which means "the players in the industrial relations field are the most important stakeholders for the programme, whereas the role of R&D units in defining the agenda has been marginal."
  - Orientation: being a regional programme, the inspiration for it "is clearly more international than national".
  - Participation: being highly design oriented, "the contents of the projects are strongly influenced by the companies themselves, and employee influence through the works councils can be considered relatively strong."
  - Infrastructure: "universities, research institutes or other educational institutes do not play any role at the project level. (…). The tradition of cooperation between consultants and academics in practice-oriented company

19 Van Hootegem, Geert; Huys, Rik, Van Beek, Gert; Beens, Ellen: In het land van Flanders Synergy. Werken en ondernemen in een innovatieve economie., ACCO, Leuven, 2008, 55 p.
Van Beek, Gert; Van Hootegem, Geert: Woorden wekken, voorbeelden strekken. Een dozijn lessen organisatieverandering in woord en beeld. ACCO, Leuven, 2008, 120 p.
Van Hootegem, Geert; Van Amelsvoort, Pierre; Van Beek, Gert; Huys, Rik: Anders organiseren & beter werken. Handboek sociale innovatie en verandermanagement. ACCO, Leuven, 2008, 203 p.

projects still seems to be very thin in Flanders when it comes to work-oriented innovations".

- Horizontal networking: "The Task Force plays a critical role concerning the possible continuation of activities in this policy area after the programme has ended".
- Resources: "The Flemish programme is rather modest in terms of material resources. (…) At the time of writing, it seems to us that the weakest link in the current Flemish approach to promoting innovative work organisation, from the perspective of triple helix thinking (…), is to be found in the marginal role of universities and other R&D units".

3.2.3. The creation of a Competence Flanders Synergy (2008-?)

At the end of 2007, ESF Flanders initiated a new call for proposals "Social Innovation". In March 2008, 16 projects were approved. The concept of this programme is very similar to the Flanders Synergy projects: a broad approach to social innovation; a high level of autonomy for the companies in the implementation process. The framework of the programme, however, is very different: there is no longer a task force as was the case in Flanders Synergy, the ESF agency being the only supervising and coordinating body. It is clear that the results of the benchmark of Flanders Synergy made by Alasoini e.a. were not taken into account in the Social Innovation programme.

More promising, however, is the adoption of a feasibility study concerning creating a competence pool; "Innovative Work Organisation". Competence pools are a specific tool in the Flemish innovation policy approach that allows focusing all existing competencies on the development of a specific innovation (usually technological). A competence pool is co-financed by the government and the companies who are member of the pool.

The feasibility study is a direct result of the Flanders Synergy programme, and is being carried out by Prof. Dr. Geert Van Hootegem of the KULeuven and his collaborators. In may 2009, the Flemish government took the decision to (co)finance the Competentiepool Flanders Synergy which has as priority to contribute to a higher performance of enterprises by means of innovative human resources development and innovative work organisation.

The success of the competence pool will largely depend on the attention given to the benchmark-findings of Alasoini (e.a.), more specifically that all social partners and other stakeholders will be envolved in the whole process and that the activities of the competence pool will focus on coordination and networking (with respect to the existing competence centers in the matter). Than one can say that with the creation of this Competence Pool, a further step in building up a basic structure for a sustainable network (according to the triple helix concept) in the field of innovative work organisation will have been set.

3.2.4. The social partners defining social innovation

In November 2008, the social partners, in a SERV-advise to the Flemish government, defined social innovation as follows: "Social innovation includes concepts and practices regarding processes in work organisation and management. Goal is to increase both performance and quality in a sustainable way. These concepts and practices are resulting out of the vision and mission of the organisation and are realised by mutual agreement with the actors in question".

Conclusions

Although the process of change in rethinking the concept of innovation and innovation policy in the direction of integrated and complimentary technological AND social innovation is a non-linear, very slow and long term one, it is incontestable that finally the quality of working life is being put on the agenda of the social partners and on the political agenda of the Flemish government.

Employee participation in ninety-five investment projects: Experience and action priorities for public policies based on observations of SME practices

Romain Chevallet

Our approach is based on an extensive study rolled out in a project group within the ANACT network involving ergonomists, organisation specialists, sociologists and labour economists[1]. The group worked on three major types of investment: the establishment or development of new information and communication technologies, the design or development of buildings and industrial investments to convert production facilities.

On the basis of a study of 95 investment project practices in SMEs, we will highlight the risks of corporate underperformance due to a lack of employee participation and insufficient acknowledgement of the actual work activity. Focusing its project on technical expertise that it does not always possess, without calling on knowledge of real operational practices, the company is required to delegate the effective running of its project to technical service providers (internal or external). This excessive empowerment combined with insufficient consideration of real operating conditions have an economic cost (the risk of failing to meet deadlines and overspending the project budget, unsuited technical and organisational solutions, etc.), as well as a social cost due to their potential impact on working conditions.

In the second section, we will use these experiences to demonstrate how an SME can be helped to regain control of its project by identifying the resource stemming from knowledge of the work activity. This can be achieved by tailoring the way in which this knowledge is used via the use of intermediary objects and user participation management (section 2).

Given the current importance of modernisation for SMEs and the opportunity to improve working conditions through investment projects, it is important that government policies incorporate an analysis of the real working activity and employee participation as criteria to ensure the success of subsidised projects.

---

1 The content of this presentation have been also written with Dominique Baradat (Aract Aquitaine) and presented in a large extent during the SELF (Société d'Ergonomie de Langue Française) congress in September 2008.

1. What the analysis of 95 investment practices in SMEs [2] shows

Financed by the Regional Council of Picardy, this study is composed of both a quantitative phase via a questionnaire distributed to 95 SMEs and a qualitative phase via semi-direct interviews held in 15 SMIs within the sample.

In both cases, the company contact was the manager of the investment project being examined. The sample companies were SMIs, 88% of which had an industrial focus. This study is not designed to achieve statistical representativeness of the corporate population or management situations but provides an *exploratory* means to identify invariants in terms of incorporating the human dimension in the implementation of investment projects in Small and Medium-Sized Enterprises.

Three types of investment projects were unders study: firstly, investments in machinery (74% of the sample), secondly, investments in information and communication technology (ICT tools) (17% of the sample) and, thirdly, investments in buildings (construction and refurbishment) (9% of the sample)

1.1. A centralised, technical project culture

The first observation in our study was that in 87% of cases, the company director (or site director) manages the investment project. The second observation was that a third of investments are made without a project team (table 1). The third observation was that when the manager gathers employees in a project team, he calls on their technical and financial skills as a matter of priority. He himself possesses the strategic knowledge and the capacity to integrate these skills.

Table 1: Level of project outreach

How the did manager proceed? (%)	**All types of investment**	**Production investments**	**Investments in ICT and buildings**
He proceeded alone	29%	35%	16%
He assembled a team exclusively comprised of internal employees	42%	47%	36%
He assembled a team composed of internal employees and external consultants	29%	18%	48%
TOTAL	100%	100%	100%

2 Study conducted by CESTP-Picardie (the Picardy Centre for Ergonomics and Work Safety) and ANACT (the French National Agency for the Improvement of Working Conditions) – (ML.Coppi, R.Chevallet, 2005) – on 95 SMEs in Picardy between 2004 and 2005.

In summary, policies governing the projects studied tended to be systematically characterised by, firstly, centralised decision-making, secondly, a dual claim over the technical and financial aspects of the project, and thirdly project managers generally lacking in technical knowledge.

1.2. Limited participation of future investment users

One of the very clear findings of the study concerns the involvement of future users in the design and implementation of the project. Companies rarely consult their employees beforehand to gauge project feasibility and forecast the impact on the different working practices. When a project team is set up, future users are called on in 45% of cases (figure 1). There is a very marked shortfall for projects concerning buildings. This result must be further qualified by the fact that the interviewees frequently and exclusively understand the term "involvement" to mean the brief training on the use of the tool organised by the equipment supplier during the roll-out. Yet we know that at this point there is very limited room for manoeuvre when it comes to adjusting the technical system and its organisation.

Figure 1: Composition of the project team

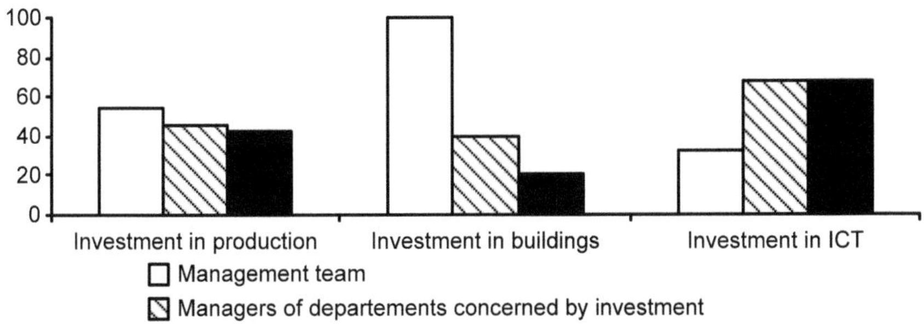

Overall, it is as if managers with strategic, technical and financial skills (or as the case may be, calling on these skills) defined a project without taking into account that the users themselves have the skills required for the smooth running of the project.

This lack of user involvement stems from a very managerial stance, namely that once the technical system has been installed the other parameters must be adjusted accordingly, with on the frontline, manpower and its organisation. This observation revealed by the statistics is confirmed in the context of interviews conducted with a number of project managers for whom the work and organisational aspects are simple variables to be adjusted after the event.

1.3. Organisation is a variable observed at the end of the project for adjustment

One of the major findings of our study shows that while only 18% of companies consider that the primary goal of investing is to improve the organisation of work, 75% of them note after the event that the investment has had an impact on the organisation. In particular, the majority of companies witnessed a change in work procedures and practices, as well as observing a change in the skill set of their employees (table 2).

Table 2: Perception of investment effects after the event

Which organisational aspect bears the main impact of the investment? Breakdown in %	
Change in work procedures and practices	48%
Change in skills	15%
Change in the functional organisational chart	13%
Multi-skilling/specialisation of staff	8%
Creation/loss of workstations	5%
Change in jobs	3%
Change in working hours	3%
TOTAL	100%

The study thus shows that the effects of an investment on the organisation tend to be perceived at the downstream stage of the project. SMEs which view the investment in principle as an opportunity to improve the organisation or certain aspects of it are few and far between.

1.4. Risks of corporate dependence and the lack of upstream project learning

Industrial investments are distinctive by the infrequent use of specifications to lay down requirements. Indeed, the offer provided by manufacturers of industrial equipment is sometimes limited and SME's negotiating leverage is extremely low. Purchases are frequently made by catalogue on the basis of a simple quote and purchase order. In the absence of specifications and a real discussion with the supplier, the company is deprived of the chance to approach and discuss the project and thereby forecast some of its consequences. In other words, upstream learning is minimal.

Table 3: Existence and development of specifications

	Investment in production (machines)	**Investment in buildings**	**Investment in ICT**
% investment which gave rise to specifications	40%	89%	83%
The specifications were drawn up by: – the internal team alone	63%	50%	47%
– the supplier alone	10%	25%	33%
– the internal team with external assistance or with the supplier	27%	25%	20%

When specifications exist, one set in five is drawn up by the service provider alone, namely in ICT projects in which a third of the specifications are drawn up by the service provider without the company's input. This situation reveals insufficient recourse to a user skill held by future users, which would however enhance the functional specifications of an ICT. The ICT project is essentially treated as a technical project with a strong emphasis on computing expertise. However, it has proven to be quite the opposite: the ICT project is an organisational project and underestimating this dimension is often the reason that such projects collapse. IT specifications do contain a technical section but also more importantly a functional section, which reflects the requirements relating to the running of the company, its organisation, work processes and user practices (Chevallet / Rocher 2003) . The functional section of specifications in information systems must be based on a user analysis concerning existing processes. It does not necessarily require calling on computing expertise to identify them. It is first and foremost a question of user competence.

Overall, the study highlights the possible risk of weakening the role of the project owner who would not invest sufficiently in the analysis and formulation of requirements. In this case, the company tends to strongly delegate this activity to an external project supervisor.

Even in summarized form, the results of our study highlight one main finding: SMIs tend to deny themselves expertise linked to operational knowledge. With project centralisation, low user involvement, a focus on technical and economic aspects and a lack of requirement specification, specific company benefits are insufficiently taken into account by the project owner. The latter then imports a technical solution and adapts, where possible, the human skills to the solution instead of calling on internal resources which, as Peteraf (1993) shows, ensure its competitive advantage (know-how, organisation).

Today, it is therefore paramount to help SMEs mobilise this expertise regarding operations and use to ensure that the investment is a technical and social success, not to mention an economic one.

2. Towards the channelling of operational skills in SME project management

Here, we will touch on several key elements, retranslated in part in three guides developed for players involved in the SME (Chevallet 2007, 2008; Bossard 2007) and regional public players in charge of financing or implementing investment grant systems in SMEs.

In the context of our public service vocation, we deem it necessary to provide free guides of around forty pages for local stakeholders, highlighting the keys to success at every stage of a project. Two guides have already been published in 2006 ("Implementing a successful industrial project in SMEs: the issue of working conditions", and "Implementing an IT project in SMEs: the issue of working conditions) and a third is scheduled to be published by the end of 2008 ("Implementing a successful design and building development project in SMEs"). Cf. Appendix.

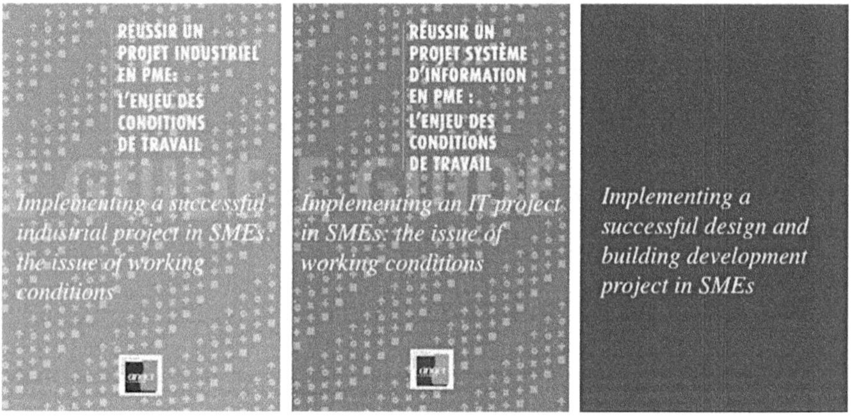

2.1. Discrepancy between the object of design and the company's core business

The first observation involves the discrepancy between the object of design and the company's core business: does the company possess technical skills and know-how with regard to the object of design?

In SMIs particularly, the industrial investment is often integrated in the core business. Technical expertise in the processing of materials or products allows a strong commitment to be made regarding the formulation of requirements concerning the project management and implementation follow-up. Yet, this theoretical knowledge of processes and equipment to be processed leads project managers to focus on the aspect they know best, namely the technical aspect. This is especially true for industrial projects.

In the case of upgrading an information system or building, the presence of skills is rarer. Despite many companies having a department or an individual in charge of IT, the set up of new systems such as ERP, workflow, CRM or Voice Picking involve new technological objects, which increases recourse to external service providers, particularly since these systems sometimes profoundly change the working activity of the users in question. Mindful of this lack of expertise, the project owner tends to focus on system compatibility, the level of technical performance to be attained and the success of data migration at the expense of organisational factors.

Architectural projects call for an even rarer range of expertise from the architect, the research and design office, the programmer, designer, etc. The company sponsoring the project can then decide whether to also purchase from these experts knowledge of operations and the activity, included in a programme or design. Here again, learning is limited in the company which delegates what it perceives to be inherent in the external service provider's expertise.

However, regardless of the nature of the investment and the available technical skills, the SME possesses its own knowledge of its business to take control of the project, while limiting the risks of dependence on an external service provider. Internal users are undeniably those who possess the knowledge on the real functioning and the future optimisation of processes. They must be involved in the different stages of the project (draft project, specifications, design studies, implementation, initiation and development). They provides knowledge of the actual functioning of the production system. The variability of the matter must be taken into account, as must the reaction of the production system to this variability and adjustments that must be made by employees; the identification of malfunctions, the updating of know-how and tips to be included in the design of the new equipment and/or to share among colleagues. On the whole, the company can call on its own specific assets (Williamson 1975). The essence of the problem for the company is to sufficiently identify these specific assets in the upstream process in order to let the project flourish and maintain control over the technical, functional, social and economic aspects.

☞ In terms of public investment support systems, it may be necessary in the preparation of investment files to identify the discrepancy between the technical object and the company's core business, assess the potential risk of dependence on external service providers and increase its awareness in this regard. The company should also be empowered to mobilise its expertise regarding work, which is as important as, if not more important than technical expertise.

2.2. The benefit of intermediary objects

This section highlights the importance of intermediary objects (plans, models, flowcharts, etc.) in investment project practices, namely in SMEs where fewer resources are able to be called on. They facilitate the upstream integration of the future technical object in an organisation, so as to anticipate the impact of changes and enhance the specifications. They are mobilised in a collective manner in order to negotiate the work and thus favour the involvement of future users in the project. On the basis of initiatives conducted by ANACT, intermediary objects (Jeantet 1996) have been proposed for all types of investment that we have previously observed:

- Wooden or cardboard models and CAD designs are media used to reposition the work activity in the industrial project setting up a comparison of points of view and representations between the different spheres of the operator and the design.
- Layout and traffic plans to map out flow movements, 3D wooden models and floor boxes are all useful media used to discuss the functioning of a space development project or architectural design (Martin, 2000).
- Logic diagrams (flowcharts) and flow mapping etc, here again the collective construction of these media provides the invaluable opportunity to contribute to both the functional and technical section of IT specifications.

Industrial project

Architectural Design

Flowcharts for IT specifications

Our groundwork has enhanced the list of intermediary objects via the "skill baseline". Recently used in the context of a large scale automation project with an automobile equipment manufacturer, upstream of business activity analyses and simulations with operators on the new processes in place, the baseline provided a means of identifying changes in professions, skills and know-how via a common "discussion medium" (used by operators and team leaders, method experts, training managers and staff representatives). Its progressive completion based on detailed engineering forged links between operators and designers and the human resources department (often granted a poor role in projects). The baseline plays the vital role of facilitating the translation between the three aforementioned functions.

In light of the question, "how can work expertise, the real functioning and the probable future be revealed", we realised that the intermediary object is a useful and inexpensive resource for any given project. It is also vital in the process of translation which requires a new technical object to be imported in an existing technical-human process (Akrich / Callon / Latour 1988) and reconciling actors with different perceptions of the design project.

☞ It seems altogether feasible for policies governing modernisation grants to encourage the use of these objects in investment projects. This could namely involve a training initiative on the part of the project manager of the SME entitled to investment support. The experience garnered by the ANACT network in collective action to support SMEs confirms this. Indeed, we have participated in several collective initiatives financed by regional councils designed to support SMEs in their industrial or IT upgrade projects alongside technical service providers. Combining collective discussions between the project leaders and individual action in companies, these public programmes result in socially and economically efficient projects. We often train project leaders in the workplace on intermediary objects: methods concerning the analysis and formalisation of processes, plan analysis, model-based simulation etc.

2.3. Helping the company to channel its operational expertise

While the project owner's role is occasional, and this is necessarily the case in an SME, the role which consists of demonstrating, channelling and integrating operations in a project may seem too infrequently used to be profitable.

The whole challenge lies in convincing SMEs that this function is less occasional than it seems, as it is useful during any change management project. The project manager, when one is clearly appointed, is too frequently in the dark about how to organise a comparison between the prescribed procedure and the reality, the general and the local, because he discovers these aspects of his role as he progress with the project he is managing. We believe that SMEs must develop this skill.

Organising and coordinating participation presupposes specific know-how to express and identify both requirements and demand linked to the activity without losing sight of the objective of the working session, while avoiding compounding the issue with claims etc (Martin / Baradat, 1998). Moreover, it must maintain involvement which is beneficial for the participants without them being lumbered with excessive responsibility. Potential collateral risks relating to the marginalisation of some users heavily involved in the project must also be managed.

☞ Also on this point, public policies governing SME investment grants may result in a contractor project manager being appointed to supervise the task, who could be entitled to training on coordination and participation within the investment project. In association with tools such as intermediary objects, this training programme could have specific features according to the nature of the investment: industrial equipment, information system or buildings.

Conclusion

We can see an increasingly *marked trend towards projects of shorter duration* and a lack of autonomy on the part of local project owners compared to parent companies due to a change of governance methods. We can see, conversely, empowerment which is often excessive as internal prerogatives are delegated to external service providers (equipment suppliers).

It seems to us that public policies, via their modernisation grants and SME investment grants (namely Regional Councils in France) can simultaneously:

- Favour the integration of working conditions in projects
- Help them to control their project, by encouraging the emergence, integration and acknowledgement of real work and use in projects.

To this end, the involvement and mobilisation of future users are vital. The use of intermediary objects, including the skill baseline, is useful to demonstrate and discuss future work irrespective of the project in question. In this way, it is a precious tool to involve users in an approach based on understanding. However, certain precautions should be taken to organise this involvement.

Finally, we think it is important to specify the mission of an *internal* project manager within the company. Adhering to objectives set by the project owner, this manager mobilises the internal expertise concerning usage and coordinates the project implementation accordingly. This role must be promoted and sufficiently equipped before and during the SME project. This role is all too often absent (as it is often managed by the project leader i.e. the manager of the SME and focused on technical aspects, lead times and budgets) or inappropriately delegated to technical service providers outside the company poorly suited to this job. This delegation heightens the risk of losing control of the project as well as losing out on learning and appropriation opportunities created through the mobilisation of internal knowledge on operational aspects.

References

Akrich, M / Callon, M. / Latour, B. (1988): A quoi tient le succès des innovations ? *Annales des Mines*, Juin, pp. 4-17 et Septembre, pp. 14-29.

Chevallet, R. / Rocher, O. (2003): Agir sur la conduite des e-projets, Edition Liaisons, 120 pages

Chevallet, R. / Coppi, M. (2005): La conduite de projet d'investissements en PME/PMI picardes : diagnostic et perspectives, Edition de l'ANACT, 69 pages

Chevallet, R., coord. (2007): Réussir un projet système d'information en PME : l'enjeu conditions de travail, Edition de l'ANACT, 44 pages

Chevallet, R., coord. (2008): Réussir un projet d'aménagement et de conception d'espace en PME: l'enjeu conditions de travail, Edition de l'ANACT, 44 pages. A paraître

Jeantet, A. (1996): Les objets intermédiaires dans la conception, Eléments pour une sociologie des processus de conception de produits, sociologie de la conception.

Martin, C. (2000): Maîtrise d'ouvrage, maîtrise d'oeuvre: construire un vrai dialogue. La contribution de l'ergonome à la conduite de projet architectural, *OCTARES, 228 pages*

Martin, C. / Baradat, D. (1998): Les paradoxes de la participation dans les projets, les journées de Bordeaux pour la pratique en ergonomie.

Peteraf, M. (1993): The cornerstones of competitive advantage: A resource-based View, Strategic Management Journal; 14(3):179-192

Appendix 1

Contents of the guide "Implement a successful information system project in SMEs: the issue of working conditions."

3 This part is an auto diagnostic tool.

Appendix 2

Extract from project sheet 4 : Specify the functional, organisational and technical requirements.

Objective

- Identifying requirements is a major step in the process of mobilisation, consultation and negotiation with users. When completed correctly, it favours the appropriation of change and facilitates recourse to the internal project manager (IT department) or external project manager (software companies, SSII, integrator consulting firms, etc.).
- Finding out the technical requirements also implies finding out the functional, organisational and HR requirements: which functionalities are needed in each system module for the current or future working activity? What are the requirements concerning changes in the organisation and professions caused by future changes in the company and/or part of its processes?

Stakeholders involved

- The project leader organises this stage and produces the required resources. It is important for the company to maintain an element of control over the identification of requirements and remain vigilant in this regard in the case of recourse to an external consultant;
- Users participate in the development of organisation-based solutions
- The members of the company management, managers of business lines, as future users and direct decision-makers for certain choices;
- The company can call on an external service provider to help it identify its functional and technical requirements and to assist with organisational and HR aspects.

Risks

- Considering the organisational and HR aspects as adjustment variables after the set up … when there will necessarily be less room for manœuvre!;
- Not taking into account the real work situations of users and progressing on the basis of a "theoretical" process;
- Causing layer upon layer of new procedures and practices after the project due to those required by the IS development, instead of revising former procedures and practices;
- Having a narrow, compartmentalised view of requirements of certain identified processes, without taking into account requirements linked to the other interfaced applications and indirectly affected users;
- Overlooking requirements linked to the system's capacity to evolve, in relation to the development of the company's activity. Risks of rapid saturation and obsolescence of the information system, of having set functionalities and being unable to make the system set up communicate with future users …

Our recommendations

✓ Use real work situations as the basis for the analysis of functional requirements, taking into account hazards, incidents, one-off cases and variations linked to the company's activity (seasonal nature, nature of the documents used, etc.).

✓ Visiting companies which have already set up a similar application, makes it easier to imagine an "unknown" situation and pinpoint requirements.

✓ Identify functional and organisational requirements on the basis of real work situations :

- do not limit the formulation of requirements to the management which often describes expected factors while users tend to describe the reality.
- collect information from users individually (interview or questionnaire) concerning critical incidents they encounter in their field of work and measure them using criteria (frequency, seriousness, consequences on the activity, etc.),
- observe the user in a work situation in terms of behaviour (gestures, movements, postures...), what is said when performing a task, what is viewed (information collected to help make decisions, etc.),
- also observe the paper documents used during

✓ Create an atmosphere whereby users participate

the activity (listing, Excel spreadsheets, post-its), and written notes made during an activity and then reused (item codes, price, etc.),
- observe and identify the requirements linked to workstation and its environment (noise, heat, etc.).

in the expression and construction of requirements to work on the different aspects of the project and create a broader view of the task. A process based analysis approach may be useful.

Example

In this wholesale SMI, the company implemented over several years an expansive project to upgrade its information system to support its growth, improve the management of the invoice flow and the shop until the decision was taken to spread the scope of computing across the board by setting up an ERP.

The majority of projects were implemented with the assistance of integrators and software companies under the aegis of two successive IT project managers.

The goals set by the management were essentially based on the set-up time (very short deadline), compliance with the IS budget, productivity and reduced processing time. No objectives were set concerning organisational or professional developments, which were nonetheless affected by these changes.

After three years of successive projects, the company experienced a major organisational crisis.

The result was an even greater compartmentalisation; departments could no longer identify their scope of activity and shrank from the responsibility of dysfunctions. Accountants and managers wary of the system and of their colleagues used their own reporting tools and photocopied invoices and purchase orders in order to file them. This became clear when one of the partners found errors in the financial reporting tables. With successive changes of applications, the result was layer upon layer of management rules and former practices.

There was no redefined organisation with users, or processes or work interfaces between departments.

Some were asked to validate the detailed specifications required for the tool setting and others took part in applying the specifications. The general atmosphere in the company deteriorated significantly.

Improvement of the performance of SMEs and their employees by participation of employees in the Region North Rhine-Westphalia, Germany – basic ideas, project examples, support structures and results

Friedhelm Keuken

1. Foreword

The Ministry of Labour, Health and Social Affairs of the federal state North Rhine-Westphalia, Germany, supports innovation strategies, especially for small and medium-sized enterprises (SMEs). Under the heading "Work-Oriented Modernisation" the different support modules of this policy are imbedded in the Programme of the European Social Fund (ESF) in North Rhine-Westphalia.

One of the support modules is "Potentialberatung" which means the support by consultation services for developing further potentials of SMEs carried out by private consulting companies which are specialised in working with SMEs. The main objective of Potential Consulting is the teaching of new management skills, methods and tools in a large number of SMEs.

Introduction to the region of North Rhine-Westphalia:

North Rhine-Westphalia (NRW) is Germany's federal state (one of 16) with the largest population and shares borders with the Netherlands and Belgium. The Ruhr area in its western part is the largest coherent economic region in Germany with 5.3 million inhabitants. About 40% of all EU citizens live within a radius of 500 km around the capital city Düsseldorf. 7 international airports and a close network of motorways and railroads are important parts of the traffic infrastructure. NRW generates 22% of Germany's GDP and is the strongest export area with 18.4% of all German exports. 36.3% of foreign investment is concentrated in NRW. 40% of all German trade fairs take place in NRW. 55 universities and colleges offer higher education for about 500,000 students. 5 of the largest 10 German universities are in NRW with Cologne University the biggest. 63 centres for technology and 27 research institutes are North Rhine-Westphalia's backbone of knowledge.

After the Second World War NRW was a growing and prosperous area with the highest concentration of heavy industry in Germany because of coal mining and steel production.

Today we still face the consequences of losing large numbers of industrial jobs without being able to substitute all of them.

To cope with these structural problems, the labour market policy of the federal state's government focuses on 5 action lines:

1. Support for young people to manage the change from school into job training and/or work
2. Integration of the unemployed into the labour market
3. Support of employees and enterprises in crisis situations
4. Promotion of business start-ups and young enterprises
5. Improvement of the competitiveness of SMEs and their employees

Introduction to the Innovative Employment Promotion Company GmbH – public equivalent body (G.I.B.):

As a federal state counselling organisation, we at G.I.B. work on the conceptual development, counselling, implementation and controlling of labour policy programmes and projects. G.I.B. acts as an interface between the federal state and the sub-regions, between programme providers and project implementers, between the state and the different players working in the municipalities, the organisations providing funding, companies and private labour market service providers.

G.I.B.'s key objective is the promotion of employment in North Rhine-Westphalia (NRW) according to the above – mentioned action lines of the federal state's government.

This paper:

This paper focuses on schemes, structures and projects to support the action line "Improvement of the competitiveness of SMEs and their employees". It describes the basic ideas, shows examples of projects, describes the support structures and presents some results of this policy.

2. The basic idea of work-oriented modernisation of SMEs

In detail, the policy to support the performance of SMEs and their employees is aimed at:

- Improvement of the competitiveness of SMEs
- Modernisation of work organisation
- Support for life-long learning

- Health and safety at work
- Improvement of the employability of the employees

The basic idea is that together management and employees work on modernising strategies on an organisational level in a participative way to improve the competitiveness of the particular SME and its employees. That means that management and staff are involved in their respective roles.

Usually the partners need external support for these processes which typically consist of the following steps:

1. Analysis of the current situation
2. Creating a medium-term vision
3. Planning of how to organise improvements and change
4. Turning the ideas into practice

In order to support such processes, private consulting companies are available to provide specific process skills required to oversee and accompany these projects.

One of the funding schemes of the policy to support the performance of SMEs and their employees is called "Potenzialberatung". This means consulting services to further develop the potential of the SMEs. This scheme provides 50% of the funding of the consultancy costs as an incentive to stimulate such modernisation projects in SMEs.

3. Project examples

3.1 Example 1: Improvement of customer requirement management in the software development department for power supply management

The first example deals with a project which was aimed at the improvement of quality management in a software company with a view to resulting in better customer service. It is an example of medium-sized company with150 employees with high-performance workplaces and highly qualified jobholders.

One of the main products of this SME is software for process management support for companies trading in the electrical power supply. The challenge of the project was to recreate the process management of the software company to make sure that products developed together with the customers meet the customer's expectations exactly. Therefore, a project team was created. The project was organised as a joint process in which management, consultant and employees were involved. The project was carried out by a core group of 15 people.

The subject of the project was the management of the interface between sales and product development. In a first step an analysis of the current situation was conducted. The main finding was the need for a renewed operational and organisational structure.

Results:

During the process a new operational and organisational structure was developed and implemented. Additionally, the decision was taken to invest in a technical tool to support the product development process. On the level of company performance sustainable growth was expected and two new full-time jobs have been created.

The project took 5 months. The consultancy fee of 15,000 € was funded in the order of 7,500 € through public money (European Social Fund). The cooperation between the company and the consultant is now continuing without public funding.

3.2 Example 2: Improvement of the controlling in company for environment protection service

This second example is a project which was aimed at the stabilisation of a small family- owned company with lower- skilled employees. The company was founded in 1966 by the father of the current owner. Today staffs of 48 are employed.

The services offered by the company are:

- Oil tank protection
- Oil tank cleaning
- Oil separating service
- Disposal of waste and oil

The economic development of the company has not always been solid but the owner was not able to put his finger on the exact causes of the problems. It was in this situation that he contacted an external consultant, a controller. The public funding of 50% of the costs which could be expected worked as an incentive to apply for a project.

A project team was created which consisted of the owner, the middle management and the consultant. As a first step an analysis of the strengths and weaknesses of the company was conducted, followed by workplace and job descriptions, respectively, and a survey of the workload of all employees.

Results:

As a first result a new operational and organisational structure was developed and implemented. On the basis of this structure a new accounting system with break-even analysis for every single service group was developed and implemented as well.

Furthermore, regular meetings of the owner with the middle management were introduced. That was a very new thing which had a positive effect on the corporate culture.

Additionally, a new pay scheme for the middle management was introduced including employee profit sharing. That last item in particular caused some concerns in the beginning. But after some time it showed positive effects in terms of company performance and wage development as well.

Another result of the project was the identification of the need for further training. Thereafter, two employees took part in a training programme on controlling.

Transparency and active information of all employees about the aims of the project were very important. The participation of the middle management was crucial for the acceptance of the project results and the changes in the company and in the workplaces.

As regards company performance, it should be stressed that the economic situation of the company has been stabilized. As a result, 6 new jobs, among them 1 new trainee job, have been created.

The project took 9 months. The consultancy fee of 10,000 € was funded in the order of 5,000 € by the public funding scheme. The cooperation between the company and the consultant is now continuing without public funding.

3.3 Common characteristics of the projects

As mentioned above, these projects are usually taken through the following stages:

1. Analysis of the current situation
2. Creating a medium-term vision
3. Planning of how to organise improvements and change
4. Turning the ideas into practice

Open two-way communication, the participation of the employees, and a process-oriented methodology of the external experts are vital for projects to succeed.

4. Support system for SME in North Rhine-Westphalia, Germany

North Rhine-Westphalia is a region with some 700,000 enterprises. 99% of all companies are SMEs (< 250 employees). SMEs employ more than 70% of the workforce.

In order to deal with the funding scheme to support SMEs and their employees in the most effective way, a network has been created with the aim of reaching a big number of companies.

A network of 120 local agencies is available for the promotion of the funding scheme and for applications by SMEs. These agencies are located with independent organisations like Chambers of Commerce, Chambers of Handicrafts (a German speciality), local agencies for economic development and local labour market agencies.

2,300 private consulting companies are available to carry out the projects. These are small companies with between 1 and 10 consultants. In terms of methodology they work in a participative and process-oriented way and use methods such as a systemic approach, an organisational development approach, TQM/ EFQM, supervision approach or other participative and process-oriented methods.

G.I.B. Services for Local Agencies and Consultants

The role of G.I.B. as a federal state counselling organisation is the information and the quality management of the network.

For local agencies and consulting companies G.I.B. provides

- Information (print media, Internet, newsletter etc.)
- Seminars and training
- Workshops for the exchange of experience

The funding system and each funded project are well monitored. This is important for any intervention on the quality management level and provides information about the projects and the whole system.

5. Results of the funding scheme "Potenzialberatung" (Consulting services for developing further potentials of SME)

5.1 Consulting offer reaches almost 10,000 companies

Potential consulting intends to give assistance to small and medium-sized companies, in particular at times when the company is undergoing change. Potential consulting continues to be on the road to success. By the end of 2007 more than 10,000 companies with a total of around 370,000 employees had made use of potential consulting in NRW.

Figure 1: Potential consulting – granting in quaterly periods cumulates Values

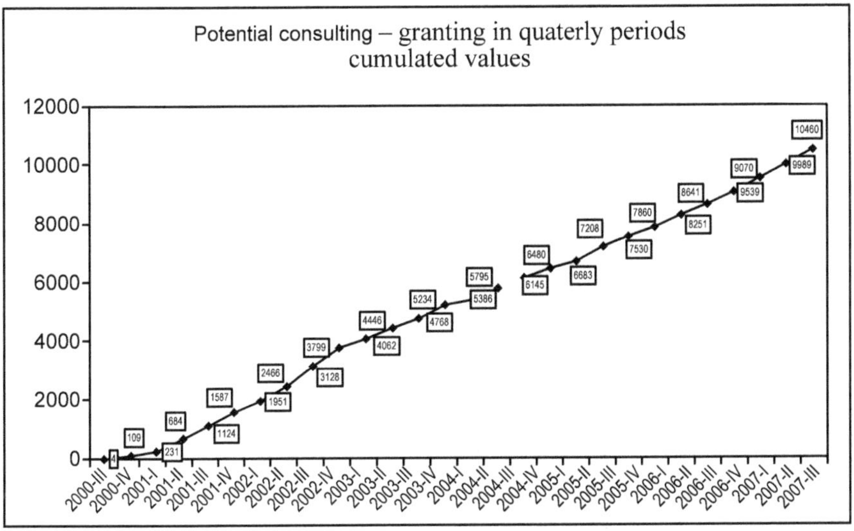

In brief:
The promotion consists of 3 to 10 consulting days for companies with up to 49 employees, 3 to 15 consulting days for companies with more than 50 staff. 50% of the real costs, up to a maximum of 500 €, are reimbursed per day of consulting.
Points of contact are the respective regional agencies
http://downloads.gib-nrw.de/Anlaufstellen.pdf

5.2 *Participating SME by size*

The objective of offering practical support to small and medium-sized companies in particular so that they are in a position to meet the market demands proactively has been achieved. The allocation according to company size shows that the envisaged target group has actually been reached.

Figure 2: Participating SME by size (no of employees) – 2000-2007

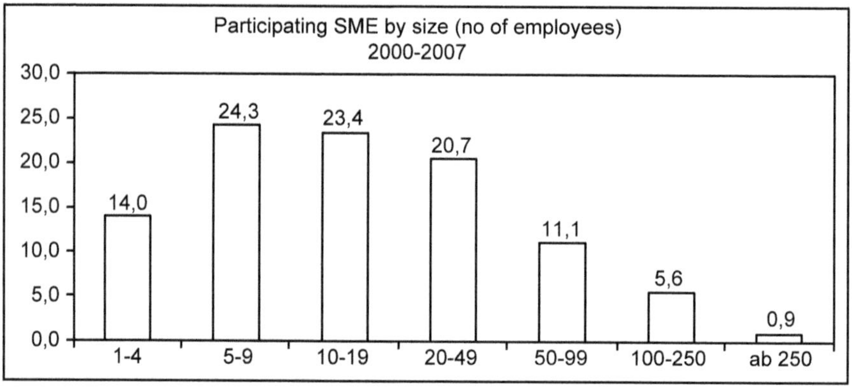

Approximately 82% of the companies participating have fewer than 50, more than 93% fewer than 100 employees. The average company size is around 33 employees.

The continuing demand on the side of small and medium-sized companies is evidence for the increasing awareness that competitiveness and employment can only be safeguarded by company modernisation.

5.3 *Participating SME by branches*

Companies from nearly all sectors participated in the potential consulting.

Figure 3: Participating SME by Branches 2000-2007

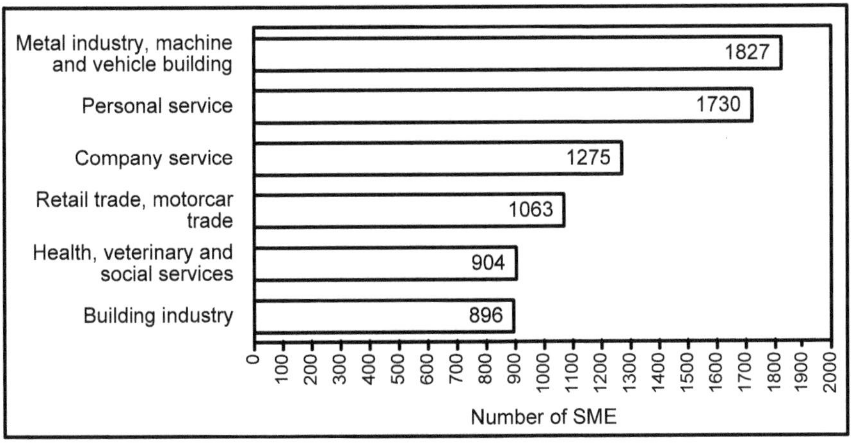

5.4 Competitiveness of companies and employment of staff – two sides of the same coin

Potential consulting aims to help companies at the same time as safeguarding and developing competitiveness and employment. According to the companies, an average increase in employment of 1.5% was achieved – in contrast to the development on federal and regional levels. The results vary according to the size of the companies. In the companies participating in the potential consulting the development of employment was better than on federal and regional levels, regardless of the actual size of a company.

Figure 4: Employment Development in PC-Companies, Companies in NRW and West-Germany

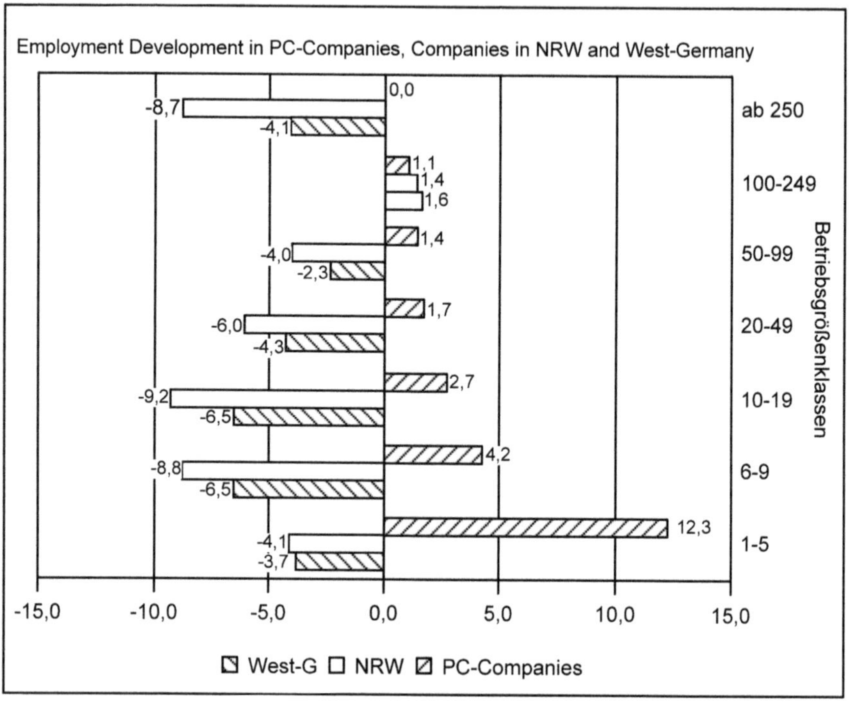

Moreover, nearly half of the participating companies in 2006 are definitely planning the development of further workplaces in the near future. In the period 2000 to 2006 this amounted to a third of the companies.

Figure 5: New work places planned according to company size

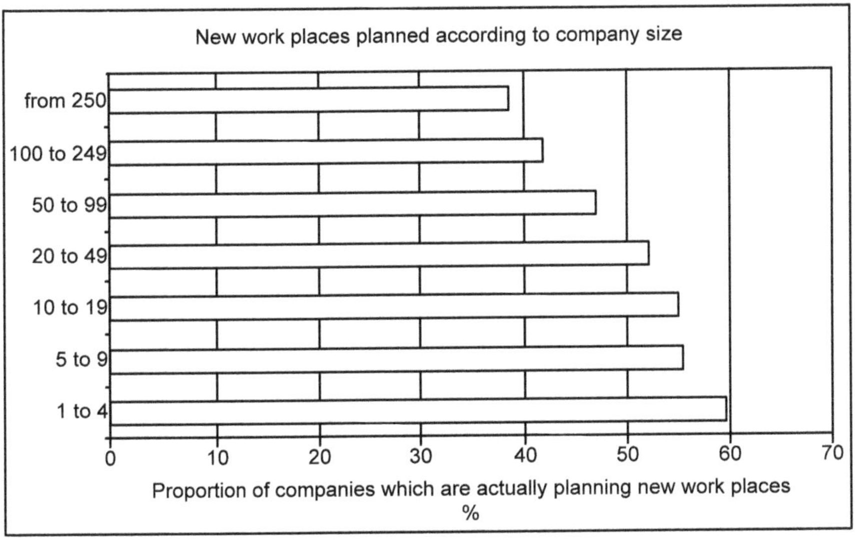

In absolute figures this means 3,812 workplaces newly created already and, additionally, 9,153 planned workplaces for the period 2000-2006.

Figure 6: Potential consulting – Newly created and additionally planned work places according to company size 2000-2006

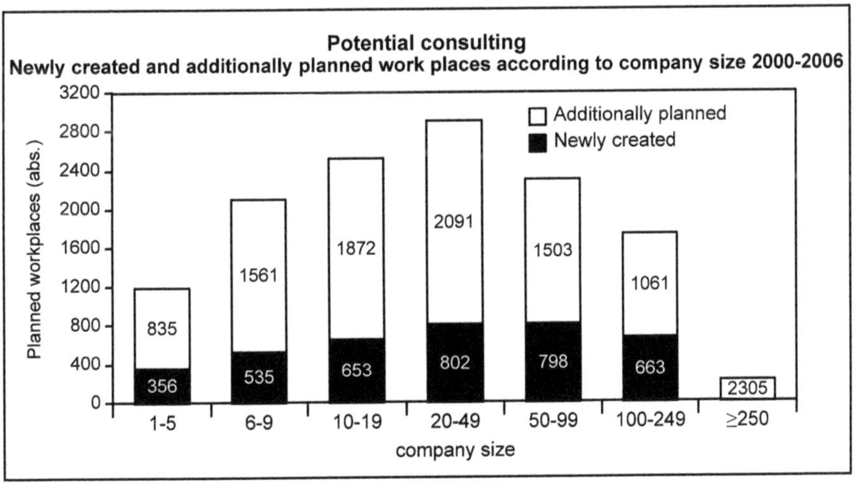

The objective of potential consulting, i.e. not only to safeguard competitiveness and employment but also to develop them wherever possible, was clearly achieved.

5.5 *Operational improvements achieved*

In most companies potential consulting also initiates first changes and achieves real operational improvements. To a great extent this creates the conditions for putting into effect the planned objectives.

Figure 7: Results being reached after 1 year

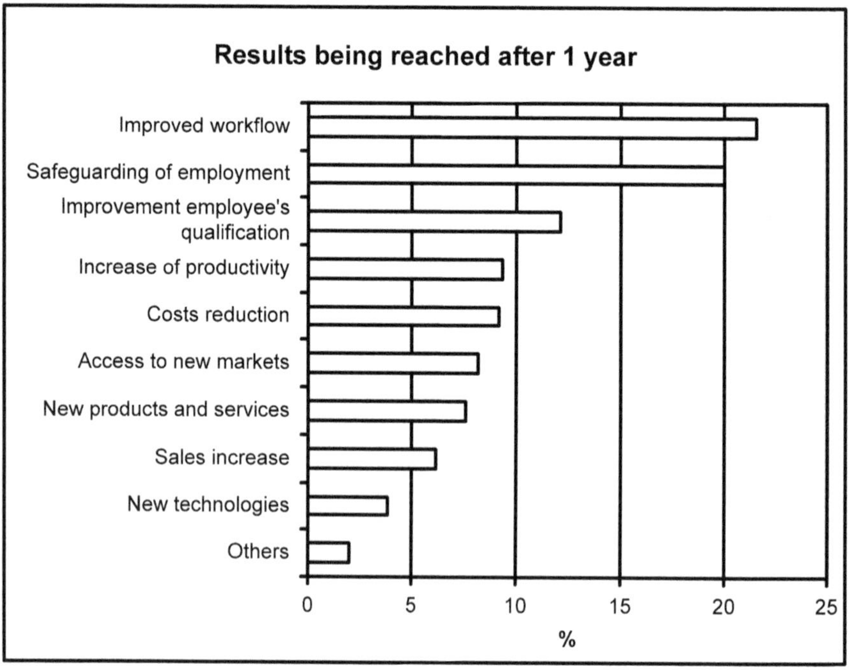

5.6 *Satisfaction with the consulting*

The participating companies give the potential consulting an extremely positive rating.

Figure 8: Potential consulting has met the expectations

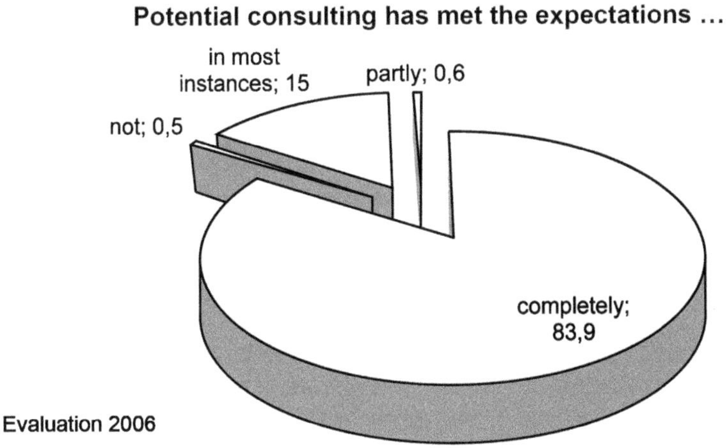

Approximately 99% of the companies state that the consulting has met their expectations fully or to a large extent, only just over 1% were less or not at all satisfied. Over time the assessment has even improved. In 2006 only 0.5% of potential consulting activities did not meet the expectations of the companies.

Figure 9: Development of satisfaction

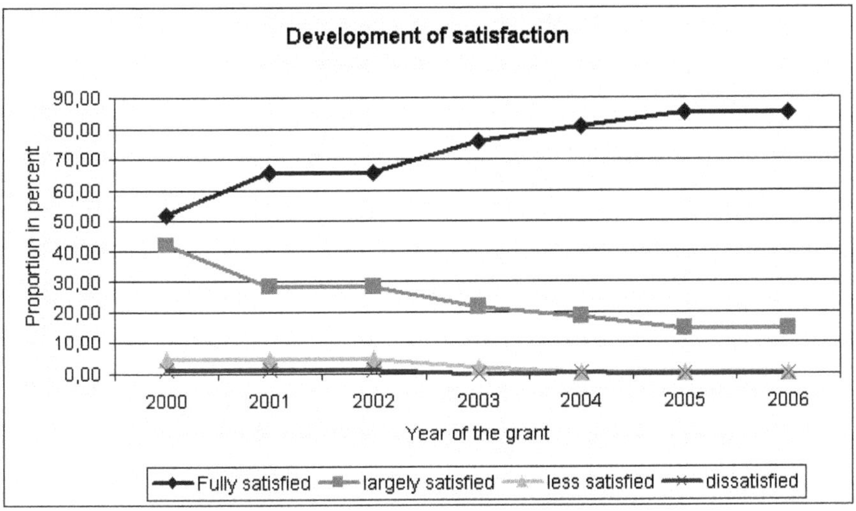

5.7 Summary

Since the beginning of the promotion in the year 2000, potential consulting has to a large extent reached the target group of the promotion instrument and, in particular, it has reached companies with a staff of 5 to 50. Potential consulting thus supports the main pillars of employment. Companies from nearly all sectors participate in potential consulting.

In contrast to the development of employment in NRW and the Federal Republic of Germany in total, where employment decreased from 2000 to 2006, employment has increased in all company size categories in the companies with potential consulting despite economic problems. In addition to the employment increase already achieved of approximately 1.5% on average, a third of the companies are planning further employment development of around 3%. Since employment started to rise again on federal and regional levels from 2005 to 2006, the employment increase in companies which have benefitted from potential consulting is even higher than in the years before.

The holistic approach of potential consulting is confirmed by the canon of the tasks most worked on: Improvement of the "structural and operational organisation", "strategic planning", the "development of market potentials/market presence" as well as "staff development" and "quality management systems". The approach of potential consulting, i.e. to improve competitiveness together with the employees (by using their know-how as workplace experts) as well as to further develop their employability has proved to be a success. The improvements agreed upon are initiated quickly and the resulting successes are achieved.

The companies have always been highly satisfied with potential consulting.

From our point of view as programme managers the most important characteristics for the success of the scheme are:

- A holistic view of the organisation
- Participation of the employees
- Process-oriented methodology of the consultants.

Making better use of potential to innovate! – some food for thought in the "Year of Innovation"

Ulrich Klotz

Sooner or later, anyone who has been covering the issue of innovation for some time – and IG Metall started doing so at the very latest in 1979 when its Executive Board adopted a very extensive resolution on trade union policy on innovation and set up its own Innovation Advice Centres – will probably ask themselves how on earth policy can promote the origination of something new and hitherto unknown.

Since roughly the mid-1970s attempts have been made at more or less regular intervals to conduct a so-called 'innovation policy'. So far all these attempts were along similar lines: groups of experts in the Chancellor's Office or relevant ministries identified this or that key technology, cross-sectional technology or technology of the future and then their development and marketing was specifically targeted by subsidy programmes. Opinions may differ as to the usefulness of such 'innovation offensives', but one thing is certain: not least for logical reasons, true innovation – which entails dreaming up and trying out hitherto unfamiliar ideas – cannot be the subject of a policy decision. On the contrary, since policy decisions are made on the basis of the knowledge available at the time, they tend to cement the research situation, rather than push back its boundaries. Frequently, subsidising something that is already familiar leads to mere imitation being described as innovation, leaving true innovation to bear fruit later on, for instance because many researchers prefer to continue working in readily subsidised areas rather than venture into uncharted territory.

Numerous powerful lobbies representing existing, familiar products and ideas past and present effectively hold sway in such groups of experts, whereas true, unforeseeable future innovation naturally has no such advocates. Incidentally, at least in the short term true innovation is not at all something that people agree on, but is instead regularly played down to begin with by the establishment as some crackpot idea that can never come to anything.

Since many previous initiatives aimed at fostering innovation turned out to be merely newly packaged conventional industrial and technology policies, it is hardly surprising that for the most part they failed to fulfil the hopes originally pinned on them. On the contrary, international comparative studies highlight Germany's weakness when it comes to innovation, a weakness that stretches back to the 1970s. Those branches of industry that still constitute the backbone of the German economy today the automotive, mechanical engineering, electrotechnical and chemical sectors – essentially owe their existence to innovative breakthroughs made in the late 19th century. Yet in virtually all current growth markets based on innovations dating from after World War Two, Germany is either insufficiently represented or even totally absent. Indeed, according to the country's central bank, the Bundesbank, Germany has now become a net importer of technology and has therefore also dropped behind other countries in terms of its economic growth.

How can you sensibly promote the creation of something – when you don't yet know what it is?

You can't get out of a 'no-hope' situation by ploughing on regardless. Instead, what's needed is a change of direction in the policy conducted up to now. In future, innovation policy must deal with innovation, not technology. Since innovation, i.e. new know-how, cannot be derived from existing knowledge and therefore cannot be as systematically planned or produced, fresh thought needs to be given to how innovation can be boosted by political means. So the question is how can we actually best foster the origination when we don't even know what it is yet?

One possible answer starts to emerge when we consider both the following questions:

Firstly, how come many of the inventions made in Germany are first taken up abroad and successfully developed into innovative products there or even further refined for additional markets? To cite but a few examples from the electronics and IT sector: key components in computers and microprocessors, inkjet printers and fax machines, walkmen, LCD flat screens or MP3 players stem from research originally conducted in German laboratories. These inventions have all given rise to markets worth billions, countless new companies and hundreds of thousands of new jobs. Yet hardly any of these firms or jobs are in Germany; most are generating wealth in the USA or Asia. This list of inventions not seized upon by Germany is virtually endless. In fact, the mass unemployment in Germany today is not least a consequence of an almost unlimited number of missed opportunities for innovation. Why is it that good ideas and inventions are so often given no chance to bear fruit in Germany?

Secondly, what makes the fundamental difference between a successful, innovative company and a less successful one? At the time of writing, a series of spectacular examples, ranging from Opel to Karstadt, are showing us that virtually every sector has both companies that are making record profits and rival businesses wrestling with problems that are threatening their very existence. It can hardly be the case that one company employs a totally different kind of people than the others, so what can explain these growing differences?

This question is taken up, for example, in the annual ExBa (Excellence Barometer) studies produced by an association of celebrated consultancy firms. These reports identify dozens of indicators which there is no room to expound on here, but can be summed up in a single statement:

Whenever and wherever successful companies in a sector are scrutinised for the differences between them and their less successful competitors, sooner or later it becomes clear that the key differences reside in the configuration of their respective work structures and processes.

The key is how work structures and processes are organised

More specifically, companies differ in the progress they have made down the path shaped on the one hand by the academic management principles set out by Frederick Winslow Taylor and on the other by the management model advocated by Peter Ferdinand Drucker.

Both Taylor and Drucker are amongst the most influential thinkers of the 20th century. Taylor's impact on corporate management in the era of expansive industrialisation is pretty well known. Taylor maintained that thinking – and hence any kind of innovation – is the preserve of the management. New ideas stemming from those carrying out the work are not at all desirable, because they could disrupt the planned flow of business.

Peter F. Drucker, on the other hand, was quick to recognise how the advent of the information age would impact on all areas of the economy and society particularly by prompting a rapid increase in the intensity of knowledge in all kinds of work. The book he published in 1946 entitled "Concepts of the Corporation" already redefined the capabilities of human beings by saying that staff are an asset to a company as opposed to mere cost factors.

Taylor still believed that "one best way" could be found for everything. Drucker saw no prospects in a dynamic world for patent recipes or single optimal solutions, maintaining that the ability to adapt constantly was crucial in a competitive context and that prerequisites for such flexibility were diversity and open communication.

Taylor applied knowledge to (simple) work and thereby made a significant contribution to the explosion in the productivity of mass-produced goods.

Drucker, by contrast, applied knowledge to knowledge because he had recognised that the real controlling resource and the absolute decisive factor of production are now neither capital, nor land, nor labour, but knowledge and that the function of the organisation will become increasingly that of making knowledge productive. According to him, knowledge is the key component in helping companies to distinguish themselves from their peers when manufacturing a product or providing a service that generates value on the market. When all is said and done, it all boils down to developing talent, for that is where competition in a knowledge-based economy takes place.

Drucker coined the term 'knowledge worker' as early as 1959, when he pointed out that as soon as their training is over, knowledge workers must know more about their activity than their boss, otherwise they will hardly be of use. In fact, part of the definition of a knowledge worker is one who knows more about their activity than anyone else in their organisation. Any organisation actively applying knowledge is increasingly dependent on specialists. Traditionally it was assumed that the boss knew what his staff were doing because he himself had done the same job just a few years previously. In an organisation based on knowledge the very opposite should be assumed, namely that bosses cannot understand the work done by their staff because they have never done it themselves. Thus, Drucker argues, knowledge is only effective when it is specialised, and specialist knowledge is productive when it is linked to the knowledge of other specialists. For this reason, knowledge workers are dependent on organisations where their know-how can be communicated and implemented in an optimal manner." (P. Drucker, The Post Capitalistic Society, p. 155 f.)

Recently, the well-known management consultant Michael Hammer said that according to Drucker's definition all of the following must be viewed – at least to some extent – as knowledge workers: a production-floor worker who is constantly confronted with manufacturing problems to analyse and solve, maintenance technicians who plan their own working day, and storeroom workers who assess the performance of suppliers. Increasingly, people like this are not the exception, but the rule. (See *WirtschaftsWoche,* 2 September 2004, p. 80)

The problem is that we are a knowledge society – but structured to work like an industrial society

In the meantime, most employees are knowledge workers in all early industrialised countries, regardless of whether they are employed by an SME or a major group. Nowadays, more than two thirds of a workforce are knowledge workers of the kind defined by Drucker. Incidentally, in this context it becomes clear that the terms ‘industrial society’ and ‘knowledge society’ are not mutually exclusive. Instead, they imply that, as with the transition from an agricultural to an industrial society, labour and everything associated with it (lifestyles, identification patterns, systems and values, etc.) is once again undergoing radical change.

The fundamental problem is that often the development of forms of entrepreneurship, organisation and work has failed to keep up with this rapid increase in the intensity of knowledge. Even today, most people – whether in companies, public institutions or other kinds of organisation – work in structures that are coloured by Taylorism, whereby management entails leading by dictate as opposed to guidance. This explains two observations. The first of these is the frequent empirical finding that only a fraction of the knowledge available in a company is actually put to use (as summed up in the old German business saying “If Siemens only knew what Siemens knows ... “.

The second observation it explains is why innovation, i.e. the process of applying knowledge to generate new knowledge – so often runs up against such stubborn obstacles. In a nutshell, new knowledge devalues old knowledge. If an organisation has been built on the founding principle that ‘knowledge is power’, then innovations will constantly become entangled in existing structures and interfere with prevailing balances of power and thereby jeopardise the privileges and benefits that go along with such power. Consequently, any innovation will invariably be dogged by both opposition and conflicts.

Hierarchically structured organisations that practise Taylorism are based on this principle. Where knowledge can be used as power instead of as a labour resource, changes rung in on the back of new knowledge will be particularly problematic. For power can also be described as a means of ignoring better arguments. An examination of a few instances of innovations that ended up not being realised in Germany soon reveals that almost all innovation is ‘bottom-up’, coming from the level in touch with the market, and it was invariably the superiors of the innovators who hampered or prevented it. In many cases the various reasons why decision-makers damage their own company in this way are banal. A new idea could highlight errors made by the superior or come from a ‘hostile’ department. Often, thinking in categories established by previous successes is a barrier to innovation, as in the case of a now defunct German manufacturer of inkjet technology, where the management rejected the technology developed by the company in the 1970s “because it can’t be used to make carbon copies”. In short, success often blinds people to something that is new. Another symptomatic example is the decline of the once glamorous computer companies Nixdorf and DEC, whose managers failed to appreciate the possibilities of PCs and therefore dismissed any corresponding developments. What’s to blame for this situation? In most instances management failings by decision-makers who fail to understand innovations, possibly because they are unable to, but nonetheless believe by virtue of their 'higher office' that they must surely know better. Such a situation pits Taylor purists directly against Drucker purists. The authors of one study crammed full of impressive case studies conclude that the exercising of authority is the key factor in determining why innovation fails ... since all ways in which authority is exercised ultimately prevent an exchange of views based on the presentation of arguments and thereby hinder the growth of knowledge. (See W. Scholl: Innovation and Information, 2004, p. 260).

In some early industrialised countries – especially Germany – these forms of labour and organisation that got in the way of innovation were perfected over decades and are now deeply anchored in companies, making them extremely intractable. Several widely respected authors have been saying this for years: In 1994, Michael Hammer observed that whereas the Germans had perfected the first Industrial Revolution, they had failed to keep up with new forms of labour and must therefore brace themselves for hard times ahead. The same year Konrad Seitz wrote that German society is mentally stuck in the Industrial Age. Drucker, who criticised managers' totally disproportionately high wages as early as the 1940s, pointed out that Taylorism in an organisation is particularly easy to spot by the treatment given to status symbols. Professor Stefan Collignon at the London School of Economics illustrates this by referring to a London investment bank that is active worldwide. The subsidiaries of this highly successful bank in all the respective countries have very flat management structures, yet the London-based CEO says that his German subsidiary sticks out as being the only one suffering constant clashes over the size of offices or the make of company car, and so on. Consequently the bank is unable to integrate Germany into its global strategy". (See *Die Zeit, 29* November 2001, p. 20). Elsewhere people recognised long ago that people cannot be motivated at all, only robbed of their motivation, which is why status symbols kill innovation.

The problem of innovation being blocked by the legacy of the Industrial Age by no means only affects German R&D departments. For innovation is something that happens every day countless times in innumerable places, namely wherever anyone does something differently to the way it was done the day before. The key factor is the additive effect of all these minor changes; that is what determines how flexible and successful a company will be as a whole.

Anyone denied important information and barred from decision-making for a long time will lose their motivation

Sooner or later, Tayloristic structures will fall victim to the behavioural patterns to which they give rise, since they promote adaptation and opportunism, the arch enemies of innovation. Joachim Gauck recently explained this in connection with labour structures in the former German Democratic Republic, saying that the people had internalised different patterns of career development, for instance that progress up the ladder could be made not only by being competent and shouldering responsibility, but by being obedient and adaptive and thereby essentially reviving ancient traditional Teutonic values. (See DLF, 8 November 2004). Tayloristic systems characterised by almost mechanical set plans, official channels, fixed responsibilities and so on – and this form of organisation still applies to many German companies today – will ultimately encounter difficulties, for sooner or later their top executives will lose touch with reality, being surrounded by sycophants as a result of their internal selection mechanisms. The result is what Weltz called 'management by Potemkin', whereby the organisation falls for its own profile. Years ago already the economist Canice Prendergast proved with mathematical precision in his "Theory of Yes-Man" why hierarchical organisation is doomed to failure sooner or later in a dynamic environment. (See the American Economic Review, 9/93).

Whenever knowledge workers are dictated to in terms of authority being exercised over them, the consequences are fatal. As Tom Peters pointed out in 1990, anyone who remains cut off from important information and decisions for a lengthy period of time loses motivation. Hierarchies are synonymous with constraints on transparency and paralyse the interest at the lower levels. The less transparent an organisation becomes, the stronger its tendency to slide into decline, because its 'grass-roots-Ievel' workers boycott it through 'internal emigration'. This has massive economic ramifications, as the annual polls conducted by the American market research multinational Gallup show. According to the latest poll (2004), only 13% of employees in Germany are actively committed to their work, 18% have already 'signed off' internally, and the remainder – a good two thirds of staff are working to rule. The Gallup researchers put the cost of lost productivity attributable to employees' lack of any emotional link to their company, e.g. as a result of an unnecessarily high staff turnover or rate of absenteeism due to illness, at a minimum of €245 billion per annum damage roughly equivalent to the German federal budget. Almost just as dramatic were the findings of a study recently published by Proudfoot Consulting, which claimed that poor leadership, especially by middle managers cost 74 working days a year per employee. Proudfoot estimates the damage caused in Germany at €158 billion, just under 8% of GDP.

Motivation is far more important than working time

These studies show that motivation is far more important than working time. Meanwhile, bearing these figures in mind, if the possibility of abolishing public holidays or prolonging working time in other ways is still being debated in Germany, this patent misjudgement of reality is just one more indication of how deeply entrenched Taylorism is in many managers' minds.

Dozens of studies on internal barriers to innovation – conducted by major consultants (KienbaumHewitt, ADL, Mercer, Droege&Comp, McKinsey and so on) – make equally informative reading. Since there is no room here to do full justice to their findings, their findings summed up in a nutshell by Peter Drucker will have to suffice: "Most of what we call management consists of making it difficult for people to get their jobs done".

A knowledge-based economy needs an open corporate culture

Are there any positives here? What is that successful, powerful, innovative companies do differently? An excerpt from a letter dating from 1989 from the legendary Konosuke Matsushita (founder of the Matsushita group) to a European colleague shows what needs to be done. Paraphrased, Matsushita said this: We will win and you, the industrial West, will lose. You cannot do anything about it because you are carriers of a fatal disease. Your companies are based on Taylor's principles. Worse still, your heads are Taylorised too. You are content running your companies by having thinkers on one side and workers carrying out their instructions on the other. For you, management is the art of smoothly transferring executives' ideas to the workers' hands.

We have analysed and evaluated the new technological and economic challenges more carefully than you, and know that the individual intelligence of the best manager – regardless of how brilliant they may be – will prove totally inadequate to face up to these challenges.

Only by drawing on the intelligence of all employees can a company ride economic ups and downs and rise to the challenges of its new environment. For this reason, our companies give their staff three or four times as much continuing training as yours. We engage in internal communication with all our employees and ask them to make suggestions about all kinds of things.

In Japan, where Peter Drucker started advising the government as long ago as the 1940s, his ideas were sown in fertile soil. Of all the companies that followed Drucker's advice particularly closely, Toyota is probably the biggest name today. With excellent quality rankings, record profits (more than €9 billion in 2003) and a market capitalisation greater than GM, Ford, DaimlerChrysler and BMW combined, Toyota is rapidly steering its way to the top of the global automotive industry. Today it is one of the best researched companies and the focus of more studies and publications than any other firm. For years now companies all over the world have been trying to copy the legendary Toyota production system. But apparently it is impossible in practice to simply import a different corporate culture based on other behavioural patterns and values. Why? Because they involve dynamic processes of change that cannot be shipped over in the way that, say, machines can.

It is enlightening to read the account given by an American manager who was selected to head up a Toyota plant in the USA, but first had to go to Japan to gain a completely new picture of himself and learn a new managerial role (see Steven Spear, Management à la Toyota, HBM, August 2004). A Toyota manager is not a boss who issues instructions to his workers and then checks up on them, but rather a coach, who constantly encourages the workforce to identify problems themselves and come up with solutions to them. In short, at Toyota all employees are regarded and duly treated as knowledge workers. And it is easy to understand why people whose accomplishments are acknowledged and who are given leeway and encouragement should then be highly motivated and produce better results.

Added value through appreciation

The way Toyota deals with its suppliers provides another indication that it has mastered the intricacies of knowledge production. No other carmaker engages in such an open exchange of opinions with other companies, which reaps rewards for all those involved. And because knowledge has different characteristics to other factors that enter into production – for instance it is a 'raw material' that grows with use – the forms of labour in a knowledge-based economy must alter fundamentally. That, in a nutshell, is what Drucker recognised and Taylor did not.

A copybook example of this process of evolution is Oticon, Denmark's global manufacturer of hearing aids, which employs more than 3,500 staff. The advent of software-based systems initially triggered something of an existential crisis for the company, but after undergoing radical restructuring Oticon managed to make the typical technologically determined change from a standardised mass product to an extensively personalisable computer application with a high service component. In the process, all hierarchies, status symbols, barriers to communication and other relicts of Taylorism were consigned to history, and today at Oticon there are no longer any established posts, just very open and highly flexible project organisation. This change has made a phenomenal cultural difference within the company, and as a result Oticon is exhausting far more potential of all its employees today than ever before. Its employees are exceptionally highly motivated and the company's results, which are way above the average for its sector, speak for themselves.

Germany, too, has examples which innovation policymakers would do well to heed. One such company is BMW, which has also been through its share of crises. In the 1980s a series of instructive projects was implemented at BMW, especially in areas to do with development. Decentralisation, a marked flattening of the company's hierarchical structure and greater room for manoeuvre all considerably improved BMW's internal knowledge logistics and its rate of success at tapping into potential for innovation. These projects also bore fruit in the long run, for BMW is in better shape today than many of its rivals.

Once again this shows us that corporate culture and behavioural patterns are substantially influenced by the respective structure – and vice-versa. Cultures cannot simply be altered, structures perhaps more so. Often it takes the advent of a crisis to force top executives to recognise the need for structural change and induce them to see the necessary measures through. If this exercise proves successful, gradually the company's culture will change – i.e. the interaction between the people within an organisation. And therein – at the level of corporate culture – lies the key to solving our problems. Instead of a boss culture in which the value of a task is defined in terms of the extent to which it benefits the boss, and instead of a culture dominated by risk avoidance and apportioning blame, what we need are open corporate cultures where minorities, alternative opinions and lateral thinkers are accepted as valuable potential sources of ideas, are duly protected and are given room for manoeuvre and support. What our companies need, instead of harmony and one-size-fits-all solutions is a culture of diversity, where different ideas about values, forms of conduct, experience traditions and views constitute a breeding ground for innovative ideas. Especially where we succeed in combining youthful exuberance bursting with ideas with the knowledge gained through experience over a long time will there be good prospects that resulting innovations will go on and be nurtured by the company and prove successful on the market. Where work processes are organised in such a way as to enable people to develop their knowledge and experience unhindered and simultaneously bring their work into harmony with the rest of their lives, this approach could also help to defuse demographic problems and stop the brain drain to countries boasting more attractive working conditions.

Incidentally, the projects mentioned above were part of the *Arbeit and Technik* (Work and Technology) research programme run by what is now the German Federal Ministry of Education (BMBF) but was started by the German Federal Ministry of Research and Technology BMFT. That programme was itself a based on a programme dating from the 1970s aimed at human ising working life. Today's framework concept for research, *Innovative Arbeitsgestaltung – Zukunft der Arbeit* (Innovative work organisation, the future of labour), unveiled in 2001, pursues even further reaching, more extensive objectives. So far more than 2,500 projects have been implemented under these ministerial programmes, which the unions helped to initiate and are monitoring closely, and they constitute a real treasure trove for anyone seeking to improve their situation at work or interested in creating new jobs on the back of innovation.

An even richer source of information and ideas is a series of Scandinavian programmes which has expended a vast, if not disproportional, amount of effort (in per capita terms) by implementing tens of thousands of projects designed to reshape people's working environments and turn them into more innovative structures. Anyone asking themselves just how Finland and Sweden, for example, have managed to halve unemployment within the space of just a few years, will find plenty of answers in these projects and programmes, amongst others.

For managers and politicians alike, fostering the ability to innovate is the key long-term objective

There is certainly no space here to explain on the basis of the above all the changes that German companies (and all other German institutions, for that matter) need to make to get the country back on the road to success, but there is no need to do so either, for Peter Drucker has already done this in the 35 books he has written over the past 60 years – which describe the situation very clearly and vividly. All we have to now is act on his advice!

Instead, let us return to the question of what policymakers can do to foster innovation. It may be impossible to directly promote, let alone take decisions about something that is unforeseeable, but we can create an environment that is a true breeding ground for innovation. To do so, we must eliminate the barriers we recognise as frequently delaying or impeding innovation.

In addition to the aforementioned barriers to innovation at company level, misplaced debates on wrong topics also constitute obstacles because they divert our attention away from what is really important. Thus, the approach of constantly focussing on costs as a factor in competitiveness – so beloved of short-sighted managers and officials – should be abandoned. That debate is dangerous because it leads us astray. After all, any attempt to compete with emerging countries purely by competing with them on costs is bound to lead us nowhere, sooner or later.

On this subject let me cite an example given by Hans-Jurgen Warnecke, who ran Rollei's plants before becoming President of the Fraunhofer Institute. When Japanese imitations started to exert pressure on the traditional camera manufacturer, it shifted production to Singapore, where the labour costs were lower than they were in Japan. This enabled Rollei to ward off the competition pretty successfully for a few years. But the Japanese launch of a new generation of electronic cameras proved catastrophic for Rollei, which had nothing to offer in response and duly went under. Warnecke: said: "We had our eye on costs and prices and neglected to invest in new developments . ... If a company wants to grow old, it must strive to stay young by constantly innovating".

As long as a country or its companies are able to offer enough innovative products and services which set it apart and that others do not yet manufacture, but do need, then even if it a high-wage country with no raw materials it will have no problem retaining its level of prosperity. Put another way, you have to always do things that others cannot yet do themselves.

What we need instead of a 'Year of Innovation' is resolute promotion of the ability to innovate. Policymakers must recognise this as their main long-term task, since the room for manoeuvre in all areas of policy depends on this to a decisive extent. In so doing they should never lose sight of the simple fact that human beings are – and will remain – the sole source of innovation. So the objective should be to encourage people, not subsidise technological artefacts. Politicians should home in on the prerequisites for ideas and innovation, or rather the breeding ground and climate in which they grow. That breeding ground is the knowledge and creativity in people's heads, i.e. the entire domain of education and training, which in Germany is also still strongly influenced in many respects by Taylorism and can hardly be deemed sufficient to meet the requirements of a knowledge society. The climate referred to above is the environment in which this knowledge is applied. An entire education will be worth precious little if the people emerging from it subsequently find themselves working in an environment where they are only able – or allowed – to put a fraction of their knowledge and skills to use. IBM's Larry Prusak put it this way: "You cannot manage knowledge like you cannot manage love, patriotism or your children. But you can set up and environment where knowledge evolves".

Innovations are mostly the result of a long and complex social process. Whether or not a new product or service turns out to be successful will depend primarily on the manner in which the associated process is shaped and how smoothly it functions. That process is also known by another name: work. In other words, the way in which work is organised will ultimately decide the success of innovations. The prerequisites for innovation include training and qualification, motivation, communication, freedom to manoeuvre and participation. Whereas authoritarian structures frequently try and cling on to traditional values and procedures for too long, qualified codetermination, for example, can certainly make a valuable contribution towards avoiding blind alleys and straying off the right track. Looking at things in this light, innovation serves as a kind of bridge between employment and the quality of labour, and only if we radically shake up our working environment will we also find ourselves capable of creating new jobs again!

Unfortunately, the issue of 'work organisation' in political debate is often considered a relic of previous efforts to improve health and safety or humanise the workplace or dismissed as 'social fiddle faddle' and filed under 'ideas that seemed good at the time', instead of being recognised as the key to a successful innovation policy. Several ongoing initiatives are perpetuating this misunderstanding, like the Federal Ministry of Economics and Labour (BMWA) initiative in which some actors seem to believe that issues to do with work organisation means carrying on where we left off in the 'glorious' 1970s, evidently because they have failed to register any of the progress made in this domain since then. This lack of awareness is also reflected in the shortcomings of our research policy. Since a mere 0.2% of the BMBF budget has been allocated to the programme entitled "*Innovative Arbeitsgestaltung*" (Innovative Work Organisation / Shaping), it is hardly surprising that the topic is hardly eliciting any response, even within the ministry itself.

In conclusion, the rather unsuccessful approaches taken up to now by German federal policy on research and technology should be discontinued. Instead, a fundamental change of direction of national activities within the framework of the current innovation initiative seems advisable. Funding is in short supply, but the shift can be achieved without allocating additional resources, merely by switching perspectives and setting fresh priorities. Instead of subsidising futile attempts to catch up with technological developments elsewhere and supporting highly prestigious major projects, we would do better to remind ourselves of where Europe's original strengths lie, as a region famous for its diversity, and above all specifically attempt to improve the conditions essential for successful technological innovation by deliberately trying to influence the social, organisational and cultural situation. This was the breeding ground that brought forth Europe's major innovations in past centuries, and it is in this way that we can hope to latch back onto the approach that led to our past successes. Since innovation takes place not just in research laboratories, but indeed everywhere, closer attention needs to be paid to the everyday goings-on in our companies. It is high time not only in our companies, but also – indeed especially – in our federal government institutions, for some innovation in innovation policy! As Peter Drucker pointed out back in 1994, if the 20th century was a century of social change, the 21 st century must be the century of social and political innovation.

III. Employee participation in Europe: propositions for designing a new research agenda

Employee participation in Europe: Propositions for designing a new research agenda – Report from Stream III

Valeria Pulignano

As rapporteur of steam III in the European workplace participation forum organized by the *Instituto per il Lavoro* (Bologna) on 24-26 September in Rome (Italy) I have been involved on reading, reflecting and providing comments on a bulk of 15 different papers covering various issues with regards to workplace participation, such as: participation at inter-company level; from a reactive to a proactive approach with regards to participation; participation and corporate social responsibility with specific reference to corporate restructuring processes; the role of participation for occupational health and safety and a good working life. The discussion which developed around the papers in the different workshops was lively and rich of stimulus. It provided to me new ideas which may be considered in order to start discussing new propositions for further research in the area of workplace participation. I will try in this paper to synthetically present these ideas while closely following the structure of the topics indicated in the forum. But before that I would like to briefly present the theoretical framework on which these propositions are constructed.

The "Cycles" of Participation and Democracy: Appraising Contemporary Trends in Workers' Participation

Since Harvie Ramsey published his 'Cycles of control' in Sociology in 1977 it has became one of the most influential work in the field of worker participation and involvement. Ramsey's theoretical framework challenged the unitarist assumption, found in much of the earlier literature on participation, that it was possible to generate a 'win-win' situation in which both management and employees benefited from participation schemes. Ramsey argued that participation initiatives in the 60 and 70 were largely misunderstood because commentators failed either to put them into historical perspective or to understand the features common to each cycle. His claim was that the participation initiatives of the period reflected the combination of shop-floor militancy that had grown in a context of full employment and prosperity, and economic pressure on employers as growth slowed and profits fell. Ramsey's argument was not that the attempts to encourage participation were futile. He stated quite explicitly that he did not consider that the democratic control of industry by those who produce its goods is a worthless pursuit. Indeed he argued that the fact that management authority was challenged periodically provided evidence of the underlying strength of calls for increased worker control. At the time 'Cycle' was written there was a good deal of optimism about the potential for participation, and Ramsey clearly saw this optimism as being based on a lack of understanding of both the cyclical nature of participation and the historical context. He observed that: "we now find ourselves back in the midst of a strong current of interests in the concept of workers' participation in management. Once more one would think the idea was new; at the very last, we are told, this time the process of democratisation is reaching an inexorable peak and this time employers really mean it" (Ramsay, 1977: 493). 'Cycles' must be understood as an attempt to correct the naïve position and optimism of those who cast their a-historical gaze upon developments in the 1970s and saw them as part of a theological process in which industry was becoming progressively more democratic. Patterns of participation have to be understood in their historical and sociological context.

The period since the publication of Cycles has witnessed political, economic, social and sectoral upheavals, with the corresponding landscape of participative practice – and its surrounding discourse – now very different from that of 1977 (Harley et al., 2005). The most visible manifestation of change has been the apparently rise in the use of employer-initiated involvement programmes, as well as joint initiatives at the inter-company level which were supported by EU legislation (see for example the European Directive 1994 on the establishment of the European Works Councils (EWCs) and the 2002 Directive on the national rights of information and consultation as well as the 2001 Directive on workers participation in a SE). Yet participative practices have apparently evolved in ways that the Cycle theory has been unable to predict: techniques have been introduced or reinforced at times of no obvious threat to management and met with active endorsement by employees and their union representative. Some literature sustain the view that participation can be introduced by employers to prevent and weaken union mobilisation attempts during period of tight labour markets (Pendlenton, 2005). However, employers themselves readily sometimes have found and find themselves opposing participative formulas which they interpret as inimical to their interests. At the EU level, for example, employers association still oppose attempt for the revision of the EWCs directive. Moreover, in the UK employers successfully resisted proposals for statutory worker directors; in Sweden employers opposed wage-earner funds; and international research point out that many multinational companies have still to implement EWCs. This suggests that participation is neither a single nor a continuous entity.

From the analytical perspective of the democratic influence but also at the more operational level, we can discern three different variants or dimensions of participation, two of which can be directly associated with management interests and the last aligned more closely with employee participation needs. The first is based on capital-sharing through employee share schemes. This is usually used by management to enhance labour performance. Profit-share schemes they work more in the United States. Across EU profit-share schemes, which relate workers remuneration to company performance, but not offer equity to employees, are much more common than share ownership. The second dimension is employer-initiated schemes and it embraces task-centred employee involvement in areas narrowly identified as being of direct interests to employees. Task involvement is here typified by direct exchanges between individual employees and managers and, as well as financial involvement, can include information, communication, consultation and job restructuring exercises, of which empowerment and team-working are well-known examples.

The third dimension of participation includes approaches that recognise and attempt to countervail the structural vulnerabilities of employees in contemporary, competitive and globalised economies by offering them regulation over employment rights that may otherwise be restricted or denied to them in a free market system. These approaches emerge directly from the efforts of employees, usually acting collectively and/or through pluralistic political programmes initiated at national, European and international level. Initiatives include support for collective representation and negotiation, works councils including inter-company structures for workers' participation, such as the EWCs, and the participation at the board level of directors or workers director (SE statute). These measures purport to influence or challenge aspects of corporate-level governance through the development of power-centred participation (Hall and Marginson, 2005). In the following sections each of the above mentioned dimensions of workers' participation will be deeply examined while attempting to provide some reflections with regards to the areas and aspects for further research.

Collective actions and/or pluralistic political programmes

Following Ramsey's proposition, it is only through the empirical investigation of the forms of inter-company employee participation and the ways they operate in practice that we can get a robust assessment of their significance and we can shed light on further developments. There is a variety of literature, in particular both survey and case study based analysis on the operation, practice and impact of existing forms of inter-company employee participation at the European level (namely the EWCs). What emerges from this bulk of study is, among the others, the attempt to assess management and employees-side views and expectations concerning the role of EWCs. In addition, it is also present an analysis aimed at explaining the different degrees of activism and influence exhibited by EWCs, focussing on issues such as the different types of EWC observable, developmental trajectories, and the key factors affecting their operation. Much of the literature confirms' Ramsay prepositions that the practice of EWC may bear only an indirect relationship to their formal remit and consultation rights, and will be shaped by a range of contingent factors (including country-sector and company specific factors, in which consideration of structure and agency interact) (Marginson and Sisson, 2004). But still some aspects remain not investigated, for example: why there has been any initiative undertaken to establish a EWC where no EWC exist? What are the problems at national or local level which constraint such activity? How all this impact on the possibility to create cross-border labour union employees cooperation? Hence, it can be argued that the effectiveness of EWCs as well as of other instruments for workers' participation at the international level (such as the International Framework Agreements or IFAs) needs to be clearly assessed. This is what emerges from the paper of Nick Hammer on the IFAs which was presented in Workshop 9 "Participation at inter-company level". In particular, how far can we consider these instruments as the foundation for organising labour strategy or rather, do we need to see – as Hammer argues – the different strategy of union organising as the precondition for the implementation of these instruments, remain as a relevant key question to investigate.

The picture, which has been painted so far about the still young experience of the IFAs conclude that these agreements have had a positive impact on the implementation of fundamental social rights. It may therefore be argued that IFAs are a useful complement to existing labour law norms. However, both studies stress the fact that the actual compliance and success of the IFA can vary considerably. Provisions for the implementation of an IFA and for their effective enforcement/monitoring seem to be important if the agreement is to have any real impact (Papadakis et al., 2008; Schömann et al., 2008). Furthermore it is recognised that no legal enforcement mechanisms exist at the global level of international labour law for the IFAs. This means that any enforcement of IFA provisions relies on the readiness of management to cooperate or on the capacity of the trade unions to compel companies to resolve complaints. So what is still under-researched is to focus on the concrete implementation of the IFAs. More specifically, it remains to be seen what determines the effective implementation, compliance and enforcement of these initiatives or instruments for employees' participation in practice. These are crucial issues whose disclosure will enable to more systematically enrich the study on the establishment of inter-company processes and structures. In this respect the paper of Nick Hammer highlights some problems with regards to the difficulty trade unions currently face in order to establish inter-company structures for employees' participation in specific sector. As the author argues this is, for example, more evident in the construction sector where a high level of decentralisation in collective bargaining is combined with a strongly segmented labour force. More specifically, in the paper of Herman Knudsen, Ole Busck, Tine Jorgensen and Jens Lind the authors claim that the extent to which the structures for employees' participation at the inter-company level can act as a collective actor, instead of operating in a fragmented way, depends on a diversity of conditions and circumstances. International literature illustrate that in some cases these structures have developed a common identity by aggregating different interests at supranational (inter-company) level. But in many others conflicting national interests seem still to override international solidarity. Some research has started to go deeply examining the nature of the factors which constrain cross-border union solidarity but still further investigation is needed. In particular, does trans-national union cooperation develop necessarily in response to hostile company strategies aimed at playing off national employees' interests against each other or is cross-border solidarity subject to the existence of particular conditions and circumstances and what are they? In other words can we expect the emergence of a counter-hegemonic block in reaction to the growing power of trans-national capital and under which conditions? More generally we need to ask: What are the obstacles and drivers to the establishment of structures of employees' participation at the inter-company level? What are the conditions and circumstances under which structures of employees' participation at the inter-company level may lead (or not) to build up collective responses and international solidarity across-borders? Do (and how) structural and agency factors account for the difference?

These are research question that need to be formulated with an attention at the capacity employees they have not only horizontally (at the inter-company level) but also vertically (across the value-chain) to set structures for employees' participation. As Rainer Greca points out in his study on the working conditions in the supply value chain in the production of textiles, toys and cars this is a critical issue which discloses strong contradictions with regards to the expectations generated in the public opinion concerning the application of European discourses and concepts, such as Corporate Social Responsibility (CSR) in the value supply chain. In the paper of Annika Lantz and Peter Friedrich on "Trade union cooperation to enhance voluntary and non voluntary mobility in the value-chains" this argument is tested more specifically with regards to forms of workers participation at the workplace. In particular, the paper warns with regards to the challenge value chains create to forms of employee participation and influence on decisions. As the authors point out "the impact of value chains can be seen as fragmentation of company-level interests' representation". In order to reduce the effects of the challenge it is stated in the paper that trade unions need to cooperate and establish coordination along the supply chain if they are to represent the interests of the employees in the partner organisations within the value chain. So the issue of cooperation and coordination assume here a different connotation than what above mentioned. It is vertically (along the supply chain) and not only horizontally (across-countries) explored. However, as Nick Hammer's study on the construction sector specifically indicates "horizontal coordination is contingent upon vertical coordination (and the weaknesses) of establishing vertical coordination". One of these weaknesses (or structural barriers) stems from the fragmentation of production as well as work and employment. These rich observations point out the need to better investigate restructuring across the value chain and its effects on the changes in work and employment. For example, one issue which has been dedicated not yet sufficient attention by international research is how restructuring across the value chain is changing work and employment. The final results of the WORKS project founded by the European Commission under the Six Framework Programme and presented in Rome on 8-9 October 2009 open in this respect new trajectory and stimulate for new research interests especially concerning employees prospects with regards to career development and prevention and rehabilitation through mobility.

It is also important to mention that although employee participation is considered a key issue in order to 'socially' cope with the forces of corporate restructuring (see the paper by Fernando Rocha on "Corporate restructuring processes and industrial relations in Spain"), in some specific circumstances restructuring shows to have negative impact on participation. For example, the study presented by Mireille Battut from the Alpha Group in Paris points out that the privatisation processes affecting public and semi-public companies entail contribute to a decrease the participation culture inside the company. More specifically, the admission of new employees to the companies, under new contractual conditions, can represent a considerable obstacle to participation. It seems possible to argue that the predisposition to participate in structures of workers' representation varies directly in accordance with the stability and security afforded by the employment relationship. From the papers presented in workshop 11 "Participation and corporate social responsibility – the case of restructuring processes", it is clear that still a lot remains to be done with regards to research concerning participation and restructuring. More specifically, as emerged from the critical discussion originated by the original presentation of Bruno Cattero in the forum, the territorial aspects with regards to restructuring, such as the role played by local actors and their participation in matter of restructuring, needs urgently to be included in the research agenda in order to better understand the dynamics and processes of change. Moreover, the management of current and future skill gaps with regards to restructuring needs also future attention. More specifically, the areas on which future research attention is needed are: the strategies and the measures aimed at coping with current and anticipated skills gaps in order to include better use of older workers, education and business linkages; lifelong learning initiatives; attraction of talent from outside the country into areas of shortage. As above indicated it also needs to be more accurately studied the role of key players – including public authorities, private agencies, employers, trade unions and other actors (e.g. NGOs) – in matter of restructuring; the nature and the extent of internal flexibility and of external transitions including the measures used. The comparative method is here seen as the more efficient one in order to fulfil the above mentioned gaps. However, the international comparison probably needs to be less categorical. For example with reference to participation and corporate social responsibility differences in the area of finance, ownership patterns, corporate law, accounting rules, boardroom practices are narrowing. The question is no longer the dispersion versus concentration (i.e. good versus weak). The diversity of the future may be more various and they may be also the necessity to think about other indicators which would allow to measure what is now considered hard to account only by using traditional indicators.

Task-involvement, participation and quality of working life

As the papers presented in Workshop 12 "The role of participation for occupational health and safety and a good working life" emphasised there has been increasing research interest on the improvement of workplace performance and its link with productivity in a context of increased global competitiveness. In particular, Herman Knudsen, Ole Busck, Tine Jorgensen and Jens Lind argue that a growing bulk of international research has looked in the last few years at the impact of the work environment on organisational productivity as well as at broad economic and social benefits of employment practices. The latter contribute to employee wellbeing and wellness which as Davide Dazzi rightly points out cannot be separated to health and safety issue. More specifically, Dazzi argues that the change in the nature of the employment contract with a stronger incidence of temporary or short term contracts leads to a more insecure workforce, which seems to be more affected by problems of stress and, therefore, with consequent difficulties with regards to its representativeness at the workplace. This is a serious challenge because of, as Maria Menèndez, Joan Benach and Laurent Vogel claim, the crucial role played by the safety representatives in the promotion of workers' occupational health in the EU.

Workshop 10 "From a reactive to a proactive approach" focused on debating what is needed in order to enhance participative and innovative capacities of employees at the workplace more generally. The extent to which combined task-involvement based practices enhance performance via opening up opportunities for autonomy and employees' participation and their impact on representative structures of participation is strongly debated. Consideration of the evidence concerning High Performance Work System (HPWs) and instruments for organisational performance (such as teamwork) show consistent and positive association between them, on which basis we should accept the hypothesis that these instruments contributes to enhance performance. However, this acceptance should be tempted by the lack of evidence concerning the processes and direction of causation. The research evidence concerning employee outcomes is far from conclusive. For example, with specific reference to HPWs we can argue that while there is evidence that HPWs practices are associated with a range of positive employee outcomes, evidence about autonomy is limited and equivocal. This, with almost the total lack of evidence that performance gains are achieved via employees' outcomes, suggests that we should regard the conventional accounts of HPWs with a measure of sprone for future research. I am not saying that HPWs never enhance autonomy, nor that they might generate performance gains via employees, but more evidence should be provided to shed light on these aspects. Without compelling evidence we cannot advance scientifically based conclusions. This aspect is summarised by Werner Fricke as "the democratic character of participation" which denotes the need to move from "dependent" to "independent autonomy" in constructing new forms of work and production organisation. The results on the working conditions of the employees are negative. As Fricke argues: "intensification of work, as the result of employees accepting the working conditions apparently determined by the market, is the price the employees pay for the illusion of self organised work, which is in fact nothing but a dependent autonomy, determined by scarse resources and the market". More specifically, Lauge Baungaard Rasmussen's paper highlights that an important aspect of "democratic participation" is the integration of interests, concerns and needs of different stakeholders in decision-making processes. For employees this implies to changing role of employees representatives, trade unions, and management in change processes. For companies, this may means involving employees in an early stage of planning processes. In this way, participation becomes essential to support a "proactive" approach which needs to be combined with "soft" or "non-binding forms of regulations" in order to increase company interests in experimenting participative workplace practices (see the paper of Tuomo Alasoini, Asko Heikkila, Elise Ramstad and Pekka Ylostalo on "Promotion of Participatory Workplace Practices through a Publicly-Funded Programme: Experiences from

Finland"). In addition, the papers of Ole Broberg and Gian Marco Campagnolo outline relevant observations with regards to the need to go beyond organisational aspects and include also "workspace" or "engineering" design processes or "modelling" when discussing the implementation of participative organisational structures in companies who aim to engage in socio-technical design processes.

Conclusions

While there is a range of potential explanations documented in Workshop 9, 10 and 11 in Stream III with regards to worker participations on one hand, on the other hand how to promote effective opportunities for employees and union representatives' participation and influence in the new changing area of employment relations and labour markets, continue to figure repeatedly as being among the most durable and consistent needs for future research. In addition, a cross-national comparative analysis of the obstacles and drivers (and their nature) of employees and union representatives' participation is needed. More specifically, it is hard to avoid the conclusion that the attempt by transnational capital to exploit the regulatory environment on one hand, and the degradation of state institutions and the decentralising and the de-institutionalising of industrial and employment relations associated with the neo-liberal ascendency in the almost last two decades on the other hand, have produced not secondary effects on the employees and their forms and processes of workplace participation. This is highlighted in the papers presented in Stream III overall. Hence, the need to investigate in the light of new research methods how to strength the relation between employee participation and employees structures of representatives participation is crucial. In this respect, more comparative (cross-national research) needs to be combined with more longitudinal studies looking at the economic, social and political effects of employees participation in order to get more inside into the complex interaction between organisational/company, sectoral and workplace structures.

References

Hall, M. / Marginson, P. (2005): "Trojan Horses or Paper Tigers? Assessing the Significance of European Works Councils", in Harley, B. / Hyman, J. / Thompson, P. (eds.) (2005): Participation and Democracy at Work, Palgrave Mac-Millan: London, pp. 204-221

Harley, B. / Hyman, J. / Thompson, P. (eds.) (2005): Participation and Democracy at Work, Palgrave Mac-Millan: London

Marginson, P. / Sisson, K. (2004): European Integration and European Industrial Relations, Palgrave Mac-Millan, London
Papadakis, K. (2008): Cross-Border Social Dialogue and Agreements. An Emerging Global Industrial Relations Framework, International Institute for labour Studies, ILO-Geneva
Pendleton, A. (2005): "Employee Share Ownership, Employment Relationships and Corporate Governance" in Harley, B. / Hyman, J. / Thompson, P. (eds.) (2005): Participation and Democracy at Work, Palgrave Mac-Millan: London, pp. 75-93
Ramsay, H. (1977): "Cycles of Control: Worker Participation in Sociological and Historical Perspective", Sociology: 11 pp. 481-506
Schomann, I. (2008): "Codes of conduct and international framework agreements: new forms of governance at company level?", Presentation to "Cross-Border Social Dialogue and Agreements: An Emerging Global Industrial Relations Framework", 29 October, Brussels.

Participation at inter-company level – Trade union cooperation to enhance voluntary and non-voluntary mobility in the value-chains

Annika Lantz, Peter Friedrich

For nearly two decades the concept of supply-chain and value-chain has had an impact on all kinds of sectors and there is a widespread belief among researchers and managers that networking and chain building have advantages for the enterprises, as well as for the national/regional sector's competitiveness. The difficulties in creating them, exploring their potential, or maintaining momentum within the networks are well documented, but have to our knowledge in the literature been discussed mainly from the perspective of the enterprise. From a trade union perspective the competitive advantages are recognized, but more often problematic issues as outsourcing and lack of influence on decisions in a complex decision-making process are raised. The impact of value-chains can be seen as fragmentation of company-level interest representation. Further, from the perspective of the trade unions, value-chains challenge the forms of participation and influence on decisions, as different trade union s might need to collaborate if they are to represent the interest of the employees in the partner organizations within the value-chain. There might however be un-known or not fully explored possibilities for employees owing to value-chain building. There might be, for example, prospects with regard to career development or with regard to prevention of health problems and rehabilitation through mobility. Different potentials for the employees are not yet fully explored, and developments in this area need to be illuminated more from both theoretical and methodological points of view.

The aim of this paper is to give input to a discussion of what the employees' advantages of value-chains might be, and to explore the potentials for trade unions' participation within value-chains. What does it take in terms of organisational solutions for trade unions' representative participation, and employees' direct participation if the potentials are to be made use of? After a brief introduction to the theoretical background, we present the results of two action-research projects carried out in cooperation between trade unions, intermediaries on the labour market, and enterprises with the general aim to enhance voluntary and non-voluntary mobility along a value-chain.

The potential of regional value-chains

Value chains and networks typically involve interaction between firms, but can also build bridges between managers, researchers, labor unions, business support organizations and intermediaries on the labor market. They offer an increasingly important method of stimulating real innovation rather than emulation: they are not only about transferring existing knowledge but about creating new levels of knowledge through the active exchange of experience and through experimentation (Lantz / Totterdill, 2004).

There are strong arguments for why innovation and learning is enhanced by regional value-chains and cooperation between academia, enterprises, labor unions, and public organizations. The individual firm can be too weak an instrument around which to build change. Innovation is intimately related to the firm's wider social environment, the semi-public sphere that defines access to knowledge, exchange of experience and shared resources. At the level of the company, and particular in SMEs, many managers and trade unions have difficulties in understanding the nature and potential of workplace innovation as the exposure to alternatives is often very limited. Yet they are often simply overwhelmed by external pressures. Access to sources of expertise relating to innovation, work organization and culture remains a serious problem for companies. New approaches cannot be implemented "off the shelf", but require a careful process of learning and negotiation. Experts with understanding and experience of these issues are rare or expensive. Changes in the outside world can within a value-chain be dealt with differently, the extended context will provide new possibilities, and when working together, the united efforts to create better conditions will be beneficial for the single company as well. Innovation of some magnitude, radicalness and novelty might be an added value, and can refer to products, services, work-place change or change related to economical restructuring and labour market.

The problem of economic restructuring and accompanying difficulties relating to the workforce (as expressed, for example, by lack of adaptability or mobility) is not a problem caused, or capable of being resolved, by a single organization or player concerned with the labor market. From this perspective we advocate that trade unions have an interest to take active part in value-chain building so to ensure that the value-chains potentials are explored and used.

Creating added value in value-chains through relation building

Relations within and between enterprises are a key factor for unchaining the potentials of value chain building (Fawcett, et al., 2005; Spekman, et al., 2002;

Peterson, 2002). The company/partner typically relates to others to gain either access to resources that it lacks itself, and/or to better be able to meet demands and changes in the market or the society. Every organization is embedded in a context, and when forming a partnership with others, this context will not only be larger, it will also be of different quality making it possible to relate to the context in new and different ways (Bessant, 2001). Relation building is facilitated by competence in communicating and relating, by shared knowledge of what characterizes a successful value chain, and platforms such as space and time to discuss internal affairs. Hence value-chains are most often referred to in a regional context.

Relations can be characterized in terms of intensity in the reciprocal giving and taking within and between partners and in terms of the qualities of their interactions. The relations with, as well as the dependence of other companies will generate two parallel organizational processes. The first is to adjust internal structures and develop internal organizational processes that fit the demands from partners. The second is to participate in the relation building between partner organizations. This is true for trade unions as well, since different trade unions need to cooperate with each other within a value-chain. The aim will be to create relations that are stable, complex, characterized by giving and taking, reciprocal adjustments, and rich in social exchange. It is in these relations the added value is created and expertise will be the product of interaction rather than as the property of the individual expert.

The partners in the value chain need to find a very precise answer to a complex question: How are they going to relate to each other and on what terms? Are the relations to be result oriented, (i.e. to accomplish a specific and predefined result) or potential oriented, (i.e. to relate and network in order to learn about and develop something which is not yet fully defined)? We believe that trade unions have an important role to play in this decision-making process. To accomplish a specific and predefined result can be to take joint effort in promoting a regional area for tourism or to make a costly promotion of for example the value of buying nationally produced food. In potential-oriented network building the advantages for the participating organizations can only be grouped into more general advantages. According to Senge and Scharmer (1996) they are to raise awareness of how the internal organizational solutions affect competitiveness, to initiate continuous improvement and support innovation, to implement knowledge from academia and generate new knowledge through action research. There might be specific issues and problems for trade unions' participation in the two above mentioned different types of network or value chain building, but as our aim is to explore potentials we focus on the process of identifying and creating these value-chains, rather than on the rationale behind the value-chain building. However, the objective (result-oriented or potential-oriented) will affect the process within the chain.

Value-chains relations are built on competence and learning

Beulens (2001; 2005) describes chain knowledge as a strategic success factor for value-chain building and distinguishes between 'knowledge about chains' and 'knowledge within chains'. Nearly all literature about value or supply chains of any kind deals with the knowledge about chains (see Heide et al., 2005; Boehlje et al., 1999) and we draw researchers attention to the fact that little empirical research has been carried out on what knowledge and competence *within* chains promotes value-chain building and in creating the added value. It is however clear that building value-chains and creating added values demand competence and organizational learning. Relating in such a way that the relations are the means to create added value, takes skill and competency in both *how to* relate and *what to relate about*. The partners within organizations and partner organizations need to define what competency it takes to develop the added value. The competence can be described as technical (production processes, work methods, technologies), procedural (knowledge of procedures for problem-solving and for ensuring goal fulfilment), contextual (how to relate to and handle the context), strategic (how to handle uncertainty and new challenges), social (how to develop the relations and how to communicate efficiently) and learning (learning how to learn).

In complex work and in most change and developmental activities or innovative work all the above mentioned types of competencies are needed. An innovation is the result of experience and knowledge exchange in collective learning processes and creative, interdisciplinary cooperation along the entire chain from idea to product/service, and maintenance (Lorenz / Valeyre, 2004).

Competence is not only to be able to successfully achieve a certain result; it is also to make use of inherent degrees of freedom in order to go beyond stipulated results through a redefinition process of the means-goal relationship in order to achieve meaningful change (Lantz / Friedrich, 2003). Enhancing individual competence in a work place setting is closely linked to degrees of freedoms, or autonomy as prerequisites for work-place learning, and organizational learning. In order for the "learning organisation" not to become a mythical phenomenon three question need to be answered when applying the concept: "Who is learning?", "Why is learning taking place?", and "What is being learned?" (Lantz / Friedrich, 2003). Whether individual learning results in organizational learning depends on if the learning results in a change of organizational structures or processes. If no such change occurs, no organizational learning has taken place. The research on organizational learning is vast, here we limit ourselves to who is learning, and what kinds of learning enhances value-chain building and added values for the employees.

So far we have argued that in the first place the support of sustainability of competencies can contribute to solving existing problems in the value chain and is a means to promote better use of its potentials and at the end even customer orientation (see Emberson et al., 2001). Secondly, the issue of competencies is the key for the generation of constructive working relationships in value-chains. It is a means for achieving the goals for chain marketing, chain logistics, quality assurance, information flows and added values for both the enterprise and its employees. This network learning enables value creation through the combination of individual competencies and it is how this learning is transformed into an asset that truly matters (Spekman, et al., 2002). New innovation research highlights the importance of all employees for successful innovations and stresses that the momentum of development lies in human work (Lorenz / Valeyre, 2004). The prerequisites for employees' work effort and hence for the developmental momentum are central. Making use of existing competencies and life-long learning along the value-chain, through fluid working relationships between the different companies, can promote creativity and innovation, strengthen organizational and individual competencies, and create understanding between actors (Diederen / Jonkers, 2001).

Trade unions' role in ensuring competence-development and life-long learning at the workplace and along value-chains

The above briefly presented theoretical background leads to the following conclusions. Building a value chain step by step and from a bottom-up approach might result in developing a potential not fully known from day one. The potential can be of innovative nature and make use of knowledge transfer between academia and practise. Building such value-chains take competence in creating stable, complex and trusting relations that are characterized by reciprocal adjustments. Making use of the existing competencies within enterprises through reciprocal relations between partners is a key factor for exploring the potential results of the value-chain and in creating its potential. If the trade unions are to be active in exploring the potentials for the employees in value-chains three critical issues need to be dealt with:

- *Trade unions need to define themselves as partners in a mutual exchange and take responsibility for creating trusting relationships so that individual and organizational learning can take place*
- *Trade unions need to influence the partners within the value-chain so that the general objective of the value chain is potential oriented*
- *Trade unions need to fully recognize the importance of both individuals' learning at the workplace and of organizational learning and find ways, both*

through indirect and direct participation, to enhance learning possibilities and rewarding competence.

So far labor unions in Sweden have in negotiations stressed the importance of workers' possibilities to learn at the workplace, both in creating working conditions that provide inherent learning opportunities and in workers' right to take part in different forms of competence-development through training and the like. From both a psychological viewpoint and a labor union perspective, interest is directed towards work conditions, since they not only provide more or less beneficial prerequisites for workers' present life circumstances – they also influence their future development potential and the potential for competence-development and lifelong learning to a considerable degree. The concept of health accommodates several dimensions, one of which is the potential for using and developing one's own resources.

Trade unions have however been passive when it comes to idea-generation of strategies for learning within enterprises and as a consequence, also in value- or supply-chains. Trade unions recognize the importance of learning and competence-development for innovation and competitiveness in order to meet the challenges of globalization, and also for the employees' long-term employability, but so far there are few examples of where the trade unions take the lead in creating such learning. Further, there are rare examples of trade union-strategies for direct participation in creating learning at the workplace. This might be due to that creating learning is a process that involves ongoing activities at the shop floor, and the trade unions' representatives within an enterprise more often have the role of a negotiator in a decision-process with management. Further, if one does not have a strategy and methods for how learning and competence-development is to be enhanced, nor the resources in terms of time and competence, it will be difficult indeed.

Two examples of value-chain building through participation

Below, we present our experience of a competency-based value chain building based on the above presented theoretical framework with the overall aim of creating value chains. The focus is on the 'building' aspect of the values (defined as several aspects of quality for product, environment and work), and on the means, which were the individual and organizational competencies. Our aim is to present practitioners, consultants and researchers with our view on what worked, and what can be improved. In the two presented cases, trade unions were important partners as to support the development of prerequisites for and the motivation of staff to participate in competence development along the value chain within food-industry in Sweden.

The first example: Life-Long Learning Along the Food Chain in Scania

The empirical facts of change and development activities in the food sector are selected from a large Swedish project, *"Life-Long Learning Along the Food Chain in Scania",* funded by the European Social Fund and the EQUAL-Initiative. The project was conducted during 2001-2006 within the food sector in Scania – an important agricultural and food region in southern Sweden. In Sweden in 1999 a total of 419,000 people (10% of the labour force) were employed in the different parts of the food chain, and most of them in Scania. There was a clear focus on building knowledge about, as well as within value chains as success factors for creating value for *both the work force and for the sector*. The keyword was competency development. This referred to organizational and inter-organizational learning, as well as to individual learning. These learning processes on different levels were considered to work hand in hand and to enhance each other (Doyle and Parker, 1999). The anticipated outcome was the development of potential-oriented relations in food chains. Although specific results were expected from sub-activities focusing on different target groups along the food chain, they were all targeted towards continuous learning as an open-ended process, where the results cannot be fully defined beforehand. The general idea was to unchain the potential of the food chain by competency development. The overall aim of the project was to:

- develop strategies for the development of human resources along the value-chain
- build relations between companies, trade unions within the food sector and intermediaries on the labour market
- create added value for both the companies and the individual employees
- involve trade unions to enhance career development and mobility along value-chains

Different sub-activities, see below, were targeted towards either a) the work force, i.e. the individual level, or b) companies and relations between companies and other organizations on the labour market, i.e. the organizational level. These activities were carried out simultaneously. The ambition was to develop the food chain to become a platform for life-long learning where learning could also take place to an equal extent by moving between workplaces along the value chain both within a company and between companies. The mobility was seen as a means to prevent long-term unemployment and for rehabilitation of employees who for different health reasons were not able to work at their workplace. The developmental activities were focusing on the creation of a regional career guidance centre for mobility and life-long learning along the food chain and career guidance actions along the food chain. Figure 1, below, illustrates the value-chain and the target groups' anticipated mobility.

Figure 1: Mobility along the value-chain.

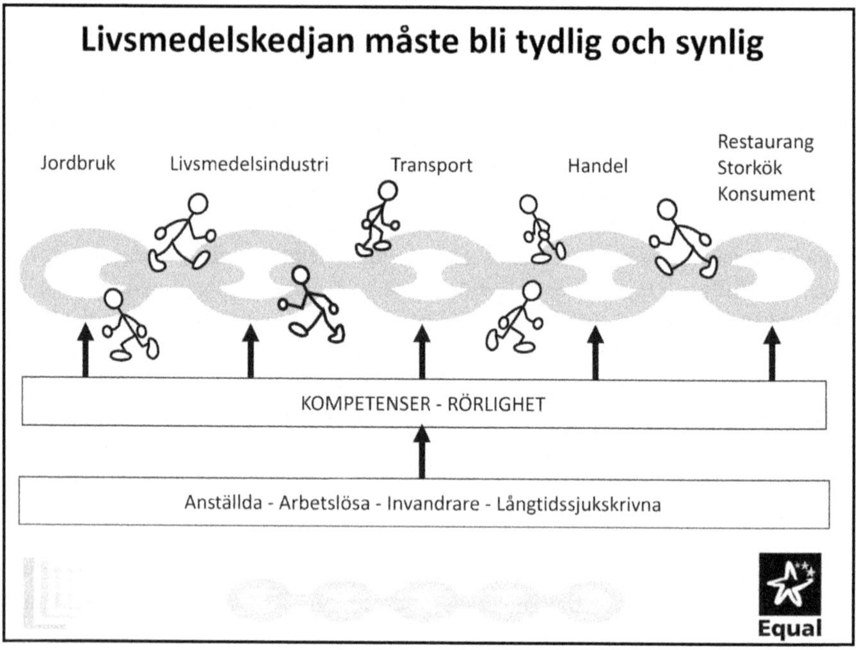

Regional career guidance centre for mobility and life-long learning

The expected outcome of the creation of a regional career guidance centre was the development of organizational excellence in networking for mobility and life-long learning along the value chain. The task of an already existing communal career guidance as a coordinator was to initiate co-operation between public organizations on the labour market (job centres and social insurance offices, training providers etc) and companies and trade unions in the region in the food sector. The aim was the creation of a stable network based on mutual understanding, the division of tasks and roles, shared responsibility for the overall gain for the society, the companies and for the individual, and partners defining themselves as "net workers for mobility". The network (mobility centre) was to be managed and coordinated by the communal career guidance centre. The means to develop the career guidance centre, and later the network, was the involvement of the staff at the career guidance centre in developing a system for assessing generic competencies, and a method for coaching mobility. The task of the career guidance centre was to coach individuals for new jobs along the food chain and to enable them to make use of the support given by the platform (the participating organizations) of mobility. Trade unions and enterprises were to help finding workplaces for the individuals and trade union representatives took the responsibility for supporting them during the introduction to the work place.

Framework for assessment of generic competencies along the food chain.

In order to enhance a shared concept of competency we developed instruments that assess competencies as a result of learning at work, and competencies that are shared and generic in the food chain. Our aim was to provide instruments that are easy to use, reliable, and valid to companies and trade unions along the food chain and to the public organizations supporting mobility on the labour market. The employees' competencies would be assessed in a similar way and their individual portfolios accepted by all partners thus smoothing the transfer between workplaces.

Trade union representatives and the researchers carried out extensive empirical research involving detailed study of the work activities that are carried out within different work places at different hierarchical levels within the food sector. Based on this research, instruments for describing an individual's *competency profile* have been developed. The profile includes *what* competencies the individual possesses to carry out the different work activities presented above, and his/her level of competency for each work activity. Competency in handling functional work tasks; disturbances; prioritizing; co-operation; organizing; quality and environmental work, is assessed on a scale that measures the extent to which an individual contributes to developing and changing his/her task. Competency in handling the organizational context is to a greater degree transferable to another workplace than functional competencies (Lantz and Friedrich, 2003).

A coordinated system for career development along the food chain.

To get a picture of all the different career paths along the food chain, information was gathered by the trade unions about every work place within the food sector in the region. The outcome, a typology of different professions along the food chain, was linked to the Internet site of the Swedish National Labour Market Board. Here jobs are described in terms of required skills and competencies, as well as the demands for the labour force (important for career guidance). The result of this linkage was a description of different career paths along the food chain, based on a common framework of competencies.

A second task was to develop a methodology and tools for coaching individuals in their career along the value chain. The coaching methodology was developed in cooperation with who, in a later phase of the project, were to carry out coaching at career guidance centres, in companies and in various networks. Trade union representatives played a mayor role in the developmental phase. The product was a ten-week training program to teach personnel involved with mobility and rehabilitation new tools and a new methodology based on networking and a competency-perspective. The coordinated system for career development was used on the different platforms and by the career guidance centre.

Partnership building between trade unions and employers in the value chain

Four different trade union organizations represented the work force in four different companies along the food chain. A trade union representative and a representative for top management/ HR department within each company formed a working relationship (tandem-partnerships). The constellation of tandem-cooperation (trade union and company representing one workplace) with other workplaces along the food chain has not been tested in Sweden before. The task of the work group (four pairs, in total eight persons) was to support employees to get new tasks within the four companies for a pilot group of eight employees (two from each company). These employees wished to get new tasks since they were either dissatisfied with their work situation, or on short-term sick-leave due to the onset of industrial diseases.

The expected short-term results were the implementation of a new type of cooperation between the different trade unions, between trade unions and companies and the launch of a new task for trade union representatives within companies. The long-term goals were to implement a shared perspective on generic competencies within the partnership, learning how to handle inter-organizational relations and knowing how to form a successful value chain.

The means for reaching these goals required the development of:

- methods for identifying "risk" individuals needing to change work as a preventive measure to avoid becoming permanently ill or unemployed,

- methods for finding, identifying and motivating employers to either exchange staff or find new tasks for the individuals,
- a definition of a new type of task for the unions as coaches for mobility,
- a shared perspective on and methods for identifying transferable skills.

The work group held regular meetings with an expert who helped to sort out issues on how inter-organizational relations could be handled and to generate ideas about how to form a successful value chain. The issues covered during the meetings were chain strategy for enhancing mobility, chain formation, chain organization, chain design, chain management and chain partnerships.

Trade union collaboration across the food-chain to enhance mobility and rehabilitation

The second project "Trade union collaboration across the food-chain to enhance mobility and rehabilitation" was led by The Swedish Food Workers' Union, and financed by Swedish Governmental Agency for Innovation Systems. The project was conducted between 2005-2007. The project was inspired by the above presented tandem-partnerships and was based on the principles and methods described above.

Trade unions representing employees in different parts of the food sector were invited to discuss the possibilities of forming tandem networks. Three different tandem-networks were built. A trade union representative with the sole task to enhance the mutual giving and taking within the tandem-networks facilitated the networks. All partners took part in a ten-week training (part time) to learn about networking, to gain a shared perspective on competence, and to learn the methodology for competence-description and for coaching. The trade union representatives had the role to coach employees who were identified as being at risk of becoming long term unemployed, or who were on long-term sick leave at their work place. The trade union representatives were supported by their tandem-partner when issues came along that needed the employers' decision or involvement.

Results

The 250 individuals who were supported by the mobility centre learned how their competencies could be made use of in a different setting. Aided by the companies along the food chain and supporting public organizations on the labour market, they explored new tasks either at a new work place, or with the current employer.

An absolute majority either got a new job or decided to go for further vocational training. But what indications do we have that this has been turned to good account by the companies along the food chain? Did they become a stable platform for life-long learning? We know that they provided work places, so in that sense we can say that the food chain became a platform for a future, and maybe, life-long career. If the individuals have control over their own career planning and development, like those taking part in the programme, they can use this as a platform for life-long learning.

Our conclusion is that by relatively simple means it is possible to use the food chain to create added value for the workforce. As long as there is one partner organization, in this case the regional career guidance centre, that assumes the role for coaching individuals along the food chain, the strategy works. However, the approach to bringing the different partner organizations together by focusing on individual coaching processes, needs to be supported by a parallel process. This involves activities on the organizational level to create a comprehension of the inherent possibilities for making use of a competency perspective to generate added value for the companies involved. *Trade unions play a central role in this work and their involvement is crucial if the activities are to be carried out.*

The short-term goals for the partnership building between trade unions and employers in the value chain were easy to evaluate. “Risk”-individuals could be identified, employers were motivated, trade unions accepted the new task and the pilot group found new work.

The long-term results are more difficult to evaluate. We know that the partnership used their inter-organizational relations as a mini labour market for finding new work places for employees after the completion of the project, and we conclude that the strategy worked. The chain organization, with issues like role division and coordination was problematic, according to the partners. The existing partnership concluded that if they were to take on the overall responsibility in the future, they should invest more in chain management. The partnership can be seen as a new organization needing its own management. The chain design proved to be functional. The companies say that they learned more about health management and used the personal contacts to solve problems of a varying nature. For example, they planned joint competency development for their HR-departments. From our perspective, the most important outcome was the finding of what it takes in mutual giving and taking of the partners if inter-organizational relations are to be built successfully.

The trade union representatives in the second tandem network coached 30 employees over a three-month period. Eight persons found new work at a new workplace within the partnership. 14 employees trained at a new workplace in order to evaluate the capacity to work, to find work motivation and take initiative to search for a new job. Meanwhile they went back to work at their workplace. Four employees were coached to come back to work at their original workplace but with different tasks. Four employees were coached but without the expected result that they would find work within the tandem-network, and got further support by the regional labour agency.

Previously, trade union representatives in Sweden have not been actively involved in supporting mobility for their members. On the contrary, the trade unions have regarded mobility as a threat to job security and have not supported the idea of life-long learning and career paths along the value chain. The trade unions very quickly adopted the new role and the Swedish Trade Union Confederation has disseminated the results and taken the initiative to start courses for trade union representatives on how to enhance mobility by building inter-organizational relations.

What did the trade union s gain?

- First, their members expressed that the trade unions did contribute to make a difference in their working lives – the membership proved to be valuable for the individual member
- The indirect participation, the individual employees being empowered to take initiative to implement meaningful changes in their carriers, enhanced the mobility and reduced the risk for members becoming unemployed
- The trade unions could influence partnerships between companies to create potentials for the employees not beforehand known
- Methods to support learning and competence development at the work place – putting words on the political agenda into action
- Self-efficacy regarding the task to help and support individual members in a challenging and difficult period in their work life

Discussion

We tried by a number of means to introduce a shared comprehension of competency within the different partnerships of organizations. What does this involve? The partnership needs expertise in defining competencies in the value-chain and not only about the value-chain, and in developing valid and useful tools. In our experience, this is a task too difficult for the companies, trade unions, intermediaries on the labour market and consultants. The partnership needs to establish a cooperation with researchers and qualified consultants within the field. Contacts with the regional universities are essential for building knowledge and the universities can have a role as stakeholders in regional innovation and development. One important task for universities can be to facilitate networking within value-chains by providing tools for describing value-chain specific methods for assessing competency.

From the individual's point of view, it is obvious that a shared competency perspective made transition between workplaces smoother. What was learned within one organization could be made use of in the next. Here we feel confident in maintaining that a competency perspective does make the abstract concept of interface tangible and that added value is made use of in the next stage in the value-chain. In some partnerships we see signs that the added value is developed further, e.g. when companies use the food chain for joint competency development. In most cases, this is not so, and we do not know if this has any bearing on the success or otherwise of our approach.

Looking back, what added value did we help create? For the workforce it is clear that an added value was created. Those who took part benefited from the different activities to enhance mobility. The value-chain perspective gave new career possibilities, which were not recognized beforehand. For the organizations it is more difficult to say. We have strong indications that they became more efficient in handling their joint task. But it is unclear if this is due solely to the shared comprehension of competency and our efforts to increase knowledge about success factors in value chains.

Our experience says that without overall management, a partnership of organizations will not form a value chain. Its main tasks are to create preconditions for effective work, to coordinate activities and to monitor the work process. This can be regarded as facilitation, but we strongly recommend the facilitator to be given a clear mandate to carry out these responsibilities. We tried different strategies, some worked better than others, but what definitely did not work was when the facilitator was missing or did not have authority. Regardless of a competency perspective, whether or not the organizations are bonded together hangs on the presence and role of a facilitator. Further, the results indicate the need for systems management, i.e. management of the interactions and the process between actors in the value chain in order to help them define what they are to accomplish, how the expected results are to be achieved and by what means. The Swedish experience is that the actors themselves cannot handle this, but need a support system to facilitate the process and bring about change. The managerial support needs to focus on the dynamics between actors, the joint process to develop new products, the joint process to produce and internal and joint competency development

One key for unchaining the value chain(s) is the competency of all those employees who are working in the different companies along the not yet "existing value chains". The problem is that most of them are unaware of their competencies, or their knowledge. They cannot describe and communicate them. They do not know if they can be developed further as they do not know their level. Moreover, they are not acquainted with other work places along the food chain, where they could possibly make use of their knowledge, qualifications, experience, etc. The key for unchaining the value chain is to increase the awareness of the employees, employers and trade union representatives of the existing competencies.

Another key for unchaining the potential of food chains is the strategies for the diffusion and introduction of the concept of a value chain. This is an overwhelming task for single companies, trade unions, intermediaries that do not seem to have this issue on their agenda.

There is a need for an agreement in the sector to value competencies as a resource for building added value and enhancing generic competencies. It is a challenge for companies. It is a great challenge for trade unions as well that politically advocate the importance of competence, but have few strategies themselves how to support it. The results indicate that the three aspects of quality are closely related to a shared concept of competency within the value chain, quality of product, quality of work environment and quality of work. The quality of work and work environment are prerequisites for a sustainable production of quality products. There is no competitive advantage in competency development or in establishing a high quality work environment if the overall goal for the production is to compete with price. Low cost prices production does not necessarily require a lot of competency development. Trade unions have for years worked for enhancing the quality of work environment and for quality of work. The link between quality of work environment, quality of work and sustainable production of quality product is however not often stressed and rarely precisely described.

Direct participation is a prerequisite if the full potential of value-chains can be explored – only those who work within them can possibly know what the potential could be, or describe the strengths as well as the weaknesses of the intra-and inter-relations within the partnership. The momentum of change lies in work activities. Indirect participation is the means to take the decision to bring change about.

Literature

Bessant, J. (2001): Using supply chains to transfer learning. (Crawley: Sussex Supply Chain Network).

Beulens, A.J.M. (2001): 'Facilitating Supply chain learning', Power point presentation at workshop "Building Chains that Win", Sydney, Australia.

Beulens, A.J.M. et al. (2005): 'Food safety and transparency in food chains and networks. Relationships and challenges. Food Control, 16, 481-486.
Boehlje, M. et al. (1999): Value Chains in the Agricultural Industries, Staff Paper # 99-10, West Lafayette: Department of Agricultural Economics, Purdue University.
Diederen, P.J.M. / Jonkers, H.L. (2001): 'Chain and Network Studies'. KLICT, 's-Hertogenbosch. KLICT/2415/RdG. [http://www.klict.org/docs/pp2415.pdf].
Doyle, M. / Parker, B. (1999): 'Achieving Supply Chain Excellence by Balancing the Economics of Production with the Economics of Cooperation', Ascet, vol 1.
Emberson, C.A. et al. (2001): 'Customer responsive supply chains: an exploratory view of concepts and definitions', Logistics Research Network Conference, Heriot-Watt University, Edinburgh, 13-14 September.
Fawcett, S.E. et al. (2005): 'The Effect of People on the Supply Chain World: Some Overlooked Issues', Marriott School. Brigham Young University, http:www.business.uiuc.edu/Working_Papers/papers/05-0118.pdf.
Heide, M. et al. (2005): 'The Paradoxical Role of Competence Development in Supply Chain Management: Empirical Findings from Norway'. Scandinavian Academy of Management (NFF) meeting, Aarhus, Danmark, august 18 -20.
Lantz, A. / Totterdill, P. (2004): Linking workplace innovation and regional development: Towards new roles for the university sector. In W Fricke, W. / Totterdill, P. (eds.)., Action research in workplace innovation and regional development, pp. 183-206. Amsterdam: John Benjamins Publishing Company.
Lantz, A. / Friedrich, P. (2003): 'Learning at the workplace: An instrument for competence assessment', The learning organization, vol 10:3, 185–194.
Lorenz, E. / Valeyre, A. (2004): 'Organisational Change in Europe: National Models or the Diffusion of a New "One Best Way"?'. DRUID Working Papers 04-04, DRUID, Copenhagen Business School, Department of Industrial Economics and Strategy/Aalborg University, Department of Business Studies.
Peterson, H.C. (2002): 'The learning supply chain. Pipeline or pipedream?' American Journal of Economics, vol 84:5, 1320-1336.
Senge, P. / Scharmer, C.L. (1996): 'Infrastrukturen des Lernens: Ûber den Aufbau eines Konsortiums lernender Unternehmen am MIT', Führung und Organisation, 65, 32-36.
Spekman, R.E. et al. (2002): 'Supply chain competency: learning as a key component', Supply Chain Management, vol 7:1, 41-55.

Managing the supply chain – corporate social responsibility or corruption and exploitation?

Rainer Greca

During the last decades, the developments of capital importance in culture, society, politics, and economy were influenced by neo-conservative thinking, namely from the Chicago school of economics (Klein 2007). In many countries all over the world –including China and Russia – the triad of privatization, deregulation, and reduction of social welfare was implemented. Evaluating the consequences of these measures, optimistic and neo-liberal proponents argue that more freedom and democracy, economic growth, and an improvement of quality of life resulted from this (Baghwati 2004), while pessimists point at post-democratic tendencies, extension of corruption and exploitation, and a growing gap between the rich and poor (Jensen 2008; Scaglia 2007).

Based on the findings of empirical studies and my own research, in this paper I will discuss the question of whether neo-liberal politics encouraged companies at the center of the production networks of toys, textiles, or cars to voluntarily start accepting greater social responsibility for the working conditions in supply chains, or if even more corruption and exploitation can now be found on workbenches worldwide.

1. Corporate Social Responsibility (CSR)

The concepts of corporate social responsibility (CSR), mainly in combination with a stakeholder-approach, is currently seen to be an appropriate instrument by the means of which companies voluntarily integrate social and environmental efforts in their business operations to promote sustainable growth and set the stage for more and better jobs. This argument particularly characterizes the policy of the European Commission: "*Through CSR, enterprises of all sizes, in cooperation with their stakeholders, can help to reconcile economic, social and environmental ambitions. As such, CSR has become an increasingly important concept both globally and within the EU, and is part of the debate about globalisation, competitiveness and sustainability. In Europe, the promotion of CSR reflects the need to defend common values and increase the sense of solidarity and cohesion.*" (European Commission 2006, 2-3). Focusing on the labor market, one can say that this argument bases itself on the neo-classical assumption that free exchange of economic activities is the pre-condition for an international maximization of welfare (Straubhaar 1994).

In 2008, in fact, 153 businesses acted on the suggestion of the European Commission and voluntarily supported the "*European Alliance for CSR.*"[1] Among these businesses are important global players like BP, Bayer, Danone, DHL, Enel, ExxonMobile, IBM, Intel, Johnson & Johnson, Microsoft, Nestlè, Nokia, Pfitzer, but also important car producers and suppliers like BMW, Ford, Daimler, Robert Bosch, Toyota, Valeo and Volkswagen. The German CSR initiative reports that 970 enterprises follow the best practice methods.[2]

Two types of instruments for the private regulation of social standards can be distinguished: (1) Voluntary commitments of companies (e.g. Codes of Conduct) and (2) International Framework Agreements (IFAs) (Kocher 2008, 198).

From an affirmative point of view, the growing number of social responsibility declarations signed and published by companies is a clear signal that privatization and deregulation have positive outcomes, because the managements of global enterprises voluntarily assume social responsibility for the working conditions not only at their own manufacturing sites but also those for their suppliers and sub-suppliers.

But the question remains open whether these initiatives really changed working conditions in compliance with international conventions – e.g. ILO convention 29, 105, 182 – or if these activities are only part of marketing strategies and have nothing to do with the real developments in the production chain.

2. Labor markets and exploitation

To examine how these initiatives have influenced the labor conditions along the supply chain, different zones, segments, and fragments of the global labor market have to be distinguished. The *theory of the labor market segmentation* (LMS) assumes that two or more segments exist, e.g. internal and external segments: The first internal segment is characterized by stable employment, high qualification, security, and good promotion, and is surrounded by a secondary internal segment with personnel qualified by on-the-job training. This secondary internal segment is itself surrounded by an external segment for low skilled work with unstable earnings (Loveridge, Mok 1979). Other concepts refer to the size of an enterprise or the qualification of the employees (Schiener 2006, 142), make a

1 Business Europe Companies supporting the Alliance for CSR www.businesseurope.eu/content/default.asp?PageID=439 1.9.2008.

2 http://www.csrgermany.de/www/csrcms.nsf/id/254CEAF0BA69F2A4C1256F030033D061 1.9.2008.

distinction between regular and irregular job markets (Pieper 2004), or emphasize the gratification level in combination with the job discrimination of women (Koch/Bäcker 2004). The concept of *balkanization* (Castel 2000) describes a two-pieced fragmentation in the working sector of societies: a shrinking but stable zone of normality with collective agreements, which allows a sustained existence. Positioned separately from this area, however, are the redundant and dispensable persons who are permanently excluded from work. A precarious zone between these poles has been established in which a plurality of flexible work is situated with contemporary staffing, minor occupation, marginal commercial independence or full employment in the low-wage sector. The labor market is divided in a number of economic branches and geographic districts where every local unit is formed by diverse patterns.

The concept of a geographical division and distribution of labor was developed in the 1970s and beyond. Wallerstein (1989) argued that in the global market economic centers, semi-periphery and periphery can be distinguished, and the tendency to export unqualified, low-wage jobs from the center to the margin can be described. Since the turn of the new millennium, Castells (2004) faces a changed situation; he argues that with the emergence of the information society qualified R&D activities are located in the core of innovative regions, skilled assembling is done in industrialized countries, while unskilled work is practiced in low cost countries, and maintenance and repair work is located in regional centers. Sassen (2001) examines different types of work corresponding to regional development in the global economy and exemplifies that, especially in global cities, the international and the local economy are drifting apart. A local economy can be integrated in the global economic system, and located in a lucrative protected zone. On the other side, however, the local shadow economy can be indicated by "gypsy cabs," referring to the fact that the poor have developed their own economy based on the conditions of low income and reduced standards of living.

Taking into regard these concepts and emphasizing the global production system, we can distinguish six zones and various segments and fragments of labor, as is illustrated in the next chart.

Extending the concept of Castel, I distinguish six zones of the labor market: (1) The *green zone* is characterized by secure, permanent and (relatively) well paid work, protected by employment law and collective labor agreements. (2) The *blue zone* is an actual growing part of the labor market illustrated by the fact that more and more enterprises hire temporary workers to create buffers in order to react flexibly to market fluctuations (Seifert/Brehmer 2008). Because temp work is characterized by lower wages, e.g. in the automotive sector, research demonstrates that qualified temporary work can achieve the necessary quality standard and avoid conflicts and work dissatisfaction only if wages of contract workers are leveled to those of regular employees. In Germany, therefore, collective labor agreements have been signed between trade union and temp agencies, especially in regions with a high demand for qualified work, e.g. in automotive clusters like Bavaria or Saxony. But in the current crises of the automotive industry the "precarious" character of this zone becomes evident again: Temp workers are fired first and temp agencies offer new contracts only in the "light blue zone" or dismiss the employees. (3) The *light blue zone* is the container for precarious forms of work characterized by low income, short-time contracts, insecure work regulations, dummy firms, and so on. (4) The *yellow zone* includes forced labor like servitude on the high seas or domestic servitude, often risky, with low wages and conditions of labor beyond formal regulations. (5) The *purple zone* covers all kinds of involuntary servitudes (e.g. in households) or activities to reduce debt bondages, which often creates permanent dependencies and everlasting living in poverty. (6) The *red zone* is characterized by old and new forms of slave and child labor.

Figure 1: Zones, segments and fragments of the labor market

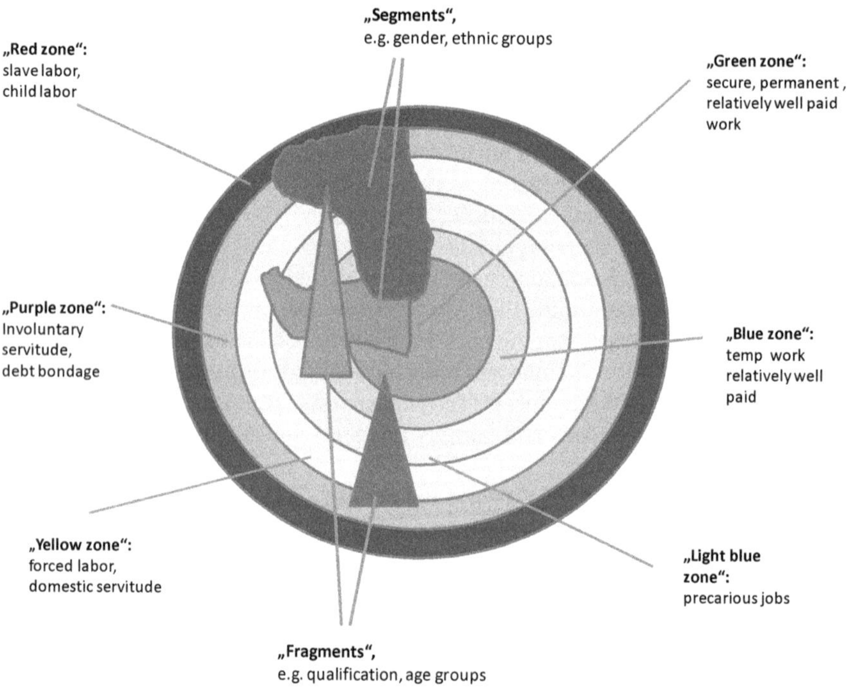

The term *market* can be applied not only to the first three zones but also to the fourth, fifth and sixth zone, although the contractors in these cases are often the taskmasters on one side and trafficking persons, groups or even state agencies on the other side – not the working people themselves who are sold as goods.

Throughout these zones, *segments* are formed, for example, by gender or ethnic clusters (such as Turkish businesses in Central Europe). *Fragments* are formed through different levels of qualification (such as engineers in the "green" and the "blue" zones) or age groups (such as elder workers or young professionals who have problems to stay in or enter the labor market).

In all of these zones exploitation of labor can take place, which can be profitable for all partners or only for the employer (Stanford Encyclopedia of Philosophy 2008). A society can be characterized as being exploitative "*when its social structure is organized so that unpaid labor is systematically forced out of one class and put at the disposal of another ... On the force-inclusive definition of exploitation, any exploitative society is a form of slavery*" (Reiman 1987, 3-4).

Three forms of exploitation can be distinguished:

(1) *Mutually advantageous exploitation* takes place if the exploited individual as well as the exploiter gains from the transactions.
(2) *Disadvantageous exploitation* refers to a negative outcome for the exploited especially in the sense that (a) rewards cover the expenses necessary to secure one's subsistence only for a certain period, or (b) rewards do not cover the subsistence of a person, although the added value produced by this person would be sufficient to sustain his or her subsistence, or (c) harms persons so that severe consequences for life and livelihood occur after a period of working (including mental or physical illness, or the death of the exploited person). Disadvantageous exploitation can be (α) relative (e.g. regarding the relation between the core and the periphery of the supply chain), or (b) absolute (e.g. in relation to the regional or national standard).
(3) *Flexploitation* bases itself on the possibility of companies to export employment opportunities to low cost countries (LCC). This causes an international concurrence between the workforces of different nations or regions whereby employees and their organizations are forced to accept the reduction of employment rights and wages and an increase of workload (Bourdieu 2004).

3. Corporate Social Responsibility – or corruption and exploitation?

Analyzing the development of the international division of labor, but also national trends, it seems that at least in some respect corruption and exploitation, not growing social responsibility, are the results of a lack of morality in business practices and a growing *organized irresponsibility* (Beck 1988) of firms and managers.

To start with the worst case: Taking the compliance of employment regulation with international conventions like the "*Protocol to Prevent, Suppress and Punish Trafficking in Persons 2000*" (Trafficking Victims Protection Act)[3], enacted by the Senate and House of Representatives of the U.S., as an indicator for growing or decreasing exploitation, the following chart demonstrates that from a world-wide perspective the human rights on the labor markets were only improved in a few countries, but the conditions were not extended or even continue to worsen in the majority of states.

---

3 Congress finds that: (1) As the 21st century begins, the degrading institution of slavery continues throughout the world. Trafficking in persons is a modern form of slavery, and it is the largest manifestation of slavery today. At least 700,000 persons annually, primarily women and children, are trafficked within or across international borders. Approximately 50,000 women and children are trafficked into the United States each year. (2) Many of these persons are trafficked into the international sex trade, often by force, fraud, or coercion. (3) This growing transnational crime also includes forced labor and involves significant violations of labor, public health, and human rights standards worldwide. (4) Traffickers primarily target women and girls, who are disproportionately affected by poverty, the lack of access to education, chronic unemployment, discrimination, and the lack of economic opportunities in countries of origin. Traffickers lure women and girls into their networks through false promises of decent working conditions at relatively good pay as nannies, maids, dancers, factory workers, restaurant workers, sales clerks, or models. Traffickers also buy children from poor families and sell them into prostitution or into various types of forced or bonded labor. (5) Traffickers often transport victims from their home communities to unfamiliar destinations. (8) Trafficking in persons is increasingly perpetrated by organized, sophisticated criminal enterprises. Such trafficking is the fastest growing source of profits for organized criminal enterprises worldwide. Trafficking in persons is often aided by official corruption in countries of origin, transit, and destination, thereby threatening the rule of law. (10) Trafficking also involves violations of other laws, including labor and immigration codes and laws against kidnapping, slavery, false imprisonment, assault, battery, pandering, fraud, and extortion. (11) Trafficking for such purposes as involuntary servitude, peonage, and other forms of forced labor has an impact on the nationwide employment network and labor market. Within the context of slavery, servitude, and labor or services which are obtained or maintained through coercive conduct that amounts to a condition of servitude, victims are subjected to a range of violations. (14) Existing legislation and law enforcement in the United States and other countries are inadequate to deter trafficking and bring traffickers to justice, failing to reflect the gravity of the offenses involved. (16) In some countries, enforcement against traffickers is also hindered by official indifference, by corruption, and sometimes even by official participation in trafficking. http://www.state.gov/documents/organization/10492.pdf.

Figure 2: Development of countries compliant with TVPA (2008)

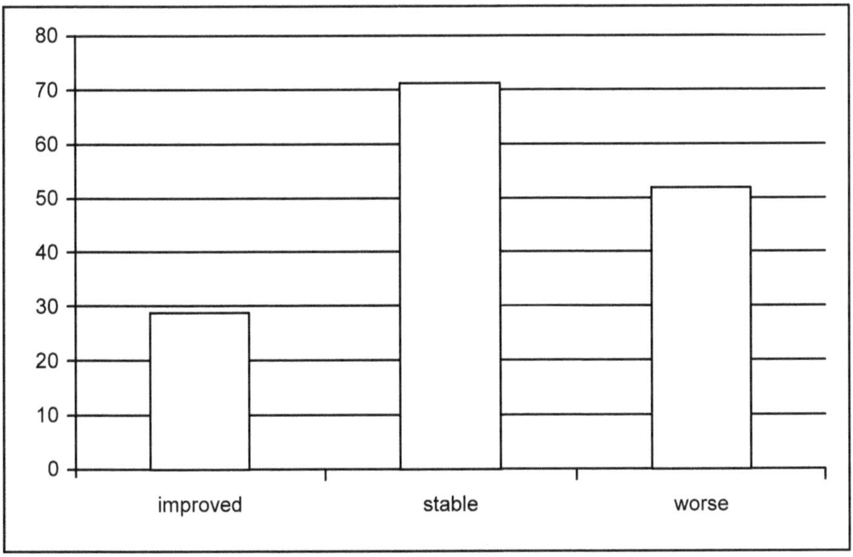

While analyzing the progress according to the Trafficking Victims Protection Act (TVPA), the U.S. Department of State reports that in 2008 the development of fundamental rights improved in 29 countries (19.1 percent of 152), remained stable in 71 countries (46.7 percent including "stability" also on a low level), but worsened in 52 (34.2 percent). From 153 countries in 2007, 29 states (19 percent) were fully compliant with TVPA, 70 (46 percent) were not complying but making significant efforts, another 40 countries (26 percent) were placed on a watch list (because changes had occurred recently), and 14 countries (9 percent) were incompliant with standards and making no efforts to improve.

A contradictory development can be found regarding the export of employment opportunities from industrialized countries to emerging nations. In collaboration with research institutes from five European countries[4], we currently study the development of the European textile and fashion industry. For centuries this business was in the core of production and occupation for many European countries. A first rapid change happened in the 1970s when production and jobs were exported to low wage countries in North Africa and Asia (Fröbel, Heinrichs,

4 http://www.ku-eichstaett.de/Fakultaeten/GGF/fachgebiete/Soziologie/lehrstuehle/Soziologie3/Projekte/Fashion.Net.

Kreye 1977)[5]. After the turn of the century this export increased, and brought new chances but also problems to the new member states of the European Community, like Romania. The Romanian government supported the re-structuring of its industry by introducing a "flat-tax" of 16 percent in certain regions of the country like Timisoara, which is close to the Hungarian and Serbian border. On the one side the positive effect was that Romanian enterprises in this sector became part of the worldwide production net of textiles and fashion, e.g. "brand-producers" from Italy and Germany contracted Romanian suppliers. Also, the automotive industry started buying textiles from Romanian sub-suppliers, e.g. for the manufacturing of seats. On the other side the negative effect was that in 2005 a quarter of all small- and middle-sized textile enterprises in Romania were closed down, because they could no longer compete with the imperative conditions in the world market. In 2006 even bigger plants were closed, which resulted in a reduction of 100,000 jobs in this sector. From a positive perspective, though, a balancing act occurred and incomes increased: In 2005 the average earnings in the region of Timisoara were about 216 Euros per month; they grew to 540 Euros per month in 2007. From the other perspective, however, the living expenses grew even more rapidly: In respect to the rent of a two-room flat, a worker's monthly earnings rarely extend. Regarding the worldwide perspective, it must be stated that concurrently the average income of a textile worker in China is only about 50 Euros per month, less than 10 percent of the costs that incurred in Romania. This price competition is used by Western European companies to put more stress on the "partners" in Romania to produce in accordance with the spinning demand and, furthermore, with high productivity and quality.

To get along with these conditions the complete structure of the textile industry in Romania changed completely: Initially, raw material was produced inside this country, which offered several job opportunities in agriculture and prefabrication. Today, because of cheaper prices in Asia, raw materials are predominantly imported with a market portion of 80 percent, while in 1989 raw materials were purchased on the internal market with a quota of 95 percent. In 2007 the value of exports in the textile and clothing sector reached a total of 2.1 billion Euros, while imports had a total of 3.9 billion Euros.

Today the curious fact is that the region of Timisoara faces full employment.[6] The low unemployment rate of 1.5 percent is caused by two facts. (1) More and

---

5 Fröbel, F./Heinrichs,J./Kreye, O., (1977), Die neue internationale Arbeitsteilung. Strukturelle Arbeitslosigkeit in den Industrieländern und die Industrialisierung der Entwicklungsländer, Reinbek.

6 „Balkanization" is a characteristic of the Romanian labor market: while in some regions with low qualification standards the unemployment rate is extremely high, also among juveniles, in other regions like Timisoara or Bucharest the unemployment rate is remarkable low.

more companies from other branches, e.g. from the automotive sector (e.g. Continental producing tires, Dräxelmaier a first tier supplier for Audi and BMW assembles wire harnesses), food industry (Nestlè produces wafers), gas production (Linde), and communication tools (Solectron produces mobile phones and gps-systems), opened production sites in Timisoara, attracted by the low tax rate and the proximity to the central European markets. (2) Another main reason for the low unemployment rate is that workers escape from unstable, flexible, low-paid work, and try to find a better-paid job abroad. Up to 3.4 million skilled Romanians are estimated to work in Italy, Spain or Germany. As a response, Romanian employers started hiring cheaper labor from the Ukraine or even China.[7] In interviews with the responsible mangers of the textile industry in Romania, these officials argued that they have no choice: either they try to cooperate with the demands of the ordering customer or shut down the factory. Managers of a first tier supplier in Germany that orders material for the seat production told us that in order to avoid contract penalties, Romanian managers transport goods to Germany in private cars, and that they allow German managers to control quality and productivity in Romania. This first tier supplier was itself forced by the OEM to improve productivity and quality, resulting in the hiring of temp workers, increased work pace, and a return to a neo-tayloristic work organization. Workers in Romania try to escape the precarious and unstable job situation because the OEM's pressure from central Europe is passed to first tier suppliers and from them to the sub-contractors in Romania who have no choice but to employ staff with flexible working conditions.

In this case, a paradox results. The growth of precarious jobs leads to high employment rates with growing income. But, on the other side, increasing living expenses and stress indicate exploitation of the "*flexploitation*"-type, and people react by attempting to run away from the scene.

Furthermore, it must be stated that exploitation and corruption is not only practiced in Third World countries or emerging markets but also in the core of the industrialized Western world.

Flexibility has become a significant characteristic of work in all industrialized Western countries, liberating people from the "iron cage" but also putting them into an instable and insecure world (Sennett 2006, 2007). One can also state that the assumption in which work in Western industrialized countries takes place in only the first three zones is wrong: Sex trafficking, domestic servitude, and forced labor can, for example, be found in the US, France, or Germany (Bales 2004). An investigation performed by Italian TV (Panorama 2008) discovered Chinese production sites in Italy where Chinese workers produce top fashion accessories

7 http://www.ba-auslandsvermittlung.de/lang_de/nn_2832/DE/LaenderEU/Rumaenien/Arbeiten/arbeiten-knoten.html__nnn=true

“made in Italy.” The workforce (in particular young and female) labored similarly to conditions in some regions of China where, for example, work schedules in the toy factories often consist of 18 hours a day and 7 days a week, and where school classes with girls are forced to work in these factories when the demand from Western enterprises is high. Hungarian colleagues reported that it is impossible to estimate the number of Chinese textile sites in the capital of Budapest. In these factories exploitation of type 2 and 3 is practiced.

This clearly demonstrates that low-wage jobs are coming back to the core of industrialized countries, either in the form of precarious work or imported by migration, corrupt entrepreneurs, or political regimes.

Precarious forms of work are widespread in Western societies of today, as is illustrated with the next chart:

Figure 3: Low-wage sector in percent of the total labor market, 2005

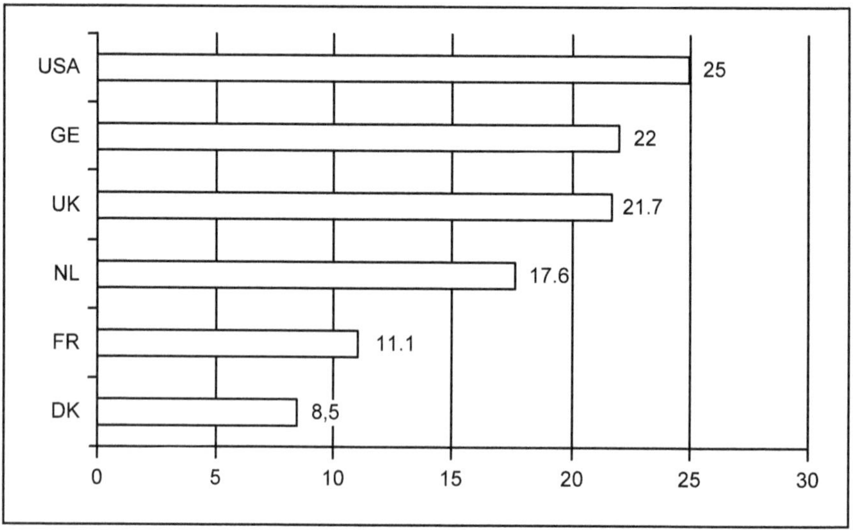

In 2005 the low-wage sector in the US had a proportion of 25 percent of the total labor market; in Germany the portion was 22 percent, in the UK, 21.7 percent, and in the Netherlands, 17.6 percent, while in France it remained at 11.1 percent and in Denmark at 8.5 percent.

Empirical research for the case of the German labor market demonstrates that precarious work conditions have grown throughout the last few decades. While labor productivity increased from 2000 to 2006 by more than 20 percent, the sector for irregular work also grew, as is illustrated in the next chart:

Figure 4: Regular and atypical work, Germany 1992-2005 (in percent of the total labor market)

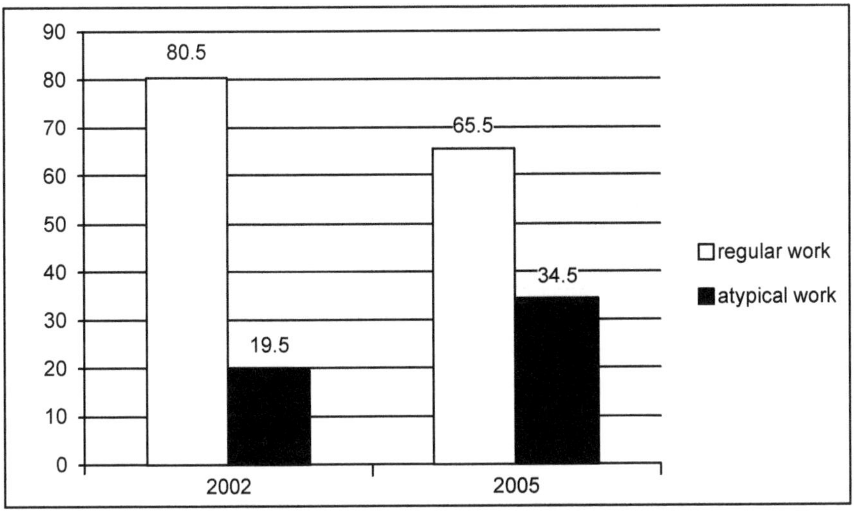

Source: Böcklerimpuls 12/2008

In 1992, regular working conditions were typical in more than 80 percent of the labor contracts; in 2005, the proportion had decreased to 65.5 percent. On the contrary, atypical work (internships, service contracts, temp work) increased from 19.5 to 34.5 percent. Temporary work contracts alone increased from about 100,000 in 1994 to more than 700,000 in 2007, and so-called mini-jobs from more than 4.1 million in 2001 to nearly 4.9 million in 2007.

Surprisingly, a growth of atypical work is also registered in those persons with a vocational qualification, which is illustrated in the next chart.

From 1995 to 2006 the proportion of employees in the low wage sector in Germany increased from 59 percent to about 68 percent. In the same period about 7 percent of workers without apprenticeships and about 2 percent of employees holding university degrees left this sector. Women (about 70 percent) are more affected than men. Astonishingly, native Germans are much more concerned by precarious working conditions (about 88 percent) than immigrants (12 percent).

Figure 5: Low wage sector by qualification, Germany 1995-2006

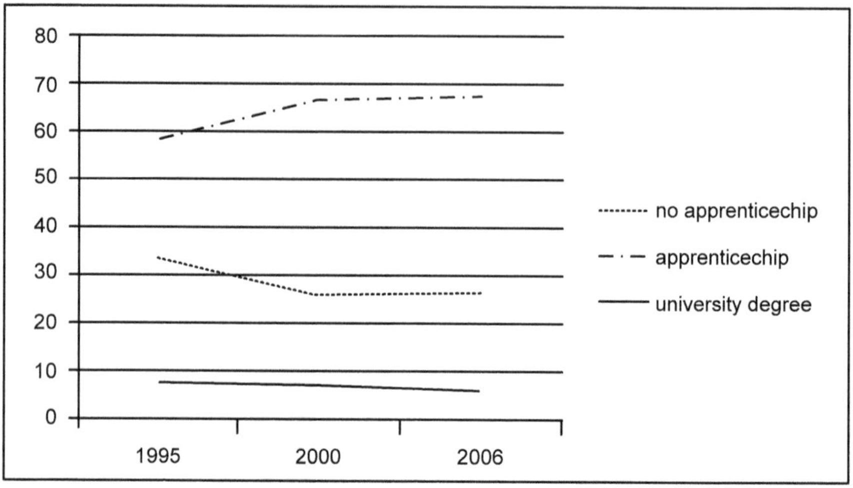

Low wages are especially an attribute of the middle-age groups, as the following chart shows:

Figure 6: Low wages by age group, Germany 1995-2006

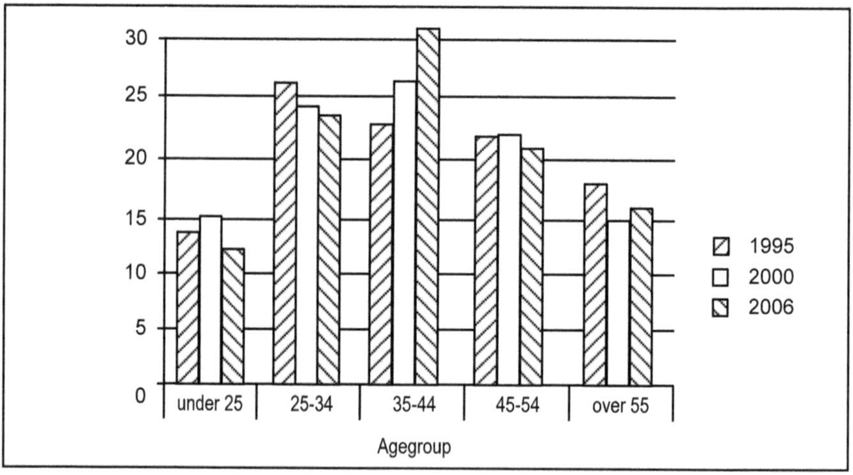

Source: Bosch/Kalina/Weinkopf 2008

In the under 25 age group the proportion of people working for low wages always remains below 15 percent. Most affected are persons in the middle-aged group of the 24- to 34-year olds (decrease from 26 in 1995 to 23 percent in 2006) and particularly in the age group of the 35- to 44-year old persons where in 2006 about 30 percent were working for low wages. Nineteen percent of the 45- to 54-year old age group and 14 percent of the over 55-year old group were earning low wages in 2006.

These facts illustrate that in the case of Germany precarious jobs also became a part of the standard expectations for the middle-classes.

4. Conclusion

It is beyond a doubt that the responsible managers of international operating businesses do not actively support the extension and conditions of work in the "*light blue*", "*yellow*", "*purple*" or "*red zone.*" But investigations in the production chain of stone (Hütz-Adams 2008), toys (Steiner 2008), sport equipment (Kamp 2008), fashion (Pflaum 2004), or textiles (Wick 2005, 2007) demonstrate that the objective to control the supply chain in accordance to CSR standards in ecological and social respect fails because of growing corruption (Eigen 2003), even if international control organizations like the ICTI try to monitor the complete production line. A report in India, for example, demonstrated that enterprises making use of child labor in the stone industry were certified as being compliant to ILO convention 182 by corrupt local authorities.[8] Market research institutes with high reputations therefore have discovered a new business, and offer an independent control of the supply chain in accordance to CSR standards (Ernest & Young 2008).

Under the pressure of global competition and extended privatization, deregulation and the lowering of social welfare, exploitation of the types 2 and 3 has increased not only in the periphery of the global economy but also in the core. "*Getting more from less*" is the philosophy of "*new outsourcing*" which characterizes the "*third revolution of added value*" (Scholtissek 2004, 11). The "*delegation of brutality*" (Schumann 2008) is not a consciously practiced measure. More or less, the leading positions in management do not feel obliged to go after financial and social aims that do not have the same value. In my own studies, I found in big companies a division of labor between responsible managers for social or ecological topics and financial management, whereby the "*logic of economic rationality*" had priority in internal discussion. Financial arguments

8 Elimination of worst forms of child labor.

and benchmarking results are to a large degree the main reasons for actual changes in the industry. Information about the finance market is communicated inside the company by financial experts, who counsel agencies and financial directors. All other dimensions are subordinated to the logic of economic rationality (Latouche 2004). Benchmarking the economic performance leads to "isomorphism", i.e. the strategies of successful operating competitors are copied (Greca 2008). Widespread concepts are dismissal of workforce, intensification of work, reduction of wages, or putting more pressure on the suppliers, which downscales the prescriptions and passes the bitter medicine to sub-contractors and so on (Deiß 2000).

Also, the motivation to join CSR initiative in most businesses is submitted to economic rationality. In a study conducted by the University of Karlsruhe about CSR practices in the 200 best-selling enterprises in Germany only 19 percent of the contacted businesses completed the questionnaire. About 35 percent explicitly refused participating in the research, and 93 did not respond all together.[9] The authors of the study sum up as a part of their findings that "*Human Rights*" as a vision for the activities of the enterprise "*is not widespread*," this also implies that suppliers are selected because of their compliance with social minimal standards (Zink u.a. 2005, 10). In a study supported by the Bertelsmann foundation, the result found that the CSR report was the least important activity in the opinion of 500 decision-makers of German businesses. Only 26 percent of the interviewed stakeholders shared the opinion that the requiring of the supplier chain to follow compliance with human rights and ecological standards would be of importance for the business (Bertelsmann Stiftung 2005, 17).

Considering the CSR concept and confronting it with research results about the development of the working conditions in the worldwide supply chains, it can be stated that the vision of a voluntary control and improvement of working conditions compliant with international standards has not become a reality. Transnational standards have had only little impact on working conditions. If working regulations were modified because of CSR, standards were implemented only in compliance with local law. It must be assumed that CSR-concepts are not adequate to manage transnational working relations, and International Framework Agreements (IFAs) do not influence the mainstream (Kocher 2008, 198, 202).

Regarding the different zones, segments, and fragments of the labor market, it can be summarized that as the workload intensifies, wages relatively decrease and working conditions worsen, and, additionally, precarious jobs are no longer offered to unqualified persons or migrants only, but instead more and more skilled, middle-

9 This is similar to the results of an investigation made by the Stiftung Warentest in Germany: Only 6 out of 14 enterprises accepted to answer to a questionnaire about ecological and social standards.

aged employees are affected. "Winners" can turn into "losers" very quickly, as currently seen with the employees of financial institutes all over the world. Corruption is a measure to stabilize volatile conditions in a liberal market: This is probably the reason why enterprises like Siemens, which originally stood for a paradigm of excellent business morality, had to change its strategies.

Adam Smith, who is often quoted to explain the argument that the market can solve all problems, was an adherent to the theory of Thomas Aquinas. Thomas' philosophy bases itself on the certainty that God has created the world and men can understand the order of the universe because the creator has given human beings the capacity to perceive the truth. The being, the truth, and the good are convertible, while the evil is interpreted as a lack of the being. The neo-liberal approach often forgets the theological character of its own model. The question is, which kind of institution can guarantee the fundamentals of the market if there is no predetermined order? The experiences of the 1980s, early 1920s (Hobsbawm 1987), and current economic developments demonstrate that in a model which relies on rational choices of profit optimizing individuals, and that separates reality from morality, the invisible hand becomes a visible fist.

Bibliography

Baghwati, J.N. (2004): In Defense of Globalization, Oxford/New York.

Bales, K. (2004): Disposable People. New Slavery in the Global Economy, Berkeley/Los Angeles.

Beck, U. (1988): Der industrielle Fatalismus: Die organisierte Unverantwortlichkeit, in: Gegengifte. Die organisierte Unverantwortlichkeit. Frankfurt a.M.

Becker, I. / Grabka, M.M. / Hauser, R. / Westerheide, P. (2007): Integrierte Analyse der Einkommens- und Vermögensverteilung, Frankfurt a.M. u.a.

Bertelsmann Stiftung (2005): Die gesellschaftliche Verantwortung von Unternehmen, Gütersloh.

Bosch,G. / Kalina, Th. / Weinkopf, C. (2008): Niedriglohnbeschäftigte auf der Verliererseite, in: WSI Mitteilungen 8/2008.

Bourdieu, P. (2004): Gegenfeuer, Konstanz.

Bundesverband der deutschen Arbeihgeberverbände (bdi) (2005): Internationale Aspekte von Corporate Social Responsibility (CSR), Praxishinweise für Unternehmen, Berlin.

Castel, R. (2000). Die Metamorphosen der sozialen Frage. Eine Chronik der Lohnarbeit. Konstanz.

Castel, R. (2001): Überlegungen zum Stand der sozialen Frage heute: Aushöhlung, Zusammenbruch oder Reorganisation der sozial abgesicherten Erwerbsarbeit.

In: Mitteilungen des Instituts für Sozialforschung, September, Heft 12, Frankfurt/M., 81-119.
Castells, M. (2004): Der Aufstieg der Netzwerkgesellschaft. Das Informationszeitalter I, Weinheim u.a..
Commission of the European Communities (2001): Green Paper: Promoting a framework for Corporate Social Responsibility, Brussels.
Commission of the European Communities (2006): Implementing the Partnership for Growth and Jobs: Making Europe a Pole of Excellence and Corporate Social Responsibility, Brussels.
Council of the European Union (2007): Joint Employment Report 2006/2007, Brussels.
Council of the European Union (2008): Joint Employment Report 2007/2008, Brussels.
Deiß, M. (2000): Flexible Beschäftigungspolitik und Arbeitsbedingungen – Deutschland, München.
Department of State (2007): Trafficking in Persons Report, U.S. Department of State Publication 11407.
Department of State (2008): Trafficking in Persons Report, U.S. Department of State Publication 11407.
Eigen, P. (2004): Das Netz der Korruption. Wie eine weltweite Bewegung gegen Bestechung kämpft, Frankfurt a.M./New York.
Ernst&Young (2008): Nachhaltige Lieferketten. www. CSR Services von Ernst & Young – Nachhaltige Lieferketten – Articles on csr-news.net.htm Zugriff 31.8.2008.
Fröbel, F. / Heinrichs, J. / Kreye, O. (1977): Die neue internationale Arbeitsteilung. Strukturelle Arbeitslosigkeit in den Industrieländern und die Industrialisierung der Entwicklungsländer, Reinbek.
Grabher, G. (1998): Urbi et Orbi. Lokale Ökonomien in Global Cities, in: Der Öffentliche Sektor, 24. Jg., Heft 2-3/98
Greca, R. (2008): The flexible response to global competition: the case of Audi and BMW, Torino.
Grimm, N., Flexibilität durch Leiharbeit: Zumutung oder Chance? SOFI Mitteilungen Nr.32.
Hütz-Adams, F. (2008): Steine des Anstoßes, Arbeitsbedingungen bei Natursteinlieferanten für Baumärkte und Küchenhersteller, Siegburg.
Hobsbawm, E. (1987): The Age of Empire 1875-1914, London.
Hofer, G. (2007): Arbeiterparadies hinter der Todeszone, in: Die Presse, Printausgabe v. 3.11.2007.
Holsmstrom, N. (1997): Exploitation, Canadian Journal of Philosophy, 7, pp. 353-69.

Jensen, A., (2008): Modernes Arbeitsrecht für das Milliardenvolk, in: Mitbestimmung7+8/2008.
Kamp, M. (2008): Unmenschliche Zustände beim chinesischen Hersteller von Puma, in: Unternehmer & Märkte, 16.6. 2008.
Klein, N. (2007): The Shock Doctrine. The Rise of Disaster Capitalism, New York, Toronto.
Koch, A. / Bäcker, G. (2004): Mini- und Midi-Jobs – Frauenerwerbstätigkeit und Niedrigeinkommensstrategien in der Arbeitsmarktpolitik, in: Baatz, D. u.a. (Hrsg.): Hauptsache Arbeit? Feministische Perspektiven auf den Wandel von Arbeit, Opladen.
Kocher, E. (2008): Corporate Social Responsibility – Instrumente zur Gestaltung transnationaler Arbeitsbeziehungen, in: WSI Mitteilungen 4/2008.
Krafczyk, E. (2006): Arbeitsbedingungen. Ein Koreaner ist fünf Polen wert, in: Stern v. 30.3.2006.
Kymlicka, W. (1989): Liberalism, Community and Culture, Oxford.
Latouche, S. (2004): Die Unvernunft der ökonomischen Vernunft, Zürich/Berlin.
Loverdige, R. / Mok, A.L. (1979): Theories of Labour Market Segmentation: A critique, Dordrecht.
Marx, K. (1961) Das Kapital. Kritik der politischen Ökonomie, Berlin.
Naim, M. (2008): Das Jahrhundert der Sklaverei, in: Cicero, Magazin für politische Kultur.
Pflaum, M. / Kerl, St. / Burckhardt, G. (2004): Zum Leben zu wenig … in: TDF – Menschenrechte für die Frau 3/4/2004
Pieper, P. (2004): Das dezentrale Lagersystem für Flüchtlinge. Zeitschrift für kritische Sozialwissenschaft, Heft 136, 34. Jg., 2004, Nr. 3.
Reiman, J. (1987): Exploitation, Force, and the Moral Assessment of Capitalism: Thoughts on Roemer and Cohen, Philosophy and Public Affairs, 16, pp. 3-41.
Sassen, S. (2001): The global city, Princeton.
Scaglia, A. (2007): Max Weber e la città democratica. Idealtipo del potere non leggitimo, Roma.
Schiener, S. (2006): Bildungserträge in der Erwerbsgesellschaft: Analysen zur Karrieremobilität, Wiesbaden.
Scholtissek, St. (2004): New Outsourcing. Die Dritte Revolution der Wertschöpfung in der Praxis, Berlin.
Schumann, M. (2008): Kampf um Rationalisierung – Suche nach neuer Übersichtlichkeit, in: WSI Mitteilungen 7/2008.
Seifert, H. / Brehmer, W. (2008): Leiharbeit: Funktionswandel einer flexiblen Beschäftigungsform, in: WSI Mitteilungen 6/2008.
Sennett, R. (2006): Der flexible Mensch. Die Kultur des neuen Kapitalismus, Berlin.

Sennett, R. (2007): Die Kultur des neuen Kapitalismus, Berlin.
Stanford Encyclopedia of Philosophy, (2008): Exploitation.
Steffen, T. (2008): Made in China, in: dasPortal, 16.8.2008.
Stiftung Warentest (2004): Unternehmensverantwortung. Sozial und ökologisch produzieren. www. test.de – Unternehmensverantwortung – Meldungen – Bildung + Soziales – Tests + Themen – Stiftung Warentest.htm Zugriff 29.8.2008.
Straubhaar, Th. (1994): Ökonomische Bedeutung grenzüberschreitender Arbeitsmigration, in: W. Weidenfeld u.a. (Hrsg.): Europäische Integration und Arbeitsmarkt. Grundlagen und Perspektiven, Beiträge zur Arbeitsmarkt- und Berufsforschung, Nr. 181, Nürnberg, S. 195-222.
Vogel, B. (2003): Leiharbeit und befristete Beschäftigung . Neue Formen sozialer Gefährdung oder Chance auf Arbeitsmarktintegration. In: Linne, G. / Vogel, B. (Hg.): Leiharbeit und befristete Beschäftigung. Neue Formen sozialer Gefährdung oder Chance auf Arbeitsmarktintegration? Arbeitspapier 68 der Hans-Böckler-Stiftung, Düsseldorf, 39-46.
Wallerstein, I. (1989): The Modern World-System III. The Second Era of Great Expansion of the Capitalist World-Economy, 1730-1840s, San Diego .
Wick, I. (2005): Nähen für den Weltmarkt. Frauenarbeit in Exportzonen und der Schattenwirtschaft. Länderbeispiele, Indien, China und Sri Lanka. Modemultis auf dem Prüfstand, Siegburg.
Wick, I. (2007): All die Textilschnäppchen – nur recht und billig? Arbeitsbedingungen bei Aldi-Zulieferern in China und Indonesien, Siegburg.
Zink, K.J. / Liebrich, A. / Steimle, U. (2005): Corporate Social Responsibility. Bestandsaufnahme in deutschen Unternehmen, Kaiserslautern.

Construction subcontracting and international trade union cooperation: what role for European industrial relations?

Nikolaus Hammer, Steve Davies, Glynne Williams

Introduction

For the construction industry, the challenges posed by European integration arise equally from the liberalisation of the product market and labour market. A series of developments, which have extended labour mobility – freedom of movement within the enlarged EU as well as the posting of workers within the EU (Cremers *et al.*, 2007; Donaghey and Teague, 2006), but also global labour mobility under Mode 4 of the GATS agreement (apart from undeclared and informal work) – have seriously threatened labour's ability to control the labour market. In addition, subcontracting – which fragments company-level interest representation – results in problems for the unions in keeping track of the product market, and has contributed to segmenting local construction workforces according to their employment and mobility status. International trade union cooperation takes place in a context where international competition – through foreign subcontractors and migrant labour – is played out at local work sites. However tenuous this grip on the product and labour market, the link between the workplace and international trade union cooperation is crucial in supporting union capacity in subcontracting chains.

The defence of labour rights and standards in the construction industry faces a series of particular challenges, which result from the specific conjuncture of regulatory regimes and the place-bound character of most construction activities. The industry is unlike other sectors: while construction activities normally have to be performed on site, the interaction of extensive subcontracting, on the one hand, and the use of various forms of mobile labour, on the other, create a functional equivalent to regime shopping. Here, complex subcontracting arrangements reinforce a heavily segmented labour market, differentiated not only with regard to pay rates but working conditions and employment statute. Compared to other industries where pay differentials are the basis for coercive comparisons and concessions, in the construction industry it is subcontracting and labour mobility that constitute implicit coercive comparisons.

In such a context, the pre-conditions for any form of international coordination of bargaining are lacking. Instead, union influence must be based on increasing control over the labour (and product) market, trying to counter the downward pressures on wages and working conditions caused by subcontracting and labour mobility. Construction unions have developed a number of international coordination initiatives. At sector level, authors have commented on the 'bottom-up' approach at bilateral and European level which aims at organising and supporting migrant workers as well as controlling migrant flows (Marginson, 2005). However, in response to more fragmented forms of production and employment, unions have also started to focus at the company level, in particular the subcontracting and value chains, where the structures and power of lead companies and contractors are used in an effort to defend labour rights and build capacity (Davies et al., 2008). In the following we discuss the particular challenges labour faces in the construction sector, discussing an International Framework Agreement in a construction MNC and contractor liability regulations, strategies that work in various ways to organise workers, develop participation and establish a form of labour market control. The conclusion explores the contribution European industrial relations could play in organising subcontracting chains.

1. Work, Employment and Labour Mobility in the Construction Sector

The restructuring of construction value chains has taken place in the context of increasing deregulation and competition. As companies have withdrawn from lower-end and labour-intensive functions, the sector has seen a growth of subcontracting as well as in informal labour, both in developing and industrialised countries. Migrant labour has risen considerably while informal employment reached 75-95% in countries such as Brazil, India and Malaysia (Wells 2007; ILO 2001; ILO 2002).

> If all of the construction workers who are employed on a casual basis, without regular contracts or any social protection, are included in the expanded concept of the 'informal economy', then it is clear that informality is now the norm, rather than the exception, in the construction industry throughout much of the developing world. (Wells 2007: 91)

A lot of the construction sector's dependence on the business cycle impacts on, and is mediated by, migrant and informal labour. In Brazil, for example, employment in construction rose sixfold, mainly fuelled by internal migration, with migrant workers constituting more than 90% of the construction workforce in São Paulo and Rio de Janeiro in 1985. While the overall proportion of migrants fell to 43% by 1996, the number of unregistered and self-employed workers rose to 74.6% by 1999, and the number of labour intermediaries also grew considerably (ILO, 2001). Employment in the Malaysian construction sector almost tripled between 1980 and 1997 (ILO, 2001: 9). Again, the role of migrant labour, labour intermediaries and subcontractors is overwhelming: according to estimates, Indonesian migrant workers constituted 80% of the construction workforce in 1992; a significant number of these workers are recruited and supervised by labour subcontractors; in 1998, 75% of foreign workers were employed by subcontractors (Narayanan and Yew-Wah, 2005; ILO, 2001).

Unions have responded in two ways, both aiming to protect fundamental labour rights and standards in their respective location. On the one hand, unions have established bilateral initiatives, for example to "protect migrant domestic workers, such as that between the Association of Progressive Labor (APL) in the Philippines and its counterpart in Hong Kong" (Asper, n.d.: 19); or initiatives trying to control labour mobility, or at least the conditions under which migrants take up employment and return to their home country. On the other hand, unions have involved themselves directly in the provision of education, information and welfare support to out-migrating and returning construction workers such as between the Filipino NUBCW and the Taiwanese NFCCW:

> such that NUBCW will undertake to facilitate sending its presently unemployed member or an employed member intending to work in the construction sites in Taiwan while the NFCCW will facilitate the acceptance of the Filipino workers in their unionised construction projects at the same time that the union in Taiwan will protect them by helping them organise a separate union for migrant construction workers or integrating them into existing union structures. (Asper, n.d.: 19-20)

In Europe, mobility in the sector has a long tradition (most recently the postwar guest worker programmes) although unions have only more recently begun to formalise cross-border cooperation. In the 1990s the restructuring of the construction value chain received an additional impetus from the influx of labour from Eastern Europe, the 'posted workers Directive' as well as the freedom of movement of workers in the wake of the 2004 accession round. Furthermore, trends of rising self-employment have played an important role within national labour markets as well as across borders (often labelled 'false' self-employment, as workers are not covered by the respective statutory protections of direct employment while *de facto* being in an employment relationship; Davies, 2008; Harvey and Behling, 2007). Thus, it is not only cross-border subcontracting and labour mobility under the freedom of movement for workers or the 'posting' of workers which resulted in pressure on existing wages and social and labour standards (Cremers et al., 2007) but also greyer and darker areas of employment with labour-only contractors, bogus self-employment, and undeclared work.

The resulting labour market segmentation poses a number of challenges for labour, both in the workplace as well as for international trade union cooperation. The place-bound nature of construction underlines the role of local labour control regimes (Castree *et al* 2004), i.e. the specific local parameters of the labour process. In other words, national differences in wages, social standards and regulations re-appear at local construction sites, and this highlights the role of the local management of a segmented construction workforce.

Again, unions have responded in a number of ways. First, bilateral union-union strategies between sending and receiving countries were devised in order to support migrant workers and, in some instances, play a part in controlling migrant flows. The German IG BAU, in particular, has concluded a number of such agreements: with their Portuguese and Italian counterparts in the late 1990s (Schulten, 1998) as well as with a range of East European unions (the British TUC concluded a similar agreement with the Portuguese CGTP-IN (Grünell and van het Kaar, 2003)). The latter agreements were placed in the context of bilateral labour treaties at government level which also established quota on construction workers from those states (Menz, 2001).

Second, unions in receiving countries have at times established information offices in sending countries, either as an initiative at national level as in the case of the Finnish unions' information office in Estonia (Lillie and Greer, 2007), or at regional level in the case of many of the Interregional Trade Union Councils between regions of the EU-15 and the 2004 accession states (Hammer 2008).

Third, the foundation of a specific European Migrant Workers' Union, at the initiative and with substantial support by the German IG BAU, constitutes another model trying to provide information, advice and support for migrant workers, and to build a union network which cooperates with other organisations and institutions dealing with migrant workers' problems (Dribbusch, 2004).

Fourth, unions have campaigned for regulation in a number of ways, at national as well as European level. Most prominent in this respect are efforts around the 'posted workers Directive' and the associated issues that were thrown up with regard to cross-border industrial action (Woolfson and Sommers, 2006). However, while these and the initiatives above are concerned with the control of the labour market, unions have also been involved in campaigns to regulate aspects of the product market, mainly at national level and mainly to do with efforts to control social and financial fraud in subcontracting arrangements. In Spain, for example, unions have succeeded in having new regulations approved which restrict subcontracting to one level for labour intensive activities, require a subcontracting register at site level, and require the transfer to 30% of subcontracted labour onto open-ended employment contracts (Cervino 2007).

Such strategies obviously have to be seen in combination and in the context of particular local labour control regimes. They promise to go some way in re-establishing control over the labour market, at times with implications for product market regulation, in particular where the incentives and parameters of subcontracting are concerned. At the same time, though, taken as such, these initiatives remain at distance from the workplace level which constitutes the very terrain of cross-border conflicts of interests in the construction sector. Thus, it may be asked whether the above forms of international trade union cooperation are in fact used in ways that increase control over the labour market where it matters, at local level, where subcontracted labour performs key aspects of the construction process.

2. Parameters of International Trade Union Cooperation in Construction

The specific characteristics of the construction sector – the mobility of capital and labour, the local and subcontracted performance of building tasks by different segments of the labour market, and continued nationally based bargaining – raise important questions about the form of international trade unionism. Four, in particular, are identified here: the appropriate level of trade union cooperation, the aims and incentives of coordination, the preconditions of cross-border coordination, as well as the specific approaches in the construction sector.

First, based on the manufacturing sector whose goods are substitutable across the sector, the sector level is generally taken to be the appropriate level of coordination for cross-border bargaining and trade union coordination (Marginson and Traxler, 2005). This assumption requires some adjustment in the face of the specific dynamics in construction. Following Commons' (1909) seminal piece the need has been highlighted for trade unions to follow market dynamics and aim for coverage of the product market. Extensive subcontracting, labour mobility, and the existence of informal labour, however, means that unions have neither control of the product market nor the labour market. In addition, cross-border worker-to-worker competition, from different segments of mobile labour, arises locally. Thus, in contrast to manufacturing, it is labour that is substitutable (rather than the goods produced), and much of the competition arising from wage differentials is played out on the local terrain (rather than across borders). In this respect, it might be suggested that the most functional level of trade union cooperation lies at the industry level between unions in sending and receiving countries, the industrial power of the lead company, i.e. the main contractor (see Riisgaard and Hammer, 2008), or at the local and site level.

This leads on to the question of the aims of cross-border trade union cooperation and the incentives unions have in engaging in such initiatives. Clearly, exerting some kind of control over the labour market means to control key aspects of labour migration and associated forms of in/formal employment, be it the number of workers who seek employment abroad or the terms and conditions under which they are prepared to work for. Even though such (cross-border) conflicts of interest arising out of labour mobility are played out at the local level, both sides have clear incentives to cooperate. While unions in receiving locations will be keen to soften pressures on wages and working conditions, unions in sending countries will be concerned about skills gaps in their labour market, the impact of chain migration from elsewhere or even the impact of returning workers over the business cycle.

With regard to international bargaining coordination, Marginson and Traxler (2005: 431) hold that an inclusive coverage that allows labour market control constitutes a precondition for such international coordination. Such coverage then enables the parties to articulate the coordination outcomes within their country or sector. Further, it is argued,

> [a]s comparative research shows (Traxler *et al* 2001), an inclusive coverage is contingent on either of two alternative arrangements: (1) multi-employer bargaining in combination with extension practices ...; (2) multi-employer bargaining in combination with high union density.
>
> '... a 'going rate' can arise only from larger key companies in a sector. In the case of highly fragmented sectors (e.g. meat-processing, building installation and building completion), where such companies do not exist, there is hardly a way of initiating cross-company bargaining coordination.' (Marginson and Traxler 2005: 435)

The fragmented character of parts of the construction sector, together with the difficulties for labour to exert control over extensive tiers of subcontracting and a heavily segmented labour market, might indicate that either of the two arrangements for inclusive coverage might not be sufficient in this case. As wages and working conditions in local labour control regimes are hollowed out from below, both extension practices and high union density (i.e. among workers with regular employment contracts) can only bite when labour is able to build control at the site level.

Fourth, given that labour faces the dual challenge of evasive and transient employer structures and a heavily segmented labour market, it needs to be asked what forms of international cooperation might allow unions to increase their control over the labour (and even product) market. While subcontracting often means that it is difficult for trade unions to identify the employer responsible for carrying out particular tasks or supplying labour, labour mobility and the transient nature of construction projects render the organisation of workers more difficult. Thus, in construction, incentives for horizontal trade union coordination are contingent on the weakness of vertical coordination; at the same time, though, the latter is faced with numerous structural barriers stemming from the fragmentation of production as well as work and employment. In this situation the EFBWW has developed what has been called a 'bottom-up' approach to trade union coordination:

> 'protecting national collective agreements from the effects of cross-border movements of labour which characterise construction (e.g. through bilateral, cross-border trade union agreements to organise and assist posted workers) whilst also establishing common reference standards for key non-wage matters (Erne 2004).' (Marginson and Traxler 2005, 427)

This approach essentially aims to establish a grip on the labour market via the control of migration, working conditions such as health and safety practices as well as services of information, legal advice and representation for workers.

However, as subcontracting and labour mobility continue to pose severe problems for unions' capacity for vertical articulation and coordination, we have seen the emergence, particularly in the construction sector, of practices that focus on lead companies' power vis-à-vis their subcontractors in order to comply with labour rights and standards. The function of the lead firm means that there is the potential for the equivalent of an extension practice across the subcontracting chain. While unions in the textiles and logistics sectors have built on strategic analyses of bottlenecks in the supply chain for organising campaigns (Quan, 2008; Lund and Wright, 2003), the position of lead contractors in the construction industry has been to control the conditions under which subcontracted work is performed. The emphasis on subcontracting chains, via a focus on collective labour rights and conditions of work and employment, therefore, promises a more direct approach to workplace or site organisation, which, at the same time, will increase labour market control and form the basis of vertical trade union coordination. In other words, attention shifts from increasingly hollowed-out sector level regulations to the lead firm which is a key actor in outsourcing and non-standard employment.

Such constraints are not confined to the European Union but, in fact, underlie the global picture of the sector. In this context, labour has focused on lead companies' power vis-à-vis subcontractors to secure labour standards in the latter. This mechanism is institutionalised in various EU countries in so-called (main) contractor liability regulations; at global level lead companies have committed their subcontractors and suppliers to fundamental labour rights in International Framework Agreements (IFAs). However, particularly in the context of the construction industry, it is obvious that the commitment to particular standards and rights does not ensure their unproblematic respect in practice.

In the following we discuss the case of an IFA in a construction MNC as well as instruments of contractor liability in a number of European countries where lead companies of one form or another are held to enforce, promote or, at least, take on liability, for fundamental aspects of the employment relationship. We explore the potential for the development of new forms of participation around these instruments, the relationship between them and different levels of participation as well as the preconditions for increasing union influence through them at the workplace.

3. Labour Rights in the Subcontracting Chain of a Construction MNC

Over the last ten years, the BWI has concluded nine International Framework Agreements with construction MNCs (see Davies et al., 2008 for more detail on the following case study; Hammer 2008) aiming to use them as a 'tool for organising' (IFBWW, 2003: 3) on the basis of efforts to inform, educate and train affiliates about the content and potential leverage of such agreements. Typically, IFAs commit MNCs to respect the ILO's core conventions on the freedom to organise and collective bargaining, non-discrimination and the use of child or forced labour. In addition, a number of agreements subscribe to ILO conventions on wages, the reduction of working time, occupational health and safety standards as well as the establishment of an employment contract; at times, MNCs commit to pay living wages. Furthermore, what is crucial for labour is that responsibilities and procedures for solving disputes, in many cases procedures of implementation and monitoring, are established, and that the provisions of the agreement are extended to subcontractors. While this extension is seen as a condition for continuous business relations in many cases, the IFAs with Hochtief, Skanska, Impregilo, and VolkerWessels see subcontractor and supplier compliance as mandatory. Thus, the BWI has tried to use the power of lead MNCs in order to extend fundamental labour rights to the subcontracting chain, to establish a platform to organise and increase control over the product as well as the labour market.

Hochtief, headquartered in Germany, sees itself as an "international construction services provider" (Hochtief, 2007a: 2) and claims to be the most international construction MNC. In 2006 86% of its sales were realised outside Europe with 80% of its workforce. The company also describes itself as a pioneer in corporate social responsibility and sustainability: it publishes a comprehensive report, audited by PricewaterhouseCoopers, and follows the Global Reporting Initiative guidelines. However, Hochtief has a dual approach to corporate social responsibility on the one hand, and industrial relations on the other. While the CSR committee is charged to implement "CSR thinking" in all Hochtief divisions, different ownership structures have an impact on the extent and depth of CSR guidelines. The Australia based Leighton, for example, which is majority owned by Hochtief and has major projects in Asia and the Gulf states, is excluded from the CSR guidelines. Equally, subsidiaries such as Hochtief do Brazil, or Turner (USA), have more discretion in applying the CSR guidelines or IFA. Also, while the IFA formally applies to all Hochtief "employees and the employees of contractual partners" (Hochtief et al., 2000), the company merely states that this represents an "undertaking" (Hochtief, 2007b: 21).

However, this varied picture does not exclude considerable managerial authority along the subcontracting chain. Hochtief operates a centre for occupational safety and health and environmental protection (OSHEP centre) which is led by the president of the General Works Council and charged to implement the OSHEP Directive throughout the Group. This centre has so far overseen the external certification of more than 50% of Hochtief's corporate units (Interview, Hochtief union official; Hochtief, 2007b, 13) and has also developed strong compliance provisions for suppliers:

> [W]e will also require contractors and suppliers to comply with a Code of Conduct which we have formulated. In this, we will, for instance, require compliance with international standards on ethical conduct, respect for the basic rights of employees and guaranteed measures regarding safety and environmental protection. There will be a provision that we have the right to check, at any time and unannounced, whether subcontractors and suppliers are complying with this planned Code of Conduct. In the event of any breaches of this, Hochtief reserves the right to terminate the business relationship. (Hochtief, 2007b: 21)

In the absence of a permanent reference group and formally organised and resourced audit procedures, implementation and monitoring of the agreement is ad-hoc and largely dependent on union organisation and vigilance. This, however, is where the structural contradictions of the IFA become most apparent: while the agreement is supposed to provide a platform for labour's exercise of organising and bargaining rights, particularly in the context of a top-down ad-hoc approach at headquarter level, this exercise in turn depends on labour organisation. Field research in Malaysia, Brazil and Ukraine has shown that unions continue to face serious problems with regard to recognition and organising at the workplace. Hochtief's tiered approach to the IFA in fact reinforces the segmentation of the construction labour market. First, its direct workforce benefits from the strength of the home-country union IG BAU in institutionalised industrial relations. Second, regional subsidiaries and joint ventures do not actively implement the agreement but take advantage of restrictions on union organisation. In Malaysia, for example, Leighton does not recognise the Union of Employees in the Construction Industry (UECI) for collective bargaining, limiting representation and recruitment to individual cases only. In Brazil, awareness of the IFA in the city-specific unions prescribed by labour law seems to be slim; in any case, only Hochtief employees are represented and organisation in subcontractors is made virtually impossible. Third, subcontractor managers are very rarely aware of the obligations under the IFA (as was the case in Ukraine). Importantly though, the fourth tier of informal labour seems to have become the largest: for example, more than 70% of the Malaysian and Brazilian construction workforce are outside an employment relationship (with a large proportion of international and internal migrants, respectively), while 55% of the Ukrainian GDP is estimated to result from undeclared work (Williams, 2007).

Problems in using the IFA for local organisation result from the structural tensions between the national industrial relations and union traditions on the one hand, and the centralised ad-hoc approach to administering the IFA on the other. In Brazil, union organisation at city, rather than workplace or national level, has made the development of a company-specific strategy difficult. In Malaysia, union fragmentation by industry, occupation and region, has focused on the core 'organisable' workforce, particularly in the context of Leighton's anti-unionism. Equally, Ukrainian unions' continued service orientation as outsourcing proceeded has limited their remit to the larger ex-state sector employers. Thus, without any supporting initiatives, an IFA cannot serve as a platform for organising in its own right. As an agreement, the IFA raises numerous questions about horizontal and vertical international practices. In the absence of worker-to-worker competition between different locations within the MNC and the subcontracting chain, however, any sustainable international/cross-border efforts at organising and trade union cooperation need to build on continuous networks and bottom-up practices of cooperation.

This case underlines the main conundrum of IFAs in practice: while reports of any infringements depend on the union presence at the workplace, subcontracting and labour mobility pose considerable obstacles for labour to establish such workplace presence. Additionally, the inconsistencies in implementation and monitoring practices, as well as the tenuous control that lead companies have over their own subsidiaries' labour relations, raise questions about the extent to which IFAs can serve as a platform to organise workplaces. In this respect, though, it is important to consider variations in using IFAs – on their own or in conjunction with other strategies, emphasising a home-country approach or more inclusively with regard to host country unions.

In the case of Hochtief, the IFA is used in an *ad hoc* manner. Here, international trade union cooperation is based on the power of the home-country union and works council, and on the power of HR management (with respect to subsidiary employers). This contrasts with other experiences. The Dutch construction unions, for example, were able to build on regular reference and monitoring groups and focused international activities around these structures: they were used to provide information on the IFA, train host country unions in organising strategies and build union networks within the respective MNC. Dutch construction unions, in particular, restructured their international projects to monitor their home country MNCs' activities in the Gulf states, and to support trade union organisation and capacity building in such countries (BWI, n.d.a; BWI, 2007a).

4. Regulation Through Contractor Liability

Historical developments of outsourcing and the emergence of complex subcontracting networks allowed firms towards the higher end of the value chain to focus on management and coordination functions. At the same time, these general contractors subcontracted labour-intensive parts of the construction process, thereby increasing competitive pressures and incentives for subcontractors to exploit social insurance and tax regulations. While such problems resulting from subcontracting highlight the failure of state regulation as well as the weakening articulation of employer associations, trade unions campaigning for a re-regulation of (sub)contractors' obligations were able to build coalitions and achieved the institution of a contractors' liability in most European countries.

Thus, countries such as the Netherlands, Germany, Finland, Austria (Bosch and Philips, 2003; Lillie and Greer, 2007; ÖGB and WKÖ, 2007; Cremers, 1998) have passed legislation that holds main contractors liable for the social insurance and tax obligations of the firms they subcontract to. Thus, legal arrangements exist specifically for the construction industry, based on the concept of value or subcontracting chains, and it is pertinent to explore to what extent such regulation might help unions in controlling the labour and product markets.

In Finland, for example, the collective agreement for the construction sector is extended by the state over the whole workforce; in addition, general contractors are liable for their subcontractors.

> ... a new law has come into effect ... allowing [labour] inspectors to fine general contractors for violations by subcontractors. Fines fall short of full liability, however, and in themselves are not seen as sufficient to prevent main contractors from using disreputable subcontractors. (Lillie and Greer, 2007: 562)

Finnish construction unions essentially exert control over the labour market by boycotting contractors noncompliant with collective agreements. While preventing boycotted companies from accessing the unionised labour market might not constitute a severe economic sanction (particularly where firms employing posted workers are concerned), it is secondary boycotts and strikes that are the central sanction in controlling the labour market. Thus, general contractors' potential benefits from engaging noncompliant subcontractors are seriously reduced, and the threat of secondary action is sufficient to control a critical mass of the labour market. This mechanism of securing the extension of collective bargaining agreements, based on a relatively high union density and the threat of secondary action, also explains why unions have no particular interest in specifically organising migrant workers.

Union officials emphasise the importance of strong site-level networks across all the contractors in the monitoring and enforcement of standards. Because most difficulties in irregular employment circumstances arise with subcontractors, multifirm, site-level union structures allow the union to keep track of subcontractors where there are less likely to be shop stewards. (Lillie and Greer, 2007: 563)

In Austria, the social partners have worked out a number of measures, specifically for the construction industry, in order to restrict the use of subcontracting for tax avoidance purposes. In 2003, the so-called reverse charge system came into force, which only entitled the general contractor to VAT deduction. Thus, other contractors in the chain are now forced to pay value added tax and cannot close their business or declare bankruptcy before having paid VAT (BMF 13 April 2004). Further, the 2007 amendment to social insurance law (67. amendment to the ASVG) made it mandatory to register workers with the social insurance institutions before their first working day (as opposed to the first 7 days so far) which, according to the calculations by the Chamber of Labour should prevent tax fraud of 300 million Euro (OTS, 2007). Most importantly, though, for labour, a contractor liability for social insurance contributions was agreed. Here, contractors are liable for their respective subcontractors' social insurance liabilities unless a) the social insurance institution attests that subcontractor companies have fulfilled all their obligations in this field in the last three years, or b) the contractor deposits 20 percent of the contract value with the social insurance institution. This system is designed to prevent the practices of so-called bogus subcontractors where workers were in fact registered with social insurance without contributions being paid. Once the institution tried to pursue the latter or even bring a court case, the subcontracting company was declared bankrupt while the workers were nominally shifted to another bogus subcontractor (ÖGB and WKÖ, 2007).

What this system of contractor liability does is ensure that social insurance contributions due are in fact paid. The main interests it serves are those of the tax payer and essentially employers in other industries which make regular payments into an insolvency fund (but tended to claim much less than the construction industry). However, while all the above are important measures in securing social wages, they do not deal with incomplete or missing registrations with social insurance or, in fact, with foreign companies (who post their workers) and whose social insurance contribution records cannot be easily verified. Thus, these regulations essentially help in controlling the local labour market if trade unions have some presence on site. Also, if irregularities are discovered unions tend to be drawn into long legal disputes with relatively little to gain.

A further important case of the regulation of subcontracting chains arises in the field of health and safety. The British Health and Safety at Work Act (1974) and relevant case law, for example, establishes health and safety obligations for employers that go beyond their workplace and ensure the protection of workers not in their employment (James et al., 2007). Still, for the moment evidence about the practical impact of such regulations remains scarce.

Thus, while regulatory structures on the social insurance, fiscal and health and safety obligations of contractors within their supply chain exist, actual implementation relies on a number of factors, not the least the resources governments make available for inspection and control. It would appear that arrangements of contractor liability in those areas constitute important institutions in order to deal with the fragmentation of more unified production structures and labour markets. Trade unions might be able to base some of their strategies to exert power in the labour market on the institution of contractor liability (which constitutes an extension mechanism of some sort), however, all the above examples indicate, that this has to be accompanied by high union density. Furthermore, extensive labour market segmentation and the existence of undeclared work require union presence and participation at the workplace and site in order to keep track of the numerous (local and cross-border) actors in the subcontracting chain.

5. Labour Strategies and Subcontracting Chains in European Construction

The cases discussed above highlight some of the potential of focussing union strategies around subcontracting chains, particularly as an avenue to develop campaigns around MNCs and beyond their organisational boundaries, as well as in linking union campaigns on working conditions across organisational boundaries (and back to the lead firm's industrial power). In the context of existing European industrial relations institutions, key issues are a) what such a focus can add to union organisation and participation at workplace level, b) what forms of international trade union cooperation could help in establishing tighter control on the construction labour market.

While the construction sector proves a relatively active example of European social dialogue (e.g. regarding the application of the Directive on posted workers) and of bilateral trade union coordination (Marginson, 2005), such strategies at sector level are not sufficient in the particular context of the sector. In this respect, the institutionalist approach needs to be expanded in two respects. With regard to construction, for example, Marginson and Traxler (2005: 435-436) hold:

> In the former case [where production and work is bound to the locus of consumption], a 'relaxed' transnational coordination is sufficient in principle, relying on a 'bottom-up' approach devised to shield national labour standards from the destructive forces of transnational labour mobility. This means that domestic regulations (i.e. an inclusive bargaining coverage and such provisions as the Posted Workers' Directive) have to 'rope in' foreign workers and thus contain competition over wages. In these circumstances, the

minimum level of transnational coordination may confine itself to exchange of information, and concerted action for favourable regulations. (The approach of the EFBWW resembles this pattern.)

We have argued, however, that while the advocated approach might be necessary, the conjuncture of subcontracting, labour mobility, non-standard employment and undeclared work puts sector level strategies in doubt. Thus, the evolving forms of participation processes in construction require a multi-level approach. A number of union strategies have focused at the company level, in fact the level of the main contractor, in order to establish structures and procedures of vertical coordination and to get a grip on the labour as well as the product market. Whereas relocation is the key mechanism for regime shopping in other sectors, the above developments allow considerable social dumping without relocation. This focus on the lead firm also has implications for international trade union cooperation. As Davies *et al* (2008: 15) argue:

International solidarity, in and of itself, cannot be the 'solution' because the most intractable problems in the industry are not primarily ones of international inequality.

Rather, it is local construction sites that provide the terrain for international worker-to-worker conflicts as well as for the coordination and management of subcontractors, in fact the terrain of local labour control regimes (Castree et al., 2004). International trade union cooperation needs to be complemented by explicit strategies of vertical coordination.

This also goes for the potential role of European Works Councils in the construction industry, which essentially establish intra-firm networks and therefore are different from the concept of subcontracting chains. While EWCs can provide an institutional platform and networks that can be extremely useful (see Pulignano 2005), they only cover the tip of the iceberg of the construction sector: i.e international contractors at the higher end of the construction value chain with employment concentrated in the first tier of the labour market, often biased towards engineering and contract management. In this respect, this focus on the legal obligations of lead firms and their power in managing labour relations can go a step towards the vertical control of the market.

However, while we have explored a number of company level instruments, from IFAs to arrangements of contractor liability in the much richer European context, the basic conundrum, already stated with regard to IFAs (Davies et al., 2008: 14), seems to hold in a broader context as well: whether to see these instruments as the foundation for organising and participation or, rather, to see workplace organisation as the precondition for the implementation of these instruments. It would seem that strategies aiming at the horizontal and vertical coordination and control of the labour market can be mutually beneficial. Without labour organisation and participation at site level, however, they both suffer from the same deficit, that is an insufficient grip on local conditions of work and employment. In a global perspective, the construction industry is a particularly pertinent example how the regulatory context restricts workplace organisation, thus, institutions such as reference groups to monitor and implement IFAs as well as regulations of contractor liability are important institutions. Without a voice at construction sites, the current state of product and labour market segmentation gives little hope that these regulations and cross-border coordination agreements can be put into practice.

References

Asper, A. (n.d.), Trade unions and workers' migration, Paper for the IFBWW-Asia Migrant Workers' Project, http://www.bwint.org/pdfs/Asiaregion.pdf [accessed 04/04/2008]

Bosch, G. / Philips, P. (eds.) (2003): Building chaos: an international comparison of deregulation in the construction industry (London: Routledge).

BWI (2007a): Interbeton is improving in the Gulf region, http://www.bwint.org/default.asp?Index=1280&Language=EN [accessed 04/04/2008]

BWI (n.d.a): Working and living conditions in Dubai are disproportionate for BWI and FNV Bouw, http://www.bwint.org/default.asp?index=662&Language=EN [accessed 04/04/2008]

Castree, N. / Coe, N. / Ward, K. / Samers, M. (2004): Spaces of work: global capitalism and the geographies of labour (London: Sage).

Cervino, E. (2007): Ground-breaking new law on subcontracting in construction sector, http://www.eurofound.europa.eu/eiro/2007/05/articles/es0705019i.htm [accessed 15/08/2008]

Commons, J.R. (1909): 'American Shoemakers, 1648–1895, A Sketch of Industrial Evolution', Quarterly Journal of Economics, 26, 39–84.

Cremers, J. / Dølvik, J.E. / Bosch, G. (2007): 'Posting of workers in the single market: attempts to prevent social dumping and regime competition in the EU', Industrial Relations Journal, 38, 6, 524-541.

Cremers, J. (1998): Liability in the case of subcontracting in the construction industry: a preliminary exploration of the question, CLR-News, 3/1998, 34-36.

Davies, S. (2008): Apprenticeships: a firm foundation. A report for UCATT (London: UCATT).

Davies, S. / Hammer, N. / Williams, G. / Raman, R. / Ruppert, C.S. / Volynets, L. (2008): Labour capacity in global subcontracting chains: evidence from a construction MNC (mimeo).
Donaghey, J. / Teague, P. (2006): The free movement of workers and social Europe: maintaining the European ideal, Industrial Relations Journal, 37, 6, 652-666.
Dribbusch, H. (2004): European Migrant Workers Union founded, http://www.eurofound.europa.eu/eiro/2004/09/feature/de0409206f.htm [accessed 15/08/2008]
Erne, R. (2004): Organised labour. an actor of Euro-democratisation, Euro-technocracy or re-nationalisation (PhD, Florence: European University Institute).
Gallin, D. (2001): 'Propositions on trade unions and informal employment in times of globalisation,' Antipode, 33, 3, 531-549.
Grünell, M. / Kaar, R. van het (2003): Migration and industrial relations, http://www.eurofound.europa.eu/eiro/2003/03/study/tn0303105s.htm [accessed 15/08/2008]
Hammer, N. (2008): 'International Framework Agreements in the Context of Global Production', 89-111, in K. Papadakis (ed.), Cross-border social dialogue and agreements: an emerging global industrial relations framework? (Geneva: IILS/ILO).
Hammer, N. (2005): 'International Framework Agreements: global industrial relations between rights and bargaining', Transfer, 11, 4, 511-530.
Harvey, M. / Behling, F. (2008): The evasion economy: false self-employment in the UK construction industry. A UCATT report (London: UCATT).
Hochtief (2007a): Annual Report 2006 (Essen: Hochtief)
Hochtief (2007b): Sustainability Report 2007 (Essen: Hochtief)
Hochtief, IG BAU and BWI (2000): Hochtief Code of Conduct in respect of the rights of its own employees and the employees of contractual partners, 15 March 2000, Berlin, http://www.bwint.org/default.asp?Index=44&Language=EN [accessed 04/04/08]
IFBWW (2003): IFBWW 'toolbox' on social dialogue and multinational companies, http://www.ifbww.org/files/startegy-mnc-en.pdf [accessed 04/04/2008]
ILO (2002): Women and Men in the Informal Economy: A Statistical Picture (Geneva: ILO)
ILO (2001): The construction industry in the twenty-first century: its image, employment prospects and skill requirements. Tripartite meeting on the construction industry (Geneva: ILO), http://www.ilo.ch/public/english/dialogue/sector/techmeet/tmcit01/tmcitr.pdf [accessed 03/12/2007]
James, P. / Johnstone, R. / Quinlan, M. / Walters, D. (2007): Regulating supply chains to improve health and safety, Industrial Law Journal, 36, 2, 163-187.

Lillie, N. / Greer, I. (2007): 'Industrial relations, migration, and neoliberal politics: the case of the European construction sector', Politics and Society, 35, 4, 551-581.

Lund, J. / Wright, C. (2003): Building union power through the supply chain: Mapping opportunities and jurisdictional boundaries in grocery distribution. Labor Studies Journal, 27: 59-75.

Marginson, P. (2005): Industrial relations at European sector level: the weak link?, Economic and Industrial Democracy, 26, 4, 511-540

Marginson, P. / Traxler, F. (2005): After enlargement: preconditions and prospects for bargaining coordination, Transfer, 11, 3, 423-438.

Menz, G. (2001): Beyond the Anwerbestopp? The German-Polish Bilateral Labour Treaty, Journal of European Social Policy, 11, 3, 253-269.

Narayanan, Suresh / Yew-Wah, Lai (2005): The Causes and Consequences of Immigrant Labour in the Construction Sector in Malaysia, International Migration 43 (5), 31-55

ÖGB / WKÖ (2007): Gemeinsame Pressekonferenz von ÖGB und WKÖ zur 'Generalunternehmerhaftung', 29/10/08 (Wien: Österreichischer Gewerkschaftsbund, Wirtschaftskammer Österreich).

OTS (2007): Buchinger: Sozialpaket bringt mehr soziale Gerechtigkeit und Sicherheit, press release OTS0178, 06/06/2007

Pulignano, V. (2005): EWC's cross-national employee representative coordination: a case of trade union cooperation?, Economic and Industrial Democracy, 26, 3, 383-412.

Quan, K. (2008): Use of Global Value Chains by Labour Organisers. Competition and Change, 12: 89-104.

Riisgaard, L. / Hammer, N. (2008): Organised labour and the social regulation of global value chains, DIIS Working Paper No 2008/9

Schulten, T. (1998): Cooperation agreement between German and Italian construction unions, http://www.eurofound.europa.eu/eiro/1998//04/inbrief/de9804259n.htm [accessed 15/08/2008]

Traxler, F. / Blaschke, S. / Kittel, B. (2001): National labour relations in internationalised markets (Oxford: Oxford University Press).

Wells, J. (2007): 'Informality in the construction sector in developing countries', Construction Management and Economics, 25, 1, 87-93.

Williams, C. (2007): Tackling Undeclared Work in Europe: Lessons from a Study of Ukraine, European Journal of Industrial Relations, 13: 219-236.

Woolfson, C. / Sommers, J. (2006): Labour mobility in Construction: European implications of the Laval un Partneri dispute with Swedish labour, European Journal of Industrial Relations, 12, 1, 49-68.

From a reactive to a proactive approach of interactive leadership

Lauge Baungaard Rasmussen

1. Introduction

A variety of participatory approaches exist. Some of them include the employees in definition, discussion and analysis of the problems. Others involve them in the design of improvements and/or in taking action. The majority of these approaches have been *reactive*, meaning that they are initiated *after* a change has occurred. However, due to the increasing levels of complexity faced by companies and institutions in today's globalization they are challenged to be more proactive in their decision making. A *proactive* approach means that planning and actions are initiated *before* a threat or an opportunity occurs. According to this rationale, the future is not just something coming. Instead, certain future possibilities can be shaped or avoided when the managers involve the employees in a continuous transformation process.

It can, however, be observed that many systems of representative employee bodies still are characterised by a defensive or passive attitude. Some employers also seem to pay attention to immediate effects only. Such an approach may create an 'organisational improvement paradox' Changes successfully implemented in one part of the company often fail to translate into gains in firm-level performance as a whole (Goodman and Rousseau, 2004). The reasons of this paradox are manifold, but some of the key-factors seem to be: (1) defensive attitudes towards change; (2) obstacles to recognize the importance of interactive rather than one-way communication and (3) lack of methods to combine short and long term perspectives and challenges.

The following questions are investigated in this paper:

- Is it possible to develop a precise conceptual framework about various forms of reactive and proactive approaches?
- Which are the different rationales for employee participation?
- How is it possible to develop and implement proactive and participatory approaches?
- Which are the possible outcomes of proactive, participatory employee approaches?

2. Reactive/proactive: a continuum rather than a dichotomy?

At least four different modes of participation can be identified as illustrated in figure 1.

The four approaches, illustrated in figure 1, differ in regards to the time-horizon and the scope of change.

A *reactive-defensive* approach (in figure 1 shown as R-D) is characterized by a non-change attitude against any novel technological, organisational, economic or political challenge. Examples are worker collectives with a strong internal cohesion and a powerful position in the organisation (Lysgaard, 1961). They fight against any change, because they fear that it may decrease their power. However, as time has passed, many of these worker collectives were defeated. Some of them – for instance the typographers and compositors – have disappeared. The economic and technological developments proved to be too overwhelming. Reactive-defensive approaches can temporary prevent change, but history shows that it is an approach, which may result in either a total collapse or more serious problems and conflicts.

Figure 1: Reactive and proactive participatory approaches

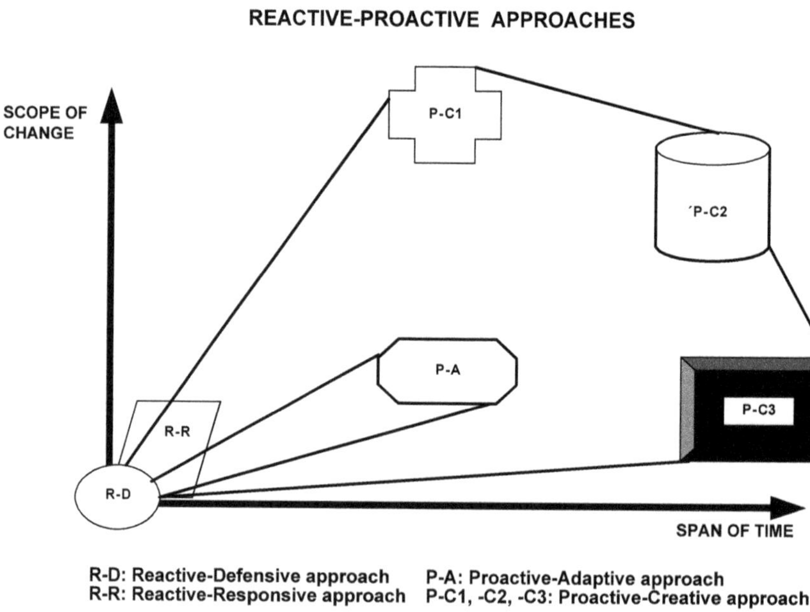

A *reactive-responsive* approach (in figure 1 shown as R-R) is focusing on needs created by changes which have already occurred. A classical example is the Hawthorne studies conducted in the 1920s and 1930s under the leadership of Elton Mayo of the Hawthorne plant at the Western Electric Company in Chicago (Mayo, 1949). With these studies the whole question of work motivation became a legitimate research issue to study. Another example is the classical socio-technical approach coined in the 1950s by the Tavistock Institute of Human Relations based on analysis of technical changes in post war British coal mines (Trist et. al., 1963). Both approaches are examples of reactive-responsive approaches. They assess a current situation, identify the existing problems, needs and unbalances, and then develop a strategy and practical action plan to meet those needs by involving the workers in the investigation and/or the solution of the problems. Reactive-responsive approaches have been the most common form of collaboration between researchers, employees and employers since the 1920s (Rasmussen, 2004; Emery and Thorsrud, 1976). In the 1960s the socio-technical projects in NOBOE Household appliances/metal and Norsk Hydro received a lot of attention in the literature (Emery and Thorsrud, 1969, 1976; Gustavsen and Hunnius, 1981). But the socio-technical approaches were not adopted by other companies in Norway at that time: "*...In their turn, the 'experimental gardens' became isolated from the rest of the organisations which even built up some kind of resistance against such a change" (van Eijnatten, 1993).* However, the socio-technical approach diffused from Norway to Sweden and Denmark during the 1970's. In *Denmark* socio-technical projects in seven firms of the Danish metal industry was carried out between 1969 and 1973 (Agersnap et. al., 1974). But the results were limited and did not diffuse to other Danish companies at that time. In *Sweden* the Swedish Employer Association (SAF) launched a new socio-technical strategy in 1975, termed 'New Factory' project. The aim of this approach was to develop more stable production systems (Argurén and Edgren, 1980; Ehn, 1988). In particular, Kalmar and Uddevalla Volvo Factories became the major symbols of this strategy in Scandinavia. Both factories followed the socio-technical principles of minimum specifications, task autonomy for the workers, fluid divisions of functions and local solutions. However, the reforms were restricted to the shop floor production level. Participation for democracy was in no sense included in this Swedish approach. Management's overall control was rather strengthened (Ehn, 1988). Similar programmes were initiated by the German humanization of working life (Humanisierung des Arbeitsleben). Most of the projects focused on reduction of stress with assembly-line production. Using the Norwegian and Swedish models they conducted experiments to introduce semi-autonomous groups and reduce machine-paced work by introducing buffer zones at the assembly-line (Fricke, 1983).

In a somewhat critical reaction to these employer-initiated projects, some action researchers and trade unions developed the so called *Collective Resource Approach.* In 1970 the Norwegian Iron and Metal Workers Union (NJMF) decided to initiate research of their own. In Sweden the DEMOS project on 'trade unions, industrial democracy and computers' started in 1975. A parallel project in Denmark was the DUE project on 'democracy, education and computer-based systems'. All these three approaches emphasized democratisation of the design process of the new computer technology and its implementation at the work places. However, the impact of these activities did not meet the initial expectations. As Ehn pointed out; "*It seemed that one could only influence the introduction of the technology, the training, and the organization of work to a certain degree. Important aspects like the opportunity to further developed skills and increasing influence on work organization were limited*" (Ehn, 1988:278). At the universities, new types of action research developed. Most of them focused on health and safety problems in the industrial sector. They were typically joint action research projects between students, local trade unions and employees at the company level. However, for some reasons it was difficult to disseminate examples of 'best practice' from one company to another.

The *proactive-adaptive* approaches (in figure 1 shown as P-A) differ from the reactive approaches. They do not focus solely on the current situation, but also try to anticipate the future situation and develop more appropriate technology, organisation and qualifications to cope with future challenges.

An example is the Peiner Project in Germany where five researchers from the Friedrich Ebert Foundation collaborated over four years with workers at the Peiner AG Screw factory to study and improve working conditions. According to Fricke (1983), the Peiner Project achieved four main results. First, the working conditions were improved in a number of ways. Secondly, worker project groups were developed whereby workers could participate in improving their working conditions. Thirdly, an approach for continual worker education was established. Fourthly, the researchers gained practical experiences with the participatory action research methods. Thus the Peiner Project as well as other Humanization projects in Germany (Ulrich, 1980; Hoppmann and Stötzel, 1981; Weltz and Lullies, 1983; Duell and Frei, 1986) demonstrated that workers are able and willing to make improvements in their own working environment, when they are offered the methods and possibilities to do so (Fricke, 2009; Fricke, 1983).

Another example is the Swedish-Danish project, UTOPIA. As an attempt to broaden the scope, the Utopia project was started in cooperation between the Nordic Graphic Worker's Union and researchers in Sweden and Denmark in 1981. A mock-up workstation was established by primitive means which could be used to simulate a computer-based page make-up. It was cheap and easy to change during the experimental process. Besides, it allowed the users to express their know-how in action, and the researcher to be actively involved during the design process. However, the method contains some pitfalls too. For instance, prototypes have a tendency to freeze users as well as researchers into a certain perspective. The result of the UTOPIA project was never implemented in a company, but the methodology of collaboration between researchers and users soon became well known in computer and social scientist circles worldwide.

A third example of researcher-user collaboration within a tool-perspective was the Danish part of the ESPRIT 1217: "*Human Centred CIM Systems*" (1986-1990). In collaboration with industrial designers of a Danish company, social scientists and system engineers developed a prototype of an Electronic Sketch Pad (ESP). This project started to focus concrete improvements of the tools used by industrial designers in collaboration with some of these designers. Later on it more long term scenarios were developed about how to improve the organisation, skills and communication between the design office and the other departments of the company (Corbett, Rasmussen and Rauner, 1991). Similar to the UTOPIA project, the direct influence of the ESPRIT project 1217 on the technology development was limited at that time. However, the methodological experiences gained from the approach influenced the teaching methods used at the Scandinavian Universities. Based on the experiences from projects like UTOPIA and ESPRIT 1217 new user oriented courses were introduced at several universities in Sweden and Denmark (Brulin, 2001; Rasmussen, 1998; Laessoe and Rasmussen, 1989).

Another type of proactive-adaptive approaches is the network approaches starting from 1985. The *Swedish national program, LOM,* (Leadership, Organisation and Co-determination) was emerging by the early 1980s and took place between 1985 and 1990. The central concepts of the LOM Program were networking, learning and democratic dialogue. The aim was to motivate collaboration and networking between the participating companies and universities. The *networking* was organised around clusters of four enterprises. The *learning aspect* focused on the capabilities to conceive new ideas. The *democratic dialogue* was defined as 'good communication', that is the capacity to engage in open discussions, all-level participation, and in reaching agreements (Gustavsen, 2001). The LOM program focused mainly on current and short term prospective problem areas, and less on more long term development possibilities.

In this respect they differ from the *proactive-creative* approach (P-C) as shown in figure 1. According to the rationale of this approach it is not possible to make exact foresights on the future, except within a very limited time-horizon. This approach builds on the premise that it is possible to shape creative and constructive strategies by creating scenarios of possible futures (in figure 1 illustrated as P-C1, P-C2 and P-C3). Another premise is that such a shaping process includes change of values, norms and behaviour throughout the organisation and hence includes all its members in a continuously learning process. The combination of participatory search conference and interactive scenario analysis is an example of a method which can be applied in proactive-creative approaches (Garibaldo, 2003; Rasmussen, 2003).The origins of the search conference can be traced back to the Tavistock Institute, namely Fred and Merrilyn Emery (Emery and Purser 1996). According to them, people are seen as subjects, entitled to have their say in their work environment. Based on this principle they structured a participative methodology termed search conference. This method has been revised by Francesco Garibaldo and his colleagues adding a diagnosis phase to the deliberative one in the classical search conference method (Garibaldo, 2003). A part of this revised search conference method has been combined with interactive scenario analysis (see figure 2).

Figure 2: The combined approach of participatory search conference and interactive scenario analysis

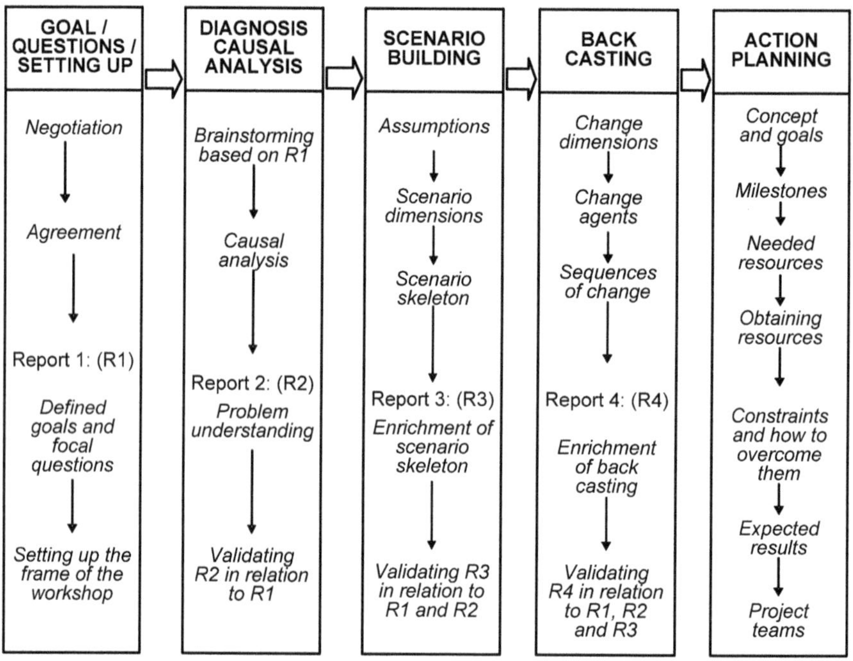

As shown in figure 2, the phases of *setting up goals* and making *diagnosis* from the search conference method are followed by the phases of *scenario building, back-casting* and *action planning* from the scenario analysis method.

This combination has been tried in practice with a promising result (Garibaldo, 2003; Rasmussen, 2003). Two of the participants of this proactive-creative workshop evaluated the outcomes as follows:

> *"It was a very satisfying experience by all the participants in terms of learning the action research methodology as a tool and the outputs of the workshop had real practical value for all the stakeholders.... Both the European and the Indian groups gained the experience of building new traditions of Action Research in India in the dairy sector. It was cross-cultural exchange between two continents on the global level."* (Mehra and Kalra, 2003).

The various phases are only briefly described in this paper, but they are more extensively described elsewhere (Rasmussen, 2003, Mehra and Kalra, 2003). The first phase, setting up the goals and questions, intends to make an agreement among the participants regarding the intended outcomes and focal questions to frame the succeeding phases. The participants are facilitated to discuss and negotiate their respective opinions. The outcome of the first phase (see figure 2) is a report (R1) framing the following phases of the approach.

Based on this framework, the next phase consists of an interactive *diagnosis* of the past and current problems and challenges facing the participants. A brainstorming session is followed by a causal analysis in which the participants are discussing how the various aspects are to be understood and related to each other. Based on this discussion, the facilitators and some of the participants draft a second report (R2) of the causal relationships between the current and prospective areas. Finally, R2 is validated according to the goals and questions mentioned in the framework report (R1).

The scenario-building phase (see figure 2) is initiated by presenting the main issues from R1 and R2. Then follows the creation of a *scenario skeleton* as an iterative process between focal questions, assumptions, scenario dimensions and features/actors in the scenario skeleton as illustrated in figure 3.

Figure 3: The interactive process of building the scenario skeleton

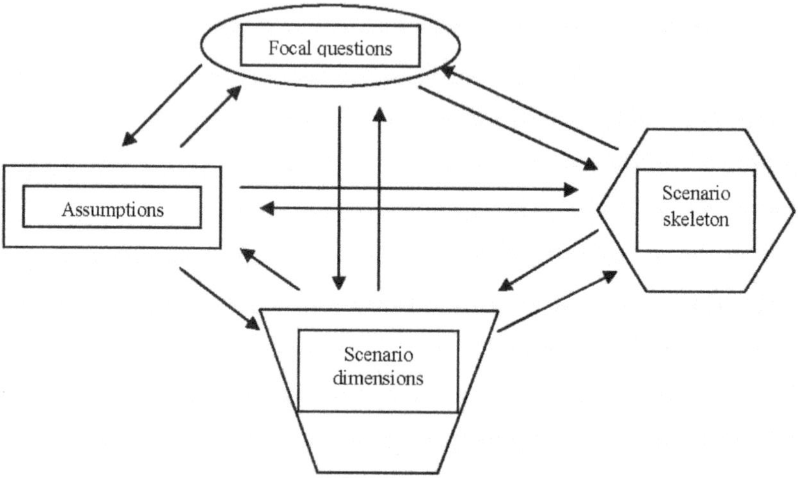

However, the scenario skeleton is an abstract structure, which needs to be enriched. The *enrichment* of the scenario skeleton (see figure 2) is like adding 'flesh and blood' to the skeleton. By the means of story-telling it is possible to enrich the skeleton by adding fictive cases of future events (Rasmussen, 2005; Boje, 2002; Johnson, 2000).

> *"... It is in the twists and turns of a written plot that one observes the workings and structural inter-relationships of the driving forces. And it is also in the twist and turns of the plot that one observes most clearly where understanding is lacking and further analysis would be productive."* (van der Heijden, 2004:258)

The enriched scenarios are described in report 3 (R3 in figure 2). They should be validated in accordance to the goals and focal questions (R1) and the analysis of the problem areas (R2) by the participants of the workshop (Alexander and Maiden, 2004).

The *fourth* phase is *back casting* (see figure 2). *Back casting* is a process of moving back from the scenarios to the current situation (Rasmussen, 2003; Keune and Gordon, 2002; Dreborg, 1996). It is a method to explore alternative development paths and their implications. Back casting implies a functional description of the possible routes and enables the development of action plans. It includes the following steps. The *first* step is to identify the *change dimensions,* for instance educational, technological, social and political dimensions. The *second* step is to identify possible *change agents.* The *third* step is to create *sequences of change* between the present and the scenarios. The *fourth* step is to create relationships between the current circumstances, the change-agent strategy, the sequences of change and the scenario. The construction of the back casting is like developing some possible 'paths' connecting the scenario with the present.

The *fifth* phase is the *action planning* phase (see figure 2). This phase is based on the results from the scenario building and the back casting process. An action plan can be *structured* as follows:

(1) The concept for action, that is, what is the overall frame of taking action?
(2) Precisely defined goals for whom and with whom?
(3) Milestones to reach the defined goals, for instance achieved changes after 3, 5 or 10 years.
(4) A list of resources needed to reach the goals, for instance money, technical advancements, training, resources and abilities for networking and so on.
(5) How to obtain the resources needed, and from whom?
(6) Expected results and the innovative aspects of these results.
(7) A list of people or institutions that may resist the planned actions.
(8) Strategies of how to overcome the resistance or opposition. For instance, the use of bargaining or the creation of powerful coalitions.

When the action plans have been developed for each scenario, they should be compared in order to identify similar or different actions. Such a comparative analysis can help the decision makers to identify which actions should be initiated depending on which scenario the participants consider the most relevant to focus on. Key linkages across time, space and themes should be identified and analysed regarding their relevance for the focal issue. Other examples of proactive methodologies are future creating workshops, interactive planning, design games, participatory SWOT and causal mapping (Rasmussen, 2008).

Possible outcomes of using proactive methodologies

Focusing on future possibilities should not be an excuse for neglecting current problems. However, using proactive approaches can help to reduce the number of 'current problems' in the future. The contextual determinants some times suggest a reactive and sometimes a proactive approach. In some cases, a reactive approach can change perspectives towards being proactive (Rasmussen, 2004). They are not mutually exclusive dichotomies, but rather a continuum of complementary approaches depending on the historical context, available resources, and the political climate.

The interactive mode of participation made possible by such a proactive-creative approach can enhance formal and informal knowledge creation and knowledge sharing (Robinson, 2003; Schwartz, 1991). Work allocation, work pacing, regeneration and social experiments presuppose participatory and proactive approaches rather than being designed by external experts without practical experiences in the work content and work relationships (Broberg, 2007; Quist and Vergragt, 2004).

In difference to forecast approaches, *one of the strengths* of a combined use of search conference and scenario workshops is that it does not pretend to predict the future. Instead it provides stories of several possible futures (van der Heijden, 2004; Alexander and Maiden, 2004; Godet, 2000). Hence, in a world characterised by many uncertainties this approach is able to cope with uncertainty, because it can help the participants to visualise and describe what might happen, *if* certain kind of trends are becoming stronger, weaker or perhaps 'overruled' by other trends (van der Heijden, 2004; Mintzberg, 1994). As they evolve over time, the scenarios are like 'laboratories' in which different strategies and development plans can be tested. *Another type of strength* is that search conferences and scenarios can provide a common platform for interdisciplinary knowledge sharing and strategy formation. For instance, scenarios may rely on knowledge from technical, social, psychological and economic disciplines as well as practical experience from managers and employees. The narrative techniques of storytelling are well suited for the creation of a mutual relationship for many bits of information. Stories are not only to be seen as effective communication devices. They are also creative tools to expose hitherto implicit anticipations or assumption. By stimulating the mind to think about different possibilities, it becomes more and more trained to move into non-conventional directions, thus improving the ability to imagine unusual situations (Lindgren and Bandhold, 2003). Hence, it may inject an element of caution, asking 'what can go wrong' if we do it in this way or in that way?

A potential risk is to develop scenarios as utopian dreams of '*paradises on earth'*, in which all kinds of problems or conflicts have disappeared. Instead they may inject naive anticipations and perhaps successive frustration. *Another type of risk* is to make '*pseudo-forecasts'*. Such a risk is overwhelming, when the scenario builders rely on almost ensured trends or mainstream thinking only. The scenarios may content no surprises or new ideas, but just represent 'conventional wisdom' in two or three slightly moderated versions. *A third kind of risk* is to *oversimplify* complex issues in order to facilitate the communication and discussion of the key aspects. Often scenarios are presented as rough skeletons without enrichment and back casting. However, such a superficial approach may turn out to be considered more like an entertaining event than a serious use of a participatory approach. *A fourth type of risk* is to generate *too many alternate scenarios*. It is quite easy to be overwhelmed with possibilities and complexities in a scenario building process. Instead, there should only be a few alternations with internally consistent or opposing pathways into the future (Wack, 1985).

Search conference and scenario analysis possess the power to break old stereotypes and enforce managers and employees to question their assumptions about how things are working. They are useful devices throughout the life cycles of system development, including for instance local community approaches, organisational development projects, human-computer interaction and health care.

The four different approaches described above rely on various economic, social and political rationales briefly described in the following section.

Different rationales for employee participation

At least three different rationales for introducing employee participation can be observed in the literature. Each of these rationales is related to the four different reactive and proactive approaches described above.

The economic rationale of employee participation

The economic rationale is based on the assumption that participation improves the employees' motivation to work effectively towards achieving the goals of the company.

Participation within this rationale aims at securing the consent and commitment of the workforce to new working arrangements. It can include initiatives which directly engage employees in planning and implementing change. In addition, influenced by such a participatory rationale, some managers seem to adopt more facilitative leadership towards their subordinates and hence try to improve their abilities to share responsibility and promote creative behaviour (Summers and Hyman, 2005; Marchington, 2000; Batt and Appelbaum, 1995). This rationale is typically underlying the reactive-responsive and proactive-adaptive approaches, depending on the conditions of the environment, the type of company, the management and the education level of the work force.

The social rationale of employee participation

The social rationale is focusing on the possible health and safety improvements as an effect of employee participation. The assumption is that active employee involvement reduces accidents and work related ill health. Another assumption is that it develops more effective risk control measures by promoting a positive and realistic health and safety culture.

The social rationale has often been associated with the proactive-adaptive approach in the literature (Rasmussen, 2004). However, often it seems to function more as a rationale for reactive-responsive approaches, though these may be changed gradually in a more proactive orientation as part of a change towards a more proactive health and safety culture (Rasmussen, 2004; Cressey and Williams, 1990). For instance the workspace design research program in Denmark has developed a proactive approach to be used by workplace consultants, managers and employees based on participatory design of healthy workplaces in industrial settings (Broberg, 2007).

The political rationale of employee participation

The political rationale is focusing on more democratic and equal relationships in organisations as an outcome of employee participation. The assumption is that a social partnership can improve the democratic attitude and behaviour of management as well as of the employees. This development is seen as a goal in itself, and not just as means to work more effectively. Such participation often forms part of the formalised system of representation in the organisation, and may be sustained by legislation, by sector or national contracts, or by agreements between the social partners. This participation approach is directly influenced by the particular industrial relations systems involved. Within this rationale it is often assumed that a situation will be improved only if employees and their representatives have access to all levels of decision making, and can successfully protect workers' rights during technological and organisational change. The political rationale is mainly associated with proactive approaches (DeLeon, 1997). Sometimes it has developed gradually from a more economic rationale to becoming a social and political experiment too (for instance Lucas Aerospace in UK in the 1970s, Cooley, 1987). However, some times there seems to be a large distance between the ideals of dialogue, participation and involvement and the actual challenges of organisational power relations. When focused with these actual challenges of power relationships, facilitation must change from handling dialogue to handling more or less openly expressed conflicts (Kristensen, 2007).

Governmental rationale of employee participation

Governmental rationale of employee participation encompasses economic, social and political rationales. It is designed to improve the national economic efficiency, health and safety level of the labour force and the democratic abilities of the employees and the managers. Comparative studies of changes in job quality (Lorenz and Valeyre, 2006; Green, 2006) and participatory approaches (Summers and Hyman, 2005) indicate, that the national institutional structures have an effect on organisation of work and numbers and level of participatory programs. However, the implementation of direct legislative intervention in the promotion of workplace participation seems to be rare. Instead, a great variety of persuasive forms of regulation are more in use (Alasoini et. Al, 2009; Forsyth et. al., 2006). An example is the TYKES Governmental R&D Program for promoting simultaneous improvements in productivity and quality of working life by funding development projects at Finnish workplaces. Similar programs are also funded by other European Governments. On a wider scale, the EU has claimed an interest in employee participation (European Commission, 2002). Currently there seems to be a wide variation between different European nations in terms of frequency and intensity of participation (Summers and Hyman, 2005). This reflects differences in culture, structure and political strategies of the social partners and their varying frameworks of national legislation. The question is, if these participatory practices across Europe will remain patchy or develop towards a larger degree of convergence? The governmental rationale seems so far mostly to be related to the reactive-responsive approach. However, it may change towards a more proactive-creative perspective, for instance challenged by the rising complexity of actual and prospective economic, environmental and social challenges facing Europe today.

Obstacles and Requirements to develop proactive approaches

The *obstacles* against proactive approaches following the literature are:

- A large hierarchy of formal management positions, where authority is defined by the position, and unconditioned discipline is expected towards the hierarchical chain of command (Debowski, 2006; EU Commission, 2002).
- A low level of informal interaction (Alasoini et al. 2010).
- A lack of available information tchnology systems to store and accumulate knowledge in such a manner, that it is easily updated and accessible to relevant stakeholders (Campagnolo, 2009; Alasoini et al., 2010; Debowski, 2006).

- The lack of education and training to enhance creative and convergent abilities among the members of the organisation (Rasmussen, 2008; Debowski, 2006).
- Poor access to proactive methods including facilitation in the use of these methods in a participatory way (Rasmussen, 2005).

Addressing these obstacles against proactive approaches makes it necessary to focus on various *requirements.* The challenge is to change values, norms and behaviour in parallel throughout the organisation, or in other words, to initiate transformational learning as shown in figure 4.

Single loop learning depends on three steps (Morgan, 1986) as shown in the smallest box in figure 4:

1. The system must be able to sense, monitor and scan relevant issues of the environment.
2. The system must be able to relate this information to the operating norms that guide the behaviour of the entities included in the system.
3. The system must be able to detect significant deviations from these norms and the initiate correcting actions when too much deviation is detected.

This form of learning corresponds to the reactive-responsive approach as it is defined in this paper. However, if the operative norms are becoming insufficient to manage the system it may include an ability to question and change the operating norms. This ability has been termed *double loop learning* (see figure 4 step 1, 2, 2a, 3) or learning to learn by Argyris and Schön (1978, 1996) and Schön (1983). This ability corresponds to the reactive-responsive approach at a higher level of complexity. The proactive-creative approach includes the ability to change not only the behaviour or the operating norms, but also the *values* behind these norms (see figure 4 step 1, 2, 2a, 2b, 3). This form of learning has been termed *transformational learning* by Hawkins (1994). For instance when a company or network of companies move from a conventional focus on profit to include values of social, cultural and environmental responsibilities too, they are changing not only actions or norms but also the values behind these norms.

Figure 4: single-loop (step 1, 2, 3), double-loop (step 1, 2, 2a, 3) and triple-loop (step 1, 2, 2a, 2b, 3) learning as different phases of transformational learning

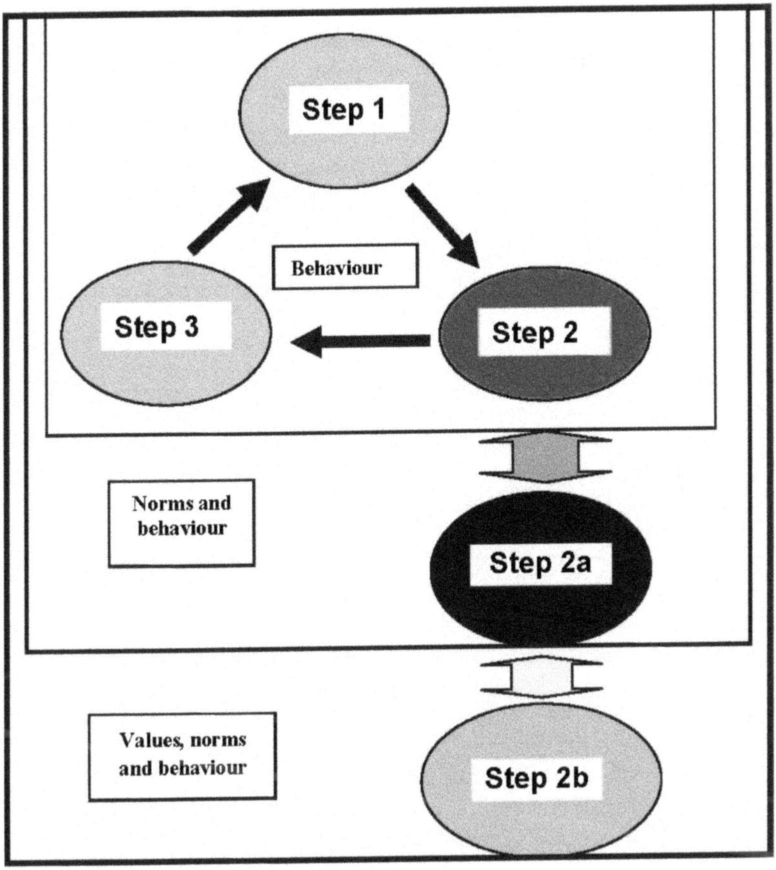

In order to make learning possible at these three different levels, the flows of knowledge must be accessible to all relevant entities of the organisation, as showed in figure 5.

Figure 5: Relationships between transformational learning and knowledge flow

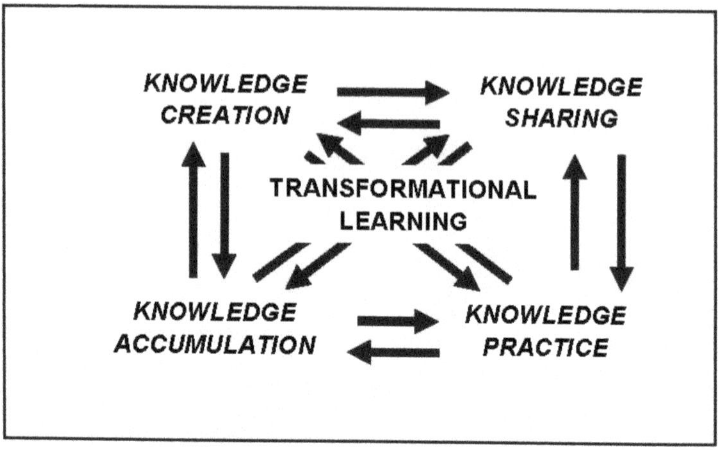

The challenge is to transform parts of tacit and explicit knowledge into a model form of knowledge, which more easily can be shared, used and accumulated (Campagnolo, 2008). Tacit knowledge, however, is typically less easy to transform than explicit knowledge captured in documents and manuals. Some aspects of tacit knowledge are impossible to replicate or too costly to imitate. In addition, tacit knowledge often includes a social dimension deeply embedded in the culture of the organisation or network of organisations. Hence, far from all knowledge can or should be transformed into a model form.

Such an unrestricted flow of knowledge can be enhanced by various devises as follows:

- The creation of learning spaces or work space laboratories where managers and employees can perform proactive-creative workshops using for instance search conferences and scenario workshops, design games, interactive planning, participatory SWOT or future creating workshops (Rasmussen, 2008).
- The creation of opportunities for networking or peer exchange between companies and knowledge institutions as a means of combining novel and already practiced ideas and knowledge (Rasmussen, 2005).
- The development of repository systems to share and accumulate knowledge created anywhere in the organisation (Debowski, 2006).
- Education and training of managers and employees to use the new opportunities and methods as means to create new forms of work organisation (Broberg, 2007; Fricke, 2010).

However, such devises are useless, when the conventional management paradigm of top-down commands continues to keep the creative abilities in the organisation in an 'iron-cage', as Max Weber termed the restrictive version of bureaucracy (Weber, 1930). Hence, an interactive leadership paradigm must accompany the implementation of proactive devises and methods. Three different forms of leadership roles should be encouraged as shown in figure 6:

Figure 6: Relationships between interactive leadership, knowledge flow and transformational learning

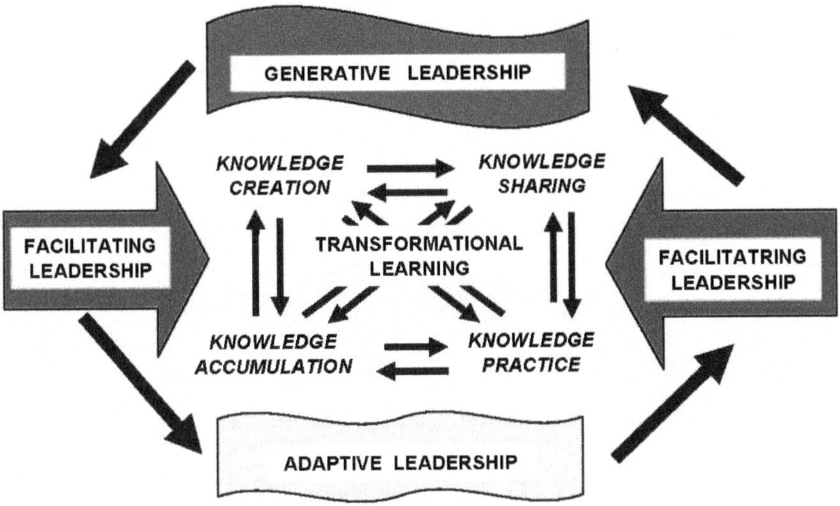

Generative leadership is focusing on the creation of structures and interaction patterns that stimulate creativity and innovation, for instance learning spaces, communication networks, repository systems and/or resources to use proactive methods.

While generative leadership is framing the structural and procedural context for creative knowledge flow (Surie and Hazy, 2007), *adaptive leadership* is a participatory and collective form of leadership that draws upon the combined knowledge of various members. It is non-positional, informal and oriented to make appropriate change of actions or norms when necessary. Adaptive leadership can occur anywhere in the organisation for instance when unexpected challenges require fast and adaptive responses. In order to ensure the dynamics between those two forms of leadership, a third form of leadership is necessary, which sometimes is termed enabling leadership (Marion and Uhl-bien, 2007). In this context the author prefers *facilitating leadership,* because it provides a more precise connection to the use of proactive approaches. As shown in figure 6, *facilitating leadership* contains two main functions. One is to guide the interaction between the generative and adaptive levels. The other main function is to ensure, that the novel ideas and experiences made anywhere in the organisation is communicated and used in the organisation. The effective outcomes of these three forms of leadership depend on the balances between four organisational principles:

- redundancy
- requisite variety
- minimum specification of rules
- multi-levelled cohesion

This is shown in figure 7.

Figure 7: Relationship between organisational principles, leadership, knowledge flow and learning

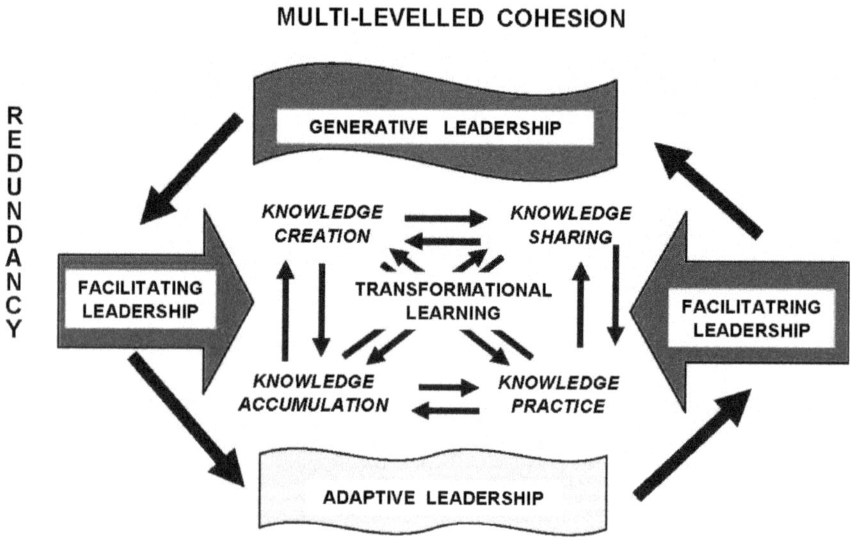

The principle of *redundancy of functions* is coined by Fred Emery (Emery and Thorsrud, 1969). Instead of spare parts being added to a system, extra functions are added to each of the entities. Each entity is able to engage in a variety of functions, rather than just perform a single, specialised function. An example is semi-autonomous work groups, where members acquire multiple skills and thus are able to substitute for each other when the need arise (Morgan, 1986). The question is, however, how much redundancy of functions should be built into each entity? In practice it is impossible for everybody to be skilled in all the jobs in the organisation.

Hence a second trait is necessary to counterbalance the principle of redundancy, namely *requisite variety*. This principle was originally coined by Ross Ashby (1960). He suggested that the internal diversity of any self-regulating system must match the variety and complexity of its environment. In an organisational context this means that all entities of an organisation should embody critical aspects of the environment thus being able to cope with the challenges they are facing or likely to face (Morgan, 1986). The combined effect of the two principles matches the reactive-responsive and proactive-adaptive approaches as defined in this paper. However, to be proactive-creative two more principles are needed: the principle of minimum critical specification and the principle of multi-levelled cohesion (see figure 7).

Minimum critical specification suggests that leaders should create conditions to enhance flexibility and creativity rather than define organisational procedures as detailed as possible. Flexibility means that roles and behaviour can respond adaptively and creatively to changes in the environment. According to the interactive paradigm, inquiry provides a much better form of proactive-creative approach than pre-designed procedures and position-fixed roles. Minimum critical specification reverses the bureaucratic principle of clear and precise description of every role and procedure in the organisation. It helps to keep the organisation adaptive and creative in relation to current and prospective challenges from the environment. However, there is a risk that it may result in chaos. Even though chaos cannot be predicted, it is possible to set up some frames to handle such a risk, namely multi-levelled cohesion.

In general, *multi-levelled cohesion* are the forces which keep the organisation together by providing a shared sense of trust not only within special groups but also across groups and sections. It provides a frame of common interpretation and meaning by sharing values, visions and occasional rituals. A high degree of division of labour and flexibility may result in fragmental groups and competing sub-cultures, and thus less cohesion. For instance, development engineers may take a different view than production engineers or people in the sales division. Employees at the shop floor may be grouped in several sub-cultures. Different ethnic groups may also give rise to different norms and pattern of behaviour. These forms of sub-cultures can contribute creatively to proactive approaches and transformational learning, but the precondition is, that they all share a sense of value or knowledge based trust across the sub-cultures as illustrated in figure 8.

Figure 8: Levels of trust stability and trust cohesion.

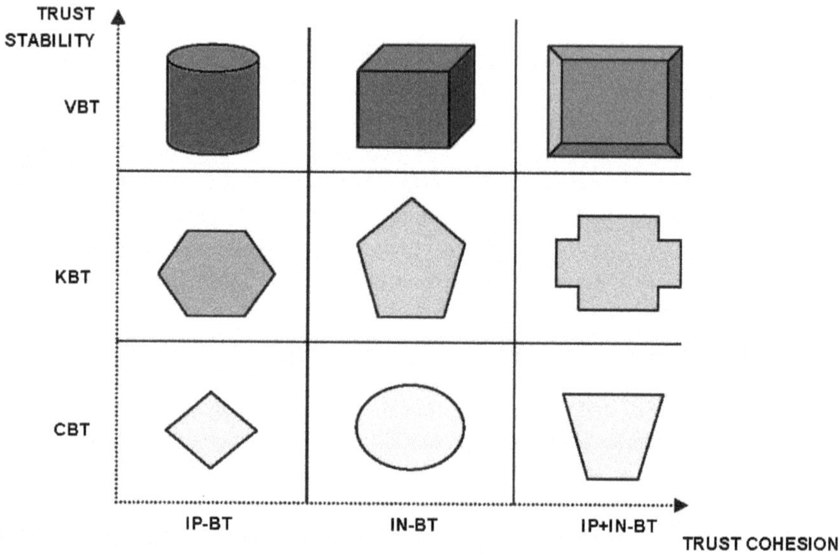

CBT: Calculus Based Trust IP-BT: Inter-Personal Based trust
KBT: Knowledge Based Trust IN-BT: Institutional Based trust
VBT: Value Based trust IP+IN-BT: Inter-Personal + Institutional Based Trust

Calculus based trust (CBT) is grounded in rewards and punishments depending on the pursuit respectively violation of the trusted agreements. Hence, CBT encourages only limited levels of knowledge sharing necessary to fulfil the formalised requirements of the contract.

Knowledge based trust (KBT) relies on knowledge about the involved actors developed through interaction over time. The assumption is that more knowledge about each other makes one able to predict the other's behaviour in a more precise way. KBT is more stable and stronger than CBT, because it is based on a more consistent understanding of why the actors is pursuing or deviating from the initial agreements.

Value based trust (VBT) means that the actors are sharing common values and interests. The common ground facilitates the sharing of knowledge, norms, needs and preferences. VBT is created either because the actors belong to similar cultural roots, or because they have recognized and learned from each other through interaction and collaboration. VBT is more stable than CBT and KBT, because sharing common values is normally associated with deeper levels of the individual or organisation than common knowledge and calculus based behaviour.

The other dimension illustrated in figure 8 is the level of *trust cohesion*. Cohesion refers to the degree in which different elements is bound together either by interpersonal, institutional or both kinds of relationships. *Interpersonal based trust (IP-BT)* is a trust relationship developed between two or more individuals based on either CBT, KBT or VBT. *Institutional based trust (IN-BT)* is formal agreements between two or more institutions independent of the persons involved. Finally, *IP+IN-BT* is trust where interpersonal as well as the institutional trust relationships are existing based on either CBT, KBT or VBT (see figure 8). The assumption is that a trust relationship becomes stronger when it develops more stable and/or more cohesive attributes, and weaker when it is developing less stable and/or less cohesive attributes. Thus the strongest trust relationship is a VBT bound together by both interpersonal and institutional relationships. The weakest trust relationship is CBT depending on interpersonal based trust relationships only. By focusing on the relationships between organisational routines and how they affect and are affected by experiential learning, it is possible to enhance the level from calculus and interpersonal based trust to knowledge and value based trust sustained at the institutional as well as at the interpersonal levels. Proactive methods like search conference, scenario workshops, future creating workshops, interactive planning, interactive design games and participative SWOT helps the participants to focus on these relationships and transform them into learning at a higher complexity level (see figure 4).

Summing up, transformational learning requires:

- An unrestricted and transparent knowledge flow between knowledge creation, knowledge sharing, knowledge practice, and knowledge accumulation anywhere in the organisation.
- A continuous and parallel interaction between generative, facilitating and adaptive leadership to ensure the unrestricted and transparent knowledge flow and transformational learning.
- A dynamic and interactive relationship between four organisational principles: redundancy of functions, requisite variety, minimum critical specification and multi-levelled cohesion. The implementation of these relationships helps to create space and surplus resources and willingness to participate in both reactive and proactive approaches of knowledge flow and transformational learning.

On the one hand, proactive methods can only be successfully applied where knowledge flow, interactive leadership and the four principles of organisation already are present to a certain extent. On the other hand, the application of proactive methods can help the members of the organisation to achieve a higher level of transformational learning.

Conclusions and perspectives

Reactive and proactive approaches are to be considered as complementary along a continuum, rather than as a mutually exclusive dichotomy. However, past and current participatory approaches tend to be reactively oriented, rather than focus on prospective needs. Some of these approaches have proved to be successful within a short term perspective as 'experimental gardens'. But often these 'gardens' have been isolated from the other parts of the organisation and created 'an organisational improvement paradox' (Goodman and Rousseau, 2004). Others have faded away as soon as the external funding of the project ended. Though not being able to survive in an ordinary organisational structure, many of them have contributed with new methodological knowledge and devices to be used in other approaches. However, more comprehensive and long term approaches are needed to cope with the rising complexity and dynamics of global and local environments. A number of proactive methods are available for instance search conferences, scenario workshops, future creating workshops, interactive planning procedures, design games and participatory SWOT. Each of them can be used to initiate organisational transformation through participatory approaches. Or they can be combined as in the example of search conference and interactive scenario analysis. Using these methods proactively enhance the integration of academic knowledge and daily experiences in a transformational learning process. The challenge is to transform implicit assumptions and experiences into explicit themes of action in order to achieve practical change and theoretical understanding at the same time. However, to be able to apply these methods successfully presupposes certain requirements and abilities of the organisations. The main obstacles against the successful use of participatory proactive approaches are lack of time and incentives, rigid hierarchies, the piece-rate payment system, the resignation of employees, and the role conflict between middle-managers and workers. On the other hand, the ideal conditions for proactive approaches are unrestricted knowledge flow, interactive leadership and the implementation of principles like redundancy of functions, requisite variety, minimum critical specification and multi-levelled cohesion and trust. When these conditions are present to a certain extent and one or some of the above mentioned proactive and participative methods are used, a higher level of transformational learning can be achieved, focusing on an interactive change of values, norms and behaviour. Participatory and transformational learning is about aligning the operational and strategic levels of change and development by using *all* the possible abilities and resources in the organisation rather than only specialised 'experts' and managers. Participatory and transformational learning approaches can no longer meaningfully be considered as approaches to only help shop-floor workers achieve better working conditions. This social rationale has to be considered as a part of a much more comprehensive rationale including the economic rationale of much more effective employees and the political rationale of less power hierarchies. Such an integrative rationale can be developed and implemented by using participatory methodologies in a proactive-creative manner, because they can enhance the cross-sector and cross-cultural understanding and promote the creative and innovative capabilities of all the participants in the organisation.

Though the practical outcomes of participatory approaches have varied during the last decades (Eikeland, 2007; Summers and Hyman, 2005), two scientifically documented evidences are still in favour of promoting participatory approaches. *The first evidence* is that the navigation in a complex and dynamic world does not only depend on the excellence and price level of the products or services, nor just its market share, networks or technology. It depends on the organisational capabilities to elicit, harness and improve the human resources resident in their employees and managers too. Only when these resources get energized and activated, the organisation becomes an innovative and effective 'player' in a complex and dynamic environment (Steger, 2007).

The second evidence is that if people don't participate in and 'own' the novel idea or solution, the implementation will be only half-hearted at best and most likely fail (Schön, 1983; Rasmussen, 2004).

Despite these evidences *further research and methodological development* are needed in the following areas:

- Concerning the question of organisational obstacles of proactive approaches, further research is needed to identify other possible obstacles, and the possible interactive relationships between them.
- Further studies are also needed of the combined use of proactive-creative methods. For instance, which methods or combination of methods can meaningfully be applied in which situations and contexts?
- Further research is needed to study how the interactive processes between generative, facilitative and adaptive levels are influencing the use and outcomes of participatory approaches.
- So far, the majority of studies of the effect of employee participation have been 'snapshots' carried out within a relative short time span. More longitudinal studies of the economic, social and political effects of employee participation are needed to gain insight into the complex interaction between organisational structure, forms of leadership, knowledge flow systems and learning practices.

References

Agersnap, F. / Møldrups, P. / Junge, F. / Brinck, L. / and Westenholz, A. (1974): Danish experiments with new forms of cooperation on the shop floor. Personnal Review, 3 (3), 34-50

Alexander, I.F. / Maiden, N. (eds.) (2004): Scenarios, Stories, Use cases – Through the System Development life Style. John Wileys & Sons, UK

Allen, C. / Cunningham, I. / McArdle, L. (1991): Employee Participation and Involvement in the 1990s. Jim Conway Foundation, Sth, S

Alasoini, T. / Heikkila, A. / Ramstad, E. / Ylöstalo (2010): Promotion of participatory Workplace Practicies through a Publicly Funded programme: Experiences from Finland. (This Volume)

Argurén, S. / Edgren, S. (1980): New factories: job design through factory planning in Sweden. Swedish Employers' Confederation (SAF), Sth, S.

Argyris, C. / Schön, D.A. (1996): Organizational learning II: Theory, Method and practice. Addison Wesley Publishing Company, US

Argyris C. / Schön, D.A. (1978): Organizational learning: A theory of action perspective. Reading M.A. Addison-Wesley, US

Ashby, W.R. (1960): An Introduction to Cybernetics. Chapman & Hall, UK

Batt, R. / Appelbaum, E. (1995): Worker participation in diverse settings: does form affect the outcome, and, if so, who benefits?" British journal of Industrial Relations, Vol. 33 (3), pp. 23-37

Boje, D.M. (2002): narrative Methods for organizational and communication research. Sage Publications, UK

Broberg, O. (2007): Integrating ergonomics into engineering: empirical evidence and implications for the ergonomists'. Human Factors and Ergonomics in Manufacturing. Vol 17, pp 353-366

Brulin, G. (2001): The Third Task of Universities or How to Get Universities to Serve their Communities!" In: P. Reason and H. Bradbury (eds.): Handbook of Action Research. pp. 440-446 Sage Publications, UK

Campagnolo, G.M. (2008): Modelling practices and participation in technological implementation: cases from the manufacturing industry. (nuneo)

Cooley, M. (1987): Architect or Bee? Hogarth Press.

Corbett, J.M. / Rasmussen, L.B. / Rauner, F. (1991): Crossing the boarder. Springer Verlag, UK

Cressey, P. / Williams, R. (1990): Participation in change: new technology and the role of employee involvement. Dublin: European Foundation for Improvements in Living and Working Conditions, Ireland

Debowski, S. (2006): Knowledge management. John Wiley & Sons, Australia

DeLeon, P. (1997): Democracy and the policy Sciences. Albany N.Y. State University of N.Y. press.

Dreborg, K.H. (1996): Essence of Back casting. Futures, 28 (9), 813-828

Duell, Werner / Frei, Felix (Hrsg.) (1986): “Arbeit gestalten, Mitarbeiter beteiligen. Eine Heuristik qualifizierender Arbeitsgestaltung”, Band 77 der Schriftenreihe “Humanisierung des Arbeitslebens”, Frankfurt/Main, Campus

Ehn, P. (1988): Work-Oriented Design of Computer Artifacts. Arbetslivscentrum, Sth. S

Eijnatten, F.M. v. (1993): The paradigm that changed the Work Place. The Swedish Center for Working Life, Van Gorcum, Assen, NL.

Eikeland, Olav (2007): “Why should mainstream social researchers be interested in action research?”, International Journal of Action Research, 3 (1+2), 38-64

Emery, F.E. / Thorsrud, E. (1969): Form and content of industrial democracy. Some experiments from Norway and other European countries. Assen: Van Gorcum, NL

Emery, F.E. / Thorsrud, E. (1976): Democracy at work; the report of the Norwegian industrial democracy program. Martinus Nijhoff, Leiden, NL

Emery, M. / Purser, R.E. (1996): The search conference. Jossey-Bass Publishers, San Francisco. US

European Commission (2002): New Forms of Work Organisation: The Obstacles to Wider Diffusion. DG for Employment, Industrial Relations and Social Affairs.

Forsyth, A. / Gahan, P. / Howe, J. / Mitchell, R. (2006): Regulating for Innovation in Workplace Production and Employment Systems: A Preliminary Discussion of Issues and Themes. Paper presented to the 3rd Australian labour Law Association National Conference, Brishane, 22-23 September, 2006.

Fricke, W. (2010): Experiences on how to enhance participative and innovative capacities of employees in action reseach provesses (This Volume).

Fricke, W. (1983): Participatory research and the enhancement of workers' innovative qualifications. Journal of Occupational Behaviour. Vol. 4 : 73-87

Garibaldo, F. (2003): Action Research Toolkit I: The Search Conference. In: Gill, K.S. and Jain, A. (eds.) Navigating Innovations – Indo-European Cross-Cultural Experiences. Vol. 1: Brandt D. (ed.): Enterprises and Cooperation networks for regional development. India Research Press, India, p. 226-240

Godet, M. (2000): The Art of Scenarios and Strategic Planning: Tools and pitfalls.

Goodman, P.S. / Rousseau, D.M. (2004): Organizational change that produces results: The linkage approach. Academy of Management Executive, 2004 18(3): 7-19. Technological Forecasting and Social Change, 65: 3-22

Green, F. (2006): Demanding work: The paradox of job quality in the affluent economy. Princeton University Press, US

Gustavsen, B. (2001): Theory and Practice: the Mediating Discourse. In P. Reason and H. Bradbury: Handbook of Action Research. pp 17-26 . Sage Publications, UK

Gustavsen, B. / Hunnius, G. (1981): New patterns of work reform: The case of Norway. The University press, Oslo, N

Hawkins, P. (1994): Organisational learning: taking stock and facing the challenge. Management Learning, vol. 25 no. 1, pp. 71-82

Heijden, K. v.d. (2004): Scenarios: The Art and Practice of the Learning Organisation. John Wiley & Sons: Chichester, UK

Hoppmann, Klaus / Stötzel, Berthold: "Demokratie am Arbeitsplatz. Ein Modellversuch zur Mitwirkung von Arbeitnehmern an betrieblichen Entscheidungsprozessen", Band 20 der Schriftenreihe "Humanisierung des Arbeitslebens", Frankfurt/Main, Campus

Johnson, B. (2000): A Story is a Promise. Blue haven publishing, Oregon, US

Kemp-Benedict, E. (2004): From Narrative to Number: A Role for Quantitative models in Scenario Analysis (www.iemss.org/iemss2004/pdf/scenario/ kemp-from.pdf)

Keune, H. / Goorden, L. (2002): Interactive back casting: a sustainable energy future for Belgium. Centre for Technology, Energy & Environment. University of Anwerpen (in Dutch)

Kristiansen, Marianne (2007) "Relational and Existential Challenges of Practicing Dialogical Action Research – Working with Social Concrete Blocks in Organizations", International Journal of Action Research, 3 (1+2), 15-37

Lysgaard, Sverre (1961): Arbeiderkollektivet. Oslo Universitetsforlag, N

Læssøe J. / Rasmussen, L.B. (1989): Human Centred Methods. Reproset, DK

Lindgren, M. / Bandhold, H. (2003): Scenario Planning: The Link between future and strategy Palgrave Macmillan UK

Lovins, A. (1976): Energy Strategy: the road not taken? In: Foreigh Affairs, pp. 186-217

Marchington, M. (2000): Teamworking and employee involvement: terminology, evaluation and context. In: Procter, S. and Mueller, F. (eds.): Teamworking. Macmillan, pp. 107-128

Marion, R. / Uhl-Bien, M. (2007): Paradigmatic Influence and leadership. The perspectives of Complexity Theory and Bureaucratic Theory. In: Hazy, J.K et al. (eds.) (2007): Complex Systems Leadership Theory. ISCE Publishing, Mansfield US.

Mayo, E. (1949): The social problems of an Industrial Civilization. (Routledge & Kegan Paul, London, UK

Mehra, K. / Kalra, R.K. (2003): Applying the Action Research Toolkits: Women Empowerment through Dairy Entrepreneurship. In: Gill, K.S. and Jain, A.

(eds.) Navigating Innovations – Indo-European Cross-Cultural Experiences. Vol. 1: Brandt D. (ed.): Enterprises and Cooperation networks for regional development. India Research Express, India. pp 259-293

Mintzberg, H. (1994): The Rise and Fall of Strategic Planning. Prentice Hall, UK

Morgan, G. (1986): Images of organizations. Sage, UK

Quist, J. / Vergragt, P.J. (2004): Back casting for Industrial Transformations and System Innovations Towards Sustainability: Relevance for Governance? In: Klaus Jacob, Manfred Binder and Anna Wieszorek (eds.): Governance for Industrial Transformation. Proceedings of the 2003 Berlin Conference on the Human Dimensions of Global Environmental Change. Environmental Policy Research Centre: Berlin pp. 409-437

Rasmussen, L.B. (1998): Learning Cultures. AI & Society, 12, 3, 134-154

Rasmussen, L.B. (2003): Action Research Toolkit II: The Scenario Workshop. In: Gill, K.S. and Jain, A. (eds.) Navigating Innovations – Indo-European Cross-Cultural Experiences. Vol. 1: Brandt D. (ed.): Enterprises and Cooperation networks for regional development. India Research Express, India. P. 241-258

Rasmussen, L.B. (2004): 'Sustainable entrepreneurship and quality of work', in F. Garibaldo / V. Telljohann (eds.), Globalisation, Company Strategies and Quality of Working Life in Europe, Frankfurt/M. et al., Peter Lang, pp. 251-278.

Rasmussen, L.B. (2005): The narrative aspect of scenario building – How story telling may give people a memory of the future. AI & Society, 19: 229-249

Rasmussen, L.B. (2008): Models for Sustainable Development – A Danish-Chinese Approach to regional development of education, work and technology based on a multi-dimensional understanding of sustainability. In: Szell, G. / C.-H. Bösling, U.Szell: Education, labour & science: Perspectives for the 21st Century, pp. 197-232, Peter Lang, Internationaler Verlag der Wissenschaften, Frankfurt a.M., Germany 2008.

Robinson, J. (2003): Future Subjunctive: back casting as social learning. Futures, 35, 839-843

Schön, D.A. (1983): The Reflective Practitioner – How Professionals Think in Action. New York, N.Y., Basic Books

Schwartz, P. (1991): The Art of the long View. Doubleday, N.Y. US

Steger, U. / Amann, W. / Maznevski, M. (2007): Managing Complexity in Global Organizations. John Wiley & Sons, London, UK

Summers, J. / Hyman, J. (2005): Employee participation and company performance. A review of literature. York publishing Design, Ltd, UK

Surie, G. / Hazy, J.K. (2007): Generative leadership: Nurturing Innovation in complex systems. In: Heckscher, C. and P.S. Adler (eds.) (2007): The firm as a Collaborative Firm. pp 349-366. Oxford University Press, UK

Trist, E. / Higgins, G. / Murray, H. and Pollock, A. (1963): Organizational Choice. Tavistock, London, UK

Ulich, Eberhard (1980): "Bericht über die arbeits- und sozialpsychologische Begleitforschung" in: "Gruppenarbeit in der Motorenmontage – ein Vergleich von Arbeitsstrukturen", Band 3 der Schriftenreihe "Humanisierung der Arbeit", S. 97-142, Frankfurt/Main, Campus

Wack, Pierre (1985): Scenarios: Shooting the rapids. Harvard Business Review. 63(6), S. 139-150

Weber, M. (1930): The Protestant Ethic and the Spirit of Capitalism. Parsons, Transl. ISBN 9780486427034 (2003)

Weltz, Friedrich / Lullies, Veronika (1983): "Innovation im Büro. Das Beispiel Textverarbeitung", Band 38 der Schriftenreihe "Humanisierung des Arbeitslebens", Frankfurt/Main, Campus

Workspace design: participation in collaborative design processes

Ole Broberg

1. Introduction

Many ergonomists and other workplace professionals are placed in consultative positions like in the occupational health service (OHS) in Denmark. The OHS system in Denmark has recently undergone a major change from being a mandatory system for companies to a system operating at a liberalized market. Throughout the years it has always been a prominent goal for the OHS units to be proactive by trying to integrate safety and health aspects into the design stage of socio-technical changes in workplaces. However, when dealing with socio-technical change processes in client enterprises, experience shows that it is often difficult for the OHS consultant to get access to and influence the design process from a safety and health point of view. In a previous study it has been shown that the ability to take on the role as a 'political reflective navigator' might be a success factor in such cases (Broberg / Hermund, 2004). However, instead of trying to 'push' safety and health into the design process, the OHS consultants could take on another role. The role as 'workspace designer' might be a new approach for integrating safety and health into workplace design processes. In this role, the OHS consultant takes a more design-oriented approach with a focus on staging the workspace design process. This might contribute to the overcoming of some of the identified obstacles to integrate safety and health into design processes (Broberg, 2007).

The Danish Workspace Design (WSD) research program is aimed to develop and trial such a potential new concept for OHS consultants to engage in design processes which imply new or changed workplaces. The notion of workspace design is inspired by the work of Horgen (Horgen et al., 1999). The workplace with work practices is seen as embedded in four dimensions: spatial, organizational, financial, and technological (SOFT), see Figure 1.

These dimensions are interdependent and in a dynamic relationship with one another. A change in one dimension may demand changes in others as well. The staging of the workspace design process is aimed at creating a dynamic coherence between work and these four dimensions of the workspace. The creation and shaping of workplaces are processes that are influenced by the actors who populate each of the four corners. The basic idea of the concept of workspace design is that actors are needed who are capable of working across the four corners, facilitating and negotiating the process of workplace-making with the different actors. These actors are staging the workspace design process, they are workspace designers. This is a job of creating shared visions among actors with different perspectives and competencies, overcoming resistance and political interests, setting up a collaborative design process, and facilitating meetings between actors from different corners in the SOFT model.

Figure 1: The SOFT model

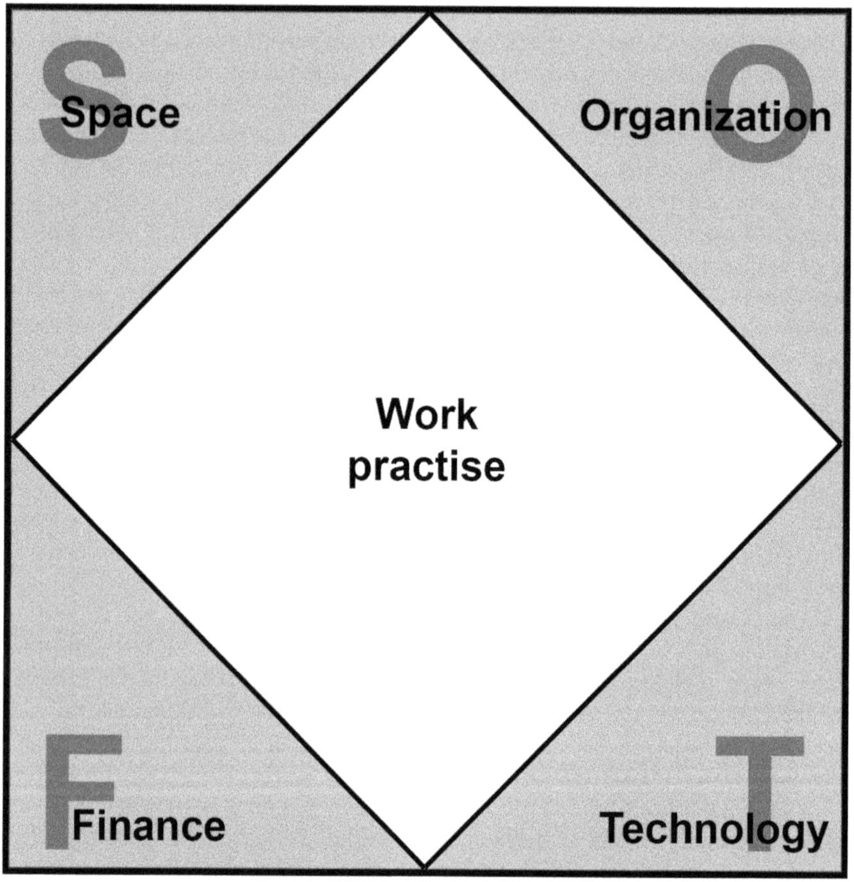

Source: Horgen et al. (1999)

Additionally, it is a core feature of the workspace design concept that staging the process is based on user participation. This implicates that methodologies and tools for user participation are important elements of the concept. And finally, the concept is aimed at helping organizations to create effective as well as sound workplaces, meaning healthy and safe work conditions and good ergonomics.

In the WSD research program the interventions in two trial cases had the form of workshops inspired by Scandinavian methods in the field of participatory design (Greenbaum / Kyng, 1991; Brandt / Messeter, 2004; Johansson et al., 2002). Hence it became an important question how to 'transmit' and sustain insights into and results from workshops into the ongoing socio-technical change project in the organisations.

The objective of this paper is to report on the trial of the workspace design concept in a case involving the design and implementation of a new mixing technology in an industrial plant[1]. The research questions based on this case study were: 1) How do participatory WSD workshops contribute to the engineering design process? 2) How are insights and ideas from workshops transmitted to and sustained in the ongoing engineering design process of an organization? 3) What sort of navigation tools is needed to be a workspace designer in an organizational context?

Finally, the paper will shortly discuss some perspectives on workers participation in socio-technical change processes. The case presented can be seen within the field of user-centred design. This philosophy and design methodology has been criticised for a micro-level approach to technology change not contributing to really new visions and scenarios of technology design (Rasmussen, 2007).

2. Research approach and the role of researchers

The test of the Workspace Design (WSD) concept took place in three case companies. In this paper I report an analysis of an industrial manufacturing case in which a company was to implement a new mixing technology in their production line. The WSD team consisted of three researchers from the Technical University of Denmark, two consultants from the Danish Technological Institute, two researchers from the Centre for Design Research, and two OHS consultants from the OHS unit that normally served the industrial manufacturer.

This team tried to take the role as workspace designer in relation to the technological change process. The team was partially split up into interventionists and follow-up researchers. The first group was responsible for the planning and completion of activities aimed at setting up a participatory design process in the company in order to optimize ergonomics and efficiency in the production facility

1 This paper is a revised version of an article to be published in International Journal of Technology Management.

being designed. The other group was responsible for establishing a baseline of data on: Basic features of the company, current production system, including ergonomics, the course of the design process so far, and the level of occupational safety and health management. This group also observed the interventions and made follow-up interviews with participants in order to clarify the effects of the intervention.

The OHS consultants were part of the first group. In this way a potential new role of the OHS consultant was developed in a mutual learning process. The idea was that the activities planned and completed in this group could be the job of the OHS consultants in their future consultancy tasks for companies.

3. Staging the workspace design process

The basic idea in the WSD research program was to trial the role as workspace designer in socio-technical change projects within different organisations. We had a theoretical idea of this role based on the SOFT model, and we had beforehand a collection of methods based on the experience gained by the WSD team members from their previous work. It was, however, during the intervention case studies that we gained experience on how to practice the role and use the methods in particular organisational and technological contexts. Based on the experience gathered from two case studies, we developed a model for a workspace designer to intervene in socio-technical change projects (Figure 2). In this model the workspace designer is seen as navigating concurrently on three different stages.

In *setting the stage* the workspace designer investigates and negotiates the frames and networks surrounding the socio-technical change project in the organisation. This will typically be based on meetings with management and representatives from the employees. Having the SOFT model in mind, the workspace designer enquires into the status of the change project by asking what in the four corners is open to alternative options and what seems to be closed. It is important to be critical as to what is declared as being closed by the involved actors. It often turns out that closed issues can be reopened. The SOFT model also points to relevant actors to be considered as participants in the intervention activities. In this phase, the workspace designer is negotiating with organisational members on the goal of the intervention, the resources to be put into the intervention, who should participate, and how insights and results from the intervention are transmitted to and sustained in the ongoing socio-technical change project.

Figure 2: The workspace design stages

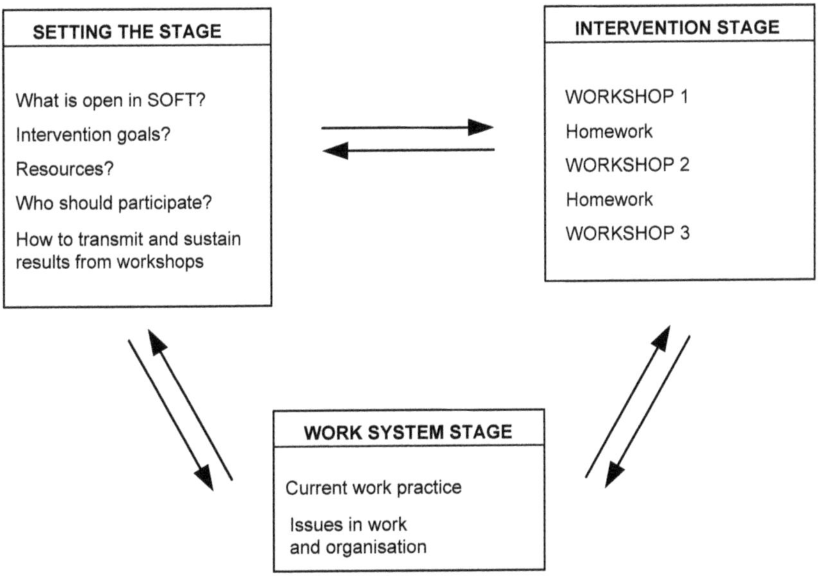

The workspace designer has to gain a basic understanding of the *work system* in the organisation or in the relevant part of the organisation in question. The issue here is to understand the basic features of the production system, work practices and working conditions. It also includes getting an idea of what is being debated in the work system, what are the current issues to be solved in the employee / management relations? Obtaining this understanding might be a concurrent process to setting the stage.

Based on the experience acquired from two cases, *the interventions* took a similar overall format. This was a format consisting of a series of workshops with intermediate periods of homework. A series of workshops must be coherent in a way which ensures that participants can see they are moving forwards towards a certain goal. The process and expected outcome of the workshop series must be presented to the participants before starting. At the same time, due to the particular organisational context and the progress of the socio-technical project, the workspace designer must be prepared to navigate. In our second case study, a public administration office, actors in the change project unexpectedly speeded up the process of designing new open space offices. This forced the WSD team to propose an adjustment in the planned series of workshops to match this speed-up. Another general experience in the intervention phase is that having two overall activities seem to work well: first, using tools and methods that are aimed at setting up a collaborative inquiry into the current work practice and workplace. Second, using tools and methods directed towards the future work practice and workplace as a result of the socio-technical change project. In the second activity it seems fruitful to emphasize the notion of 'laboratory'. Participants in the workshops are inquiring into several possible futures, they are doing experiments with the future workplace (Binder, 2007).

After a presentation of the industrial manufacturer case study the model in Figure 2 will be used to give an account for the WSD navigation and intervention in this particular context.

4. The industrial manufacturer case

The company is manufacturing so-called socks for the renovation of piping, especially sewage piping. The key process at the company is the impregnation of socks with chemical mixtures that allow the socks to harden up when installed in piping. The mixing of chemicals into different prescriptions takes place in batch processes located in the mixing plant. The production system implicates much manual handling of barrels and bags by the 4-5 operators. Exposures to vapours and dust are also part of a work environment that is considered to be problematic by all parties involved in the company.

The production management and the company safety organization initiated the socio-technical change project. In different contexts the reason to start the project was stated as being one of the following two or a combination of them both: 1) The production capacity had to be increased due to a growing number of orders, 2) The current production facility suffered from severe work environment problems, and an official order from the Danish Work Environment Agency was under its way. The company engaged two external design engineers as consultants to the project. They first worked on a project replacing the current batch technology with new batch technology. During their work, however, they identified a German machine supplier who was able to develop continuous working machinery for the mixing process. It was subsequently decided that they should opt for this solution, and the two design engineers drew up a requirements specification for such machinery. The new production system would be a closed system with automatic inflow of raw materials, thereby improving some aspects of the work environment considerably.

At the time of the WSD intervention the new mixing machine was specified and ordered. During the process of building the machine the supplier was participating in his own workshop. The design engineers had made two proposals for the layout in the empty production hall where the new machinery was to be installed. Both proposals were based on an optimization of the piping in the new facility, as the length of the pipes could be a critical factor due to a risk of hardening up of raw materials in the pipes.

Table 1 gives an overview of the WSD activities in this case, showing the three stages at which the WSD team was navigating.

Table 1: Workspace design activities at the industrial manufacturer

Stage	**Activity**
Setting the stage	Two meetings with the project manager. Signing of agreement on collaboration.
Work system	Work environment screening by WSD team walk-through in current production facility
Work system	WSD team interview operators, production planner and production manager
Setting the stage	First meeting with participation of the two consulting design engineers.
Work system	WSD team members doing a walk-through with operators taking photos for a workbook.
Setting the stage	Presentation of intervention plan to project manager and design engineers and allocation of tasks.
Intervention: Workshop 1	Presentation of workbooks. Layout design game based on proposal from design engineers (meeting room)
Homework	The operators design their layout
Intervention: Workshop 2	Layout design game based on operators' proposal (meeting room)
Setting the stage	Meeting with OHS coordinator and production planner on planning of use scenarios.
Work system	Meeting with project manager and OHS coordinator. Identification of incidents in current production system.
Intervention: Workshop 3	Use scenario with focus on work procedures, machinery and layout (production hall)
Homework	Contact to machine supplier
Intervention: Workshop 4	Use scenario with focus on OHS conditions in the new facility (production hall)

5. Setting the stage

In starting up the WSD project we had difficulties in recruiting companies that were willing to serve as trial cases. The industrial manufacturer company was recruited due to one of the OHS consultants in the team. Her husband had a job in the corporation, which owned the company. She gave him a pamphlet describing the WSD project. He, in turn, gave this pamphlet to the occupational health and safety coordinator in the company. The OHS coordinator then contacted the WSD project manager, and a meeting was set up. The participants were: The WSD project manager and one of the OHS consultants, the OHS coordinator of the company and the production manager, who also was the project manager of the technology project. Shortly after this meeting, a new meeting took place due to some uncertainty in the WSD team as to whether the company in question would be an appropriate case. Some team members were afraid that too many decisions were taken; leaving only limited space for the intervention. This time the meeting was between a consultant from the Danish Technological Institute and the OHS consultant from the first meeting. The agenda was to clarify the current status of the socio-technical change project and mutual expectations and requirements. The meeting resulted in a formal agreement on collaboration. The agreement stated that the company would receive assistance to ensure the best possible working conditions in the new facility and to enable a process of workers' participation and involvement. The agreement also stated that a contact between the machine supplier and the WSD project should be established. On the other hand, the agreement ensured the WSD project the "rights" to trial tools and methods, and to disseminate the results. The overall goal of the WSD activities in the company was stated: ".. to ensure a holistic shaping of new or redesigned workplaces which are healthy for the employees and effective for the company".

The WSD team represented by the OHS consultant presented a plan for two workshops that were to focus on the layout of the new production hall. This was the result of the inquiries into the current socio-technical change process in the company. In the WSD team we had discussions on the 'closed' and 'open' issues in the change process. The new machine was being built in the workshops of the German supplier, and this seemed to be a closed issue in the meaning that it would be difficult to change the specifications and alter the machine. But the layout in the empty production hall seemed to be open to alternatives. The two design engineers had made two proposals for the layout, but nothing was decided. The plan was presented to the project manager and the OHS coordinator, and we requested the project manager to enlist the two external design engineers in the workshops. The project manager agreed on that.

6. Work systems

In order to gain an insight into the work system and work environment of the company, the WSD team completed a walk-through with the operators and the safety representative of the mixing plant (work environment screening). This was followed by interviews with the operators, the production planner and the project manager on the working of the current production system, including normal incidents that had to be handled. Finally, the WSD team took a walk-through with the operators and a digital camera. The operators were told to pick out motives from the production system based on the following code: Things that are considered problematic and hence should not be transferred to the new production system (red), things that work well and should be retained in the system (green), and things that require attention (yellow). Twelve photos were then selected to a workbook. The workbook was placed in the control room for a period of one week. In this period the operators commented on the photos by using the colour code in drawing and writing. The safety representative and the OHS consultant prepared similar workbooks.

7. Interventions

The intervention by the WSD team was organized as two collaborative events, each consisting of two workshops. Each workshop had duration of approximately three hours. The events were design games (Horgen et al., 1999; Johansson et al., 2002; Brandt / Messeter, 2004) aimed at staging the meeting between the production management, two consulting design engineers and three employees of the mixing plant. The design game format was aimed at facilitating a collaborative design process between these actors. In the first event the workshops were focusing on the layout of the new plant in which the new mixing machine was to be installed. In the second event the two workshops were organized as use scenarios, aiming at simulating work processes and ergonomics in the new plant.

7.1 The layout design game

The first event was a layout design game that took place in a meeting room in the company. As a starter to this workshop, the workbooks were presented by the OHS consultant, the safety representative and the operators to give an overview of known, but also not hitherto identified, problems. Important issues were added as ‘one-liners’ to a compilation, which was put on the wall in the form of a poster. Next, the design engineers shortly presented how the new machine was working.

Figure 3: The layout design game

The WSD team had produced game boards and gaming pieces. During the two workshops, the participants were sitting around a game board placed in the middle of the table (Figure 3). The game board was a sketch of the floor plan of the existing mixing plant and the adjacent hall in which the new mixing machine was to be placed. Coloured cardboard pieces represented different artefacts in the plant. A WSD team member was designated as game master, and he instructed the participants that the purpose of the design game was to set up a collaborative design process on the layout of the new mixing plant. He also stressed that the workshop was a sort of a 'laboratory' in which participants had the opportunity to explore different layout possibilities.

In the first workshop the game board was based on the design engineers' proposal for layout. This layout was printed to the game board and was not moveable. The coloured gaming pieces represented different issues in relation to workplace design, work tasks, and equipment. The participants filled them in during the game. In this way, all the participants could make enquiries to the design engineers' proposal and this procedure resulted in a number of possible solution proposals to identified problems. At the end of the workshop homework was scheduled to the second workshop. The design engineers should check up on some machine features, the production manager and the OHS coordinator should investigate into regulations on fire and chemicals. Finally, the production manager suggested that the operators should work on a new proposal for layout.

The second workshop started with reports from the production manager and the design engineers on their homework. Next, the operators presented their layout proposal step-by-step at a game board with moveable gaming pieces, each representing machines and equipment. During the game they explained their reasons and ideas and a collaborative design process started up. In the end, the game board was representing a layout including many of the operators' proposals, but during the collaborative design process other things had been changed.

Figure 4: The layout game board

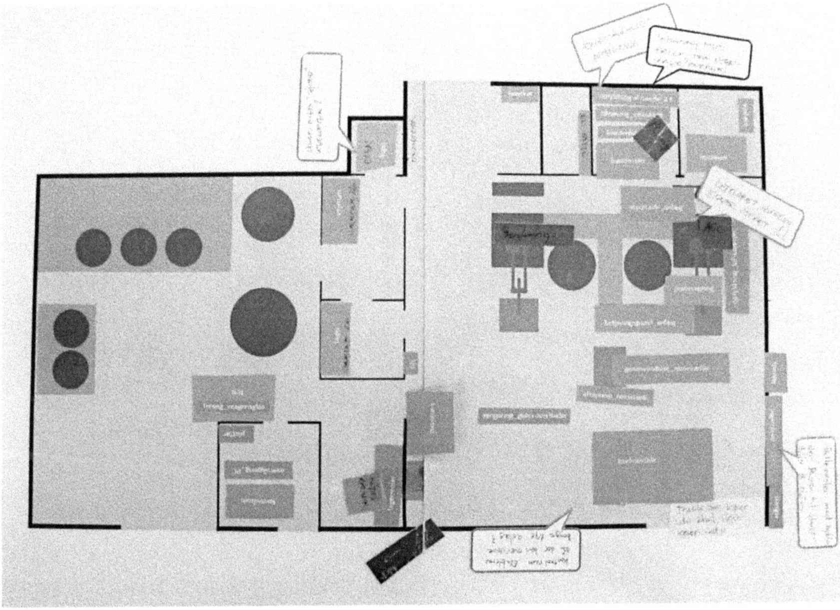

In short, the outcome of the layout design game was a proposal for the layout of the new mixing plant that was quite different from the two proposals originally made by the two consulting design engineers. Especially, the work practice experience and ideas brought in by the employees had a profound influence on the new proposal for layout and also included important aspects of ergonomics. The employees were able to highlight things that had not been considered by the design engineers. The design engineers had not considered maintenance and storage. Such facilities were part of the new lay out design. The physical product of the layout design game was the game board with a floor plan on which the cardboard pieces illustrating the machine and other artefacts were placed in new ways (Figure 4).

Figure 5: Use scenario in the production hall

7.2 The use scenario workshops

In the second collaborative event a use scenario was set up by the WSD team. The idea was to explore more closely the ergonomics and future work practice related to the operation of the new mixing machine in the surroundings designed during the layout workshops. Simulating future work processes through scenarios taking place in the empty hall designated for the new mixing plant did this. The WSD team produced two artefacts to facilitate the use scenario. The first was a 1:20 scale model of the new plant with movable representations of machines and devices (Figure 5). The second was the placement of tape markers on the floor, representing the machines and new walls in the empty hall according to the results of the layout game. The scale model was placed on a table in the empty hall, and the use scenarios started out by having the participants standing around the model. At the same time, it was possible to move around in the new mixing plant by looking at the tape markers on the flooring. The WSD team applied two different kinds of use scenarios. In both cases the participants were the production management, the two consulting design engineers, and three employees from the mixing plant. A WSD team member was game master.

7.3 Use scenario with incident cards

At the first use scenario the production manager and the employees were asked by the WSD game master to go through the process of what would be expected to be a normal production scenario with the new machine. By doing so they were pointing to the scale model. Then the WSD team had prepared incident cards on which realistic production incidents were described. These events had been identified through interviews with employees and production management and were based on experience acquired from the operation of the existing mixing plant. An example is the following instruction: "You have started the weekly cleaning process. Suddenly you spot a leaky valve. Approximately five litres of fluid have spilled out on the floor, and it is still leaking. It smells like an organic solvent. What do you do?" The idea was to open up for a collaborative inquiry of how actual production events could be handled at the new mixing plant with a machine based on new principles. The employees took turns taking a card, and together the employees discussed how they would deal with this event in the new facility. The other participants joined the open reflection by answering questions or putting forward their points of view. WSD team members continuously registered the identified potential problems and ideas to solve them on flip charts. During this session, the production manager made an 'on-the-spot' design decision because he realized that a vacuum tank had to be moved from one room to another. Afterwards the flip charts were systematized by the WSD team in a document and handed out to all participants. All items from the flip charts were placed in three categories: Hall layout, the technical system, and work procedures. Items requiring further investigation were registered too and persons to be responsible for the homework were appointed.

7.4 Use scenario simulating workplace assessment

The second use scenario took place in the same setting as the first with the same participants. Now the work environment and ergonomics in the new mixing plant were to be investigated with the aim of being proactive. The workshop was staged by the WSD team with the following scenario: "The new plant has now been running for two years, and today the OHS consultant comes for a visit to carry out a workplace assessment". A workplace assessment is a systematic mapping of the work environment and measures and is mandatory according to Danish law.

Figure 6: Simulation of workplace assessment in the production hall

The OHS consultant was then taken on a walk-through of the new plant by the employees (Figure 6). Moving around the tape markings at the floor and looking at the 3 D scale model did this. During the tour, the OHS consultant asked a lot of specific questions on work procedures, workplace design, equipment and personal protections. All participants reflected openly upon these questions, and potential problems and ideas for solutions were registered by the WSD team, and afterwards were systematized in a document and handed out to the participants. This time, the items were categorized by rooms at the new mixing plant, e.g. the control room, the mixing room, the chemicals storage room. Based on the two use scenario sessions, the production manager made several changes to the requirements specifications for the new facility. A vacuum tank was moved from one room to another. The machine supplier was asked to modify a detail in the machine allowing for mixing additives when the machine is operating. In an evaluation of the workshops he stated: *I am sure we have saved a lot of resources by doing it in this way. Otherwise we would have to make changes afterwards.* The OHS consultant stated: *Overall, it was a really good session. It was fantastic effective to envisage the future production system and the work in it. The workers were much more engaged, maybe because they were expected to contribute.*

8. Participatory WSD contributions to the socio-technical change process

How did the participatory WSD workshop sessions contribute to the design of a new production line in the mixing plant? As mentioned in the introduction, the trial of the WSD concept may be seen as an intervention in a technology design project to promote more humanistic technology (Badham et al., 2001; Garrety / Badham, 2004). Actor-network theory (ANT) offers a framework for understanding the manner in which new socio-technical objects come to be built or assembled. ANT focuses on technology in the making (Latour, 1987). In this framework technology design projects are understood as a process of changing networks of social and technical relations. The role of technology designers are discussed by introducing the concept of "script" (Akrich, 1992). When engineers are designing a machine or a production system they make hypothesis about the context in which the machine or system is to be used. They define users and prescribe how users associate with the technology. As stated by Akrich:

> A large part of the work of innovators is that of "inscribing" this vision of (or prediction about) the world in the technical content of the new object. I will call the end product of this work a "script" or a "scenario". (Akrich, 1992, p. 208)

This is in line with the concept of "configuring the user". Configuring during the design process includes defining the identity of future users, and setting constraints upon their likely future actions in relation to the object (Woolgar, 1991). Both concepts are based on a distinction between the projected user and the real user, and thus the designer is working with different representations of the user.

In this specific case, however, the practise of the WSD concept implied that the real users were involved in inscribing their visions of the new production line in the script. The two design engineers were under way with a script which was not very specific about the users of the new production facility. They were mostly concerned with optimizing the piping, and hence the work of the operators was not articulated. In this way it is hard to say that a configuration of the user had taken place. The engineers were designing the technical system and leaving the work tasks unidentified. The layout design games, and later on the use scenarios, became a reframing of the design object in the engineering design process, hence developing a "stronger" script setting up more explicit the relationships between the new machine and the operators. Bringing in the work practices of the operators and their reflections on conduct in the new system enlarged the design object to include a redesign of the new production facility, work procedures, equipment, cleaning, maintenance and a number of work environment features. This contrasted to the original work of the design engineers, which primarily focused on piping and layout of the technical components.

The use scenarios explored the new production system as a result of the design process in the layout game workshops. The set-up of the scenarios was a mixture of two main media for simulation (Daniellou, 2006): Experimental simulation based on a prototype and a narrative simulation where participants built up an oral account of feasible ways of carrying out the future tasks. The use scenario with incidence cards proved to be a collaborative inquiry of the characteristics of the new production system adding to the script. Playing the scenarios revealed the difference between the employees' tasks and their conduct (Daniellou, 2005). The employees were not talking and reflecting about their formal tasks. They were talking about the difficulties they could foresee in the new production system and were thinking aloud about how to deal with these problems. By reflecting on the feasibility of conduct, a lot of factors were identified, factors that the design engineers and the production manager had not considered in the design of the new system.

How could the WSD workshops contribute to the process of shaping a script? Instead of working with representations of users, the designers were collaborating with the actual future operators of the facility in the WSD workshops. Seen from a social learning perspective, the workshops contributed to set up a temporary learning space in which the daily power relations, expert roles and decision-making processes receded. The WSD team set up the rules for the workshops, which all participants were to stick to. This learning space was also perceived as a laboratory in which experiments took place. The experiments were about a collaborative inquiry into the initial plans of the design engineers and subsequently a collaborative design process of the production facility based on inputs from future operators, design engineers, production management and the OHS consultant. By the design games the WSD team facilitated the meeting and initiated mutual learning processes between these actors from different corners of the SOFT model. The game board and the pieces, the scale model and the tape markings in the production hall were operating as appropriate 'boundary objects' (Wenger, 2000), allowing usable connections between different work practices. The workshop rules and these artefacts enabled multiple practices to initiate a collaborative design process because the artefacts could be comprehended and interpreted by all participants. The abstract term of "learning space" even became very tangible when we experienced the power of setting up the use scenarios in the actual production hall. An operator stated:

> It is really a good idea to bring people from different departments together in a room with sufficient time to discuss design and layout in-depth. And the icing of the cake was to be situated in the actual production hall instead of a meeting room. The design engineers, one of them a little bit reluctantly, also recognized the effect of the workshops. One of them stated: The starting point was to optimize the piping. Quite other things are now in focus, and the facility will look very different than designed from the beginning.

8.1 Transmitter devices between workshops and engineering design process

Setting up a temporary learning space or a lab was important to facilitate a collaborative design process. It was even more important, however, that the outcomes of the workshops were "transmitted" to daily life in the organization in order to enter into the engineering design process. It turned out that artefacts like the final version of the layout game board and a systematic compilation of documents served as important "transmitter substances". These artefacts contributed to sustain the insights and ideas from the workshops in a transparent way for all participants. The game board was a collaborative design product. It was a way of sustaining what at the end of the workshop was a shared understanding of the layout of the new mixing plant. The project manager himself was an important 'transmitter actor'. He used the transmitter substances to revise the requirements specification document, and by so doing he made the final transformation of workshop results into ordinary organizational documents in the engineering design process.

Sticking to the lab metaphor, Latour (1987) has coined the concept of inscriptions and inscription devices in his study of laboratory work and the construction of scientific facts (Latour, 1987; Latour / Woolgar, 1979). Inscription devices transform pieces of matter into written documents. As stated by Latour / Woolgar:

> More exactly, an inscription device is any item of apparatus or particular configuration of such items which can transform a material substance into a figure or diagram which is directly usable by one of the members of the office space" (Latour / Woolgar, 1979, p. 51)

The transmitter substances between the workshops (labs) and the engineering design process can be looked upon as inscriptions. Inscriptions are images of different kinds that have been extracted from laboratory instruments to appear cleaned, redrawn, and displayed (Latour, 1987). In our case, inscriptions were needed to transform the insights, ideas, and proposals from the workshops into details that could enter into the engineering design process. The layout game board became such an 'inscription' which was usable for the actors in the engineering design process. The game board transformed the layout experiments and collaborative design among the participants into a figure or drawing. This figure was placed in the company, and it was referred to after the workshops as the design of the new mixing plant. After leaving the lab, the game board inscription entered into what had been termed a political career (Henderson, 1999). The game board model entered into the political network of the company as a visual representation of the new facility that can be used by actors to garner support for the project.

The WSD team acted like an inscription device in producing inscriptions (PostIt's, bullet points at paper, gaming pieces) from the workshops (the lab) that can be transferred and understood in the engineering design process. The workshop sessions were like a lab, and instruments/inscriptions devices were needed to provide a visual display of the results of the experiments in the lab. The many processes taking place in the lab had to be partly de-contextualized in order to move them out of the lab.

The inscriptions from the use scenarios were compilations. It was, however, a transformation of the bullet points and other writings that had been recorded on flip charts during the scenarios. This text was analyzed and categorized by the WSD team and compiled in a schematic representation. The WSD team became the inscription device that recorded workshop activities and transformed them into figures in the form of systematized compilations of design requirements. The compilation format turned out to fit well with the engineering way of working, as it represented design requirements and proposals in a form that left the detailed design to the engineers. In the case of the layout game board, this inscription was constructed by the workshops participants themselves as the result of a collaborative design process.

8.2 Workspace designer navigation

In this case, the WSD team tried to act like a workspace designer. In order to understand the navigation needed in practising the workspace design concept, we constructed the model in Figure 2. The model sprang up based on our practical experience from two cases. In staging the workplace-making process, the workspace designer has to navigate at the three different stages.

When setting the stage, it was, in this case, important that the company contacted us and asked for help. They were motivated, partially because of pressure from the Labour Inspection, and partially because they were genuinely interested in learning how to involve the employees in socio-technical change projects. For the WSD team it was crucial that an alliance with the production manager, who was also the project manager of the technology design project, was in place right from the beginning.

The WSD team proposed that the project manager focus on the layout in two workshops to which he agreed. The team requested that the project manager ask the two external design engineers to take part in the workshops. Had the project manager not entered into this alliance, their attendance would have seemed doubtful. The project manager also approved that the design engineers' proposals could be subjected to a re-evaluation in the workshops. Further, the production manager showed his commitment by revising the requirements specification document based on results from the workshops.

The WSD team was navigating on behalf of a projected workspace designer; a task that in the future might be the task of the OHS consultants. One of the OHS consultants participating afterwards got a new position as occupational health and safety manager in the case company. In a follow-up interview she stated:

"It is a super product for an occupational health service to put on the market in relation to all kinds of changes in a company. In my new position as OHS manager I would engage a consultant to perform the WSD methods. I think it is important to have other persons manage the process who are not them selves engaged in the change process. I have strongly recommended the methods to others since my participation. It is a way of engaging the employees in an active manner".

9. Conclusions

The industrial manufacturer case showed how the WSD concept might contribute to an engineering design process. The WSD team took the role as workspace designers and by using participatory methods in workshops achieved a tangible impact on the technology design project. The layout was changed, new work procedures emerged, and measures related to the ergonomics and work environment were identified and specified in the design requirements. The technology project is not yet implemented in the company. Therefore, we are not able to demonstrate the effect of the WSD concept. The design plans, however, have been changed considerably with the acceptance of all the actors.

The design object, and therefore the script, changed from primarily focusing at piping and layout of the technical components to include work processes, procedures, and work environment factors. In the role as workspace designer it was important for the WSD team to make sure that the achievements in the workshops were transmitted to and sustained in the ordinary engineering design process. In this case it turned out that the artefacts such as the layout game board and compilations of ideas and requirements from the use scenarios served as appropriate transmitter devices or inscriptions. In taking the role as an inscription device, it seems important for the workspace designer to identify appropriate inscriptions as input to the engineering design process if the workshop results shall have a chance to impact on the further design process.

From a workers participation point of view, the WSD concept enables a real proactive form of participation. The workers were involved before the technology project was implemented. The proactive approach, however, is very fragile and highly dependent upon the moment that the workers are invited to participate. In the industrial manufacturer case the machine design was nearly completed at the time of the WSD intervention. The safety organization is the institutional participatory scheme in Danish companies. Hence, it seems to be very important that the workers' safety representatives are well informed about planned socio-technical changes. In the reported case, the safety representative was also a participant in the WSD interventions. This mixture of direct and representational participation seemed to be beneficial. In several occasions the safety representative was the foremost advocate for safety and health issues whereas the other operators often pursued a more production-oriented agenda.

This case, seen as user-centred design, confirms the micro-level approach to technology design. One should remember, however, that the aim of the WSD concept is to create effective as well as healthy workplaces when an organization undertakes a socio-technical change process. Therefore, it is at the micro-level technology design is handled. The idea is not to develop new alternative technologies for a market. The idea is to learn an organization participatory ways to explore and experiment with different socio-technical configurations when planning and designing a change. In a strategic perspective, we are learning OHS consultants and units to master the participatory WSD concept, and by that disseminate the approach to a wider number of organizations.

Acknowledgements

The Workspace Design research program is partially funded by the Danish Work Environment Research Fund.

References

Akrich, M. (1992): The de-scription of technical objects. In W.E.Bijker / J. Law (eds.), Shaping technology/building society: studies in sociotechnical change (pp. 205-224). Cambridge MA: MIT Press.

Badham, R. / Garrety, K. / Kirsch, C. (2001): Humanistic redesign and technological politics in organisations. Journal of Organizational Change Management, 14, 50-63.

Binder, T. (2007): Why Design:Labs? In Design Inquiries 2007 (Stockholm: 2nd Nordic Design Research Conference.

Brandt, E. / Messeter, J. (2004): Facilitating collaboration through design games. In A. Clement (ed.), (pp. 121-131). New York: ACM.

Broberg, O. (2007): Integrating ergonomics into engineering: Empirical evidence and implications for the ergonomists. Human Factors and Ergonomics in Manufacturing, 17, 353-366.

Broberg, O. / Hermund, I. (2004): The OHS consultant as a 'political reflective navigator' in technological change processes. International Journal of Industrial Ergonomics, 33, 315-326.

Daniellou, F. (2005): The French-speaking ergonomists' approach to work activity: cross-influences of field intervention and conceptual models. Theoretical Issues in Ergonomics Science, 6, 409-427.

Daniellou, F. (2006): Simulating future work activity is not only a way of improving workstation design. In R.N.Pikaar, E.A.P.Koningsveld / P.J.M.Settels (eds.), Meeting Diversity in Ergonomics (pp. -5pp.). Amsterdam: Elsevier.

Garrety, K. / Badham, R. (2004): User-centered design and the normative politics of technology. Science, Technology, & Human Values, 29, 191-212.

Greenbaum, J. / Kyng, M. (1991): Design at Work: Cooperative Design of Computer Systems. Chichester: Lawrence Erlbaum Associates.

Henderson, K. (1999): On Line and On Paper. Cambridge MA: The MIT Press.

Horgen, T.H. / Joroff, M.L. / Porter, W.L. / Schön, D.A. (1999): Excellence by Design: Transforming Workplace and Work Practice. New York: John Wiley & Sons.

Jensen, C.B. (2006): The wireless nursing call system: Politics of discourse, technology and dependability in a pilot project. Computer Supported Cooperative Work, 15, 419-441.

Johansson, M. / Fröst, P. / Brandt, E. / Binder, T. / Messeter, J. (2002): Partner engaged design: New challenges for workplace design. In Participatory Design Conference (Malmö.

Latour, B. (1987): Science in action. Cambridge MA: Harvard University Press.

Latour, B. / Woolgar, S. (1979): Laboratory life: The construction of scientific facts. Princeton: Princeton University Press.
Rasmussen, L.B. (2007): From human-centred to human-context centred approach: looking back over 'the hills', what has been gained and lost? AI & Society, 21, 471-495.
Wenger, E. (2000): Communities of practice and social learning systems. Organization, 7, 225-246.
Woolgar, S. (1991): Configuring the user: the case of usability trials. In J.Law (ed.), A Sociology of Monsters (pp. 57-99). London: Routledge.

Experiences on how to enhance participative and innovative capacities of employees in action research processes

Werner Fricke

1. Concept of participation and of employees' innovative capacities

To avoid possible misunderstandings I want to make clear from the very beginning my understanding of the terms participation and employees' innovative capacities as elaborated in the following text:

I am speaking of **employees' innovative capacities** (or innovative qualifications) as we met them in several action research projects exclusively in the sense of capacities to develop social and organizational innovations like democratic participation or industrial democracy. I am not relating to technical or economic innovations (increasing productivity, e.g.). There is of course a positive relationship between broad participation and the innovative capacities of organizations and enterprises (see e.g. Palshaugen 2000) but this is not my perspective in this paper. In our present context participation means direct participation of those concerned in an open democratic process, based on employees' innovative qualifications and participative interests. Democratic participation is a value in itself; it cannot and should not be legitimated by its contribution to increase an organization's productivity and efficiency, because this argumentation ignores or tries to restrict the human and political value of democratic participation.

I understand **direct participation of those concerned** as complementary to institutional forms of co-determination, as we find it in different forms in many European countries. Participation does not only give employees a voice but above all a chance to engage in and to influence organizational change processes according to their interests.

This implies that I understand participation as **democratic participation**. It is necessary to stress the democratic character of participation since management developed so called participative strategies, which seem to meet the employees' interests in a higher degree of autonomy at work but instead lead to nothing but "dependent autonomy" (Peters 2001) which makes employees accept the working conditions apparently determined by the market. Intensification of work is the price the employees pay for the illusion of self organized work, which is in fact nothing but a dependent autonomy, determined by scarce resources (time and personnel) and the market.

A third dimension of direct democratic participation is its character as an **open process**, which marks its difference to institutional forms of democratic participation as, e.g., co-determination. Open processes of direct participation must however not be understood and organized as alternative to institutional forms of co-determination. The relationship between both forms of participation is twofold: Institutional forms of participation such as co-determination may be strengthened and intensified by participative engagement of employees: works councils are in a better position to negotiate with management when they can rely on and cooperate with an active workforce[1]. On the other hand direct participation may profit from protected spaces in organizations guaranteed by institutional forms of co-determination.

In addition to its political, organizational and institutional dimension participation has clearly an **anthropological dimension**, which means: to participate is a genuine and very basic desire of any human being: We all want to have a chance to influence the living and working conditions, i.e. the social context of our lives, be it at work or in other social fields. Although we experience the social conditions and working conditions as a set of institutions and rules that determine our life and work, we have nevertheless altogether created these social institutions[2], and we insist in being not only determined by, but also in being creative subjects of our living and working conditions. Many research experiences from the field of workers' participation in industry and working life demonstrate that this basic desire to participate does in fact exist (Fricke u.a. 1981; Fricke 1983; Reason 2002[3]; Kristiansen / Bloch-Poulsen 2005; Kristiansen 2007), but at the same time most of these publications report on difficulties to

1 In many enterprises the passivity of large parts of the workforce creates problems for both works councils and trade unions, not only in terms of legitimacy but also by weakening their bargaining power. Direct participation of workforces may revitalize trade unions on enterprise level as well as in society. Modern trade unions in many countries have realized the positive effects of direct democratic participation; they try to enhance it in the economy, sometimes however not yet sufficiently within their own organizations in relation to their members.

2 The chance to influence living and working conditions is of course not equally distributed among employees and citizens. Those in power have by far greater chances to shape the institutions and rules at work and in society. This is why processes of democratic participation in organizations are confronted with power and power relations. The unequal distribution of participative chances is however not at all an argument against the existence of a general human interest in democratic participation.

3 Peter Reason additionally mentions an ontological dimension of participation: Humans are part of nature and cosmos; participation is the overall principle of co-existence. Bruno Latour is thinking about a parliament of fish: fish as well as nature in general should have a voice when concerned by any developments resulting from human decisions (Latour 1999).

enhance participation processes, because employees hesitate or are reluctant to engage in these processes for different reasons.

How can we understand this obvious contradiction between the basic need (Bedürfnis) to participate and the fact that in concrete situations employees often hesitate or refuse to engage in participation processes?

I can see several reasons for these contradictory empirical findings: (1) Participation is not easy. It demands considerable efforts from practitioners as well as – by the way – from action researchers. As open participative processes often run into conflicts with organizational routines, hierarchical structures and institutionalized labour relations they afford courage and creative power of actors engaged in participative endeavours. (2) Participation needs time; if there are no time resources provided by the organization (enterprise) the participants have to invest time additional to their working time or they have to reorganize their work flow in such a way that some time resources become free for participation. (3) Participative processes are learning processes. To engage in theoretical and practical discourses in order to understand (theoretical discourses) and to develop actions and ways to change (practical discourses) is hard work. (4) Employees often experience that participation does not lead to practical results which meet their interests. Participation however is not just dialogue; it must also have practical consequences.

(5) Participation is based on what we have called "innovative qualifications" (Fricke et al. 1981; Fricke 1983; Fricke 2009). Innovative qualifications are different from professional qualifications. They indicate the capacity and the interest to engage in processes that aim at improving one's living and working conditions. As many action research projects on participation in industry have proved any employee as a potential subject of his/her working and living conditions owns these innovative qualifications. This innovative capacity may be and often is suppressed by the actual working conditions (hierarchy, monotonous work processes, market driven work organization, dependant autonomy), but it may be revitalized and developed under certain conditions. Very often it is this long term suppression of participative qualifications which is the main reason why employees hesitate to engage in participative processes.

This is my basic thesis for this paper. In the following sections I want to report on some of our research findings which demonstrate how innovative qualifications may be developed and enhanced (section 2), while in section 3 I will reflect the conditions under which democratic participation may be enhanced in industrial organizations.

2. How to enhance participative and innovative capacities

In our action research projects the enhancement of workers' innovative qualifications was part of a multidimensional process combining participation, change, learning, reflection and dialogue. Workers and researchers were cooperating in joint action and reflection processes. Both partners participated in theoretical discourses, aiming at understanding the situation, and in practical discourses, aiming at generating action and change. This is crucial: Enhancement of innovative qualification is not possible as an isolated process of learning and education. Innovative qualification which aim at influencing one's working (and living) conditions according to one's interests can only be developed by training participation in change processes.

Anybody who tries to organize participative processes in an industrial organization must be aware of the fact that at present it is not the workers (dependent employees) who in industry decide on their working conditions. These decisions are taken by other groups, such as (top) management, experts like engineers or (perhaps) change agents, to a certain extent also middle management and supervisors. Distribution of power is unequal in industry. This is why any attempt to introduce democratic participation must start by creating some public space for employees and their representatives as a precondition for becoming subjects of development, change and decision processes in their organization – sc. in cooperation with other groups of the organization, not workers alone.

In a humanization project we (five researchers from an independent research institute) negotiated about such a public open space for participation processes with the management of an enterprise from metal industry in Northern Germany. As management was unsatisfied with the innovative capacity of middle management they agreed to organize a participative process by which 45 male and female, both German and migrant workers from one department were given the chance to elaborate concepts to improve their working conditions according to their interests and (this is substantial) to engage in and control the implementation of their ideas. If there would occur some rationalization effects in addition to humanization of working conditions, these effects would be shared at equal parts between the enterprise and the employees; the enterprise guaranteed that no jobs would be lost.

This agreement was possible because of some special conditions:

- there were a strong works council and influential trade union members from the supervisory board who supported the negotiations with management

- The humanization programme provided financial resources to buy working time for the participating employees for group discussions and seminars outside the enterprise.

These were clearly special conditions. The idea of our action research project was however to develop a process of democratic participation which may serve as an example to demonstrate how innovative qualifications and democratic participation may principally be enhanced and realized in industrial contexts. I will discuss in section 3 which of the conditions that enabled the participation process in our action research may be realized under normal economic conditions, i.e. without support from state financed development projects.

When we contacted the 45 workers for the first time we met them in deep frustration and passivity. We tried to motivate them to participate in a development process to improve their working conditions, but they answered: "Nothing has changed here throughout the past 30 years, and there will nothing change in the future". These are sentences you never forget.

We did however not give up, visited the workers at their workplaces during six weeks and asked each of them three questions:

- please describe and explain your work
- do you have any critique on your working conditions?
- What do you want to change?

These are very simple questions, but the attitude behind is of basic importance: The researchers learnt to listen to the workers, to understand their view of the situation and their interests to improve their working conditions.

Our main intention however was to initiate a learning process which should enable the employees to learn by reflection as well as by action to unfold their participative and innovative capacities (innovative qualifications). We were convinced that in order to start and to participative in such a process the employees first had to develop a perspective transcending their actual work places and working conditions. The danger we wanted to avoid from the very beginning was to restrict the employees' innovative capacities to being purely reactive-responsive to the existing working conditions[4]. According to our leading hypothesis innovative qualifications include employees' own perspectives about how to run their lives and how to organize their work.

It was and is a fact that to develop alternative (i.e. democratic, participative, self-determined) perspectives to design and change work is not possible from

---

4 The categories "reactive-responsive" versus "proactive" as divergent orientations in participative processes are developed in Lauge Rasmussen's contribution to this volume.

within the current working conditions, as long as they are characterized by time pressure, stress, heavy work load, alienation. As the reflective heart of our participative development process, we have therefore designed four one week seminars outside the work place, in which all 45 workers had the opportunity to take part, which they did with the only exception of one female worker.

Especially the first seminar had the function to enable the participants to look at their work from a distance and from their own perspectives which – as it turned out – had to be developed. We met the workers in a personal situation that was characterized by

- isolation and lack of solidarity; under conditions of a piece rate wage system each of them worked for him/herself in a kind of competition
- a high degree of physic and psychic stress
- lack of experience and capacity to learn and reflect both individually and jointly (partly due to negative school experience)
- frustration and experience of failure (none of them was ever asked for any idea to improve their working conditions; they had no idea how to implement proposals for better working conditions).

I will describe here briefly the three main steps of this first seminar in order to demonstrate in which way we encouraged and enabled the workers to look at their work from a distance and develop a new, innovative perspective as a precondition and a first step to participate in a change process according to their own interests[5].

In the beginning we asked the workers to inform each other about their personal history and their present situation, about their wishes and hopes for their future and about their personal work experiences: "What do I feel when I return home from work"? In the same way the researchers presented their personal history, future expectations and work experiences.

The idea of this sequence was to enable all participants to recognize and encounter each other as persons with their individual experiences, interests, desires and characteristics. New personal contacts and communication developed beyond the roles of colleagues at work. We took two days out of the five days' seminar to make the persons with all their individual richness visible behind their role as colleagues at work. This was in our concept a necessary condition for enabling workers to create their own perspectives and engage jointly in a participative change process according to their interests.

---

5 For details of the seminar sequences see Fricke et al. (1981), p. 163-216.

The second sequence of the seminar dealt with ideas about an alternative conceptualization of work. We asked the workers to imagine "how I want my work and workplace to look like after 10 years", and we encouraged them to think utopian, i.e. not to consider the difficulties and barriers that might hinder the realization of their ideas. "We want to elect our supervisors for limited periods of time", "we want to change the wage system from piece rate wage (Einzelakkord) to payment per time, so that we know in the morning/in advance how much we will have earned at the end of the day/week/month" or "we want to sit during work at our machines": These were some of the utopian wishes of workers, who suffered from hierarchy, whose incomes were subject to factors beyond their influence and who worked standing at machines eight hours a day, five days a week, twenty days a month for ten, twenty or thirty years. Regardless their successes or failures it was however important that they started the change process from utopian thinking – in a pro-active way, as Rasmussen puts it (Rasmussen 2010).

Some of these desires were met during the project (new construction of machines to reduce the work load), some others after fifteen years (payment per time), some not up to now (election of supervisors).

This utopian sequence was dedicated one day.

Finally the workers selected those ideas which they considered to be realistic under the given circumstances in the enterprise. This selection was based on a systematic presentation of all the ideas and critique the researchers had collected during the first six weeks of the project when we were asking the three before mentioned questions. Together with the new perspectives gained during the first two sequences this feedback was a breakthrough at the beginning of the participative process. The workers suddenly realized the productive force of their ideas, and they learned that they would be able to develop their innovative qualifications under the following conditions:

- there was a realistic chance to implement their ideas
- they started to trust this opportunity (chance)
- they started to communicate with each other (so far they communicated indirectly, through the group of researchers only).

After we had presented the whole body of the workers' innovative ideas they were discussed during the last two days of the seminar, and three fields of change activities were agreed upon: wage system (wage per hour instead of piece rate system), work load (reduction of noise and monotony e.g.) and technology (machines that allow the worker to sit during work, e.g.). These fields were elaborated by three working groups which had the possibility to meet during working time for two hours twice a month.

The working groups met a lot of difficulties and resistance especially from middle management. Engineers and supervisors experienced the workers' initiatives to engage in change processes concerning work organization and technology as competition; they regarded the maintenance of a continuous process of innovation their field of activity, although they were not able to meet top management's expectations in this respect since quite some time.[6] In the beginning of the process middle managers succeeded in fact to slow the participative process down, but after the first half year the workers' engagement in the working groups gained momentum, and many proposals how to improve the working conditions were conceptualized and later implemented under the workers' control.

During the first six months of the participative process there was, however, still another factor that hindered the process: The workers had no idea about the procedures necessary to get their proposals accepted by works council and top management. They lacked any knowledge about and experience with the institutional framework of the enterprise decision making process. According to the legally fixed co-determination structures and procedures works council and top management had to negotiate and agree about any proposal that was elaborated by the working groups. This procedure did not only need time, it was also alien to the workers' thinking. They had to learn that it was not sufficient to have a good idea and to elaborate it until practicability, but that they had to take into account the institutional context of the enterprise decision procedures.

This was a difficult new perspective for the workers; it afforded patience, knowledge, tactical thinking and a considerable amount of time. After the first six months many of the workers were disappointed and frustrated because none of their ideas had been realized so far. The second seminar was therefore designed to make them acquainted with the institutional setting of the enterprise and the co-determination procedures in order to give them a realistic time feeling for the rest of the change process.

On the other hand they experienced the institutions of works council and co-determination as a complementary and helpful context of the participative process they were engaged in. Direct democratic participation could not be realized in a capitalist setting without an institutional context of co-determination and an active works council. The members of the works council on their part learned that a participative work force, activated by processes of direct democratic participation strengthened their position in joint decision making processes with management.

6 In fact top management's main motivation to accept our research group to initiate and organize a participative change process was their discontent with middle management's innovative performance.

Back to the working groups. They provided space for both reflecting and steering the process and for elaborating concrete change proposals with the professional (sometimes reluctant) assistance of engineers and other experts. The proposals were discussed and decided upon by joint committees of management and works council within the normal structure of co-determination and, when accepted, implemented under the control of the workers.

It is not necessary to go further into details here; I will only point out the most crucial preconditions of how to enhance workers' innovative qualifications.

a) In order to engage in participative change processes workers (employees) must have and trust the chance, to take part in deciding on the aims of a change process. Without such a realistic and at the same time pro-active perspective based on utopian thinking they will not be able to overcome their passivity and frustration, which results from the experience that their voices are not heard and – if heard – that their ideas are only implemented when they meet the interest of the enterprise and its owners, while their own interests are widely neglected. In other words: Dependent employees will only engage in participative change processes if their results are compatible with their interests.
b) Due to mainly three factors innovative qualifications of dependent employees are submerged. These factors are the unequal distribution of power, the usual division of labour and especially the lack of communication and discussion between isolated employees. They are altogether responsible for the fact that employees are not accustomed since years to use their innovative qualifications with the consequence of losing trust and confidence in their innovative and creative potential.
c) Starting from a situation of passivity and lack of self-confidence innovative qualifications can only be developed and enhanced by processes of active learning and action. We did this in our humanization project by enabling the workers to look at their work from their personal perspectives and by then integrating phases of learning (reflection, dialogue) and of action (implementing what has been learned in change processes). The message is that democratic participation cannot be developed, innovative qualifications cannot be enhanced but by practicing them, i.e. by practice or even better: by reflective practice.
d) Learning processes of this kind are very different from those in traditional learning structures characterized by top-down-teaching, by separation of learning and action. Necessary are self determined learning processes, which are part of change processes in organizations based on dialogues and communication between participants.
e) The processes of joint learning and joint action had to be organized in such a way, that professional and innovative qualifications of workers were able to

influence the process by dialogues with representatives of other groups of practitioners (middle and top management, experts). It is crucial in this respect, that instead of position, power, eloquence or special knowledge dominating the process all participants should have equal opportunities to take part in dialogues and following change processes. The aims of change processes have to be agreed upon, not decided by power or expert knowledge. These are crucial conditions for the enhancement of workers' innovative capacities and for using them in participative change processes.

This is easy said, but difficult to be done. A crucial question is whether it is possible in capitalist organisations to create the necessary conditions for the enhancement and use of innovative capacities. This will be discussed in section 3.

The main problem is that dependent employees have to develop and use their innovative qualifications in work situations characterized by unequal distribution of power, by rigid division of labour and/or processes of continuously growing intensification of work; all these elements of modern work organisation result in complex forms of work load, both physically and psychologically[7]. None of these conditions of work are favourable conditions to enhance communication and dialogue at the work place. In the contrary: Very often employees find themselves in a situation of isolation; communication at work is normally restricted to questions of daily life during the breaks (which is important to communicate about) and to work related communication (which is often automated or reduced to signals and "instrumental communication"[8]), while critical and innovative reflections about improving the working conditions do not take place (Glissmann 1999) and seem to be impossible.

During the Swedish LOM programme[9] (1985-1990) a set of criteria on democratic participation has been developed and used in so called dialogue conferences in which all groups of employees had a chance to participate. If one takes

7 See the latest report on work load by Dublin Foundation for the Improvement of Living and Working Conditions, Dublin 2002.

8 Habermas makes a difference between communicative and instrumental action; according to him work belongs to the sphere of instrumental action. I think this separation is politically dangerous. In order to enhance democracy at work via democratic participation elements of communicative action, such as dialogue and reflection between individuals with equal rights have to and may be realized in working life. My own research, several humanization projects and work life programmes in Scandinavia have demonstrated that it is in principle and under certain conditions possible to introduce elements of industrial democracy into the world of instrumental action or – as we may say more concretely – into the world of economy driven by profit oriented finance market capitalism.

9 LOM is the acronym for Leadership, Organisation, Medbestemmelse (Mitbestimmung).

these criteria seriously and implements them as a guide for dialogues between employees in an enterprise or organization including top management (i.e. under realistic conditions), it becomes obvious that the main challenge for democratic dialogues is the unequal distribution of power in any organization.

The criteria of democratic dialogues are the following (Gustavsen 1992, p. 3/4):

1. The dialogue is a process of exchange: ideas and arguments move to and fro between the participants.
2. It must be possible for all concerned to participate.
3. This possibility for participation is, however, not enough. Everybody should also be active. Consequently each participant has an obligation not only to put forth his or her own ideas but also to help others to contribute their ideas.
4. All participants are equal.
5. Work experience is the basis for participation. This is the only type of experience which, by definition, all participants have.
6. At least some of the experience which each participant has when entering the dialogue must be considered legitimate.
7. It must be possible for everybody to develop an understanding of the issues at stake.
8. All arguments which pertain to the issues under discussion are legitimate. No argument should be rejected on the ground that it emerges from an illegitimate source.
9. The points, arguments, etc. which are to enter the dialogue must be made by a participating actor. Nobody can participate "on paper" only.
10. Each participant must accept that other participants can have better arguments.
11. The work role, authority, etc of *all* participants can be made subject to discussion – no participant is exempt in this respect
12. The participants should be able to tolerate an increasing degree of difference of opinion.
13. The dialogue must continuously produce agreements which can provide platforms for practical action. Note that there is no contradiction between this criterion and the previous one. The major strength of a democratic system compared to all other one is that it has the benefit of drawing upon a broad range of opinions and ideas which inform practice, while at the same time being able to make decisions which can gain the support of all participants.

The following criteria are most difficult to be realized under realistic conditions in enterprises/organizations:

- it must be possible for all concerned to participate
- all participants are equal
- work experience is the basis for participation
- all arguments which pertain to the issues under discussion are legitimate
- each participant must accept that other participants can have better arguments
- the work role, authority etc of *all* participants can be made subject to discussion – no participant is exempt in this respect.

Trying to implement these criteria in democratic dialogues under realistic working conditions meets heavy resistance and difficulties[10]. To give a few examples: Marianne Kristiansen reports about dilemmas action researchers experience when they try to organize democratic dialogues (Kristiansen 2007, p. 19-31): Practitioners do not have sufficient time to engage in dialogue sessions during work – should the researchers accept them refusing to participate, should they try to convince them to participate in spite of their time restrictions or should they risk conflicts with management to reach an agreement providing sufficient time for reflection and dialogue seminars[11]?

Another example: Top managers are reluctant to have their work role or authority subject to discussion although they claim (and are convinced) that their organization is guided by democratic principles and allows dialogues on any topic. They erect a taboo in their organization: There is a difference between ideal and reality, but this difference must not be touched in dialogues. When this nevertheless happens in a seminar a tension arises that is bodily felt: "We have experienced a very strong or sometimes very offensive energy in the room when conflicting perspectives have clashed ... we have reacted bodily by perspiring, freezing, by a rapid pulse – or by becoming wide awake almost like animals sensing dangers" (Kristiansen 2007, p. 28).

Kristiansen and her co-researcher Bloch Poulsen have encountered what they call a social concrete block. "We understand social concrete blocks as man made, unproductive relational patterns that over a period of time stiffen into unquestioned assumptions (taboos: WF) and alienated organizational patterns which are taken for granted (Kristiansen, Bloch-Poulsen 2005, p. 282). ... It is our experience that part

10 There is however little evidence in literature about such difficulties. Researchers, also action researchers, prefer to report success stories, not the difficulties and the compromises they made in organizational change processes. Marianne Kristiansen, who has great experience in dialogic action research without however explicitly using Gustavsen's criteria of democratic dialogue, is an exception.

11 This is what we did in our humanization project on democratic participation (Fricke et al. 1981).

of the unspoken often hardens into a social concrete block" which can become a more or less dominant part of an organizational context" (Kristiansen 2007, p. 29).

I have chosen these examples in order to demonstrate that the conditions which hinder dependent employees to develop and use their innovative qualifications cover a wide range from lack of time to very sophisticated forms of power in organizations. It is difficult enough to provide organizational conditions for democratic participation and use of innovative potential such as time, space and favourable structures (co-determination) in enterprises, but the greatest challenge is certainly the unequal distribution and undemocratic use of power in organizations. The situation complicates, because it is not only the use of power as such, which creates problems, but to a much greater extent it is the wide range of power related strategies reaching from apparently anonymous forms in market driven work organizations (it is the market, not personal decisions that determine working conditions) via open ways, incorporated in hierarchical structures up to hidden (sometimes even unconscious) forms embodied in unquestioned assumptions and alienated organizational patterns (social concrete blocks). These are very deep rooted obstacles against any learning and change process, built on innovative qualifications and democratic forms of social relations.

3. Conditions and strategies to realize democratic participation in capitalist organizations

My point is not a vision of organizing working life free of power, which is not realistic. My point is to reflect on and enhance possibilities of a democratic use of power, which allows for democratic dialogues and a reflective practice in working life, at least for steps into this direction as far as possible in capitalist organizations.

In the late 1970 it has been demonstrated by our and several other humanization projects (Ulich 1980; Fricke et al. 1981; Hoppmann, Stötzl 1981; Weltz, Lullies 1983; Duell, Frei 1986) that democratic participation is possible in industrial organizations under certain conditions. Within these participative processes and as their driving force innovative qualifications were developed. New knowledge was created by all groups of participants including researchers. And we have proven that at least temporarily open public spaces may be created within normal structures of capitalist enterprises – open spaces, which may be used for democratic dialogues and participative change processes. Finally and last not least the projects have investigated and demonstrated, which conditions are indispensable to realist at least initial stages of democratic participation, to enhance workers' innovative qualifications and to allow joint reflection and democratic dialogues in real industrial settings.

These indispensable conditions are:

a) strong co-determination institutions and active works council members who are able and willing to realize, test and use opportunities to extend the institutional forms of co-determination by open participative processes
b) integration of self-determined learning opportunities, based on joint reflection and action, into participative change processes
c) creating open spaces for democratic dialogues (see below)
d) time resources for dialogue meetings (seminars or working groups)
e) financial resources for implementing innovative concepts/ideas
f) in the long run the extension of legal co-determination beyond its representative institutions and regulations in direction of open participative processes.

These minimum conditions for the enhancement and use of innovative capacities within democratic participation processes may be established in contexts of capitalist organizations. This has been demonstrated not only by several projects from the German programme "Humanization of Living and Working Conditions" and by some tariff agreements in Germany[12] but also by a series of Scandinavian Work Life programmes since the 1960s. We must however bear in mind that the conditions for democratic participation in industry today are less favourable than they were 30 years ago; this holds true for German contexts as well as for Scandinavian programmes. Nevertheless there is empirical evidence that processes of democratic participation can considerably influence the cultural climate of organisations in industry (Unternehmenskultur; see Benthin, Brinkmann 2008; Fricke 2008). I will especially draw upon examples from Scandinavian action research projects which demonstrate that participation of all groups of employees in theoretical and practical dialogues may result in the establishment of open spaces in enterprises.

The Norwegian action researcher Oyvind Palshaugen reports on institutions which have been developed and implemented by two action research projects in Norwegian enterprises in order to enhance broad employee participation. The first one is the so called development organization. In addition to the usual work organization, which any enterprise has established to organize the daily work flow a development organization was created. A development organization consisted of different discussion forums which gave elected representatives of all

12 Under conditions of co-determination and tariff autonomy with active and strong trade unions agreements on time for education as part of the working time are possible: some years ago in some German enterprises (e.g. Volkswagen AG) such agreements have been realized; some decades ago agreements on leave for education (Bildungsurlaub) have been introduced and are still in use. Similar agreements should be possible in Scandinavia and do perhaps exist.

groups of employees from shop floor to top management the opportunity to discuss middle and long range perspectives of enterprise development, which means: they had to think of and elaborate innovations to enhance the future growth and development of their enterprise. Palshaugen points out that broad participation in development organizations did not only strengthen the competitive advantage of the enterprise but that it provided also an opportunity to train for and to enhance participatory democracy at the workplace. He concludes. "Local development organizations in the enterprises … could function as a very forceful measure for

- increasing the competitive advantage by increasing the innovative capabilities and thereby the overall productivity, and
- to do this in a way that makes optimum use of the whole range of local conditions for improvement and innovation – cultural and technological ones,
- and finally, to come closer to realizing the promise which has always been made, that capitalism should allow for a more democratic development also *within* working life – by permitting any member of the work organization to participate in the task of improving the enterprise's competitive conditions" (Palshaugen 2000, p. 253).

The democratic dimension of participative enterprise development strategies is clearer elaborated in another publication by Oyvind Palshaugen in which he is discussing the possibility to create public spheres in enterprises as spaces for a discourse democracy at work. In 1982 the two main Norwegian Labour market parties signed an "Agreement on Enterprise Development". "The general purpose of the Agreement was to encourage efforts at improving the competitive force of the enterprises by means of enterprise development projects based on extensive participation by the employees" (Palshaugen 2002, p. 164). Based on this agreement a series of enterprise development projects was performed in Norway which all started with so called dialogue conferences. These dialogue conferences constituted a kind of public sphere within the enterprise in which all employees had "the freedom to express any opinion both on what the problems are and what the future of the enterprise should be …" (l.c., p. 182).

Dialogue conferences and the discussion forums within development organizations provide space for employees to train their innovative qualifications by practicing democratic participation – under the condition however that the criteria of democratic dialogue are observed and that the employees have the possibility to influence and control the implementation of their ideas in a change process. As we found in our action research project dialogues have to be binding, i.e. they must have practical consequences. "The dialogue must continuously produce agreements which can provide platforms for practical action", number 13 of the rules for democratic dialogue says (see above). If there is no chance to have their ideas realized employees will not be motivated to engage in participation processes or democratic dialogues (Fricke et al. 1981).

To create public spheres in enterprises opens perspectives for industrial democracy in an economy that is based on private ownership of capital and the right of capital owners and their management to direct their enterprises (Direktionsrecht). Co-determination is an institution to introduce some public elements into enterprise decisions, too; it limits the private character of the enterprise to a certain (though very limited) extent. In a historical perspective both, participative institutions and processes should be understood as strategies to continue and complete historical development that has its roots in 17th and 18th century. When the emerging bourgeoisie was about to emancipate itself from the feudal state system their base for social and political independence was private business, which they were permitted to run. At the same time they created a public sphere *outside* their private businesses (and families) and until today the bourgeois and capitalist insists in separating the public sphere in society from his private business. This historic development has a lot of implications; one of the most challenging and threatening is the growing domination of public and social affairs by private capitalist business. I do not want to discuss this implication here. I simply want to point to the fact that to restrict economic activities to a private sector does not follow any genuine economic logic – it is just a historical fact, which may be revised by creating and using public spheres in enterprises with the perspective of enhancing industrial democracy.

This is however impossible without people, workers, employees who engage in participative processes based on their innovative qualifications. Besides the creation of democratic institutions the greatest difficulty they have to master is and will be the continuous effort to engage in democratic dialogues within structures determined by unequal distribution of power. This power, be it personal or institutional, is very deep rooted and embodied in social concrete blocks, organizational routines and taboos, in personal attitudes, differences of education, eloquence etc as pointed out above. Dependent employees need their innovative qualifications, a lot of personal courage and the perspective of change in their interest to engage in such complicated and challenging processes of democratic participation.

Which are the innovative qualifications employees need for engaging in participative change processes? In our action research practice we met the following:

- The ability to discuss and agree upon joint interests, values and aims
- Solidarity
- The energy and trust to overcome their passivity resulting from long term experience of failure

- The ability to engage in utopian (pro-active) thinking and consequently to develop alternatives to the existing reality
- Courage to engage in democratic dialogues with supervisors, top management and experts on an equal base
- To know and to use their legal rights
- To reflect their situation and engage in reflective action; in action research terminology: To engage in theoretical and practical discourses.

To sum up:

Innovative and participative capacities of employees may be enhanced by

- giving employees a voice and a chance to influence change processes according to their interest and by that
- restoring their trust in their genuine innovative qualifications, which have often been suppressed since years
- providing favourable conditions such as financial and time resources, public spheres for democratic dialogues
- organizing a process of joint learning, reflection and action, i.e. a practice to develop and make use of participative capacities
- providing an institutional frame to protect public spaces in private enterprises from interventions by those in power; co-determination and similar participative institutions are in this sense complementary to direct participation
- as far as research is concerned: listen to practitioners; engage in theoretical and practical discourses with them; refrain from othering businesses (Eikeland 2007), i.e. do not make practitioners an object of research, but a partner; be responsible – in one word: do action research.

References

Benthin, Rainer / Brinkmann, Ulrich (Hrsg.) (2008): "Unternehmenskultur und Mitbestimmung. Betriebliche Integration zwischen Konsens und Konflikt", Frankfurt/Main, Campus

Duell, Werner / Frei, Felix (Hrsg.) (1986): "Arbeit gestalten, Mitarbeiter beteiligen. Eine Heuristik qualifizierender Arbeitsgestaltung", Band 77 der Schriftenreihe "Humanisierung des Arbeitslebens", Frankfurt/Main, Campus

Eikeland, Olav (2007): "Why should mainstream social researchers be interested in action research?", International Journal of Action Research, 3 (1+2), 38-64

Fricke Else / Fricke, Werner / Schönwälder, Manfred / Stiegler, Barbara (1981): "Qualifikation und Beteiligung", Band 12 der Schriftenreihe "Humanisierung der Arbeit", Frankfurt/Main, Campus

Fricke, Werner (1983): "Participatory Research and the enhancement of workers' qualifications", Journal of Occupational Behaviour, 4, 73-87

Fricke, Werner (2008): "Demokratische Beteiligung. Fundament einer Unternehmenskultur von unten" in Benthin/Brinkmann (Hrsg.) "Unternehmenskultur und Mitbestimmung", Frankfurt/Main, Campus, S. 373-390

Fricke, Werner (2009): "Innovatorische Qualifikationen. Ihre Entfaltung und Anwendung im Prozess des Lernens und Handelns in Arbeitssituationen" in: Axel Bolder, Rolf Dobischat (Hrsg.) "Eigen-Sinn und Widerstand", Wiesbaden 2009, VS, S. 179-206

Glissmann, Wilfried (1999): "Assertion of Employees' Interests d the new Autonomy of Work", Concepts and Transformation. International Journal of Action Research and Organizational Renewal, 4 (1), 83-105

Gustavsen, Björn (1992): "Dialogue and Development. Social Science for Social Action: toward organizational renewal", Assen/Maastricht, van Gorcum

Hoppmann, Klaus / Stötzel, Berthold: "Demokratie am Arbeitsplatz. Ein Modellversuch zur Mitwirkung von Arbeitnehmern an betrieblichen Entscheidungsprozessen", Band 20 der Schriftenreihe "Humanisierung des Arbeitslebens", Frankfurt/Main, Campus

Kristiansen, Marianne (2007): "Relational and Existential Challenges of Practicing Dialogical Action Research – Working with Social Concrete Blocks in Organizations", International Journal of Action Research, 3 (1+2), 15-37

Kristiansen, Marianne / Bloch-Poulsen, Jörgen (2005): "Midwifery and Dialogue in Organizations. Emergent, Mutual Involvement in Action Research", München und Mering, Rainer Hampp

Latour, Bruno (1999): "Das Parlament der Dinge. Für eine politische Ökologie", Frankfurt/Main, Suhrkamp

Peters, Klaus (2001): "Individual autonomy in new forms of work organization", Concepts and Transformation. International Journal of Action Research and Organizational Renewal, 6 (2), 141-158

Palshaugen, Oyvind (2000): "The Competitive Advantage of Development Organizations", Concepts and Transformation. International Journal of Action Research and Organizational Renewal, 5 (2) 237-255

Palshaugen, Oyvind (2002): "Discourse Democracy at Work. On public spheres in private enterprises", Concepts and Transformation. International Journal of Action Research and Organizational Renewal, 7 (2), 141-192

Rasmussen, Lauge Baungaard (2010): "From a reactive to a proactive approach", (this volume)

Reason, Peter (2002): "Justice, Sustainability, and participation", Concepts and Transformation. International Journal of Action Research and Organizational Renewal, 7 (1), 7-29

Weltz, Friedrich / Lullies, Veronika (1983): "Innovation im Büro. Das Beispiel Textverarbeitung", Band 38 der Schriftenreihe "Humanisierung des Arbeitslebens", Frankfurt/Main, Campus

Ulich, Eberhard (1980): "Bericht über die arbeits- und sozialpsychologische Begleitforschung" in: "Gruppenarbeit in der Motorenmontage – ein Vergleich von Arbeitsstrukturen", Band 3 der Schriftenreihe "Humanisierung der Arbeit", S. 97-142, Frankfurt/Main, Campus

Appendix

We were asked by the coordinator of our working group to suggest some very urgent research questions concerning the enhancement of employees' participative capacities. These are my suggestions:

Research Questions

Research is necessary on different levels of society:

1. In Organizations

How to combine institutional forms of labour relations (co-determination, e.g.) with open, direct forms of democratic participation (Fricke 1983)?

How to create public spaces in organizations/enterprises? Examples: to integrate development organizations into classical organizational structures, parallel to work organization (Palshaugen 2002).

For researchers: To engage in theoretical and practical discourses with actors from organizations/enterprises instead of studying their situation or advising them (Eikeland 2007: "Othering business"). Joint action and research instead of applied research and counselling.

2. On regional level

How to organize learning and development processes between enterprises, research and public administration on regional level? (Gustavsen 2008) The idea is to generate institutions for dialogue, joint learning and regional development which care for sustainable and democratic development processes by cooperation between different regional actors (generative results of research; see Alasoini 2008 and Arnkil 2008)

3. On national level

On national level it is important to have social coalitions which support research and development strategies to generate democratic procedures of development on regional level rather than political decisions from the centre. Research and development programmes must be accompanied by public debates on all levels of society. Top down strategies, originating from the central bureaucracy are too far from social reality at local and regional level.

4. Research on Trade Union Renewal

Trade Unions and direct democratic participation: May the enhancement of direct democratic participation contribute to Trade Union renewal (a) as social partner in the field of industrial relations (b) as a social organisation in socio-political contexts (c) as a social movement?

- dd participation of members within trade unions
- dd participation of employees in organizations/enterprises

Research questions

Which are the conditions to enhance dd participation of employees/of TU members? (Training, exercise, cooperation between research and TU, employees and TU members, especially action research by joint theoretical and practical dialogues)

Which are the barriers and obstacles?

Which actors may contribute to enhance dd participation?

In which way does dd participation

- of employees
- of TU members

enhance organisational renewal change of Trade Unions? Can dd participation and institutional forms of co-determination be organized in a complementary way (i.e. direct participation supports and strengthens institutional forms of co-determination)?

This research may be performed in different fields:

- for special trade unions (IGM or Ver.di in Germany)
- in selected organizations
- on national level
- on international level (due to specific national contexts and institutions opportunities for dd participation in working life and TU organizations will be different from country to country)

Promotion of participatory workplace practices through a publicly-funded programme: experiences from Finland

Tuomo Alasoini, Asko Heikkilä, Elise Ramstad, Pekka Ylöstalo

Introduction

This paper examines to what extent participatory workplace practices can be promoted through a publicly-funded programme. The empirical material consists of data from 117 workplaces that participated in development projects funded by the Finnish Workplace Development Programme TYKES between 2004 and 2008. The overall aim of the TYKES programme is to promote simultaneous improvements in productivity and the quality of working life (QWL) at private and public workplaces in Finland.

This paper starts with an overview on arguments which state that QWL on the decline in many industrialized countries, the most notable exception to this trend being the Nordic countries. While finding some evidence in favour of this 'Nordic exceptionalism' in comparative analyses, this paper highlights that even the Nordic countries are not immune to the enforcing effects of the new phase of global competition. This discussion is followed by an examination of possible policy options to counteract this trend. The general conclusion is that 'soft' forms of regulation are probably the most efficient approach available to increase companies' interest in experimenting with participatory workplace practices.

The empirical part of this paper examines the results of the High-Involvement Innovation Practice Survey, which is intended to monitor changes in workplace practices achieved through development projects of the TYKES programme. The changes are monitored by comparing the situation at participating workplaces both at the beginning of the project and at its conclusion, and by analysing management and personnel responses separately. This paper looks at the effects of the projects on employees' opportunities for direct participation and supporting managerial and organizational practices.

The Quality of Working Life in Comparative Perspective – Does the National Infrastructure Matter?

According to many influential authors on the subject, we are witnessing a long-term trend of degradation in QWL in industrialized nations (e.g. Beck, 2000;

Head, 2003; Rifkin, 1995; Sennett, 1998). In this debate, the main driving force is economic globalization, supported by increasing liberalization and deregulation of the product, financial and labour markets, rapid progress of information and communications technologies and declining powers of the trade unions. Some recent comparative studies, however, have suggested that the Nordic countries form an important exception to this general trend, as employees in these countries still enjoy a reasonably high QWL.

Dobbin and Boychuk (1999) compared the level of job autonomy experienced by management and workers in four Nordic countries (Denmark, Finland, Norway and Sweden) and three English-speaking industrialized countries (Australia, Canada and the United States). The comparison was based on responses from people who hold full-time jobs (N = 7,496) in each of the countries in the 1980s. The study showed that the job autonomy experienced by both management and workers, measured in terms of their capacity to design their own work processes and make key, non-routine decisions, was greater in the Nordic countries than in the English-speaking countries, even after standardizing the main background variables. The authors concluded that one can speak of national employment systems, each with its own logic affecting the organization of work. They also considered that the Nordic countries embraced what could be termed a skill-governed system, as distinct from the rule-governed system characteristic of the English-speaking countries, particularly in regard to management, workers' opportunities for training and co-determination, and job security.

Gallie (2003) used the 1996 Employment in Europe survey to examine the contention that there are differences in QWL between the Nordic countries and other European countries. The survey consisted of responses from 6,163 employees in 14 EU countries. The study's principal hypothesis was that the Danish and Swedish active policies on working-life reform, supported by high union density and consensual industrial relations, are reflected in a higher QWL than for other European countries. He made the assumption that the same applies to Finland, though to a lesser degree. For the most part, the study results supported the hypothesis of a distinctive 'Scandinavian pattern'. The Nordic countries stood out from the other countries especially in terms of the quality of work tasks, employees' opportunities for participation and consultation, and employees' opportunities for training. On the other hand, no clear difference was found in career opportunities. In addition, and in contrast to Finland and Sweden, the job security position of Danish employees was no better than in the other countries.

Lorenz and Valeyre (2006) analysed data from the third Survey on Working Conditions by the European Foundation of Living and Working Conditions, conducted in 2000, to examine the extent to which forms of work organization are converging in Europe. The data consisted of the responses of 8,081 employees working in companies employing at least 10 people. By using a multiple correspondence analysis on 15 organizational variables they built up a typology of four clusters, which they called 'discretionary learning', 'lean', 'Taylorist' and 'traditional' forms of work organization. The distinguishing features of the discretionary learning organization model were an advanced level of autonomy and task complexity, good learning opportunities offered by the work and ample problem-solving needed in the work. The other main modernization strategy, based on the lean organization model, contained some of the same features, but also contained more constraints on autonomy and laid more emphasis on formal team work and job rotation, and precise quality norms and quality control.

The analysis by Lorenz and Valeyre indicated that forms of work organization vary considerably across sectors and occupational categories. There were also significant differences in the diffusion of the four forms of work organization across the European countries in the study. The discretionary learning organization model was most widespread in the Netherlands, Denmark and Sweden, and to a lesser extent Finland, Germany and Austria. The lean organization model was most in evidence in the UK and Ireland, while the Taylorist form was most widespread in the Southern European countries. Adoption of the discretionary learning and lean organization models, i.e. the most dynamic forms of work organization, had a significant positive association with the level of R&D expenditure of the countries concerned, which may indicate that there are country-wise differences in the degree to which companies are positioned at the high-technology or high-quality end of product markets. This, however, did not explain the choice made between the adoption of a discretionary learning or a lean form of work organization. The main explanation provided by the authors for this choice is that the level of regulation of the labour market is positively associated with the level of institutional support for establishing discretionary learning forms of work organization: first, collective coordination of the labour market serves to buffer distributional conflict and helps maintain collaborative, high-trust labour-management relations that are an important prerequisite for broad participation of employees in developmental and innovation-promoting activities in companies; second, it provides a more solid foundation for companies to make extensive investments in training and other activities to enhance employees' skills.

In his volume entitled *Demanding Work*, Green (2006) undertook secondary analyses of a number of surveys that had examined changes in job quality in Western industrialized nations – mainly the United Kingdom, the United States, Germany and Australia – in the last twenty years. The concept of job quality used by Green is a particularly broad one that includes the following elements: the skills needed for the job, the work effort, the personal discretion of workers over their work tasks and forms of participation in workplace decisions, the pay received, occupational health and safety, job security and job satisfaction. His general conclusion is that job quality has deteriorated in many respects in Western industrialized nations in recent years. He also highlights certain exceptions to this conclusion, namely the Nordic countries, and particularly Finland. Green's view is based largely on development trends regarding the task discretion available to workers. Whereas in the United Kingdom, for example, task discretion has decreased dramatically in recent years in many issues, it has remained more or less unchanged in Finland.

The comparative studies referred to above indicate that national institutional structures have an effect on the organization of work. This is reflected in different aspects of QWL. Dobbin and Boychuk (1999) suggest that these structures have strong, mutually supporting systemic properties. They talk of national employment systems that are highly institutionalized, each with a different equilibrium between its various sub-systems (management, training, collective bargaining, job security), and which have the capacity to reproduce themselves, thus also displaying a high level of structural inertia. Megatrends, such as the globalization and networking of the economy and the development of information and communication technologies, percolate through these structures in different ways, depending on the country in question. The new management doctrines concerning such megatrends do not therefore have a mechanical influence but instead take on hybrid forms at national level on the basis of local (re)interpretations.

The argument on mediating role of national institutional structures is supported by two recent Finnish studies. Statistically reliable data that represent the employed labour force at Finnish workplaces employing at least 10 people (N=1,117) show that employees' experiences of the effects of teamwork on their own work are surprisingly positive, especially when put into a comparative perspective with the much more contradictory findings of many studies carried out in the English-speaking industrialized countries. The main explanation given by Niemelä and Kalliola (2007) to the highly positive accounts is the institutional characteristics of the Finnish system of industrial relations that fosters the implementation of teamwork in a cooperative way, combined with the overall high level of trust prevailing in Finnish society (see also Castells and Himanen, 2002; Pesonen and Riihinen, 2002). In another recent study, Kalmi and Kauhanen (2008) analysed the effects of workplace innovations on employees' (N=4,104) experiences of job intensity, job influence, job security, job satisfaction and the level of stress as well as the level of pay, based on the Quality of Work Life Survey carried out by Statistics Finland in 2003. The results indicate that workplace innovations, such as self-managed teams, employer-provided training, incentive pay and procedures for information sharing, were mainly associated with beneficial outcomes for employees. The authors of this study, too, refer to special characteristics of the Finnish industrial relations environment, which they consider apt for mutual gains from workplace innovations.

Such national institutional structures, which in Finland and in the other Nordic countries have had a positive influence on QWL as shown in the studies referred to above, are, however, also subject to changes themselves. The positive effect of these systems on QWL in the future is not a foregone conclusion but will require their constant development on the basis of a common understanding among the parties concerned. The new kind of managerial rhetoric associated with the megatrends referred to above has already taken root widely in the Nordic countries. In Sweden, many researchers have noted that the former 'Swedish welfare model' has weakened in recent years to the extent that it no longer generate positive impacts on QWL (e.g. Huzzard, 2003; von Otter, 2004). A similar debate has been held in Finland, too. In a study that generated considerable public discussion, Siltala (2004), for example, highlights what he sees as 'the recent deterioration in working life', noting that 'global hypercompetition' is leading to diminished opportunities for self-regulation at work for the vast majority of Finnish employees.

Siltala's gloomy conclusions concerning the collapse of 'Finnish exceptionalism' are partly supported by the annual time-series data provided by the Working Life Barometer studies of the Ministry of Employment and the Economy, which clearly demonstrate that the positive trend in employees' opportunities for exerting an influence at work halted in Finland in the early 2000s and has since turned into a decline at both private and public workplaces (Ylöstalo and Jukka, 2008). Despite the positive results of the two studies referred to above concerning the effects of teamwork and other workplace innovations on employees, the overall occurrence of participatory workplace practices in Finland seems to be now on the wane, rather than on the rise.

Policy Options in the Promotion of Workplace Innovation

It is possible to make a distinction between different types of policy approaches in the promotion of innovative development in working life. On the most general level, we can talk of 'hard' and 'soft' forms of regulation. The former concept refers to legislative intervention, which, in turn, can be further divided into two types. Direct legislative regulation focuses directly on workplace practices, whereas in the case of indirect 'hard' legislation changes in workplace practices are pursued indirectly through changes in the product market and the labour market, for example. 'Soft' regulation refers to non-binding policy intervention. Also 'soft' regulation includes different variations, ranging from general policy frameworks and recommendations (weak forms) to the provision of information on 'best practices' and training and education to managers and employees (medium-strong forms) and, further, to advisory and consultancy services, benchmarking tools and grants and subsidies to companies (strong forms).

An analysis made by Forsyth et al. (2006) shows that the use of direct legislative intervention in the promotion of workplace innovation is rare. What we find, instead, is a great variety of persuasive, 'soft' forms of regulation. A 'soft' approach can be a useful policy option, especially in situations where the objects for change (workplaces) are heterogeneous, processes leading to desired changes (workplace innovations) can take different shapes and means used in the promotion of changes (new workplace practices) are of sensitive nature (Trubek and Trubek, 2005).

For many companies, the threshold for actively searching for workplace innovation is considerably high. This may be due to the following reasons, among others (Betcherman, 1997; Business Decisions Limited, 2002; Ichniowski et al., 1996):

- Lack of information: companies may lack knowledge on how to promote workplace innovation.
- Lack of competence: companies may be well equipped with information, but they may lack competence to bring about necessary changes.
- Lack of motivation: management does not have a special incentive to actively promote workplace innovation, because the pressure on the part of customers, competitors or any other stakeholder group is not strong enough.
- High risks related to changes: the high level of risk may stem, for example, from long pay-back times of the investments made in the promotion of workplace innovation, volatility of the product market and the operational environment, or the possibility of leaks included in the actions taken (e.g. immediate imitation by competitors or loss of trained key personnel due to labour turnover).

The viability of the different policy options distinguished above is dependent on what are the main reasons for companies' insufficient activeness in the promotion of workplace innovation. Weak forms of 'soft' regulation may be enough, if it is solely a matter of lack of information. Medium-strong forms are needed in cases where a company lacks information or competence. If the major obstacle is in the motivational area or related to the high level of risk, stronger forms of 'soft' regulation, combined with indirect forms of legislative regulation, may be required.

A study by Business Decisions Limited (2002) on the obstacles to wider diffusion of new forms of work organization that was carried out in 10 EU countries in the early 2000s indicated several apparent and underlying factors. Among the workplaces that did not apply new forms of work organization as defined in the study, the biggest obstacles concerned motivational factors. Motivational factors were also mentioned as the main reason for problems that emerged during the implementation phase among the users of new forms of work organization, while also factors related to lack of competence played a role. Another study that was later undertaken in Finland brought similar results (Ylöstalo, 2005). Both studies give support to a view that in most cases effective promotion of workplace innovation would call for stronger means than proving solely general policy guidelines, information or training and education.

Promotion of Participatory Workplace Practices in a Programme Context

In the following, we first take a look at the Finnish Workplace Development Programme TYKES as an example of a strong form of 'soft' regulation. After that, we examine whether it is possible to promote participatory workplace practices through a publicly-funded programme and reverse the trend towards decreased employee influence at Finnish workplaces.

TYKES (2004-2009) is a governmental R&D programme, coordinated by the Finnish Funding Agency for Technology and Innovation Tekes and implemented in cooperation with the social partners, for promoting simultaneous improvements in productivity and QWL by granting funding to development projects at Finnish workplaces. TYKES is a continuation to an earlier programme that was implemented in two phases, in 1996-1999 and 2000-2003 (Alasoini, 2004; 2007). Support from the programme focuses on the work input of the experts (consultants, researchers and researcher-developers) used in the projects. So far, more than 900 projects have been funded, covering over 3,000 workplaces of all sizes, both in the private and public sector.

The workplace-level objective of TYKES is to help workplaces adopt managerial and organizational practices that will enable them to develop in a way conducive to *qualitatively sustainable productivity growth.* Productivity growth can be considered qualitatively sustainable when it subsumes improvement of QWL. This is manifested in greater opportunities for development and exerting influence at work for personnel, increased wellbeing at work, and strengthened internal cooperation and trust within the work community. In practice, in about 70% of concluded development projects, clear improvements in both productivity and QWL can be shown (Ramstad, 2007).

Many studies and earlier development projects have highlighted good practices that have helped introduce qualitatively sustainable productivity growth in different kinds of workplaces. However, successful workplace-specific solutions are typically just that – workplace-specific and hence unique. The results of successful development projects cannot generally be transposed from one workplace to another without modification.

New managerial and organizational practices can collectively be described as social innovations, and it may be assumed that their capacity for being transposed is governed by the same factors as the diffusion of innovations in general. Rogers (2003) mentions the following principal factors related to perceived attributes of innovation: the relative advantage of the innovation; its compatibility, with the potential adopter's current way of doing things and with social norms; the simplicity of the innovation; the ease with which the innovation can be tested by a potential adopter; and the ease with which the innovation can be evaluated after trial.

In the case of new managerial and organizational practices, these contributing factors are usually not present to such an extent that the practices could be mechanically transposed from one context to another. More commonly, solutions implemented in one workplace function as *generative ideas* for the others. What this means is that earlier solutions and models prompt new ideas and serve as inspiration and encouragement for self-motivated development work. Translating generative ideas into functional practices requires local redesign by the adopter (Alasoini, 2006). Successful redesign requires from the adopting workplace a retrospective, collaborative and investigative analysis of its own mode of operation.

Because of this, it was decided not to draw up a list of good practices in TYKES as a blueprint to be applied in development projects. Instead of helping workplaces adopt one-off solutions, the programme approach has been that it is more sensible to define characteristics that can help workplaces undertake continuous development.

Generally speaking, there are three such characteristics that are given considerable importance in TYKES (Alasoini et al., 2008). *Firstly,* the workplace must have development competence regarding products and services, production processes, work organization, management, and so on. *Secondly*, the workplace management and personnel must have the capacity and the willingness to commit to genuine cooperation in development. Broad employee participation in development aiming at qualitatively sustainable productivity growth is of the utmost importance. Through such participation, the development competence of the entire organization improves, there is more commitment to the solutions generated, and the scope of the development broadens. Solutions are also better because they take into account those dimensions of QWL that are important for employees. *Thirdly,* the workplace must be able to use external networks competently to support its development measures as necessary. The use of external experts brings complementary knowledge in support of development work, and often enhances innovativeness of new solutions and enables more comprehensive change taking place at the workplace (Ramstad, 2008).

All these three characteristics are important. One might think that the third of them could compensate for a lack of development competence at the workplace itself, but this is only partly true. Small workplaces in particular cannot, and need not, have competence in all areas of development important to them. What is more relevant is to know where and how such competence can be found when required. The need for improving the workplace's own development competence derives on the one hand from the workplace needing to be able to determine realistically at the strategic management level what kind of development measures it requires in order to attain the goals set; the measures must be governed by a strategy and the goals derived from it instead of blueprints offered by outside experts. On the other hand, such a need also derives from the fact that most workplace development measures are typically conducted alongside everyday work in a gradual and tacit improvement of products and work processes. Without the existence of such development competence and measures based on it, it may be difficult to implement more radical reforms at the workplace when needed.

As operating environments become increasingly complex, fluid and unpredictable, workplace competitiveness is increasingly dependent on the capacity for continuous improvement. This means that the focus in workplace development policies must be not on searching for one-off solutions but on changing the whole workplace mode of operation.

The High-Involvement Innovation Practice Survey and the Data Used

The High-Involvement Innovation Practice Survey is aimed at a selected group of workplaces participating in TYKES development projects, both at the beginning of the project and at its conclusion. The survey is given separately to a representative of management (usually production or personnel manager) and of the largest personnel group (usually chief shop steward or staff representative) using an online form. The purpose of the survey is to investigate high-involvement innovation practices – i.e. managerial and organizational practices that support continuous improvement and broad employee participation – at the workplaces, viewed by the two parties, and to monitor the effects of the projects on the use of these practices. The monitoring data is derived from differences between the entry and exit surveys. Workplaces are selected for the survey using the following five criteria: at least 10 employees participate in the project; at least 25% of the workplace personnel participates in the project; the funding received by the workplace from the programme is at least EUR 10,000 (EUR 5,000 in the case of a local government workplace); the duration of the project is at least 10 months; and no more than three workplaces are selected for the survey in each project. The purpose of these criteria is to pinpoint the workplaces that participate in development projects the most intensively.

The analysis here is focused on the effects of the projects on employees' opportunities for direct participation and supporting managerial and organizational practices. Opportunities for participation are examined by analysing (1) decision-making structures and (2) the role of work teams at the workplaces concerned. The supporting managerial and organizational practices comprise (3) information sharing at the workplace, (4) personnel competence development, (5) the role of supervisors in supporting employees and (6) cooperation between management and personnel in development. The comparison is made between the results of the entry and the exit survey, and, in cases of remarkable differences in view, also between responses of management and employee representatives.

The comparison only includes workplaces that have so far responded to both the entry and the exit survey; the number of responses is 189 and 162, representing 107 projects and 117 workplaces. The entire entry survey material consists of 723 responses to date (response rate 74%), and the entire exit survey material consists of 225 responses (response rate 59%). The share of responses by management and personnel representatives differ from one another in the various materials, and the potential bias in the distributions when making analyses with the combined material (i.e. examining the responses by management and employee representatives together) has been eliminated by using appropriate weighting coefficients.

The material under comparison was compiled from very different workplaces. 57% were private-sector workplaces, 24% was in local government, 14% from the third sector, and the rest were from agriculture and forestry and central government. The workplaces included in the material under comparison employ a total of 115,000 people, of whom more than 11,000 have actively participated in TYKES development projects. About half of the workplaces have more than 100 employees.

Empirical Analysis

Decision-Making Structures

Firstly, this paper examines changes in decision-making structures of the participating workplaces by making use of the 'responsibility index', developed by the Nordic 'Flexible Enterprise' project (NUTEK, 1999). This index was used in the project as one of the main criteria in making a distinction between 'flexible enterprises' and 'traditional enterprises'. We do not use the index as such; instead, we examine decision making at the workplaces through seven items included in the index separately.

In the High-Involvement Innovation Practice Survey, the respondents are asked who usually makes a decision in different matters. The given alternatives are 'the employee herself/himself', 'a group or a team', 'a supervisor or middle management', 'top management', 'someone else' or 'the question is not applicable'. Following a classification developed by Klein (1991), decision making in a modern team-based work organization can occur in three different ways. Decision making is *centralized* in case a manager makes the decision, or the decision is based on a rule or procedure. Decentralized decision making can take place in two different ways. In *independent* decision making responsibility is delegated to individuals, whereas in the case of *collaborative* decision making the team comes to a decision. The following analysis looks at changes in decision making on both dimensions, i.e. whether decision making is centralized vs. decentralized and whether decentralized decision making takes places individually vs. collaboratively.

To study to what extent participation in a project has resulted in a more flexible decision-making structure at the workplace, the following regrouping of responses was made: Cases in which decision making is usually available for individual employees or work teams are considered as an indication of a decentralized decision-making structure (DEC) in the issue concerned, while the cases where the primary decision-maker is top management or 'someone else' are classified as an indication of centralized decision making (CEN). Cases in which decision making is usually the priviledge of supervisors or middle managers are classified as intermediate (INT). Because there are not statistically significant differences between management and personnel responses, it is not feasible to discuss them separately at this point.

A great majority of the workplaces have a decentralized structure for decision making in daily planning of an individual employee's work task (Table 1). In about half of the cases, employees or teams usually make decisions on weekly planning as well. Supervisors and middle managers play the utmost role especially in the follow-up of results, purchasing and quality control, while the role of top management is emphasized in the development of production or services. A comparison between the entry and exit surveys indicates that the most notable change is an increased decision-making power by supervisors and middle managers. Their role is reinforced in all the seven items under investigation. A clear shift towards decentralized decision making has taken place only in the development of production and services.

Table 1: Decision-Making Structures at Workplaces

	ENTRY SURVEY, %				EXIT SURVEY, %			
	DEC	INT	CEN	**ALL**	DEC	INT	CEN	**ALL**
Daily planning	74	25	1	**100**	71	27	2	**100**
Weekly planning	50	47	2	**100**	49	48	3	**100**
Follow-up of results	13	72	15	**100**	14	76	10	**100**
Quality control	32	46	22	**100**	32	51	17	**100**
Purchasing	19	54	27	**100**	19	60	21	**100**
Maintenance	32	42	26	**100**	30	43	27	**100**
Production/service development	19	37	44	**100**	26	39	35	**100**

Entry survey, N=184-186
Exit survey, N=143-145

Next, we take a look at changes *within* decentralized decision making, i.e. to what extent decisions are delegated to individual employees vis-à-vis work teams. Figure 1 shows a considerable upsurge in collaborative decision making as work teams now are responsible for an increasing number of issues at the workplace.

The greater role played by work teams is seen especially in weekly planning (increase of 6.9 percentage units), quality control (increase of 5.0 percentage units) and the development of production and services (increase of 5.6 percentage units). One could argue that individual autonomy enjoyed by individual employees is increasingly being replaced by collective autonomy of work teams at workplaces where the degree of task interdependence is increasing in line with the introduction of process-oriented work system design (cf. also Klein, 1991). Decrease of individual autonomy, indicated as the share of cases in which the employee herself/himself usually makes a decision, is most clearly observed in daily planning (decrease of 5.9 percentage units), weekly planning (decrease of 8.0 percentage units) and quality control (decrease of 4.6 percentage units).

Figure 1: Change in Individual and Collaborative Decision Making between the Entry and Exit Surveys (entry survey minus exit survey, in percentage units)

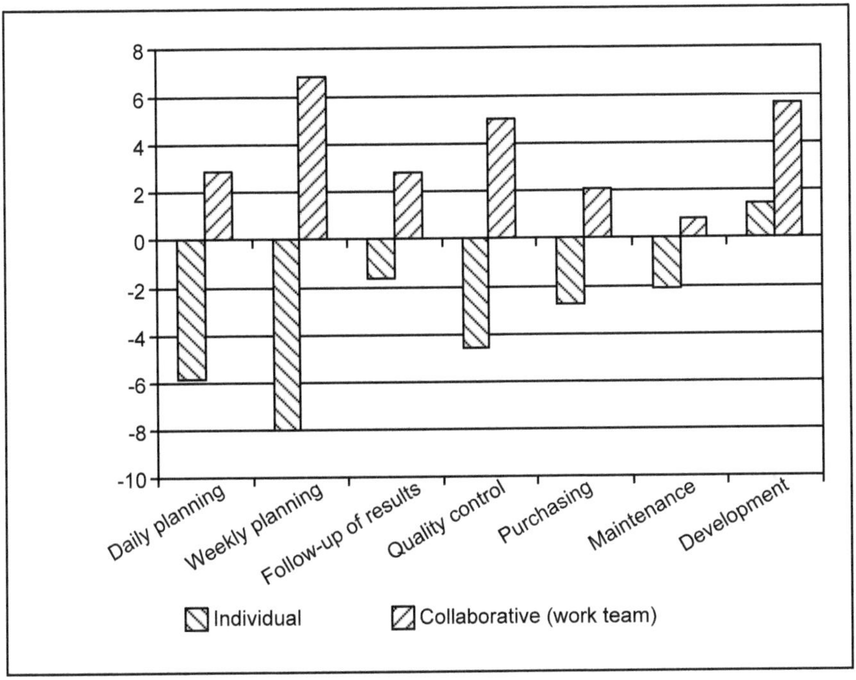

The above analysis shows that change in decision making is advancing on two tracks at the reformed workplaces. On the one hand, supervisors and middle managers are gaining increased influence in operational decision making. This change seems to be taking place mainly at the expense of top management. At the same time, collective autonomy by work teams is increasingly substituting for individual autonomy by employees. Next, we take a closer look at changes in the role of teamwork at the workplaces concerned.

The Role of Work Teams

Teamwork is a widespread phenomenon at Finnish workplaces these days: in the entire entry survey material only 11% of the respondents state that no-one at their workplace works in a team, cell or other group. The roles and responsibilities of teams, however, differ greatly from one workplace to another. According to the study by Kalmi and Kauhanen (2008), for instance, while most employees in Finland participate in teams, the share of those working in self-managed teams in 2003 accounted only for around 10% of respondents. Self-managed teams in their study were defined as teams that select their own leader and decide on the internal division of responsibilities.

The High-Involvement Innovation Practice Survey characterizes teams with nine features. The respondents are asked in the survey how well these features correspond with the features of the teams found at their workplace. The different options available are: 1=not at all, 2=not very well, 3=to some degree and 4=well. Table 2 shows the statistical means of the responses in the entry and exit surveys. Neither in this case are there statistically significant differences between management and personnel responses.

In the case of eight of the nine features, the means of the exit survey are higher, indicating a change towards a more versatile role for the teams. The greatest differences concern direct contacts both with other teams at the workplace and with parties outside the workplace (e.g. customers, subcontractors and suppliers), all of which have increased substantially. The main exceptions to the general trend are flexible division of work within the teams, where the change is only slightly in a positive direction, and the selection of team members, where there is a slight change towards an opposite direction. Statistically significant differences between distributions of the entry and exit surveys can be found in three of the nine items.

Table 2: Characteristics of Work Teams (only includes responses from those workplaces that have teams)

Scale (1=does not describe work teams at all – 4=describes work teams well)	ENTRY SURVEY Mean	EXIT SURVEY Mean	
Decide on their day-to-day and weekly tasks themselves	3.07	3.17	
Are responsible for the quality of their work themselves	3.49	3.64	$p<.05$
Members perform several different tasks in the team	3.43	3.49	
Choose their own members	1.99	1.94	
Choose their own leaders	1.91	2.07	
Have direct contacts with other teams at the workplace	3.07	3.28	
Have direct contacts with parties outside the workplace	2.57	2.88	$p<.01$
Develop their operations continuously	2.92	3.09	$p<.05$
Develop products and services	2.65	2.81	
N	165-168	143-147	

Information Sharing

Information sharing at the workplace is the first of the four supporting managerial and organizational practices under examination. Table 3 demonstrates that there is a statistically significant difference between the entry and exit surveys in two questions concerning personnel's knowledge on the key results targets at the workplace. Once again, differences between management and personnel responses in both surveys are small.

Table 3: Information Sharing at Workplaces

	ENTRY SURVEY	EXIT SURVEY	
Scale (1=very poor – 4=very good)	Mean	Mean	
Personnel's knowledge on the key results targets of the whole workplace	2.46	2.79	p<.001
Personnel's knowledge on the key results targets of their own work unit	2.77	3.04	p<.001
N	187	159	

Increased awareness of the key results targets in the exit survey may be partly explained by the fact that any development project, in itself, requires increased openness and transparency in order to lead to success. It remains an open question whether this change achieved during the course of project will lead to a more sustainable change in information sharing practices at the participating workplaces.

Personnel Competence Development

Practices to develop personnel competence are monitored by two questions. The first question concerns the proportion of employees at the workplace who have an individual training and development plan. Secondly, the survey examines participation in employer-paid training in the last 12 months.

The entry survey indicates that only 19% workplaces have drawn up an individual training and development plan for the majority of their personnel (Table 4). In the exit survey, this figure has gone up to 30%. It is worth noting that the percentage of workplaces where no employee has such a plan has dropped significantly (46% to 28%). The difference between management (MGMT) and personnel (PER) responses found in the entry survey remains in the exit survey.

On the whole, there is a statistically significant difference ($p<.01$) between the results of the two surveys.

Table 4: Proportion of Personnel with an Individual Training and Development Plan

	ENTRY SURVEY, %			EXIT SURVEY, %		
	MGMT	PER	**ALL**	MGMT	PER	**ALL**
All	12	9	**10**	19	13	**16**
More than half	12	6	**9**	18	11	**14**
No more than half	36	34	**35**	40	44	**42**
None	41	51	**46**	23	32	**28**
Total	100	100	**100**	100	100	**100**
N	95	88	**183**	79	78	**157**

Participation in training paid for by the employer has also increased between the two surveys, though the difference between the two surveys is not statistically significant (Table 5). The percentage of workplaces where the majority of employees have participated in training has clearly increased. In the entry survey, 52% of workplaces had provided training for the majority of employees within the past year. This figure has gone up to 60% in the exit survey. As in the previous question, the difference found between management and personnel responses in the entry survey still exists in the exit survey.

Table 5: Proportion of Personnel Participation in Training Paid for by the Employer

	ENTRY SURVEY, %			EXIT SURVEY, %		
	MGMT	PER	**ALL**	MGMT	PER	**ALL**
All	31	24	**27**	39	25	**32**
More than half	30	21	**25**	29	27	**28**
No more than half	34	45	**39**	29	43	**36**
None	5	11	**8**	3	5	**4**
Total	100	100	**100**	100	100	**100**
N	94	92	**186**	79	79	**158**

Role of Supervisors in Supporting Employees

The supervisory structure can play either a coercive or an enabling role with regard to employee performance at the workplace (Adler and Borys, 1996). In the High-Involvement Innovation Practice Survey, the focus is exclusively on the enabling role of supervisors. The survey examines through three statements how management and personnel representatives consider the role of supervisors supporting employees at work and encourage their learning and opportunities for initiative and development. Respondents have four options in the questionnaire: 1=disagree completely, 2= disagree partly, 3=agree partly and 4=agree completely.

Examination of the results of the entry and exit surveys indicates a slight, but not statistically significant, change towards a more supportive role for supervisors (Table 6). The most interesting result, however, is that there prevails, in both the entry and the exit survey, a statistically significant difference between management and personnel responses. One possible explanation to this gap is that management and employee representatives use different standards when making assessments on managerial practices at the workplace, or that they have different expectations concerning what is 'good management'.

Table 6: Role of Supervisors in Supporting Employees

Scale (1=disagree completely, 4=agree completely)	ENTRY SURVEY Mean			EXIT SURVEY Mean		
	MGMT	PER	**ALL**	MGMT	PER	**ALL**
Support and encourage employees at work	3.21	2.83	**3.02**	3.33	2.88	**3.11**
Encourage learning and development of employees at work	3.31	2.84	**3.08**	3.38	2.93	**3.16**
Encourage employees taking initiative and develop new procedures	3.28	2.82	**3.05**	3.28	2.92	**3.10**
N	93	92	**185**	79	76-78	**155-157**

Cooperation between Management and Personnel in Development

The fourth set of supporting managerial and organizational practices concerns labour-management relations at the workplaces through four statements. The options available for the respondents are the same than in the previous section. As in the case of the supervisory structure, there is a slight, yet not statistically significant, change towards higher trust and more collaborative relationships between management and personnel (Table 7). Here again, there exists a consistent difference of level between responses submitted by management and personnel representatives. In spite of the fact that personnel representatives have a more critical view on the state of labour-management cooperation than those of management, the workplaces participating in the TYKES programme, on average, have a relatively collaborative systems of employee relations. For example, in the exit survey the proportion of personnel representatives that agree partly or completely with the statement 'management takes a constructive approach to personnel proposals' is as high as 76%.

Table 7: Cooperation between Management and Personnel in Development

Scale (1=disagree completely, 4=agree completely)	ENTRY SURVEY Mean			EXIT SURVEY Mean		
	MGMT	PER	**ALL**	MGMT	PER	**ALL**
Relationships between management and personnel are open and confidential	3.06	2.68	**2.87**	3.25	2.67	**2.96**
Management and personnel engage in genuine development cooperation	3.13	2.72	**2.93**	3.18	2.85	**3.01**
Management takes a constructive approach to personnel proposals	3.40	2.87	**3.14**	3.51	2.90	**3.20**
Personnel takes a constructive approach to management proposals	3.00	2.81	**2.91**	3.10	2.90	**3.00**
N	94	91-92	**185-186**	78-79	76	**154-155**

Summary and Conclusions

This paper revolves around the issue to what extent participatory workplace practices can be promoted through a publicly-funded programme. Conclusions drawn in the following are based on a comparison between the results of the entry and the exit survey of the High-Involvement Innovation Practice Survey developed by the Finnish TYKES programme. Employees' opportunities for participation were examined by analysing the level of decision making in seven issues at the workplace, the role of work teams in nine issues and a number of supporting managerial and organizational practices.

The empirical analysis, based on results from 107 concluded development projects and 117 workplaces that participated in the projects, indicates a two-way trend in the pattern of decision making at the reformed workplaces. On the one hand, supervisors and middle managers are strengthening their role in operational decision making; on the other hand, the responsibilities of work teams are expanding. Another set of questions, which takes a closer look at the characteristics of work teams, shows that teams at the reformed workplaces have increased direct outward contacts and broader responsibilities in quality control and development. A comparison between the entry and exit surveys also shows a clear advance in the use of information sharing and personnel competence development practices at the reformed workplaces. In issues related to the enabling role of superviors and the state of labour-management cooperation, there exists a statistically significant difference of level between views by management and personnel representatives. Also here we can notice a slight, but not yet statistically significant, change towards a more supportive role for supervisors and more collaborative labour-management relationship at the reformed workplaces, according to both management and personnel responses.

Are the results described above supportive to a view that it is possible to promote employees' opportunities for participation through strong forms of 'soft' regulation, such as development programmes? An answer to this question depends on two matters, in particular.

Firstly, the empirical analysis did not show a clear shift towards decentralized decision making, with the exception of the development of production and services. At the same time, work teams were increasingly substituting for individual employees in issues where decision making is decentralized. The decisive issue, then, is how work teams operate in practice, i.e. how democratic is their internal division of labour and how decisions are made within the teams. A tentative conclusion is that a changeover to a team-based work system can be combined with increased employee participation on condition that sufficient supportive managerial practices in, for example, information sharing, personnel competence development and enabling supervisory work are in place, equipping *all* members of the work teams with sufficient information and increased skills and competencies on an equal basis. Unfortunately, our data do not allow us to examine this issue here in greater detail. Future research will hopefully shed more light on the preconditions for participatory structures within work teams; an issue which has been discussed previously elsewhere, too (e.g. Kirkman and Rosen, 1999; Procter and Burridge, 2008).

The second conditional issue is how durable the improvements attained are. As previous experience with many development projects shows, it is often easier to achieve one-off improvements than bring about processes of sustained development at workplaces with the help of a publicly-funded intervention (Alasoini, 2006). An important indication of sustained development would be the fact that simultaneous improvements can be monitored in several workplace practices. This argument stems from a view that workplace practices have system-like characters and there exists significant complementaries between different practices (e.g. Pettigrew et al., 2003; Roberts, 2004). Success in attaining sustained development towards participatory workplace practices would probably call for a system-based view on the object for development in publicly-funded programmes and projects. Future research on this issue, too, would be needed.

References

Adler, P.S. / Borys, B. (1996): 'Two Types of Bureaucracy: Enabling and Coercive', Administrative Science Quarterly 41(1): 61-89.

Alasoini, T. (2004): 'The New Finnish Workplace Development Program (TYKES-FWDP) as an Approach to Innovation', Concepts and Transformation 9(3): 279-295.

Alasoini, T. (2006): 'In Search of Generative Results: A New Generation of Programmes to Develop Work Organization', Economic and Industrial Democracy 27(1): 9-37.

Alasoini, T. (2007): 'The Finnish Workplace Development Programme as an Expanding Activity: Results, Challenges, Opportunities', pp. 9-41 in J. Pelletier (ed.) Intervention Practices in Firms. Lyon: Anact.

Alasoini, T. / Heikkilä, A. / Ramstad, E. / Ylöstalo, P. (2008): 'High-Involvement Innovation Practices at Finnish Workplaces', International Journal of Productivity and Performance Management 57(6): 449-459.

Beck, U. (2000): The Brave New World of Work. Cambridge: Polity Press.

Betcherman, G. (1997): Changing Workplace Strategies: Achieving Better Outcomes for Enterprises, Workers and Society. Ottawa: Government of Canada and OECD.

Business Decisions Limited (2002): New Forms of Work Organisation: The Obstacles to Wider Diffusion. Brussels: European Commission, DG for Employment, Industrial Relations and Social Affairs.

Castells, M. / Himanen, P. (2002): The Information Society and the Welfare State: The Finnish Model. Oxford: Oxford University Press.

Dobbin, F. / Boychuk, T. (1999): 'National Employment Systems and Job Autonomy: Why Job Autonomy Is High in the Nordic Countries and Low in the United States, Canada, and Australia', Organization Studies 20(2): 257-291.
Forsyth, A. / Gahan, P. / Howe, J. / Mitchell, R. (2006): Regulating for Innovation in Workplace Production and Employment Systems: A Preliminary Discussion of Issues and Themes. Paper presented to the 3rd Australian Labour Law Association National Conference, Brisbane, 22-23 September 2006.
Gallie, D. (2003): 'The Quality of Working Life: Is Scandinavia Different?', European Sociological Review 19(1): 61-79.
Green, F. (2006): Demanding Work: The Paradox of Job Quality in the Affluent Economy. Princeton: Princeton University Press.
Head, S. (2003): The New Ruthless Economy: Work and Power in the Digital Age. New York: Oxford University Press.
Huzzard, T. (2003): The Convergence of the Quality of Working Life and Competitiveness: A Current Swedish Literature Review. Stockholm: National Institute for Working Life.
Ichniowski, C. / Kochan, T.A. / Levine, D. / Olson, C. / Strauss, G. (1996): 'What Works at Work: Overview and Assessment', Industrial Relations 35(3): 299-333.
Kalmi, P. / Kauhanen, A. (2008): 'Workplace Innovations and Employee Outcomes: Evidence from Finland', Industrial Relations 47(3): 430-459.
Kirkman, B.L. / Rosen, B. (1999): 'Beyond Self-Management: The Antecedents and Consequences of Team Empowerment', Academy of Management Journal 42(1): 58-74.
Klein, J.A. (1991): 'A Reexamination of Autonomy in Light of New Manufacturing Practices', Human Relations 44(1): 21-38.
Lorenz, E. / Valeyre, A. (2006): 'Organisational Forms and Innovative Performance: A Comparison of the EU-15', pp. 140-160 in E. Lorenz and B.-Å. Lundvall (eds.) How Europe's Economies Learn: Coordinating Competing Models. Oxford: Oxford University Press.
Niemelä, J. / Kalliola, S. (2007): 'Team Membership and Experiences of Work in the Finnish Context', Economic and Industrial Democracy 28(4): 552-588.
NUTEK (Swedish Agency for Economic and Regional Growth) (1999): Flexibility Matters – Flexible Enterprises in the Nordic Countries. Stockholm: NUTEK.
Otter, C. von (2004): Swedish Working Life – Searching for a New Regime. Stockholm: National Institute for Working Life.
Pesonen, P. / Riihinen, O. (2002): Dynamic Finland: The Political System and the Welfare State. Helsinki: Finnish Literature Society.

Pettigrew, A.M. / Whittington, R. / Melin, L. / Sánchez-Runde, C. / Bosch, F.A.J. van den / Ruigrok, W. / Numagami, T. (eds.) (2003): Innovative Forms of Organizing: International Perspectives. London: Sage.

Procter, S. / Burridge, M. (2008): 'Teamworking and Performance: The Extent and Intensity of Teamworking in the 1998 UK Workplace Employee Relations Survey (WERS98)', International Journal of Human Resource Management 19(1): 153-168.

Ramstad, E. (2007): 'Unresolved Couple? The Relationship between Performance and the Quality of Working Life and the Role of Development Approach', pp. 93-108 in J. Pelletier (ed.) Intervention Practices in Firms. Lyon: Anact.

Ramstad, E. (2008): Innovation Generating Model – Simultaneous Development of Work Organization and Knowledge Infrastructure. Reports of the Finnish Workplace Development Programme 65. Helsinki: Tekes.

Rifkin, J. (1995): The End of Work: The Decline of the Global Labour Force and the Dawn of the Post-Market Era. New York: Putnam.

Roberts, J. (2004): The Modern Firm: Organizational Design for Performance and Growth. Oxford: Oxford University Press.

Rogers, E.M. (2003): Diffusion of Innovations. 5th edition. New York: Free Press.

Sennett, R. (1998): The Corrosion of Character: The Personal Consequences of Work in the New Capitalism. New York: W.W. Norton.

Siltala, J. (2004): Työelämän huonontumisen lyhyt historia: muutokset hyvinvointivaltioiden ajasta globaaliin hyperkilpailuun [A Short History of the Deterioration of Working Life: Changes from the Era of Welfare States to Global Hypercompetition]. Helsinki: Otava.

Trubek, D.M. / Trubek, L.G. (2005): 'Hard and Soft Law in the Construction of Social Europe: The Role of the Open Method of Co-ordination', European Law Journal 11(3): 343-364.

Ylöstalo, P. (2005): Työn uudet organisointitavat: Käyttö ja käytön esteet yksityisellä ja julkisella sektorilla [New Forms of Work Organization: Use and Obstacles to Use in the Private and Public Sectors]. Reports of the Finnish Workplace Development Progamme 39. Helsinki: Ministry of Labour.

Ylöstalo, P. / Jukka, P. (2008): Työolobarometri: lokakuu 2007 [Finnish Working Life Barometer: October 2007]. Publications 16/2008. Helsinki: Ministry of Employment and the Economy.

Employee involvement in health and safety at work

Davide Dazzi

Work transformation and risk profiles

The world of work is undergoing continuous changes. If we had to assess the road of work based on its "milestones", the present times might be referred to as the third great revolution[1]. After the industrial revolution dating from the 18th and 19th centuries, the Taylorist management scientific organization model and the Fordist production model emerged, centered on mass consumption and standardized products with demand led by supply. The third great revolution is characterized by the shift from the Fordist to the post-Fordist production model, in turn characterized by a leaner, more flexible and *just in time* production, where supply is led by the changing market conditions: the production level depends on the volatility of demand, thus introducing a close relationship between production and consumption. There was a shift from *mass production* to *lean production,* where technological development became a lever to invest on in order to maintain one's competitiveness on the market.

If on the one hand, the technical-scientific development became the instrument for the establishment of the post-Fordist production model, on the other hand, globalization, or better a global market has created the reference context by reshaping the balance between demand and supply and by stimulating a constant variability of the market. In a globalized market, where everything is more accelerated and where competitiveness depends on enterprises' ability and timeliness to ad just to the changing market needs, it becomes necessary for enterprises to act in a lean and flexible way. The industrial production structure shifts away form the vertical model, by *outsourcing* those non *core* business activities (and especially the *labour intensive* activities), an by developing a close network of enterprises linked to the industrial *core asset,* and interconnected by a complex set of service and supply relationships, inevitably leading to high business birth and death rates. At the same time, the small and medium sized enterprises, especially those working in the industrial sector, have become increasingly more networked to reach the necessary critical mass to engage in joint innovation projects.

The need for flexibility is not only imposed by the corporate production structure but also by the work organization and by the bargaining configuration

1 With reference to the Hungarian economist and philosopher Karl Polany.

itself. Suffices it to think of the collective bargaining of the different Member States, or of the role played by working hours flexibility or by the European Social Dialogue, or the controversy raised by the working hour Directive or the Bolkestein Directive on domestic market services, to understand how the work organization trend is *especially* going towards flexibility. Also with reference to labour contracts are concerned, a flexibilization process of labour relations is now taking place and the debate on *flexicurity* is the most recent expression of this phenomenon and the increase in the number of atypical workers is an evidence of that (during the 2000-2006 period in the 25-EU Member States, the *non standard* work growth rate was 2.4%, although at different speeds, by Country, age and gender)[2]

Health and safety at work has not remained unaffected by all these significant changes that have occurred in the world of work. The range of risks has also changed along with the various organization and legislative changes. In the past, a special attention was paid to physical fatigue and the repetitiveness of operations, whereas at present, the workers' health and safety representatives are not only faced with a further increase of "traditional risks", but also with new ones. Workers are now obliged to adjust to the new market conditions without any actual safe and longstanding jobs, thus with a disruption of the qualitative balance between social and work life, breaking away from the Ford-Keynesian compromise between subordination and full safety and getting closer to the "flexible man" notion by Sennet[3].

Hence, there has been a shift away from traditional work to new "emerging" forms of work or "emerging" performances expected from traditional employees. Technical and technological development has been accompanied by a whole set of electronic communication and control systems that have had a major impact on work organization and have changed risk profiles, by increasing the nervous fatigue load on workers.

The knowledge of impact and effects that new forms of work organization have on workers' health and safety conditions at the workplace, on the dimension of workers' psychological, physical and social wellbeing must necessarily take into account the new changes that have occurred on the labour market and its setup. A "new" form of participation in the labour market, namely the female participation, is now also emerging. The increase of the female employment rate, also encouraged by the same European employment strategy, now opens the door

2 ETUI-REHS, Benchmarking Working Europe 2007.

3 Sennet R., The Personal Consequences of Work in the New Capitalism, Norton & Company, 1998 (Sennet R., The Personal Consequences of Work in the New Capitalism, Norton & Company, 1998, Feltrinelli, 2001).

to a greater occupational disorder rate affecting women workers in particular, such as allergies, infectious diseases, neurological, liver and skin problems. A further element to be taken into consideration is the demographic growth of the labour force, with a growing number of older employees. The latter are affected by higher specific risk profiles, also due to rapid technological and organizational changes, which they are not familiar with. Hence, the reorganization of the continuous training system and, more specifically, in the area of health and safety at work to provide all employees with the necessary tools to work safely. A further demographic aspect that has an impact on safety at the workplace is immigration. Migrant workers usually are usually hired in labour intensive compartments of the manufacturing system, where the work accident rate is higher.

The health and safety system is an open system and as such it should be intended according to a policy perspective. It is not enough to observe the work accident phenomenon to identify the weaknesses and strengths but it is necessary to adopt a systematic and multidisciplinary approach according to the philosophy of social determinants, which is now widely spread at the European level. The work accident phenomenon should not just be observed and its causes do not only lie in what is statistically defined as "material agent". Work accidents also depend on other factors, such as social, cultural, age-related and "institutional" factors. They cannot be ignored when effective preventative policies, strategies or actions are to be designed.

Work conditions in Europe

The fourth survey on work conditions that has been carried out by the European Foundation for the Improvement of Living and Working Conditions of Dublin highlights that in addition to ongoing physical distress factors, further significant psychosocial elements are now also emerging[4].

Over the past few years, work intensity – namely hectic paces, busy agendas and deadlines – has increased especially among highly skilled workers. In 2005 46% of European labour force (EU25) stated that they worked at hectic pace during at least three quarters of their working hours (in 1990, in EU12, the per-

4 Starting from 1990, every five years, the European Foundation for the Improvement of Living and Working Conditions (Dublin) has carried out surveys aimed at collecting information on the perception that European employees have about their own working conditions (physical and social environment, work organization, working hours, health and safety etc. ...). During the second six-month term of 2005, 30 thousand employees from 31 countries (EU25, Bulgaria and Romania, Croatia, Turkey, Switzerland and Norway) were interviewed.

centage did not exceed 35%). In the European manufacturing sector, namely 40% of employees stated that their work pace depended on the machinery speed. More than half of the interviewed employees (56%) worked according to a timetable set by their own company, without any possibility to change it. To a much lesser extent, 25% stated that they could decide freely when they wished to take a break. An increase in work intensity is not offset by an equal increase in freedom to decide about work organization.

As far as physical risks are concerned, 62% of the labour force stated that during 25% or more of their working hours they were obliged to carry out repetitive hand and arm movements[5] (+4% as against the previous survey), whereas 20% of workers stated that they hade to handle heavy burdens during all their working hours or for most of the time. The survey by the Dublin Foundation also included specific questions on the social environment. These surveys also indicate that a rather alarmingly high rate of 5% of employees have suffered a form or another of abuse, stalking or harassment at the workplace: young women workers are the main victims, especially in the large-sized enterprises in Northern European countries. The physical violence rate has also worsened: it has increased from 4% in 1995 to 6% in 2005. In summary, in most cases, employees complain about the outbreak of "traditional" forms of abuse and the inexorable increase of psychological and social disorders, i.e.: backache (29%) and muscular pain (28%) as well as stress and fatigue (27%). The concerns expressed both by employers and employees' representative organizations have led the European social partners to sign the Framework Agreement on work-related stress in 2004 and of the and Framework Agreement on harassment and violence at work on April 26th, 2007.

European strategies for health and safety and employee involvement

Over the past few years, the national international regulatory trends at the workplace health and safety area have shown a growing attention to the development of health and safety system management methods. The traditional regulations, centred on a prescriptive approach, regarded employees as passive individuals subject to rules and regulations. The far too evident constraints of this kind of "*top down*" approach have spurred the development of new systems in furtherance of a participatory approach: employees and employers' involvement in *Occupational Health and Safety Management (OHSM)*. Hence, there was a shift from a prescriptive and compulsory approach to prevention-oriented provisions through

5 In Bulgaria and Romania the same percentage reaches 74%.

the regulation of a safety management process by means of an active involvement of business stakeholders.

The Framework Directive 89/391/EC and the following specific Directives are the regulatory source of reference for the new Community approach. The new Community Directive envisages a management system for a work environment organization based on a set of measures that, on the one hand, oblige employers to carry out a risk assessment and, on the other hand, the other stakeholders to establish a preventive dialogue for the adoption and use of prevention tools.

The Framework Directive on health and safety is based on 4 fundamentals whereby employers are obliged to guarantee the employees' health and safety:

- Occupational risk prevention programme and constant updating of prevention provisions
- Risk assessment
- Protection and prevention services
- Employee involvement

Employee involvement in the Framework Directive on health and safety

Occupational health and safety is a theme that has often been taken into account in the EU social policy through the adoption of a large number of Directives, which have then been transposed into several national legislations. The EU policy has thus contributed to define a common platform of rights and duties, which become an essential point of reference for national policies regulating the health and safety system. In spite of their highly significant regulatory and organization role, Directives are a necessary but not sufficient condition, at a European level, to guarantee a real improvement of living and working conditions. To start with, a few weaknesses can already be detected in their legislative form. As a matter of fact, Directives are the synthesis of a decision-making process that might at times require compromises among the various partners, which might end up weakening the consistency and convergence of provisions to be implemented. The effectiveness of a set of measures in the area of safety at work is not just a question of legislative form: no top-down approach can indeed lead to an actual improvement working conditions but the thrust should come directly from employees themselves.

The Framework Directive 89/391/EC has envisaged a greater employee involvement in many Member States, by recognizing a primary role to be played by preventive strategy and by obliging them to cooperate with other health and safety key stakeholders for the continuous improvement of living and working conditions. Participation also means implementing "balanced" information and consultation practices, in compliance with specific practices and legislations. The right to be consulted and to put forward proposals concerns:

- Actions having an impact on the safety system
- Appointment of people responsible for prevention services
- Outsourcing risk assessment services
- Training organization

Employee engagement practices in the area of health and safety were already in place in various member States even before the implementation of the Framework Directive, but they were very different from one another since they expressed different industrial relations cultures. From the participation point of view, the impact of the Framework Directive has varied from country to country. In Italy, for instance, the Workers' health and safety representative (Rls) as well as the Unitary Union Representative Body (Rsu)have been appointed, whereas in the UK the Government was obliged to extend all health and safety representation rights to all workers, even in those cases where there already were Union Representative Bodies. In France, the EU legislation has extended the powers of the so-called *Comité d'hygiène, de sécurité et des conditions des travail* (CHSCT), whereas in Sweden no particularly innovative factors have been introduced into the already existing system.

In 2004, the European Commission published the results of the implementation of the provisions set out by the Framework Directive and by the specific Directives on health and safety at work (COM(2004) 62 final). The European survey stems from the national relations, which take into account social partners' viewpoint, from an expert report and from the control activities of the transposition of Directives and their implementation in all business sectors. The EU Commission expresses a general positive opinion concerning the impact of the European legislation on the national rules and regulations and on its practical implementation in the economic and business fabric as well as in the specific public institutions. The Commission is aware of a few difficulties of implementing the directive in Small and medium sized enterprises (SME's) and in the Public sector mainly due to:

- Differences/difficulties in carrying out systematic risk assessment
- Difficulties/ Differences in the protection and prevention services
- Corporate organization structures
- Poor employee involvement

The Commission Communication lists a few possible causes for a low degree of direct employee participation:

- A general lack of knowledge vis-à-vis the new participation rights;
- A preference towards practical and occasional solutions by employees' representatives;
- A generalized fear that the further commitment towards the issue of safety might take time away from other activities and is mainly confined to mainly administrative activities;
- The delegation of responsibilities to employees' representatives or to specific representative bodies reduces the individual engagement in the are of health and safety at work. In those countries that are characterized by a co-management culture, a negative trend emerges: the more structured and defined the representative participation system is, the larger the number of bodies and committees dealing with health and safety will be and less likely will be for employees to be directly involved in the definition of prevention policies at the workplace;
- Employees and their representatives feature a knowledge *gap* in the area of health and safety in comparison with their employers or company experts. This *gap* becomes even wider when SME's are taken into account;
- A generalized lack of interest by employees in the issue of safety at the workplace.

Wellbeing at the workplace

The changes that have occurred in the world of work, also in terms of organization and contracts and the consequent changes on the labour market have led to a transformation of living and working conditions and of the risk profiles. Work accidents and occupational diseases, although still being among the priorities pursued by health and safety policies, now run the risk of no longer covering the whole spectrum of work conditions. Work accidents are the clear evidence of inappropriate and incorrect organization and relational processes. Yet, these inadequacies do not always become evident. Health and safety policies that are merely oriented to the reduction of work accidents and occupational illnesses take only one part of the picture into account, neglecting the various components, or better psychosocial and organization determinants.

Following the European Council of Nice held in December 2000, which urged the European Commission to implement a "real" Community strategy in the area of health and safety based on the "*definition of common comparable objectives*", in

2002 the European Commission launched the Community strategy "*Adapting to change in work and society: a new community strategy in health and safety at work 2002-2006*" (COM(2002)118). The Community strategy has introduced a global approach to workers' wellbeing at the workplace including not only physical risks but also moral and social ones (i.e. stress, depression, violence, harassment) and takes into account the changes of work. In order to meet the new objectives, the European strategy envisages three main categories of measures:

- Adjustment of the legal framework and production of new legislative provisions related to emerging risks
- Fostering the social dialogue, the exchange of best practices, comparative analyses, spreading of social responsibility and effective systems
- Integration of workplace health and safety practices to other Community policies: wellbeing at the workplace cannot be promoted only by means of health and la safety policies but it should be integrated and enhanced also through other European policies (employment, public health, trade, transport), thus leading to a multidisciplinary and wide-ranging set of actions.

Participation in the new European strategy for health and safety (2007-2012)

In line with a practice launched back in 1978, in February 2007, the European Commission adopted a new five-year strategy (2007-2012): "*Improving quality and productivity at the workplace: 2007-2012 Community strategy in the area of health and safety*". Without considering in this context the ambiguity of the title itself, centred on a link between the corporate productivity and the work-related health, the Commission's Communication leaves room to a few doubts. Apart form defining a few numerical Community objectives to be reached to reduce the number of industrial injuries and occupational diseases, towards which trade unions, employers' organizations and governments have shown a few doubts during the discussions in the preparatory phase, the European strategy systematically avoids the issue of employee representation, but it then refers to it under the recommendations on "health capital", thus taking up an individualistic vision of health as an investment to be managed that does not take into account the implications of the social determinants. In this case the Commission Communication confines itself to inviting social partners to take into account the issue of health and safety in the framework of the sectoral social dialogue, this being a field of action of European industrial relations which is not very suited to deal with such a general theme.

The new strategy has not enhanced the strategic role that can be played by employee involvement even though this was one of the priorities put forward by the Employee Group of the Consulting Committee for health and safety of Luxemburg (2006) faced with the European Commission Communication(2005) on social policy including all the projects related to the health and safety strategy for the 2007-2012 period. The Advisory Committee considers the employees' representatives for health and safety an essential element that is not yet widely spread. In spite of the prevention and organization role, in most European countries, a remarkable percentage of employees does not enjoy this form of representation. Without a structured representative body of employees any attempt of participation in the occupational health and safety system will be stultified. The mere existence of such a representative body is of course not enough to imply a real participation.

Early in 2008 the European Parliament published a Resolution where it expressed its opinion about the European Commission Communication, with the intention not only to share the approach and objectives defined by the Community strategy but also to introduce new initiatives, including corrective actions. More specifically, the European Parliament's Resolution urged the Commission and the Member States to "*guarantee a better implementation of the already existing legislative tools in the area of health and safety at work*" by "*all the means at their disposal*", including "*a greater employee involvement at the workplace*". In addition to the idea that "*employee representation plays a major role in any policy in the area of health and safety at work*" and "*that the positive link between the presence of occupational health and safety representatives and a better performance that cannot be ignored*", the European Parliament urged the Commission and the Member States to "*promote the participatory approach and make sure that possibly all male and female workers have access to these representatives*"[6].

Direct and representative participation in the management of the occupational health and safety system

Changes of work necessarily affect the participatory procedures at the workplace between management, employees and trade unions. Under this approach, direct and representative participation are regarded as essential tools to enhance work quality and competitiveness, with reference to the literature centred on *best work practices*, which the European Union often refers to (*Green Paper – Partnership for a New Organisation of Work*, 1997). The expression representative participation refers to joint consulting practices between social partners, co-determination, collective bargaining, social dialogue practices, with reference to the culture and his-

6 European Parliament Resolution dated 15/01/2008 on the 2007-2012 Community strategy for health and safety in the workplace.

tory of national industrial relations. On the other hand, direct participation mainly refers to direct employee involvement, without any representation constraint.

In general, the involvement of employees in the occupational health and safety system management can be defined as: co-operative or conflictual. In the former case, employees and their representatives support employers in the domain of occupational health and safety by sharing their experiences and co-operation:

- External experts do not necessarily know everything in detail. Employees and their representatives can contribute to identify actions and priorities in the corporate safety system management
- The practical knowledge of the manufacturing process seems to be important for a real implementation of solutions in the area of health and safety
- If employees and their representatives are involved in the identification of problems and problem-solving, it will be more likely that they are more willing to adopt and comply with safety regulations. The involvement of employees and their representatives improves the cost/benefit analysis in the filed of health and safety: maximization of benefits at minimum costs.

In the conflictual scenario, the involvement of employees and their representatives is necessary since it acts as counterpart to employers according to an antagonism logic between health and safety system management and business profit. The employee involvement thus plays a balancing role in an efficiency oriented corporate policy, where actions in the area of health and safety are often regarded as costs.

The two approaches – the collaborative and conflictual ones – are intertwined and overlapping in enterprises and they emerge according to the different industrial relations contexts and cultures. Both participatory approaches are useful to make employers and managers aware of the relevance of work conditions. In a participatory approach employees have more tools and resources than in a conflictual approach.

The different climate in relations between employers and employees necessarily affect the various forms of participation. There is a wide consensus, in literature, on the individual employees' initiatives and problem solving attitudes at work. At the same time, representative participation in health and safety system management can take place in a collaborative or conflictual manner (Frick K., Sjostrom J., 2006). From the collaborative point of view, the complexity of occupational health and safety issues suggests indirect participation forms, since employees' representatives can be specifically trained and have more time and skills to understand specific problems. Also from a conflictual point of view, indirect participation allows to exert a more effective lobbying even on the management who is most reluctant in implementing occupational health and safety rules.

The recent results of a research carried out by ETUI-REHS (European Trade Union Institute for Research, Education, Health and Safety) called "The Impact of

Workers' health and safety representatives on occupational health: a European perspective (the EPSARE project)" show how the main approach adopted by the European Union for the promotion of employee involvement in the health and safety system management is the election of workers' health and safety representatives[7].

In spite of the lack of a systematic collection of data, it has been estimated that in the EU-27 Member States, there is more than one million *workers' health and safety representatives.* Most of the time, the workers' health and safety representative is a worker with a sound work experience, usually a trade union member, even though in a few countries the industrial relations system allows the election of non unionised employees. In summary, four different types of the election can be identified:

- workers' health and safety representatives directly chosen by employees
- workers' health and safety representatives appointed by employees' representation bodies (i.e. works council, etc.)
- workers' health and safety representatives elected by the trade union
- works council acting as the health and safety representation body

In most EU Member States, health and safety representatives are entrusted with extended powers, either through legislation or negotiation. Even though the Framework Directive is now 20 years old and is the starting point for employee involvement, it should be noted that still today it provides the necessary framework for the full implementation of employees' health and safety representatives' rights and functions.

In addition to the election of workers' health and safety representatives, a further form of representation of workers' health and safety representatives is the setting up of health and safety Committees (such as in France). Committees are made up of employers and employees' representatives engaged in the improvement of safety conditions at the workplace.

Over the past few years, research in the area of employee involvement in safety – in spite of the limited number of studies in the field – has shown that forms of direct participation in the area of health and safety have not often led to positive results for employees' occupational health. The surveys that have been carried out so far show that in cases where no forms of representative participation exist, the forms of direct participation, recommended at times by employers, are nothing but a cosmetic façade: in a few countries, such as the United Kingdom and Denmark, specific rules have been adopted aimed at fostering the organization

7 Menéndez M., Benach J., Vogel L., title "The Impact of Workers' health and safety representatives on occupational health: a European perspective (the EPSARE project), *ETUI-REHS (European Trade Union Institute for Research, Education, Health and Safety),* Brussels, 2008.

of forms of direct participation in enterprises without any representation mechanisms. Without a strong and organized participatory structure, employers have broader leeway for manoeuvre towards employees thus unilaterally imposing limits to the employee information and consultation procedures.

Employee involvement: what motivations

Different motivations push employees or their representatives to become involved in decision-making and management processes in the area of health and safety. The main motivations can be grouped in three macro-categories (Shearn P, 2004):

- *Improvement of psychosocial and organizational development.* The participatory propensity of enterprises may depend on their willingness to overcome a few organization or information gaps. Employee involvement stimulates and strengthens social learning, through which information is collected according to a *bottom up* approach and them made available for the design of policies and actions in the area of health and safety. Employees have the knowledge and experience to improve their work conditions and to reduce risk situations. A possible result of a social learning improvement might be the monitoring of occupational accidents or *near misses*, i.e. preventive measures to avoid the occurrence of any future accidents. Employee involvement does not only allow an organization improvement, but it also triggers off a greater commitment at the workplace and employee satisfaction;
- *increase of productivity and efficiency.* In spite of an indirect link between employee involvement and productivity increase, it is still possible to observe a link between employee involvement and improvement in health and safety, which translated into a reduction of occupational accidents, absenteeism and insurance premiums. The increase in employee satisfaction and motivation at work, induced by participatory schemes also translated into a better quality and productivity at work;
- *legal obligations and rights.* Motivation encouraging employee involvement is the moral and ethical thrust allowing employees to become involved in the decision-making processes at the workplace. This a principle that is now shared by the democratic society but it is not always fully recognized and enforced. In other words, employee involvement is a way through which employers and employees' interests coincide to reduce conflictual elements in an industrial relations context.

In this paragraph, evidence is provided showing that a few forms of social dialogue have contributed to an improvement of work conditions in the different Member States. In this case, the term "social dialogue" refers to all the types of formal dialogue between partners, discussions, consultation, negotiations and joint actions undertaken by the corporate representatives (management) and by elected employees' representatives. Employee involvement is thus mainly shifted towards indirect forms, consistent with a representative principle. The data, which is reported, refers to a Report by the European Foundation for the Improvement of Living and Working Conditions of Dublin whose title is "*Working conditions and social dialogue*" (2007). The Report analyses the relationship between social dialogue and work conditions at the national, sectoral and plant level, taking into account the quantitative and qualitative analyses carried in the different Member States. The Report is intended to highlight how advanced forms of social dialogue lead to positive effects on work conditions. This paragraph will focus only on the most significant cases that have actually led to a substantial improvement in terms of health and safety at work.

A survey carried out by the Belgian trade unions on 3,000 employees working in small and medium sized enterprises highlights the link between the presence of trade unions and the lobbying exerted by employees in decision-making processes in the area of health and safety within the enterprise[8]. The greater the union density, the greater the influence of employees on management. The survey does not only underscore the important role played by trade unions in fostering an effective participation in occupational safety issues, but it also opens a further debate on "contractual" issues: main determinant that "explains" this link is the employment status, namely only *standard employees* (i.e. full-time workers with an open-ended labour contract) can actually have an impact on decision-making processes. The so-called *non-standard employees* have a much weaker or absolutely marginal impact on them. Furthermore, the survey points out that the information flows in the area of health and safety at work are better where trade unions are present. The same conclusion has been reached by a survey carried out by the Bulgarian trade union on behalf of ILO (International Labour Organization)[9]. In particular, the positive impact of social dialogue on health and safety at work leads to an easier access to training on occupational safety issues and to an effective participation of trade unions in the development of policies and regulations.

---

8 Available at the Url: http//www.hiva.be/docs/rapport/R1043a.pdf.

9 Available at the Url: http://www.ilo.org/public/english/region/eurpro/budapest/social/safety_cd/index.htm.

According to a further survey carried out in Finland in 2004 by the Finnish Institute of Occupational Health and by the Ministry of Health and Social Affairs, the debate launched on the maintenance of work ability (MWA) at work by groups composed of employees and managers' representatives, and by health and safety services has led to a very positive effect at the workplace, and in particular improvements have been recorded in the are of: physical health, more cooperative working climate, better work conditions and reduction of absenteeism. Synergy and cohesion reached by groups jointly has allowed to launch effective activities in furtherance of maintenance of work ability.

The quality of the occupational health and safety system necessarily depends on, among several other factors, the management favourable approach. A further survey carried out by the Norwegian Research Institute FAFO based on interviews to employer and employee representatives underlines how the presence of the social dialogue is linked to the willingness by the management to shoulder greater responsibility towards sick or disabled employees by adjusting the work environment to better suit their needs. Furthermore, the survey concludes that in those cases where there is an advanced form of social dialogue the issues related to the work environment and to absence sue to sickness reasons will more likely be part of the business agenda[10].

The benefits stemming from the social dialogue are not only limited to an improvement of the physical conditions of the work environment but also of the psychosocial dimension. A few studies have shown that the social dialogue has a favourable impact on the management and it helps it be relieved from work-related stress. Several research reports have been published by the *Health and Safety Executive* (HSE- United Kingdom) and, in particular, on different approaches to manage stress (*Beacons of excellence in stress prevention*) through participation mechanisms. The *Stockton Borough Council* has adopted a partnership approach for stress prevention and the promotion of wellbeing, creating groups of employee supported by experts and trade unionists. A similar approach has been undertaken by the *London Electricity*, a regional energy agency, to foster the reintegration of employees in the workplace after a sickness leave. In view of such a reintegration, a dialogue is opened between the worker himself, a consultant, a Human Resources representative, a Production Manager and a trade union representative to agree on possible changes to be introduced in the work load, the behaviour, the task execution speed and in all those factors that might become a threat.

---

10 Available at the Url: http://www.fafo.no/pub/rapp/542/542.pdf.

According to a comparative analysis of Workers' health and safety representative and Health and safety manager at the European level by ISPESL (National Institute of Occupational Safety and Prevention), it clearly emerges that new organization and relational provisions laid down by the European Framework Directive have been mainly transposed into national legislation and negotiation practices. A more explicit spirit of renewal clearly stems from the broadening of a more balanced participation, as envisaged by the Framework Directive. The various systems based on bilateral works committees or groups, which are especially established in Northern Europe, are now laid down in all national legislations, except for Italy, which has appointed the joint industry boards to establish this link between the trade unions and the various employers' associations[11]. Therefore, this renewal effort has not led to a homogeneous situation. For instance, in most cases the very small sized enterprises are not obliged by law to appoint a specific occupational health and safety representative, except for Italy and Sweden. In Italy, area delegates are appointed in the craft, building and trade sectors, although to a limited extent; in Sweden, the regional delegates have claimed the right for all workers to be represented, even in enterprises with less than 5 employees. In Italy, the territorial representative for health and safety (RLST), where it has been appointed, is perceived as an advantage in view of the improvement of safety conditions at work. According to a research carried out by the Institute per il Lavero (The Institute for Labour) in (2005)[12] on behalf of EBER, Enter Bilateral per l'Artigianato in Emilia-Romagna (joint industry board), 77% of employees stated that they knew about the presence of a territorial representative for health and safety. At the same time, the research has allowed to investigate also the perception of enterprises towards the Rlst representative: 69% of interviewed craft firms stated that they met the Rlst representative and almost all of them (more than 90%) judged the meeting "sufficiently useful" or "very useful".

In Sweden the positive effects stemming from the introduction of territorial representative for health and safety can also be pointed out in terms of work accident prevention. A clear example might be that of bakeries, where work accidents often take place, with hand injuries caused by the use of machineries.

11 ISPESL, Comparative analysis of the profiles such as the Workers' health and safety representative and the Prevention and Protection Services representative in the legislation transposing the EU Directives in the field of health and safety by the EU Member States, 2003.

12 Bonora C., Dazzi D., Il sistema sicurezza EBER visto dalle imprese e dai lavoratori, Ente Bilaterale Emilia-Romagna, Bologna, 2005.

Together with the Labour Inspectorate, the regional representatives for health and safety have pointed the risks and hazards related to the use of machineries not equipped with the necessary protection guards. The immediate result of the information campaign was a rapid reduction in the number of sickness leaves following an occupational accident caused by the improper use of machineries. (with a decline from 2,500 during the 1989-1992 period to 1,500-2,000 in the 1993-1996 period).

The 2006 Swedish research on the regional representatives for health and safety in the building, manufacturing and services sector, carried out on behalf of the Swedish Union Confederation (LO), pointed out that 94.8% of respondents believe that the role played by the regional representatives has substantially contributed to improve the work environment[13]. Furthermore, the survey highlights the widespread conviction that both the management and employees confine themselves to a mere passive role in the area of working environment, and in particular in the area of health and safety at work, by leaving the greater responsibility to the regional representatives for health and safety. The research outcomes underscore the role played by the employees' health and safety representatives also beyond the corporate environment and are able to meet the requirements deriving from new manufacturing fabrics that are increasingly more characterized by fragmentation processes. A further survey carried out in 2002 described another awareness-raising campaign launched by the Swedish trade unions from the building sector aimed at showing the advantages deriving from a better work environment. The main result of the research was the acknowledgment of the importance of the role played by the regional and local safety representatives and the need for a better coordination among them.

With reference to SME's a few Danish research studies have pointed out areas to be improved in terms of participation in the occupational health and safety system. A report by the National Centre for Health promotion at the workplace (NCSA) dated 2004 highlighted the poor knowledge and experience or methods on how to promote issues related to health in SME's. Similarly, another Danish study performed by the Centre for Alternative Social Analysis (CASA) in 2001 in the services sector highlighted that the themes related to the work environment were not under the responsibility of the Safety Committees but occasionally dealt with by the management, without any formal agreement with the employees representatives. According to the research, the lack of a formal dialogue indicates the level of priority attached to occupational safety by the management: Safety Committees are a cost for enterprises and tit is always difficult to find employees willing to take part in these Committees.

---

13 Available at the Url: http://www.lo.se/home/lo/home.nsf/unidView.

Conclusive remarks

A few conclusive remarks will be outlined, starting from the information that has been provided in this report, which can launch a debate among social partners and public actors, at the national and European level.

First of all the extent of literature on the direct and indirect benefits deriving from a greater employee involvement in the area of health and safety at work suggests that a greater investment should be made from this point of view, especially in the framework of the European strategy. The evidence shows the need for a greater impact to be held by representative participation in an area where knowledge and experience play an absolutely key role. Hence, it is fundamental to extend workers' health and safety representative rights where they are not yet enforced and to foster their development. Direct participation by itself is not enough to contribute to an effective improvement of work conditions. This statement does not exclude a broadening of direct participation forms adequately linked to other representative participation forms.

Several studies underline the relevance of the role played by trade unions and of a strategic trade union approach for an ongoing and lasting improvement of male and female workers' conditions. In general terms, the trade union strategies at the European level concerning health and safety, and in particular the role played by the workers' health and safety representative, can be grouped into two categories. The first one consists in strengthening the role played by the workers' health and safety representative through a greater and better training or through the promotion of networked information platforms. The second trade union strategic line consists in the integration of the safety representative functions within the company level union representation structure, thus benefiting already consolidated bodies. The adoption of such a strategic line as against another one depends on the national industrial relations culture and they can often cohabitate.

In the event of territorial representatives for health and safety or other forms of employee involvement even in small and very small-sized enterprises, on the one hand their relevance emerges within the framework of the health and safety system and their ability to having a positive impact on work conditions. Participatory practices in the area of occupational health and safety in small-sized enterprises become an increasingly more urgent need faced with the continuous fragmentation processes of the European manufacturing system and as a reaction to the continuously high work accident rate. Thus a large number of enterprises and employees risks being excluded. The examples of Italy and Sweden can stimulate the development of participatory solutions also in manufacturing areas where trade unions do not have a capillary presence and to promote participation forms that go beyond the mere company borders. (territorial, site, sector representatives).

The growth of contractual flexibility and of labour relations inevitably produces an impact on the employee involvement system, as a whole, and on the issue of occupational health and safety, more specifically. Data show a prevalence of standard workers vis-à-vis non standard standard workers policies in the area of safety at the workplace. It is therefore necessary to identify in a direct and representative way the numbers of employees who are hired with flexible contractual configurations.

References

Antonioli, D. / Pini, P. (2005): Partecipazione dirette, partecipazione indiretta e innovazioni tecno-organizzative. Alcuni risultati per il sistema locale di Reggio Emilia, maggio 2005.

Bonora, C. / Dazzi, D. (2005): Il sistema sicurezza EBER visto dalle imprese e dai lavoratori, Ente Bilaterale Emilia-Romagna, Bologna.

European Commission (COM (2004) 62 final): February 2004, Brussels.

European Foundation for the Improvement of Living and Working Conditions (Eurofound) (2008): Annual review of working conditions in the EU 2007-2008, Dublin.

European Foundation for the Improvement of Living and Working Conditions (Eurofound) (2007): Working conditions and social dialogue, Dublin.

European Foundation for the Improvement of Living and Working Conditions (Eurofound) (2005): Fourth European Working Conditions Survey.

Declaration by the workers' group part of the Advisory Committtee on health and safety of Luxemburg (2006): in *Quaderni 2087* "Europe. Health and safety, trade unions. The strategies for the next 2007-2012 period", n. 9, novembre 2006.

ETUI-REHS (2007): Benchmarking Working EUrope.

Fondazione Rosselli (2005): Sicurezza sul lavoro: benchmarking delle principali tendenze in atto in alcuni paesi dell'Unione Europea, febbraio 2005.

Frick, K. / Sjostrom, J. (2006): Factors influencing worker and safety reparticiation – How to understand the OHS participation process, *National Institute for Working Life*, Stoccolma.

ISPESL (2003): comparative analysis of Workers' health and safety representative and of the Prevention and protection service in the legislation for the transposition of EU Directives in the field of health and safety by EU countries.

Menéndez, M. / Benach, J. / Vogel, L. (2008): denominata "The Impact of Safety Representatives on occupational health: a European perspective (the EP-

SARE project), ETUI-REHS (European Trade Union Institute for Research, Education, Health and Safety), Bruxelles.

Sennet, R. (1998): The Personal Consequences of Work in the New Capitalism, Norton & Company (Feltrinelli, 2001).

Shearn, P. (2004): Workforce Participation in the Management of Occupational Health & Safety, Report number HSL/2005/09, Health & Safety Laboratoty, September 2004.

Vogel, L. (2007): A critical review of the 2007-2012 European strategy with reference to Occupational Health & Safety, in Quaderni 2087, n1., February 2007.

Workers' participation – How to develop further the European Social Model

György Széll

Pre-remark

There are a number of fundamental questions we have to ask ourselves, before we are able to come to grips in regard to the future of the European Social Model. Apparently we also have to inquire about the role of Europe in a globalising world. Today we are facing a number of challenges, which grew over the last couple of decades, but have materialized only over the last couple of months. Just a week before the opening of the Third Congress of the European network "Regional and local development of work and labour" the biggest financial and economic crash since the Black Friday 1929 has shuttered the economic model of deregulation at any price and the attempt to destroy the welfare state. Apparently we are at a new beginning, hopefully for better, although those, who are mainly responsible for this disaster, which destroys dozens of millions of jobs, the economies of a whole generation, try to blame the state. Actually there were since many years already a number of warnings that this neo-liberal economic system, which declared war to the trade unions and workers' participation, is not sustainable – neither economically, financially nor socially or environmentally. In 1986 the movie "Wall Street" characterised the financial system with its elements of corruption and megalomania quite precisely. It may be also reminded of another quite pertinent Canadian movie in the same year: "The decline of the American Empire". This all in the highlight of the Reagan administration and its Reaganomics. The most successful financial speculator, George Soros, published in 1998 a book with the significant title "The crisis of global capitalism. The open society endangered", where he warned of the risks of an uncontrolled financial system. I published in 1987 an article with a scenario for 2000, where I forecasted the crisis of autumn 2008. (English translation: Széll 1990) Apparently I was partly wrong, as I put it eight years too early. However, most probably – besides the fascination of a round number – the break-down of the Soviet system in 1989/1990 gave ultra-liberal market capitalism another few extra years.

The management of the financial crisis today, however, is more concerned to save the big companies instead of taking the occasion for a fundamental turn-around. The old recipe: privatisation of profits and socialisation of losses. The former chief-economist of the World Bank, Nicholas Stern, who became well known, as he published last year the first account of the costs of neglecting environmental protection, published in December 2008 an article, where he argued that the crisis is a unique chance to save the planet.

History

Trying to set the stage for a further European Social Model we have first to look back. As Warren Buffet, the richest man in the world, said: We can only learn lessons from the past. So what has changed in regard to our topic over the last 150 years, since 1945, 1968, 1989, and 2000? Apparently the dates are not neutral, and we may take other options. In 1858, after some failed revolutions in Europe, perhaps the most important element was that Prussia entered the international scene, first unifying and establishing the Second German Reich, and then building up huge industry and military. The second important element is the unification and ending of the inner frontiers of the United States of America about the same period. The German model, to catch up with the leading economies and imperialist powers – i.e. the British and French empires – was a modernisation from the top, played on two different fronts, expansion outwards and pacification inwards: the introduction of the Bismarckian welfare state and the interdiction of the Social-Democratic Party (SPD). The outcome was terrible, as we all now, two World Wars and the Holocaust (Wehler).

Fascism and Stalinism were both based on the passive participation of the masses (Gramsci). Another important innovation was the system of Fordism, developed in the USA, combining mass production and mass consumption, i.e. participation was reduced to it.

After the Second World War Fordism spread over to the other industrialised nations, including Japan. In Germany the "social market economy" was designed as a third way between socialism and capitalism. The biggest political and economic experiment in the 20th century was the creation of the European Union in 1958 with its predecessor the European Community of Coal and Steel in 1951. It is largely successful, although the realisation of a European Social Union is still lagging far behind.

In the Third World some countries experimented with other forms of industrialisation and welfare state (China, India, Cuba, North Korea, Algeria, Tanzania – just to name a few), however, mostly failed. China changed in 1978 to the so-called "socialist market-economy" with the destruction of most of its welfare system (Széll / Kamppeter / Moon, 2009).

1968 was not only for my generation a fundamental watershed, but for future generations as well. It was the starting point for a large democratisation process.

Until then democracy stopped at the factory gates. The famous slogan "To dare more democracy" of the then German Chancellor and Peace Nobel Prize winner, Willy Brandt, was a marking stone.

The implosion of the Soviet system in 1989/1990 gave way for the integration of some of its European satellite states into the EU, for the others a fall back into more or less authoritarian structures. The end of history, as declared by Francis Fukuyama in 1992, did fortunately not take place, although a new era of deregulation and military conflicts started, and did not end so far.

At the beginning of the new century, or the new millennium the fifteen Millennium Goals by the United Nations, the Lisbon Agenda for the EU, and the Decent Work campaign by the International Labour Organisation were launched. There was a slogan of the beginning of the Pacific Century with the rise of China in accordance with its past grandeur.

The questions

Some fundamental questions first, before we proceed further:

1. Is there one European Social Model?
   For sure there are – as already studies in the 1970s demonstrated – quite a number of variations (IDE 1981), due the differences relating back to history, culture, power etc. However, some clusters are discernible: Nordic, Anglo-Saxon, Central European and Mediterranean – before 1990 there existed also the Yugoslav one. Although these differences are still quite marked, we can conclude in comparison to namely the U.S.-American or also the Japanese model there are some distinctive features, which make it that we may speak on the global level of a European Social Model.
2. What kind of participation are we looking for? Again there are quite substantial differences. Namely we may differentiate between financial participation, participation in decision-making and on different levels, direct or representative participation, ad hoc or permanent participation (Kester / Pinaud 1996).
3. Double participation: Participation within the company and as a citizen and/or consumer. These roles may be contradictory at some times. The task is to overcome this kind of schizophrenia.
4. What is the role of experts? Participation in decision-making has become through globalisation and the differentiation of the workforce so complex that workers and their representatives need special training and/or advice from experts to come to grips with decisions about future investments, off-shoring, environmental issues, human rights etc. Although it may be still true, what

the former general secretary of the French CFDT once said: "The worker is the real expert concerning his work."

I have put the following questions to the panellists during the plenary session:

1. What are in your eyes the main elements of Workers' participation?
2. What have been the main successes and failures of workers' participation in Europe over the last decades?
3. How do you define the European Social Model?
4. Who are the main actors to promote Workers' participation in Europe?

You may read their answers by themselves.

The challenges

During a conference "Which European Social Model?", which was co-sponsored by the European Foundation for the Improvement of Living and Working Conditions, in Aix-en-Provence in September 2001, I presented a paper on "Fifteen challenges for a European Social Model" (Széll 2002a), which is in my eyes still up-to-date. Let me just pick up some of the issues:

1. The environment – is still the biggest challenge. And since the movie by the former US-American Vice-president and Peace Nobel Prize winner, Al Gore, "An inconvenient truth" and the report by his co-Peace Nobel Prize laureate, the International Panel on Climate Change (IPCC), there is no doubt that environmental protection is the biggest challenge for humanity. We only have an opening of another ten years to fix the challenge (Hennicke 2009). All empirical studies prove that it is only with the participation of all concerned that this challenge may be overcome (Széll 2004a). However, even after the progress, which has been made by the European Union in this regard over the last two years, and the election of Barrack H. Obama as President of the U.S.A. the prospects look rather grim for a Kyoto II-convention in 2009 in Copenhagen, not to speak of the ongoing pollution and depletion of the seas and rivers, the lack of drinking water, the waste disposal etc.
2. Gender equality is the next big challenge, not only – as the late Chairman Mao Dze Dong put it: "Women are half of heaven" – but because without the active participation of women in all realms of life, not at least in environmental protection, there will be no social justice, no decent work, no future.
3. All organisations (political, social, trade unions) are in a deep crisis in regard to recruiting new members, especially from the younger generation. The problem

concerns as well the low qualified and the most highly qualified strata of society. It seems that the dominant economic system with its focus on "Sex and shopping" has resulted to a large degree of depolitisation and individualisation, which has been analysed by Alexis de Tocqueville already more then 170 years ago.

4. In regard to trade unions they have certainly partly to blame themselves, as they still remain largely blue collar, male unions, which are not only in the EU quite diverse, due to their historical legacies. Besides, quite often they seem to be more concerned to compete among each others than to struggle together for their common targets, if they are politically or sectorally differently oriented, which leads to a number of unnecessary conflicts and by that to the weakening of the whole labour movement. To that adds the lack of training, competence and quality of many union officials. And the employers contribute to these difficulties their part as well. E.g. Peugeot and Siemens, two of the biggest companies in the world, financed until recently "yellow unions". Definitely the trade unions have to restructure themselves. But big – as the mergers of the past years show – is not always beautiful and successful. The mergers in Germany with as result the biggest single unions in the world (IG Metall, ver.di) had as a collateral damage the formation or strengthening of smaller unions of a guild type (pilots, train conductors, health sector). On the other hand the European Trade Union Confederation (ETUC) has made substantial progress since the enlargement of the EU. And another very positive development is the creation of the unified International Trade Union Confederation (ITUC) in 2006, seventeen years after the break-down of the Soviet Empire. This gives hope for a new élan. Since then the presence of the trade union movement on the international scene has much progressed.
5. The weakness of the labour movement is mirrored by the weakness of the employers' associations. Quite a number of companies in the new economy do not associate themselves with employers' associations, thinking they can save the fees, and they are better off without binding collective agreements (Széll / Bösling / Hartkemeyer 2005).
6. This phenomenon is particularly pronounced within the new EU-Member States, where employers' associations in the period of really existing socialism did not exist. The strategy in these countries is still to make the pie bigger to share some of the benefits, instead of going for sustainability.
7. After the implosion of the Soviet system there was much fear of a large East-West migration. This happened only partially, as the freedom of movement was restricted for the first years after the entry of the new Member States. Nevertheless migration is quite an issue as the illegal flux from non-EU States is still very strong, and as all EU Member States face a decrease of population, notably the active population (Széll 2002b).

8. In regard to participation and the European Social Model there are many obstacles to overcome, even within the EU, as the European Social Union is far from being realised, i.e. that not only social rights can be easily transferred. And the full recognition of diploma, which started with the Bologna-process ten years ago, is not yet established everywhere.
9. Social security is still largely a national affair. One of the reasons of the negative referenda in France and The Netherlands in regard to the EU Constitution Treaty was just the defence of the national social security systems against liberalisation strategies on the EU-level. This fear seems to had reasons as for two decades the neo-liberal strategies focussed on the destruction of the welfare state. However, on this concrete point the refusal of the EU Constitution Treaty was wrong: It would have brought more social rights than the Nice-Treaty. And the famous Plan B by Jacques Delors – with better social protection – was a myth. Even now the problem is who controls the social security system? The drive for privatisation was very strong. Especially the pension funds, which are already now the biggest institutional investors, are playing the game on the international markets – with all the risks we know now. And the pension funds of the big US-American car makers are one of the reasons of their bankruptcy. The only real alternative to state bureaucratic control of the social security system is the social economy, the fastest growing sector in the world – without the risks of the dominant sector.
10. That brings us to the concern of globalisation. Here the main actors are the WTO, IMF, World Bank, G8 and OECD. The driving force in this process, the financial sector, is not regulated at all, as we just noticed in the banking crisis in autumn 2008 and as George Soros monitored previously.
11. One answer to the unregulated globalisation is continental regionalisation, of which the EU with all its flaws is still the most successful model, namely with its own currency, the Euro. Mercosur, ASEAN and SARC are modelled after the EU, and even in North-East Asia China, Japan and South Korea try to establish their own union with its own currency.
12. Although the shareholder dictatorship has been questioned during the last couple of months, those who profited most of it, blame the state of failure and not their own business. So, the European alternative, the stakeholder democracy, has to struggle hard to overcome this ideology.
13. One of the means of shareholder dictatorship to increase profits to a maximum is outsourcing, off-shoring, and delocalisation. Although this strategy may bring benefit to new EU-Member States, the emerging economies and Third World countries, the price is rather high, because outsourcing, off-shoring, and delocalisation does not only mean lower salaries, but less social protection, non-respect of human rights and the environment. In so far participation

in decision making is a pre-condition for decent work and sustainability instead of social and environmental dumping.

14. The results of uncontrolled and unregulated globalisation are precarisation and dualisation of the workforce. No standard, life-long labour contracts any more for an increasing part of employees, mainly the young ones. The "Generation Praktikum" (generation internship) in Germany and elsewhere is a symbol of this trend. Apparently the precarisation does not only affect the quality of life and working-life but also the possibilities of life-long learning and participation, and with it the quality of products and services.
15. That this process could so easily be implemented without much resistance by the concerned is certainly due to the cultural hegemony of the media industry. That a tycoon like Silvio Berlusconi came twice to power, based on his ownership of large parts of the TV-industry, in a civilised country like Italy is a scandal. Here the analysis by the US-American media-sociologist Neil Postman with his book "Amusing Ourselves to Death" from 1984 is more up-to-date than ever. His thesis that everything in our societies, even politics, becomes entertainment is convincing. That does not mean that everything of new global information and communication technologies, e.g. Internet, contributes to this trend. Our scientific conferences and publications, the World Social Forum and its regional and national off-springs would not have been possible without the new media and technologies.
16. Education (general, vocational, university training) is in a crisis as well. Europe – except Scandinavia – is far from its target to invest 3% of its GDP into science and research. In international comparisons it is lagging behind even of emerging nations like South Korea or China. Expenditure for education and science is in general still regarded as costs and not as an investment into the future. However, in the OECD countries 40+% of a generation are today university graduates. So not only the future managers and elites are trained there, but a large part of the workforce. So university training has to give them the qualification for participative management and participation in decision making. But economics and business are not taught in secondary schools – not to speak of primary schools –, although everybody will be part of it. An essential precondition to have a future for a participative European Social Model is that teachers and university faculty have these competencies and are unionised themselves. There is still in most countries a long way to go, as – when they are unionised – it is mostly in kind of professional, guild-like associations with rather conservative ideologies.

Conclusions

The world has not only changed in regard to the topics mentioned in the paragraphs above on the challenges, but also concerning the structure of the economy. The Lisbon agenda speaks of a knowledge-based society. The biggest economic sectors in the world today are agriculture, IT, health/care, entertainment, tourism – which are at the same time the weakest in regard to unionisation.

Performance is certainly the issue of today, but also quality. And quality of life and working life are actually the most important targets, as the economy is not an end in itself. (Széll / Ehrig / Staroske / Széll 2009) To reach a sustainable company, economy and society, which are the targets of the Rio and Lisbon agendas, environmental Kaizen is an important tool (Széll 2004a). To realize them we need a kind of socio-cultural revolution. Part of it is Corporate Social Responsibility, which includes the environment as well (Széll 2006; Széll / Laasch / Wittstock 2009).

A fundamental element of this socio-cultural revolution is trust. Trust is the basis of all human society and relations, although it has been largely lost during the last couple of decades of casino capitalism, as also the crash of the last couple of months proves. The state, which has been dismantled during this period, because regarded as ineffective, has become again the only institution, into which citizens and consumers have trust.

The civil society, which has been destroyed as well, being replaced by crude individualism, is the other institution, on which the reconstruction of the economy and society at large has to be based on.

In the last years benchmarking and best practice have become tools to modernize the economy and business. But as we know against Taylorism there is no one best way. The optimal solution depends on the socio-historical context of each institution. The Open method of co-ordination within the EU is a flexible answer to this. The target of adaptation to or overcoming the challenges has to be a win-win situation, where there are collateral benefits instead of damages.

"Think globally, act locally!" was the slogan in the 1970s and 1980s. That is truer than ever today. And our international network Regional and Local Development of Work and Labour in its tenth year of existence, is a – although modest – answer.

The old dream – from hetero- via co- to self-management – is on the agenda again. There is empirical prove since long that participative companies and those with social responsibilities perform much better than the others. (Garibaldo / Telljohann 2004) So the question stands, why are these principles not applied everywhere, if the power of market and the *homo oeconomicus* prevail? Again recent economic research – honoured by diverse Nobel prizes – as well as the recent developments in the world economy demonstrate that the economy is far from being as logical as the main stream neo-classical textbooks pretend. Keynesianism was already an answer to this widespread market failure.

The obstacles are ideological, and are ignorance, i.e. cognitive dissonance. It is power relations within business and the economy, which prevail and are termed by the German author Günter Ortmann (1995) as micro-politics. There the role of academia comes in for training and research. Human Resources Management, change management, quality management, and environmental management are already partial answers in this process of Enlightenment. Fortunately there are a number of companies and institutions, which are run by an enlightened management and driven by enlightened economic, political, social and cultural actors. It is a dialectical process. As Karl Marx described it 160 years ago: "In the womb of the old society the new one is born". History may proceed as the procession in the town of Echternach in Luxemburg: two steps forward, one step back. Hopefully we are now at the moment of two steps forward, and the European Social Model is part of it.

References

Busch, K. / Széll, G. et al. (eds.) (2000): Ways to Social Peace in Europe. Osnabrück, Secolo.

Fukuyama, F. (1992): The End of History. New York: The Free Press.

Garibaldo, F. / Telljohann, V. (eds.) (2000): The role of intermediate institutions: The case of Research Institutes Concerned with Work and Labour. Milano, Franco Angeli.

Garibaldo, F. / Telljohann, V. (eds.) (2004): Globalisation, Company Strategies and Quality of Working Life in Europe. Frankfurt/M. et al., Peter Lang.

Garibaldo, F. / Telljohann, V. (eds.) (2006): Nuove forme di organizzazione del lavoro e relazioni industriali. Dov'è l'Italia?, Rimini, Maggioli.

Harrisson, Denis / Széll, György / Bourque, Reynald (eds.) (2009): Social Innovations and Labour. Frankfurt/M. et al., Peter Lang.

Hennicke, Peter (2009): 'Increasing Resource Productivity:A possible win-win strategy to protect resources, climate and jobs', in Széll, G. / Ehrig, Detlev / Staroske, Uwe / Ute Széll (eds.): Quality of Life & Working Life in Comparison. Frankfurt/M. et al., Peter Lang.

Industrial democracy in Europe (IDE) International Research Group (1981): 'Industrial democracy in Europe. Differences and similarities across countries and hierarchies', Organization Studies 2 (2): 113-129.

Kester, Gérard / Pinaud, Henri (eds.) (1996): Trade unions and democratic participation in Europe: A scenario for the 21st Century, Aldershot et al., Avebury .
Lammers, C.J. / Széll, G. (eds.) (1989): International Handbook of Participation in Organizations. Vol. I: Organizational Democracy – Taking Stock. Oxford, Oxford University Press.
Marx, K. (1989): Capital. Harmondsworth, Penguin, 3 vols.
Nicolaou-Smokoviti, L. / Széll, G. (eds.) (1994): Participation, Organisational Effectiveness and Quality of Working-Life in the Year 2000. Frankfurt/M. et al., Peter M. Lang.
Ortmann, Günter (1995): Formen der Produktion. Organisation und Rekursivität. Opladen, Westdeutscher Verlag.
Postman, N. (1985): Amusing Ourselves to Death. Viking-Penguin, New York.
Soros, G. (1998): The crisis of global capitalism. The open society endangered. New York, Public Affairs Publisher.
Stern, Nicholas (2008): 'La crise, une chance pour sauver la planète', Le Monde, 14/15 décembre, p. 16.
Sünker, H. / Farnen, R. / Széll, G. (eds.) (2003): Political Socialisation, Participation and Education: Change of Epoch – Processes of Democratization. Frankfurt/M. et al., Peter Lang.
Széll, G. (1988): Participation, Workers' Control and Self-Management. Trend report and bibliography. London, Sage, Current Sociology, vol. 36, # 3.
Széll, György (1990): '2000 AD: X Goes to Work', European Labour Forum, 1990, # 1: 27-29
Széll, G. (ed.) (1992a): Concise Encyclopaedia of Participation and Co-Management. Berlin / New York, de Gruyter.
Széll, G. (ed.) (1992b): Labour Relations in Transition in Eastern Europe. Berlin / New York, de Gruyter.
Széll, G. (ed.) (2001): European Labour Relations. Aldershot, Gower, 2 vol.
Széll, G. (2002a): 'Fifteen Challenges for a European Social Model', in György Széll / Gian-Primo Cella (eds.), The Injustice at Work: An International View on the World of Labour and Society. Frankfurt/M. et al., Peter M. Lang, pp. 588-606.
Széll, G. (2002b): 'Migration and Globalisation', in University of Piraeus (ed.), Essays in Honour of Professor Litsa Nicolaou-Smokoviti, Piraeus, 2002, vol. III: 1683-1691
Széll, G. (2003a): 'Industrial Democracy', in W. Outhwaite (ed.), The Blackwell Dictionary of Modern Social Thought, Oxford, Blackwell, pp. 288-290.
Széll, G. (2003b): 'Workers' Council', in W. Outhwaite (ed.), The Blackwell Dictionary of Modern Social Thought, Oxford, Blackwell, pp. 742-744.

Széll, G. (2004a): 'Environmental Kaizen: Environmental Protection as a Process', in György Széll / Ken'ichi Tominaga (eds.): Environmental Challenges for Japan and Germany – Interdisciplinary and Intercultural Perspectives, Frankfurt/M. et al., Peter Lang, 2004: 253-268.

Széll, G. (2004b): 'Sociology and Industrial Democracy', in N. Genov (ed.), Advances in Sociological Knowledge – over half a century, Wiesbaden, VS-Verlag, pp. 396-418.

Széll, G. (ed.) (2006): Corporate Social Responsibility in the EU & Japan. Frankfurt/M. et al., Peter Lang.

Széll, G. (2007) : 'La participation des travailleurs dans les entreprises allemandes en crise', Personnel & Gestion, N°7/Août, pp. 5-9.

Széll, G. / Bösling, C.-H. / Hartkemeyer, J. (eds.) (2005): Labour, Globalisation and the New Economy. Frankfurt/M. et al., Peter Lang.

Széll, G. / Bösling, C.-H. / Széll, U. (eds.) (2008): Education, Labour & Science – Perspectives for the 21st Century. Frankfurt/M. et al., Peter Lang (vol. 10 of the series Labour, Education & Society).

Széll, G. / Cella, G.-P. (eds.) (2002): The Injustice at Work: An International View on the World of Labour and Society. Frankfurt/M. et al., Peter M. Lang.

Széll, G., Chetty, D. / Chouraqui, A. (eds.) (2002): Participation, Globalisation & Culture – International and South African Perspectives. Frankfurt/M. et al., Peter M. Lang.

Széll, G. / Ehrig, Detlev / Staroske, Uwe / Széll, Ute (eds.) (2009): Quality of Life & Working Life in Comparison. Frankfurt/M. et al., Peter Lang (in the series Labour, Education & Society).

Széll, György / Cornforth, Chris / Blyton, Paul (eds.) (1989): The State, Trade Unions and Self-Management. Issues of Competence and Control, Berlin / New York, de Gruyter.

Széll, G. / Kamppeter, Werner / Moon, Woosik (eds.) (2009): European Social Integration – A Model for East Asia? Frankfurt/M. et al., Peter Lang, 2009 (in the series Labour, Education & Society).

Széll, G. / Laasch, Oliver / Wittstock, Jürgen (forthcoming): Managing CS(E)R – A Comprehensive international-interdisciplinary Textbook of Corporate Social Responsibility (for Sustainable Development).

Széll, G., Schlatermund, H. / Széll, U. (eds.) (1993): Arbeitsorientierte Wissenschaft und Forschung in den Neunziger Jahren in Europa – Labour Oriented Science and Research in Europe in the Nineties. Osnabrück, Secolo.

Tocqueville, Alexis de (1965): Democracy in America. Commager, Henry Steele [ed.]. London et al., Oxford Univ. Pr. (repr. from 1835).

Wehler, H.-U. (1987-2007): Deutsche Gesellschaftsgeschichte. München, Beck, 5 vol.

Authors

Tuomo Alasoini
Tekes – Finnish Funding Agency for Technology and Innovation, Helsinki, Finland

Davide Antonioli
University of Ferrara, Italy

Mirella Baglioni
University of Parma, Italy

Karina Becker
University of Jena, Germany

Paul Berckmans
Foundation Innovation & Work, Brussels, Belgium

Szilvia Borbély
Institute of Social and Economic Research of Trade Unions, Budapest, Hungary

Ulrich Brinkmann
University of Jena, Germany

Ole Broberg
DTU Management Engineering, Lyngby, Denmark

Romain Chevallet
ANACT – National Agency for the Improvement of Working Conditions, France

Steve Davies
University of Cardiff, United Kingdom

Davide Dazzi
Istituto Ricerche Economiche e Sociali dell'Emilia-Romagna, Bologna, Italy

Wolfgang Dunkel
ISF München, Germany

Thomas Engel
University of Jena, Germany

Werner Fricke
Institute for Regional Cooperation, Wieren, Germany

Peter Friedrich
Fritz Change AB, Stocksund, Sweden

Francesco Garibaldo
Bologna, Italy

María Gonzalez
University of Oviedo, Spain

Rainer Greca
University of Eichstätt-Ingolstadt, Germany

Nikolaus Hammer
University of Leicester, United Kingdom

Asko Heikkilä
Finnish Ministry of Employment and the Economy, Helsinki, Finland

Friedhelm Keuken
G.I.B. – Innovative Employment Promotion Company, Bottrop, Germany

Ulrich Klotz
IG Metall, Frankfurt, Germany

Norbert Kluge
ETUI-REHS Brussels, Belgium

Nick Kratzer
ISF München, Germany

Wilfried Kruse
Sozialforschungsstelle Dortmund, Germany

Annika Lantz
University of Uppsala, Sweden

Salvo Leonardi
Istituto Ricerche Economiche e Sociali, Rome, Italy

Jan Kees Looise
University of Twente, Netherlands

Loris Lugli
Istituto Ricerche Economiche e Sociali dell'Emilia-Romagna, Bologna, Italy

Maria Matey-Tyrowicz
Warsaw, Poland

Massimiliano Mazzanti
University of Ferrara, Italy

Sonia McKay
Working Lives Research Institute, London Metropolitan University, United Kingdom

Guglielmo Meardi
University of Warwick, United Kingdom

Wolfgang Menz
ISF München, Germany

Ralf Niemann
ArcelorMittal, Bremen, Germany

Patricia Nieto Rojas
Universidad Carlos III de Madrid, Spain

Paul Oehlke
Cologne, Germany

Paolo Pini
University of Ferrara, Italy

Anna Pollert
Bristol Business School, University of the West of England, United Kingdom

Erik Poutsma
Radboud University Nijmegen, Netherlands

Valeria Pulignano
Kathokieke Universiteit Leuven, Belgium

Elise Ramstad
Tekes – Finnish Funding Agency for Technology and Innovation, Helsinki, Finland

Lauge Baungaard Rasmussen
DTU Management Engineering, Lyngby, Denmark

Ekaterina Ribarova
Institute for Social and Trade Union Research-Sofia, Bulgaria

György Széll
University of Osnabrück, Germany

Volker Telljohann
Istituto Ricerche Economiche e Sociali dell'Emilia-Romagna, Bologna, Italy

Jochen Tholen
Institute Labour and Economy, University of Bremen

Nicole Torka
University of Twente, Netherlands

Alan Tuckman
University of Nottingham, United Kingdom

Stefano Tugnoli
Istituto Ricerche Economiche e Sociali dell'Emilia-Romagna, Bologna, Italy

Ulke Veersma
University of Greenwich, United Kingdom

Sigurt Vitols
Wissenschaftszentrum Berlin, Germany

Michael Whittall
Technical University of Munich, Germany

Jan Ekke Wigboldus
SBI training and consultancy and University of Twente, Netherlands

Peter Wilke
WMP consult Hamburg, Germany

Glynne Williams
University of Leicester, United Kingdom

Pekka Ylöstalo
Finnish Ministry of Employment and the Economy, Helsinki, Finland

Arbeit, Bildung & Gesellschaft
Labour, Education & Society

Herausgegeben von Prof. Dr. György Széll, Prof. Dr. Heinz Sünker, Dr. Anne Inga Hilsen und Dr. Francesco Garibaldo

Bd. 1 György Széll (ed.): Corporate Social Responsibility in the EU & Japan. 2006.

Bd. 2 Katja Maar: Zum Nutzen und Nichtnutzen der Sozialen Arbeit am exemplarischen Feld der Wohnungslosenhilfe. Eine empirische Studie. 2006.

Bd. 3 Daniela De Ridder: Vom urbanen Sozialraum zur kommunikativen Stadtgesellschaft. 2007.

Bd. 4 Heinz Sünker / Ingrid Miethe (Hrsg.): Bildungspolitik und Bildungsforschung: Herausforderungen und Perspektiven für Gesellschaft und Gewerkschaften in Deutschland. 2007.

Bd. 5 Anja Bastigkeit: Bildungsbiographie und elementarpädagogische Bildungsarbeit. 2007.

Bd. 6 Antônio Inácio Andrioli: Biosoja versus Gensoja. Eine Studie über Technik und Familienlandwirtschaft im nordwestlichen Grenzgebiet des Bundeslandes Rio Grande do Sul (Brasilien). 2007.

Bd. 7 Russell Farnen / Daniel German / Henk Dekker / Christ'l De Landtsheer / Heinz Suenker (eds.): Political Culture, Socialization, Democracy, and Education. Interdisciplinary and Cross-National Perspectives for a New Century. 2008.

Bd. 8 Francesco Garibaldo / Volker Telljohann (eds.): New Forms of Work Organisation and Industrial Relations in Southern Europe. 2007.

Bd. 9 Anne Marie Berg / Olav Eikeland (eds.): Action Research and Organisation Theory. 2008.

Bd. 10 György Széll / Carl-Heinrich Bösling / Ute Széll (eds.): Education, Labour & Science. Perspectives for the 21st Century. 2008.

Bd. 11 Francesco Garibaldo / Philippe Morvannou / Jochen Tholen (eds.): Is China a Risk or an Opportunity for Europe? An Assessment of the Automobile, Steel and Shipbuilding Sectors. 2008.

Bd. 12 Yunus Dauda: Managing Technology Innovation. The Human Resource Management Perspective. 2009.

Bd. 13 Jarmo Lehtonen / Satu Kalliola (eds.): Dialogue in Working Life Research and Development in Finland. 2009.

Bd. 14 György Széll / Werner Kamppeter / Woosik Moon (eds.): European Social Integration – A Model for East Asia? 2009.

Bd. 15 Benedicte Brøgger / Olav Eikeland (eds.): Turning to Practice with Action Research. 2009.

Bd. 16 Till Johannes Hoffmann: Verschwendung. Philosophie, Soziologie und Ökonomie des Überflusses. 2009.

Bd. 17 Denis Harrisson / György Széll / Reynald Bourque (eds.): Social Innovation, the Social Economy and World Economic Development. 2009.

Bd. 18 Werner Weltgen: Total Quality Management als Strukturierungsaufgabe für nachhaltigen Unternehmenswandel. 2009.

Bd. 19 György Széll / Ute Széll (eds.): Quality of Life and Working Life in Comparison. 2009.

Bd. 20 Francesco Garibaldo / Volker Telljohann (eds.): The Ambivalent Character of Participation. New Tendencies in Worker Participation in Europe. 2010.

www.peterlang.de

www.ingramcontent.com/pod-product-compliance
Ingram Content Group UK Ltd.
Pitfield, Milton Keynes, MK11 3LW, UK
UKHW021830100926
8556IPUK00004B/248

9 783631 589434